RULING ONESELF OUT

Ruling Oneself Out

A Theory of Collective Abdications

Ivan Ermakoff

Duke University Press ▪ Durham & London ▪ 2008

© 2008 Duke University Press
All rights reserved.

Typeset in Minion by Tseng Information Systems, Inc.

Library of Congress Cataloging-in-Publication Data appear
on the last printed page of this book.

CONTENTS

TABLES

FIGURES

PREFACE

"Nothing is so treacherous as the obvious" — Schumpeter (1976 [1942], 235)

History is punctuated with critical decisions, decisions that engage one's fate and the fate of others, decisions that people make in a mist of darkness, the darkness of their own motivations, the darkness of those who confront and challenge them, and the darkness of what the future has in store. This book is about decisions of this kind: collective abdications. The peculiarity of the collective abdications I am examining is that they were formally sanctioned by an explicit decision — a vote. A further peculiarity is that they meant the renunciation of democracy.

Abdication is different from surrender. It is surrender that legitimizes one's surrender. It implies a statement of irrelevance. When the act is collective, the statement is about the group that makes the decision. The group dismisses itself. It surrenders its fate and agrees to do so, thereby justifying its subservience. This broad characterization sets the problem. Why would a group legitimize its own subservience and, in doing so, abdicate its capacity for self-preservation?

1

The time and the setting: 23 March 1933, the Reichstag building, Berlin. The building had been partially destroyed by arson three weeks earlier, on the night of 27 February. It still bore the marks of the fire, and the persistent smell of charred rubble lingered in the corridors. Clara Siebert and her colleagues of the Center party parliamentary delegation had convened in the room in which they usually held their meetings. It was a little before 6 P.M. The delegates were now leaving the building. Because of the damage caused by the arson, the parliamentary session was temporarily taking place in another building, the Kroll Opera House, situated a few blocks away. The session was about to resume after a three-hour intermission. Though the place was familiar, the circumstances were not.

The representatives of the Center party were about to vote on an enabling bill (the "Law for the Relief of the People and of the Reich") that allowed Hitler's cabinet to issue, independently of the parliament, decrees deviating from the Constitution. In effect, the bill was a constitutional mandate. Hitler had enjoyed executive and legislative powers since his appointment as premier (chancellor) by the president of the Republic, Hindenburg, on 30 January 1933. The enabling bill granted Hitler the right to legally discard the constitutional framework of the Weimar Republic. In light of the Nazis' explicit political agenda, there was no doubt that this was the goal intended by the bill. The new regime would clearly be authoritarian in nature. Nothing guaranteed that basic individual rights would be protected.

The session began. The first speaker to take the rostrum at the Opera was the chairman of the Social Democratic party, Otto Wels. The Social Democrats, Wels explained, had suffered considerable persecution since Hitler's appointment as chancellor, and after having experienced such persecution the Social Democratic Party could not be expected by anyone to vote for the bill. The Social Democrats held fast to the basic principles of a government based on law. Hitler responded to Wels's speech with immediate violence aimed at the representatives of the democratic camp. "Springing like a beast thriving to tear apart its prey" (Wirth), Hitler castigated the Social Democrats for coming too late. The fate of the Social Democratic party, Hitler explained, was sealed. The party would be cast into the dustbin of history.

Then came the turn of Ludwig Kaas, the Center party chairman, to explain his party's vote. Both the tone and content of his speech were different; Kaas spoke of the work of national salvation that had to be accomplished. The Center party consented to vote for the enabling bill, provided that the government would base its policies on the three principles outlined by the chancellor (Hitler) during the first reading of the law: the reconstruction of the state; the recognition of the Catholic and the Protestant confessions as the pillars of the state; and the preservation of the Länder. Kaas's explanation was followed by similar statements from the leading representatives of the other parties that had opposed the Nazis in the past. At 7:30 P.M. the vote took place and the die was cast. Hitler's enabling bill was passed by a majority of 444 to 94. The two-thirds majority required for any constitutional change was met, and this although the Nazi party and its allies in the government represented only 53 percent of the votes in parliament. The 94 "no" votes were cast exclusively by the Social Democratic representatives.

2

The passing of Hitler's enabling bill by the German Reichstag in March 1933 meant termination of the constitutional organs of the Republic and formally marked the end of a constitutional system of democratic representation. In voting for this bill, non-Nazi members of the Reichstag not only relinquished their constitutional authority but also validated, by an act of collective approval, the legitimacy of their own dismissal. Their withdrawal from the political arena went along with an explicit and formal transfer of constitutional rights. Hitler was in effect given a free hand to legally bury the democratic Constitution of Weimar.

The first explanation which comes to mind regarding this event is that political actors do not legitimize their own subservience if they are not coerced to do so. Threats and intimidation thus explain abdication. This claim is a factual one and needs to be assessed accordingly. Regarding March 1933 this argument, on the surface, has considerable merit. Hitler had been at the helm of the state since the end of January 1933. In addition to Hitler, three other National Socialist leaders held ministerial positions in March 1933: Frick supervised the Ministry of the Interior; Göring was minister of aviation and commissarial minister of the interior for Prussia; and after 7 March Goebbels was added to the team, at the head of the Ministry of Propaganda. The three were instrumental in curtailing freedom of the press—the government imposed bans on newspapers that criticized the government too harshly—and in using state repression against political opponents.

The Reichstag fire on 27 February—which the government promptly attributed to a Communist plot—provided Hitler with a political opportunity to increase his arbitrary power. With Hindenburg's seal of approval, on 28 February Hitler issued an emergency decree that suspended basic civil rights and allowed the government to assume the powers of any Land government that proved unable or unwilling to restore public order. Nazi thugs harassed their opponents with seeming impunity. They hoisted the swastika over official buildings, ransacked union and party locals, and jailed and brutalized journalists and politicians who had opposed them in the past. Violence and intimidation suffused the political climate and marked the rapid transition from a formally democratic constitutional setting to an arbitrary and authoritarian political system of rule.

Fear is a convenient explanation of abdication, because it offers a simple, readily available, and commonsensical solution to the problem. Yet the apparent obviousness of the explanation is deceptive. Implicit in the coercion explanation is the notion that threats are naturally effective, that they produce enough fear to incapacitate any attempt at resistance. This assumption is more problematic and paradoxical than it may seem. Groups also decide to resist in the face of coercive pressures, and threats of reprisal sometimes have effects opposite to those intended, yielding cohesion among those under challenge and providing them with a new impetus to resist. In assuming that credible threats are bound to produce fear, one overlooks an intriguing question: When do credible threats produce submission?

The coercion explanation also conceals a paradox. Hitler and his henchmen did not temper their efforts to frighten their opponents in parliament. This observation suggests two interpretations. One is consistent with the coercion explanation and the conclusion that the Nazis were successful: German democrats were fearful of reprisals and coercion worked. The other interpretation points to the paradoxical significance of such threats: Why did the Nazis feel it necessary to exert pressures until the very conclusion of the vote? Why did they invest so much energy in threatening their opponents? Was this not, on their part, an indication that in spite of their threats of reprisal, they had no guarantee about the outcome?

The paradox of coercion is that it often highlights what it attempts to suppress: the possibility of resistance. In relying extensively on threats and intimidation, one acknowledges the irreducible character of the other party's capacity for decision; and the more coercive the threats, the greater the acknowledgment that resistance is a possibility. Ultimately, actors can choose to disregard the threats that are deployed against them. They can decide to challenge the odds. At the final moment, the decision is theirs. That is why acquiescence can never be assumed away as a foregone conclusion. That the threats were quite real in March 1933 cannot account for abdication. Rather, it reminds us that the outcome could have been different.

3

We cannot fully account for this relative indeterminacy without focusing on the moment of the decision. Doing so implies exploring what made these decisions critical from the actors' *own* point of view. Two observations stand out. First, the actors in March 1933 related their decision to their peers'. Witnessing their world crumbling, they turned their eyes to political affiliates expecting them to provide guidance and meaning. Second, uncertainty was pervasive. Commitments and dispositions lacked a firm grounding. Opinions were vacillating. The group did not know where it stood.

The theory of collective alignment developed throughout this inquiry draws a connection between these two observations and conceptualizes them as the defining features of a type of collective conjuncture. Individuals fluctuate because (1) they are concerned about the behavioral stance of those whom they define as peers and (2) they do not know where these peers stand. Individual oscillations are the seismograph of collective perceptions. Their uncertainty fluctuates with the degree of irresolution imputed to the group. Actors are uncertain about themselves because they are uncertain about their peers.

Mutual uncertainty as a result describes a situation in which the members of a group face the same decision, are uncertain about their peers' preferences regarding the decision to be made, and expect to pay a high cost if their action is at odds with the action of the other group members. In this situation individual consequences are interdependent, and action preferences are conditioned by this interdependence. Uncertainty is a key feature of the group situation: individuals realize how difficult it is for them to ascertain their position relative to that of their peers and, as a result, how difficult it is to assess the risks involved. The uncertainty becomes mutual when individuals realize not only that they experience the same state but also that they share this awareness.

In such situations, being mutually aware that they experience the same predicament, individuals realize that they share an interest in forming concordant beliefs about their own collective behavior. For this purpose, they need information about the group's future stance. They can acquire this information in two ways. Through their interpersonal contacts individual actors get pieces of information about one another's behavioral preferences. This information is localized. It constitutes their local knowledge. On the basis of this local knowledge, actors attempt to assess how the group might behave as a whole.

Public statements, for their part, provide actors with information about their own collective preference if they are in a position to interpret these statements as reflecting the group's stance. They tacitly coordinate their expectation about the group by assuming that others share their interpretation. The thrust of the analysis is to explain how they come to this conclusion. I advance the hypothesis that the key to the possibility of such a convergence process is the group's knowledge of the properties of those who take a public stance. This knowledge in turn is conditional on their prominent status.

4

Four concepts provide the analytical moorings of this theoretical framework: alignment, reference group, threshold, and prominence. These conceptual bearings echo one another and set a constellation of functional relations. *Alignment* is the core concept. The argument I have just outlined points to a theory of collective alignment. By alignment I mean the act of making oneself indistinguishable from others. As a collective phenomenon, alignment describes the process whereby the members of a group facing the same decision align their behavior with one another's.

Alignment is *sequential* when actors make their decision after having observed how many others opted for each option. *Local knowledge* prevails when actors rely on the information gathered through face-to-face interactions to assess the preference distribution and likely stance of the group facing the challenge. *Tacit coordination* describes the process whereby actors coordinate their beliefs about the group's future stance by drawing inferences from events that are common knowledge, such as the behavioral stance adopted by prominent actors in a public setting. Group members tacitly coordinate their beliefs about their own collective stance when they are confident that they have reached an informal consensus about themselves. They determine their behavioral preference in light of inferences about the group they assume to be widely shared.

Underlying this threefold category is a basic distinction between behavioral and inferential processes of alignment. Sequential alignment is serial and based on observation. Local knowledge and tacit coordination are inferential mechanisms. These two types are incompatible. Either actors align because their information is perfect—they know that their threshold is met: enough actors have already committed themselves to one stance—or they infer the most plausible outcome and make their choice accordingly. Local knowledge and tacit coordination, on the other hand, may have congruent effects. Therefore the local knowledge and the tacit coordination scenarios are not mutually exclusive. Local knowledge orients individual actors' assessment of the group stance if it helps them reduce their uncertainty. But individuals may also amplify their mutual uncertainty through their interpersonal contacts.

The notion of alignment implies the notion of a reference group. Individual actors determine their behavior by reference to a group. This group can be based on status distinctions or formal criteria of membership, or it can be ad hoc. If it is ad hoc, individuals define the reference in light of the problem that confronts them. In any case, the individual actor actualizes this reference to others in the process of making his decision. His reference group is the collective entity onto which he projects a definition of the situation and from which he derives an interpretive frame for assessing the risks involved.

Both the definition of a reference group and the decision to align a behavioral stance with the stance of other group members point to the notion of "individual threshold." This is the third critical concept. The notion of individual threshold describes an individual actor's propensity to choose one course of action depending on the absolute or relative number of those opting for this line of conduct (Granovetter 1978, 1422). The threshold metaphor captures the image of a tipping phenomenon: this number, or proportion, tips this actor over from one line of conduct to another. It refers, furthermore, to a specific action. For instance, a German parliamentarian's opposition threshold in the context of Hitler's enabling bill is this actor's propensity to cast a "no" vote as a function of the number, or proportion, of the members of his party delegation who choose this line of conduct.

If this propensity is an individual characteristic—i.e., if it reflects a bundle of idiosyncratic features: the actor's sensitivity to risks, his inclination for the different options at hand, and the extent to which he values his affiliation with the group—it is also, as Granovetter (1978, 1436) pointed out, context dependent. An actor's assessment of the risks involved depends on the features of the situation he is experiencing. The terminology of the notion is counterintuitive. An actor whose opposition threshold is high is unwilling to oppose the legal endorsement of a prospective Nazi dictatorship unless a high proportion of those whom he views as his peers oppose this prospect as well. Hence a high opposition threshold means a low individual propensity for opposition.

This brings me to the fourth concept: prominence. Individuals coordinate their stance by forming beliefs about the group which they assume to be commonly shared. The clue to the tacit character of coordination lies in this last clause: actors assume their inferences about the group to be commonly shared. They draw these inferences from events that are common knowledge. In the present case, these events are statements made in a public forum by one or several group members about their own action preference. The key claim is this: statements of this kind *indirectly* shed light on the group's preference when there is ground to believe that the author or authors of the statements make their own stance conditional on that of the group.

Why is prominence so crucial? If the author of the statement is anonymous—I use the feminine to designate this actor—group members have no clue for collectively assessing whether this actor might choose one or the other option depending on the proportion of her peers opting for one line of conduct. In other words, they have no clue for figuring out the value of her action thresholds. If, on the other hand, this actor is prominent, both conditions are no longer a priori problematic. This actor took a stand on multiple issues in the past, either because her group responsibilities compelled her to do so or because she is inclined to take a public stand. These statements generated attention. They had "resonance." They are the source of her prominence.

The more frequent and recent these public stands, the more likely her prominence. Prominence is an individual property that only exists through the beliefs of those who endorse it. A prominent actor enjoys salience in the eyes of her peers. These in turn know it. The record of this prominent actor's past public stands is part of the group's common knowledge. Group members establish her political profile from this record. In addition, they can reasonably believe that the conclusion they draw from this record regarding her present inclination is also widely shared. This last point answers the question. Prominence is crucial because it makes possible the disclosure of threshold values. This disclosure makes alignment cognitively possible.

5

At this point, to avoid any misunderstanding about the status of these theoretical claims, two possible objections need to be discussed. The discussion allows me to outline how historical research and conceptual abstraction, including the type of abstraction that can be transposed in formal terms, can be combined to further their own requirements. The first objection invokes the exceptional character of the case as a pretext to call into question the scope of the argument. In other words, the theory is primarily a theory of the case. Its scope is limited to the confines of the case. The second objection is based in the opposite view. Here the problem is the explanation of the case. In confining the analysis to the moment of decision, we forget about the context. I discuss each objection in turn and, in the process, specify the terms of the dialogue.

To the first objection (the theory is a theory of the case), my response is twofold. First, the empirical investigation unfolded throughout the following chapters probes two paradigmatic cases, not one, of collective alignment. Consider the decision by the National Assembly of the French Third Republic to transfer constitutional authority to Marshal Pétain in July 1940. On the afternoon of 10 July 1940, a great majority of deputies and senators—569 parliamentarians, about 85 percent of those who took part in the vote—endorsed a bill that vested the premier of the time, Marshal Pétain, with full powers, "not merely the full powers by which many 1930's prime ministers had legislated by decree during crises, but explicit authorization to draft a new constitution" (Paxton 1972, 30).

This event is as unique and irreducibly singular as the constitutional devolution of March 1933. Pétain was premier since 17 June 1940. He had been appointed in the midst of a military disaster. With this vote French parliamentarians signed a blank check to him, legalizing their own political ousting and the political collapse of the Republic. The decision was, again, a collective abdication. The next day Pétain abolished the legislative power of the parliament, repealed the constitutional article stipulating that the president of the Republic is to be elected by the National Assembly, and adjourned the existent chambers *sine die*. Political leaders suspected of opposition were arrested two months later. Anti-Semitic decrees were enacted in October 1940. The Vichy regime soon committed itself to a policy of collaboration with Nazi Germany.

Interestingly, as chapters 3–5 outline, the vote of 10 July 1940 elicited explanations similar to those that historians and actors have proposed to account for the Reichstag decision of 23 March 1933: French parliamentarians were fearful of possible reprisals; they were mistaken about the political implications of the bill; and they were ideologically contaminated by an authoritarian zeitgeist that overshadowed the end of the 1930s. These explanations overlook the significance of the event as a moment of initial decisions, and they fail to pay due attention to the actors' uncertainty, their qualms and oscillations.

With the exception of the small clique that actively pushed for passage of the bill, the great majority of those who voted for the power transfer did not want a regime politically aligned with Nazi Germany. The crucial factor underlying the collective abdication of the French National Assembly on 10 July 1940 was not threats, blindness, or ideological propensities but the dynamic of expectation formation that took shape among parliamentarians in Vichy. French parliamentarians endorsed the power transfer when they realized that no one would oppose it. They rationalized their decision by portraying it as the only viable and acceptable course of action.

6

My second response to the objection that the theory is primarily a theory of the case relates to the substance of the theory. Although my empirical focus is on dramatic cases of abdication, the theory elaborated in this book is a theory of collective alignment. This theory applies to a broad class of collective situations and outcomes. The situations are ones in which individuals experience a behavioral dilemma which they assume is shared by others. Similarly, the theory of inferential alignment applies whenever this mutual interdependence translates into mutual uncertainty. The penultimate chapter (chapter 10) demonstrates that these situations are independent of institutional context and group configuration. The argument about processes of collective alignment is therefore not limited to formally defined groups. Nor is it restricted to the parliamentary setting. In this sense, the theory has no time and space. It stands on its own, and needs no empirical referent to set forth its claims and counterclaims.

Because my primary focus is on processes of alignment and their conditional factors, the theoretical framework elaborated in the following chapters provides analytical leads to investigate not only collective abdications but also cases that do not fit the coercion argument, that is, cases in which groups collectively decide to confront coercive pressures, in spite of all indications suggesting that the group will be crushed (e.g., the student uprising in Kwangju, South Korea, in May 1980). Additionally, since this theory of alignment is not conditional on specific group configurations and institutional contexts, it can shed light on abdications that did not have a formal sanction. The universe of investigation is any situation in which one or several groups confront the possibility of collective persecution and have to decide whether to endorse the prospect of abdication. As a result, the theory can account for the apparent willful consent to a dreadful fate.

7

Thus, this book takes as objects of investigation two historical instances of collective abdication: those at the Kroll Opera House in Berlin on 23 March 1933 and at the Grand Casino in Vichy on 10 July 1940. The framework is comparative, but the method is not. My unit of analysis is not the historical case, but the individual actors who partook in the collective decision. The primary focus is on the collective interactions that took place within the time and space referents constituting each event.

But why two events instead of one? And why these two events in particular? The first answer is: historical significance. This point deserves close attention. For now I state my claims in an apodictic fashion. The analytical and empirical underpinnings of these claims will become fully apparent once the inquiry has been completed. That is why I return to the issue in the concluding chapter (chapter 11).

In sanctioning the legality of a new system of political rule, the delegation of constitutional powers to Hitler on 23 March had two significant impacts. First, the legality of the power transfer crucially undermined the prospect of effectively mobilizing against a Nazi takeover of the state. The parliamentary decision of 23 March stated that Hitler now had the right to define the rules of the game, and there was no doubt that these rules would buttress the Nazis' political domination. Second, the parliamentary abdication of 23 March prompted a wave of rallying in support of the new rule. Since the transition was legal, one could expect groups that had always demonstrated their respect for constitutional legality to now acquiesce in the new rule, even though some, such as the German bishops, had opposed Nazism in the past on ideological grounds. Both effects demonstrate the gain in political legitimacy acquired by Hitler in the spring of 1933 and the Nazis' capacity to implement a totalitarian regime within a few months.

Similar observations apply to the political impact of the parliamentary decision of 10 July in Vichy. In the subsequent months no one seriously challenged Pétain's right to establish a regime of personal rule with a strong reactionary ideology. His constitutional mandate authorized him to do so. Political opposition on legal grounds was therefore excluded. Similarly, the decision to initiate a policy of state collaboration with Nazi Germany initially encountered passivity and acquiescence among the former political élite (Baruch 1997, 577–78). Again, people abode by these policy decisions under the assumption that since these decisions emanated from a duly invested ruling élite, they would receive widespread acceptance. The legality of the transition had a legitimizing effect.

The second motivation for an in-depth examination of these two events is their paradigmatic status. The collective decisions of March 1933 and July 1940 lay bare in an exemplary fashion a problem—the problem of collective abdication—that has been overlooked in studies of democratic breakdowns and political transitions. These events are ideal-typical cases: they approximate pure cases of critical decisions in situations of collective and mutual uncertainty. Hence they provide us with a magnifying lens for examining the dynamic of collective interactions that are likely to emerge in such conjunctures. Transition processes are punctuated with confrontation moments of this kind, and—such is my claim—to understand the outcome of these transitions we need to understand the outcome of these confrontation moments.

This conclusion redirects our attention to instances of democratic collapse in which collective abdication was a significant aspect of the transition process. Consider the passing of the "Acerbo bill" by the Italian parliament on 20 April 1923 that granted Mussolini the right to amend the constitution and allowed him to legally take over the Italian state. Or consider the collapse of the Czech Republic in January 1948, or even the granting of full powers to de Gaulle in July 1958, which marked the end of the French Fourth Republic. In all these cases political challenge was intense and uncertainty rife among democrats. At some point, acquiescence and a willingness to compromise with the challenger got the upper hand. I hypothesize that the signals provided by prominent actors through their public behaviors were the key to consensus formation and political alignment.

The point is not confined to political breakdowns in the modern age. In July 1672, in a context of military disaster and popular unrest, the representative assembly of the Dutch Republic (the States-General) granted full powers to the Prince of Orange and endowed him with the title of military commander, or Stadholder (Geyl 1964, 128). William's appointment did not give him the equivalent of a Roman dictatorship: it was not meant to be a temporary arrangement motivated by military emergency. The appointment implied a transformation of "the structure of power" (Israel 1995, 802)—a reallocation of powers among groups competing for the control of the state. At the time of the transfer, the military situation was dire: the Dutch Republic was at war with France and England. The armies of Louis XIV occupied three of the seven provinces of the Republic. There is no doubt that the emergency loomed large in the republican representatives' decision. But it is also worth asking why the republican representatives endorsed the prospect of a state infused with a monarchical principle of sovereignty.

Nor is the argument confined to transitions from democracies to dictatorships. Several moments punctuated the process that led to the rapid demise of socialist regimes in Eastern Europe in 1989. At these critical junctures, the members of the ruling élite faced an intractable choice: either reassert the primacy of socialist rule or open the door to a possible regime transformation (Pfaff 2006, chapter 7). The challenge was extreme and each option bore considerable risks. Again, if we follow the analysis developed here, we would expect the members of the ruling élite to have striven to overcome the strategic dilemma they faced by forming mutual beliefs about their future behaviors. An interesting question is the extent to which the public stances adopted by the state leadership influenced this process of belief formation.

8

There remains the issue of context. For the practice of historical research and the ethos of the discipline the issue is critical. Abstracting the event from its historical context is a crucial mistake. The discipline of history, as we are reminded by Goldthorpe (1991, 212), following E. P. Thompson, is "the discipline of context." In narrowing the focus down to the actors' experience of the decision process, am I breaching the ethos of the discipline?

But what is the "context"? Are we talking about diffused ideological beliefs, the legacy of past and current conflicts, the structure of social relations, or political institutions? Most often, we mean all of these bundled together. As a result, we do not mean much. Intuitively, the "context" refers to factors beyond the reach of individual actors, factors which define actors' understanding of the realm of the possible and from which they derive schemas of interpretation, implicit or not, that help them to assess others' behaviors as well as their own behavioral choices. The contextual quality of these factors lies in their collective significance. Actors get enmeshed in these beliefs and presuppositions often because they impute them to others. This collective makeup is essential to a shared sense of possibility and constraint.

This definition has methodological implications. Lurking in the back of the reference to the context is a call for a historical anthropology of collective representations that can capture the specificity of collective motives and beliefs. If we take this methodological imperative seriously, the only way to pin down the "context" is to examine how actors collectively define the situations they experience, which presuppositions they mobilize for this purpose, how they reconsider their beliefs if at all, and whether this subjective process affects their behavioral stances. I identify three realms of possible contextual factors inherited from the long run and the immediate circumstances: institutional constraints and organizational resources, the structure of political conflicts, and ideological beliefs.

To what extent do the institutional and organizational characteristics of the setting in which actors interact constrain their capacity for coordination? Do patterns of cleavages, antagonisms, and alliances that have endured over time structure the way in which groups assess the tactical options available? Is there ground to believe that shared ideological categories shape actors' political doxa to the point of determining which strategic options they deem thinkable? Institutions, conflicts, and ideology, broadly defined as contextual factors, are causally significant if they are motivationally relevant, that is, if they provide information and schemata of interpretation which individuals deem relevant to their dilemma and decision. Assessing this relevance requires examining actors in the process of making their decision. For this purpose I reconstitute actions, interactions, webs of subjective beliefs, and assess which beliefs were behaviorally of consequence.

The surprising observation emerging from this analysis is how little impact these different factors have on actors' ultimate decisions. A pervasive sense of indeterminacy lingers throughout these meetings. This indeterminacy reflects actors' mutual uncertainty. Those who go through this uncertainty de facto agree to make their choice conditional. As they realize that their peers have no firm preferences, they decide to leave their choice in abeyance until an informal consensus takes hold of it and decides for them. Mutual uncertainty thus prevails, independent of the organizational context. For as I outline in chapter 7, German and French parliamentarians confront their dilemma in significantly different institutional and organizational settings. Party delegations in the Reichstag are clearly defined and display strong behavioral cohesion. The parliamentary setting of the French Third Republic is made up of loosely defined affiliation groups.

These contrasting organizational and institutional contexts have different implications for patterns of interactions. Whereas the German delegates primarily met with the members of their own affiliation group, French parliamentarians were involved in out-group ties. As a result, the configuration of reference groups is different across these two events. For German parliamentarians, the reference group is the party delegation. For French parliamentarians, the Assembly as a whole emerges as a reference group "by default," partly produced by the circumstances. Given this major difference in the organizational configuration of interpersonal ties, we would expect individuals in the more "structured" environment to rely more on the prospect of coordination and to be less subject to the mutual character of their uncertainty.

Nothing indicates that this was so. True, the German delegates met with this expectation in mind. Nonetheless, the sense of the dilemma overwhelmed them as the decision moment came closer and as they realized how much of their political ethos they would be giving away through their acquiescence. French parliamentarians for their part were at a loss to figure out whether coordination would effectively take place given the organizational breakdown of their affiliation group. The scope of their uncertainty had less clear-cut boundaries. Still, it crucially undermined their resolution and motivated their wait-and-see stance. The broader observation suggested by this comparative insight is that the type of challenge imposed upon actors shapes how group members define and frame the situation beyond institutional and organizational factors (chapter 10).

9

This brings me to the issue of sources. The theory that I develop in this book encompasses three hypothetical scenarios: sequential alignment, local knowledge, and tacit coordination. We cannot differentiate these scenarios in light of their outcome. All three can in theory produce unanimity or quasi-unanimity. Thus the focus should be on the processes of decision making and on the behavioral indicators differentiating these processes. Sequential alignment prevails when actors react to group-level indicators that reveal levels of commitment. Alternatively, these actors rely on their local knowledge if they pay primary attention to the information conveyed by interpersonal contacts. They engage in tacit coordination when they relate to their peers indirectly, in the process of acknowledging the revealing quality of their statement.

To probe the empirical soundness of these different hypotheses, we need a kind of evidence documenting actors' subjective states as they make their decision. Only actors, those who were involved, can provide us with evidence of that kind. Consequently, the data basis that I constituted for the purpose of this inquiry incorporates multiple sources: (1) contemporary accounts whatever their format (diaries, letters, published articles, explanations of votes before an audience), (2) published memoirs, (3) unpublished accounts, (4) verbal testimonies before a jury or inquiry commission, and (5) written accounts requested by a jury or a commission. In addition, I draw on information provided by witnesses and informants who were in close contacts with those who took part in these decisions. Appendix A offers a synoptic overview of these sources. Depending on the group under consideration, the data bases of personal testimonies constituted for each case represent between 20 percent and 30 percent of the reference population.

These sources vary considerably in terms of format and length. Some are a few handwritten notes scribbled on a piece of paper. Others are letters, diaries, accounts and memoirs. The time of their production also differs widely: some were written at the time of the event, others a few hours afterward, still others months later. This heterogeneity can be a liability or a resource. It is a liability if the sources are not comparable. It is a resource if it provides multiple points of entry to probe the empirical soundness of alternative hypotheses. Appendix A further elaborates this point. I draw on actors' accounts for different heuristic and demonstrative purposes, depending on their timing and formal characteristics. Contemporary accounts such as letters and diaries are very helpful to debunk ex post rationalizations. Accounts, whether retrospective or contemporary, that have a full-fledged narrative structure not only highlight fine-grained factual observations but also situate them in a chronological temporality that is critical to assessing a behavioral mode versus an inferential mode of alignment.

10

As the preceding remarks make clear, this book researches historical processes as much as it elaborates theoretical claims about decision making and collective interactions. To this end, it incorporates different levels of analysis and different interpretive idioms. Drawing on a range of analytical tools—formal, quantitative, and hermeneutic—applied to a variety of historical sources, I combine these interpretive idioms within and across individual chapters. This dialogue across genres is geared to greater analytical specificity for the purpose of investigating the complexity of the cases. In the process, both theory and history gain in intelligibility and leverage. The benefits derived from an immersion in complex cases through an engagement with theoretical claims abstract enough to lend themselves to formal formulations set the terms and requirements of this dialogue.

The specifics of historical cases compel formal theory to tackle research questions that initially fall outside its purview. Consider the issue of reference groups. As I document in chapter 7, actors bereft of a behavioral script gauge the extent of their mutual interdependence and their uncertainty as they interact through interpersonal contacts. The question then is how they construct their beliefs about the group given this awareness. This question calls for analyzing the relational configuration of reference groups and draws attention to the cognitive makeup of belief formation. These dimensions go beyond models of interactions cast in strategic terms. In this respect, an immersion in the maze of historical processes from the participants' point of view expands the realm of inquiry of decision theory.

A close scrutiny of the dynamics of collective processes that seeks to document the subjective and interactive dimensions of these processes—in the same way that ethnography seeks to document the dispositions of the subjects—contributes to refining theoretical explorations in another respect. The close-up draws attention to conditional factors, at the level of groups and institutions. In the present instance it is because the circumstances of the vote were dramatic that they offer a particularly vivid image of how individuals deal with a decision-making problem characterized by choice interdependence and high potential costs. The critical character of the decision provides a magnifying lens through which to explore the factors conditioning different "logics of the situation" (Popper 1961, 149) when the members of a group experience mutual uncertainty.

Conversely, formal theory enhances our historical understanding of collective processes by furthering the search for specificity. Here the input is twofold. For one thing, the formal lenses of decision theory help interrogate broad explanatory categories which we often use out of convenience, from a synoptic and stylized point of view, because their meaning seems quite obvious. Ideology and coercion are prime examples (chapters 3 and 5). In inviting us to examine how these categories translate in terms of actors' dispositions, schemes of representation, and motivations, formal theory hones our attention to the "noise" of history, these apparent "small" details that actually can carry considerable analytical weight and historical significance. In addition, the focus on decision parameters restores the range of actors' subjective orientations toward their future. I reconstruct the temporality of these subjective orientations to elucidate the dynamics of collective abdication in two subsequent chapters (chapters 8 and 9).

Formal modeling serves a second methodological purpose. To reconstruct an actor's subjective orientations, I use a type of evidence produced by the actor herself (memoirs, letters, personal testimonies, narrative accounts), and as a result bound to remain fragmentary, sometimes contradictory, or truncated. One way to deal with this problem is to employ the historian's critical method: examine the evidence in the same way a judge probes the exhibits of a case, juxtaposes testimonies one against the other, situates their authors, and identifies possible motives for falsification. Another way to confront the incomplete character of this evidence is to relate it to formal insights about possible logics of action.

Insights developed deductively provide not only antidotes to the historicist bias inherent to any retrospective analysis but also indications about which bits of information to seek. They provide a grid of reading which can help uncover clues that go unnoticed in a literal reading, clues which often actors provide incidentally, in passing, without being aware of their causal significance. As I will show throughout this inquiry and as I point out in Appendix A, personal statements say much more than their authors assume.

11

The following chapters accordingly call into question a strict division between theory and empirics. Each tackles an analytical issue and weaves empirical observations. Chapter 1 provides a chronological account from afar and poses the problem of historical significance. Probing the legal architecture of the bills submitted to the German and French parliaments, chapter 2 defines the problem of abdication. These two chapters set the stage. A group of actors abdicates when these actors collectively relinquish their capacity to defend themselves and formally acknowledge this incapacity. In explicitly depriving themselves of the right of self-defense, these actors legitimize their future subservience.

Part II of the book discusses three commonsensical explanations of collective subservience — explanations that relate collective abdications to either the fear of retaliation, misjudgment, or ideological contamination. Showing that these prevailing explanations are either incomplete or misleading, the analysis calls for greater specificity. The first explanation presumes that credible threats and, more broadly, coercive pressures necessarily produce subservience. Consequently, this interpretation cannot account for collective resistance in the face of credible threats of persecution (chapter 3). The explanation, that abdication is based in misjudgment, takes actors' most common retrospective justification at face value — they had not fully realized what the stakes were — thereby obfuscating the extent to which the actors experienced their decision as a dilemma *at the time of the decision* (chapter 4). As for the ideological collusion explanation, it obfuscates the extent to which actors realize that in abdicating they relinquish basic values (chapter 5).

Underlying these three interpretations is a similar conception of historical causality — one that shares some of the basic postulates of what Abbott (1988, 169) has termed the "general linear model": a conception of the social world as made up of broad causal entities, the assumption that big events can only be produced by big causes and the absence of sequence effects. The starting point is a contextual variable: the balance of power between two or several groups (coercion), collectively shared misrepresentations (miscalculation), or pervasive ideological affinities (ideological collusion). This variable summarizes the context and affects the group as a whole, thereby producing individual propensities to choose one option or the other. Typical in this regard is the coercion argument. Pressures and intimidation "act" on people in the same way an external force would act on a material object. Fear is the outcome. It comes to dominate the group and determine collective behavior. In this framework, individual actions are the translation of broad exogenous factors.

The argument developed in parts III and IV builds on and expands this critique. In part III, I lay out an explanatory framework accounting for both acquiescence *and* opposition (chapter 6), and I probe the empirical sound-ness of the behavioral alignment hypothesis (chapter 7). Chapter 6 presents the core hypotheses of the theory in light of the empirical observations pre-sented so far. This chapter specifies the general class of collective decisions (of which the constitutional challenges of March 1933 and July 1940 are two spe-cific instances), presents the notion of individual threshold, conceptualizes the notion of reference group, distinguishes between the three types of alignment processes that I outlined above (sequential alignment, local knowledge, tacit coordination), and defines prominence.

The class of decision that I am considering has two main features. First, the decision is risky. Individuals face options the consequences of which can be extremely costly. Second, whichever option is chosen, isolation is the worst possible outcome. This means that publicly disclosing one's preferences is also risky. In this situation the members of the group under challenge face imper-fect information and, to the extent that they remain trapped by it, experience uncertainty. Given the terms of the challenge, they seek to overcome their un-certainty by aligning their line of conduct with that of their peers. I elaborate the distinction between behavioral (i.e. sequential) mechanisms of alignment and inferential ones (i.e. local knowledge and tacit coordination). For this purpose I draw on the concepts of reference groups and individual thresholds. One contribution of this analysis is to highlight the factors conditioning the likelihood of each process.

Chapter 7 examines the extent of sequential alignment and raises the issue of the relevant reference group for making this assessment. I show that when German and French parliamentarians confronted their decision, they referred their stance not to their constituents but to those whom they identified as their parliamentary peers. In Berlin the parliamentarians' reference group was the members of their party delegation. In Vichy parliamentary delegations col-lapsed from an organizational point of view and parliament as a whole be-came the reference group. The empirical examination allows me to consider whether in the process of interacting with one another, actors converged on a similar assessment of the situation. The upshot of this analysis is paradoxical in light of the sequential alignment argument: interpersonal interactions, far from assuaging actors' qualms and hesitations, led them to realize the mutual character of their uncertainty.

Part IV narrows the focus down on inferential mechanisms. Inquiring into the twists and turns of actors' subjective assessments, I delve into the tempo-rality of the interactive process. Chapter 8 documents the emergence of a col-lective stance in favor of acquiescence among the Center party parliamentary delegates. Two factual observations stand out in this account. First, the context of the delegation meetings in Berlin brought these actors' sense of dilemma to the fore. Second, the Center party delegates resolved their mutual uncertainty in light of the behavioral cues provided by their most prominent peers. Chapter 9 lays bare widespread collective oscillations among French parliamentarians in Vichy and traces these oscillations back to the public statements of highly visible members of parliament.

Part V addresses the issues of scope and significance. In chapter 10 I examine the extent to which the theory of collective alignment discussed in this book is indebted to the specifics of the two paradigmatic cases providing the empirical leads. I show that the peculiar characteristics of these events magnify processes we might otherwise overlook, and that they help us further our understanding of preference instability and ambivalence. Chapter 11 reconsiders the issue of historical significance from the broader point of view of the theory of collective alignment. I expand the scope of the argument by conceptualizing these events as public statements delivered by a collective actor in a situation in which groups have to decide which line of conduct they should adopt vis-à-vis the powers that be. The event is significant because as a public statement, it elicits shared expectations about acquiescence.

The primary focus of these chapters is on rank-and-file group members. Actors who enjoy prominence, as I define the term in chapter 6, face strategic constraints different from those of their rank-and-file colleagues as a result of their prominent status. Explaining their stance requires additional hypotheses. In terms of length, analytical qualifications, and evidence, the discussion of these hypotheses is beyond the scope of this book. As a result, this analysis will be the subject of a subsequent inquiry.

A brief note on organization and design: in the course of this inquiry, I go back to the same facts and events several times, each time with a different lens in hand. This design — which departs from the convention of narrative exposition and, in this respect, is peculiar — translates in formal terms the interdisciplinary character of this inquiry. It also reflects the requirements set by the blending of different research idioms, and acknowledges the complexity of its object. As the previous considerations make clear, I put different accounts of abdication to the test. These accounts belong to different disciplinary genres. They often differ with regard to the factual observations deemed worthy of analytical attention. They also differ in terms of scales. The greater the scope, the greater the scale: single claims bundle many processes and actors at once. Hence the greater the scope, the lower the magnifying effect of the lens used to this effect. Conversely, the lower the scope, the greater the visibility.

This explains why I adopt different lenses depending on which explanation

I put to the test. I adjust the level of specificity, and hence the lens, to the type of argument being considered. I start with the least magnifying lens of factual narrative in terms of regime breakdown. I end with the most magnifying lens in identifying interactions and subjective states. Similarly, I document inter-active processes from different angles, combining a quantitative assessment with a phenomenological inquiry. In procedural terms, both approaches stand far apart. Most often they defiantly look at each. In the present case, thick descriptions and quantitative analyses converge on the same assessment and outline the significance of tacit coordination.

ACKNOWLEDGMENTS

Over the past few years I have been very fortunate to benefit from the crucial support of several people. I would like to express my gratitude to them.

This inquiry originated in a dissertation defended at the Department of Sociology of the University of Chicago. I am particularly thankful to the four members of the dissertation committee—Andrew Abbott, Adam Przeworski, William Sewell, and George Steinmetz, who chaired this committee—for the opportunity to engage in an interdisciplinary dialogue that was as inspiring as it was formative. I owe special thanks to George Steinmetz for his staunch support and to David Laitin for providing references and advice and for creating, conjointly with George Steinmetz, the opportunity of the Wilder House weekly workshops. It is at the Wilder House that I presented the first outline of what was at the time a bare research project. I am also very grateful to Jim Fearon for taking the time to read portions of the dissertation and for providing comments. While at Chicago I was the recipient of a ssrc dissertation fellowship and a Wilder House/CASPIC MacArthur fellowship, which allowed me to do research abroad and complete the dissertation.

The second institution which provided considerable help and resources for the nitty-gritty of research work is Nuffield College at Oxford University, where I was Prize Research Fellow for eighteen months in 1997–99. The college granted me the time and resources to investigate more archival material in Germany and France and to reexamine the architecture of my argument about collective alignments. I want to thank in particular Tony Atkinson, the warden of Nuffield College, for his constant support—especially for organizing the conference on democratic stability in May 1999; Robert Gildea, for agreeing to be the discussant of the paper that I presented at this conference; and Michael Bacharach, Duncan Gallie, Diego Gambetta, Roberto Franzosi, Ian McLean, Gerry Mackie, and Federico Varese, for their warm welcome and our numerous discussions.

I wrote the manuscript while in Madison. Interacting with faculty members and students in sociology there has been extremely rewarding in many respects, because of the democratic spirit that pervades the place, the intellectual vividness of the seminars and the attention to hard-nosed empirical research. Through salary support during the summer of 2003 and a very generous Vilas Young Investigator Award, the College of Letters and Science and the Research Committee of the Graduate School at the University of Wisconsin provided key financial support to complete archival work. James Montgomery, Pam Oliver, and Erik Olin Wright provided written comments from which I greatly benefited. I am very grateful to Chas Camic, Mitch Duneier, Mustafa Emirbayer, Adam Gamoran, Phil Gorski, Chuck Halaby, Doug Maynard, Alberto Palloni, Joel Rogers, Gay Seidman, and Larry Wu for their support, and to the students of Erik Wright's seminar, who in the fall of 2002 read several chapters and through their perceptive remarks generated a very fruitful seminar session. My late colleague Steve Bunker had been incomparably friendly since my arrival in Madison, and I have a vivid memory of the time spent in the company of him and his wife Dena Wortzel.

At different stages of this research I was invited to present aspects of my work to various audiences whose questions have always been helpful: the University of Bielefeld (Zentrum für interdisziplinäre Forschung, Bielefeld, October 1998), the Marc Bloch Center in Berlin (January 1999), the Seminar on Theories of Groups at Oxford University (St Johns College, May 1999), the École des Hautes Études en Sciences Sociales at the Vieille Charité in Marseille (June 1999), the University of Chicago (Comparative Politics Workshop, February 2001), Columbia University (Historical Dynamic Workshop, November 2001), the Center for European Studies in Madison (November 2003), the Pierre Mendès France University in Grenoble (Sociology Department, June 2004), and Yale University (Comparative Politics Workshop, December 2004).

This inquiry is based on research in numerous national and local archives in Germany, France, and the United States. For their helpfulness I wish to thank the archivists of the Hoover Institution Archives in Stanford, the Archiv für Christlich-Demokratische Politik, Konrad-Adenauer-Stiftung (Sankt-Augustin), the Archiv der sozialen Demokratie der Friedrich-Ebert-Stiftung (Bonn), the Bundesarchiv (Koblenz), the Haupstaatsarchiv in Stuttgart, the Historisches Archiv of the city of Cologne, the Institut für Zeitgeschichte in Munich, the Kommission für Zeitgeschichte in Bonn, the Archives of the city of Paris, the French National Archives (CHAN, Paris), the Bibliothèque Nationale, the Fondation Nationale des Sciences Politiques (Paris), the Office Universitaire de Recherche Socialiste (OURS, Paris), the Musée Historique Henri

Queuille (Neuvic, Corrèze), and the Archives Départementales of Aude (Carcassonne), Charente (Angoulême), Charente-Maritime (La Rochelle), Corrèze (Tulle), Isère (Grenoble), Finistère (Quimper), Rhône (Lyon), Sarthe (Le Mans), and Seine-Maritime (Rouen). I am thankful to Doris and Wolfgang Lauff for their kindness and hospitality during my numerous visits to the Bundesarchiv in Koblenz.

The comments I got from two anonymous reviewers through Duke University Press were exemplary for their relevance and willingness to seriously engage the claims elaborated in this book. I would like to express my deep thanks to Julia Adams and George Steinmetz for their written comments, and for the meeting they organized with the editorial board at the University of Michigan in Ann Arbor in March 2003. I also want to thank Reynolds Smith, the acquisitions editor at Duke for the social sciences, for his confidence in the project and most particularly Julia Adams for her enthusiasm, insights, and commitment. I was very fortunate to have received cogent and precise comments on the final manuscript from William Patch of Washington and Lee University and to benefit from his expert knowledge of the Center party, the Christian Trade Unions, Heinrich Brüning, and, more broadly, contemporary European history. The preparation of the index was a collaborative affair, to which Matthew Dimick contributed with diligence and competence.

Florence Vatan's perceptive critiques and comments throughout these years were of immeasurable assistance. As this book came close to its final version, she very carefully read the whole manuscript and, with her usual incisiveness, made very pointed remarks about specific arguments. Max and Tonio, our two sons, did not hesitate to ask sound, irreverent, probing, skeptical, nagging, joyful, and punned questions when necessary. I bow before their joie de vivre.

A NOTE ON CITATIONS

For this type of inquiry, primary sources (produced by actors themselves) have a very different status from historiographical accounts or theoretical references. To avoid confusion about the type of source being quoted and to allow readers to figure out which type of evidence is being adduced, I use the following convention. When I quote a primary source, whether archival or published, I cite the reference in a note. For published personal accounts, I indicate the author's last name, the title of the book or booklet, and the page number: Blum, *A l'échelle humaine*, 83. For personal statements and items that remain unpublished, I indicate the institution where this archival source is held, the city, and the name of the archive—whether personal or administrative—and identify the document. For instance: Kommission für Zeitgeschichte, Bonn, Tagebuchaufzeichnungen von Clara Siebert, 94. I identify all references to published historiographical monographs and, more broadly, academic references *in the text* by last name of author, year of publication, and pagination when appropriate.

All translations are mine unless otherwise noted.

PART I

The Stage and the Problem

Chapter 1

Actors and Events

When shall we start? Events are nominal constructs. Their referents are bundles of actions and decisions that analysts and commentators abstract from the flow of historical time. This abstraction is based on a variety of criteria—temporal contiguity, causal density, and significance for subsequent happenings—routinely mobilized by synthetic judgments about the past. Because events are temporal constructs, their temporal boundaries can never be taken for granted. They take on different values depending on whether we derive these boundaries from the subjective statements left by contemporary actors (Bearman et al. 1999) or construct them in light of an analytical relevance criterion derived from the problem at hand (Sewell 1996, 877).

This last point—causal time has different temporalities depending on our analytical agenda—comes out with particular force in the present case. If we approach March 1933 and July 1940 as instances of regime breakdown, a plausible option is to take the chronology of the political regimes as temporal referents. If we construct them as parliamentary events, the temporal setting of legislatures provides a lead. If we define them primarily as collective decisions, causal time is likely to be harnessed to the interactive processes underlying the decision. Different conceptual definitions induce different empirical foci and different temporalities. The narrower the focus, the narrower the scope that we might impute to the temporal frame.

This correlation is only indicative. Depending on which aspect of collective interactions we conceptualize as causally relevant, this temporal scope can substantially shrink or expand. Consider the appraisal by Maier (1972, 193) of the vote by the Center parliamentary delegation on 23 March 1933 as a "belated post-scriptum" (*ein spätes Postskriptum*) to the cultural conflict between German Catholics and the central state inaugurated by Bismarck's antichurch policies in 1871 (Kulturkampf). If we endorse this appraisal, the adequate historical chronology, which allows us to comprehend March 1933, overflows the political context of the 1930s and more broadly the temporal setting of Weimar. Historical analyses that place primary emphasis on actors' belief systems in the reconstruction of political developments often adopt such a grand scale as they unfold their explanatory narrative (Sontheimer 1962; Mosse 1964; Sternhell 1996).

In the following chronological exposition I leave open the choice of a temporal frame. My points of departure are arbitrary: the presidential election of 1932 and the outbreak of war in September 1939. These starting points do not prejudge the definition of an adequate temporality; I will discuss this issue subsequently, in chapter 11, after having explored the collective and structural facets of the events under consideration. In this chapter these chronological points of entry serve expositional purposes. I introduce the actors and the stage. Some of those introduced are collective actors (parties, unions, social groups). Others hold key state positions (presidents, chancellors, premiers, ministers).

This chapter also tackles the significance of these events. In the present case, significance can be assessed from different, and not necessarily complementary, standpoints. One is heuristic. The event lays bare processes and causal mechanisms that we usually do not observe with such distinctive clarity. It has a revealing or magnifying quality. The other standpoint is historical. Here "significant" equates to "having consequences." This definition builds on an insight by Sewell (1996, 262): events transform structures. Herein lies their specificity as temporal happenings and their *sub specie* quality as historical events. From this perspective, the significance of an event is commensurate with its impact on structures and subsequent historical developments.

THE GERMAN CATASTROPHE

I consider groups involved in processes of political contention as well as actors who because of their position in the state apparatus have substantial decisional power and influence. Some groups—political parties, unions, and duly organized interest groups—can be formally constituted. The organizational emergence of these groups can be traced to a founding act. Others do not have this organizational visibility. They are not regulated by explicit charters and formal rules of membership. Yet actors constantly use them as referential categories to make sense of their political interactions and social relations. These groups define principles of collective and motivational identities. Actors identify themselves and others in light of this classification scheme. The imputation of group identities onto others goes along with assumptions of shared interests, common understandings, and group solidarity.

The landed aristocracy in Germany in the 1930s is a case in point. Since the last third of the nineteenth century, this social group had been breeding a class of high-ranked civil servants (Carsten 1990, 120). Although their world-view was closer to bourgeois and modern values than their social background would suggest (Steinmetz 1993, 104–7), these actors often defined themselves by reference to the landowning aristocracy, and members of other classes defined them in these terms. Marshall Hindenburg, the president of the Republic since 1925, was the Junker par excellence. He was Prussian, a landowner, full of the social prejudices of his class, and a great soldier, the hero of the battle of Tannenberg. In 1932 Hindenburg stood for a second presidential mandate. The election was scheduled for March (first round) and April (second round).

In the constitutional framework of the Weimar Republic, the president has considerable power. He is elected for a seven-year term through a popular vote (Articles 41 and 43). He "appoints and dismisses the chancellor of the Reich and, on the latter's recommendation, the Ministers of the Reich" (Article 53).[1] By virtue of Article 25, he alone has the right to dissolve parliament (the Reichstag). No provision prevents him from dismissing the chancellor, even if the chancellor has the confidence of the parliament (Finn 1991, 145). Consequently he can circumvent legislative control through the expedient of dissolution. Article 48 authorizes him to "take the required measures to reestablish public safety and order when in the Reich public safety and order are greatly disturbed or endangered" and to resort to armed force if necessary.[2] When this happens the parliament's room to maneuver is limited to demanding a revocation of emergency action. Given these decisional and political prerogatives, the election of the president was a major political event.

An Embattled Stage

The first ballot of the presidential election took place on 13 March. It pitted Hindenburg against Thälmann, the chairman of the Communist party; Duesterberg, nominated by the nationalist Right; and Hitler. When Hindenburg bade for a presidential mandate seven years earlier, in 1925, the leadership of the Social Democratic Party vigorously opposed him, depicting him as the instrument of social reaction. In March 1932 Social Democrats endorsed him with the slogan "smash Hitler, vote Hindenburg" (Harsch 1993, 179). This shift in position was a direct consequence of the threat that Hitler had posed to the Republic since September 1930. Two years earlier the Nazis were a "negligible

1. *Verfassungsgesetze* 1926, 22.
2. Ibid.

quantity" (Heiber 1993, 158). Between 1924 and 1928 they won less than 3 percent of the popular vote at the national level. The parliamentary elections of 14 September 1930 were a political cataclysm. Getting 18 percent of the popular vote, the Nazi party swept "into the mainstream of German politics" (Childers 1983, 140) and became the second-largest party in parliament (107 seats) after the Social Democratic party (143 seats).

Although preceding elections at the regional level in 1930 had signaled that the Nazis would make significant electoral gains, the electoral takeoff of September 1930 dumbfounded contemporary observers. The Nazis had been political outcasts for years. They were now major political players. This outcome could never have been achieved without the political alliance forged in 1929 with the mainstream nationalist Right against the Young plan — a redrafting of Germany's reparation payment. At the initiative of the press magnate Alfred Hugenberg, who had been elected a few months earlier (October 1928) at the head of the German National People's Party (Deutschnationale Volkspartei, or DNVP), several right-wing organizations (the Stahlhelm, the Landvolk party, the German League, and the Nazi party) formed a Reich Committee for the German Referendum against the Young Plan in July 1929. Through their association with this committee Hitler and his party gained not only considerable visibility but also credentials of political respectability on which they capitalized first in regional elections and then, in a spectacular fashion, at the parliamentary elections in September 1930.

When Hindenburg was making a bid for a second presidential mandate in March 1932, the threat posed by the radical Right to the Republic had become so formidable that Hindenburg was now the Republic's bulwark. The Right-Left cleavage does not fully capture the political significance of the presidential contest of March 1932. The political landscape was fragmented into three antagonistic blocs and a host of less easily identified splinter and regional parties. On the far right stood the national opposition, ideologically and dogmatically opposed to the Republic and parliamentary democracy in the name of radical nationalism. Two main parties carried the flag: the German National People's Party and the Nazi party.

The German Nationalists were the heirs of the conservative parties from the imperial era pre-1914 (Wilhelmine Germany). One wing of the party opposed any compromise with the Republic; the other was ready to adopt a constructive opposition stance and to participate in forming republican governments (Neumann 1965 [1932], 61). German Nationalists identified with the counter-revolution in the 1920s. Between 1924 and 1928, as the regime stabilized, they played the game of parliamentary politics, taking part in two coalition cabinets (in 1925 and 1928) and voting a watered-down version of the law for protecting the republic (1927). Hugenberg's election at the head of the party (in October 1928) marked the political revival of dogmatic opposition to the Republic.

Hugenberg's political efforts to rally the radical Right under the banner of the national opposition culminated in the organization of a mass meeting in Bad Harzburg on 11 October 1931. The list of those who participated in this demonstration offers a useful indication of the spectrum of forces that at the end of 1931 united in an uncompromising offensive against the republican regime. In addition to the German Nationalists, those attending included the Stahlhelm (an association of ex-servicemen), the Nazis, representatives of the pan-German movement, agrarian members of the Reichslandbund, and a handful of industrialists, as well as two former members of the high administration: von Seeckt, former minister of war and now deputy of the German People's Party (Deutsche Volkspartei), and Schacht, former president of the Reichsbank (Feuchtwanger 1993, 257). The meeting did not have the impact that Hugenberg reckoned it to have, but Hitler did make a strong showing, getting most of the public attention. Furthermore, the two parties failed to agree on a common candidacy for the presidential election to take place a few months later.

The Constitutionalist Camp

Opposed to the radical and antidemocratic Right formed by the Nazis and the German Nationals were three main constitutionalist parties. They rallied behind Hindenburg in the presidential election of March 1932 and remained strongly committed to the Republic: the Social Democrats, the German State party (Deutsche Staatspartei, or DStP), and the Center party (Zentrum). The Social Democratic Party (Sozialdemokratische Partei Deutschlands, or SPD) had made the defense of the republican regime and parliamentary democracy one of its political priorities since September 1930. A few days after the results of the elections that month, the Social Democratic deputation announced that "the threat posed to democracy directly by the fascists and indirectly by the Communists required that the SPD's first concern be to secure democracy, constitutional government, and parliament" (Harsch 1993, 86). Their endorsement of Hindenburg's candidacy to a second mandate was explicitly motivated by the goal to avoid splitting the republican vote and, in doing so, to bar Hitler from the road to the presidency (Harsch 1993, 179).

At the center-left stood the German State party. The state party played a role in the foundation of Weimar. Its members and leading representatives were bourgeois democrats and liberals (Jones 1988, 377). They reached their greatest electoral gains in January 1919 with a little less than 19 percent of the popular vote. From then on, their political significance constantly declined, reaching 3.8 percent of the popular vote in September 1930. State party representatives clearly identified with the Republic and consistently denounced Nazism.

The third pillar of the Weimar Republic in the 1930s was the Center party. The party was born in the context of rising anticlericalism soon before the Kulturkampf—the struggle over cultural policy that pitted the political and religious representatives of German Catholics against Chancellor Bismarck in the 1870s (Kalyvas 1996, 210–13). As a consequence of the conditions that prevailed during its creation, the Center historically viewed the defense of German Catholics' interests as its primary political mission. However, it did not define itself as a confessional party and one could not correctly define it as such (Neumann 1965 [1932], 43). Significantly, after the war, the Center leadership contemplated acquiring the new name of Christian People's party (Christliche Volkspartei) to assert its identity as an all-encompassing party (Bracher 1970, 72). The Center was a conglomerate of social groups and political factions, some leaning to the conservative Right, others to the democratic Left (Neumann 1965 [1932], 42, 44).

In the 1920s the defense of the Weimar constitution was a staple of political Catholicism. The national Center party manifest of 1927 explicitly endorsed the principle of republican institutions (Neumann 1965 [1932], 48). Several of its prominent members were "republicans from reason" (Vernunftrepublikaner) who through the course of the Republic's troubled history became strongly committed to parliamentary democracy (Cary 1996, 131). When in the 1930s the threat posed to republican institutions by the radical Right became ominous, this commitment took a more dramatic turn. Center members opposed Nazism not only because it was anti-Christian and inhumane, but also because the Nazi movement threatened the Republic (Dirks 1969, 9).

Three Blocs

The political stance taken by the Communist leadership in the 1930s adds an additional line of cleavage to the conflict between the national opposition and the constitutionalist camp. The party system was primarily divided between three blocs: the authoritarian, the democratic, and the communist (Lepsius 1978, 36). The Communist party (Kommunistische Partei Deutschlands, or KPD) was engaged in "no less implacable a struggle against the Republic than were antidemocratic forces on the far-right" (Peukert 1992, 268). The sixth congress of the Comintern held in Moscow in July–September 1928 prohibited any form of collaboration with Social Democrats, under the pretense that reformist socialist parties were truly fascist. Accordingly, the leadership of the KPD dropped the policy of a "proletarian common front" and launched an all-out offensive against the "social fascists."

Semiloyalty

This presentation of the Weimar party system classifies political stances in a two-dimensional space structured on the one hand by the Left-Right continuum and on the other hand by the distinction drawn by Linz (1978) between "loyal" and "disloyal" members of the polity (29). *Loyal* actors abide by the rules of the constitution and consider them valid principles of regulation. *Disloyal* actors strive to subvert the constitutional framework. While loyal actors regard the constitutional rules as the grounding principles regulating political interactions, disloyal actors use the constitution to advance political goals that ultimately imply the destruction of this constitutional framework.[3] This does not mean that loyal actors are impervious to the notion of constitutional change. The changes that they might consider are intended to strengthen the constitutional framework.

Two small parties on the right of the Center party can be characterized along these lines as loyal to the constitutional framework (Opitz 1969, 95). The explicit program of the Christian-Social People's Service Party (Christlich-sozialer Volksdienst, or CSVP) was to protect "the state against the resurgence of radicalism—left and right—to create a bourgeois counterweight to the influence of Social Democracy" (Jones 1988, 367) and more broadly to effect a Christian regeneration of German political life (Opitz 1969, 100; Jones 1988, 353). The Conservative People's Party (Konservative Volkspartei, or KVP) aimed to "provide a German version of Tory democracy, popular conservatism prepared to participate constructively in affairs of state" (Feuchtwanger 1993, 228). Both parties splintered from the German Nationalist People's Party in reaction to its political dogmatism on the regime issue.

The distinction between loyal and disloyal actors points to a third, in-between category: *semiloyal* actors. One of the characteristics of semiloyalty

3. Linz (1978, 29–30) specifies several litmus tests of loyalty to a democratic regime while noting that these tests may not apply during crises: (1) a public commitment to legal means of gaining power and the rejection of the use of force, (2) the rejection of any "knocking at the barracks" for armed force support, (3) the acceptance of parties that have the right to rule owing to the support they receive from the electorate, and (4) the refusal to curtail the civil liberties of the leaders and supporters of parties attempting to exercise constitutionally guaranteed freedoms.

is a "willingness of political leaders to engage in secret negotiations . . . with parties they themselves perceived as disloyal" for the purpose of probing the conditions of a governmental coalition (Linz 1978, 32). Semiloyal political forces develop ambiguous strategies that betray an absence of commitment to the constitutional organization of the regime. The dividing line between loyalty, semiloyalty, and disloyalty shifts across time. Linz (1978) notes for instance that "the crisis situation creates the conditions for the emergence of semiloyal political forces" (33).

Actors loyal to the regime at one point may reveal themselves as semiloyal at another point. Similarly, semiloyal actors may shift to disloyalty because of a change of leadership. The German People's Party (Deutsche Volkspartei, or DVP) is a case in point. The DVP was the counterpart of the German State party on the right. It was a bourgeois party deeply involved in managing governmental affairs in the second half of the 1920s. In the campaign for the parliamentary elections of 1930, the German People's Party took a strong anti-Nazi stand. From 1931 on, however, the party chairman, Dingeldey, adopted a more conciliatory stance toward the "national opposition" of Hugenberg and Hitler (Jones 1988, 416).

The distinction between loyal and disloyal members of the polity helps to characterize the political stance of several small parties whose conceptions of the national political order is often far from clear. Parties organized along regional lines: the Bavarian People's party (Bayerische Volkspartei, or BVP), the German Party of Hannover (Deutsch-Hannoversche Partei, or DHP), and the Bavarian Peasants' League (Bayerischer Bauernbund, or BBB) demonstrated little attachment to the Weimar Constitution. They vested their political stakes in the provisions buoying the regional and particularistic interests they were defending. The same broad characterization applies to splinter parties that advocated and lobbied for the material interests of specific social groups. Examples included the Christian-National Peasants' and Farmers' Party (Christlich-Nationale Bauern- und Landvolk Partei, or CNBLP) and the Business Party (Wirtschaft Partei, or WP), which defined itself as the defense group of middle class economic interests and shared with the CNBLP and the DVP an inclination toward accommodation with the Nazis (Jones 1988, 413).

The picture that emerges from this overview is fragmented and polarized. Fifteen parties gained political representation in the Reichstag with the election of September 1930 (table 1).[4] As a result of the upsurge in political extremism, the disloyal opposition (Communists, German Nationalists, Nazis) represented a little less than 40 percent of the seats. The radical Right tallied

4. *Statistisches Jahrbuch für das Deutsche Reich*, vol. 52 (Kolb 1988, 194–95).

Table 1   Parties and the Weimar Republic, September 1930–July 1932

	Number of Seats	Percentage of All Seats
Loyal		
Social Democratic Party (SPD)	143	25
German State Party (DStP)	20	3
Center Party (Zentrum)	68	12
Christian Social People's Service (CSVP; Volksdienst)	14	2
Conservative People's Party (Konservative Volkspartei)	4	1
Bavarian People's Party (BVP)	19	3
Total, loyal parties	268	46
Semiloyal		
German People's Party (DVP)	30	5
German Peasants' Party (Deutsche Bauernpartei)	6	1
Rural League (Landbund)	3	1
Christian National Peasants' and Farmers' party (CNBLP)	19	3
German Party of Hannover (Deutsche Hannoversche Partei)	3	1
Business Party (Wirtschaftspartei)	23	4
Total, semiloyal parties	84	15
Disloyal		
Communist Party (KPD)	77	13
German National People's Party (DNVP)	41	7
National Socialist Party (NSDAP)	107	19
Total, disloyal parties	225	39
Total, all parties	577	100

Source: *Reichstag-Handbuch, Wahlperiode 1930.*

one fourth of the parliamentary representation. Parties whose loyalty to republican institutions could be increasingly questioned represented about 15 percent of the parliamentary mandates. This political arrangement prevented the formation of any workable majority and led to unstable cabinets. In 1931 Brüning governed by emergency decree.

State Crisis

In the first round of the presidential election Hindenburg won 49.6 percent of the votes and Hitler finished second with 30.1 percent (Bracher 1964 [1955],

475). When the two faced off in the second round, four weeks later, on 10 April 1932, Hindenburg was elected for a second presidential mandate with 53 percent of the popular vote while Hitler got 36.8 percent (Bracher 1964 [1955], 478). The leadership of the Social Democratic Party interpreted this outcome as an indication that the republican regime was regaining strength (Harsch 1993, 180). A few days later (on 13 April), the democratic constitutionalist camp found another source for optimism in the publication of a presidential decree dissolving the Nazi paramilitary troops (the SA). The government would no longer tolerate Nazi violence. The crackdown on Nazi militias was in effect reversing a directive — issued by the defense minister Groener a few weeks earlier (29 January) — that had allowed the recruitment of National Socialists into the army (Reichswehr).

This optimism was short-lived; several events shattered hopes of political stabilization and consolidation. The first event was Hindenburg's publication on 15 April of a letter to the defense minister of the Brüning cabinet, General Groener, in which the president demanded in substance that the republican paramilitary organization, the Reich Banner (Reichsbanner), be banned along with the Nazi paramilitary organizations. The Reich Banner stood for a united defense of the republic and saw protection of the Weimar constitution as its duty (Eyck 1963, 371). Although the majority of its members were members of the Social Democratic Party, several representatives of the German State party and the Center party sat on its national executive committee (Rohe 1966, 274). In asking to ban this organization, Hindenburg was in effect turning his back on those who had elected him. Groener responded to his letter by denying that the evidence cited by Hindenburg proved that the Reich Banner was subversive, and the minister of the interior did not ban the organization.

The second event was the regional state elections of 24 April in Prussia, Bavaria, Württemberg, and Anhalt. The election results confirmed the Nazi party's electoral gains. The outcome in Prussia was particularly troublesome for the constitutionalist camp because Prussia was a republican bulwark. At the time of the election, the government of the regional state was a coalition cabinet headed by a Social Democrat, Otto Braun. In the state election the Nazis and Communists together obtained nearly half the votes. The Nazis raised their representation from 9 to 169 seats while the Social Democrats lost about one third of their popular votes (Orlow 1991, 159). The parties of the Weimar coalition (Social Democrats, Center party, and German State party) no longer commanded a parliamentary majority. Given the political configuration of the Prussian parliament, no solution seemed possible except a black-brown (Center-Nazi) coalition. Otto Braun stayed in office at the head of a caretaker cabinet.

Brüning's Dismissal

Hindenburg's decision to dismiss Brüning from the chancellorship on 31 May 1932 took most political actors by surprise (Bracher 1964 [1955], 517). In Brüning's place Hindenburg appointed an obscure politician, Franz von Papen, at the head of a reactionary government composed for the most part of reserve officers with no party ties—four of them resigned from the German National People's Party (DNVP) to mark their independence from party politics—and no parliamentary mandate (Feuchtwanger 1993, 280). The event triggered months of political instability, conflicts, and deadlock. Soon after his appointment, Papen accused postwar governments of promoting a welfare state "which sapped the moral fiber of the nation" (Evans 2004, 285; Eyck 1963, 401). He failed to obtain the support of most political parties except the German Nationalists. The Nazis conditioned their toleration of the new cabinet on the dissolution of parliament and the rescinding of the decree banning Nazi paramilitary formations. The presidential decree pronouncing the dissolution of parliament was issued on 4 June, the decree lifting the ban on the SA on 16 June.

Coup against Prussia

Political violence was tremendous in the following weeks. From mid-June until 18 July about one hundred people died in street fights. More than one thousand were wounded, most of them in Prussia (Feuchtwanger 1993, 287; Schumann 2001, 320). On 17 July a street battle between Communists and parading Nazis in Altona (Hamburg) caused the deaths of eighteen civilians (Eyck 1963, 409). On 20 July von Papen, invoking the rise in political violence, informed the members of the Prussian government that a new presidential decree appointed him, by virtue of paragraphs 1 and 2 of Article 48, national commissioner for Prussia. This new decree granted him the power to relieve Prussian ministers of their offices. The Reich chancellor assumed the functions of premier while the Prussian police were placed under the command of a Reich commissioner. The new authorities imposed a state of emergency in Berlin and the province of Brandenburg. The Social Democratic leadership pointed out that the constitution offered no legal basis for such a move, and that this presidential decree ipso facto amounted to a coup deposing the minister-president, Otto Braun, and his interior minister, Carl Severing. Rather than call for a general strike and measures of resistance, Social Democrats decided to challenge the constitutionality of the presidential decree before the German Supreme Court, the Staatsgerichtshof (Evans 2004, 286–87).

July 1932: Nazi Electoral Landslide

The elections of 31 July were a defeat for the Social Democrats (21.9 percent of the votes against 24.5 percent in September 1930) and a clear victory for the Nazis. With 37.4 percent of the vote (compared with the 18.3 percent obtained in September 1930), the Nazi party received 230 seats out of 608 in the new Reichstag (table 2). The Communist party won 14.6 percent of the votes and 12 new seats (increasing the size of its delegation from 77 to 89). The new parliament displayed greater political polarization. The disloyal opposition represented almost 60 percent of the parliamentary mandates. Within the constitutionalist camp the Center party and the Bavarian People's Party remained stable, while other middle-of-the-road and splinter parties (the German State Party, The Christian-Social People's Service) suffered significant losses. The parties that located themselves between these two camps and occasionally flirted with the radical opposition on the Right were wiped out. As parliament got more polarized, it also got less fragmented.

Violence erupted as soon as the results became known. Negotiations between the Nazi leadership and the president's office for the formation of a new government ended abruptly on 13 August when the president's office issued a statement indicating that the president refused "most emphatically" Hitler's demand to be granted the chancellorship (Eyck 1963, 427). On 12 September, at parliament's second business meeting, party delegations voted on a motion of no-confidence in the government. The only party delegations voting against this motion were the German Nationalists (DNVP) and the German People's Party (DVP). The motion was approved by a vote of 512 to 42 with 5 abstentions, as von Papen announced a new presidential dissolution decree at the rostrum. Elections were set for 6 November 1932.

November 1932: The Nazi Tide Is Ebbing

The results of the November elections showed a significant decline for the Nazi party, which lost 14.9 percent of the votes received three months earlier; its share of the popular vote decreased from 37.4 to 33.1 percent. By contrast, the Nazis' Communist and German Nationalist competitors within the disloyal camp increased their share. The Communist party registered a gain of 13.2 percent (0.6 million votes) in winning 16.9 percent of the ballots, increasing its representation in parliament from 89 to 100 seats. The German Nationalists and the German People's Party polled over a million more votes than they had got three months earlier and gained 9 seats for a total of 63 (52 DNVP and 11 DVP). The parliamentary stalemate remained unresolved. Constitutionalist

Table 2   Parties and the Weimar Republic, July 1932–November 1932

	Number of Seats	Percentage of All Seats
Loyal		
Social Democratic Party (SPD)	133	22
German State Party (DStP)	4	1
Center Party (Zentrum)	75	12
Christian Social People's Service (Volksdienst)	3	*
Conservative German's Party (Konservative Volkspartei)	1	*
Bavarian People's Party (BVP)	22	4
Total, loyal parties	238	39
Semiloyal		
German People's Party (DVP)	7	1
German Peasants' Party (Deutsche Bauernpartei)	2	*
Rural League (Landbund)	2	*
Christian National Peasants and Farmers' party (CNBLP)	1	*
Business Party (Wirtschaftspartei)	2	*
Total, semiloyal parties	14	2
Disloyal		
Communist Party (KPD)	89	15
German National People's Party (DNVP)	37	6
National Socialist Party (NSDAP)	230	38
Total, disloyal parties	356	59
Total, all parties	608	100

* = less than 0.5 percent
Source: *Reichstag-Handbuch VII, Wahlperiode 1932.*

parties saw their share of the vote slightly decline. The Social Democratic Party obtained 20.4 percent (versus 21.6 percent in July), the German State party 1 percent, and the Center party 11.9 percent (versus 12.5 percent in July).

Papen engaged in fruitless negotiations with party leaders to probe their willingness to support the government. When it appeared that these negotiations were bound to fail, he resigned on 10 November. Upon his resignation Hindenburg refused again to entrust Hitler with the chancellorship, and on 2 December he appointed General Schleicher, who served as Papen's minister of defense and had no political affiliation. Schleicher's policy declaration criticized both capitalism and socialism and announced plans for job creation as well as concessions to the trade unions. Local elections in Thuringia on 4 December confirmed the electoral decline of the Nazi party. The liberal *Frankfurter Zeitung* expressed the same view: "The mighty National Socialist assault on the democratic state has been repulsed" (quoted by Turner 1985, 313).

Hitler Chancellor

However, Schleicher proved unable in the following weeks to find a workable parliamentary majority and resigned on 28 January. Two days later Hindenburg appointed Hitler chancellor of a coalition government composed for the most part of members of the German National People's Party (DNVP). Papen held the title of vice-chancellor. Hugenberg, the chairman of the German Nationalists, was minister of the economy and alimentation. Apart from Hitler, two Nazis had ministerial portfolios. Wilhelm Frick supervised the Ministry of the Interior; and Hermann Göring was minister of aviation and minister of the interior for Prussia. On the day following his appointment, Hitler requested—against Hugenberg's wishes—that the president dissolve parliament. Hindenburg issued a presidential decree to this effect which set the date of the new election on 5 March.

The Campaign for the Republic

The electoral campaign took place under restricted conditions. On 4 February Hindenburg signed an emergency ordinance authorizing the prohibition of newspapers or public meetings "that abused, or treated with contempt, organs, institutions, bureaus or leading officials of the state" or broadcast false information that might "endanger the vital interests of the state" (Craig 1978, 572).

Throughout the campaign the representatives of the constitutionalist parties (Social Democrats, Center party, German State Party) along with the Bavarian People's Party and the Christian-Social People's Service denounced plans for dictatorship, asserted a strong constitutional stance, and condemned Nazism. In a programmatic speech delivered on 5 February 1933, the chairman of the Center party, Ludwig Kaas, explained that the Center party was fighting for "a system of law that fits the grounding principles of a truly Christian and conservative state leadership. . . . The worst Parliament is still better than cliques intriguing in the antechambers."[5] On 18 February in Würzburg, the former chancellor Heinrich Brüning denounced politicians "who only believe in power" and described their belief as "the most perverse one that can be imagined; it

5. *Kölnische Volkszeitung*, 6 February, 2.

leads . . . to an abyss without end." The Center was aiming at the "salvation of [the] Constitution." It fought for "Liberty, Law and the Homeland."[6]

Measures of intimidation and persecution stepped up after the burning of the Reichstag building on the evening of 27 February. On 28 February Hitler issued an emergency decree "for the protection of the people and the state" which bore Hindenburg's signature and abolished basic civil rights conferred by the Constitution. Article 2 of this decree allowed the national cabinet to assume the powers of any Land government that proved unable or unwilling to restore public order.[7] Articles 4 and 5 ordered the execution or imprisonment of persons charged with certain crimes such as failure to adhere to the provisions of the decree, assassination attempts on the life of the Reich president and members of the government, treason, arson, or incitement to riot.

Portraying the arson of the Reichstag as a Communist plot, Nazi ministers used these emergency powers to arrest thousands of Communist representatives and activists, and harass democratic parties. In spite of this highly coercive context and the limitations imposed on the constitutionalist parties' capacity to campaign effectively, the Social Democratic party and the Center party held firm, and the Nazis did not achieve an absolute majority in parliament (table 3). They won 45 percent of the votes and succeeded in electing 288 delegates (out of a total of 647). Hitler remained dependent on his governmental partners to command a simple parliamentary majority. If the Communist delegates were deprived of their elective mandate—they were either jailed or had fled the country—the Nazis controlled 51 percent of the parliamentary seats, and in conjunction with German Nationalists, the parliamentary representation of the Hitler cabinet rose to 60 percent (table 4).

The Kroll Opera House, Berlin, 23 March 1933

The parliamentary session opened on 21 March with a ceremony in Potsdam. On the same day the government released the text of the "Law for the Relief of the People and of the Reich" (*Gesetz zur Behebung der Not von Volk und Reich*). This bill—which was to be submitted to parliament two days later—was an enabling bill with extensive powers including the power to change the constitution: "the national laws enacted by the Reich government can deviate from the Constitution, insofar as they do not affect the institution of the Reichstag and the Reichsrat as such" (Article 2).[8] Articles 3 and 5 of the bill specified that

6. Reproduced in *Hitlers Machtergreifung*, 79.

7. *Reichsgesetzblatt* 1933, I, 83 (reproduced in *Das "Ermächtigungsgesetz" vom 24. März 1933*, 26).

8. *Reichsgesetzblatt* 1933, I, 141.

Table 3   The Parliamentary Election of 5 March 1933

	Number of Seats	Percentage of All Seats
Loyal		
Social Democratic Party (SPD)	120	19
German State Party (DStP)	5	1
Center Party (Zentrum)	73	11
Christian Social People's Service (Volksdienst)	4	1
Bavarian People's Party (BVP)	19	3
Total, loyal parties	221	34
Semiloyal		
German People's Party (DVP)	2	*
German Peasants' Party (Deutsche Bauernpartei)	2	*
Total, semiloyal parties	4	1
Disloyal		
Communist Party (KPD)[1]	81	13
German National People's Party (DNVP)	53	8
National Socialist Party (NSDAP)	288	45
Total, disloyal parties	422	65
Total, all parties	647	100

* = less than 0.5 percent

[1] The candidates of the Communist party remained on the ballot although they were de facto excluded from political representation as a result of the systematic repression launched against them (Repgen 1988, 215–17).

Source: *Reichstag-Handbuch VIII, Wahlperiode 1933*, 71.

the chancellor was in charge of "ratifying" (*ausfertigen*) the laws enacted by the cabinet and that this Act would be in effect until 7 April 1937 for a period of four years.[9] In sum, the bill granted the government the power to enact legislation independently of parliament. Furthermore, it permitted changes in the basic principles of the constitutional framework.

Since this bill opened the way for constitutional changes, it could not be passed without a two-thirds majority. In the newly elected Reichstag, the constitutional majority was 432. Assuming that the German Nationalists would endorse the bill, Hitler needed at least 91 more votes to pass the law "for the Relief of the People and the Reich." Even if he could reasonably expect to receive four "yes" votes from the German People's Party (DVP) and the German Peasants' Party (Deutsche Bauernpartei), which took a clear-cut pro-Hitler

9. Ibid.

Table 4   Distribution of Seats in the Reichstag in the Absence of Communist Delegates, March 1933

	Number of Seats	Percentage of All Seats
Loyal		
Social Democratic Party (SPD)	120	21
German State Party (DStP)	5	1
Center Party (Zentrum)	73	13
Christian Social People's Service (Volksdienst)	4	1
Bavarian People's Party (BVP)	19	3
Total, loyal parties	221	39
Semiloyal		
German People's Party (DVP)	2	*
German Peasants' Party (Deutsche Bauernpartei)	2	*
Total, semiloyal parties	4	1
Disloyal		
German National People's Party (DNVP)	53	9
National Socialist Party (NSDAP)	288	51
Total, disloyal parties	341	60
Total, all parties	566	100

* = less than 0.5 percent

stance during the electoral campaign, he still needed the endorsement of a major constitutionalist party. The Center party had 73 deputies in the new parliament, the Bavarian People's Party 19, and the Social Democrats 120.

The bill discussion and vote were set for 23 March. The parliamentary session started at 2:00 P.M. with a report by the Nazi delegate Stöhr on a proposal to modify the regulations concerning parliamentarians' leaves of absence. According to this proposal, presented by the parties of the governmental coalition, "the chairman of parliament can exclude from the debates for a period up to 60 business days anyone who does not take part in the parliamentary sessions, the committees' meetings and the votes without a leave of absence or due to an illness that in fact does not impede one from participating [in the debates]." Delegates excluded by virtue of the preceding provision would "be considered as present."[10] The proposal was endorsed.

10. As Bracher (1962, 159) points out, this last provision made the regulation an "incredible legal fiction" intended, first, to prevent deputies from making a parliamentary vote unconstitutional by stepping out and, second, to facilitate the expulsion of political opponents from parliament.

Hitler then went to the rostrum and presented the justification for the government's bill. Throughout the fourteen previous years, he declared, the German people had "suffered a decadence beyond imaginable proportions." The goal of a reform of the Reich had to be the design of a Constitution that bound "the will of the people with the authority of true leadership." The government of the national revolution considered that its fundamental duty was to "prevent these elements, who consciously and purposefully negate the life of the nation, from having any influence on its formation." A radical moral reformation would be pursued. Race and blood would become again a source of artistic inspiration. Viewing both Christian confessions as "the most important factors that consolidated nationhood," the government would create and secure "the conditions of a truly deep and spiritual religiosity." In passing the bill submitted to them, the parties represented in parliament would make the continuation of peaceful developments in Germany possible.[11] Hitler ended his speech at 3:12 P.M. The session was adjourned for three hours to let the party delegations deliberate.

Parliamentarians convened again at 6:16 P.M. The chairman of the Social Democratic Party was the first to speak: Otto Wels mounted the stairs of the tribune and explained that his party would vote against the bill. Hitler responded to this speech with considerable violence (in essence: the German Social Democracy's moment has passed; your fate is sealed). After Hitler's response, around 7:00 P.M. the chairman of the Center party, Ludwig Kaas, went to the rostrum to announce that his party would vote for the bill. "The Center party holds out its hand to all, including previous enemies, who are willing to ensure the continuation of the work of national salvation."[12] The chairmen of the State party, the Bavarian People's party, and the Christian Social delegations went along. These parties would cast a "yes" vote. At 8:00 P.M. on 23 March the bill passed.[13] Hitler had constitutional powers.

11. *Verhandlungen des Reichstags*, vol. 457, 26–32, reproduced in *Das "Ermächtigungsgesetz" vom 24. März 1933*, 55–62.

12. *Verhandlungen des Reichstags*, vol. 457, 37.

13. *Verhandlungen des Reichstags*, vol. 457, 40. In announcing the results Göring, acting as chairman of the Reichstag, reduced the quorum from 432 (two-thirds of the mandates in the newly elected assembly) to 378, thereby de facto pronouncing the Communist mandates void. There was no legal basis for such a decision (Biesemann 1987, 288; Repgen 1988, 215–20; Schneider 1968 [1953], 419). This change of quorum did not affect the outcome. Historiographic accounts (e.g. Bracher 1962, 158; Matz 1989, 145) presume the exclusion of the Communist mandates from the total tally of the votes when they state that Hitler needed 38 votes in addition to those of the governmental majority (or 34 assuming that he would get the votes of the German People's party and the German peasants' party) to have the bill passed (see table 4).

LEGAL REVOLUTION

What is the significance of this event? Analyses that focus on the Nazis' coercive capacity state that the enabling bill made no key difference. From a
real political standpoint, given the balance of forces a "no" vote would have
changed nothing (Repgen 1967, 13). Hitler was resolute to pursue his political agenda through violence if necessary and he already yielded considerable
executive power. Bracher (1962, 158) epitomizes this analysis. The key event
that decisively altered the balance of power and provided the Nazis with the
tools to suppress their opponents was the issuance of emergency decrees on
28 February, not the enabling bill. The dictatorial powers granted to Hitler by
virtue of the emergency decrees destroyed the institutional foundations of
democracy. Winkler (1989, 906) concurs: in March 1933 the constitutional state
of Weimar no longer existed; it had been invalidated by the emergency decrees
of 28 February. Therefore the historical significance of the power transfer of
23 March is limited.

At odds with these assessments cast in realist terms are numerous statements
asserting the importance of the event. Morsey (1960, 353; 1977, 115, 151) speaks
of "the turning point of the enabling bill" (*Wendepunkt Ermächtigungsgesetz*).
Matz (1989, 146) evokes a "decisive session" (*entscheidende Sitzung*). For Volk
(1987) the emergency decrees of 28 February *and* the passing of the enabling
act of 23 March are the two milestones that "provided Hitler with all the means
to launch a systematic takeover of state power" (1). Hörster-Philipps (1998)
portrays the acceptance of the enabling bill as "a decisive moment in the construction and the consolidation of the national socialist regime" (429).

If the event is decisive, we have to conclude that it will alter subsequent
developments. It will have important consequences. Yet, assessments cast in
terms of realpolitik suggest that the power transfer of 23 March had no significant impact on Hitler's capacity to carry out his political goals. For now I
leave open the question of whether these different assessments contradict one
another—this will be the subject of the concluding chapter—and I set forth
the following claims. Hitler had the coercive and legal capacity to expand his
power. Yet as will become clearer in chapter 2, his margin of maneuver would
have been much narrower in the absence of the enabling bill, and the margin
of maneuver of his actual and potential opponents within and outside the state

---

This presumption about the de facto exclusion of the Communist mandates seems to have
been widely shared at the time. This probably explains the computations set forth by these
historiographic accounts.

apparatus would have been much greater. The historical character of 23 March lay in this legal process of assuming power. The enabling bill gave way to a *legal revolution*.

For this was a revolution. The Nazi leadership reshaped state institutions by destroying the federal structure and by making executive power independent of any political supervision. By the same token, the Nazis excluded or gradually marginalized political actors who until then had been involved in managing governmental affairs. State power became the exclusive domain of the chancellor and his affiliates. The change in state structure went along with a process of élite displacement. The peculiarity of this political revolution is that it implied no breach of constitutional legality. From a formal standpoint, the statutes were fulfilled. "For sure, what had taken place in [February and March] was a revolution, but this revolution was clean and legal and therefore distinguished itself in a pleasant way from the 'detestable odor' of the November [1918] revolution" (Thamer 1986, 280).[14]

The bill was an act of political foundation. Laying the constitutional groundwork for a new political order, the "legal revolution" of March 1933 had legitimizing effects. In providing the Nazi leadership with the justification of legality, passage of the bill enabled Hitler to secure the loyalty of the state apparatus and contributed to stabilizing the Nazi regime (Böckenförde 1961, 218; Thamer 1986, 280; Winkler 1989, 906). This explains why the Nazi leaders attached great importance to the legal character of their mandate (Schneider 1968 [1953], 426) and were eager to have the bill passed. They could expect to derive great political benefits from this vote at a time when they were not in full control of the state apparatus. Endorsing the bill was the "cardinal mistake of political Catholicism in 1933," because of the prestige and the aura that it provided to Hitler (Repgen 1967, 24).

Contemporary and retrospective statements betray an awareness of this historical significance. On the day of the vote, before the Center parliamentary delegation, the chairman of the Center party acknowledged the crucial importance of the moment.[15] The Center deputy, Joseph Wirth, characterized the parliamentary sessions of 21 and 23 March as "historical" and spoke of the "decisive hour" of the enabling bill.[16] The German Nationalist representative, Edmund Forschbach, depicted 23 March as a fateful day (*schicksalsschwerer*

---

14. Several authors (Bracher 1966, 117; Jasper 1986, 138; Linz 1978, 76; Richter 1986, 104) invoke the legal revolution category to account for the specificity of the event.

15. Bundesarchiv, Koblenz, Nachlaß Kaiser N1018/246, 53.

16. See the title of his manuscript: "The Historical Sessions of Parliament of 21 and 23 March 1933" (*Die historischen Reichstagssitzungen vom 21. und 23. März 1933*), Bundesarchiv, Koblenz, Nachlaß Wirth N1342/133.

Tag).[17] These actors described the moment as decisive and their decision as portentous because more or less explicitly, they grasped its consequences. The representative of the Christian-Social People's Service (Volksdienst), Paul Bausch, portrayed the vote for the enabling bill as a "grave political mistake" (*ein schwerer politischer Fehler*).[18] "Every one of us, who either as a publicist or as a 'politician' was forced to make decisions that he regretted afterwards, has made mistakes. Yet, the word is still too weak for the acceptance of this law [the 'Ermächtigungsgesetz'] and even the word 'afterwards' misses what were my feelings; for I already knew at that time that I would never be able to erase this 'yes' from my life" (Theodor Heuss, former German State Party deputy).[19]

DEFEAT AND BREAKDOWN: THE TERRIBLE YEAR

Contemporary legal scholars of the 1930s are quick to point out the peculiarity of the transition by systematically using the notion of "legal revolution" to describe the institutionalization of Nazi rule, or in the Nazis' parlance the *synchronization* (*Gleichschaltung*), that took place in the spring of 1933 (Bracher 1962, 88).[20] The legal-revolutionary oxymoron brings about, in capsule form, a unique feature of a type of political transition in which a group of actors uses "constitutional institutions against their clear intent" (Linz 1978, 77). March 1933 is not a unique and exceptional case. With similar relevance, the category of "legal revolution" applies to the collapse of the French Third Republic in July 1940.

War

In the summer of 1939 prospects of war with Nazi Germany were looming. In March 1939, violating the agreement which had been reached a few months earlier at the Munich conference in September 1938, Hitler had occupied Czechoslovakia and continued to pursue his aggressive expansion to the East. War seemed unavoidable unless Hitler was given a free hand. The conclusion of a nonaggression pact between Germany and the Soviet Union on 23 Au-

17. Archiv der Konrad Adenauer Stiftung, Sankt Augustin, Nachlaß Forschbach, I-199, "Vier Tage," 9.

18. Bundesarchiv, Koblenz, Nachlaß Bausch, N1391/11, letter to Zoeller, chief editor of *Echo der Zeit*, 26 February 1958.

19. Heuss, *Die Machtergreifung und das Ermächtigungsgesetz*, 23.

20. In a premonitory fashion, Carl Schmitt published an article in July 1932 in which he examined the possibility of a constitutional jurisprudence that could forestall Hitler's "legal revolution" (Bendersky 1983, 423; Finn 1991, 177).

gust 1939 dramatically aggravated this prospect, since Hitler could then attack Poland without having to fight on two fronts.

War broke out on 1 September 1939 after Hitler's invasion of Poland. The French premier, Édouard Daladier, reacted to the event by summoning the Chamber of Deputies and the Senate on the following day. In his speech before parliamentarians, Daladier expressed both the government's wish for conciliation and its determination not to let Hitler's aggression "be accomplished." Both houses voted the war credits by a show of hands. According to the minutes reported in the state's official bulletin (*Journal Officiel*), this show of hands was unanimous.[21] The next day (3 September), the British and French governments declared war on Germany. From this moment on political developments in France were inextricably enmeshed with and attuned to the chronology of external events: the fall of Poland at the end of September 1939, the Finno-Soviet armistice in March 1940, and the German offensive against French armies in May 1940.

After the invasion of Poland by Soviet and German armies, the leadership of the French Communist Party denounced the war as one between imperialist powers and called for peace negotiations. On 26 September Daladier's cabinet dissolved the Communist party, dismissing Communist mayors and municipal aldermen for the sake of "public order and general interest" and replacing them with special delegations (Bonnefous 1967, 124). The banned Communist deputies present in Paris reorganized their parliamentary delegation as the "Worker and Peasant Group" and addressed to the chairman of the Chamber of Deputies, Édouard Herriot, a Radical party member, a letter demanding that the expected German-Soviet peace proposals "be examined with a willingness to establish a fair peace" (Bonnefous 1967, 125). Maurice Thorez, secretary general of the party, deserted from the French army on 4 October. Warrants for the arrest of all members of the "Worker and Peasant Group" were issued on the following day. On 16 January 1940 the Chamber of Deputies stripped Communist deputies of their mandate almost unanimously, 521 to 2 (Bonnefous 1967, 126).

Throughout these few months the French high military commander refrained from taking any military action, and in March 1940 Daladier came under fierce criticism for having failed to help Finland after the Soviet Union attacked it. Daladier resigned on 19 March. President Albert Lebrun called on the conservative Paul Reynaud, former minister of finance in the Daladier cabinet, to form a new government. This new government included conservatives, Socialists, and Radicals (Daladier was minister of war) and was ex-

---

21. *Journal Officiel*, 2 September 1939, 1950.

Table 5   Vote for the Reynaud Cabinet in the Chamber of Deputies, 22 March 1940

		Yes	No	Absten-tion	Absent	Total
Left	Union Populaire Française (former communists)	13	0	0	0	13
↑	Parti Socialiste (SFIO)	154	1	2	0	157
	Union Socialiste Républicaine (USR)	22	0	4	1	27
	Gauche Indépendante	9	0	7	0	16
	Groupe Républicain Radical et Radical-Socialiste (Radical Party)	34	10	69	3	116
	Gauche Démocratique et Radicale Indépendante	1	29	4	2	36
	Groupe Démocrate Populaire	7	0	7	0	14
	Alliance Démocratique	6	23	12	1	42
	Groupe Agraire Indépendant	3	6	1	0	10
	Groupe Indépendant d'Action Populaire	10	1	0	4	15
	Républicains Indépendants et d'Action Sociale	3	19	2	2	26
	Indépendants Républicains	5	3	2	0	10
↓	Fédération Républicaine	1	54	2	2	59
Right	Parti Social Français	0	10	0	0	10
Total		268	156	112	15	551

Source: *Journal Officiel, Chambre des Députés, Annexe au procès-verbal de la séance du vendredi 22 mars 1940*; Rossi Landi (1971, 226–28).

pected to prosecute the war more forcefully. On 22 March it received a vote of confidence in the Chamber by a margin of 268 to 156 — a margin which political observers viewed as extremely narrow given the high proportion of abstentions (111).

This vote reveals the fragmentation of the Third Republic parliamentary scene and the lack of group cohesion.[22] A significant proportion of these groups were ad hoc groupings that had little collective existence except on paper. Groups that were not ad hoc, on the other hand, had to deal with a structure of incentives and constraints that played against their cohesion.

22. I define cohesion in behavioral terms as a group's propensity to adopt a unanimous or quasi-unanimous stance. There may be cohesion without discipline, that is, without the explicit attempt on the part of some members in the group to have others align with a group directive.

Deputies were elected through a double-ballot system with single-member districts. Elections were therefore uninominal and district based. In this electoral system politicians had an incentive to personalize their political mandate and develop a patron-client relationship with their local constituents (Kreuzer 2001, chapter 2). Their political fortunes were contingent on their ability to preserve this relationship, which had precedence over group obligations. Party nominations were not so crucial. The groups' leaderships in turn often lacked the resources to effectively sanction disobedience. Hence these groups were structurally weak (Le Béguec 2003b, 258–59).[23]

The fragmented character of political affiliations was particularly visible among those located between the two poles of the parliamentary gamut: the self-proclaimed "moderates" (modérés), the "Radicals," and groups that gravitated between the Radicals and the Socialist Left. The modérés may well be defined as republicans who castigated any form of political extremism. Typical in this regard were the representatives of the Democratic Alliance. These politicians traditionally endorsed the model of a centrist mediation between parties (Audigier 1995, 154). They were conservatives and proponents of the "juste milieu" (Audigier 1997, 231). For them the political vocation of the Alliance was to be the rallying point of all the republicans endorsing liberalism (Sanson 1978, 329, 333). In more pragmatic terms, they did not exclude collaborating with members of the radical-socialist party (Groupe républicain radical et radical-socialiste) in government.[24]

These modérés were scattered among numerous loosely organized clusters with "little political consistency," to use the characterization by Le Béguec (2003b, 258) of the Indépendants Républicains (see also Delbreil 1990, 219–20; Pinol 1992, 310–11). Often the names of these groups changed from one legislature to the other. In 1932–36 the Républicains indépendants et d'action sociale labeled themselves the Groupe républicain et social (Mayeur 2000, 189). To further complicate the distinction of political affiliations, these names were misleading if interpreted literally, because of the explicit reference to the "left":

23. Until July 1910 groups in parliament had no official recognition and could not pretend to have organizational existence. Parliament modified its own rules to make possible the formation of commissions on the basis of lists set up by the groups. This change implied that the size of the groups should be known and the groups officially recognized (Le Béguec 2001, 190–91; Waline 1961, 1182–86).

24. The groups I have just listed were registered in the Chamber of Deputies. Their equivalents in the Senate were the Democratic and Radical Union (Union Démocratique et Radicale, or UDR), and the Republican Union (Union Républicaine). The Union Démocratique et Radicale was founded in November 1924 and provided a bridge between the Radicals of the Gauche Démocratique and the moderates of the Union Républicaine (Le Béguec 2003b, 254).

e.g. the "Independent, Radical and Democratic Left" (Gauche démocratique et radicale indépendante) and the "Democratic Alliance of Republicans from the Left" (L'Alliance démocratique des Républicains de gauche, or Alliance) (table 5). Contrary to what these labels might suggest, both had no political affinity whatsoever with the "left."

Similarly, the radical-socialist party—often abbreviated as Radical party—was not politically radical. The name derived from cleavages that emerged in the 1880s among Republicans, at a time when consolidation of the republican regime was still an issue. Radical republicans opposed opportunist republicans by aggressively emphasizing the republican principles that oriented their political action. As a result of this political history, the Radical party became identified with the republican regime in general and the Third Republic in particular. It was the party whose interests were one and the same with the interests of the republican regime, of which it was the staunchest champion (Berstein 1982, 591). Radicals were "fiercely" (Berstein) attached to the accomplishments of this regime, such as separation of church and state (laïcité), a free and obligatory secular education, and equality of social opportunities. In the 1930s their "prime concern was defending republican institutions against the supposed menace of the right-wing leagues" (Larkin 1988, 53). One resilient ideological motto constitutive of their political identity was the rejection of both extremes (Puyaubert 2005, 105).

It is significant that even in groups that had an organic tie with a political party—the Alliance, the Republican Federation, the Radical party—political individualism set the tone. Not all the deputies of the Alliance and the Republican Federation were affiliated with the group that bore the name of their party in the Chamber of Deputies (Mayeur 1984, 301; Sanson 1978, 328).[25] Furthermore, both parties granted their deputies freedom to vote as they wished. Consequently, these groups were constantly exposed to centrifugal tendencies—what Kreuzer (2001, 6) aptly terms "fluid functionalism." The Républicains indépendants et d'action sociale, for instance, were a splinter group from the Republican Federation. These deputies constituted their own group in parliament to reassert their commitment to political liberalism at a time when their Republican Federation colleagues seemed to drift toward political intransigence (Delbreil 1990, 275; Mayeur 2000, 189).[26]

25. This observation holds for the Senate as well. The thirty Alliance senators divided themselves between the Union Républicaine and the Union Démocratique et Radicale (UDR).

26. Fragmentation concerned representatives elected on a platform grounded in Social Catholicism as well. In the Chamber these representatives were affiliated with the Young Republic (Jeune République), which was part of the "Independent Left" (Gauche Indépendante),

Between the Radicals and the Socialist Left stood the "Independent Left" (Gauche indépendante) and the Republican Socialist Union (Union Socialiste Républicaine, or USR). Both were loosely defined clusters of splinter groups and personalities located outside of the Socialist party and the Radical party (Burrin 1986, 274; Mayeur 1984, 318). Originally the core of the Republican Socialist Union was constituted of former Socialist representatives excluded from the party because of their advocacy of a strong national state at the expense of the traditional tenets of the Socialist doctrine (Hohl 2004, 78). At the end of the 1930s, however, the USR, like the Independent Left, had been attracting politicians who did do not want to submit themselves to party discipline and pursued a political and governmental career outside the boundaries of traditional parties.

In this institutional landscape the exceptions were the delegations of the Communist party, the Socialist party and the French Social party (Parti Social Français, or PSF). As I mentioned earlier, the Communist delegates were stripped of their mandate in January 1940. Those who in the fall of 1939 resigned to protest the party leadership's defense of the German-Soviet pact created the French Popular Union (Union Populaire Française, or UPF) in December 1939 (Rossi 1948, 444–45; Rossi-Landi 1971, 141). As for the delegates of the Socialist party (Section Française de l'Internationale Ouvrière, or SFIO), they formed in 1936–40 the largest political group registered in the chamber (147 members).[27] Although they identified themselves as Marxist and revolutionary, their political stance was reformist and anticlerical, with a strong emphasis on republicanism. Some of their representatives were involved in managing government affairs during the First World War. In May 1936 the victory of a leftist electoral coalition (the Popular Front) led to the formation of the first Socialist government of the Third Republic, headed by the party chairman, Léon Blum.

The French Social Party was the heir of the Croix de Feu, a paramilitary organization whose political appeal was based on anti-parliamentary slogans and the denunciation of national decadence and corruption. This organization consistently called for implementing a strong regime. The Croix de Feu was suppressed by a governmental decree in 1936 because of its paramilitary

---

the Popular Democratic party (Parti Démocrate Populaire, or PDP), the Independents of Popular Action (Indépendants d'Action Populaire), who came from Alsace-Lorraine, and the Independent Republicans of Social Action (Républicains Indépendants et d'Action Sociale) (Hilaire 1992, 541).

27. Unless otherwise specified, I use the label Socialist to designate the members of the SFIO parliamentary groups in the Senate and the Chamber of Deputies. The SFIO was the French Section of the Workers' International (Section Française de l'Internationale Ouvrière).

nature. Colonel La Rocque, its leader, decided to convert his movement into a regular political party (the Parti Social Français, or PSF). Beginning in 1937 the party leadership repeatedly indicated that the PSF did not call into question parliamentary democracy. These disclaimers notwithstanding, the members of the PSF were among the most vocal critics of parliamentary institutions and clearly in favor of a more authoritarian and nationalist polity, even if in their public views the strengthening of the state did not mean a break with the republic and the democratic form of the regime (Machefer 1978, 309, Mayeur 1984, 376; Nobécourt 1996, 639–51).[28]

Prodromes of a National Revolution

The German offensive began on 10 May. Within five days the German armies broke through the defenses of the Meuse (Jackson 2003, 37–54). Reynaud appointed Marshal Pétain vice-premier on 18 May. On 12 June the commander in chief, General Weygand, informed the government that the military situation was desperate and that an armistice was necessary. The German armies entered Paris on 14 June as the government was fleeing for Bordeaux. On 17 June a public statement announced that in the present grave circumstances, the Council of Ministers, on the proposal of Paul Reynaud, considered that the government of France should be vested in a prominent personage having the unanimous respect of the nation. As a result, Reynaud submitted the resignation of the members of the cabinet to the president of the Republic. Albert Lebrun accepted their resignations while paying tribute to the patriotism that inspired them, and immediately called upon Pétain, who accepted the duty of forming a new government.[29] Shortly afterward, at 12:30 P.M., Pétain delivered his first message to the nation: "It is with a sad heart that I tell you today that we must stop fighting."

The French government signed an armistice with Germany on 22 June. The armistice divided the metropolitan territory into two zones separated by a demarcation line that ran from Lake Geneva to Tours and then headed south-

28. There has been considerable debate about La Rocque's and his affiliates' ideological profile. Rémond (1982, 206, 211–14) interprets The Croix de Feu and the Parti Social Français as a variant of the Bonapartist tradition, anticipating de Gaulle's party after the war. Milza (1987, 133–42) emphasizes the lack of a Fascist program. In contrast, Irvine (1991, 282–95) outlines these movements' revolutionary and anticapitalistic strands, while Soucy (1995, 116–18) questions La Rocque's commitment to democratic principles. For Passmore (1997, 19, 295), the PSF ceased to be Fascist when it moved away from paramilitary activism. Beyond definitional criteria, this debate engages methodological and substantive issues, as Dobry (1989, 513; 2003, 18–21, 34–35) points out. I will address these issues further in chapter 3.

29. *Le Temps*, 18 June 1940.

ward to the Spanish border. The German military occupied the northern part, while the southern part was free from the Germans' military presence. This division was motivated by the continuation of war with England and was to be temporary. In theory the French government remained sovereign in the occupied zone with the exception of the Alsace-Lorraine, which the German Reich annexed. In practice French administrative services in the occupied zone were expected to conform to the requests of the German military authorities (Azéma 1984, 46).

On the evening of 25 June Pétain publicly justified the armistice: France had been militarily defeated. "From this point on, we have to turn our efforts towards the future. A new order begins. . . . We need to restore France. Our defeat stems from our looseness. The spirit of pleasure destroys what the spirit of sacrifice has erected. I invite you first to participate in a moral and intellectual restoration."[30] Since Bordeaux was in the occupied zone laid out in the armistice with Germany, the government left the city at the end of June, first for Clermont-Ferrand and then for the spa town of Vichy in the center of France. Among other advantages, the city had many hotel rooms. In addition, no national figure politically dominated the area (Paxton 1972, 18; Cointet 1993, 18–20). On 5 July the news was released that the Chamber of Deputies and the Senate were summoned "to vote on a bill permitting the government of Marshal Pétain to give France the new Constitution required by the circumstances."[31]

The vice-premier, Pierre Laval, disclosed the text of the government bill before the deputies and senators on 8 July: "The National Assembly confers all powers upon the Government of the Republic under the authority and the signature of Marshal Pétain, President of the Council [i.e. the prime minister], to promulgate by one or more acts the new Constitution of the French State. This Constitution will guarantee the rights of Labor, Family, and Homeland. It will be ratified by the Assemblies it will have created."[32] The text expounding the motives for the bill referred to the necessity of a "national revolution" in which France, "in the bitterest moment in its history . . . ought to see the conditions of its salvation." The government needed "to have all powers necessary to make decisions, to take initiatives, and to engage in negotiations." That is why it asked parliament "to trust Marshal Pétain, President of the Council, to promulgate under his signature and his responsibility, the fundamental laws of the French State."[33]

30. Ibid., 27 June 1940.
31. Official statement as reproduced by the *Dépêche de Toulouse*, 5 July 1940.
32. Reproduced in Michel (1966, 61), trans. Humphrey Hare (Aron 1958, 81–82).
33. *La Dépêche de Toulouse*, 10 July 1940, 1.

The bill opened the way for constitutional reforms. To be passed it required a majority in the "National Assembly," that is, the Chamber of Deputies and the Senate convening together. The government orchestrated a two-step process. The first step conformed to Article 8 of the constitutional law of 25 February 1875: "The Chambers have the right, by separate resolutions, taken in each by a majority of votes, either spontaneously, or on the demand of the President of the Republic, to declare that there is need for a revision of the laws of the Constitution."[34] Accordingly the cabinet requested that the two parliamentary chambers, in separate sessions, cast a vote on a single clause motion "declaring that there is need for a revision of the laws of the Constitution." This vote was to take place on the following day (9 July). The second step was the meeting of the National Assembly proper. Because a majority in each chamber opted to vote in favor of this proposal for revision, both chambers gathered as a "National Assembly" on 10 July to decide on the constitutional bill submitted to them by Laval on behalf of the government.

Vichy, the Grand Casino, 10 July 1940

On the morning of 9 July, around 9:30 A.M., the chairman of the Chamber of Deputies, Édouard Herriot, a Radical, opened the meeting of the chamber by honoring the memory of the deputies who had died in action, rendering homage to Marshal Pétain, announcing that the government was submitting a bill, and referring the bill to the Commission of Universal Suffrage for approval in conformity with parliamentary regulations. The commission immediately convened and the session was suspended for the duration of this meeting. One hour later, Jean Mistler, a Radical, presented his report on behalf of the commission. "The country has become aware of the necessity, if we want to rebuild France, to reform profoundly its political institutions." The twenty-three members of the Commission of Universal Suffrage had "unanimously" decided to approve the proposal of the government, so that the parliament could facilitate "the immense effort required for the reconstruction of the country, in accordance with Republican order and legality."[35] The Chamber of Deputies passed the bill by a vote of 395 to 3.

The session of the Senate, at 4:00 P.M., followed the same course. The chairman, Jules Jeanneney, celebrated parliamentarians killed on the field of battle

34. Translation by Humphrey Hare (Aron 1958, 101). The French Third Republic did not have a constitution in the proper sense of the term. The short text that served in its stead was composed of three laws voted by the National Assembly (the Chamber of Deputies and the Senate) on 24–25 February and 16 July 1875.

35. *Journal Officiel*, Chambre des Députés, Séance du 9 juillet 1940, 814.

and assured Marshal Pétain of his "veneration." Then the Legislative Commission of the Senate examined the government draft bill for about one hour. The spokesman of the commission, Jean Boivin-Champeaux, a conservative, read his report before the Senate. The commission concluded that the procedure was "legal and in order: it conforms with precedent, with the sole exception that the previous revisions of 1879, 1884, and 1926, were only partial, whereas today you have to envisage a total remolding of our institutions." The object of the session, Boivin-Champeaux explains, was not to "get to the root of the matter" but rather "to speak out for the principle of revision," about which "everyone agrees." The Senate endorsed the motion by 229 to 1.

Two meetings were planned for the next day. In the morning deputies and senators would discuss the government motion during a meeting closed to the public. They would vote on the bill in the afternoon at a meeting open to the public. At the opening of the morning session, two senators from the ex-servicemen group, Jean Taurines (from the conservative Groupe de l'Union Démocratique) and Maurice Dormann (no affiliation), presented a proposal signed by a number of other ex-servicemen. Their proposal introduced the principle that the new constitution should be ratified by the nation. Laval agreed to the amendment: "The Constitution will be ratified by the nation and applied by the Assemblies it will have created" would replace the sentence "The Constitution would be ratified by the Assemblies it has created." Then Laval attacked England for having led France into the war and murdered French sailors at Mers-el-Kébir.[36] He denounced the previous government for having overlooked national interests out of political bias. And he explained that the government proposal was "the condemnation, not only of the parliamentary regime, but also of everything that was and can no longer be."[37]

The session of the National Assembly in the afternoon proceeded rapidly. In his capacity as president of the Assembly Jules Jeanneney opened the meeting and read a telegram from several parliamentarians who found themselves in Algiers at the time of the vote. Following the government's instructions,

36. On 3 July 1940 a British fleet shelled the French ships anchored in the harbor of Mers-el-Kébir in Algeria, after the French government rejected an ultimatum enjoining these ships "to go to distant colonial ports, join the British or scuttle itself" (Paxton 1972, 56). More than 1,260 French sailors were killed during this attack.

37. "[Le projet du Gouvernement] est la condamnation, non seulement du régime parlementaire, mais de tout ce qui a été et ne peut plus être." *Événements* I, 488. The *Journal Officiel* did not reproduce the minutes of this meeting, attended only by parliamentarians. The minutes are available along with several other documents in the report published after the war by the parliamentary Commission of Inquiry set up to investigate the events that occurred in France between 1933 and 1945. This report (hereafter *Événements*) also included the hearings of the commission.

these parliamentarians had sailed from Bordeaux to North Africa before the conclusion of the armistice on the steamer *Massilia*. The telegram protested the administrative hurdles that prevented them from attending the vote. After the reading of the telegram, Édouard Herriot, the chairman of the Chamber of Deputies, made a short announcement in which he explained that these parliamentarians left "because they had been instructed to do so by the government." Laval took note of this declaration while contrasting the attitude of those who left with that of Marshal Pétain, who declared: "Whatever happens, I for myself will stay among my fellow citizens." Laval added, "One cannot serve France by leaving it."[38]

After this incident the conservative Fernand Bouisson, former president of the Chamber of Deputies, requested that the government's bill be given priority treatment. When Jeanneney began to determine the number of votes required to reach a simple majority, Senator Mireaux, from the conservative Groupe de l'Union Démocratique, interjected to propose that the majority be calculated according to the number of those present and not according to the number of mandates in the two Assemblies.[39] His motion was adopted by a show of hands. The session was then suspended at 2:50 P.M. — it had started at 2:05 P.M. — to let a special commission, made up of the Senate's Legislative Commission and the Chamber's Commission of Universal Suffrage, examine the legality of the bill submitted by the government.

The commission first heard Laval, who confirmed that the bill would be modified as suggested in the morning session and asserted that the two chambers would be maintained "until the new Assemblies foreshadowed by the new Constitution will be created." In the course of his explanations before the commission, Laval also indicated that no parliamentary committee would decide on the new constitution and that the right to become French after one generation would be called into question: "France needs to be governed exclusively by Frenchmen."[40] The commission "unanimously" adopted the bill with the exception of four votes.

The session resumed at 5:20 P.M. Senator Boivin-Champeaux, in his capacity as spokesman of the Special Commission, delivered the report of the commission on the bill submitted to the National Assembly. "[This bill] gives to the

---

38. "Quoiqu'il arrive, moi, je resterai au milieu de mes concitoyens . . . ce n'est pas en quittant la France qu'on peut la servir." *Journal Officiel*, Annales de la Chambre des Députés, 16ème Législature, Débats parlementaires, Sessions ordinaires et extraordinaires de 1940, Séance du 10 juillet 1940, 822.

39. Ibid., 823.

40. "Compte rendu de la séance tenue par la Commission constitutionnelle de l'Assemblée Nationale, le 10 juillet 1940," reproduced in *Événements* I, 498–502.

government of Marshal Pétain full executive and legislative powers. It provides these powers without restrictions, in the largest possible sense. . . . Second, this bill gives the government constitutional powers."[41] Boivin-Champeaux went on to point out that the new constitution would be ratified by the nation. Finally he raised the issue of the future institutions: "What will be this new constitution? We only know what was exposed to us in the statement of motives, the terms of which, by the way, we can only approve: homeland, labor, family. The image of France would not be complete if it did not also include the freedoms for which so many generations have fought [Applause]."[42]

The bill was put to a vote and passed by 569 to 80, with 21 abstentions (table 6):[43] "The National Assembly confers all powers on the Government of the Republic, under the signature and authority of Marshal Pétain, President of the Council, to promulgate by one or more acts, the new Constitution of the French State. This Constitution will guarantee the rights of Labor, Family, and Homeland. It will be ratified by the nation and applied by the Assemblies it will have created."[44]

The "French State"

The next day (11 July) Pétain promulgated several "constitutional acts," whereby he abolished the legislative power of the parliament, repealed the constitutional article stipulating that the president of the Republic ought to be elected by the National Assembly, adjourned the existent chambers *sine die*, and appointed himself "Head of the French State." These constitutional acts gave him "authority to carry out all executive and legislative acts, except declarations of war, without referring to the Assembly" (Paxton 1972, 32). This promulgation, the style of which was reminiscent of royal edicts ("We, Marshal Pétain . . ."), marked the legal birth of what is known as the Vichy regime.

The category of legal revolution captures the peculiarity of one type of regime breakdown that is not restricted to Germany in March 1933 or France in July 1940. Italy 1924, Czechoslovakia 1948, France 1958, Poland 1989, East Germany

41. "[Ce texte] donne au Gouvernement du Maréchal Pétain les pleins pouvoirs exécutifs et législatifs. Il les lui donne sans restriction, de la façon la plus étendue. . . . Le texte donne en second lieu, au Gouvernement, les pouvoirs constituants." *Journal Officiel*, Séance du 10 juillet 1940, 824.

42. Ibid.

43. Calculated on the number of those who officially attended the session, the majority requested to pass the bill was 336.

44. *Journal Officiel*, Débats parlementaires, 11 July 1940.

Table 6   Breakdown of the Vote in the National Assembly, 10 July 1940

		Yes	No	Absten-tion	Absent (Passengers aboard the *Massilia*)	Other Absent	Total
Left	Union Populaire Française (UPF; former communists)	7	3	0	1	2	13
	Parti Socialiste (SFIO)	87	29	6	8	23	153
	Socialist Party (SFIO; Senate)	3	7	0	0	4	14
	Union Socialiste Républicaine (USR)	20	0	0	0	7	27
	Gauche Indépendante	5	6	0	1	4	16
	Groupe Républicaine Radical et Radical-Socialiste (Radical Party)	65	13	3	12	19	112
	Gauche Démocratique, radicale et radicale-socialiste (Senate)	106	14	8	1	17	146
	Gauche Démocratique et Radicale Indépendante	31	0	0	0	4	35
	Groupe Démocrate Populaire	11	2	0	0	1	14
	Union Démocratique et Radicale (UDR)	25	0	0	0	6	31
	Alliance	34	2	1	0	5	42
	Groupe Agraire Indépendant	8	0	0	0	2	10
	Groupe Indépendant d'Action Populaire	10	0	0	1	4	15
	Républicains Indépendants et d'Action Sociale	23	1	0	0	2	26
	Union Républicaine	41	0	1	0	17	59
	Indépendants Républicains	6	0	0	1	4	11
	Action Nationale, Républicaine et Sociale	11	0	0	0	6	17
	Fédération Républicaine	43	0	2	2	11	58
Right	Parti Social Français	7	0	0	0	3	10
Not affiliated		26	3	0	0	9	38
Total		569	80	21	27	150	847

Sources: *Journal Officiel, Chambre des Députés, 22 juillet 1948: Annexe au procès-verbal de la séance du mercredi 10 juillet 1940*; *Dictionnaire des parlementaires français*; Sagnès (1991, 568).

1989 are amenable to the same characterization. The choice of an empirical category has conceptual implications. When we refer to revolution we think of a process and an outcome. The process describes the emergence of a situation of "dual" (Trotsky 2001 [1932], 225) or "multiple" (Tilly 1975) sovereignty, in which different blocs exercise state-like functions and advance "effective, competing and mutually exclusive claims to the state" (519). Public authority is divided into one or more power centers that obtain practical recognition for their claims to exclusive legitimacy from important segments of the population at large (Aya 1979, 45).

When legal revolutions occur, state sovereignty is not fragmented into several blocs. We do not observe blocs pitted against one another and mobilizing under their wings an army of militants, supporters, or subjects. The revolutionary character of the political process lies in its outcome: a change in state and authority structures. In focusing on outcomes, however, we tend to lose sight of the collective processes that make the oxymoron—the revolution is *legal*—possible. To fully account for this paradoxical character, we need to shift away from the generic category and focus on these collective processes. The transition to an authoritarian regime is legal because groups formally abdicate their political capacity.

Chapter 2

Constitutional Abdication

He that performeth first, has no assurance the other will perform after; because the bonds of words are too weak to bridle men's ambition, avarice, and other Passions. — Hobbes (*Leviathan*, I, 14)

1

These collective decisions enact a power transfer and open the way to a change in the state structure. The change is legal and revolutionary. It is legal with regard to the process of decision implementation, and revolutionary with regard to its outcome. How much of the revolution is contained in the law? To what extent does the legal character of the transition process beget its revolutionary outcome? The scope of the constitutional mandate determines the extent to which the power transfer is a foundational act for the revolution to come. If the scope is limited, then we may have to revise the notion of legal revolution. The oxymoron is deceptive if the law cannot justify the revolution.

From a formal standpoint, the bills voted in March 1933 and July 1940 qualify the devolution of constitutional rights. Parliamentarians do not simply say: "We give you the right to write and implement a new constitution." They say: "You have the right to design constitutional rules under the following qualifications." The March 1933 bill states that the president's rights "remain unchanged" and that the institution of parliament will be preserved. The July 1940 bill indicates that the new constitution will be ratified by the nation. At first sight, it seems that these specifications pose limits to what the challenger can legally do. Hitler cannot suppress the president's decisional rights. Nor can he, according to the bill, suppress parliament. Since the mandate is qualified, one could also argue that the power transfer is limited.

This view is plausible, but mistaken. A close analysis of the legal architecture of the March 1933 bill and of the "silences" of the text voted in July 1940 shows that these qualifications are pro forma. They adorn the unconditional character of the power transfer. Once the bills are stripped of formal paraphernalia, they appear for what they are: devolutions without warrantees, constitutional blank checks. In each case parliament transfers the right to define rules allocating decisional and representational rights—constitutional rules—to a political challenger. This challenger has a free hand to discard the existent constitutional structure and set up political institutions in which his arbitrary power is unchecked.

2

These few remarks bring the puzzle into relief. Groups that abdicate their constitutional authority abdicate their capacity to determine their own fate. They consent to abandoning their right to setting regulating principles for themselves. Once this constitutional authority has been transferred without institutional guarantee the challenger cannot, properly speaking, abuse his power. Any constitutional act falls within the scope of the delegation. Therefore the challenger cannot credibly commit himself not to abuse his power. His verbal promises, whatever they may be, have no binding quality.

Note furthermore that constitutional requests disregarding accountability and institutional guarantees would have little raison d'être if they were not motivated by an authoritarian agenda. What is the point of requesting unrestricted constitutional capacity if not to maximize power? Groups faced with such requests have good reasons to suspect that the claimant harbors authoritarian goals. His demands are revealing of a broader political project: he seeks unrestricted power. Legal interpretations confined to formal issues miss the point if they do not take into account this political subtext. A legal exegesis reveals the scope of the power transfer. A political interpretation lays bare its underlying agenda and motivations.

Both observations raise the issue of the rationality of such decisions. I illustrate the problem through the analytical device of a stylized game between the constitutional claimant (the "challenger") and those subject to his challenge (the "target actors"). This formal approach normatively concludes that in the absence of an institutional compromise ex ante and if the target actors behave rationally, for them opposition is the best response. They have no guarantee that their basic rights and interests will not be crucially endangered once the power transfer is completed, and they should expect that the challenger will strive to monopolize state power. This conclusion is based on three restrictive assumptions: (1) There is uncertainty as to the outcome of a showdown between the two parties. (2) The exclusive character of the challenger's claims to state power is public knowledge. (3) The challenger and the target actors have mutually exclusive interests. Each of these assumptions suggests in counterpoint a possible explanation of the outcome.

LEX REGIA OR CONDITIONAL TRANSFER?

> The government requested a total and unconditional power delegation.
> —Erwin Respondek, former Center party delegate[1]

Hitler's enabling bill has five articles. Article 1 stipulates that the right to amend the constitution is granted to the government, not the chancellor. Article 2 excludes from the cabinet's competence decrees pertaining to "the institution of the Reichstag and the Reichsrat as such," and preserves the constitutional prerogatives of the Reich president, including the right to dismiss the chancellor and the supreme command of the army. Article 5 fixes the duration of the bill at four years and confines the right of constitutional amendment to the existent cabinet: the "bill will expire once . . . the present government is replaced with another one."[2] These provisions can be interpreted as restricting the scope of the power transfer. Brecht (1944, 99) argues, for instance, that the act of delegation implied by the bill is not a *lex regia*, a transfer of sovereignty to one single man, since it is restricted in several respects. Is that the case? Can these provisions be viewed as legal and reasonable safeguards against absolute power?

Article 2: The Rights of the Reich President Remain Unchanged

As mentioned in chapter 1, the Weimar constitution granted considerable powers to the Reich president. In stating that the rights of the president remained unchanged,[3] the enabling bill apparently preserved this hierarchy of rights and offered a safeguard against the chancellor's arbitrary power. Erwin Respondek, former Center Reichstag delegate, made precisely this point: "First, the wording of the enabling bill was important. Second, the bills that would be enacted by the cabinet in virtue of Article 2 could deviate from the Constitution, to the extent that they did not deal with the institutions of the Reichstag and the Reichsrat, and the rights of the Reich president. [The enabling bill did not] grant the 30 January cabinet full powers without restrictions. On the contrary, the full powers were granted within the limits set by the grounding institutions of the Constitution."[4]

---

1. "Die Reichsregierung forderte jedoch eine absolut selbständige Vollmacht." Bundesarchiv, Koblenz, Nachlaß Schwertfeger, N1015/255, Das "Ermächtigungsgesetz," April 1947, statement by Respondek, 1.
2. *Reichsgesetzblatt*, 1933, I, 141.
3. Ibid.
4. Bundesarchiv, Koblenz, Nachlaß Wirth, N 1018/32, Das "Ermächtigungsgesetz," statement

This literal reading of Article 2 overlooks the key issue. By virtue of article 1, the government under the responsibility of the chancellor had the right to enact bills independently of the supervision of the president. The point is crucial. Heretofore the drawing up and promulgation of the bills passed by parliament was the president's special right. He had now lost this exclusive privilege. One could object that he did not lose it to the benefit of the chancellor, since Article 1 granted the right to amend the constitution—and, by extension, the right to enact bills independently of parliamentary supervision—to "the government." The chancellor bore the responsibility of the government, however. The permanence of the cabinet was tied to his person. Individual resignations and cabinet reshuffles would not affect the power delegation.[5] Therefore the power delegation voted by parliament applied "not to the totality of the cabinet, but to Hitler personally" (Becker 1961b, 200).

If the president did not de jure lose the right to issue emergency decrees, Hitler had the power to thwart the enactment of such decrees by refusing to countersign them. Consequently the full powers requested from parliament restricted the functions of the Reich president to purely "representational ones" (Becker 1961b, 200). This is the paradox of Article 2. It provided a "guarantee" that obfuscated a fundamental change in the structure of decisional rights. Once it was acknowledged that the enabling bill substantially restricted presidential prerogatives (Schneider 1968 [1953], 423), the provision stating that the rights of the Reich president remain unchanged lost much of its significance and could not be interpreted as a restriction that would effectively check Hitler's legislative and executive capacity.

This fundamental change did not elude the attention of actors well versed in the intricacies of power struggles. One German Nationalist deputy in the Prussian parliament, Edmund Forschbach, revealed the dismay caused among some of his reactionary friends by the provision allowing the chancellor to promulgate bills without the president's supervision and assent. "[Edgar] Jung was incensed by the fact that according to the draft of the bill, the right to promulgate and publish laws—which, in the Weimar constitution, belonged to the Reich president—was to be handed over to the Reich government."[6] In a meeting of the German Nationalist delegation on 20 March, Alfred Hugen-

---

by Respondek, April 1947, 3. This statement is also in the Nachlaß Schwertfeger, Bundesarchiv, Koblenz, NL Schwertfeger, N1015/255.

5. For instance, as Schneider (1968 [1953], 421) points out, Hugenberg's resignation from the Ministry of Economy and Alimentation at the end of June 1933 did not represent a change in government.

6. Konrad Adenauer Stiftung, Sankt Augustin, NL Forschbach, I-199, 014/1, "Vier Tage," 1.

berg emphasized the same point, noting that the bill implied a change in the position of the president of the Reich. While until now the president had the responsibility to issue emergency decrees, the proposed bill dispensed with his cooperation. Laws would be decided by the cabinet and promulgated by the chancellor.[7]

Blank Check

Thus an analysis of the overall architecture and logic of the bill shows that the chancellor (Hitler) could legally neutralize or circumvent the restrictions contained in Article 2. These restrictions were mainly formal. This conclusion justifies the characterization of the bill as a blank check (*Blankovollmacht*) (Becker 1961a, 195, 200; Junker 1969, 183; Morsey 1977, 152) and the decision of the Catholic parties as an act of "self-dismissal" (*Selbstaufgabe*) (Volk 1990, 53). Through their consent to the enabling bill, the Catholic parties "eliminated themselves" (*Die katholischen Parteien . . . [haben] sich ausgeschaltet*) (Volk 1990, 51). They sanctioned their own removal (Junker 1969, 188).

The historical significance of the bill should also be assessed from this perspective. This was not the first time that the Reichstag was being asked to vote on a bill allowing the government to deviate from normal legislative proceedings (Bracher 1962, 83). Parliament had passed several enabling acts in 1923–24 permitting the government to issue emergency ordinances concerning economic and fiscal matters (Finn 1991, 199). Hitler's enabling bill, however, was quite different in nature. The bill's provisions offered "no guarantee against

---

7. Bundesarchiv, Koblenz, Nachlaß Martin Spahn N1324/175, 13–14. (Spahn, who took these notes, added in parentheses that Hugenberg on this issue expressed himself in a "very unintelligible way" and that because of this Spahn was not sure whether he had rendered his words appropriately.) Along the same lines, on 21 March 1933 the president of the district court of Leipzig, Dr. Wagner, wrote to German Nationalist representatives to point out that according to the bill the chancellor could now promulgate laws against the will of the Reich president. This meant that through such a bill, the chancellor could simply designate a successor after the Reich president died. Wagner mentions his German Nationalist credentials and indicates that he took cognizance of the content of the bill in the press. His letter suggests three amendments: (a) all ministers must sign new laws, (b) the Reich president must enact them and the minister must countersign them, (c) a new Reich president should be elected according to the provisions of the constitution. The German Nationalist Reichstag delegate Schmidt-Hannover has a copy of this letter in his personal papers, Bundesarchiv, Koblenz, Nachlaß Schmidt-Hannover, N1211/34: letter from Wagner, 21 March 1933. In his diary on 18 March Reinhold Quaatz, a member of the DNVP Reichstag delegation, mentions the prospect of an enabling bill to "completely eliminate [*ausschalten*] Hindenburg." Quaatz, *Die Deutschnationalen und die Zerstörung der Weimarer Republik*, 243.

interference with the power of member states, with the organization and functioning of political parties, with the position of the judiciary, and with other vital elements in the political structure of the country" (Watkins 1939, 125).

Hitler was asking the non-Nazi delegations in Parliament to approve in advance any legislation he would deem necessary. The power transfer had therefore an unconditional character (Matz 1989, 144). "In the scope of powers granted and in the elimination of parliamentary restraints, the Hitler enabling bill was without precedent under the Weimar Constitution" (Watkins 1939, 124). Hoerster-Philips (1998, 429) remarks in this regard that if the emergency decree of 28 February invalidated parts of the constitution, civil liberties, and the rights of the regional states, Hitler's enabling bill on the other hand disposed of the Constitution as a whole and removed the power of parliament. It called into question the very substance of a democratic and parliamentary state (Böckenförde 1961, 218). The four-year limit of application could fool no one. Devolution of constitutional powers to Hitler and his cabinet was bound to seal the constitutional death of the Weimar Republic. It implied the "legal burial of the Republic" without the honors of the state, as the *Frankfurter Zeitung* put it a few days later.

RATIFICATION

> My [July 1940] vote was strictly conditioned by the two following
> considerations: a) The power delegation was granted to the government of
> the Republic. This implied the future permanence of the republican design of
> the government. b) According to the final version of the bill, the Nation will
> ratify the new constitution. In the initial bill, this ratification was to be carried
> out by the assemblies it will have created. Therefore, I had the three following
> guarantees: a) the republican regime will continue, b) the nation will ratify and
> c) there will be no constitution before sovereignty is recovered.
> —René Besse, centrist deputy from the Democratic Left[8]

Besse's explanation for his vote was typical of the evidence invoked by those who described the vote as a conditional power delegation and a "swindle." On 11 July Pétain issued several constitutional acts that dispensed with the republican form of the regime. Parliamentarians who referred to a swindle argued that these acts had no legal validity, since the National Assembly transferred the power to write and promulgate a constitution to the "government of the Republic." As a result, Pétain had no mandate to get rid of the republican

8. Archives Nationales, Dossiers du jury d'honneur, Paris, AL5300, dossier René Besse, letter to the honor jury, n.d.

regime. Along these lines, Henri Becquart, a far-right deputy of the Republican Federation, explained that "on 11 July, not on 10 July, was the law breached and the Republic overthrown in defiance of the bill passed on July 10 by the National Assembly."[9] The conservative senator Jean Boivin-Champeaux developed a consonant argument: on 10 July parliamentarians were voting for the permanence of the republican regime to be ratified by the nation.[10]

All Powers . . .

This interpretation does not stand up to a closer examination. First, the constitutional mandate conferred on the government was de facto a transfer of constitutional authority to Pétain, since the government's responsibility was placed under his authority. The bill acknowledged this transfer of authority with the following wording: "The National Assembly confers all powers on the Government of the Republic, *under the signature and authority of Marshal Pétain*, President of the Council . . ." (my emphasis).[11] Second, the government under the authority and signature of Marshal Pétain has "*all powers . . . to promulgate* by one or more acts, the new Constitution of the French State" (my emphasis). Therefore the constitutional acts of 11 July 1940, whereby Pétain appoints himself head of the French state and adjourns the existent chambers sine die, cannot be deemed illegal.

Is not "ratification by the nation" a sufficient guarantee against the emergence of a nondemocratic regime? The silence of the bill on this issue is eloquent. Pétain has a mandate to promulgate constitutional acts *before* the nation ratifies them. There is no indication about the conditions under which the nation would ratify the new constitution. Nor is there any indication about the procedures of this ratification. During the meeting with the National Assembly "constitutional commission" on the afternoon of 10 July, members of the commission ask Laval for details on the ratification process. Laval replies that he cannot provide these details.[12] In the absence of further specifications, these issues fall within the scope of the constitutional mandate.

Public statements at the time of the decision betray an awareness of this lack of guarantees.[13] It is significant in this regard that in his report before the

9. Becquart, *Au temps du silence*, 212.

10. *Événements* VII, 2199–2200.

11. *Journal Officiel*, Séance de l'Assemblée Nationale du 10 juillet 1940, 823.

12. The minutes of this meeting are reproduced in *Événements*; for this specific exchange see 500–501.

13. For instance, on 5 July in a public meeting attended by Laval, the conservative deputy Marcel Héraud underlined the blank spots of the bill: "Which reform do you intend to realize?

National Assembly right before the bill was put to a vote, the conservative senator Jean Boivin-Champeaux raised the problem of the "transition period" and expressed the *wish* that the existent assemblies would continue to function while simultaneously acknowledging that the decision would rest with the government, since the bill left the issue open.[14] The bill and the text laying out the motivations for it (*exposé des motifs*) made no statement about the nature of the regime to come. There was no official commitment to preserve the republican format.[15] Nor was there an official commitment to preserve individual freedoms.[16]

Self-deposition

The bill stated it plainly: It was a delegation of full powers—executive, legislative, constitutional—to one single man. Personal testimonies acknowledge the scope of the delegation. The centrist deputy Paul Boulet described Laval's bill as "requesting from the members of the [National] Assembly that they relinquish their constitutional powers in order to hand them over to one man."[17] Léon Blum emphasized that "Laval planned to request a power delegation left

---

You did not tell us. . . . About the constitution that you anticipate, I only know the verbal aspect: Labor! Family! Homeland! Authority! These are high-sounding words which I read on electoral leaflets and which could serve to defend the Republic as well as to fight it. Furthermore, we even ignore who will be in charge of writing and promulgating the constitution. Will it be Marshal Pétain? Will it be you, Laval? After we divest ourselves of our power, the strongest or the boldest could take hold of it" (Archives Nationales, Dossiers du jury d'honneur, Paris, AL5316, file Héraud, draft of the speech delivered by Héraud submitted to the honor jury. Héraud voted "yes" on 10 July). In his diary the conservative senator Pernot also notes how uncertain political developments look at this point (Pernot, "Que nous réserve l'aventure?," *Journal de guerre*, 106).

14. *Journal Officiel*, Séance de l'Assemblée Nationale du 10 juillet 1940, 824.

15. In the commission of universal suffrage that meets on the morning of 9 July, Pierre Trémintin, deputy of the Parti Démocrate Populaire, requests an amendment to the bill voted on 9 July—the bill stating the necessity of a constitutional revision (see chapter 1). This amendment explicitly refers to the "preservation of the republican form of the regime." Laval, according to Trémintin, turns down this request. Archives départementales du Finistère, Archive Trémintin, Quimper, handwritten notes on the "Projet de Résolution," 104 J 5.

16. In the meeting of the constitutional commission of the National Assembly on the afternoon of 10 July, before the vote, the senator Boivin-Champeaux deplores the fact that the government text made no reference to individual freedoms. His colleague Pierre Masse asks for a qualification: "After the last sentence: 'This constitution will guarantee the rights of Labor, Family and Nation' could we add: 'and individual freedoms'?" Laval dismisses this request (*Événements* IV, 501; quoted by Wieviorka 2001, 63).

17. Paul Boulet's testimony before the Committee of Inquiry set up after the war (*Événements* VII, 2213).

blank, a total and global delegation to the benefit of Marshal Pétain."[18] Contemporary actors and witnesses were in no way mistaken about the political significance of this vote: given the scope of the power devolution, it amounted to an act of political hara-kiri, "one without precedent."[19]

The regional newspaper *Le Petit Dauphinois* reported on 9 July, "The next meeting [of the National Assembly] will witness the deputies countersign their own *abdication* act and attend the funeral service of the regime that fell into abeyance."[20] In his diary the conservative senator Jacques Bardoux remarked about the vote: "An icy hush welcomed the ballot whereby parliament willfully voted its immediate *deposition*"[21] (my emphases). The Socialist deputy Louis Gros was even more blunt: "Parliament purely and simply committed suicide. . . . The Third Republic was dead. . . . This was a total abdication."[22]

The scope of the power delegation and its unprecedented character explain why initially Paul Baudouin, the minister of foreign affairs in Pétain's cabinet, had serious doubts about the success of Laval's initiative. Baudouin thought that these plans were dangerous, since they "could only succeed if 480 senators

18. Blum, *Mémoires*, 71. The Socialist deputy François Camel observes in his contemporary notes: "[10 July] In spite of protests and questions, it was impossible to get precisions on the new constitution and the rights of the nation in the new regime" (François Camel, *Ultimes Paroles*, 32).

19. Bardoux, *Journal d'un témoin de la Troisième*, 405; Paul-Boncour, *Entre deux guerres*, 280.

20. Quoted by Calef (1988, 420–21). For Azéma (1984, 53) and Cointet-Labrousse (1987, 29) the vote was a parliamentary "hara-kiri."

21. Bardoux, *Journal d'un témoin de la Troisième*, 405.

22. "Le parlement venait purement et simplement de se suicider. . . . La Troisième République était morte" (Gros, *République toujours*, 65). "C'était donc une abdication totale . . ." (68). A few days after the vote, the Socialist deputy François Camel makes the same assessment: "Parliament abdicated in disgrace" ("Le Parlement a abdiqué dans la boue!") (Camel, "Ultimes Paroles," 31, statement read on 23 July 1940 before the members of the local SFIO cell in Saint-Girons). Several parliamentarians refer to the vote as an act of "political suicide": "Parliament committed suicide" ("Le parlement s'est suicidé"), Archives Départementales du Rhône, Archives Emile Bender, Lyon, 64 J 6, 273; "suicide through persuasion" ("suicide par persuasion"), Paul-Boncour, *Entre deux guerres*, 284. As early as 2 July, Déat in his war diary evokes the "hara-kiri" which Laval is requesting from senators and deputies (Archives Nationales, Paris, F7 15342: Déat, Journal de guerre, 362). De Monzie's journal, published in 1941, mentions laval's harangues to "those committing suicide in parliament" ("les suicidés du parlement," *Ci-devant*, 263). In his personal notes the conservative deputy Flandin refers to the assemblies having abdicated "without honor" ("les assemblées abdiquaient sans grandeur") (Bibliothèque Nationale, Paris, Archives Flandin, Don 31357, box 127: "notes de base pour les mémoires"). As these last two examples show, those who voted "yes" also describe the decision as an "abdication." The Radical deputy Camille Briquet, for instance, explained after the war that this "abdication" was a "necessary sacrifice" (Archives Nationales, Dossiers du jury d'honneur, Paris: dossier Briquet, AL5302).

and deputies agreed to commit suicide."[23] Significantly, no one protested when the day after the vote Pétain promulgated constitutional acts that allowed him to assume the new office of "Head of the French State" (Michel 1966, 68; Paxton 1972, 32). The Radical deputy Lucien Galimand, who voted "yes," confirms this point. "The first constitutional acts, as well as Pétain's broadcast message neither surprised nor scandalized anyone."[24] This absence of reaction casts doubt on the ex post suggestion that Pétain's constitutional acts "betrayed" the mandate granted by parliamentarians, and that it was a breach of confidence and a "coup" (Édouard Herriot). No one protested on 11 July, most probably because everyone knew that legally and politically, parliament had signed a blank check to Pétain.

COMMITMENT AND ABDICATION

> Who? Why? (Foreign Policy?) Which guarantees? Whose responsibilities? No one knows — Handwritten notes dated 9 July 1940 by Ernest Pezet, deputy of the Popular Democratic party[25]

> "Où nous conduit-on?" ["Where are we being led?"]
> (Albert Rivière, exchange with Chautemps, July 8, 1940, Vichy).[26]

The Terms of the Challenge

Consider a collection of actors who interact. Their interactions are regulated by a set of formally codified rules. One actor ("the challenger") requests the right to redefine these rules. This right can only be granted by a definite proportion of those who are directly concerned by the challenge (the "target actors"). Target actors face the following dilemma. They have to decide either to acquiesce in the challenger's demands or to turn them down. In turning down these demands, they engage in a direct showdown with the challenger. In acquiescing in the transfer of constitutional powers, they entitle the challenger to transform the state and control its coercive resources. The challenger will acquire the right to alter the rules regulating processes of power allocation and political competition. Since institutional arrangements condition political power — that

---

23. Baudouin, *Neuf mois au gouvernement*, 222, see also 227. Baudouin favored instead a solution according to which Pétain would be granted full powers to govern, a new government would be appointed, and the chambers would be recessed indefinitely.

24. Galimand, *Vive Pétain! Vive de Gaulle!*, 65.

25. Fondation Nationale des Sciences Politiques, Paris, Archives Pezet, handwritten note, "Vichy—9 juillet 1940," P E 6, dossier 1.

26. Archives Nationales, Paris, papiers d'Albert Rivière, AB/XIX/4238/1/dossier 1, 229.

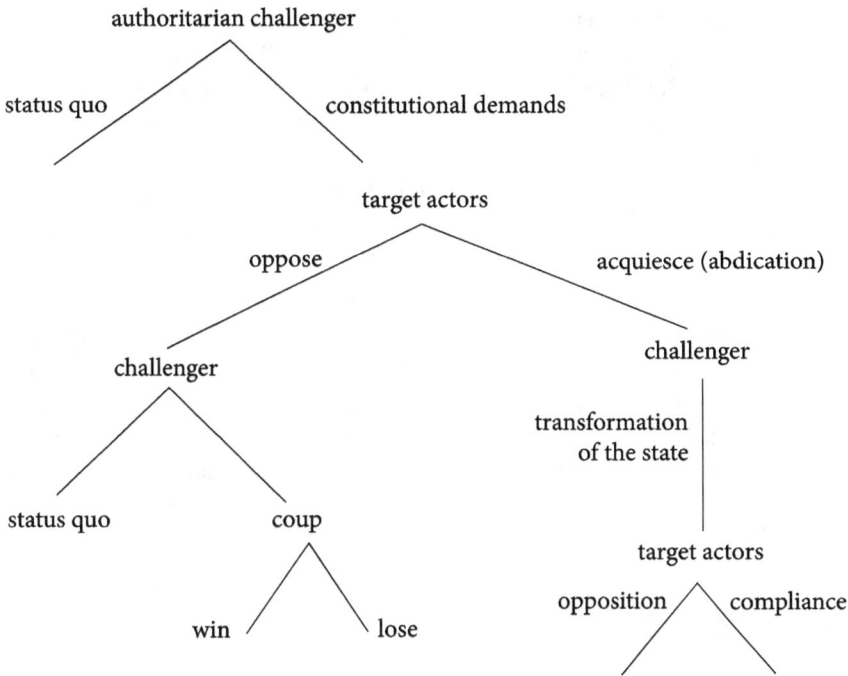

Figure 1 Abdication game

is, the probabilities that "particular interests will be realized to a definite degree and in a specific manner" (Przeworski 1987, 67) — target actors are engaged in a struggle that bears upon their very capacity to realize their interests.

This dilemma may be represented in abstract as a three-round game (figure 1). First the challenger discloses his constitutional demands. Then the target actors choose between turning down these political demands (*opposition*) and endorsing them (*constitutional abdication*). If the target actors turn down the challenger's constitutional request, two scenarios are possible: either the challenger backs off (*status quo*) or he decides to go ahead and impose his claims by force (*coup*). If target actors acquiesce in the challenger's constitutional request, the latter has free rein to transform the state.

The target actors' decision whether to oppose or acquiesce in the challenger's demands is a function of what they expect the challengers to do once their constitutional request has been fulfilled (Fearon 1993). The key point is that the challenger's political demands (1) are exclusive and (2) bear upon constitutional rules. The challenger asks to be the exclusive depositary of political sovereignty and to be granted the right to determine how the game will be played in the future. The challenger claims the authority to judge how and to what extent he will use the state's coercive resources. He does not commit himself to any specific institutional arrangement. In Przeworski's terms (1987, 64), there is no "institutional compromise"; there is no institution binding the parties to a certain type of outcome. The transition from one regime to another is not "negotiated."

In these conditions target actors should expect that if they abdicate, the challenger will attempt to push his advantage as far as possible and, for this purpose, will implement policies maximizing his own power. They have no guarantee that the challenger will refrain from abusing his power once he has consolidated his hold over the state. Moreover, opposition to the challenger will be less likely to succeed after the power transfer. Since target actors have no guarantee that their basic interests will be unaffected in the process, the challenger cannot credibly commit himself to a policy of self-restraint. Nominal promises will not do. Hence constitutional abdication is a suboptimal choice. Target actors have a sufficient motive to turn down the challenger's bid for exclusive power (see the addendum to this chapter).

Validity

The lack of warrantees highlights the peculiarity of these collective decisions. Neither in March 1933 nor in July 1940 is the challenger compelled to abide by specific rules and principles. Guarantees are given orally if at all. Target actors have every reason to believe that the challenger will strive to monopolize state power and that their own capacity for resistance will be even more limited after the power transfer is completed. Yet they do consent to the devolution. Everything happens as if there were no commitment problem or, to be more precise, as if this problem were of no consequence.[27]

In abdicating the right to define constitutional rules, the target actors precommit themselves to endorsing an institutional outcome about which they will have no say. They tie their hands, but in a way that makes it very different from the type of precommitment that Elster (1984, 37) details with the parable of Ulysses and the sirens. In requesting that his companions attach him to the mast, Ulysses voluntarily abdicates the capacity to decide for himself. This abdication is temporary. It will last as long as the sirens' singing lasts. Furthermore, his abdication enhances his future capacity to act, since if he were not tied to the mast, his ruin would be sealed. The crew has no interest in taking

---

27. In this respect, the parliamentary decisions of March 1933 and July 1940 go counter to the basic rationality of a constitutional framework. The challenger's promises not to hurt others are not credible, since he is not constrained "to obey a set of rules that do not permit leeway for violating commitments" (North and Weingast 1989, 804).

advantage of the situation, since they need his expertise for the rest of the trip. Hence his decision to have himself tied is rational.

In the realm of institutional decisions pertaining to constitutional practices, the equivalent of Ulysses's decision is a constitutional dictatorship. Confronted with a crisis jeopardizing its continued existence, the members of a representative institution agree to voluntarily hand over lawmaking authority to an executive office. A constitutional dictatorship is "temporary and self-destructive" (Rossiter 1948, 9). It remains in effect as long as the crisis is serious enough to jeopardize the polity. The members of the representative assembly suspend the constitution to save it from being permanently destroyed. The purpose of the suspension is to dispense with the crisis. The Roman dictatorship provides the paragon of this model of power devolution. In an emergency, the republic officials called upon a citizen and endowed him with absolute powers. In this model of power devolution, the transfer of absolute powers is designed to preserve the constitution.

Constitutional abdications are a different matter. Here one does not abdicate for the purpose of preserving oneself. Rather, one abdicates the capacity to preserve oneself. The delegation of capacity opens the door to the possibility of organized servitude. These few observations also outline in what sense constitutional abdications differ from the power transfers conceptualized by Coleman (1990, 207–16). In Coleman's framework individuals transfer their right of control over their action to one another, and by derivation to the group constituted of themselves, so that they can pursue mutual interests. The transfer is a prerequisite for a type of collective action geared to a collective good. This transfer is not unilateral: I transfer my right to others assuming that others do the same.

Consider the decision whether or not to rush to an exit door if a fire alarm is sounded in a theater (Coleman 1990, 207). A priori, it is in the interest of each individual actor in the room to rush to the exit to maximize his chances to get out. In rushing, however, this individual actor motivates other people in the room to rush as well, and if the move is collective, there is a jam: the probability of getting out gets dramatically lower. Coleman analyzes the decision not to rush as a transfer of right: the actor acknowledges the right of the group to control his action. The transfer is conditional—it makes sense as long as there is no rush to the door—and mutually beneficial: it enhances the group's collective ability to increase its welfare. By contrast, the transfers of right investigated in this book are *unconditional* and a source of collective *incapacity*.

The political rationality of these collective decisions is thus in question (Duverger 1982, xiii). The problem underlies the debate about the constitutional validity of these power devolutions. From a formal standpoint, the enabling acts of March 1933 and July 1940 are legal power transfers, since they involve no departure from the requirements of the constitution (Jackson 2001, 134; Prélot 1972, 25–26). According to this conception, the political transitions that took place in 1933 and 1940 are constitutionally valid. Theorists of constitutional law, such as Carl Schmitt (1933, 458) and Kaisenberg (1933, 461), took advantage of this formal reading of the constitutional framework to legitimize the legal foundations of the "new state."

One could of course question this legality in light of the conditions in which the decisions were made. The legal rationale runs as follows: whenever threats and coercion are involved, the decision is not free and consequently actors' decisions cannot adequately be described as their own.[28] Beyond the argument about the conditions of a free vote, it is possible to question the rationality of constitutional abdication. The issue is whether legal decisions that lack the substantive requirement of a rational decision can be considered valid. As early as September 1940 René Cassin challenged the "absurd" decision of a constitutional devolution. A representative assembly has no mandate that allows its members to divest themselves of their constitutional authority. It cannot lawfully alienate its constitutional sovereignty. Transfers of constitutional powers such as those allegedly carried out in March 1933 and July 1940 are null and void.[29] They have no substance.

This legal critique rests on a metaconstitutional understanding of the right to amend the constitution. It assumes that the members of a representative assembly are bound by what Finn calls the "constitutive principles of constitutionalism": (1) executive power is to be restricted by "structural limitations and procedural guarantees" and (2) "government is based upon reason" (Finn 1991, 29). Failure to respect these grounding principles invalidates the assembly's decision.

Between a formal reading of the decision and a reading in terms of foundational principles the gap is unbridgeable, for the two readings rely on incommensurate principles of judgment. Both can be said to be true depending on the frame of reference taken into account. One takes as a reference the formal

28. This is, for instance, the view adopted by Léon Blum (*Mémoires*, 93) and Badie (*Vive la République*, 51).

29. Archives Nationales, Paris, Archives René Cassin 382 AP 31. See also the "déclaration organique complétant le Manifeste du 27 octobre 1940" in Musée Historique Henri Queuille, Neuvic, Archives Henri Queuille C I, dossier 2: "la dite assemblée, abdiquant une compétence qui lui appartenait à elle seule, s'est bornée à prendre la décision, aussi inconstitutionnelle qu'insensée, de confier à un tiers un véritable blanc-seing, à l'effet d'élaborer et d'appliquer lui-même une nouvelle constitution."

content of constitutional provisions, the other the constitutive principles of constitutionalism. The issue is bound to remain moot and the debate unresolved as long as the discussion is confined to arguments of constitutional law. The more fundamental question relates to the conditions under which a political commitment may be considered valid. What is the significance of a contract in which one party reserves for itself the right to define the content of its provisions?

THREE SCENARIOS

The analysis sketched above describes how target actors should behave given the problem at hand and the configuration of the game: target actors should reject the challengers' claims to constitutional power. This conclusion is based on three assumptions: (1) There is uncertainty as to the possible outcome of a showdown with the challenger. (2) Target actors are rational actors and they adequately decipher the challenger's effort to gain absolute power. (3) The challenger and the target actors have mutually exclusive interests. If the target actors expect the cost of a confrontation with their challenger to be unbearable, or if they believe that they are bound to be defeated, there is no commitment problem. The credibility of the challenger's promises becomes secondary to more immediate concerns (see the addendum to this chapter). Similarly, the conclusion drawn from the model does not hold if target actors fail to rationally gauge the situation or if they perceive their challengers' interests to be compatible with their own.

Each of these three assumptions is the negative of a possible explanation of abdication. The first explanation states that target actors abdicate because they are certain to be defeated. The cost of confrontation is perceived as so high that it precludes opposition. According to the second explanation, target actors do not follow a rational rule of decision. They misjudge their challenger's intentions by trusting, for instance, his promises of self-restraint. In this view, abdication results from miscalculation. The third explanation calls into question the assumption that target actors and their challengers have mutually exclusive interests. It sees abdication as stemming from a convergence of interests. The following pages briefly elaborate each of these scenarios in theoretical terms.

Coercion

The coercion thesis portrays abdication as a *forced* choice. Target actors foresee no way out of the standoff. They have no other reasonable choice. Two variants of this scenario might be considered. In the first, the target actors yield to the challenger's demands because they expect to be defeated if they oppose the challenger.[30] In abdicating, these actors anticipate and endorse the prospect of their defeat. Abdication is the "preemption of dethronement" (Elster 1985, 420). The second variant focuses on the expected cost of opposition. The target actors yield to the challenger because they expect that the conflict with the challenger as a result of their noncompliance would leave them worse off than if they complied with his demands. Abdication is a lesser evil.

Miscalculation

The miscalculation scenario calls into question the assumption that target actors correctly assess the implications and significance of their decision. They either believe that abdicating will provide them with future bargaining leverage (tactical miscalculation) or are mistaken about the true intentions of their challengers (strategic miscalculation). Tactical miscalculation means that the target actors are not mystified about the challenger's ultimate agenda — absolute power — but assume that their abdication will allow them to preserve their capacity for counteraction. Strategic miscalculation means that the target actors assume the challenger will not abuse state power once granted constitutional sovereignty. In either case, the target actors misjudge the outcome of a transfer of constitutional powers and give credence to their challenger's nominal assurances.

Collusion

The discussion so far rests on the hypothesis that the challenger and the target actors have conflicting interests. It may be, however, that the target actors agree to transfer their constitutional sovereignty because they view their political agenda as overlapping with the challenger's. Accommodation is motivated by the prospect of a mutually beneficial modus vivendi. The most plausible hypothesis in this regard is an ideological one. The target actors overlook the threat inherent to absolute, unchecked power and collude with the challenger because they have similar ideological interests, broadly defined as the value vested in models of social relations. In devolving their constitutional authority, the target actors seek to fulfill these ideological interests.

---

30. In formal terms, $p = 0$ (see the addendum to this chapter).

ACTORS AND ARENAS

In the previous analysis I made two restrictive assumptions that deserve further discussion. First, I assumed that the challenger and the target actors were unitary actors. For the challenger this simplification is acceptable. One single actor—the claimant—is expected to benefit from the power transfer. This transfer, once actualized, makes state power a personal attribute. Those who actively support the challenger—the challenging party—share the goal of state takeover. Their political preferences can be assumed to be homogeneous in this respect. For the target actors, however, this homogeneity assumption is unrealistic. The only reason so far for subsuming them under the same category is that they share the position as the bearers of constitutional authority. They collectively hold the right to decide on the rules allocating representational and decisional rights (constitutional rules). There is no reason to assume homogeneity with regard to other structural dimensions (class locations, status, political preference).

The second simplifying assumption concerns the modeling of the game. In focusing on the interaction between challenger and target actors, I have considered one arena of interactions and sidestepped factors which, although exogenous to this arena, may turn out to be relevant to understanding constitutional abdications. Actors simultaneously involved in different arenas may be confronted with noncongruent stakes that lead them to forsake their interests in one arena to preserve their interests in another (Tsebelis 1990, 4). If the target actors are political representatives and the challenge is directed at them because of this political status, two additional arenas need consideration. One encompasses the interactions with groups that because of their position in the structure of socioeconomic relations, wield considerable economic power. The other is the relationship between each target actor and his constituents. In the following chapters I will examine different facets of these arenas to explore whether and how the strategic games played in each may have affected the outcome.

The bills of March 1933 and July 1940 were examples of *constitutional abdication*, broadly defined as a formal decision by means of which a group or representative assembly transfers to an external agent the right to define the rules allocating decisional and representational rights. I cast this definition in broad terms to underline that the issue of constitutional abdication may apply to any situation in which collective interactions are regulated by a set of explicit institutional rules that no single actor can pretend to change at will. Constitutional challenges in parliamentary democracies represent one case. Decisions about governance structure in groups, organizations, and institutions are another.

I have so far advanced three hypothetical scenarios of constitutional abdications. (1) Target actors abdicate out of coercion. (2) They abdicate because they misunderstand the significance and the implications of the showdown. (3) They abdicate because they consider that their interests are to a certain extent congruent with those of the challenger. These scenarios are causally descriptive. None can be dismissed out of hand. Are these scenarios mutually exclusive? There is a priori a difference in kind between yielding to threats, behaving on the basis of misconceived premises regarding the challenger's intentions, and reflecting self-consciously on future courses of action.

My goal in the following chapters is to examine how well the three hypotheses fare when confronted with the two paradigmatic cases that form the foci of this investigation. Did those who abdicated in 1933 and 1940 yield to threats of retaliation? Did they believe that their challengers would not pursue a strategy of power monopolization? Or did they think that despite the lack of any institutional agreement, a modus vivendi could be reached with the challenger? Answering these questions requires that we pay close attention to actors' own assessment of the situation and their interests.

ADDENDUM

Payoffs are determined by (1) the utility attached to the outcome and (2) the expected cost of a direct confrontation. To simplify matters, I suppose that for both sides the utility of prevailing in the showdown is 1, and losing is worth 0. The target actors prevail if the constitutional order is preserved. The challenger prevails if he gets the political capacity to implement an alternative power structure that suits his thirst for state power. Several courses of action are theoretically possible, depending on whether the target actors oppose the authoritarian challenger's constitutional demands (figure 2).

Opposition

If the target actors oppose the challenger's request for a constitutional blank check, the challenger may decide to comply with their decision (status quo) or resort to a coup de force to overrule it. Let us assume the probability that the challenger backs off to be a and the probability that he imposes his request by force to be $1 - a$. In this last case, I designate the costs of a violent confrontation for the target actors to be r and that for the challenger to be c. The probability

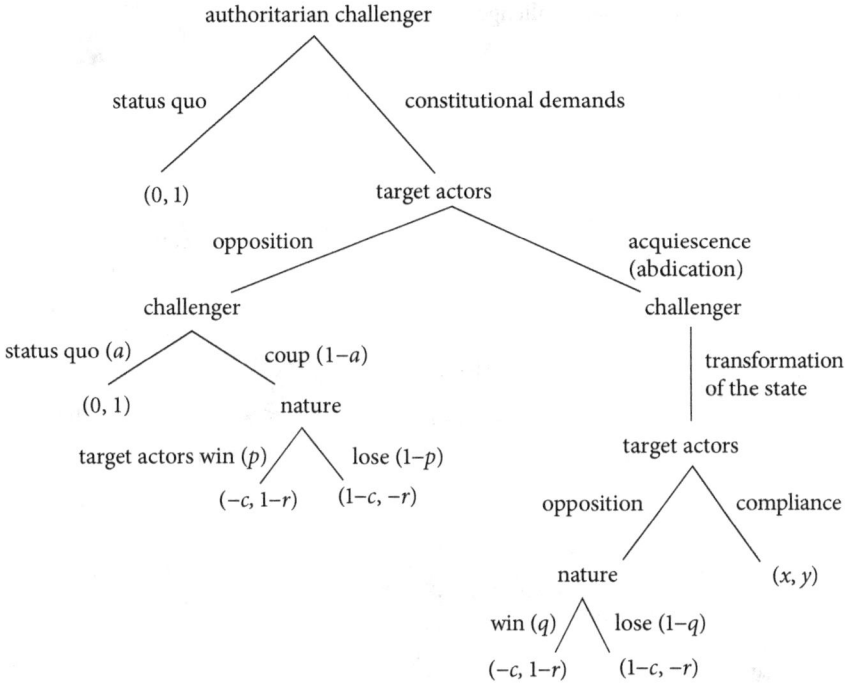

Figure 2 Constitutional abdication or opposition?
Note: The first payoff is that of the challenger and the second that of the target actor.

that target actors win an open confrontation is p and the probability that they lose $1 - p$.

The expected payoff of opposition for target actors in the case of a coup is $p(1 - r) + (1 - p)(-r) = p - r$. For the challenger the expected payoff of this scenario is $1 - c - p$ (figure 3).

Acquiescence (Constitutional Abdication)

If the target actors abdicate, the authoritarian challenger has the right to transform the state structure. The challenger implements a state structure that maximizes his power. I assume that in this scenario the payoff for the target actor is y and that for the challenger is x. The target actors face the following choice: either oppose this structural change or comply with it. I designate by q the probability that the target actors win an open confrontation if they decide to challenge the new state structure.

authoritarian challenger

status quo

constitutional demands

(0, 1)

target actors

opposition

acquiescence
(abdication)

challenger

challenger

status quo (*a*)

coup (1–*a*)

transformation
of the state

(0, 1)

(1–*c*–*p*, *p*–*r*)

target actors

opposition

compliance

(1–*c*–*q*, *q*–*r*)   (*x*, *y*)

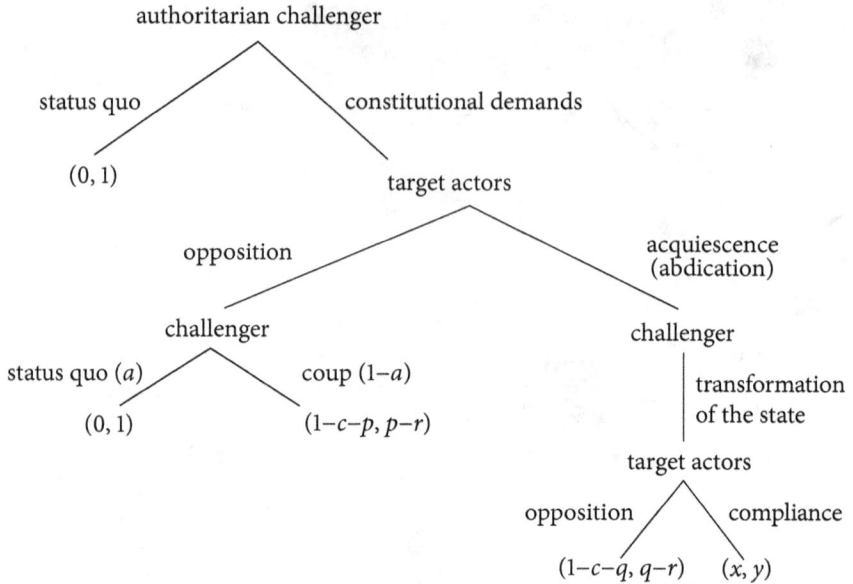

Figure 3   Expected payoffs

The expected payoff of opposition for target actors after the challenger has transformed the state structure is: $q(1-r) + (1-q)(-r) = q - r$. For the challenger the expected payoff of a confrontation with the challenger is $1 - c - q$ (figure 3).

As Fearon (1993) has shown, this model emphasizes that if the target actors and the challenger have mutually exclusive interests ($y = 1 - x$), opposition is the best reply for the target actors. This proposition rests on two observations. First, the target actors should expect that if they abdicate, the challenger will implement an institutional framework designed to maximize his control over the state. He will push his advantage to the point where he can still command the acquiescence of those who have abdicated, that is, up to the point when $y = q - r$. Second, the challenger will have a greater control of state coercive resources after the power transfer than before. Target actors will have less leverage to oppose policies detrimental to their interests. The probability of a successful opposition will be lower after the challenger has been granted a constitutional mandate. Therefore the expected payoff of opposition after the transfer of constitutional powers is lower than the expected payoff of opposing the challenger's constitutional request ($q - r < p - r$).

This deduction is premised on the terms of the power transfer: The challenger asks for the right to define the rules of the political game and does not commit himself to any institutional compromise. After having been granted the right to devise a new constitution, the challenger can implement rules that maximize his power. The target actors, on the other hand, lack a guarantee that their interests and security will not be crucially affected in the process. Abdication implies for them the possibility of subjection. In the absence of an institutional compromise securing their basic interests, these actors have a sufficient motive not to transfer their constitutional powers and to reject their challenger's claims. The lack of institutional guarantee should induce the target actors not to comply.

This conclusion rests on three assumptions. First, the probability of winning a direct confrontation with the challenger is greater than 0 ($p > 0$) and the expected cost of opposition lower than 1 ($r < 1$), that is, this cost is not prohibitive. Second, the target actors are rational actors; they correctly anticipate that the challenger will pursue a strategy of power monopolization. Third, the target actors and the challenger have mutually exclusive interests ($y = 1 - x$).

PART II

Subservience, Common Sense

1

Coercion: actors collectively abdicate because they fear possible retaliations. Miscalculation: actors abdicate without fully realizing the consequences of their decision. Ideological collusion: they abdicate because they have been contaminated by an ideology—i.e., a system of value-laden beliefs about the social world—that leads them to disregard their group interests. In chapter 2 I deduced these three hypothetical explanations from a formal analysis of the commitment problem inherent to any devolution of constitutional authority. These are plausible explanations. Yet one could argue that since the move was deductive, this causal mapping remains an intellectual exercise without much empirical grounding.

This reservation would be unwarranted. Factual accounts—whether they belong to the genre of the autobiography or fulfill the methodological standards of a historiographical inquiry—constantly invoke these three explanations when they attempt to make sense of the outcome. These three claims map out the universe of arguments that actors and historians have proposed in the past. Rarely do accounts hinge on one single explanation. Most often they invoke several at once. Each explanation, furthermore, advances a claim about motivations: threats produce fear, ignorance makes individuals less self-reflexive, ideological affinities nurture their good faith. As a result, accounts that draw on multiple explanations at once end up invoking multiple motivations. Pervasive fears went along with resignation. Hopes coexisted with apprehensions. Ideological biases contributed to misconceptions.

Not only are these three explanations ubiquitous. They also enjoy all the trappings of the commonsensical. Once they have been made, they go without saying. Of course, we are told, parliamentarians' decisions reflected coercive pressures. In the confusion of the time, they did not fully comprehend the implications of their act. A zeitgeist loaded with prejudice, wishful thinking, and political biases was leaving its mark on political inclinations and bearings. The exceptional context—marked by the specter of violence—crystallized latent political leanings. Coercion, miscalculation, and ideological collusion delineate our common sense of collective abdication and constitute elementary units of explanation in the constellation of factual accounts. We need therefore to start here. Is this common sense the ultima ratio of processes of abdication? Do we have reasons to be suspicious?

2

Because factual accounts so often rehearse, combine, and restate these three basic explanations and because they have the allure of common sense, we need to have a close look at the validity of the claims being made and at their internal consistency. The purpose of the next three chapters is to probe the empirical and analytical soundness of the common sense of abdication. To do so I isolate each argument from the other two and lay bare its underlying logic and core assumptions. This conceptual stylization guides my empirical inquiry. I treat each explanation separately as an ideal-type. This is an artifice of presentation that can easily be viewed as an artifact, since most accounts are de facto mongrel ones drawing on several claims at once. One does not necessarily find these types so well delineated in factual accounts. Similarly, I do not assume that these explanatory ideal-types summarize the historiography. Historical accounts are multivocal. They convey the complexity of events by invoking multiple causal factors, and they describe this causal web by retracing the actors' points of view, actions, and beliefs. Types, by contrast, are intended to provide blueprints and expositional clarity.

3

This is not purely an exercise in refutation. The critique of common sense yields three positive insights for a theory of collective abdication. First, the coercion argument is always incomplete. We have to explain why coercion produces its effects in some cases and not others. Second, miscalculation is self-deception. This self-deception is sustained by a collective process of belief construction that needs to be spelled out. Third, actors experience their decision as a dilemma when the decision is not for them ideologically obvious. If there are oscillations and hesitancy, then one cannot say that ideology provides the key to the outcome. Ideology should rather be seen as creating a universe of historical possibilities.

Chapter 3

Coercion

"Coactus tamen voluit"[1]

1

Max Weber (1978 [1922]) notes that "people may submit from individual weakness and helplessness because there is no acceptable alternative" (214; quoted by Przeworski 1991, 54). This explanation dominates retrospective and historical accounts of March 1933. In their retrospective explanation of their votes, former parliamentary delegates from the Center party outline that the alternative was either acquiescing in Hitler's rule and, in doing so, making possible the restoration of law and order, or facing the revenge of thousands of bloodthirsty Nazi activists who only waited for this pretext to indulge in political violence. "Opposition . . . could have served no other purpose than to crown the Republic with the halo of a martyr's death" (Watkins 1939, 126).

In February and March 1933 Nazi threats and pressures were blatant. The electoral campaign was bathed in violence and intimidation. After the Reichstag fire, the Nazi leadership invoked the emergency decrees of 28 February to put the state's repressive apparatus on their side. Their violence now had the official stamp of the state, and they made clear how they intended to treat people who had dared to oppose them in the past: dismissals from the civil service, embezzlement charges, imprisonment, and physical abuse—the means were varied, but the goal was the same. The Nazis tried to intimidate and scare. They hinted at massive layoffs among the civil servants affiliated with the Center party if the Center parliamentary delegation turned down their demands. On the day of the vote, Nazi activists demonstrated outside the Kroll Opera House, where the parliamentary session took place. In the meeting room they filled the banks reserved for external observers.

The thrust of the coercion thesis is that individuals act against their will (or preference) under the injunction of another actor. "One party surrenders

---

1. "Although coerced, it was still his will" (Weber 1978 [1922], 334).

any part of its interests to an adversary while the adversary benefits from the sacrifice without giving up anything" (Bueno de Mesquita and Lalman 1992, 102). Coercion readily solves the problem away and has the rhetorical force of the obvious. When constraints are overwhelming, groups under challenge feel powerless. If one simultaneously considers the circumstances and the outcome, the diagnosis seems beyond dispute. The Center party delegation yielded to Hitler's political demands for his exclusive benefit.

2

Yet there was in fact opposition. The Social Democratic delegation unanimously voted against the bill. Several members of the Center delegation opposed a "yes" vote in the delegation meetings that preceded the vote. If coercion is the prime explanation, opposition becomes unintelligible unless we interpret it as an act of foolishness — heroic foolishness, foolish heroism — or as an indication that actors have nothing to lose because whatever they choose, they expect to be annihilated: better to die with honor than to die with shame.

Both interpretations are unwarranted. Social Democrats could have voted "yes" or, more plausibly, abstained. Their collective "no" vote was an act of defiance toward the new power holders. This vote reasserted an oppositional stance. Undoubtedly, dignity considerations were a part of the Social Democrats' motivations. For the democratic Left and more broadly the constitutional camp, endorsing Hitler's enabling bill implied reneging oneself. But the vote was not simply a moral statement, the reassertion of a principled stance. Nor was the moral repulsion elicited by Nazism the only motivation at work. Opponents of the bill gauged their capacity to limit Hitler's powers and to influence future political developments. For these representatives, the moral rejection of Nazism could not be decoupled from strategic considerations about the political impact of a legal endorsement of Hitler's constitutional claims. A "yes" vote could only enhance Hitler's capacity to establish a Nazi dictatorship. It was therefore morally unjustifiable *and* strategically dubious.

These few remarks about opposition in the context of March 1933 invite us to question the equivalence between external conditions and group behavior and consequently the explanatory logic of the coercion thesis. A close analysis of the range of strategic assessments and political stances adopted by Hitler's opponents in March 1933 shows, first, that actors confronted with the same situation do not spontaneously come up with the same strategic assessment and, second, that they do not necessarily derive the same behavioral implications from this strategic assessment. In March 1933 one could believe the game to be over and yet oppose the bill to signify the rejection of any compromise with the Nazis. Conversely, one could believe that the game was not over and that the best way to prepare the ground for future opposition was to deprive Hitler of the legal resource of a constitutional enabling bill. More strikingly, the same assessment of the situation may motivate different behavioral choices. In March 1933 Joseph Wirth (Center party) and Theodor Heuss (German State Party) viewed Weimar as dead. So did Ludwig Kaas (Center party, chairman). Wirth and Heuss advocated an oppositional stance. Kaas chose acquiescence.

Motivations do not always fit the constraints that the coercion thesis would lead us to expect. This point is indicative of a broader analytical problem that bears upon the definitional criteria used to assess the explanatory power of the coercion factor. "Whenever one actor acquiesces to the demands of another actor, then we say that the acquiescing party has been (tacitly) coerced" (Bueno De Mesquita and Lalman 1992, 102). This definition captures the gist of the coercion argument and reveals its logic. There is coercion whenever actions in response to external demands do not fit initial preferences. That is, the outcome identifies the phenomenon. Furthermore, whenever coercion provides the main interpretive key, the "power" of this explanation lies in the contrast between actions and preferences. Hence the outcome provides the explanation. As a result, it is not clear what remains of its explanatory power. Its value is mainly descriptive. It characterizes the outcome. We can reasonably presume that cost expectations may have played a role. This presumption does not tell us, however, why they did play a role.

At first glance, the situation faced by constitutionalist parties in March 1933 is a prima facie case of coercive constraint. I show that even in this case we should not assume that credible threats necessarily produce their effects and generate subservience. March 1933 is a test case, because of the prevalence of pressures and intimidation. If in this particular instance we have reasons to question the coercion thesis, then a priori we have reasons to question the soundness of any account that explains a collective stance as the byproduct of coercive threats. The point is not to deny the possible effects of threats. Rather, it is to ask: when do threats produce their effects?

3

The coercion thesis takes on a peculiar twist in the case of the French parliamentarians: if the element of threat is not absent in Vichy in July 1940, these threats take the form of vague and unsubstantiated rumors. Threats, as a result, lack agency. They are around, but no one knows for sure who are the agents and who are the principals. This observation raises two questions. First, to what extent do actors lend credence to these diffuse threats? Second, do these rumors significantly affect their decision? A survey of the range of beliefs and attitudes prevalent among deputies and senators present in Vichy confirms that we cannot deduce strategic assessments and behavioral stances from external conditions. There were actors who behaved as if they had grounds to be fearful even though the threats were far from obvious. Actors who had the most to fear, on the other hand, took the prospect of retaliation lightly.

By the same token, this analysis provides us with a clue for addressing the incompleteness of any account that posits coercion as the primary causal factor. People communicate rumors as they interact. These collective processes of interactions are transformative. Actors modify their beliefs and their understanding of a situation as they communicate with others who feed them with rumors. That is, rumors have amplifying and transformative effects because they are interactive. Between the "facts" that initiate the process — or the external conditions — and the collective by-product, the lack of connection may be blatant. This suggests that the effects of coercive pressures are ultimately conditional on interactive processes. Threats do not work as such. They work when groups allow themselves to be impressed. Consequently, credible threats may prove ineffective — they do not produce their intended effects — while less believable threats may significantly contribute to subservience.

THE NAZIS ASSAULT DEMOCRATS

> I had the feeling that if the Nazis were let loose, on the same evening a huge slaughter would have taken place in Berlin, and this concerned not only the delegation to which I belonged, but also the members of the Social Democratic Party, insofar as one could get hold of them. I was totally convinced of this. One had to see the grim faces [of the Nazis].
> —Wiedemeier, former Center party deputy[2]

> We were not dealing at the time with a lawful constitutional situation, but with a true revolution ... and for us the question was not whether we could contain this revolution with parliamentary procedural rules. The question was more basically how we could avoid a civil war and a Saint-Bartholomew night.
> —Oskar Farny, former Center party deputy[3]

2. Wiedemeier's testimony before the inquiry commission of the parliament of Bad-Württemberg, Beilage Nr. 77 vom 1. April 1947 zu den Sitzungsprotokollen des Württembergisch-Badischen Landtags, Wahlperiode 1946–1950, Beilage-Bd 1, 96.

3. Farny's letter to *Die Zeit*, 25 March 1953, in response to an article entitled "Der Mythos des Ermächtigungsgesetzes" published in this newspaper, Archiv der Konrad Adenauer Stiftung, Sankt Augustin, NL Farny, I-468, 001-1.

Violence and Blackmail

In March 1933 the Center delegates had good reasons to believe the Nazis capable of massive retaliations. Since Hitler's assumption of power at the end of January 1933, the Nazis had systematically used violence as a tool of propaganda, governance, and persuasion. They launched their electoral campaign with the feeling that they could harass their opponents with impunity. Their primary targets were Communists and Social Democrats. As the campaign grew in intensity, they also directed their efforts against the Center by violently disrupting Center meetings, challenging orators, and threatening sympathizers and the rank and file. Stegerwald, former labor minister in Brüning's cabinet (April 1930 to May 1932) was slapped by National Socialists in Krefeld on 21 February (Forster 2003, 590). Bloody incidents occurred in Hamburg and several neighborhoods of Berlin (Neuköln, Spandau, and Moabit).[4] In a public speech on 22 February, Lauscher denounced the terror campaign against Center orators.

To this violence the state added its own violence. Paragraph 9 of the presidential decree "for the protection of the German people" (*Verordnung des Reichspräsidenten zum Schutz des deutschen Volkes*), signed by Hindenburg on 4 February, allowed Göring, acting as minister of the interior in Prussia, to suspend newspapers whose comments were deemed offensive to the dignity of the government. As early as 9 February the government banned for a few days various newspapers affiliated with the Center,[5] and started dismissing civil servants who were members of the opposition, including the Center party (Morsey 1977, 105).[6] State violence and measures of intimidation reached an even higher pitch with the issuance of the emergency decrees of 28 February. Since these decrees authorized the detention of anyone considered a threat to public order, "terrorism gain[ed] official sanction" (Patch 1998, 294). The government jailed Communist and Social Democratic representatives in the

---

4. *Germania*, 23 February 1933.

5. The bans against the press are listed in the electoral newsletter *Wahldienst* 32, Archiv der Konrad Adenauer Stiftung, Sankt Augustin, NL Wegmann, I-366, 001-4. This list is completed in *Wahldienst* 43, 1 March 1933, Archiv der Konrad Adenauer Stiftung, Sankt Augustin, NL Siben, I-586, K021, "Der Terror wütet weiter."

6. The German State party and the Christian-Social People's Service party were not immune from state-sponsored repression. For the German State party see Bundesarchiv, Koblenz, NL Külz, N1042/19, Politische Informationen und Notizen, 5 March 1933. For the Christian-Social People's Service party, Archiv der Konrad Adenauer Stiftung, Sankt Augustin, NL A. Schmidt, I-115, 005/2, circular letter, 9 March 1933.

name of state security and indefinitely banned their newspapers.[7] Parliamentary immunity was nonexistent.[8]

Violence did not abate once the electoral campaign was over. A few days after the election results were published, the Nazis took over public buildings, ransacked union and party locals, hoisted the swastika alongside the old imperial flag on newly conquered buildings, and brutalized journalists and politicians who had challenged them in the past (Evans 2004, 341).[9] Frick, the Nazi minister of the interior, proceeded to remove from their positions high-ranking civil servants and regional state executives who could oppose the government. The Center delegate Clara Siebert reports in her recollections of these few days: "On March 8, the Nazi flag is hoisted on the castle, the parliament [of the regional state of Bade], the post office and the city hall. On the 9th, Wagner [a local Nazi] becomes representative of the Minister of the Interior and Reich executive commissar for Bade."[10]

Credible Threats

As the vote came closer, threats became more precise. In a cabinet meeting on 7 March, Göring explained that "it would be best to tell the Center that all its civil servants will be laid off if it does not vote for the enabling bill."[11] Nazi newspapers bandied about open threats. On 21 March the news agency of the NSDAP stated: "this time the decision of the Reichstag will determine, not the fate of the government, but the weal and woe of parties themselves, whose future stands in their own hands. Parties should have no illusion: a rejection of the bill will mean a declaration of war, which will be taken up by the gov-

---

7. *Anpassung oder Widerstand*, 180.

8. In a letter to the chairman of the Landtag of Württemberg, Wilhelm Keil (former SPD Reichstag delegate) and Pflüger protested against the arrest of their colleague Ulrich right after a Landtag meeting on 15 March 1933. Friedrich-Ebert Stiftung, Bonn, Nachlaß Keil, Mappe 34, letter to Schmid, 17 March 1933, signed by Keil and Pflüger.

9. In several letters addressed simultaneously to Hindenburg, Papen, Frick, Göring, and Blomberg (13 March, 15 March, 20 March), the national executive committee of the Free Trade Unions systematically listed acts of violence perpetrated against union cadres and members (Archiv der sozialen Demokratie der Friedrich-Ebert-Stiftung, Bonn, ABI-ADGB, NB 625). In his unpublished memoir, the SPD Reichstag delegate Arthur Crispien mentions that he would always carry his gun whenever he left his apartment (Archiv der sozialen Demokratie der Friedrich-Ebert-Stiftung, Bonn, Nachlaß Crispien, Erinnerungen, 12).

10. Kommission für Zeitgeschichte, Bonn, Tagebuchaufzeichnungen von Clara Siebert, Arch. 46, 94.

11. *Akten der Reichskanzlei: Die Regierung Hitler*, vol. 1, no. 44, 162. See also Morsey (1960, 356; 1977, 119).

ernment."[12] The Nazis were saying in substance: "We have no qualms, and we will retaliate if necessary." The threat was credible: Nazi ministers made clear how they intended to treat their opponents and they had the coercive resources to bring this threat about.[13] Coercive pressures were therefore blatant, cynical, and credible.

Immediate Circumstances

On the day of the vote (23 March) several thousand Nazi activists gathered in the streets adjacent to the Kroll Opera House, in which the parliamentary sessions were to be held. Inside the building Nazi activists vociferated in the tribunes. Carl Severing, SPD delegate and former minister of the interior of the Prussian government, mentioned that "their presence heightened the threatening tone of the announcements [made by those outside]."[14] "The room had been decorated with swastikas and other ornaments. The diplomats and external observers' banks were full. As we entered to take our seats at the extreme left, SA and SS members took place in a half circle at the exits and along the walls. Their countenance did not portend anything good" (Wilhelm Hoegner, Social Democratic deputy).[15] Nine SPD delegates had been jailed in March.[16] Arthur Crispien, Wilhelm Dittman, Otto Landsberg, and Philipp Scheidemann, who had to face personal threats, crossed the border.[17]

12. *Hitlers Machtergreifung*, 163. Zentrum newspapers such as *Germania*, the *Kölnische Volkszeitung*, the *Neue Badische Zeitung*, and the *Pfälzische Volkszeitung* reproduced this statement.

13. Treviranus, *Das Ende von Weimar*, 367–68. One aspect of this strategy of intimidation was to indict politicians holding organizational responsibilities with charges of mismanagement and corruption. Expecting such charges, Andreas Hermes, the leader of the Federation of German Christian Peasants' associations, resigned from his Reichstag mandate on 17 March and was jailed three days later (Morsey 1960, 356). In her unpublished memoirs his wife, Anna Hermes, notes that the purpose of this indictment was to incapacitate him politically. Archiv der Konrad Adenauer Stiftung, Sankt Augustin, Nachlaß Hermes, I-090, 160, F/II/2: Fragmente der Lebenserinnerungen, 135.

14. Severing, *Mein Lebensweg*, 386.

15. Hoegner, *Der schwierige Außenseiter*, 93. In his unpublished autobiographical notes, Erich Wienbeck, German Nationalist Reichstag delegate in March 1933, makes similar observations about the location of the SA in the room and its members' menacing glance. Bundesarchiv, Koblenz, KLE 627 Wienbeck, 272. See also Ernst Lemmer's recollections (*Manches war doch anders*, 171–72). Lemmer was a parliamentary delegate of the German State party in March 1933.

16. Josef Felder provides the list in his memoirs. Felder, "Erinnerungen an Weimar, die schwäbische Sozialdemokratie und Hitlers 'Machtergreifung,'" 181.

17. Letter by Crispien to the executive committee, "An den Parteivorstand," n.d. (most prob-

It is no surprise that in these conditions Center delegates remember the event as full of threats and intimidation. Joseph Wirth knew about how the Nazis had treated some SPD functionaries and representatives. He also knew that he was directly exposed: "I was being told: 'you will be arrested during the night.'"[18] Clara Siebert recalled that a few hours before the bill was put to the vote, the members of the Center parliamentary delegation were echoing prospects of civil war. "I was hearing around me delegates speaking of a looming civil war. 'There will be no restraint, if we do not agree to a transfer of powers. The streets will no longer be under control.'"[19] Her colleague, the prelate Ulitzka, made similar remarks: it "was terrible when the representatives in this session had to undergo the pressure of the SA and the SS."[20] Carl Bachem observed in his personal notes that a vote of rejection from the Center party would have entailed the liquidation of the party.[21] The majority of the Center party representatives, explained the former Center deputy Jacob Kaiser, believed that if they did not endorse the enabling bill, "the Reichstag would have been dissolved on the very same day again and even greater political turbulence would have followed."[22]

Lack of a Real Alternative

There are two strands to the coercion thesis. One invokes direct threats to individual actors' physical and psychological integrity. When actors refer to the prospect of a bloodbath, a "Saint-Bartholomew night" (Oskar Farny), had they turned down Hitler's demands, they invoke this variant of the thesis. Concerns for the immediate future overrode any other consideration. Acquiescence is a coerced choice since the alternative is a bloodbath. The decision is not free. The

---

ably end of March 1933); handwritten letter from Scheidemann, 17 March 1933, Archiv der sozialen Demokratie der Friedrich-Ebert-Stiftung, Bonn, Nachlaß Dittmann, Mappe 21.

18. Bundesarchiv, Koblenz, Nachlaß Wirth, 1342/18.

19. Kommission für Zeitgeschichte, Bonn, Tagebuchaufzeichnungen von Clara Siebert, abridged in Das "Ermächtigungsgesetz" vom 24. März 1933, 137.

20. Reported by Webersinn (1970, 192), and quoted in Das "Ermächtigungsgesetz" vom 24. März 1933, 150.

21. Stadtarchiv Köln, Cologne, Nachlaß Bachem 950, handwritten observations, 25 March 1933, published in Morsey (1960, 431). Bachem was not directly involved in the debates. Having been a Center representative, he knew the main actors of the drama and had an insider's knowledge of the party.

22. Bundesarchiv, Koblenz, Nachlaß Kaiser N1018/246, 3. See also Friedrich Meinecke's testimony. The day before the vote, Meinecke asked a Center delegate he knew: "You are going to vote against, aren't you?" The delegate shrugged and replied: "Then it will be even worse!" (Meinecke Die deutsche Katrastrophe, 127; quoted by Morsey 1977, 252).

second strand invokes the certainty of being defeated in a direct showdown. Here the assessment takes a broader scope. Opposition would have changed nothing. It would not have prevented Hitler from reaching his goals. These two strands are often interwoven in accounts that invoke the weight of the circumstances. The certainty of being defeated in a direct showdown goes along with the certainty of being retaliated against. Yet we should analytically distinguish the two. Actors may deny that fear and apprehension for their personal security play a role in their decision, and yet justify a vote of acquiescence by pointing out that there is no plausible alternative.[23]

Historical accounts simultaneously refer to these two strands when they describe the Center delegates' motivations. Emphasis has been placed by Morsey (1977) on the threat of reprisals and an "atmosphere of terror" (144), by Bracher (1962) on the circumstances in which the enabling bill was passed, "under the pressure of naked violence, thwarting the expression of a free decision" (166),[24] by Brecht on the expectation of many Center party members of an "orgy of cruel acts" ("*Orgie von Grausamkeiten*") if they did not acquiesce,[25] by Schulz (1992, 598) on the Center leadership's concern for the fate of civil servants affiliated with the Center and the oppressing effect of the Nazi blackmail, and by Watkins (1939, 125) on the effectiveness of the purge of Communists as a tool of propaganda that scared and neutralized the opposition.

The realist interpretation of coercion underscores the lack of alternatives.[26] Hitler had all the cards in his hand and was determined to impose his will in any case. The "capitulation of the Reichstag" (Bracher 1962, 158) was a case of *force majeure*. The situation left no real alternative (Becker 1961b, 202; Becker 1963b, 156). This conviction prevailed in the Center party circles (Bracher 1962, 159). A vote of rejection would have changed none of the political developments. Not only would Hitler have repressed parliamentarians (Winkler 1989, 206), he would also have continued his march toward absolute power. The emergency decrees of 28 February had already destroyed democratic rights. In

23. This is, for instance, the argument developed by August Wegmann, former parliamentary delegate of the Center, in a letter to Repgen regarding an article published by Repgen in 1966 on the enabling bill (Konrad Adenauer Stiftung, Sankt Augustin, NL Wegmann, I-366, 040-2, letter to Repgen, 9 July 1966). Wegmann refutes the suggestion that Center delegates voted for the enabling bill because they were fearful. He reiterates his critique of Repgen's analysis and value judgment in a letter to Fonk, 5 April 1971, Konrad Adenauer Stiftung, Sankt Augustin, NL Wegmann, I-366, 040-2.

24. Brecht, *The Political Education of Arnold Brecht*, 304.

25. Ibid.

26. Jakob Diehl, "Das Ermächtigungsgesetz," 5 October 1946 issue of *Allgemeine Zeitung*, Konrad Adenauer Stiftung, Sankt Augustin, NL Diehl, I-139, 024/2; Stadtarchiv, Köln, NL Schwering, Best. 1006, no. 141.

short, in March 1933 parliament did not seal its own death. Rather parliament was pushed toward its death (Jasper 1986, 137). The vote for the bill was a way of conjuring up a worse threat: a full-fledged Nazi revolution.

THE POSSIBILITY OF RESISTANCE

If the case is so compelling, why do actors refuse to go along? Not everyone acquiesces in threats and pressures. If one is bound to be deposed, can opposition be anything other than a futile gesture? This point lays bare a key assumption of the coercion thesis. There is no room in the coercion argument for a strategic determination of opposition. Since actors are bound to be defeated and the expected cost of open defiance is unduly high, resistance can only be a "heroic" gesture, heroic but futile (Watkins 1939, 26). It is an act of foolishness in that it is foolish not to protect oneself. When the focus is primarily on the prospect of violence, opposition seems either incomprehensible or the expression of a value commitment strong enough to overcome the possibility of having to face violence. The decision to struggle takes the form of a struggle between apprehension and honor.

Undoubtedly, value considerations were present in the motivations that underlay a "no" vote on 23 March. When this motivation is prevalent, the problem is to understand why *groups* would choose the path of collective heroism when acquiescence is a safe option (and can be justified as a case of force majeure). For this purpose, we cannot take for granted the assumption that coercive constraints necessarily yield similar strategic assessments. Intense political showdowns are laden with uncertainty, and at different points in time individuals assess outcomes and developments differently. Nor can we simply assume, as the coercion thesis leads us to do, that actors who have the same definition of a situation make the same behavioral choices. Both points invite us to question the coercion thesis and, down the road, allow us to examine why some groups are more vulnerable to threats than others. My purpose here is to show that the coercion explanation assumes more than it explains, and that we need additional hypotheses regarding the conditions under which coercion is effective and threats produce fear.

The Sense of Honor

> One can take our freedom and our lives, but not our honor. After the persecution that the Social Democrat Party has recently experienced, no one can fairly demand or expect that it will vote for the enabling bill as here

introduced. . . . The Weimar Constitution is no Socialist Constitution. But we hold fast to the basic principles of a government based on law [*Rechtsstaat*].
—Otto Wels, chairman of the German Social Democratic Party, speech before parliament on the afternoon of 23 March 1933[27]

Contemporary witnesses were impressed by the moral force of this statement. "Wels showed considerable courage. During the chancellor's speech he already interjected several times. The speech is not devoid of a national tone" (Joseph Wirth, Center delegate).[28] "'Defenseless but not without honor' [Wels] spoke with dignity and gravity" (Clara Siebert, Center delegate).[29] "I wished the ground would have swallowed me up, for Wels' attitude was *politically* and *morally* the only possible one" (Jakob Kaiser, Center delegate, March 1933; my emphasis).[30] "I have to admit that, as I was listening to the courageous speech of Otto Wels, I was envious of the political attitude of the SPD (Paul Bausch, delegate of the Christian Social People's Service)."[31]

Wels's explanation of his vote was a moral statement. That is why it impressed contemporary witnesses. The Social Democrats' vote of rejection was motivated by a sense of impossible compromise between their political ethos and Nazism. Endorsing Hitler's enabling bill would mean reneging oneself, one's profession of faith, the meaning of one's political activism, as well as betraying one's constituency. The moral significance of the refusal to yield is all the more salient when actors are aware of the dangers that await them. In March 1933 German Social Democrats were the Nazis' main political target, and their position was, as Watkins (1939, 125) points out, "particularly insecure." After the Reichstag fire, "strenuous efforts were made to implicate them in the alleged Communist conspiracy" (Watkins 1939, 125).

This moral character of the decision also takes special significance when exit is a possible option. In March 1933 several Social Democratic delegates (Karl Höltermann, Otto Buchwitz, and Heinrich Ritzel) suggested that the delegation should not partake in the vote.[32] Collective absence in this particu-

27. *Verhandlungen des Reichstags*, vol. 457, 33–34, trans. adapted from Brecht, *The Political Education of Arnold Brecht*, 428.

28. Bundesarchiv, Koblenz, Nachlaß Wirth N1342/133, "Die historische Reichtagsfraktion vom 21. u. 23. März 1933," 23.

29. Kommission für Zeitgeschichte, Bonn, Tagebuchaufzeichnungen von Clara Siebert, 113.

30. Conversation with Kaiser-Nepgen after his return from Berlin in March 1933, quoted by Kosthorst (1967, 172).

31. Bausch, *Lebenserinnerungen*, 120. Ernst Lemmer (delegate of the German State party) evokes "a powerful speech that shook us all" (*Manches war doch anders*, 170).

32. Buchwitz, *50 Jahre Funktionär der deutschen Arbeiterbewegung*, 149; Felder, "Mein Weg," 37; Hoegner, *Der schwierige Außenseiter*, 129.

lar context can have two meanings. It may be a symbolic protest against the conditions under which the vote is taking place, or it amounts to implicit abstention and, consequently, passive acquiescence. In this last case the delegates seek to avoid making a decision. Unless they explicitly portray their absence as a protest decision, abstention through absence is amenable to these different readings and, given this ambiguity, the delegates cannot avoid the suspicion that they are acquiescing without acknowledging their acquiescence. In March 1933 the Social Democratic delegation ruled out this possibility and collectively opted for an unambiguous choice.

Split in the Center Delegation

Moral considerations are also present in the political stance advocated by members of the other constitutionalist parties on 23 March. In his recollections of the event Brüning recalls himself interpolating his colleagues' sense of honor. "Even if we agreed now, our newspapers will disappear, we will lose our schools and our youth will fall into the hands of the Nazis. It was better in these conditions to sink with honor, rather than to have singular individuals experience this fate little by little."[33] Fritz Schäffer, chairman of the Bavarian People's Party in March 1933, provides a retrospective account that strikes a similar chord: "The question was how the [political parties] were to die, whether they were going to fall in battle or whether they would be liquidated like dogs."[34]

However, considerations of political strategy come to the fore in primary sources. The Center parliamentary delegation met twice on 23 March. The first meeting took place in the morning, three hours before parliament convened. In this first meeting of the Center delegation, Brüning stated his opposition to a "yes" vote. Brüning's opposition hinged primarily on the absence of political and institutional guarantees: "There is no guarantee that the Hitler government will keep its promises."[35] Brüning felt "obliged to lay bare his reservations and the possible dangers [of a "yes" vote]. He took a stand for the election of Hindenburg by arguing in the first place that the latter was the guarantor and the trustee of the Constitution. Now the Constitution as a whole is exposed to the greatest dangers, especially since Hindenburg came to terms with the enabling bill."[36] Beyond considerations of honor, strategic assessments motivated Brüning's oppositional stance.

33. Brüning, *Memoiren*, 658.
34. Bundesarchiv, Koblenz, Nachlaß Schäffer N1168/9, letter to Ministerialrat Dr. Messner, 20 March 1947; mentioned by Altendörfer (1993, 768).
35. *Protokolle*, 23 March, parliamentary delegation, no. 750, 631.
36. Ibid.

In the second meeting of the Center parliamentary delegation, which took place in the afternoon, Joseph Wirth and Ludwig Kaas, the chairman of the party, vented their political divergences over past coalitional choices. In the course of this meeting Ludwig Kaas proposed that a ballot be taken.[37] Delegates were asked to write down their name and their vote preference on a sheet of paper, and about fourteen delegates indicated their opposition to a "yes" vote. The number and identity of these delegates have been a subject of contention: the document that listed the votes was destroyed afterward. It is however possible to identify the fourteen "no" votes by cross-checking the sources available:[38]

Fritz Bockius	Josef Joos
Eugen Bolz	Jakob Kaiser
Heinrich Brüning	Johannes Schauff
Friedrich Dessauer	Hermann Joseph Schmitt
Josef Ersing	Christine Teusch
Heinrich Fahrenbrach	Helene Weber
Heinrich Imbusch	Joseph Wirth[39]

37. "On the proposal of Dr. Kaas, [the delegation] proceeds to a vote, which does not yield any unanimous outcome." *Protokolle*, 23 March, parliamentary delegation, no. 751, 631. See also the Tagebuchaufzeichnungen von Clara Siebert, reproduced in *Das "Ermächtigungsgesetz" vom 24. März 1933*, 137, and the Nachlaß Kaiser N1018/246, 53, Bundesarchiv, Koblenz.

38. I draw on secondary and primary sources. On the basis of private letters and, apparently, oral testimonies, Morsey suggested a few names in 1960 (162) and a longer list in 1977 (140). Several relevant documents are reproduced in *Das "Ermächtigungsgesetz" vom 24. März 1933*, including a statement by Schauff dated 1934 (135). Christine Teusch evokes thirteen or fourteen opponents and gives several names including her own (testimony in Prégardier and Mohr eds. 1991, 73). In addition to these documents, I take into account the following primary sources: Kaiser's written statement after a visit by Theodor Heuss in April 1958, Bundesarchiv, Koblenz, Nachlaß Kaiser N1018/246, "Ermächtigungsgesetz"; and a statement by Johannes Schauff available at the Archiv Johannes Schauff, Institut für Zeitgeschichte, Munich, ED 346, no. 24. In his written statement of 1958 Kaiser mentions fifteen votes against the bill and five abstentions. Among those who abstained, according to Kaiser, were Brüning and Dessauer. Among those who voted "no": Joseph Wirth, Jakob Kaiser, Heinrich Imbusch, Heinrich Fahrenbrach, Helene Weber, and probably Josef Ersing.

39. One controversial issue is the attitude of the former labor minister and union leader Adam Stegerwald. Christine Teusch includes him among the "yes" votes (testimony in Prégardier and Mohr eds. 1991, 73). Several accounts (Morsey 1960, 162; Aretz 1978, 78; Hörster-Philipps 1998, 423) describe Stegerwald as an opponent. Patch (1985, 223) and Cary (1996, 139) state that Stegerwald's stance is "unknown." However, Jakob Kaiser's personal testimony explicitly indicates that at the afternoon meeting of 23 March, after having stated that "he was against the bill," Stegerwald confronted him, reproaching him his inexperience. Kaiser narrates this episode in observations dictated to his secretary in 1958 (Bundesarchiv, Koblenz, Nachlaß

Assessing the Future

It is not incidental that on 23 March, mentioning seventy years of struggles for "Truth, Law, and Freedom" — the old political motto of the Center party — Brüning referred to the memory of Windthorst, the great Center leader who led the fight against Bismarck during the Kulturkampf.[40] Windthorst was the symbol of resistance to the religious persecution carried out by the Prussian state (Morsey 1997, 147–50). In recalling Windthorst's politics and suggesting that the political tradition of the Center demanded resistance, Brüning was not only promoting an attitude of opposition. He was also identifying a strategic line of conduct.[41] The alternative, thus, was to organize opposition on religious grounds along the lines defended by the Catholic leadership before 1933: defense of individual rights, defense of the rule of law, defense of the constitution of Weimar.[42]

At this juncture the Nazis had not taken over the state apparatus yet. They had made considerable political inroads, but they still had to share state and governmental responsibilities with their reactionary allies. The conjuncture was still one of high contention. A "no" vote was politically significant insofar as it would give opponents within the state apparatus the political resources to oppose Hitler's claims to absolute power. The oppositional stance taken by Brüning and several Center parliamentary delegates closely involved in the Catholic workers' movements (Joos, Hermann Joseph Schmitt, Kaiser, Fahrenbrach) can be interpreted along these lines.[43]

Kaiser N1018/246, "Ermächtigungsgesetz"). In his biographical sketch of Stegerwald, Morsey identifies him with the "yes" camp (Morsey ed. 1973, 214). Forster's detailed account of Stegerwald's stance in March 1933 concurs with this assessment (Forster 2003, 594–95). Kaiser's testimony and Stegerwald's own stance in the morning meeting of the parliamentary delegation on 23 March (which I analyze in chapter 8) strongly suggest that Stegerwald should be counted among the "yes" voters. I did not include Otto Gerig in this list of "no" voters, although Brüning mentioned him among the opponents to the enabling bill of 23 March in a conversation with Hanna Gerig and her son in 1955. Archiv der Konrad Adenauer Stiftung, Sankt Augustin, Nachlaß Hanna Gerig, I-088, 001, Mappe 6, 002, Mappe 11. I found no other testimony corroborating this assertion.

40. Brüning, *Memoiren*, 657–58. See also the statement: "In the weeks about the time of Easter, the only way I could draw attention to the perils lay in my recalling of Windthorst's strategy" (Brüning, *Memoiren*, 664).

41. See the analysis in Böckenförde (1961, 222): "There was however another behavior, which today strikes us as a solitary sign of clear-sightedness and tough determination." Böckenförde refers to Graf von Galen's decision to resign from his parliamentary mandate in the Prussian Landtag to avoid having to endorse the enabling bill submitted by the Nazis.

42. On this point see *Katholische Kirche und Nationalsozialismus*, 50.

43. I will theorize this claim further in the concluding chapter.

These few observations complement the point made in chapter 1 about the historical significance of the event. The aim was not to prevent Hitler from having power. He already had executive power. Rather the aim was to hamper the Nazi leadership's capacity to monopolize state power. With a constitutional enabling bill, the road to a state monopoly was wide open. Being able to preserve the pretense of legality, Hitler was able to secure the allegiance of the state apparatus and to curtail his opponents' political capacity. That is why passage of the enabling bill significantly consolidated the prospect of a Nazi dictatorship (Böckenförde 1961, 218). And that is why contemporary actors (Heinrich Brüning, Jakob Kaiser, Theodor Heuss) immediately perceived passage of the bill as a major political mistake.

SENATUS CONSULTE

Power Vacancy

It is always tempting to relate the exceptional character of an event to the exceptional character of the circumstances that surround it. In July 1940 the situation was rife with exceptional circumstances. France had been militarily defeated. By virtue of the armistice concluded on 22 June, the German army occupied half of the country. In these conditions, the argument goes, deputies and senators could not reasonably dismiss Pétain. There was no other reasonable course of action. This view provides the subtext of most accounts interpreting the collapse of the Third Republic as the sanction of a military failure. Ferro (1987, 133), for instance, argues that even if parliamentarians were technically free to vote, politically they were not. German troops were camping only a few miles away. A "no" vote would have had the significance of a vote of no confidence. It would have entailed Pétain's resignation. Such an outcome would have opened the door to unpredictable and probably appalling decisions on the part of the Germans. It would have been a leap into the abyss.[44]

This interpretation of the event points to the danger of a power vacancy and the necessity of a dictatorial government in times of military occupation. Some parliamentarians apparently lent credence to this scenario. Two hours before the afternoon meeting, on 10 July the deputies Paul Goussu and François Saudubray, both from the Sarthe département and the centrist Parti Démocrate Populaire,[45] asked the old senator and Radical leader Joseph Cail-

44. The essayist Maurice Martin du Gard, who was in Vichy in July 1940, offers the same interpretation (*Le chronique de Vichy*, 40).

45. The département is an administrative unit comparable to the county in the United States, under the authority of a prefect (*préfet*).

laux for his advice. To their surprise Caillaux replied that voting "No" would be a gross mistake: "The armistice is signed. In refusing to vote [for Pétain], you call [the armistice] into doubt, you repel it, and under these circumstances! This means exposing our unfortunate country to Hitler's demoniac furor."[46] Thus given the constraints of the time, parliamentarians had little choice.

Why a "Constitutional Revolution"?

The problem with this interpretation is that the situation created by the armistice did not require a devolution of constitutional powers. Nor did it imply the implementation of an authoritarian regime. Paxton (1972) makes this point with exemplary clarity: "Although the armistice of 25 June had made a diplomatic revolution, nothing obliged France to make a constitutional one. An armistice regime administering France just to keep essential services functioning during the interim period, as in Belgium and Holland, was a valid alternative" (30).[47] The conservative leader Flandin initially approached the issue in these terms when he arrived in Vichy. Pétain's cabinet could be granted extensive executive powers to deal with the consequences of the military occupation in the same way as the previous governments had been granted dictatorial powers to deal with the war.[48]

Two counterproposals drafted in Vichy by the conservative senator Jean Taurines and the Radical party delegate Vincent Badie granted Pétain the role of a Roman dictator, required by the necessities of the time, without compromising on republican principles. In the same vein, Flandin suggested that the two chambers appoint Pétain president of the Republic in place of Albert Lebrun.[49] Therefore there is no reason to assume that the only possible choice in July 1940

46. This statement is reported by the deputy of the Popular Democratic party Paul Goussu (Fleurieu 1951, 281). See also the account sent by Goussu to the honor jury in September 1945, Archives Nationales, Paris, Dossiers du jury d'honneur: dossier Goussu, AL5314. François Saudubray confirmed the substance of this exchange in an interview in 1981, Archives Départementales de la Sarthe, Le Mans, Archives Caillaux, 39 J, interview of François Saudubray by Michel Rosier, La Vie mancelle, April 1981, n 203.

47. Dates concerning the armistice with Germany can be confusing. When Paxton mentions the "armistice of 25 June," he is referring to the date when this armistice was implemented. The armistice with Germany was signed on 22 June and took effect on 25 June, after the signature of the armistice with Italy (Jackson 2001, 128).

48. Louis Noguères's diary, Événements VII, 2236. Pierre-Étienne Flandin was premier in 1933–34 and minister of foreign affairs in 1936. In 1940 he was chairman of the conservative Alliance group in the Chamber of Deputies and a leader of the parliamentary Right (Wileman 1990, 170–72).

49. Bibliothèque Nationale, Paris, Archives Flandin, Don 31357, box 127: note dated 10 November 1945.

was between granting Pétain full constitutional powers and dismissing him from office (and in doing so facing the risk of a German backlash). In short, Caillaux's legal reasoning was mistaken. Rejecting the government's bill did not imply calling into question the armistice. Nor did it imply the resignation of Pétain. According to Berl's testimony, Pétain did not tie his political fate to that of Laval, whom he was prepared, in case of failure, to disavow.[50] Interestingly, Caillaux himself, if we are to believe Paul-Boncour's testimony, was aware that another course of action could have been devised.[51] More to the point: the debates in Vichy did not hinge on the issue of the armistice. "People did not part ways on the basis of who was for the armistice and who was against" (Boulet, deputy of the gauche indépendante).[52] Significant in this regard was the wording of the counterproposal drafted by Badie. While explicitly rejecting any power transfer that would "ineluctably lead to the disappearance of the republican regime,[53] the signatories of this counterproposal agreed to give Pétain "full powers to bring about a policy of public safety and peace."[54] Hence, these parliamentarians opposed the prospect of an authoritarian regime while acknowledging the "peace" brought about by the armistice. This was a state of fact. The armistice had been signed; it was a *"fait accompli"* as numerous actors outline in their testimonies.[55] Challenging it could not be the issue.

50. Berl, *La Fin de la IIIe République*, 188.

51. "[Caillaux] had seen [the crucial point]. But he did not insist. I regret his silence. . . . The great authority he had over the Senate could have helped us. With an ironic gaze behind his monocle, he alluded to the possibility of using a forgotten procedure: Senatus-consulte" (Paul-Boncour, *Entre deux guerres*, 257). The term designates a decree enacted by the Senate under the French Second Empire.

52. Paul Boulet's Testimony, *Événements* VII, 2223. Boulet voted no.

53. "Les parlementaires soussignés . . . refusent à voter un projet qui, non seulement donnerait à certains de leurs collègues des pouvoirs dictatoriaux, mais aboutirait inéluctablement à la disparition du régime républicain" (Badie's testimony, *Événements* VIII, 2271).

54. "Les parlementaires soussignés [. . .] estiment qu'il est indispensable d'accorder au maréchal Pétain qui, en ces heures graves, incarne si parfaitement les vertus traditionnelles françaises, tous les pouvoirs pour mener à bien cette oeuvre de salut public et de paix" (Badie's testimony, *Événements*, 2271).

55. And "as a *fait accompli* it was broadly accepted" (Paul Boulet's testimony, *Événements* VII, 2223). It must be noted that the reference to the armistice as a "fait accompli" comes under the pen of politicians with different political sensibilities. "The issue was not to approve, or disapprove of, the armistice. This was a fait accompli" (Ernest Pezet, deputy of the Parti Démocrate Populaire who voted yes; Archives de la Ville de Paris, Paris, Archives Raymond-Laurent, memorandum by Ernest Pezet: Déchéance civique: Observations à titre personnel d'un député DP," n.d., D 51 Z 72). "As for the allusion to peace, we were before a *fait accompli*" ("Quant à l'allusion à la paix, nous étions devant un *fait accompli*," Badie, Radical deputy who voted no, *Vive la République*, 47). "The armistice was a given fact (*un fait acquis*)" (Maurice Voirin, Socialist deputy who voted yes, *Le Scrutin du 10 juillet 1940*, 43).

In a letter to de Gaulle dated October 8, 1943, the Radical deputy Galimand made this point very clearly: "What does a "yes" vote mean? . . . In July 1940, the armistice was signed, and had been implemented for a few weeks. The chambers did not have to give a verdict on this act which sadly was final. A "Yes" vote therefore does not mean having approved capitulation, its explicit or secrete provisions. Only a demand of constitution change was submitted to the Assembly."[56] Emmanuel Berl, who had the leisure of observing the events in Vichy without being a participant, offers a consonant testimony: "The Armistice? Whether one blamed or approved it, it had been signed two weeks earlier, and no one among those who had deplored it, were thinking of calling it into question."[57] Congruent with this interpretation is the fact that only a small number of the parliamentarians' vote explanations and testimonies mention, implicitly or not, the armistice as a motivation for the vote (27 out of 223, that is, 12 percent).[58]

It is not surprising that the issue of the power transfer, not the significance of the vote with regard to the armistice, should have been central to the deliberations. For deputies and senators the key issue was whether Pétain could be granted a constitutional mandate allowing him to discard republican institutions and whether they, as republican representatives, could take the risk of

56. Galimand, *Vive Pétain! Vive de Gaulle!*, 75–76. See also Becquart's incidental remark about the report on the government bill read before the final vote by Boivin-Champeaux on behalf of the Commission of Universal Suffrage: this report, Becquart notes, did not even touch upon the issues of the armistice and foreign policy "because these issues were not at stake." Becquart, *Au temps du Silence*, 249.

57. Berl, *La Fin de la IIIe République*, 211.

58. This estimate takes into account implicit as well as explicit references to the armistice. Implicit references relate the vote to the experience of the defeat, such as in this statement by Fernand Talandier: "at the end of June, I had seen the shameful rout of the French army" (Archives Nationales, Dossiers du jury d'honneur, Paris: dossier Talandier, AL5331). Talandier's explanation can be interpreted as implicitly suggesting that through his choice he was endorsing the armistice. Explicit references are straightforward. Albertin Fabien, a Socialist deputy, explains that "those who were hostile to the armistice on June 17 hesitated to call it into question on July 10, when it had been fully implemented" (Archives Nationales, Dossiers du jury d'honneur, Paris: dossier Fabien AL5295). Charles Reibel, a conservative senator, states that he "only viewed the armistice as a temporary necessity" ("L'armistice ne m'apparaissait que comme une nécessité temporaire") (Archives Nationales, Dossiers du jury d'honneur, Paris: dossier Reibel, AL5327). The number of testimonies that refer to the possibility of a German backlash is also relatively low: 42 out of 223, or 19 percent. There is a significant overlap between reference to the armistice (explicit or not) and reference to possible German retaliations: 24 percent of the accounts invoking the threat of the Germans also refer to the need for peace; 37 percent of the accounts invoking the armistice point to the possibility of a German backlash. All told, accounts that invoke the armistice, the German threat, or both amount to 21 percent of the total of vote explanations.

legalizing the transition to an authoritarian regime designed on the model of Nazi Germany or Fascist Italy.[59] These few observations suggest that Caillaux's political and legal considerations were not prevalent in the parliamentarians' decision. Interestingly, the two Christian democratic deputies who asked for Caillaux's advice did not expect him to provide them with such a rationale. Caillaux's justification for a "yes" vote came to them as a surprise. As Paul-Boncour put it: "The problem was to know whether we were going to relinquish to one man, whoever he was, this constitutional power that belonged to the Nation only and to its representatives."[60]

MILITARY OCCUPATION

As early as 4 July Pierre Laval, appointed vice-premier two weeks earlier, had evoked the threat of "labor camps." "If Parliament does not acquiesce, Germany will impose all these measures with the immediate consequence of the military occupation of the whole territory."[61] Hitler and his associates never indicated that they had an interest in what was going on in Vichy in July 1940 (Miquel 1995, 176). Nor did they suggest at any point that they cared about which regime was installed in France.[62] In spite of this lack of threats and pressures on the part of the Nazi leadership, French parliamentarians may have nonetheless been concerned about the possibility of retaliation from the German military authorities.

59. Badie, *Vive la République*, 47.

60. Paul-Boncour, *Entre deux guerres*, 265.

61. Taurines, *Tempête sur la République*, 10. On this point see also the testimonies of Louis Gros (*République toujours*, 57), Louis Noguères (*Événements* VII, 2232), Vincent Badie (*Événements* VIII, 2273), and Jules Moch (*Rencontres avec . . . Léon Blum*, 274).

62. On 5 July, concerning this issue, Noguères notes in his diary the discrepancy between Laval's statements in Vichy and Pétain's public announcement (*Vichy, July 1940*, 31–32). Noguères most likely has in mind Pétain's asserting on 25 June: "the government remains free. France will only be administered by Frenchmen" (reproduced in *Philippe Pétain: Discours aux Français*, 65). The Nazis' lack of interest in the issue of regime change was public. On 12 July the newspaper *Le Nouvelliste de Lyon* translated a German radio broadcast on the political situation in France: "We have little interest in the intense discussions of the parliamentarians in Vichy. France's attempt to build a new government cannot deflate our attention from the main fact: our victory opened the way to a settlement that will hold for centuries. We may doubt the need for, and sincerity of, France's constitutional reform. We request France to definitely renounce its domination on territories outside of its vital space and to leave Germany the task of rebuilding Europe on the ruins created by the Versailles treaty" (Archives Départementales du Rhône, Lyon, Archives Émile Bender, 64 J 6, "Un commentaire allemand sur la situation politique en France"). Paxton (1972) notes that "Vichy's first hundred days . . . took place without close, direct German supervision" (48) and that "the National Revolution was not "imported on German tanks" in any direct sense" (142).

One variant of the argument invoking the pressures of the circumstances grounds the collective decision in the "traumatic experience" of the defeat and the exodus. Not the expected cost of a possible backlash but the *coup de massue* of the disaster motivates acquiescence: deputies and senators "*approve en masse* ["*plébiscitent*"] an armistice that fits the desperate situation which they perceive on the ground. The vote of 10 July bears the mark of this empiricism" (Wieviorka 2001, 45; my emphasis). Regions that experienced the war do not oppose the power transfer. Conversely, the greater the distance from the battlefield, the greater the propensity to adopt an oppositional stance (46). Stated in specific terms: "the more representatives have been in contact with war, the weaker their willingness to resist" (Wieviorka 2001, 46).

How shall we assess the impact of the "exposure to war" and its disasters? Sixty-five of the seventy-five servicemen present in Vichy voted "yes" (Wieviorka 2001, 45). This means that the proportion opposing the power transfer was slightly greater among the parliamentarians who had just served in the army (10 of 75, that is, 0.133) than among their colleagues without a combat experience (70 of 574, that is, 0.122). In statistical terms, the difference between these proportions is insignificant. In other words, these figures do not back up the claim that the experience of war and defeat predisposed parliamentarians to endorse the power transfer. There is no significant correlation between this experience of war and a propensity to vote yes.[63]

What about the impact of German occupation? If parliamentarians were most impressed by the factual evidence of the defeat, we would expect a posi-

---

63. According to Wieviorka (2001), the presence of these servicemen "in Vichy had a devastating influence on their colleagues" (45). Quoting Pomaret, Wieviorka observes that these servicemen, through their testimonies, confirmed the impossibility to pursue the fight (Pomaret, *Le dernier Témoin*, 196). In describing their experience, they converted many of their colleagues to the necessity of an armistice. However, the relevance of this testimony by Pomaret is problematic if the point is to back up a claim about the vote *in Vichy*. Pomaret was a proponent of the armistice in Reynaud's cabinet as he readily admits in his recollections. Having become convinced that it was necessary to put an end to the "effusion of blood," he was also more likely to give more weight to testimonies and facts that justified the position he had taken (Pomaret, *Le dernier témoin*, 107). Further—and more important—the experience Pomaret is describing in the quote mentioned above takes place in Bordeaux before the conclusion of the armistice, between 16 and 18 June, *not in Vichy*. He is evoking the situation before the conclusion of the armistice about three weeks before the vote in Vichy. Thus, Pomaret's testimony does not contradict the observation by many actors that in Vichy "the armistice was no longer the issue" (Abel Gardey, Radical senator: Archives Nationales, Dossiers du jury d'honneur, Paris: dossier Gardey, AL5313). The issue did not emerge as a salient line of cleavage. In this regard, the case of the Socialist deputy Tanguy Prigent is worth pondering: he volunteered to serve in a fighting squad, witnessed the debacle, endorsed the armistice in June as a result, and voted "no" in Vichy (Bougeard 2002, 104–7).

Table 7 Voting Behaviors and Military Occupation

	Yes	No	Abstention	Total
South of the demarcation line	208	45	17	270
Expected	*229*	*32*	*9*	
Military-occupied zone	361	35	4	400
Expected	*340*	*48*	*13*	
Total	569	80	21	670

Pearson Chi-square: 26.20; df = 2; p = .000
Note: This table presents correlations with the votes officially recorded in the *Journal officiel*. I identified eight parliamentarians who were present in Vichy but decided not to vote. For consistency I do not take them into account in computations of voting behavior. Including these informal abstentions does not change results and estimates.

tive correlation between the fact of having witnessed firsthand the German occupation of the country and a "yes" vote. Similarly, we should expect the fear of a German backlash to have been greatest among the representatives from regional districts (*départements*) under German military control. At first sight, these expectations are borne out: representatives of districts located in the militarily occupied zone were 2.2 times more likely to vote "yes" than their colleagues in the free zone: the odds of voting "yes" are 10.3 (361/35) in the militarily occupied zone and 4.6 (208/45) south of the demarcation line ("free zone") (table 7).

On closer examination, the correlation proves tenuous and frail. The military occupation effect reflects in part differences in the geographical distribution of the political propensity to vote in favor of the power transfer. As may be seen in table 8, there were relatively more representatives from the right in the occupied zone. These representatives were more likely to vote "yes" on 10 July regardless of the military occupation. Thus, controlling for political affiliation reduces by more than 40 percent the odds of voting "yes" rather than "no" in militarily occupied districts. More to the point: controlling for political affiliation makes the coefficient of the German occupation factor insignificant at the 20 percent level (table 9). A multinomial logistic regression also reveals that contrary to what we could have expected, parliamentarians were less likely to abstain than to vote "no" in the occupied zone.[64]

64. In probing the causal relevance of the coercion argument through a regression analysis, I am taking over the underlying analytical premise of this argument, that is, the assumption that individual actors are independent monads subject to the broad causal influence of coercive pressures. In this regard, the coercion argument is not fundamentally different from the miscalculation and the ideological collusion arguments. These three standard explanations

Table 8   Political Camps and Military Occupation

	Free zone	Military-occupied zone	Total
Left	82	61	143
Expected	*58*	*85*	
Center	132	135	267
Expected	*108*	*159*	
Right	56	204	260
Expected	*105*	*155*	
Total	270	400	670

Pearson Chi-square: 64.57; df = 2; $p = .000$

Note: Some départements were only partially occupied by the Germans. I coded as "militarily occupied" those in which the Germans were in hold of the main administrative center (*chef lieu*).

A NOTE ON POLITICAL CLASSIFICATIONS

The previous discussion refers to a tripartite distinction between left, center, and right. Classifications of this kind can easily appear ad hoc, arcane, unsubstantiated, or arbitrary. My purpose here is simply to clarify its underpinnings. The lexical birth of the right-left distinction harks back to the first months of the French Revolution (August–September 1789), when the members of the National Assembly, conflicting on the issue of the king's veto, spatially divided themselves (Gauchet 1992, 398–400; Rémond 1982, 19; Sirinelli and Vigne 1992, xii). At this point, however, according to Gauchet (1992, 400–401) the distinction remained primarily topographical: since it was at odds with an ideology banning the prospect of factional dissensions, it failed to produce a principle of identification.[65] This invention proper took place after 1815, under the Restoration, when topography served to capture political cleavages (Gauchet 1992, 402–8). It survived the following decades with ups and downs until it became, at the dawn of the twentieth century and the time of the Dreyfus affair, a referential category (Gauchet 1992, 413; Sirinelli and Vigne 1992, xv).

The left-right dichotomy thus belongs to the longue durée of political representations in France. Its resilience is constitutive of its evocative power. Any at-

---

share a linear understanding of social causality as analyzed by Abbott (1988, 169–181): coercion, shared misconceptions and ideology—defined as a value-laden representation of the social world—shape collective outcomes independent of the dynamic and sequence of collective interactions.

65. Hence with regard to the ideological genealogy of the left-right antagonism, Gauchet (1992, 401) describes the summer of 1789 as a "false start" rather than a "birth."

Table 9 Coefficients from the Multinomial Logistic Regression of Vote on Assembly (Senate = 1), Military Occupation, and Political Camp (N = 670)

	Model 1				Model 2 [a]			
	Yes vs. No		Abs. vs. No		Yes vs. No		Abs. vs. No	
Variables	Parameter Estimates	Odds Ratio	Parameter Estimates	Odds Ratio	Parameter Estimates	Odds Ratio	Parameter Estimates	Odds Ratio
Political camp								
Left					-2.83*** (0.50)	0.06	-2.04** (0.84)	0.13
Center					-2.10*** (0.45)	0.12	-1.52** (0.79)	0.22
Military occupation	0.82*** (0.24)	2.28	-1.17** (0.60)	0.31	0.32 (0.26)	1.38	-1.48** (0.62)	0.23
Assembly	0.42 (0.26)	1.53	0.57 (0.51)	1.77	0.24 (0.31)	1.27	0.39 (0.57)	1.48
Intercept	1.38*** (0.19)		-1.18*** (0.35)		3.61*** (0.50)		0.51 (0.76)	
-2*log likelihood	32.103				75.55			
χ^2	29.05***				81.03***			
Degrees of freedom	4				8			

[a] The improvement of fit between model 1 and model 2 ($\chi^2 = 51.98$, d.f. = 4) is significant at the 0.1% level.

* $p <= .10$, ** $p < .05$, *** $p < .01$

Note: For an explanation of the Left-Center-Right typology, see the text.

tempt to lay bare its political content can start with a few basic considerations. First, both notions are relative. One does not exist without the other (Rémond 1982, 31). Second, they define a system of binary oppositions. The right opposes the left and vice versa. Third, these oppositions are ideological. They imply different normative visions of the world. These visions have a semantic and symbolic consistency of their own. Hence, to speak of the left versus the right is to enter the realm of ideological representations. Any reference to the dichotomy asserts the prevalence of a doctrinal standpoint.

I define the "right" as designating representations of the social world that owe their consistency to two regulative ideas—regulative in a Kantian sense, in that these ideas organize and direct representations. The first is the idea that the hierarchy structuring social relations is a natural one—whether this hierarchy is derived from a transcendent order, inherited from tradition or generated by market relations—and that as a result, it has a legitimacy of its own. In short, those with high status are entitled to their status, and to higher responsibilities. The second regulative idea is the transposition of the first in the realm of political action. If social hierarchies are naturally grounded, any action that breaches this natural order portends ominous disruptions. Political action is to be conservative, and the responsibility of politicians is to make sure that human affairs are conducted in accordance with the basic principles of the order embodied in natural hierarchies.

The worldview expounded by the left rests on opposite premises. Social relations are pervaded with inequalities and arbitrary power. The notion that these inequalities are inevitable, necessary, or justified is unacceptable. Any depiction of the social hierarchies that make these injustices possible as naturally grounded is a mystification that benefits in the first place those who have an interest in maintaining an unequal distribution of resources. The correlate of this representation in the realm of political action is that for the sake of social justice, reforms directed at the structure of social relations are required. The politicians' responsibility and mission is to devise the right decisions to remedy injustices. There are different variants to this conception, depending on the scope that politicians impute to structural reforms and their modus operandi. (Who are the agents of reforms? How accountable are they? Is implementation exclusively a top-down process?)[66]

This is an abstract definition and as such remains wanting, for two reasons. First, it is devoid of historical time. It turns the distinction into a distinction

---

66. In this presentation, I started with the right and define the left as its negative. No precedence is attached to this order of presentation. I could have started with the left and defined the ideological contours of the right by contrast. As mentioned earlier, both notions are relative.

of essence and expels the time of conflicts and competition. Political identities cannot be assumed to be fixed and essential, as Passmore (1997, 4) and Dobry (2003, 36, 45) observe. The logic of political competition leads actors to constantly redefine their position. Second, this abstract definition does not pay attention to the pragmatics of politics, such as the way actors exercise their decisional power or their propensity to strike deals and form alliances. Focusing on the pragmatics takes us away from the substantialist postulates of an atemporal distinction and points to the issues of the political center and the gradation of positions.

Descriptions of the political space in terms of the left-right topography hints at the possibility of a "center." What is the center in this descriptive framework? We could say that by definition the center is in between. Therefore, it incorporates normative elements of both the left and right camps: order is to be preserved, but reforms addressing distributive inequalities may be necessary. From this perspective the center might well be an ideological no-man's-land: it merges the contraries and has no consistency proper and no place to stand. Instead, I define the center in terms of dispositions and practices. The center belongs to those who, as they exercise power and political responsibilities, make compromises with both sides. Pragmatism is their distinctive mark.

The definition of the center points to a second issue: how shall we measure degrees and variations? We need a gradient superimposed on the basic left-right dichotomy. Individuals and groups define themselves as located more or less on the right and more or less on the left. The reference to the pragmatics of power and political compromise provides the clue. Pragmatism reflects the extent to which actors view their conception of the world as exclusive and, by way of consequence, the extent to which they assert the need for political action exclusively geared to this conception. Actors who display a propensity to strike deals with "the other side" and shun an exclusive definition of their practice can be said to be closer to the center.[67]

Two tentative methodological conclusions can be inferred from this presentation. First, a classificatory grid in terms of the left-right distinction needs to specify its temporal referent. It loses meaning if it pretends to be outside the time of political conflicts and cleavages. My temporal focus in the present case is the sixteenth legislature of the Third Republic (1936–40), and more specifically the period 1938–40. The formation of Daladier's government in April

67. See Gauchet (1992): "If there is a Center, this means that each of the lateral camps is itself the subject of radical tendencies" (433). The characterization by Bernard (1998, 8–9) of the modérés as fundamentally "pragmatist" is consonant with the definition of the center proposed here.

1938 is a moment of ruptures (within the Popular Front) and realignments (Prost 1977, 38).

Second, we need to disentangle actors' definitions of themselves from the dynamic of relations of competition and conflicts. For this purpose, the factorial analysis by Prost (1977) of voting behaviors during the sixteenth legislature is particularly helpful. Prost's study underscores that in the first months of Blum's cabinet (summer 1936), the camps were clearly drawn (27). A few deputies from the Radical party, the Republican Socialist Union, and the Independent Left expressed dissent through abstention votes. Subsequently, these dissident voices became more numerous, and they adopted positions in between the two antagonistic poles of the political space (Prost 1977, 34–35). After the formation of Daladier's government (April 1938), a distinctive center emerged, made up of Radical deputies as well as members of the Republican Socialist Union and the Independent Left. On the right the group around the Republican Federation and the French Social party, characterized by their intransigence toward the left, remained firmly in place. Those commonly identified as the "modérés" (see chapter 1) were situated in the same location of the left-right gradient. On the left stood the Socialist and the Communist parties.

The classification of left, center, and right that I use in the logistic regression discussed earlier is based on the results of this factorial analysis. The "right" thus comprises the French Social party (the Parti Social Français, or PSF), the Republican Federation, the Independent Republicans of Social Action (Républicains Indépendants et d'Action Sociale), the Independent Republicans, and the Popular Democratic party (Parti Démocrate Populaire, or PDP), the Independents of Popular Action (Indépendants d'Action Populaire), as well as the "modérés" of the Alliance and the Democratic Left. In the Senate I identified as the "right" the Democratic and Radical Union, the Republican Union, and the Group of National Social and Republican Action. The "left" comprises Socialist (SFIO) deputies and senators as well as the members of the French Popular Union (former Communists). As for the "center," it encompasses the Republican Socialist Union and the Independent Left in addition to Radical deputies and senators.

Shifting from an assessment of objective positions to an assessment of actors' self-definitions—the subjective space of classification struggles—is unproblematic in many cases. For instance, members of the Republican Federation had been flirting with antiparliamentary mass organizations (Jeanneney 1978, 348–49; Irvine 1979, 123; Hutton, Bourque, and Staples 1986, 286). They obviously had no qualms situating themselves on the right. At the opposite pole, the SFIO delegates viewed themselves as belonging to the left. As for the Radicals, they had for years been divided "between a progressive and a conservative wing, the latter primarily concerned with order and good government, the former continually inspired by the attempt to bring about greater social justice through institutional reform" (Hazareesingh 1994, 211). Their involvement in the Popular Front situated them more on the left. The break with their former leftist allies in November 1938 marked a shift rightward and put them back in the center (Berstein 1978, 294–95; Puyaubert 2005, 118).[68]

In other cases, subjective self-definitions are discrepant with objective positions. The discrepancy is particularly evident for three groups: the Republican Socialist Union (Union Socialiste Républicaine, or USR), the Independent Left (gauche indépendante), and the Popular Democratic party (Parti Démocrate Populaire, or PDP). The explicit purpose of PDP representatives was to be at the center of the political spectrum (Delbreil 2000, 354). Members of the Republican Socialist Union defined themselves as leftist at the end of the 1930s, as did many representatives of the Independent Left (Cointet 1978, 266, 271). This discrepancy between positions and self-representations in part reflected the diversity and lack of cohesion of these groups (Cointet 1978, 271; see chapter 1). The analysis by Prost (1977, 40) shows, for instance, that while a small number of USR deputies throughout the legislature voted along with the Socialist party, their colleagues had more widely dispersed positions in the political space.[69]

What about the Alliance? Is there ground to argue that at the end of the 1930s, Alliance deputies and senators stuck to a vision of themselves as representing a middle way between left and right? I draw a distinction between the Gauche Démocratique and the Alliance in this regard. In the Gauche Démocratique coexisted Radicals and friends of the Alliance (Mayeur 1984, 380). These representatives did not want to cut ties with the Radicals (Mayeur 1984, 277). Members of the Alliance, on the other hand, adopted more intransigent positions vis-à-vis the left after 1936. The victory of the Popular Front shifted the party rightward (Audigier 1997, 325–27; Sanson 2005, 103). Some started to view Fascist regimes as a bulwark against the threat of Communism (Sanson 1978, 333).[70]

68. In 1937 Albert Sarraut defined his party as representing "the fair center" (le juste milieu), "enabling France to avoid the division between two blocs, Left and Right dominated by extremes" (Mayeur 1984, 310).

69. Not surprisingly, the historiography offers divergent assessments of these groups' political profile depending on the standpoint adopted. Whereas Burrin (1986, 337) characterizes the Republican Socialist Union as a group of the center, Michèle Cointet (1993, 41) and Jean-Paul Cointet (1978, 271) evoke "marginals from the Left." Passmore (1997, 14, 16) classifies the Popular Democratic party within the right along with the Republican Federation, the Democratic Alliance, and the French Social party, while Mayeur (1984, 305) defines it as belonging to the center.

70. This shift in position does not mean that Alliance deputies and senators had developed

Thus classifying the groups registered in parliament by considering the way actors situated themselves invites us to recode the Republican Socialist Union and the Independent Left as part of the left and the Popular Democratic party as well as the Gauche Démocratique as part of the center. Interestingly, this new classification grid leaves the conclusions of table 9 unchanged: controlling for political affiliation reduces by about 40 percent the odds of voting "yes" rather than "no" in militarily occupied districts and makes the coefficient of the German occupation factor insignificant at the 15 percent level. The assessment of the impact of military occupation conditional on political affiliations is not affected by the way we classify these groups.

RUMORS

"Beware . . ."

In July 1940 the promoters of the bill (Laval and his associates) spread the rumor that Weygand, chief of the armies and defense minister in Pétain's cabinet, was planning a coup and would surely assume power if the deputies rejected the government's bill.[71] On 10 July an impressive cordon of policemen ("gardes mobiles") encircled the building in which the Assembly convened (Sadoun 1982, 38).[72] Léon Blum was insulted in the streets and his close asso-

---

antidemocratic dispositions. Flandin even considered the participation of some of his party colleagues in Blum's second cabinet (Audigier 1997, 343). His colleagues defined themselves as republican and remained committed to a worldview antithetical to Fascism (Sanson 1978, 339; Wileman, 1990, 172).

71. "There were rumors circulating, not in a precise, official fashion, but we were being told: 'If you do not vote tonight, general Weygand will be here and you will be dispersed by force!'" (Paul Boulet's testimony, *Événements* VII, 2223). The conservative senator Bardoux learned of these rumors in a conversation with Rivaud (Bardoux, *Journal d'un témoin de la Troisième*, 402). "In the corridors of Vichy, sinister rumors circulated" (Maxence Roldes, Socialist deputy: Archives Nationales, Dossiers du jury d'honneur, Paris: dossier Maxence Roldes, AL5329). Émile Fouchard wanders among small groups: "Here people are speaking of Laval, here they are speaking of Weygand, elsewhere of German troops located in Moulins" (Fouchard's testimony in Marielle and Sagnès 1993, 57).

72. Desgranges, *Journal*, 393; Montigny, *De l'armistice*, 69; Becquart, *Au temps du silence*, 211; Fouchard's testimony in Marielle and Sagnès (1993, 57): "the casino is surrounded by several police trucks: gendarmes, mobile guards, and police; people say that opponents could be arrested at the end of the parliamentary session." Albert Rivière evokes "armed patrols" (Archives Nationales, Paris, AB/XIX/4238/1/ dossier 1, Papiers d'Albert Rivière, 239). Noting the presence of armed soldiers in his day-to-day account of the events (most probably written during the war), the centrist deputy Ernest Pezet speaks of an "18th Brumaire atmosphere," a reference to Bonaparte's coup on 10 November 1799 (Fondation Nationale des Sciences Politiques, Paris, Archives Pezet, handwritten notes, "éphémérides," PE 6, dossier 1, 9).

ciates feared for his security. The extreme Right leader Jacques Doriot, a former Communist, shouted to the Socialist senator Marx Dormoy, former minister of the interior in Blum's cabinet: "We are out to get you!" (Miquel 1995, 192).[73] Marquet, minister of the interior, advised the Socialist deputy Jules Moch to abstain if he wanted to avoid dire consequences.[74] After having indicated to Ybarnegaray, minister in Pétain's cabinet, that he was going to vote "no," the Socialist deputy Vincent Auriol heard him reply: "For God's sake. Do not do that!" — "And so, I answered laughing, I won't sleep in my bed tonight?"[75]

Thus pressures and threats were present in the Vichy context. The question is: How effective were these threats? To what extent did they affect the outcome? Several historical accounts suggest that those who voted "yes" on 10 July were motivated by the fear of reprisals (Aron 1958, 132; Bouju and Dubois 1986, 123; Shirer 1969, 955). Léon Blum offered a similar explanation: Fear, he argued, was the primary motivation at work, the fear of Doriot's gangs, of Weygand's soldiers, and of German armies.[76] According to Sadoun (1982, 36) and Sagnès (1991, 559), the threat of a military dictatorship had a considerable influence on the vote of the parliamentarians. Weygand was known for his connections with the Far Right.[77] Parliamentarians may thus have been tempted to opt for a less adventurous choice, embodied in the tandem of Laval and Pétain (Sadoun 1982, 36).[78]

73. "Doriot and his gangs of militiamen were pacing the streets, up and down . . . Strange atmosphere" (Renaitour, *La Mémoire fidèle*, 143). Renaitour, a deputy of the *gauche indépendante*, abstained.

74. "We are subject to blackmail. Marquet, Minister of the Interior, suggested that I not show up since I was still mobilized in the army. Otherwise, I could suffer for it" (Moch, *Une si longue Vie*, 161). "Blackmail, the abominable blackmail was wrapping each one of us. Echoes of threats, of threats of all kinds, were wandering around" (François Camel, *Ultimes Paroles*, 33). A gendarme tells Fouchard, after Fouchard told him that he was going to vote against Laval's bill: "Well, tonight, you will sleep in jail!" (Fouchard's testimony in Marielle and Sagnès 1993, 57). Moch, Camel, and Fouchard voted "no."

75. Auriol, *Hier . . . demain*, 128.

76. Blum, *Mémoires*, 84–85.

77. Ibid., 84. While emphasizing Weygand's professionalism, Bankwitz (1967, 280) also notes the "ubiquity" at the end of the 1930s of rumors involving him in authoritarian plans. These rumors were part of Weygand's public image (Bankwitz 1967, 281–82).

78. This is the explanation propounded by the conservative deputy Édouard Barthe, who was also questeur in the Chamber in 1940. "I am intimately convinced that several hundreds of parliamentarians, including myself, at first hesitant, were led to grant their trust to the 'loyal Pétain' out of fear for the reactionary Weygand" (Barthe, *La ténébreuse Affaire du "Massilia,"* 39, quoted by Sagnès 1991, 559). However, this explanation is questionable. Badie observes that Barthe was one of the most active supporters of the bill in July 1940. Moreover, in Vichy Barthe signed the "Bergery motion," which called for the transfer of constitutional powers and the implementation of a "national and social order" in France (Hoover Institution Archives, Stanford,

Dubious Credibility

This interpretation calls for several observations. First, Laval and his support-ers directed their explicit threats at those who had consistently advocated re-sistance to Hitler's *coup de force* in 1938–39. Laval's and Pétain's entourages were insidiously castigating these political leaders for steering the country into war and defeat. Yet on 10 July these representatives — chief among them Léon Blum — rejected the bill. If indeed threats and pressures were the decisive factor influencing the parliamentarians' decision, shall we conclude that those who rejected the bill on 10 July 1940 were less aware of the dangers entailed by their choice? In the present case, parliamentarians who were the most exposed to threats of retaliation decided to disregard them.

Second, that French parliamentarians may have collectively lent credence to Laval's menaces requires explanation. As Blum points out in his recollections of the event, had parliamentarians reflected only for one moment about the different scenarios that Laval and his confederates were outlining for them, they would have realized how implausible these scenarios were. There was no tangible reason for believing that a coup would be staged against parliament. Laval was obviously trying to mystify his audience. "The seditious plan im-puted [to Weygand] was obviously a complete fabrication. Those who hawked it with the most sincere anxiety were incapable of indicating on which fact, on which sign they relied to make such an imputation. . . . The march of Ger-man tanks onto Vichy was no more likely than the *raid* of Weygand's riders" (Blum).[79]

Nor was the position of republican representatives hopeless. Ferro (1987, 127) remarks that the "Doriot gang" was not very impressive: a handful of men. Blum himself notes that those who wanted to oppose the government's bill had little reason to fear the worst if they collectively resisted. "Was the risk quite real? Was it anything other than a bugbear for feeble minds? Laval might retaliate against a few isolated opponents, but would he on the evening of the vote throw a couple of hundreds of deputies and senators into jail?"[80] There-

---

Fonds Bergery). It is therefore extremely unlikely that the experience of pressures, if there were any, played a role in his decision.

79. Blum, *Mémoires*, 85–86. Taurines implicitly acknowledged this point when on 7 July he replied to Laval, who had told Jacquy and Taurines that he would resign if their counterproposal was passed and that Weygand would implement a dictatorship. "During the so-called informal meetings in the Senate, in order to have the 1875 constitution revised, you brandished the bogey of the Germans. Tonight you are brandishing that of General Weygand. Tomorrow, what will you find?" *Événements* VIII, 2334.

80. Blum, *Mémoires*, 85–87.

fore if we are to assume that parliamentarians felt indeed constrained by the prospect of reprisals, we have to explain how these threats may have become credible in the first place.[81]

■   ■   ■

The coercion scenario obfuscates acts of resistance. It cannot explain why actors who have every reason to expect retaliation do turn down a challenger's demands for constitutional powers. Despite all appearances in retrospect, acquiescence in March 1933 and July 1940 was not a foregone conclusion, and it is misleading to assume that there was an inexorable necessity leading to collective abdication in either instance. In this respect the coercion thesis misrepresents the relative indeterminacy of the conflicts originated by the political showdown and the complexity of the motivations at work.

This last point explains Carl Severing's dismissal of the contention that a "lack of personal courage was ultimately the reason for the delegates' acquiescence." The circumstances were indeed dreadful. Severing, an SPD delegate in March 1933, was in custody when Göring gave the order that he be freed so that he could cast his vote. He had to go through the Nazi crowd that had gathered in front of the Kroll Opera House. "We want the enabling bill. Otherwise it will be nasty." "What the mass of heavily armed members of the so-called services in charge of order, the SA and SS, meant by nasty, they made it clear."[82] Voting "no" in these conditions required considerable "political and personal" courage. But those who decided to pass the power transfer did not necessarily lack this courage.[83]

81. Regarding the Vichy episode, Warner (1968) notes that "it would be a gross oversimplification to attribute [Laval's] success to a mixture of bribery and threats" (210). Paxton (1972, 24–25), reaches the same conclusion: invoking the threat of a military coup or the threat of German armies became a convenient excuse after the war for exculpating the "fault" or "mistake" of the vote of 10 July. Miquel (1995) also observes that "in order to explain the massive victory of the 'Yes' vote, one has to call upon other factors than the exceptional and tumultuous circumstances of the vote. No violence was exerted from outside. As for the Germans, they in no way interfered with the debate" (176). See also Burrin (1986, 337), Wieviorka (2000, 97: "no mythological explanation—plot or fear—explains the vote granting full powers"), and Cointet (1993, 36: "it is doubtful that there were objective reasons for fear in this charming spa city").

82. Archiv der sozialen Demokratie der Friedrich-Ebert-Stiftung, Bonn, Nachlaß Severing, Mappe 28, no. 37, 1.

83. "Yet, I would not accept the idea that a want of personal courage was the ultimate reason for the delegates' acquiescence." Archiv der sozialen Demokratie der Friedrich-Ebert-Stiftung, Bonn, Nachlaß Severing, Mappe 28, no. 37, 1.

Chapter 4

Miscalculation

1

In uncertain conjunctures, miscalculation about the consequences of one's actions is always a possibility. As a result, when political actors make decisions that in retrospect appear to have been politically self-defeating, they can easily invoke the uncertainty of the situation as an explanation for their mistake. This explanation has two advantages which make it highly popular. First, it is plausible and commonsensical. Everyone would agree that in troubled times, decisions are difficult to make because their consequences are difficult to assess. Second, the miscalculation-qua-uncertainty argument does not jeopardize the moral integrity of the decision maker. If uncertainty indeed is the main culprit, honor is safe and intentions unstained. Thus, this explanation has the advantage of sounding true *and* of providing a morally acceptable account that one can rationally endorse for oneself and for others.

2

The miscalculation argument is ambiguous, however, for it can mean two things. First, it connotes ignorance and the possibility of deception induced by ignorance. People know little about the challenger's true plans. The challenger in turn misleads people about his intentions and future plans. French parliamentarians often rely on this explanation. In July 1940, they explain, Pétain deceived people. The trust placed in him was almost universal. Pétain was a fatherly figure. Everyone expected that he would take the nation under his wing and show the way out of disaster. The ignorance argument is less frequent in Reichstag deputies' accounts, in part because Hitler never disguised how he intended to exercise state power. When German parliamentarians invoke ignorance, they invoke it regarding the prospect of a totalitarian regime. Hitler shrouded his claims to state power in the guise of radical nationalism. For many conservatives, this was familiar ground. One could not expect that the Nazis would attempt to brutally suppress all forms of pluralism.

But ignorance is not the only possibility. Actors may well be aware of the challenger's agenda, and decide nonetheless that they have something to gain by endorsing his political demands. Retrospectively, the decision amounts to a failed bet. It was a tactical mistake. In Vichy in July 1940 some may have believed that Pétain would be able to foil Laval's maneuvers and thwart any prospect of a political alignment with Nazi Germany. They misjudged the balance of forces among the new power holders. In Germany in March 1933 the political bet took various forms. Reactionaries of all stripes could hope to use Hitler for their own purpose as the agent of a radical transformation of the power structure along authoritarian lines. Their mistake was to believe that they would still be able to manipulate him. Conservatives for their part bet that Hitler, now chancellor and vested with the highest political responsibilities, would behave like a statesman, and would display the moderation and the sense of responsibility that can be expected from a statesman.

3

These observations raise different questions. One concerns the factual validity of the claim of ignorance. Is there ground to argue that neither Hitler nor Laval disclosed his true agenda before requesting constitutional powers? The answer is no. Hitler had made clear that under his rule there would be no room for political dissent. In Vichy, Laval spelled it out: "Make no mistake! We are now living under a dictatorship!" France would have to align its political institutions and its foreign policy with those of Nazi Germany.

Did political actors know about this? Here the answer is positive. During a meeting of the Center party's parliamentary delegation on 20 March, the party chairman, Ludwig Kaas, mentioned that in the future the Center would have to abandon the terrain of political struggles and confine itself to religious and cultural issues. Two days later, the former chancellor and minister of the interior Joseph Wirth warned his colleagues in the delegation of what they should expect if Hitler consolidated his power: the suppression of all liberties and all elementary individual rights. French parliamentarians, for their part, were shocked to hear Laval advocate a reversal of alliances and political institutions negating their republican traditions.

4

Actors who acknowledge that they were aware of the threat explain simultaneously that their decision was tactically motivated. The bet consisted in yielding to the challenger's demands to consolidate their position. Center leaders convinced themselves that in voting for the enabling bill they increased their party's chances of organizational survival and a modicum of political influence. French parliamentarians convinced themselves that Pétain would preserve a republican regime despite Laval's repeated allusions to a nondemocratic agenda. In each case the bet failed because of misjudgment (Hitler was shrewder than his political opponents believed him to be) or deception (Pétain breached the terms of the contract with parliamentarians who trusted him).

The puzzle in these accounts is less the bet than the assumptions that made it possible. In abdicating their constitutional authority, parliamentarians were abdicating all political leverage. Oral promises remained oral. What could be the validity of such promises once the challenger had been granted a mandate to redesign political institutions according to his will? To view the bet as plausible, one had to abdicate a substantial amount of critical judgment. This is the puzzle: actors who by profession were trained to assess opportunities and threats came to believe that the challenger would be nice enough to restrain himself and not abuse the resources of his power. Miscalculation was voluntary blindness and wishful thinking. In March 1933 and July 1940 parliamentarians did not properly "miscalculate." They decided to deceive themselves. Catholic representatives came to believe in the fiction that Hitler would behave like a statesman. French parliamentarians convinced themselves that future institutions would not fundamentally depart from republican principles.

Any attempt to grasp the tactical reasons that actors provided to themselves to justify their vote stumbles therefore on the following difficulty. Actors knew that they would have no control over the challenger's future actions. Yet they behaved as if they would be able to retain some leverage over political decisions. The problem lies in this choice for self-deception. Voluntary blindness, as Elster (1983, 149) points out, is inherently paradoxical. How can one decide to be blind? How can one decide to forget what one knows? I will not specifically address the question in this chapter. My purpose in discussing the miscalculation argument is to lay the ground for a possible theory of self-deception: in March 1933 and July 1940 miscalculation and wishful thinking were both collective phenomena. The collective dimension of the phenomenon provides the key to its resilience and phenomenological effectiveness.

THE IMPOSSIBILITY OF IGNORANCE

In 1933 no one knew which direction Hitler was going to take after having taken over power, for its programmatic statement was moderate and full of appeasing assurances. At this point in time, no one could imagine that the people had fallen into the hands of a swindler and liar of such historical proportion.—Oskar Farny, former member of the Center party parliamentary delegation in 1933[1]

One cannot reproach the NSDAP leaders for concealing their ultimate goals.
—*Der gerade Weg*, 1 March 1933[2]

The Agenda Disclosed

In November 1931 the police in the state of Hesse seized Nazi documents—the "Boxheim papers"—that laid out the plans for an armed emergency by the Hessian SA in case of a Communist uprising (Evans 2004, 274).[3] The Boxheim papers confirmed suspicions that the Nazis were willing to resort to extreme political violence (Hömig 2000, 435). The point became obvious again in the summer. The July campaign for the Reichstag elections provided the Nazis with an opportunity to intensify their direct confrontation with their political opponents and more particularly with Communist militants. On the last day of the campaign in Koenigsberg (31 July), the local SA went on a bombing and killing spree. Ten days later, on 10 August, five uniformed members of the SA savagely murdered a young Communist laborer in front of his mother in Potempa, a village of Upper Silesia. Four of the perpetrators were brought to trial and on 22 August sentenced to death pursuant to a recent emergency decree against political terror. Hitler sent them a telegram saying that for him it was a question of honor that they be freed.

That Hitler wanted to destroy democracy was no secret. Moreover, his failed coup in Munich in November 1923 had earned him two years in prison. As he explained on 25 September 1930 before the state tribunal (*Staatsgerichtshof*) at the trial of three army officers accused for high treason because of their membership in the Nazi party, his tactic was to achieve state power legally. In contrast to the 1920s, a coup was no longer on his agenda. The overthrow of Weimar remained his goal, however (Watkins 1939, 53; Finn 1991, 163). "Denunciation of the evils of parliamentary government had always been a staple of National socialist agitation. From the beginning their appeal to the elector-

1. Archiv der Konrad Adenauer Stiftung, Sankt Augustin, NL Farny, I-468, 001-1. Farny wrote these notes after the war in response to a denazification questionary.

2. *Der gerade Weg*, 1 March 1933, 3: "Der positive Katholik wählt grundsätzlich." This newspaper openly acknowledges its Catholic readership. Archiv der Konrad Adenauer Stiftung, Sankt Augustin, Nachlaß Scherer, I-046, 002/3.

3. Severing, *Mein Lebensweg*, 328. These papers stated that "opposition would be threatened with death." Archiv der sozialen Demokratie der Friedrich-Ebert-Stiftung, Bonn, Nachlaß Severing, Mappe 29, "Vor zwanzig Jahren," 1.

ate had been based on the promise of absolutism" (Watkins 1939, 121). Buch-heim (1961) brings this point home: "In light even of the worst measures which will be taken later against the Church, one cannot reproach Hitler to have breached his governmental statements. Those who had ears to listen should not have abandoned themselves to illusions on March 23" (503).

ASSESSING THE THREAT

So the plan had been laid out. Were these announcements clearly understood by members of the constitutionalist parties? Early on, leaders of these parties denounced the Nazis' authoritarian goals. At the end of 1931 Theodor Heuss, a leading member of the German Party of the State, published under the title "Hitlers Weg" a thorough analysis of the Nazi phenomenon and a vigorous de-fense of republican institutions (Jones 1988, 435). On 24 February 1932, during the Reichstag debates that opened the presidential campaign, the chairman of the German State party delegation, August Weber, accused the National So-cialists of "having traveled the route of political murder." Eyck (1963) indicates that this charge was met "with such a wild display that the session was immedi-ately adjourned" (358). Two days later Weber proceeded to substantiate his accusations. The Nazis left the chamber before he began to read his report.

Many electoral statements indicate that the Center leaders were clearly aware of the Nazis' long-term goals. On 5 July 1932 the Center party deputy, Johannes Bell, stated in an electoral meeting that the fight revolved around issues of "existence and non-existence."[4] In his speech before the party's cen-tral committee in Berlin on 5 February 1933, Kaas accused the two government partners (the Nazis and the German Nationalists) of being united only in their hatred of dissenting opinions.[5] On 12 February Eugen Bolz, prime minister of the state of Württemberg and Center parliamentary delegate in the Reichstag, declared that the conception of the state being implemented by Hitler's gov-ernment placed the state above any individual right and that this conception was in "absolute contradiction" with Christian views. No compromise was possible with such a conception. It called only for frontal opposition.[6]

As the electoral campaign proceeded, the Nazis demonstrated how they

4. Bundesarchiv, Koblenz, Nachlaß Bell N1272/12, *Westdeutsche Landeszeitung*, 5 July 1932, no. 182. In the fall of 1932 Hermann Dietrich, chairman of the German State party, adjudged that the Nazi party's exclusive goal was the takeover of state power. This explained the Nazi leader-ship's lack of principled commitment and the lack of a clear policy program. Bundesarchiv, Koblenz, Nachlaß Dietrich N1004/224, "Die Nationalsozialisten," 1.

5. *Kölnische Volkszeitung*, 7 February 1933.

6. Ibid., 15 February 1933.

intended to exercise state power. The Center leaders increasingly denounced the suppression of any legal opposition.[7] On 22 February in Cologne, Lauscher castigated the monopolization that was taking place, explaining that the Nazi party was behaving as if the state was its possession and that as a result, the fight against the Nazis was becoming the fight against the state, a situation without precedent.[8] In the Center information bulletin dated 24 February, Kaas hinted at the risk of a party dictatorship.[9] In a speech delivered in Cologne on 1 March 1933, he pointed out the Nazis' attempt to monopolize state power: "*everything gets monopolized. . . . But . . . we will not tolerate that one monopolizes Germany from the political viewpoint of a party, and that one defames any opposition to this truly unjustified claim for monopoly*" (my italics).[10]

Whether they wanted to acknowledge it or not, Center delegates were aware of the stakes. They knew that the Nazis were aiming at the destruction of what they, the Center party, had stood for: constitutional rights, basic freedoms, political representation, parliamentary institutions, and a Christian ethos. The electoral campaign of February–March—the suppression of the freedom of the press, Nazi violence, intimidation, calumnies—gave them a taste of what lay ahead. The Center party literature—leaflets, internal memos, press releases from the party, literature for the activists—showed an unmistakable intuition of the threat.

The Prospect of the "Total" State

Here is the warning released by the executive committee of the Center party on the eve of election day (5 March): "A serious word at the last hour. There is danger! The German people is supposed to be taken by surprise through an enormous propaganda. . . . The election of March 5 . . . is a trial of strength . . . A disastrous politics of arrogance, slogans, and the unreserved suppression of free opinion and dissent has started. Power is supposed to prevail over law

7. The Nazis restricted the freedoms of press and gathering as early as the beginning of February 1933. The *Kölnische Volkszeitung* was banned on 5 and 7 February. Brüning mentions this fact in his speech of 18 February in Würzburg.

8. "For this party the government is not only an ally or a protector; it is more than that; it is the other side, the second Ego of the party; both feel that they form one entity; both make their power resources (*Machtmittel*) available to each other. In attacking the party one confronts today not only its own irregular formations, but also the state's power resources. This is the totally new and . . . the extreme danger of the present situation." *Kölnische Volkszeitung*, 23 February 1933.

9. Kommission für Zeitgeschichte, Bonn. Nachlaß Dessauer FD 12, no. 7136.

10. *Kölnische Volkszeitung*, 3 March 1933. My italics.

and freedom. Truth can no longer be voiced. Free opinion is even denied to the leaders of the Catholic people. You have also a sense of what is at stake."[11] As early as 9 February a political leaflet drafted for Catholic women raised the prospect of a dictatorship: "We are calling for an electoral fight of decisive consequences, one which the Center party has never been through. . . . Truth, Liberty, Justice! . . . We are fighting for the personal freedom against Communist terror and national socialist oppression! We are fighting for justice! Never was justice more threatened than now. Never was the German state more in danger to fall under the rule of dictatorial power and violence."[12]

To illustrate the implications of the Nazi challenge to state power, the Center party literature drew an explicit parallel with the Soviet Union. "Who now substitutes the brutal fact of power in place of law and uses law only to cast a beautiful window dressing on this power, in the long run undermines the fundaments of all state and social life and promotes a conception that has come to dominate in the Bolshevist Soviet Union, a conception for which law is only a means of the political struggle" (Press service of the Center party, electoral memo no. 20, 20 February 1933).[13] In a remarkable description of the totalitarian conception of the state, the journal of the party, *Das Zentrum*, denounced the call for a "total state" (*totaler Staat*): "We witnessed the grotesque spectacle: those who internally destroyed the state authority through their demagogic agitation, raised the demand of an all powerful state to the utmost. In contrast to the pre-war time, in which one coined the concept of the so-called omnipotent state, one calls now for the total state. While in the omnipotent state the weight is on the completeness of its power and lasting capacity for intervention, the total state emphasizes the actual and effective incorporation of all aspects of life."[14]

11. Konrad Adenauer Stiftung, Sankt Augustin, ACDP, Nachlaß Wegmann, I-366, 001-4, one-page statement, signed: "The executive committee of the Center party" (*Der Vorstand der Zentrumspartei*), n.d.

12. Konrad Adenauer Stiftung, Sankt Augustin, Nachlaß Wegmann, I-366, 001-4. The circular to the women's councils (Frauenbeiräte)—signed Helene Weber—strikes the same chord: "The Center party needs to fight for the freedom of the German citizen, for the personal freedom and for the social freedom, of which a dictatorial state leadership wants to deprive him." Konrad Adenauer Stiftung, Sankt Augustin, Nachlaß Wegmann, I-366, 001-4, Reichsfrauenbeirat der Deutschen Zentrumspartei, Berlin, 9 February 1933.

13. Konrad Adenauer Stiftung, Sankt Augustin, Nachlaß Feilmayr, I-150, 031-4, Wahldienst no. 20, 21 February 1933.

14. Konrad Adenauer Stiftung, Sankt Augustin, Nachlaß Feilmayr, I-150, 032-2, "*Das Zentrum*, nos. 1–2, February 1933, Der 'Totale' Staat." Although the article makes no explicit reference to the Nazis, it is a political indictment of their political philosophy. The passage I have just quoted is followed by a critique of Carl Schmitt's Friend-Enemy (*Freund-Feind*) theorie. The 1 March 1933 issue of *Merkuria*, journal of the German association of Catholic merchants'

Equally significant are the references to Fascist Italy in communications internal to the Center circles. At the beginning of March 1933 a "strictly confidential" four-page memo intended for the Center party cadres refers to the fate of the Catholic party in Italy and to rumors that the Center party will be subsequently eliminated.[15] On the evening of 20 March, after the first meeting of the Center parliamentary delegation, the lack of freedom in Italy and the suppression of free speech are the subject of a conversation between Clara Siebert, Helene Weber, and Else Peerenboom.[16] Italy foreshadowed the political future of Germany. As Wirth mentions in his personal notes, there was no lack of information about what to expect from the Nazis.[17] Clara Siebert's testimony emphasizes that she gauged the extent of the Nazi threat on 9 March 1933, when she learned that a Nazi regional leader had been appointed Reich commissar for the state of Baden. "Then I knew what awaited us, Catholics, and what awaited the Center."[18]

TACTICAL BARGAINING

Thus the Center leadership had gauged the threat. In light of this threat, the tactical justifications for bargaining with Hitler in March when he claimed full powers without constitutional bounds were of three sorts. First, the enabling bill put an end to the state of exception inaugurated by the emergency decrees of 28 February and the suppression of all individual rights. Since the bill did not call into question the Reich president's right of veto, it preserved the president's political capacity. It created a legal framework which in place of further revolutionary developments would restore law and order. Second, the Center leaders used their bargaining position to extract assurances on the scope of power being delegated. They strove to ensure that they would preserve some influence on the political process and that Catholics' fundamental rights— both religious and cultural—would not be endangered by the new state. Third, Center leaders expected that Hitler's demagoguery would not sustain the test

organizations, elaborates similar themes, contrasting the Catholic conception of human rights with the ideological foundations of the calls for "an authoritarian state" and "total state." Stadtarchiv Köln, Nachlaß Teusch, Best. 1187, 234.

15. Konrad Adenauer Stiftung, Sankt Augustin, Nachlaß Bormann, I-352, Mappe 9, "Streng vertraulich," 1.

16. Kommission für Zeitgeschichte, Bonn, Tagebuchaufzeichnungen von Clara Siebert, Arch 46, 99.

17. Bundesarchiv, Koblenz, Nachlaß Wirth N1342/133, "Die historische Reichtagsfraktion vom 21. u. 23. März 1933," n.d., 1.

18. Kommission für Zeitgeschichte, Bonn, Tagebuchaufzeichnungen von Clara Siebert, Arch 46, 94.

of governmental politics. Failing to implement his political program, he would lose his popular support and his power would soon collapse.

In the end each of these tactical bets failed. The bet on Hitler's moderation faltered when it became clear that he was determined to turn the state into a party state excluding all dissent. The bet on Hitler's concessions regarding the independence of the judges, the powers of the Länder, and Catholics' religious and cultural rights proved to be a fool's deal. Hitler did not keep his promises. The Center party disappeared and Catholics' religious and cultural autonomy was soon jeopardized. As for the bet on Hitler's failure to implement his program, it turned out to be dramatically ungrounded.

Binding Hitler to a Rule of Law

The emergency decrees of 28 February suspended constitutional provisions pertaining to civil liberties and individual freedoms. The government had full powers to repress subversion writ large. The state of exception had become the rule. Moreover, the Nazis held an absolute majority in parliament. Therefore the prospect of rescinding these decrees through parliament was ruled out. By granting Hitler full constitutional powers, one could hope to prepare the ground for the restoration of law and order. Having his demands fulfilled, Hitler would no longer need to resort to emergency measures. The bill would put an end to the state of exception. It would bind the Nazi leadership to a more moderate and reasonable course of action.[19]

This tactical rationale was predicated on two assumptions. One was that the enabling bill provided legal resources to check Hitler's claims to absolute power. Because the enabling bill was theoretically limited to four years and did not call into question the Reich president's right of veto,[20] in theory the Reich president was still the "guardian of the constitution" and had the capacity to check Hitler's power if necessary. Constitutional authority was formally granted not to Hitler but to his cabinet. Brüning argued retrospectively that

19. This is for instance Brecht's contention: most members of the Center Reichstag delegation still hoped, through their acquiescence, "to bind the Nazis to a more reasonable course of action and to set limits to an irrepressible movement" (Brecht, *Mit der Kraft des Geistes*, 305). See also the interpretation by Winkler (1989): "The representatives of the bourgeois middle parties, who without exception voted for the *Ermächtigungsgesetz*, were not only afraid for their life and the existence of the party organization. Indeed, they also hoped that the *Ermächtigungsgesetz* would give satisfaction to Hitler and, as a result, would consolidate the 'state' against the 'movement.' They yielded to unprecedented pressures as well as to their own wishful thinking" (906).

20. On this point see chapter 2.

the Reich president might be able within "two or three months to undertake actions against Hitler."[21]

The second assumption was that Hitler represented the "moderate," the "orderly" side of Nazism. In voting for the enabling bill, the Center representatives were making a gesture of goodwill and appeasement. Thereby they hoped to strengthen within the Nazi movement the "party of order"—the contingent of Nazi leaders who sought to put an end to the political turmoil and reaffirm the authority of the state—against the "party of revolution." The belief in Hitler's statesmanhood and moderation conditioned the belief in the possibility of an orderly transition, as well as the belief that he would fulfill his promises and that non-Nazi political organizations might be allowed to survive.

A Quid Pro Quo

In the morning of 20 March, three days before the vote on the enabling bill, a Center delegation composed of Kaas, Stegerwald, and Hackelsberger met with Hitler to study under which conditions the Center would agree to confer full powers upon the government. In bargaining with Hitler, Center leaders were attempting to extract concessions from the latter on issues which fundamentally bore upon Catholics' rights as a religious minority. Since the government was resolute to carry out its authoritarian plans, was it not more sensible to save whatever could still be saved? Through acquiescence, Center leaders could hope to secure a lesser evil (Hürten 1992, 186). A retreat on the political front was better than a general defeat. With the enforcement of the emergency decree of 28 February, the Center party had no stronghold left to defend. Kaas's tactic was to preserve the chances of retaining some influence on the course of the "national revolution" and to substitute the reduced political power of the party for guarantees about the central points of its program (Becker 1963b, 157).

Moreover, in voting for the enabling bill the Center delegates would allow their party to avoid direct repression. In a manuscript written a few years after the event, Wirth describes how in the meeting of the Center parliamentary group on 23 March, he finally yielded to the argument advanced by the representatives of the Christian trade unions: the acceptance of the bill could allow them to keep their organizations alive for a few years.[22] Heuss mentions that some members of the executive committee of the German State party (Staats-

21. Brüning, *Reden und Aufsätze eines deutschen Staatsmanns*, 259.
22. Bundesarchiv, Koblenz, Nachlaß Wirth N1342/133, 12.

partei) believed that the party could survive under the new regime, with its network of small groups of faithful members. A vote of rejection would jeopardize the survival of the party.[23]

The Prospect of Hitler's Failure

Coupled with this tactical assessment was the belief that Hitler would not be able to implement his demagogic program and, as a result, would soon lose popular support. From Brüning's perspective, many of those who voted for the *Ermächtigungsgesetz* in March 1933 expected Hitler's official responsibility to destroy his popularity.[24] Elaborating the reasons for his vote, the former Center Reichstag delegate Erwin Respondek remarked that he had not been the only one to think that the nationalistic demagoguery of the government would achieve no miracle.[25] Paul Bausch, a member of the small delegation from the Protestant Christian Social People's Service (CSVD), made the same point: "there was hardly any member of the democratic groups who believed that the Nazi domination would last for a long time. All those whom I knew were of the opinion that this system would fail within a short time in face of the harshness of the political reality."[26]

THE POSSIBILITY OF BLINDNESS

Erwin Respondek's explanation for his vote (April 1947) provides a synthetic summary of the tactical miscalculation argument. First, the enabling bill was not a blank check granting Hitler full powers. The fundamental institutions of the constitution set limits to his power. In short, Hitler was not entitled to do whatever he wanted. Second, even if Hitler decided to transgress the limits of his mandate, the rights of the Reich president remained a last guarantee. The Reich president had sworn to fulfill his role as guardian of the constitution. The Center delegates believed that they could let the national experiment fol-

---

23. Bundesarchiv, Koblenz, Nachlaß Heuss N1221/82, letter to Dr. Kurt Hiller, 12 April 1947.

24. Brüning, *Reden und Aufsätze eines deutschen Staatsmanns*, 253.

25. Bundesarchiv, Koblenz, NL Schwertfeger, N1015/255, Das "Ermächtigungsgesetz," April 1947, statement by Respondek, 2. A copy of this five-page statement is in the personal papers of Josef Wirth, Bundesarchiv, Koblenz, Nachlaß Wirth N1342/32.

26. Bausch, *Lebenserinnerungen und Erkenntnisse eines schwäbischen Abgeordneten*, 121. In an interview with Gotto and Knopp, Heinrich Krone, Center Reichstag delegate in March 1933, explains that he believed a Hitler dictatorship would not last long. Archiv der Konrad Adenauer Stiftung, Sankt Augustin, Nachlaß Krone, I-028, 006/5, interview with Knopp and Gotto, 6.

low its course until it collapsed, so that the way for reasonable politics would be free again.[27]

All these reasons are plausible. How sound are they? This question is two-pronged. First, do these arguments adequately describe actors' tactical motivations at the time? Second, to what extent did actors believe in their own justifications? The first question is motivated by the observation that several members of the Center party who opposed a vote in favor of the enabling bill on 23 March—chief among them Brüning and Joos—retrospectively used some of these arguments to justify the vote of the Center delegation. The second question requires examining in detail the actors' state of mind at the time of decision. At issue is the credibility of the tactical reasons the delegates invoke for themselves.

Retrospective Justifications

In his talk with the historian Rudolf Morsey in 1963, Joos formulated an explanation of the vote similar to Respondek's. Most Center representatives, Joos explained, were clearly aware that the emergency decrees of 28 February had fundamentally altered the rules of the political game and the exercise of democratic rights. In these conditions their primary goal was to obtain from Hitler the guarantee that some of these measures would be rescinded and the Constitution would not be discarded.[28] In his recollections, Joos indicates that he agreed to vote for the enabling bill when the Center delegation was given assurances against the misuse of the bill, assurances that were to be confirmed in writing by Hitler and Hindenburg.[29] Brüning made the same argument in 1947 when he attested to the confidence of Hindenburg's collaborators that the enabling bill would not put into question the president's constitutional rights.[30]

In explaining that the vote for the enabling bill was not a jump into the abyss, that Hitler's mandate would be checked by the Reich president, Hindenburg, and that they had received assurances to this effect, Joos and Brüning endorsed a view that became the former Center delegates' semi-official stance on the event after the war. The striking fact is that both Joos and Brüning opposed

27. Bundesarchiv, Koblenz, NL Schwertfeger, N1015/255, Das "Ermächtigungsgesetz," April 1947, statement by Respondek, 4.

28. Conversation with Rudolf Morsey broadcast on 13 November 1963, Kommission für Zeitgeschichte, Bonn, Nachlaßsplitter Joos, Archiv IV, box 1. On this point see also the text entitled "Der Wortbruch beim Ermächtigungsgesetz," Kommission für Zeitgeschichte, Bonn, Nachlaßsplitter Joos, Archiv IV, 3–4.

29. Joos, *So sah ich sie, Menschen und Geschehnisse*, 92–93.

30. Brüning, *Reden und Aufsätze eines deutschen Staatsmanns*, 253.

a "yes" vote on 23 March. Brüning justified his opposition by arguing that the conditions capable of holding the government to its promises were lacking. He did not disguise his view that the enabling bill was "the most monstrous thing that [had] ever been asked from parliament."[31]

Underlying the political rationale for a vote of rejection was a negative assessment of the political implications of a legal power transfer. The vote sanctioned the Nazis' political victory and consolidated their takeover of the state. Guarantees were lacking, a point reiterated by Brüning in some of his recollections of the event: the "superficial guarantees" contained in the Ermächtigungsgesetz concerning the Reichspräsident, the Reichstag, and the Reichsrat remained meaningless as long as the provisions of the emergency decrees that infringed civil and political freedoms were not rescinded.[32] For this purpose, Brüning explained, he insisted upon obtaining a written commitment from Hitler that the guarantees would be met.[33] In the absence of these guarantees Hitler's oral promises lacked credibility.

These few observations indicate that we should not let ourselves be deceived by tactical justifications provided post factum. Wirth, Joos, and Brüning were among the most consistent opponents of the enabling bill. They voted "yes" along with the other members of the Center parliamentary delegation after agreeing to abide by the delegation's discipline of vote. Yet the reasons they provided for the vote ex post blur their initial motivations. Brüning's insistence on the guarantee issue and his pressures to obtain a written commitment from Hitler before the vote suggest that he did not believe Hitler's promises. Hitler's oral assurances were not credible because no one had the capacity to hold him to his word.

Facts and Judgments

Wirth, Joos, and Brüning had to convince themselves that their decision made sense *despite* their initial decision to oppose it. Behind their justification lurks the need for sensible reasons. The observation invites us to reconsider the tactical reasons for a "yes" vote in a different light. Did Center parliamentarians who leaned toward a "yes" vote on 23 March really believe in what they were saying? Were they truly convinced that they might be able to consolidate their position? Or did they catch these arguments in the same way a drowning man catches a lifebuoy, because they had no other justification available?

31. *Protokolle*, 23 March, parliamentary delegation, no. 750, 631.
32. Brüning, *Reden und Aufsätze eines deutschen Staatsmanns*, 261.
33. Brüning, *Reden und Aufsätze eines deutschen Staatsmanns*, 262.

Contradictory Expectations

In the early afternoon of 20 March, Kaas reported to the executive committee of the Center party Reichstag delegation the content of the talks which
he, Stegerwald, and Hackelsberger had had with Hitler in the morning. Kaas
ended his report by noting that the government was determined to carry out
its plans but that the way was open for further negotiations.³⁴ These last remarks concerning Hitler's determination to overlook any obstacle were not
incidental. Kaas reiterated the point two days later in a meeting with the Center parliamentary delegation a few hours before the crucial vote. Even if the
government did not get a two-thirds majority, it would carry out its plans by
other means.³⁵ In sum, whether the Center opposed the bill or not would not
make much difference. Hitler would achieve his ends. According to the Center
delegate Ulitzka, this opinion was shared by his colleagues in the delegation:
people knew that Hitler would interpret the law in his own way.³⁶

The problematic nature of a deal with Hitler lies in these contradictory beliefs. How could the Center representatives believe that Hitler would remove
any obstacle *and* that his assurances were credible? If they believed that Hitler
would pursue his agenda at all costs, then they had no reason to think much
of his promises. The problem is compounded because, as Brüning made clear,
the Center party had no guarantees that Hitler would fulfill his promises, and
had no institutional leverage to hold him to his word.

Viewing the vote for the enabling bill as a quid pro quo with Hitler therefore
implied a significant amount of wishful thinking. Center representatives had
to believe either that Hitler would not take advantage of his constitutional
power to shape a Nazi state or that he would fail in his attempt to take over
the state apparatus. Miscalculations often betrayed a willingness to deceive
oneself. Significantly, Carl Severing blurs the distinction between miscalculation and self-deception when he assesses the motivations that underlay a
"yes" vote: "Political mistakes led to this pitiful outcome. Almost all bourgeois
parties found themselves trapped in a series of self-delusions [*eine Reihe von
Selbsttäuschungen*]. . . . The Center was the victim of a similar delusion when,
through the words of its chairman, Dr. Kaas, it expressed the opinion that

34. *Protokolle*, 20 March, parliamentary delegation executive committee, no. 742, 622.
35. *Protokolle*, 23 March, parliamentary delegation, no. 750, 630.
36. Reported by Webersinn (1970, 192), and quoted in *Das "Ermächtigungsgesetz" vom 24.
März 1933*, 150. Equally worth noting is Reinhold Maier's contention that his colleagues in the
German State party delegation to the Reichstag did not expect Hitler to abide by the terms of
the enabling bill. "Der Bericht des Untersuchungsausschusses," partly reproduced in *Das "Ermächtigungsgesetz" vom 24. März 1933*, 154.

Hitler's explanations in the March 23 Reichstag session would become the fundamental and practical guidelines for the implementation of the legal work which the Center expected."[37]

What remains puzzling is the Center representatives' awareness of the threat of a party state. Obviously, the political developments that had taken place in Germany since the election results of 5 March and the Nazis' display of violence were powerful reminders of Fascism's rise to power in Italy. If we want to account for the Center representatives' willingness to view the vote as a bargain with Hitler along with their awareness of the Nazi threat, we need a different line of inquiry, one that reverses the direction of causality between beliefs and decisions. According to this alternative interpretation, the Center representatives first decided that a compromise with Hitler was possible. This decision led them to overlook the possibility of a fool's deal. A memo from 1946 in defense of the Center vote unknowingly pointed to the problem: "the Catholic parties' 'Yes' was not a thoughtless capitulation. Rather, it was a decision to consent with all reservations, a decision *based on trust and faith*" (my emphasis).[38]

CLASS AND COMPROMISE

We are thus back to the original problem: did the Center representatives have good reasons to believe that they could find a modus vivendi with Hitler? Which interests might have shaped their belief that a compromise was possible? In examining this aspect of the problem, I want to investigate motivations that are only imperfectly captured by the tactical reasons provided by actors to themselves and to others. My focus now is on the possible influence of class interests, defined as material interests determined by class positions. In the following discussion, class positions refer to actors' occupation and their position within the structure of production.

Analyzing Marx's different takes on the bourgeoisie's willingness to abstain from state power, Elster (1985, 419–21) mentions several motives for political

37. Archiv der sozialen Demokratie der Friedrich-Ebert-Stiftung, Bonn, Nachlaß Severing, Mappe 28, no. 37, "NWDR Köln," 3: text of a radio broadcast. In the same text Severing describes the incapacity to adequately assess the political situation and the logic of Hitler's demagoguery as a "political fault" (*eine politische Schuld*). Schwertfeger (1947, 314), makes a similar assessment.

38. Kommission für Zeitgeschichte, Bonn, Nachlaß Wollf, GW I 2 n, "Das Ermächtigungsgesetz," 3. See also Ernst Lemmer's acknowledgment that this decision was made "in the foolish hope that Hitler's dictatorship would remain within legal bounds" (Lemmer, *Manches war doch anders*, 170).

abdication. Power holders may abdicate to preempt dethronement. They may transfer power to an adversary with the expectation that the responsibilities of exercising power will induce this adversary to restrain himself. I have already discussed these two hypotheses. The "pre-emption of dethronement" argument remains wanting as long as it does not explain how actors form their beliefs about their future welfare. The belief in the "taming" qualities of the exercise of state power amounts to wishful thinking if there are clear indications that the challenger is resolute in pursuing an authoritarian agenda.

Elster (1985, 419, 421) also points to a lack of trust in one's ability. I will not examine this hypothesis, for it obviously lacks relevance in the present case: the groups which abdicated power in 1933 and 1940 had exercised state responsibilities and suffered from no competence complex. Rather, I will focus my attention on an alternative explanation which views actors' attitude toward power in terms of opportunity cost. The basic idea is that in highly confrontational situations, holding power is costly because it exposes one to direct attacks from various contenders and undermines one's ability to realize one's material and class interests. The notion of "opportunity cost" is compatible with diverse motivations, such as the desire to improve one's bargaining position in the confrontation with a third party, the desire to defuse opposition onto another group, or the call for an arbiter.

In addition to the opportunity cost hypothesis, I consider a further line of inquiry. In this second scenario, actors holding economically dominant positions, such as landowners and industrialists, realize that democratic institutions open the door to political movements threatening their socioeconomic dominance. Consequently, these economically dominant actors seek to implement institutions which bar the workers' movements and the Left from governmental responsibilities. They view the rise of a mass-based radical movement on the far Right as a political opportunity to defeat their enemies on the Left for good, and to substitute oligarchic institutions for democratic ones. In this case, the compromise with the challenger is not purely tactical. Economically dominant groups believe that their political goals are congruent with those of the authoritarian challenger, since both want to discard parliamentary institutions.

Opportunity Costs

In *The Collapse of the Weimar Republic*, Abraham (1986) develops the argument that in the context of the economic crisis of the 1930s, fractions of dominant classes came to the conclusion that the fragmented democratic setting of Weimar did not allow them to reconcile their divergent interests. Two weaknesses prevented these groups from implementing their own political solution to the crisis. First, dominant groups could not rely on a broad mass movement of their own to further their political claims. They were, to use Abraham's expression, "politically inadequate" (xlix). Second, dominant groups were embroiled in intractable internal conflicts that sapped their ability to realize their interests and undermined republican institutions, ultimately contributing to their demise. Economically dominant groups were no longer interested in monopolizing state power and saw "no other way out of the crisis acceptable to them" than an alliance with fascism (Abraham 1986, xvi).

Underlying this historical argument is a theory of political abdication. Class fractions which enjoy socioeconomic dominance and lack the support of a mass-based political movement are willing to abdicate their hold over the state when they realize that their conflicts are collectively self-destructive. The argument is based on two premises. One is that these groups behave as collective actors. They have the political resources to collectively decide on one course of action, and to commit their members to this course of action. The second premise is that these groups are rational. They have the capacity to devise a rational solution to their collective plight. To avoid the destructive consequences of their internal fighting, they decide to tie their hands and let an arbiter decide their collective fate in their place. Precommitment prevents them from getting embroiled in conflicts that pit them against one another. As in Elster's parable of Ulysses and the sirens (1984, 88–102), precommitment precludes weakness of the (collective) will.

In this scenario there is no problem of collective action and no problem of agency—that is, no disjuncture between objective interests as determined by the structure of production and the political translation of these interests. This argument assumes collective rationality on the part of the propertied élite and their constituencies. The deal concluded with the challenger is grounded in a clear awareness of class or class fraction interests. Much could be said about the factors—both organizational and social—that affect actors' collective capacity to devise, implement, and sustain collective precommitment. In many historical instances similar to this one, precommitment to an external arbiter may never see the light, for the simple reason that no group or group member has the political clout or resources required to mobilize other group members and other groups.[39] Moreover, this argument leaves us in the dark regarding the factors which condition the propertied élite's belief that it can bring to power the authoritarian challenger and significantly check his power.

---

39. This is the classic free-rider problem analyzed by Olson (1965, 2). Marwell and Oliver (1993, 52–57), have shown that this problem is overcome when there exists a critical mass of group members with enough pooled resources to make participation beneficial.

These analytical objections notwithstanding, is there evidence that in the dramatic and conflict-laden context of March 1933, groups which endorsed the power transfer to Hitler viewed him as the arbiter who could settle their differences? Concerning the Center party, two observations motivate this question. First, conflicts between interest groups were rife in the Center party. At different points in its history these conflicts seriously endangered the unity of the party. For instance, in September 1927 the Center finance minister in Marx's cabinet, Heinrich Köhler, proposed a substantial salary hike for civil servants. Köhler's bill elicited the vigorous opposition of the leaders of the Christian unions and their representatives in the parliamentary delegation, who denounced the bill as too costly and as restoring pre-war pay differentials between workers and civil servants. When the bill was put to a vote in December 1927, the head of the Christian miners' union, Heinrich Imbusch, opposed it while a third of the delegates, many of them workers' representatives, abstained (Becker 1961a, 368; Patch 1985, 119–21). Bachem's contention (quoted by Morsey 1966, 69) that "the Center Party embraced all classes" and was able to "harmonize within its own ranks the inevitable conflicts of interest" obviously did not reflect the situation that prevailed at the end of the 1920s.

The second observation is that the Center representatives were concerned by the rise of class conflicts within and outside their party. It is in part to overcome the destructive effects of these conflicts that at the party convention of December 1928 many delegates decided to elect a prelate, Ludwig Kaas, to the chairmanship (Patch 1985, 138–39). Similarly, as Germany became embroiled in an intractable political crisis in the second half of 1932, the Center leadership seriously considered forming a government above parties. In October 1932 Kaas invited all responsible party leaders to form an "emergency and majority community" (*Not- und Mehrheitsgemeinschaft*) for the sake of the country (Morsey 1960, 327).[40] On 1 January 1933 he published an article in the Catholic press calling for the advent of a strong man who would reunify Germany.[41] The notion that class and political conflicts could be overcome with the appointment of a government transcending party divisions was therefore central to the Center's political repertoire in the last months of the Weimar Republic.

Yet there is no indication that this motive played any significant role in the decision of 23 March. Center delegates did not see in Hitler the man capable of settling class divisions and conflicts. They viewed him as a threat to their own security and most basic interests. The campaign for the elections of 5 March and its aftermath had smashed the illusion of a "coalition of all men of good will" which Kaas had evoked in the fall of 1932. Violence and cynicism now

40. *Germania*, 18 October 1932, no. 290, 4.
41. *Kölnische Volkszeitung*, 2 January 1933.

had the last word. The Nazi leadership's efforts to suppress dissent made it hard to believe that their action would soothe social antagonisms instead of exacerbating them. Moreover, Center leaders were now concerned about the possibility that the new state might attempt to suppress Catholic organizations. Hitler was therefore not a choice, but a threat.

The opportunity cost hypothesis proves no more illuminating with regard to the parties representing dominant business and agrarian interests in parliament. Recall the thrust of this argument: dominant groups face a situation so rife with antagonisms that they no longer want to be in the frontline. These groups—or rather their political representatives—leave the responsibility for harsh political decisions to others, and decide to "cultivate their gardens." Interestingly, this is the strategy that Brüning suggested to Alfred Hugenberg, the head of the German National People's party (DNVP), during a meeting which took place at the end of August 1931. The economic crisis, Brüning explained, would last until the summer of 1932, and the government would have to take unpopular measures for one more year after the end of the crisis. The nationalist Right would be in a better position if it entered the government after the economic crisis receded.[42] Hugenberg, however, had no intention to shun state power (Patch 1998, 189). His primary objective was to get rid of the parliamentary system of Weimar, and he needed state power for this purpose as well as Hitler's support.[43]

Social Reaction and Fascism

This brings me to the second explanation in terms of class interests. According to this explanation, in times of intense class antagonisms economically dominant groups compromise with mass-based radical movement from the Right to defeat their leftist opponents and implement nondemocratic institutions. Along these lines, Abraham (1986) points to the collapse at the end of the 1920s of the social compromise that underlay Weimar's stability. The onset of the Great Depression "revealed a contradiction between the demands of democracy and the needs of capitalism" (1986, xv). The "democratic arrangements of the Republic, its tenuous system of class cooperation, extra parliamentary compromise and corporatism" (1986, xlix) became incompatible with the requirements of private accumulation in a capitalist economy. Industrial-

42. Brüning, *Memoiren*, 375. Patch (1998, 188), offers a detailed analysis of this meeting.

43. Brüning reports the following statement by Hugenberg during a private exchange in November 1930: "I am more convinced than ever that I was always right. Germany stands in the middle of the collapse that I predicted.... Therefore I must combat you and the whole system." Brüning, *Memoiren*, 210, quoted and translated in Patch (1998, 112–13).

ists viewed the social and political concessions granted to social democracy as too costly.

Accordingly, dominant industrialist groups put an end to their previous conciliatory stance and called into question the compromise implemented with the Social Democrats after 1923. In abandoning their program of conciliation, these groups created the conditions of an intractable political stalemate and an opening for the Nazis (Abraham 1986, xv). Further, dominant industrialist and agrarian groups compromised with the National Socialists in 1932 "to maintain what was theirs and improve their future prospects" (Abraham 1986, xvi).

Since the vote on the enabling bill was a vote on political institutions, the Marxist theory of political abdication has potential relevance and can be extended legitimately to the parliamentary decision of 23 March. The validity of the thesis is conditioned on the existence of a direct influence of dominant economic groups on non-Nazi and non-Socialist parties represented in the Reichstag. Does this argument highlight the cleavages that took shape on the issue of the enabling bill? Is there evidence suggesting that parliamentarians were expressing class interests when they opted for abdication?

If we consider the class constituency of the parties represented in parliament, the Marxist thesis has much empirical credibility. There is a broad correlation between how the parties voted in the Reichstag on 23 March 1933 and the socioeconomic profile of these parties. The German Nationalists and the DVP—the parties that embodied political reaction and voiced the interests of business groups in parliament—endorsed the power transfer without apparent qualms. The Social Democrats, on the other hand, who had stuck to a policy of defending the material interests of the working class, opposed the power transfer to Hitler. The Center represented a median position: in previous years the party had made governmental coalitions with both Social Democrats and bourgeois parties. Since 1930, however, the party leadership overall had granted support to a deflationary policy that hurt workers' economic interests (Morsey 1960, 299).

The attitude displayed by the DNVP representatives in particular seems quite consistent with their previous strategy. From the time of Hugenberg's election to the chairmanship of the party (October 1928), the leadership of the DNVP pursued a strategy of subverting Weimar and frontally opposing the parties which supported the Republic. This strategic goal had incited Hugenberg from 1928 on to seek a political alliance with the Nazis and to provide financial support to them. From this perspective, the vote of the enabling bill was the coronation of these political efforts.

When we look more closely at intraparty cleavages, however, this first approximation becomes quite problematic. Cleavages within parties on the enabling bill did not reflect clear-cut class interests. A fraction of the German Nationalist leadership considered amending the enabling bill in a restrictive sense. The evidence concerning the relationship between the socioeconomic position of the Center representatives and their stance is inconclusive. Most union representatives endorsed a "yes" vote, even though workers were less likely than other social groups represented in the Center delegation to advocate acquiescence in Hitler's rule, as I will indicate below. As for the SPD, the conclusion is paradoxical: it is union leaders who suggested a conciliatory stance vis-à-vis Hitler before the vote.

Split within the German Nationalists

On 20 March, three days before the vote, the German Nationalist (DNVP) delegation met in Berlin. In the meeting Hugenberg described the content of the bill. Several prominent members of the delegation were critical toward it, and the debate hinged upon which strategy to adopt to avoid being completely marginalized by the NSDAP. Some delegates advocated a fusion with the Nazi delegation, while others considered the possibility of joining forces with the Center to amend the bill.[44] What is striking about this debate is that it reveals the DNVP representatives' acute awareness that they were standing on the verge of being wiped from the political map. At this point the DNVP leadership was not playing the Hitler card to advance its own strategic interests. It was desperately in search of a strategy that could check Hitler's political claims.

The Center Delegation: Social Origins and Political Stances

Do class fault lines offer a predictor of political cleavages on the enabling bill? Answering this question requires first that we identify the sociological profile of the Center parliamentary delegation. For this purpose I rely on the biographical information provided by several directories and on autobiographical accounts.[45] I distinguish six occupational groups: (1) workers, (2) farmers, (3) delegates endowed with economic capital and economic power (landowners, industrialists, executive managers, and businessmen), (4) professionals and independents (lawyers, editors, writers, executives), (5) civil servants and teach-

---

44. Bundesarchiv, Koblenz, Nachlaß Martin Spahn N1324/175, minutes of the DNVP parliamentary delegation, 20 March, 15.

45. *Inventar zu den Nachlässen der deutschen Arbeiterbewegung; MdR: Biographisches Handbuch der Reichstage; MdR: Die Reichtagsabgeordneten der Weimarer Republik in der Zeit des Nationalsozialismus.*

Table 10   Vote Inclination on 23 March and Class Origin

	In Favor of "Yes" Vote	In Favor of "No" Vote	Total	Percentage of Delegation
Workers	8	4	12	17
Farmers	6	0	6	8
Economically dominant groups (landowners, industrialists, executives, managers, businessmen)	8	1	9	13
Professionals and independents	10	4	14	19
Civil servants and teachers	21	4	25	35
Religious groups	5	1	6	8
Total	58	14	72	100

χ-square = 4.29, d.f. = 5, p = .50

ers, and (6) members of the church hierarchy (priests and prelates). Delegates who identified themselves as workers owed their party responsibilities to their activism as union representatives or as leaders of Catholic organizations.

Civil servants and teachers formed the bulk of the Center delegation (table 10). Combined with professionals and independents, they represented more than half of the Catholic parliamentary delegation. A little less than one fifth of the delegation had a working-class background. In terms of class identities the Center parliamentary delegation was therefore quite heterogeneous. Does this information highlight the delegates' vote inclinations?[46] Workers were twice as likely as nonworkers to favor a "no" vote (table 11). If in addition to union representatives and former union representatives we consider Josef Joos and Hermann Joseph Schmitt, delegates who were not workers but viewed themselves as the traditional political representatives of Catholic workers as a result of their leadership positions in the Catholic clubs (Patch 1985, 65), the odds of advocating a "no" vote for the representatives of the workers' movement become four times higher. Conversely, the representatives from the economically dominant classes as well as teachers and civil servants were half as likely as their colleagues to advocate a "no" vote.

Given the small numbers involved, the significance of these differences remains open to question (table 11), and we need additional evidence to assess

46. In chapter 3 I mentioned the circumstances under which the delegates expressed their preferences for the vote on the power transfer on 23 March, and the list of those who, given the sources available, we can reasonably assume took a position against the enabling bill.

Table 11 Odds of a "No" Vote in Meeting of Center
Delegation, 23 March 1933, by Occupational Group

	Odds Ratio	p-value
Workers versus non-workers	2.23	0.25
Economically dominant groups	0.43	0.45
Civil servants	0.62	0.46

the extent to which class cleavages may have played a role in the decision of 23 March. Did Center representatives affiliated with economically dominant groups readily endorse Hitler's political claims? Did they envision their endorsement as a way of undermining the political influence of workers' unions? The minutes of the meetings of the parliamentary delegation executive committee indicate that during the committee's meeting on the morning of 23 March, Kaas mentioned rumors "in certain industrial circles, according to which the Center would not put up enough resistance." He "protested against these [charges], pointing out that if these circles had put up a fraction of the efforts [deployed by the Center leadership], something could perhaps still be done on the side of the Reich president."[47]

It is not clear to which "industrial circles" Kaas is referring, but his remark goes counter to the thesis that business interest groups in general brought pressures to bear on the Center leadership in favor of a conciliatory stance toward Hitler. However, this observation should not obfuscate the fact that the very few Center deputies who publicly displayed their support for the power transfer represented economically dominant groups within the Center delegation. These delegates were Alfred Hackelsberger (an industrialist from Baden), Oskar Farny, and Florian Klöckner. In the summer of 1932 these delegates had been instrumental in making the Center Party Committee for Commerce and Industry endorse Papen's cabinet. Their political support for Papen contradicted the Center's official stance (Patch 1985, 223).[48] In February 1933 they greeted a cabinet which they hoped would curb the influence of the trade unions (Patch 1985, 223).[49]

---

47. *Protokolle*, 23 March 1933, Vorstand, no. 748, 629.

48. Bundesarchiv, Koblenz, Nachlaß ten Hompel N1133/21, letter by Hompel to Fonk, 3 August 1932.

49. The 3 April issue of the newsletter of the Center Party Committee for Commerce and Industry describes the vote on 23 March as a positive act of collaboration that firmly grounds the Center party in the national camp. Kommission für Zeitgeschichte, Bonn, Nachlaß Fonk, Archiv 7, "Mitteilungen der Handels- und Industrie-Beiräte der Deutschen Zentrumspartei, 3 April 1933, 1.

By contrast, delegates affiliated with the workers' movement formed the core of the small minority which two hours before the final vote advocated opposition to Hitler. All the union officials who opposed the power transfer held leading positions in workers' organizations: Heinrich Fahrenbrach (chairman of the textile workers' union), Heinrich Imbusch (chairman of the Christian miners' union), Jakob Kaiser (leading member of the league of Christian unions), and Josef Ersing (secretary of the Christian unions for the district of South Germany). In a meeting that took place a few days before the parliamentary discussion of the enabling bill, the leading circles of the Catholic workers' clubs for western and southwestern Germany, based in Cologne, decided to send a resolution to the Center parliamentary delegation asking the delegates not to endorse the power transfer.[50] Accordingly their representatives in the delegation, Joseph Joos and Hermann Joseph Schmitt, took an oppositional stance.

Nevertheless, two thirds of the union representatives who were deputies in parliament declared themselves in favor of a "yes" vote during the delegation's meeting on the afternoon of 23 March:

Stegerwald of the league of Christian unions
Johannes Becker of the Christian construction workers' union
Peter Schlack, former union official and head of the consumers'
    cooperatives
Karl Schmitz, chairman of the Christian metal workers' union
Peter Tremmel, chairman of the Christian factory workers' union
Otto Gerig, member of the German nationalist Union of Commercial
    Employees (DHV)
the union officials Johann Ernst, Fritz Kuhnen, Franz Riesener, and Franz
    Wiedemeier (Kosthorst 1967, 171)

Division prevailed. Stegerwald sharply criticized Kaiser for his opposition to the bill, arguing that he was too young and had too little experience to be able to correctly assess the matter.[51] Toward the end of the meeting Josef Ersing, the secretary of the Christian unions for the district of South Germany, left to consult with union leaders and representatives of the farmers' associations who were present in the Reichstag building.[52] These representatives, Ersing explained to his parliamentary delegates, "asked him—despite everything—to

50. Kommission für Zeitgeschichte, Bonn, KAB Archiv, F III, 1.c, memorandum by Willy Heitkamp, 1 May 1966, no. 319.

51. Bundesarchiv, Koblenz, Nachlaß Kaiser N1018/246, "Ermächtigungsgesetz," no. 53.

52. The parliamentary sessions took place in the Kroll Opera House, but the Center delegation was meeting in the Reichstag building.

assent to the power transfer out of love for the people" (*aus Liebe zum Volk*).[53]
The divisions among union representatives on 23 March relativize an interpretation in terms of class interests. Class antagonisms tell us only part of the
story. All social groups consented to the prospect of a "yes" vote, including the
representatives of the workers' unions.

SPD Union Representatives and Hitler

The evidence regarding the debates that took place within the Social Democratic delegation is also quite striking. The union leaders affiliated with the
SPD (the ADGB: *Allgemeiner Deutscher Gewerkschaftsbund* or General German
Trade Union Federation) were willing to play the card of conciliation. After
the election of 5 March the leadership of the ADGB "hoped to convince Hitler
that the Free Trade Unions [the other denomination of the ADGB] were not incompatible with his national revolution" (Harsch 1993, 231). In the meeting on
14 March of the SPD National Executive Committee, Otto Wels, the chairman
of the party, pointed out that the unions were distancing themselves from the
Social Democratic Party, and expressed his concern that union members in
the parliamentary group (around forty delegates) might be tempted to defect
when the Reichstag convened a few days later.[54] On 20 March the national
council of the ADGB stated in a letter to Hitler its readiness to collaborate
with the new state. The social tasks of the unions, the letter explained, had
to be fulfilled "whatever the nature of the regime" (*gleichviel welcher Art das
Staatsregime ist*).[55]

There is therefore no clear-cut relation between actors' class interests and
their positions on the enabling bill. In March 1933 several German Nationalist
representatives viewed the Hitler option as a threat serious enough to suggest
amending the enabling bill. Within the parliamentary Center delegation, no
social class distinguished itself as a bastion of resistance. In all occupational
groups a majority declared itself for a vote endorsing the transfer of constitutional powers to Hitler. As for SPD representatives, the line of cleavage which
took shape in March is the opposite of the Marxist prediction. Not middle-

53. Bundesarchiv, Koblenz, Nachlaß Wirth N1342/133, 12.

54. *Anpassung oder Widerstand*, meeting of the (SPD) National Executive Committee, 14
March 1933, 172. This political evolution of the ADGB leadership is acknowledged in an issue of
Politisch-gewerkschaftlicher Zeitungsdienst dated 6 March, Archiv der sozialen Demokratie der
Friedrich-Ebert-Stiftung, Bonn, ADGB Restakten, NB 241 b.

55. *Die Gewerkschaften in der Endphase der Republik*, document 189, 866; *Gewerkschafts-
zeitung*, 25 March, 117, quoted in Matthias (1960, 178) and in *Anpassung oder Widerstand*, meeting of the (SPD) National Executive Committee, 14 March 1933, 171 n. 16.

class representatives but union representatives favored reaching some kind of accommodation with Hitler. This tactical move was motivated by an attempt to ensure the survival of union organizations, not by a Marxist reading of Hitler's takeover of the state apparatus. These few observations suggest a conception of the event in which actors define their stance along lines that are not adequately captured by class-based cleavages.

THE SUSPENSION OF DISBELIEF

Hitler disclosed his political agenda before he assumed power. Pétain was far more ambiguous. His programmatic statements amounted to vague calls for moral regeneration, combined with a covert condemnation of leftist social policies—those of the electoral coalition that had gained a parliamentary majority four years earlier (the "Popular Front"). Consequently, the claim that Pétain abused the parliamentarians' confidence rings true. Since Pétain did not say much about future policies and institutions, parliamentarians who voted for the power transfer can easily argue that they were mistaken or deceived about his intentions. "I was the victim of a swindle aggravated by an abuse of trust."[56] This statement by the conservative deputy Becquart summarizes a vindicatory stance that one finds often in parliamentarians' accounts.

Yet we cannot take this claim at face value. True, Pétain did not lay out a program. But this was part of the problem. Parliamentarians did not know for sure what Pétain was up to. There were, moreover, ominous signs. Measures were taken against those who had consistently argued for a policy of resistance vis-à-vis Hitler. Many statements in Vichy betrayed a spirit of revenge against the Popular Front. The supporters of the bill signaled whom they viewed as their political enemies. Although Pétain did not publicly take a position in July 1940, he let others speak on his behalf, chief among them Pierre Laval, whom he appointed vice-president of the Council of Ministers on 23 June. Laval, for his part, was explicit about the agenda which underlay the government's bill: France had to align with totalitarian countries. On this point there was no ambiguity.

"We Were Cheated"

Most of those who voted for Pétain in July 1940 later explained that they were misled by the wording of the bill and Laval's assurances regarding the con-

---

56. "Je fus victime d'une escroquerie aggravée d'abus de confiance." Becquart, *Au temps du silence,* 258.

ditions of its application. Confusion was the order of the day. It was easy in these conditions to be misled by the tandem of Laval and Pétain.[57] Castagnez, a Socialist deputy, stated that "dictatorship was implemented in violation of the unanimous will of the French people's representatives."[58] The Socialist deputy Février added that "the members of the Parliament have been ignominiously deceived. Their vote granted power to the 'government of the Republic.' They could not surmise that the title of Marshal of France was compatible with perfidy."[59] When on 11 July Pétain proclaimed himself "Chief of the French state," the argument goes on, he usurped his mandate. Laval and Pétain betrayed the confidence that republicans had vested in them.

Thus the deception has a twofold significance. First, there was a breach of legality. Pétain did not legislate as the head of the "government of the Republic." He appointed himself "Head of the French state" by virtue of the constitutional acts of 11 July. These acts amounted to a "coup," as Herriot describes them.[60] In a letter to de Gaulle dated 8 October 1943, Lucien Galimand (former Radical deputy from the Seine) makes the same argument: the enabling bill provided Pétain and Laval with a restricted delegation of power. Their action went beyond the mandate they had received. Laval's promise to keep parliament in place was not fulfilled.[61] Parliamentarians were voluntarily deceived: "Laval had not yet revealed himself and most of us had not yet reconstructed the web that the party of the Defeat had woven for several years" (Becquart).[62] For Février the bill was breached by the very man in charge of applying it.[63]

---

57. Many letters written by former Socialist deputies and senators after the war bring forward an explanation along these lines. Archives OURS, dossiers Léon Bon, François Blancho, René Boudet, Ernest Esparbes, Roger Lefèvre, Charles Saint-Venan. Some explicitly say that they were mistaken (Albert Mennecier, Auguste Muret, Marcel Régis). This is also the explanation provided by the secretary general of the Socialist Party, Paul Faure, who however did not take part in the Vichy meetings. Faure, *De Munich à la Libération*, 15.

58. Castagnez, *Précisions oubliées*, 13. Castagnez also underlines that Pétain did not have in July 1940 the reputation of an apprentice dictator. On this subject, he refers to the judgments by de Gaulle, Blum, and Reynaud (9–10).

59. Février, *Expliquons-nous*, 33.

60. "On the 11th, the veil is torn apart. The breach of trust is perpetrated. The coup is manifest, brutal, cynical" (Herriot, *Épisodes*, 148). The Radical senator William Bertrand develops a similar interpretation. Archives départementales des Charente-Maritime, La Rochelle, archive William Bertrand, 23 J 20.

61. Galimand, *Vive Petain! Vive de Gaulle!*, 76. Galimand's letter is in Félix Gouin's personal papers, Archives Nationales, Paris, Archives Félix Gouin AJ 72 520 dossier 5. Becquart states that Laval's promise was the "tip (pourboire) given to the Assemblies so that they consent to this abdication" (*Au temps du silence*, 224).

62. Becquart, *Au temps du silence*, 230.

63. Février, *Expliquons-nous*, 28.

Second, there was a breach of trust and confidence. In the words of the far-right deputy Becquart, it was "only in light of the events that followed [the vote] that parliamentarians realized in which trap they had been led."[64] The image of a swindle comes up again and again in testimonies. Boivin-Champeaux was adamant about the meaning of the constitutional acts of 11 July: "This is a scam" ("c'est une escroquerie!").[65] The Socialist deputy Monnet extended the point to the whole Vichy regime: "The Vichy experience proved to be a monstrous swindle. . . . Had they known how their votes were going to be used, most of the parliamentarians that voted for the Pétain-Laval's bill would have certainly modified their attitude."[66] Boully summed up this pronouncement about the power transfer when he stated that "the Republic has been sacrificed from July 1940 to 1944 because of the Pétain government's remarkable treason."[67] "The Assembly was odiously deceived by Pétain" (Raymond-Laurent, deputy of the Popular Democratic Party).[68]

The subtext of these accounts is that deception was only possible because parliamentarians lacked information relevant to their decision. Had they known the government's intentions, they would have rejected the bill. They had to vote on the spot without being well informed. Most of them had not attended the meetings which had taken place in Bordeaux—before the government moved to Vichy at the end of June—and at which Laval and his accomplices had been honing their political offensive. They did not know what the government intended to do.[69]

It is this last claim that we need to examine closely. Was there actually a lack of information about the political goals that motivated the bill? I question this assumption in light of two observations. First, the government's public statements and initiatives before the Vichy meeting revealed that it aimed to settle old scores. Professional politicians could hardly have missed this political message. Second, Laval and his affiliates did not disguise their plans. They made no secret of the undemocratic character of future institutions.

64. Becquart, *Au temps du silence*, 193.

65. *Événements* VII, 2210.

66. Archives OURS, dossier Monnet.

67. Boully, *Mémoire à mes juges*, 19. See also Marcel Vardelle's opinion: "In a paper written in August 1942, speaking of the elected to parliament who had voted the wrong way, I wrote: "to these [representatives] one can reproach the foolish imprudence of believing that Pétain, Laval and Co were French and honest." Archives OURS, dossier Vardelle.

68. Archives de la ville de Paris, Archives Raymond-Laurent, "Brève explication du vote de Vichy," D 51 Z 72. In a letter to de Gaulle, Raymond-Laurent's colleague in the Popular Democratic Party, abbot Desgranges, is as assertive. Archives de la ville de Paris, Paris, Archives Raymond-Laurent, Letter by Desgranges to de Gaulle, 16 February 1945, D 51 Z 72.

69. Becquart, *Au temps du silence*, 257.

What seems rather surprising in retrospect is the genuineness with which Laval and the supporters of an authoritarian solution explained what they were up to. No doubt they viewed the political situation as propitious to an initiative of this sort. But their confidence led them to be particularly open and unrestrictive about the general philosophy of the political future they were hoping to implement. They seemed to ignore the possibility that politicians accustomed to years of republican and parliamentary traditions, and people who just had been at war with Germany and Italy, might feel repelled by the prospect of becoming vassals of a regime modeled on totalitarian Germany.

The Revenge of the Vanquished

There were clear signs that some were out to settle old scores. On 9 July during the Chamber session the far Right deputy Tixier-Vignancourt (affiliated with the group of the Independent Republicans) requested that a motion calling for "the punishment of those responsible for the disaster" be adopted by the Chamber. In the course of his exchange with the chairman of the Chamber, Herriot, Tixier-Vignancourt nominally cited the former prime minister (Paul Reynaud).[70] In the private meeting of the national Assembly (on the morning of 10 July), Laval openly attacked Blum for having failed to secure an alliance with Italy.[71] Vichy marked the comeback of those such as Laval who had been relegated to the margins of political life in 1936.[72]

In the meetings that took place in Bordeaux, some parliamentarians disclosed their eagerness for political revenge against those whom they castigated as "bellicist." As early as 18 June, when the government was still in Bordeaux, some parliamentarians (Marquet, Spinasse, and Bergery among others) were promoting a reform of political institutions in informal meetings (Burrin 1986, 328).[73] At the beginning of July a newspaper owned by Laval in Clermont-Ferrand (the *Moniteur*) started a campaign for the constitutional revision. In the issue of 2 July Laval wrote: "This is a new chart, a new status, a new organic law that the country is waiting for . . . a new constitution, freed from all that paralyzed us, all that weakened us."[74]

70. *Journal Officiel*, Chambre des Députés, 815.

71. Compte-rendu de la séance du 10 juillet 1940: Séance du 22 juillet 1948 du bureau du Conseil de la République, 489.

72. Blum, *Mémoires*, 70.

73. See on this point the testimonies of Vincent Auriol (*Hier . . . demain*, 69) and François Camel ("Ultimes Paroles," 31).

74. Quoted by Beau de Loménie (1951, 365).

The Anti-Republican Agenda

> At the Casino of Paris [i.e. the room in which the July 10 vote was taken], I asked the representatives of the nation, senators and deputies, to vote for a bill which put an end, not only to parliamentary activity, but also to a regime.
> —Laval, 11 July 1940[75]

> No one could have been mistaken. No member of the assemblies liable [to the decision] could claim that he did not know where he was being led, and that Mr. Pétain and Laval have exceeded their powers. Things were tragically clear, not equivocal, when Mr. Laval requested absolute powers and France and the Republic were handed over to him.
> —Auriol, Socialist deputy, former finance minister in Blum's first cabinet[76]

Laval's Announcements

The new government would design institutions modeled on totalitarian regimes. Laval made this point as early as 4 July, when he started to hold informal "information meetings" separately with deputies and senators. "Pierre [Laval] asserts that parliament needs to be dissolved, that the constitution needs to be reformed and 'aligned with totalitarian states.' He even mentions the establishment of 'labor camps' and if Parliament does not consent to it, he adds, it is Germany that will impose this measure upon us and this would immediately result in the occupation of the whole country" (Taurines, conservative senator who voted "yes").[77] Laval also presented the same views in a meeting with deputies on the same day.[78]

On 5 July Laval reiterated the political agenda that motivated the power transfer: "The point is not for the government to apply a so-called remedy or to proceed to a so-called reform while maintaining on the whole what exists. No. We want to destroy the totality of what exists. Then, once this destruction is accomplished, we want to create something else that will be entirely different from what has been, from what is. It's got to be one thing or the other: either

---

75. Quoted by Auriol, *Hier . . . demain*, 110.

76. Ibid.

77. Taurines, *Tempête sur la République*, 10, reproduced in *Événements* VIII, 2330. Laval's statement had a considerable impact on Taurines: immediately after the meeting, "in the street, among the crowd that had overwhelmed Vichy, these puzzling words still resonated in my head: 'alignment with totalitarian states,' 'labor camps'" (Taurines, *Tempête sur la République*, 10). This testimony is confirmed by the Radical senator Paul-Boncour (*Entre deux guerres*, 254).

78. Blum, *Mémoires*, 68. Noguères's testimony, *Événements* VII, 2221; Manent quoted in Odin, *Les quatre-vingts*, 32, and Sagnès (1991, 560).

you will accept what we are asking and you will align with the German Constitution and the Italian Constitution, or Hitler will impose it on you . . . There are
no more parties and there will be from now on no room for any party, or rather
there would be soon only one party: the party of all French, a national party
that will provide the supervisors (*cadres*) of national activity . . . we are paying
today for the fetishism that chained us up to democracy" (Louis Noguères's
written transcription of Laval's speech).[79]

These statements did not go unnoticed. In his diary under the date 5 July,
the president of the Republic, Lebrun, noted that Laval's enterprise was not "a
small one. It is a matter of abolishing the constitution of 1875 and substitut-
ing with it a regime that, while denying being inspired by foreign examples,
actually implements an authoritarian system, a totalitarian one, mixed with
national-socialism and fascism. Nothing less!"[80] Additional meetings took
place on 6 and 8 July, and each time Laval developed his argument in favor of
an authoritarian regime.[81]

Particularly significant was his programmatic speech on 8 July. The Socialist deputy Vincent Auriol, who voted against the power transfer on 10 July,
described the speech as follows: "In this private meeting in the small Casino,
in the absence of stenographer, Laval revealed his plans, clearly, without re-
luctance. . . . I took some notes, and my recollections are all the more faithful
that his words appalled me. Laval first read the text of the bill. . . . But soon
the horizon gets unveiled. Laval comments on the text. . . . In the same way
Germany after the 1918 defeat adopted the political regime of the victorious
nations, now we need to adapt our institutions to those of the victor. Parliamentary democracy lost the war; it needs to disappear to leave the ground to
an authoritarian regime, a hierarchical one, national and social."[82]

Auriol's account is corroborated by the testimonies of conservative and
centrist deputies who voted "yes." Henri Becquart reported similar statements
almost word for word. "Since parliamentary democracy wanted to engage the
fight against Nazism and Fascism, and since it has lost this fight, it ought to
disappear."[83] Laval, explained Becquart, attacked England and "finally asserted
the necessity of a change of regime, not because of its shortcomings and its

---

79. Louis Noguère's testimony, *Événements* VII, 2231–32.

80. Lebrun, *Témoignage*, 104.

81. Paul-Boncour, *Entre deux guerres*, 265; Jeanneney, *Journal politique*, 92; Pernot, *Journal de guerre*, 97. In his diary the conservative senator Pernot evokes Laval's totalitarian views (101).

82. Auriol, *Hier . . . demain*, 104–9.

83. Becquart, *Au temps du silence*, 174.

being worn away, but because of its defeat.[84] In his diary under the date 8 July, the conservative senator Bardoux imputed to him the following statements: "France now must align itself with totalitarian countries; we must implement a totalitarian regime French style."[85] Laval was remarkably candid about his political agenda.[86] Furthermore, he remained so publicly, before a large audience.

The Bergery Declaration

Laval's public statements and press reports were not the only piece of information that parliamentarians had at their disposal. In the early days of July the centrist deputy Gaston Bergery wrote up a "declaration on the National Assembly," co-signed by twenty of his colleagues in the Chamber of Deputies.[87] This statement of a few pages, which became known subsequently as the "Bergery manifesto," offered a political assessment of the causes for the disaster, delineated the broad lines of a policy of renovation, and invited deputies and senators to endorse the government bill without reservation. For the authors of the declaration, the causes of the disaster lay in the decadence of political mores, the prevalence of party interests over the interests of the nation, the incompetence of the political leadership, and an inconsistent and misguided foreign policy. With the war declaration, which as the manifesto pointed out only Bergery in the Chamber and Laval in the Senate tried to oppose, with the support of a courageous minority, "the regime was on the way to its fall, dragging along with it the nation."[88]

The Bergery declaration also laid out a plan for the future. Reconstruction would be the first task. Germany had an interest in collaborating with France, but its attitude would depend on the French government's willingness to col-

84. "I say and repeat: a regime that brought about war and defeat is not qualified to make peace." Becquart, *Au temps du silence*, 174.

85. Bardoux, *Journal d'un témoin de la Troisième*, 400.

86. The centrist deputy Raymond-Laurent underlines Laval's call for a revision not only of the constitution but of France's foreign policy as a whole (Raymond-Laurent, *Le Parti Démocrate Populaire*, 148). See also the testimony of the Radical deputy Gaston Manent, who most probably confuses 7 July for 8 July: "July 7. The 3 P.M. meeting started at 4 P.M. Laval arrived late accompagnied with the senators Fourcade and Mireaux. In substance he told us that we had to align with totalitarian countries" (Manent, "Une explication de vote," reproduced in *Événements*, 2260).

87. "Déclaration sur l'Assemblée nationale," Hoover Institution Archives, Stanford University, Gaston Bergery Papers, box 12.

88. Ibid., 2.

laborate with the victor. This change in foreign policy required a change of regime. "The military disaster . . . is but the catastrophic expression of the corruption of the regime."[89] The authors of the declaration agreed to devolve upon Pétain full powers to promulgate a new constitution implementing a political order that had to be "authoritarian," "national," and "social."[90] They defended themselves against the charge that this new regime would be a "servile copy" of national socialism by noting that the move toward a national form of socialism was universal: "France will know how to extract from its substance a regime which will be compatible with those of all continental Europe but which will bear the mark of its own genie."[91]

The declaration was quite clear and the direction of the change unmistakable. With the military victory of Germany, continental Europe was dominated by totalitarian regimes. Calling for the implementation of institutions "compatible with the regimes of continental Europe" left little doubt about the nature of these institutions. The point was driven home by the use of three key words: authoritarian, national, and social. The Bergery declaration spelled out the policy choices that Laval laid out in his meetings with parliamentarians. Political alignment with totalitarian countries, collaboration outside within the framework of a new European order dominated by Germany, institutional alignment inside: "The outline of the new order sketched by Bergery was amenable to diverse interpretations. Linked with a policy of collaboration with Nazi Germany, however, this outline took on a significance that could mislead no one" (Burrin 1986, 336).

Thus in crucial respects the political agenda of those who supported the power transfer was unambiguously clear. Before the Vichy meeting Pétain's cabinet had taken measures against political actors who could be expected to oppose a policy of collaboration with Hitler. Mandel's arrest, the threats against Blum, the appointment of radical pacifists to governmental positions, the harsh criticisms against parliamentarians who had sailed to northern Africa—all of this reeked of political revenge and indicated which type of regime lay ahead (Wieviorka 2001, 64). Furthermore, Laval's public statements as well as the political program outlined by his most fervent supporters (Bergery's "Declaration on the National Assembly") made clear that what was envisioned was a model of polity inspired by totalitarian countries.

89. Ibid.

90. "A written constitution is but the sanction of a deep change in mores. . . . The new (political) order must be an authoritarian order. . . . Authority is required to preserve the freedom of the state. . . . Second, the new (political) order must be national." Ibid., 2–3.

91. Ibid., 3.

Exposure

Yet we cannot exclude a priori the possibility that because of the circumstances and the organizational mess in Vichy, a large number of parliamentarians had not taken cognizance of Laval's statements and as a result were mistaken about the motivations underlying the power transfer. Clearly those who had followed the government to Bordeaux in June and had witnessed Laval's efforts to oppose the departure of the government and parliamentarians to Northern Africa, as well as those who had attended the earlier meetings with Laval, knew what to expect. What about the others, all those who had not been in Bordeaux or arrived late in Vichy? Could it be that they did not have the information and the time to assess the political motivations of Laval's plans for constitutional reforms?[92]

Several observations cast doubt on this hypothesis. A significant proportion of deputies and senators were in Bordeaux and had witnessed Laval's intrigues there (table 12).[93] The same was true of the "information meetings" in Vichy between 5 and 8 July, during which Laval was most explicit about his agenda. About one fifth of those who voted on 10 July had attended Laval's presentation on 5 July, as had one third on 6 July and a little less than half on 8 July (table 12). Thus about half the deputies and senators who voted on 10 July had firsthand knowledge of the political motivations behind the bill. The way this information was communicated in interpersonal contacts was quite diffuse. In their personal testimonies Louis Noguères, Vincent Badie, and Louis Gros explained that right after their arrival in Vichy, colleagues informed them of Laval's plans. "5 July . . . Those who had been here for a few days were asserting that the Pétain government was ready to suppress Parliament and to implement a Fascist regime."[94]

92. The Socialist deputy Gaston Allemane, who later on will take an active part in the resistance movement against the Germans, notes that he arrived in Vichy without any knowledge of what happened in Bordeaux (Archives Nationales, Paris, Dossiers du jury d'honneur: dossier Allemane, AL5295). A few other parliamentarians (Maxime Fauchon, AL5311; Ernest de la Framond, AL5313; Édouard Fuchs AL5313; Jean Maroger AL5321) make the same point in their retrospective accounts. Henri Becquart, a conservative deputy, sums up this explanation as follows: "The deputies who were arriving had not attended the meetings in which Laval had dropped his mask by furiously opposing the government's departure for Africa" (Becquart, *Au temps du silence*, 153–54).

93. Prélot (1972, 23–24), mentions somewhat fewer than one hundred parliamentarians. According to Rimbaud (1984, 44), the correct number is between 150 and 200. Édouard Barthe mentions a meeting gathering eighty people, most probably on 22 June. Barthe (*La ténébreuse affaire du "Massilia,"* 27).

94. The testimonies of Louis Noguère (*Événements* VII, 2230), Badie (*Événements* VII, 2269), and Gros (*République toujours*, 54–55), are congruent. The Radical deputy André Liautey argues

A comparison of the roll calls indicates that about 8 percent of the parliamentarians who voted on 10 July had not voted on 9 July (tables 12–13), most probably because they were not in Vichy yet. Interestingly, there is no noticeable difference across types of votes. Among the "no" votes the proportion of latecomers is 6 percent (table 13). This proportion is 8 percent among the "yes" votes: only forty-six parliamentarians who voted "yes" on 10 July did not vote on 9 July. Several of these parliamentarians arrived in Vichy on the evening of 9 July. This means that only a tiny fraction of those who cast a ballot on 10 July might have had to make their decision on the spot, without a clear knowledge of the political motivations behind the bill. These different observations clearly support the contention that exposure to relevant information was not a key problem.[95]

The last piece of evidence against the claim that parliamentarians were misinformed is Laval's speech during the meeting of the National Assembly that took place *on the morning of 10 July*, a few hours before the vote and behind closed doors. Laval watered down his assertions in part to defuse the opposition that he had elicited two days earlier.[96] Still, he was remarkably explicit about the political significance and implications of the bill. First, he contrasted democracy to "France," implying that one (France) had been sacrificed to the benefit of the other (democracy). Then he was emphatic in condemning parliamentary democracy and asserting a need to break with the past.[97] Finally, he pointed to Italy and Germany as ideological models. A new faith, he stated,

---

that he tried to alert his colleagues about the threat (Archives Nationales, Paris, Dossiers du jury d'honneur, dossier Liautey, AL5319). A letter dated 29 June to Léon Blum mentions that "Marquet, Laval and several others do not dissimulate that they want to convert us to the Hitlerian way of life" ("Marquet, Laval et pas mal d'autres ne dissimulent qu'à peine leur intention de nous convertir [au mode de vie hitlérien]"). Fondation Nationale des Sciences Politiques, Paris, Archives Blum, Notes manuscrites pour les mémoires, 3 BL 2, dossier 2, sous-dossier 2, letter dated 29 June 1940.

95. The Socialist deputy Maurice Voirin is a case in point. He arrives on the morning of 10 July. "Those who, like me arrived in the morning of 10 July were immediately informed by newspapers and conversations." Maurice Voirin, "Le scrutin du 10 juillet 1940," memorandum dated 20 September 1944 in Fondation Nationale des Sciences Politiques, Paris, Archives Pezet, P E 6, dossier 1.

96. Becquart describes this speech as a "revised version, edited and corrected—according to the indications provided by his agents—of the speech he had delivered two days earlier [on 8 July]" ("Ce fut la réédition, revue et corrigée selon les indications de ses agents, de son discours de l'avant-veille"). Becquart, *Au temps du silence*, 217.

97. This bill is "the condemnation not only of the parliamentary regime, but also of all that was and that can no longer be" ("[Le projet du gouvernement] est la condamnation, non seulement du régime parlementaire, mais de tout ce qui a été et ne peut plus être"). *Compte rendu sténographique de la séance privée des membres de la chambre des députés et du sénat tenue à*

Table 12   Attendance in Bordeaux and Vichy: Chronological Assessments

	Deputies	Percentage of Voters on 10 July	Senators	Percentage of Voters on 10 July	Total	Percentage of Voters on 10 July
Bordeaux					100–110	12–16
Vichy						
4 July	100–110					
5 July	60–110	15–25	50–60	25	120–140	18–21
6 July			70–100	30–42	200	30
8 July	150–200	35–47	80–100	33–42	220–300	33–45
9 July	400	93	225	94	625	93

Sources: [Bordeaux:] Archives Nationales, Paris, Dossiers du jury d'honneur: Dossier Colomb, AL5304; Barthe, *La ténébreuse affaire du "Massilia,"* 27. Estimates on 4 July: Archives Nationales, Paris, F⁷ 15342, Déat, Journal de guerre, 367; Barthe, *La ténébreuse affaire du "Massilia,"* 37: "July 4: meeting at 16:30: about one hundred parliamentarians." Estimates regarding the number of deputies on 5 July: Louis Noguère's testimony, *Événements*, VII, 2230. According to Déat, more than a hundred deputies attended the meeting (Archives Nationales, Paris, F 15342, Déat, *Journal de guerre*, 369). Estimates regarding the number of senators on 5 July: Pernot, *Journal de guerre*, 92; Vallat, *Le grain de sable de Cromwell*, 136. Vichy Senators, 6 July: Noguères, *Événements*, 2234; Pernot, *Journal de guerre*, 94. Estimates of the total number of parliamentarians present in Vichy on 6 July: Vallat, *Le nez de Cléopatre*, 184. On 6 July Galimand improvised a short speech: "In the hall of the Casino, transformed into a Versailles palace, I saw again several hundred of my colleagues, friends or adversaries . . ." ("Dans le hall du Casino, transformé en palais de Versailles, je revis quelques centaines de collègues, amis ou adversaires . . .)" (Galimand, *Vive Pétain! Vive de Gaulle!*, 47). Estimates of the number of deputies present on 8 July: Auriol, *Hier . . . Demain*, 99. The Socialist Ernest Laroche assesses that two hundred deputies attended the information meeting for the deputies on 7 July (*France during the German Occupation*, 364: letter to Mrs. Laval, 26 November 1955). Estimates of the number of senators on 8 July: Bardoux, *Journal*, 400. Estimates of the total number of parliamentarians on 8 July: Raymond-Laurent, *Le Parti Démocrate Populaire*, vol. 2, 148. In his handwritten notes the conservative deputy Laurent Bonnevay estimates that about three hundred deputies and senators attended the meeting on 8 July (Archives Départementales du Rhône, Lyon, Archives Laurent Bonnevay, 10 J 20, "L'Assemblée Nationale du 10 juillet 1940"). Estimate of the attendance on 9 July: roll call for votes in the Deputy Chamber and the Senate on the need to revise the constitution (see chapter 1).

needed to be built on the idea of nation.[98] Individual rights would be secondary to the superior interest of the nation.[99] "Make no mistake, we are now living in a dictatorship."[100]

Vichy le 10 juillet 1940: Séance du 22 juillet 1948 du bureau du Conseil de la République, Chambre des députés, Paris, 487–88, quoted in chapter 1.

98. Ibid., 489–90.
99. Ibid., 490.
100. Ibid., 491.

Table 13   Absentees on 9 July

Vote on 10 July	Did Not Vote on 9 July	Total	Ratio
"No" votes	5	80	0.06
"Yes" votes	46	569	0.08
Abstentions	2	21	0.10
Total	53	670	0.08

The substance of this speech comes through in many independent personal testimonies by parliamentarians on both sides of the fence: "apology of totalitarian countries" (Raymond-Laurent, "yes" vote), "condemnation of the parliamentary regime (Becquart, "yes" vote), "Laval did not disguise the support he expected from the Germans" (Ramadier, "no" vote). He advocated an "alignment" with totalitarian regimes (Louis Gros, "no" vote; Auriol, "no" vote).[101] Ignorance, therefore, is problematic. Laval's audacity and explicitness explain why the collective decision of 10 July puzzled many opponents and observers:[102] "No one could have been mistaken" (Auriol).[103]

Paul-Boncour summarizes the problem well:

> How many among these well-informed politicians can seriously pretend that they have been deceived? At most they could invoke as attenuating circumstances the disarray of the minds after the defeat, and the difficulties of the situation. However, they could not ignore that their vote implied not only the overthrow of the republican regime, but also the acceptance of the capitulation and the armistice as well as the abandonment of our alliance regardless of France's solemn engagements. They could not ignore that the solution that was being proposed to them, had been rejected with horror by governments such as those of Belgium, Holland, Yugoslavia and Norway. By the way, in the preparatory debates, Laval was particularly explicit, and he never disguised the fact that at issue was a change of regime in order to align with totalitarian countries

101. Raymond-Laurent, *Le Parti Démocrate Populaire*, 153; Becquart, *Au temps du silence*, 221; Ramadier, "Vichy (juillet 1940)," 51; Gros, *République toujours*, 60; Auriol, *Hier . . . demain*, 105.

102. See for instance Laurent Bonnevay, letter to Jean Odin, 17 December 1945, reproduced in Odin, *Les quatre-vingts*, 217–19; Le Gorgeu, letter to Jean Odin, 29 December 1945, reproduced in Odin, *Les quatre-vingts*, 229.

103. "Personne n'a pu se méprendre." Auriol, *Hier . . . demain*, 107.

and to modify the foreign policy in the direction of a collaboration with the enemy.[104]

* * *

Actors often account for their choice by invoking either their ignorance or the challenger's cunning. These claims call for different types of assessment, and the preceding discussion took pains to develop several observations. The first is that information about the challenger's agenda in Germany and France was public and widely shared. Hitler and his lieutenants revealed the totalitarian and exclusive nature of their political goals before they assumed power. In Vichy the different factions that supported the government bill publicly indicated that they planned a diplomatic and institutional alignment with Germany.

The second observation addresses the claim that the devolution of constitutional powers was a bet that failed. Center representatives argued that with their "yes" vote they intended to bind Hitler to a rule of law, and to secure some guarantees about the scope of his constitutional mandate. But Hitler proved to be a master liar with no scruples. French parliamentarians emphasized that by their vote they granted constitutional authority "to the government of the Republic" under the authority of Marshal Pétain. According to the provisions of the bill, the new constitution would be ratified by the nation. These two provisions were sufficient indications that arbitrary power would be limited.

The problem with these tactical justifications is that they give short shrift to the lack of guarantees about the challenger's future actions. In voting for the power transfer, parliamentarians agreed to voluntarily deprive themselves of the right to legally challenge the government's political decisions. The issue surfaced in the debates which preceded the vote. In March 1933 the guarantee issue motivated Brüning's opposition to endorsing the enabling bill and his request of a written letter from Hitler specifying his commitments. In July 1940 concerns about the design of future institutions underlay attempts to alter the government bill to maintain some form of external control, however dim this control might be.

In both cases legislators realized the risks inherent to the decision. Yet in acquiescing they behaved as if they could safely ignore the problem. They hoped for an outcome that made little sense in realist terms, given the information available and the content of the bill. This discrepancy between the good reasons they had for questioning the challenger's assurances and the tactical justifications which they ultimately provided to themselves for justifying a "yes" vote remains striking. Delegates endorsed the belief that the challenger would

104. Archives Nationales, Paris, Archives Paul-Boncour 424 AP 39.

not abuse his power despite the evidence to the contrary. In these conditions tactical justifications amounted to wishful thinking and self-deception.

This observation opens up two possibilities. One is that actors who voted "yes" actually confused tactical and strategic interests. They assumed that they and the challenger had similar political goals. The decision to transfer full powers to the challenger was not a tactical bet but one piece of a broader political plan. Drawing on Abraham (1986) and Patch (1985), I have translated this hypothesis into class terms. Economically dominant groups and their representatives in parliament backed up the challenger's political claims because they saw in the challenger's offensive against parliamentary democracy an opportunity to get rid of a political system which did not effectively preserve their material interests.

If we narrow the focus to the Center parliamentary delegation, it appears that the handful of delegates who proved eager to actively collaborate with Hitler in March 1933 were politically and sociologically affiliated with business circles. In playing Hitler's game these circles hoped to settle old scores with the unions (Patch 1985, 223). An analysis in terms of class antagonisms therefore captures some of the motivations at play. However, this explanation does not tell us why the political representatives of economically dominant groups believed that their material interests would be secure in a political system under the exclusive or quasi-exclusive control of the challenger. Moreover, an explanation in terms of class antagonisms cannot account for the extent to which the enabling bill received support from all social groups represented in parliament, including Center delegates representing the workers' movement.

The other possibility is that self-deception was the byproduct of actors' ideological beliefs, broadly defined as the set of interrelated and collectively shared beliefs that account for actors' value commitments. Systematic evidence of self-deception may point to the existence of biased beliefs that distort judgment and undermine the capacity to critically assess a situation. These biases have all the more phenomenological force when they form a system. In both March 1933 and July 1940 tactical decisions were predicated on a political assessment of the situation. Moreover, in both March 1933 and July 1940 actors persevered in holding to a set of beliefs about the challenger's future actions in spite of accumulating evidence that contradicted these beliefs. They behaved as if they systematically underestimated the threat represented by the challenger, and this mistake was collectively endorsed. The systematic *and* collective character of this bias points to the possible effect of ideology. I now examine this hypothesis.

Chapter 5

Ideological Collusion

1

Times of crisis: crisis of democracy, crisis of the liberal idea of man, economic and social crises. For democrats, the age was placed under an ominous sign. Totalitarian regimes were making converts. In the political vulgate of the time, the debility of parliamentary democracy, its inherent failure, had wide currency. Parliamentary democracy had failed because it had nurtured internal strife and decadence. It lacked the vitality, the spiritual energy, and the political resources necessary to reform a society bled white by the decline of ancestral solidarities and the triumph of petit bourgeois individualism. Eras faced with heroic challenges require regimes of heroic grandeur, and democracy lacked grandeur. Momentum was on the side of dictatorships and totalitarian regimes.

This cultural crisis has been thoroughly documented (Stern 1963, Sternhell 1996 [1986]), and my purpose here is not to summarize the analysis. Rather, I want to address the argument that the cultural and ideological context of the interwar years undermined democratic convictions to the point of rendering them ineffective. This argument goes as follows. Contamination begot political collusion. Democrats were breathing an air vitiated by antidemocratic themes and slogans. As the crisis of democracy became part and parcel of the political rhetoric of the time, even democrats lost their faith. Their commitment to democratic institutions weakened, becoming either tenuous or dubious. As they faced the ultimate challenge, they suddenly realized that they had nothing to defend. Their stance proved ideologically powerless. Hence they abdicated. The democratic idea was dead. Democrats yielded to the prospect of an authoritarian regime without a fight.

2

An argument framed in terms of ideological contamination suggests that constant exposure to a challenging ideology has insidious effects. Such exposure undermines commitments, subverts political beliefs, and prepares the ground for renunciation, defection, or turnarounds. In the 1930s democrats bathed in a cultural and intellectual context that was too biased and pervasive to leave them unaffected. The political doxa had become colonized by the denunciation of the evils of democracy in general and parliamentary democracy in particular. This antidemocratic zeitgeist was the ideological matrix of the transition from democracy to an authoritarian regime.

Two sets of questions come to the fore. First, was there ideological contamination? Had the antidemocratic ideologies made significant inroads in the political repertoires of those who identified with the regime? Did the political culture and traditions of the groups under challenge have ideological affinities with the challenger? The perspective here is genealogical. I map the ideological profiles of different groups, their intellectual milieus, and their political culture, to identify possible filiations between them. In doing so I take for granted the main assumption made by an ideological collusion argument: groups can be defined in ideological terms, and the reasons for actors' political behaviors are to be found in the ideological setup of their group of affiliation.

The second set of questions refines the focus of my argument. I examine whether the ideological affinities posited by the contamination thesis capture the cleavages that emerged among the parliamentarians at the time of the decision. Is there a connection between the groups' political culture and individual choices? Can we pin down the effect of ideological predispositions on the process of decision making? Both sets of questions allow me to explore the mental landscape of the actors involved. As I indicated in the Preface, we cannot analyze historically situated decisions without identifying actors' presuppositions, implicit assumptions, and commonsensical beliefs.

3

If we assume the point of view of intellectual history, contamination seems quite plausible at first. There were indeed points of contact between the political culture of the groups under challenge and some of the themes aggressively publicized by their challenger. For instance, among German Catholics and Center representatives, the call for implementing a corporatist social order free of class conflicts could easily drift into a diffuse critique of liberalism and parliamentary democracy. Similarly, both Catholic publicists and radical nationalists celebrated "the community of the people" (*Volksgemeinschaft*) as the ultimate yardstick of politics. In France political conflicts and controversies in the second half of the 1930s were overshadowed by the denunciation of national decadence and internal subversion. A new political order was needed, one which would restore political authority and renovate the nation.

This assessment of the ideological landscape is misleading, however, as long as it is not qualified. During the Weimar period Catholic representatives opposed the Nazis on ideological grounds. The Christian worldview could not be reconciled with racist and totalitarian conceptions of the polity. In France the great majority of parliamentarians did not envision political renovation outside the boundaries of the Republic. In both cases the ideological landscape was far less one-dimensional and determinative than a retrospective account might suggest. The "spirit of the time" and the political culture of the groups under examination contained antidemocratic elements, but also elements that precluded accommodation with a totalitarian project. As a result, accounts that only emphasize factors of ideological congruence offer a truncated representation of the zeitgeist.

This last point takes on a particular significance when we shift focus to the decision process. Both in March 1933 and in July 1940 actors experienced the choice they had to make as an excruciating dilemma. As personal testimonies point out, it was for many the most difficult decision they ever had to face. Had contamination been so pervasive and effective, individual actors would have had no ground to view their decision as a problem. Furthermore, individual choices cannot be strictly deduced from the political culture associated with groups of affiliation. Ideological lines of cleavage only imperfectly account for the fault line between opposition and abdication.

The question is whether this lack of fit reveals a substantial source of variance that cannot be captured by an argument cast in terms of ideological determination. My argument is that the disjuncture between ideology and decision was indeed significant and that we miss a key political dimension of the event if we rule it out as the noise of history, because the collective decision reshuffled previous lines of cleavage. The implication is more important than we may think at first. In 1933 and 1940 the "ideology" and political culture of the groups being challenged provided arguments for *and* against acquiescence, for *and* against opposition. With regard to the decision, therefore, ideological representations were relatively indeterminate. They could be invested with quite different motivations, which is another way of saying that they offered poor guides for action.

THE NATION VERSUS THE LIBERAL STATE

There are several strands to the argument that the Center party's decision to politically collaborate with Hitler in March 1933 was ideologically motivated. The first strand refers to the pervasive influence of a reactionary ideology characterized by antiliberal and organicist conceptions of politics. This analysis traces the ideological roots of Catholic antiliberalism back to the traumatic experience of the French Revolution. The second strand underlines the lack of deep democratic or republican convictions among German Catholics: many Catholic representatives, both religious and political, only reluctantly endorsed the Weimar republic. They viewed it as a lesser evil: no wonder that they did not oppose its legal demise. The third strand points to the force of nationalist feelings and the way the mystique of the national community played out among Catholics in the political context of the spring of 1933.

These different strands correspond to different temporalities. The ideological critique of modernity and liberalism discloses a belief system forged by decades of doctrinal developments. Here the search for ideological motivations becomes as a genealogical inquiry. The second strand draws attention to the era inaugurated by unification (1871) and the introduction of a parliamentary system. Finally, the reference to the nationalist mystique that took hold in Germany in 1933 refers to a time span of a few weeks.

Historical accounts that address the issue of Catholics' attitude to Hitler in 1933 often invoke multiple time frames at once.[1] In doing so they lend credence to the notion that at the critical juncture of March 1933, different ideological beliefs and predispositions resonated with one another. From this it seems easy to conclude that ideology overdetermined the choice to collaborate with Hitler. There was no want of reasons for Catholics to endorse an authoritarian alternative. This point is ultimately an empirical claim which needs to be investigated as such. For purposes of clarity, I will present and discuss the different variants of an argument cast in ideological terms in the order of increasing temporal specificity.

Antiliberalism

German Catholics were vulnerable to the subterranean force of a reactionary ideology in two respects. As Catholics they rejected the modern world and its political (liberal) implications. Their model of society was a hierarchical corporate order in which cooperation between professional groups would substitute for class conflicts. The intellectual forebear of this attitude to modernity was the reactionary critique of the French Revolution and the vision of an organic society in which individual freedoms and interests are subsumed under the well-being of the community. Nineteenth-century Catholic thinkers (Joseph de Maistre, Louis de Bonald) were at the forefront of the ideological fight against liberalism (Holmes 1993, 16–32). Liberalism was held up to public obloquy because it extolled political freedoms and the critical exercise of

---

1. See for instance Böckenförde (1961, 219, 233).

political reason. Liberalism generated monstrous political developments, i.e., developments that went "against nature": they promoted individualism and destroyed the natural order.[2]

Furthermore, German Catholics were also Germans. That is, they lived in a society characterized by the permanence of "pre-industrial traditions" and the "reactionary predilections of traditional elites." These predilections allowed for the periodic resurgence of "authoritarian continuities" which vitiated liberal democracy (Eley 1986, 11). This ideological background, it is suggested, allowed for political collusion with the authoritarian Right, and highlights how and why in the spring of 1933 Catholic leaders came to view companionship with the National Socialist regime as possible. First, this pervasive antiliberalism led Catholic leaders to close themselves to reality and to judge the political conjuncture according to doctrinal principles (Böckenförde 1961, 237). They took refuge in a mental attitude characteristic of "the thought process of any ideology" (Böckenförde 1961, 237). Eschewing a realist assessment of the danger, Catholic representatives precipitated their fall.

Second, between the fight against "the liberal spirit" promoted by radical nationalists and a "natural law" conception of the political order, a terrain of agreement could easily be found (Böckenförde 1961, 237). There was a "certain consistency" in the decision to associate with National Socialism (Böckenförde 1961, 238). Catholic leaders, it is argued, surrendered to Hitler because they were not entirely immune to an antiliberal frame of mind and an organicist conception of the nation. They were all the more inclined to give credence to the Nazis' political claims that their political tradition had a strong antiliberal component.

The Regime Issue

Given this ideological background, it is not difficult to understand how the military defeat and overthrow of the monarchy might have fueled a political resentment that became a chamber of resonance for an ideology of national redemption, Caesarism, and "cultural despair" (Stern) rooted in the intellectual critique of liberalism and parliamentary democracy (Stern 1961, xxix; Mosse 1964). Weimar bore the stigmata of a regime that had been generated by military defeat. Parliamentary democracy was seen as the culprit responsible for the decision to endorse the humiliating peace imposed by the Versailles treaty. To make matters worse, Weimar was incapable of quenching internal subver-

2. Along similar lines, it has been argued that Roman Catholicism rests on a belief system which is authoritarian in nature and as a result inconsistent with democracy. The classic formulation of this thesis can be found in Lipset (1981, 72).

sion. Conflicts of interest opposing social groups against one another were rife. Liberal democracy was the heyday of national disintegration and decadence.

Most lay and religious representatives of the Catholic camp partook in this political assessment. Many had experienced the collapse of the monarchy as a tragedy. "The antidemocratic thought, which had intellectually neutralized the ideological bastion—in any case quite weak—of the liberal democracy of Weimar, was certainly not the common lot of political Catholicism. This antidemocratic thought found nonetheless enough Catholic supporters who believed that they had to get rid of the parliamentary regime at almost any price" (Sontheimer 1963, xix). The rejection of Weimar dovetailed with a pervasive antiliberalism. Some within the Catholic camp were not immune to the idea that the price paid for maintaining parliamentary democracy was too heavy.

In some Catholic quarters this rejection of parliamentary democracy took the form of an "ideology of the Reich": Germany had a sacred mission to fulfill, which could only be brought about by a new *Reich* (empire). According to Breuning (1969, 151), the promoters of this Reich ideology represented a small group. But their influence was considerable, because their theories echoed Catholics' disillusionment about Weimar, their longing for a hierarchical social order, and their antiliberal conception of the state. Dirks (1969, 18) estimates that much of the strength of conviction (*Überzeugungskraft*) of this ideology was due to its combination of theology, politics, and contestable historical insights.

One can interpret the ambivalence of the Center party leadership toward the regime issue as indicating its lack of commitment to parliamentary democracy. Within the ranks of the Center party, the republican design of the regime remained an issue of contention throughout the first years of the Republic. As late as December 1927 Wilhelm Marx, chairman of the party and chancellor at the time, explained at a meeting of Center press associations that the Center was neither a republican nor a monarchist party but a "constitutional party." In adopting this stance, he admittedly was reiterating the position he had taken at the Kassel party congress in 1925 (Knapp 1967, 210; Becker 1969, 68). Catholic publicists affiliated with the Center party cultivated this political ambivalence. For instance, Georg Schreiber, prelate and parliamentary representative of the Center party, foregoes any clear-cut endorsement of the democratic regime when in a book published in 1930 he spells out the political platform of his party.[3]

Theological conceptions inherited from Pope Leo XIII (1878–1903) could

---

3. See for instance the following statements: "We do not want to despair over, and become estranged from Democracy.... The Center party supports the state, it supports the people, it supports the church for they belong to one another." Schreiber, *Zentrum und Reichspolitik*, 9, 10.

furthermore justify conciliation with an authoritarian regime. While revolutionary violence is against the law of nature, the state is an expression of natural law (Junker 1969, 36). The faithful have a duty to obey the rule of the state in order not to disrupt the peace of the community. Leo XIII made the indifference of the church toward state structure a point of doctrine grounded in natural law (Böckenförde 1961, 234–35). Consequently, while the existence of the Center party was only compatible with a state structure based on party representation, the Catholic church did not face this constraint: it could coexist with any state, whatever its form, as long as the state did not frontally call into question the church's essential principles and existence (Junker 1969, 37). For several historians (Junker 1969, 128; Sailer 1994, 31, 143–56) this point is key to understanding lay and religious leaders' acceptance of Nazi rule after March 1933. In March 1933 Hitler was the legitimate power holder. It was the duty of Catholics to consolidate state institutions and avoid chaos.[4]

The Mystique of the Nation

Catholic leaders had always emphasized that their primary goal was to serve the Volksgemeinschaft and to overcome class-based antagonisms. At the same time, the Center party leadership was involved in an ideological fight against the radical nationalists' attempt to appropriate the category of the "nation" for their own sake. In the Center party political culture, the nation was not exclusive of any particular social or religious group. The community of the people encompassed all social groups and confessions. In the context of the "national revolution" of the spring of 1933, so goes one version of the collusion argument, Hitler manipulated to his profit Catholics' longing for a strong and conservative state. The Center party leadership fell prey to the "mystique of the nation" in a time of turmoil and rapid political transition.

Nationalist Effervescence

In his policy statement of 1 February 1933, Hitler set the goal of his cabinet: "national recovery" (*nationale Erhebung*). The "Marxists" and their fellow travelers had exercised state power for fourteen years. The result was a "field of ruins."[5] The time of reconstruction was to begin. Soon after the result of

4. The memo in Gustav Wollf's papers explicitly refers to the "catholic doctrine of the state" (*katholische Staatsauffassung*) to justify a stance of conciliation in March 1933. Kommission für Zeitgeschichte, Bonn, Nachlaß Wollf, GW I 2 n, "Das Ermächtigungsgesetz," 1.

5. Appeal of the government on 1 February 1933: "The Reich president, Marshal von Hindenburg, has called upon us to provide the nation with the possibility of a new rise made possible

the elections of 5 March became known, Nazi activists throughout Germany stormed their political opponents' offices. They hoisted the Nazi flag on governmental buildings along with the old imperial flag. A "national revolution," the government proclaimed, was in march. These political developments came to a climax with the opening of the parliamentary session in Potsdam on 21 March, which the governmental press publicized as "the Day of Potsdam." "Goebbels staged a symbolic rite over the coffin of Frederick the Great in the Garrison Church of Potsdam in the presence of Hindenburg and the Crown Prince. The pretence was maintained that the National Socialist ammunitions were being subordinated to the common goal" (Bracher 1966, 122).

The Center leadership behaved as if it endorsed this reading of the situation. In his public letter to Hitler on 5 March protesting against calumnies published in the Nazi press, Kaas referred to the unity (*Einheitlichkeit*) of the "national will" (*nationales Wollen*) (quoted by Junker 1969, 171). After 15 March Center newspapers took over the concept of the "national revolution," either to signal their endorsement or to call for its stabilization. In his speech before the Reichstag on 23 March, Kaas evoked the work of national salvation that lay ahead.

The connection then can be easily made between the nationalist effervescence that characterized the celebrations of Potsdam and the political stance adopted by the Center party delegation two days later. Catholic representatives, the argument goes, became embroiled in the "mystique" of the national revolution (Bracher 1962, 147). Overwhelmed by the national fervor displayed by Hitler, and misled by his ability to address Catholics' patriotic feelings (Buchheim 1960, 24), Catholic leaders were mesmerized by a collective mood which overwhelmed traditional boundaries. In this mystical conjuncture marked by the extolling of the German nation, they failed to discern the imposture of the "national revolution." They failed to decipher Hitler's game under the guise of conservative nationalism (Buchheim 1961, 497, 501). Buchheim (1961, 497) speaks of the "fascination" produced by Hitler's national call. According to Junker (1969), on 23 March Kaas "identified the idea of rallying together (*Sammlungsgedanke*) [a Center party electoral slogan] with the national appeal of these days" (176). Sailer (1994, 185–86) notes that in negotiating with Hitler, Kaas was yielding to "nationalist watchwords."

---

by our unanimous agreement.... The Marxist parties and their fellow-travellers had 14 years to show their ability. The result is a field of ruins." *Hitlers Machtergreifung*, 36–38.

The Community of the Nation

Between the organicist ideal of a Christian society and the mystical vision of a national community, the affinity seems beyond doubt. Notions such as Volksgemeinschaft, on which the Nazis drew extensively in the spring of 1933 as "master frames" of their political agenda, were also being used by Center leaders to justify their own programmatic claims. Hitler exploited what was common to the system of values of National Socialism and Catholicism: both declared their allegiance to the state, their willingness to promote the nation, and their critique of Marxism and liberalism. These commonalities facilitated the illusion of a possible convergence in the Catholic camp in 1933. Ideological affinities, including in some quarters anti-Semitism, nurtured strategic blindness (Lill 1990, 138).

The Legacy of the Kulturkampf

The ideological prevalence of the nationalist thematic was also significant in an indirect way: Catholics felt vulnerable to the charge of not being truly Germans. They suffered from an "inferiority complex" on the national issue. This complex paralyzed them vis-à-vis their National Socialist challengers (Harcourt 1938, 31, 34).[6] This situation was in part the legacy of the Kulturkampf (Becker 1963b, 160; Morsey 1960, 361–62, 366).[7] German Catholics were eager to be perceived as "national" in order to "compensate" for their confessional belonging (Böckenförde 1962, 228). Their endorsement of the new state and their efforts to find a terrain of agreement with Hitler reflected their desire to be finally recognized as true members of the German nation. Their political alignment in 1933 was a "post-scriptum to the Kulturkampf," to borrow an expression from Maier (1972, 193; Morsey 1977, 144).

Catholics were all the more likely to protest their national loyalty if they were portrayed as antinational by their political opponents. As early as 5 February Kaas felt compelled to recall the "national" credentials of the German Catholics in a speech before the leading committee of the Center party in Berlin.[8] Göring in a speech in Essen on 8 March denounced the black international, comparing it with the Socialist International and the International of Money. Around mid-March the Nazi press contended that the Center party

6. See the standpoint of Eberle presented in *Die schönere Zukunft* (Harcourt 1938, 75).

7. The Kulturkampf was the anti-Catholic campaign launched by liberal parties and Bismarck in the 1870s.

8. *Kölnische Volkszeitung*, 6 February 1933.

had been sold to the French (Morsey 1977, 120). This caused Kaas and Eßer to address a protest to Hitler and Göring. Morsey (1977, 120) notes that Kaas's and Eßer's protests were dictated by the fear of being castigated as enemies of the Reich. As a result of these attacks, the theme became more and more prevalent in Center representatives' public statements and in the press.[9]

GERMAN CATHOLICS AGAINST NAZISM

The ideological factors mentioned so far lend credence to the idea that Catholic leaders struck a deal with Hitler because they lacked democratic convictions, shared with the radical nationalists a rejection of the liberal state, and embraced an organicist conception of the national community. If at this point we were to draw a conclusion, the diagnosis would be unmistakable: collusion was overdetermined by a system of beliefs embodied by a political culture and crystallized by the doctrinal teaching of the Church, which postulates that since the state is grounded in natural law, it commands obedience. The form of the state as such does not matter as long as it does not contradict the essential principles of the Christian faith.

The diagnosis is unequivocal. Yet it is misleading, for it provides a partial representation of the set of ideological and political beliefs which Catholic representatives—both religious and lay—mobilized in their attempt to deal with the Nazi phenomenon. First, the Catholic opposition to Nazism before March was ideologically grounded. Bishops denounced National Socialism's racialized vision of the world and its denial of the sacred character of the individual person. They adamantly emphasized that the Nazi worldview was incompatible with the Church doctrine. Their condemnation was unambiguously moral and political. Second, there is no straightforward relation between actors' organicist and nationalist convictions and their political stance on the enabling bill. The right wing of the party, represented by men like Kaas, Brüning, Stegerwald, and Kaiser, was identified as reactionary and the least

9. On 8 February in Cologne Josef Ruffini (secretary general of the Center party in the Rhine region) raised the possibility of a Kulturkampf (*Kölnische Volkszeitung*, 9 February 1933). Less than one week later, Bolz in a speech delivered in Ulm also mentioned the issue (*Kölnische Volkszeitung*, 15 February 1933). Ulitzka released an article on the matter through the Center party news agency, the *Pressebüro Krauss* (Bundesarchiv, Koblenz, Nachlaß Bell N1272/16). On 15 February an article in the *Rheinpfälzer* denounced the "insinuation that the Center party and the *Bayerische Volkspartei* were enemies of the Reich and unreliable in national terms" ("Verdächtigung der Reichsfeindigkeit und der nationalen Unzuverlässigkeit der BVP und des Zentrums"). Two days later, an editorial in the *Kölnische Volkszeitung* entitled "The Mistake of Bismarck" warned against excluding the Catholics from the second phase of the revolution (quoted by Junker 1969, 174). Kaas raised again the issue on 3 March in the *Vossische Volkszeitung*.

committed to the Republican regime. Yet several of its prominent members were among the few who advocated a "no" vote on 23 March.

The Doctrinal Condemnation of Nazism

We, Christian Catholics, do not recognize any religion based on race, but only the authority of Christ over the world.[10]

As early as September 1930, when the Nazi movement emerged as a serious political challenge to the Weimar Republic, the Catholic hierarchy took a firm stand against any compromise with National Socialism.[11] In 1931 German church leaders imposed upon Catholics a ban on membership in the National Socialist Party. Members of the Nazi party were not allowed to attend mass and were not entitled to a religious burial. As late as 28 February 1933, in the midst of the electoral campaign, these religious leaders reiterated their warnings against Nazism, and newspapers affiliated with the Center party reminded their readers that condemnation of the National Socialist heresy by the church was still in effect (Morsey 1977, 108).[12]

In the 1930s the Catholic denunciation of the spiritual threat of Nazism was unambiguous. The Catholic hierarchy took a strong position against the racist and *völkisch* views of National Socialists because these views called into question central tenets of the Catholic doctrine of morality (Lill 1990, 136). Not only National Socialists' racism but also their claim that the "party was the totality" was a key issue of contention for Catholic spiritual leaders (Lill 1990, 138). As the bishop of Mainz put it in a statement clarifying the Catholic assessment of

10. Cardinal Bertram's New Year's Eve proclamation, "A Public Statement in a Grave Hour" ("Ein offenes Wort in ernster Stunde"), published in *Tremonia*, 1 January 1931, quoted in *Katholische Kirche und Nationalsozialismus*, 15–19.

11. In addition to this particularly important public statement by Cardinal Bertram, mention should also be made of the statements by the episcopal ordinariat of Mainz on 30 September 1930 (Harcourt 1938, 14–15); the pastoral instructions of the Bavarian episcopate in February 1931; and the proclamations of the bishops of Cologne (*Kölnische Volkszeitung*, 7 March 1931), Paderborn (*Tremonia*, 17 March 1931), the northern region of the Rhine (23 March 1931), and Berlin (20 March 1931). The pastoral letter for the parliamentary elections of 31 July 1932 (Böckenförde 1961, 217; *Katholische Kirche und Nationalsozialismus*, 41) and the statement of the Bavarian episcopate on 7 September 1932 (Harcourt 1938, 26) touched upon the same issue. These statements were broadly publicized (for instance in the April 1931 issue of the Center journal *Der Weckruf*). Their diffusion was not restricted to religious circles within the Church. They were intended for a large audience. Publicists reproduced them (for instance Nötges in 1931: "Nationalsozialismus und Katholizismus," published in Cologne; see *Katholische Kirche und Nationalsozialismus*, 21).

12. *Katholische Kirche und Nationalsozialismus*, 58–70.

Nazism at the end of September 1930, there was a fundamental incompatibility between the two worldviews (Harcourt 1938, 15).[13] Kaas endorsed this ideological assessment before the Center party executive committee in November 1930 (Becker 1963a, 85).

The important point is that spiritual Catholic leaders were in no way deceived by the pseudo-Christian profession of faith of National Socialist leaders (Harcourt 1938, 15). In the summer of 1932 German bishops explained that the dictatorship pursued by the National Socialists could only have the most ominous prospects for the interests of the Catholic Church (Volk 1990, 50).[14] They adopted the same position during the electoral campaign of February 1933.[15] Their task was facilitated because Hitler had never really disguised his antagonism toward the Catholic Church (Harcourt 1938, 50–58).

The programmatic statement of Hitler's government on 1 February 1933 did refer to Christianity as "the foundation of our morals" and made a perfunctory injunction of God (May God the Almighty . . .). But as Breuning (1969, 176) points out, assurances of this sort hardly produced a swing in Catholic quarters. On 17 February 1933 the major Catholic associations issued a statement in which they explained that if Hitler's government were to consolidate power, it would implement "a civil order in which arbitrariness and partiality [would] take the place of justice and group interest [would] be more decisive than the common good."[16] Catholic representatives did not pay serious attention to the religious references in Hitler's programmatic statements (Breuning 1969, 176; Buchheim 1961, 497).

Hence before 1933 religious Catholic leaders had correctly assessed the ideological nature of the Nazi movement and the spiritual threat that it embodied. They were clearly aware that the totalitarian aims of Nazism represented a deadly threat to the very principle of the Catholic church. Hitler's ultimate goal was not only to subsume religion to race but also to substitute a "German church" for the Catholic church. This goal could not be achieved without a new Kulturkampf. National Socialist references to Christianity, bishops explained, should not mislead the faithful about the kind of Christianity being envisioned (quotations in Harcourt 1938, 15, 17, 23). Thus before March 1933, German bishops viewed the rift between National Socialism and the doctrine

13. See also the attacks against National Socialism published by the abbot Moenius in the *Allgemeine Rundschau* (Harcourt 1938, 77).

14. Akten deutscher Bischöfe, 844.

15. On 20 February 1933 German bishops published a letter calling Catholics to vote for the Center party and to shun "agitators." This veiled reference designated both Communists and Nazis. Repgen (1967, 22) points out that the wording of this letter followed almost literally that of the electoral letter of 1932.

16. *Germania*, no. 47, 16 February 1933, 1.

of the Catholic church as unbridgeable. If one strand of the Catholic worldview emphasized a hierarchical and organicist conception of the political order, another placed primary emphasis on the importance of individual rights and the respect of the individual person, since the individual person is the epitome of the humanity created by God.

The ideological analysis of Nazism developed by Eugen Bolz before the representatives of the Swabian Center party on 12 February summarized these fundamental points of contention. Bolz stressed that the Nazis and their allies promote "a new concept of the state, a concept which says: the state can and is entitled to do everything. The individual is nothing and means nothing. This means actually absolute denial of any individual freedom. Such a doctrine is in absolute contradiction with the doctrine of natural rights, and with our Christian conception. I cannot understand how Catholics could partake in such a conception of the state, since in the end it implies that no freedom can subsist also with regard to religious matters."[17]

The Party of the Constitution

What about the argument that the Center parliamentary delegates were not truly committed to the constitutional ethos of Weimar? By the end of the 1920s not only had Center leaders come to terms with the idea of parliamentary democracy (Ruppert 1986, 84); they also believed that the constitution of Weimar had to be defended—even though it needed to be amended— against radical challenges from the Right and the Left because it preserved the interests of the Catholic minority.[18] The Center manifesto of 1927 made this clear: "There is for us no other reality in terms of the state than the German Republic and its symbols."[19] Center leaders who had been critical of the Republic, such as Stegerwald, Bolz, and Brüning, had become "republicans

17. *Kölnische Volkszeitung*, 15 February 1933, 2.

18. How then should we interpret the ambivalence displayed by the Center political leadership on the issue of the Republic? According to Evans (1981, 264), this ambivalence fulfilled primarily a tactical purpose. It reflected a conscious effort to win back those who had defected from the party at the beginning of the 1920s, when the Center endorsed the republican framework of Weimar. "The split in the ranks of political Catholicism was largely caused by differing attitudes toward the Republic and toward cooperation with Social Democracy and so all party pronouncements were worded with utmost care to express support of the Weimar Constitution and existing governments without showing undue devotion to republican principles" (264).

19. Quoted in Breuning (1969, 152). Repgen (1963, 18) suggests that this profession of faith resonated within the Catholic people. In a statement written in July 1929, Wilhelm Marx, leading member of the Center and former chancellor, described the Weimar constitution as "undoubtedly a great step forward" since it emphasized religious freedom. Stadtarchiv Köln, Nachlaß Marx, Best. 1070, no. 43, 82–85.

from reason" (Becker 1980, 4; Cary 1988, 506; Sailer 1994, 117; Patch 1998, 10; Hömig 2000, 87).[20]

In this regard the programmatic speech that Kaas delivered at Münster on 17 October 1932 is worth noting. "Germany will be fundamentally democratic or it will not be."[21] For more than two hours Kaas took pains to specify the ideological stance of the Center on the regime issue. On the one hand, he called for a more authoritarian state. On the other hand, he reaffirmed the democratic stance of the Center and the necessity of a normal political life for political parties. This ideological assertion of the Center's democratic commitment came right after the question "What is our stance in this electoral fight?" (*Wo stehen wir in diesem Kampf?*) and before a discussion of foreign policy, economic policy, and "experiments with the constitution." The speech also denounced totalitarianism, with a clear emphasis on the fundamental value of individual rights, and defended Weimar: "this constitution has had vital tasks and it has fulfilled these tasks."[22] The Weimar constitution closed the revolutionary era and consolidated peace and freedom.

Center representatives entered the electoral fight of February 1933 under the banner of "Truth, Law and Freedom" (Morsey 1977, 105) and throughout the election campaign took an adamant constitutionalist stand. The Center was the party of the constitution (Junker 1969, 78). It was opposed to breaching the constitution and to bringing about change by force (Morsey 1966, 77; Junker 1969, 55). Thus to suggest that Catholic representatives voted for the enabling bill in March 1933 and de facto legitimized Hitler's political claims because they were not immune to antidemocratic prejudices gives short shrift to their commitment to the constitutional framework.[23]

---

20. Patch (1998, 24–38) records this shift in stance with Brüning in the early 1920s. Stegerwald, who was said to belong to the right wing of the party, devoted the bulk of his speech at the Catholic Convention (*Katholikentag*) in September 1927 to praising a Republic which "had brought parity for Catholics" (Cary 1988, 464). When Wilhelm Marx stated in 1927 that the Center was a constitutionalist and not a republican party, he was contradicted by Wirth and the delegation chairman, Theodor von Guérard, a member of the Center's right wing, who "insisted that the Center was a republican party" (Knapp 1967, 210). Similarly, Brüning's eulogy for the former SPD chancellor Hermann Müller on 20 March 1931 betrayed a pro-democratic stance (Patch 1998, 149).

21. "Deutschland wird ein Staat demokratischer Grundhaltung sein oder es wird nicht sein." *Germania*, 18 October 1932, no. 290, 2.

22. "Diese Verfassung hat ihre lebenswichtige Aufgabe gehabt und erfüllt." Ibid.

23. One could still object that the Center party was less committed to the constitution of Weimar than to formal legality. In voting for the enabling bill on 23 March 1933, Center representatives could claim to remain faithful to their pledge to constitutional legality. This formal reading overlooks the political implications of the event.

The Right and the Left

It is possible to probe the claim that underlying reactionary longings motivated accommodation with Hitler at another level by looking at the cleavage between the right wing and the left wing of the Center party. The "left" designated those who in the first decade of the Weimar Republic advocated a political alliance with the Social Democrats as the only way to stabilize the Republic. Wirth was their most prominent representative. At the end of the 1920s he received the support of Joos, Dessauer, and Krone among others (Knapp 1967, 210; Knapp 1973, 167).[24] The "right wing" viewed German conservatives as natural political allies and shunned any political arrangement that could be seen as advancing the cause of social democracy. This was the position imputed to Kaas, Brüning, and in the 1920s Stegerwald (Morsey 1960, 295; Morsey ed. 1973, 212).

If an explanation in terms of political affinities were significant—that is, if Catholics' political endorsement of Hitler in March 1933 were primarily the outcome of a lack of "democratic substance," to borrow an expression from Morsey (1960, 413)—we should expect ideological distance to be a relevant factor, and we should expect that those within the Center who politically were closest to the conservative right would also have been the most strongly inclined to collaborate with the Nazis. Along these lines, Arnold Brecht argues that the cleavage between the "left" and "right" wings within the Center highlights the fault line that emerged on 23 March.[25]

Yet this interpretation is far from being convincing. Brüning, Kaiser, and Graf von Galen were regarded by their party colleagues as representatives of the right wing of the party (Morsey 1960, 325). From 1930 on "Jakob Kaiser took the lead in efforts to demonstrate that the program of the Christian unions alone offered a true synthesis of 'national' and 'social' values" (Patch 1985, 207).[26] In his recollections Joos observed that Brüning's commitment to the Republic was questioned within the Center party: "those who were in

24. In an interview with Gotto and Knopp, Heinrich Krone portrays himself as a member of the republican wing of the party while emphasizing that in the 1930s the Center party was fully committed to the Republic (Archiv der Konrad Adenauer Stiftung, Sankt Augustin, Nachlaß Krone, I-028, 006/5: interview with Knopp and Gotto, 3–4). In August 1932 Johannes Bell published an article in the Nationale Zeitung that identified him as belonging to the left wing of the Center party (Bundesarchiv, Koblenz, Nachlaß Johannes Bell, N1272/12).

25. Bundesarchiv, Koblenz, Nachlaß Arnold Brecht, N1089/127, Manuskript der Memoiren, 482.

26. Jakob Kaiser constantly refers to the imperative of "national unity" in his electoral speeches of February and March, outlining the political necessity to integrate Catholic workers in the "community of the nation." See for instance his speech on 22 February 1933 as well as the speech reproduced in the Kölnische Volkszeitung, 25 February 1933.

the Center party were designated as particularly favorable to democracy . . . adopted a somewhat reserved attitude because they did not exactly know what Brüning's position was."[27] On 23 March 1933 these actors took a stance at odds with what an ideological reading of the event would lead us to expect (Cary 1988, 536). Conversely, Center delegates who affiliated themselves with the left wing, such as Bell, Krone, and Wegmann, on 23 March 1933 opted for conciliation.[28]

Thus it is not clear *how* the ideological prevalence of schemes such as "national Volksstaat" may have induced Center representatives to acquiesce in Hitler's political demands in March 1933. The Catholics and the National Socialists understood notions such as Volksgemeinschaft in very different terms. For the National Socialists, the national community was a community based on soil and blood. For Catholics, the Volksgemeinschaft referred to a classless society by opposition to an authoritarian state (Morsey 1977, 23; Evans 1981, 277). As such it defined the "central concept of an egalitarian ideology" (*Zentralbegriff einer Ausgleichsideologie*) (Becker 1969, 69). This explains why in February 1933 Center representatives challenged Hitler's government claim to speak on behalf of the nation. The two parties which had taken over political power on January 1933, Joos explained in a speech delivered on 7 February, in no way could pretend to represent the nation as a whole.[29]

PEACE AGAINST NATIONAL DECADENCE

The political challenge directed at parliamentary institutions was a European phenomenon in the 1930s. France was no exception. The extreme Right started to mobilize against republican institutions in 1932. After a series of corruption scandals involving politicians, the movement reached a political climax with the riot of 6 February 1934, in which thousands of demonstrators threatened to storm parliament. For its harshest critics, parliamentary democracy did not work well. It fostered political instability and was corrupt. The regime

27. Kommission für Zeitgeschichte, Bonn, Nachlaßsplitter Joos, Archiv IV, box 1.

28. Consistent with these observations is the absence of a systematic correlation between the right-left division within the party—as was commonly perceived at the time—and the cleavage that emerged after March 1933 between those who promoted and those who opposed accommodation with Hitler. Morsey (1977, 268) questions Muckermann's suggestion that "being on the left of the party" was a factor conducive to a resolute stance vis-à-vis coercive pressures at the end of the spring of 1933. The debates brought about by the vote on the enabling bill and the subsequent question of collaboration with the Nazis, far from confirming the political significance of the division between "left" and "right" within the party, redefined political cleavages.

29. *Kölnische Volkszeitung*, 8 February 1933.

had to be reformed in an authoritarian sense. Parliamentary democracy was a degenerate system. Dynamism and audacity were on the side of authoritarian regimes.

Against the nefarious influence of a cosmopolitan culture and against internal subversion, a strong state reasserting the values of national belonging and national identity was needed. Nationalist conservatives castigated "the Jews" for their alleged lack of attachment to the nation and propensity to be politically subversive. For these national conservatives Judaism was one facet of Marxism, and many of them viewed Nazi Germany as a bulwark against the spread of communism. Intransigent pacifists, for their part, suspected foreign and French Jews of pushing for war in an effort to oppose Nazism (Birnbaum 1992, 214–15; Jackson 2001, 107; Jelen 1988, 214–21; Schor 1992, 48). The war with Germany and ultimately the defeat were thus blamed on the Jews.

This critique of democracy found a broad echo among conservative circles after the electoral victory of the Popular Front in June 1936 (Hoffmann 1974, 32). If indeed parliamentary democracy could make a leftist coalition led by the Socialist party electorally victorious, then something was definitely wrong with it. Faced with what they perceived as a fundamental threat to their interests, conservatives of all stripes did not disguise their sympathy for regimes that had succeeded in eradicating political subversion. Between this antidemocratic spirit and the zeitgeist of the conservative revolution, the parallels are patent: rejection of mass democracy and parliamentary institutions, cultural pessimism, glorification of the state as the medium of moral renewal, coupled with an authoritarian form of government.

There was, however, a crucial difference. The nationalism of the opponents of democracy in Germany was aggressive. This radical and antidemocratic nationalism was also directed at the political settlement of the Versailles treaty. By contrast, pacifism loomed large in the antidemocratic constellation that took shape in France in the course of the 1930s. A war against Germany could only benefit the Soviet Union and the spread of communism. It meant opening the door to the possibility of a leftist revolution. War was a matter of internal politics. Those who supported a firm stance against Germany's territorial pretensions in the East were de facto playing the game of the communists. In Vichy in July 1940, it is argued, this pacifist stance made an unexpected alliance with authoritarian longings elicited by the social fear of 1936 and nurtured by the denunciation of moral and cultural decadence. The conjunction of these different motivations characterizes the ideological matrix that presided over the vote of 10 July.

The Longing for an Authoritarian State

> Projects were swarming . . .

As Paxton (1972) writes, "projects for new French institutions swarmed around Vichy in July 1940" (29). General Weygand, the minister of national defense, submitted to the government at the end of June a short "manifest" that condemned class struggles, moral decline, a spirit of pleasure and carelessness, and demographic and national decadence. In the same text Weygand also denounced a political regime (parliamentary democracy), which he viewed as given over to cosmopolitan compromises and Masonic influences, and as the main cause of the disaster. A "new social regime based on the confidence and the collaboration between workers and employers" was needed. The new political élite had to "hark back to the cult and the practice of an ideal summarized by these few words: God, Homeland, Family."[30] On 5 July the conservative senator Bardoux sent to Pétain a letter expounding his plans for constitutional reforms, which included among others the election of local assemblies by occupational groups, the regulation of confidence votes, and the right of dissolution.[31]

Both Weygand's and Bardoux's plans remained confidential. Bergery's programmatic statement, on the other hand, was widely publicized in the form of a parliamentary motion. As indicated in chapter 4, this motion called for implementing new institutions, modeled on those of the victor, even though they were supposed to retain a distinctive French character. Finally, there was the official statement exposing "the motivations for the bill" distributed to parliamentarians before the vote: "France has to acknowledge and accept the necessity of a national revolution. . . . The government needs to have all powers required to decide, undertake and negotiate."[32] Protection of family against

---

30. "The old order" ("l'ancien ordre des choses") that is a "political regime of masonic, capitalist and international collusions, led us to where we stand now . . . Class struggles divided the country, hindered any profitable work and allowed the overbids of demagoguery. . . . The decline of natality . . . led us to define our territory with an inadmissible proportion of northern-African, colonial and foreign contingents. . . . Family needs to be honored again. The wave of materialism that submerged France, the spirit of pleasure and easiness ("esprit de jouissance et de facilité") are the deep cause of our weaknesses and of our renunciations. We need to hark back to the cult and the practice of an ideal summarized by these few words: God, Homeland, Family" (Weygand, *Mémoires*, 298–99). According to Pomaret, minister of the Interior in the Pétain cabinet (until 27 June), Weygand transmitted this manifest to Pétain on 28 June (Pomaret, *Le dernier témoin*, 254).

31. Bardoux, *Journal d'un témoin de la Troisième*, 393–98.

32. Archives Départementales de l'Isère, Grenoble, Archives Justin Arnol, 37 J 40: Projet de loi constitutionnelle, Exposé des motifs.

"morale and intellectual perversion," control and arbitration of social groups, development of a corporatist organization of the economy, collaboration between employers and employees, and restoration of value hierarchy: the statement was playing the same chords as the reform plans I just mentioned.

Weygand, Bardoux, and Bergery wrote up their plans and manifestos independently. Taken together, their texts sketch a political project with a clear reactionary bent. Their common denominator was a reaction against what was perceived as a crisis of the state (decline of its authority) and a moral crisis (class struggles, spirit of pleasure, cultural decadence), both sanctioned by the military defeat. They varied with regard to their reference to republican principles. Bardoux did not envision political structures that would not be republican. Weygand and Bergery were obviously in favor of an authoritarian state freed from democratic control. As for the official programmatic statement expounding the motivations for the bill, this statement left the form of the future regime in the dark. Mention was made of "a national representation" that would collaborate with the government, but the way this national representation would be designated was not specified. Nowhere was the future state characterized as republican, which could easily be interpreted as an indication that it would not be so.

State Reforms

These plans for national renovation were of course motivated by the catastrophe of May–June. But they did not come from nowhere. There had been considerable talk about reforming the state since the mid-1930s, as external threats became more ominous and political instability nurtured the rise of an ideological critique of parliamentary democracy (Cointet 1993, 31). The major goal of the reform plans elaborated at the time was to reinforce and consolidate executive power. The suggested means were diverse: a social reorganization along corporatist lines, an extension of the right to dissolve parliament, extension of the referendum procedure, transfer of competences to regional and local assemblies, and the rationalization of parliamentary work (Cointet 1996, 38). The unmistakable goal of these institutional proposals was to enhance the authority of the executive branch.

But the "crisis of the thirties" went beyond these plans for state reforms. It was marked by the gradual disintegration of the "republican synthesis" (Hoffmann 1974, 32) which Cointet (1996, 26) characterizes as the marriage of parliamentary democracy and economic liberalism. It is in the realm of intellectual productions that the symptoms of a crisis of democratic ideals became particularly visible. A survey by Lindenberg (1990) of the intellectual landscape during this period leads to the same diagnosis: "the republican idea was quite sick" (16). Analyzing the avatars of Fascist ideology in France in the interwar period, Sternhell (1996 [1986]) concludes that the antiliberal and organicist tradition had "impregnated [French] society to a far greater degree than is generally admitted" (x). The national, antiliberal, antimaterialist, and anti-Marxist reaction was intended to be a political *and* moral revolution. These intellectual currents were diffuse. They were nonetheless, Sternhell suggests, influential insofar as they accustomed political actors to the idea of authoritarian alternatives.

Material Interests and Political Legitimacy

In a text written in 1940, Marc Bloch (1990, 197) remarked, "one could hardly exaggerate the emotion that the advent of the popular Front caused in 1936 among the ranks of the well-to-do, even among the men who seemed to think the most freely." Employers and their political representatives had been humiliated by the sit-ins that followed the electoral victory of the Popular Front and by the social gains brought about by the Matignon accords (June 1936). The experience of the Popular Front left the French bourgeoisie not only "anxious" and "dissatisfied" but also "bitter" (*aigrie*) (Bloch 1990, 197). Some were tempted to throw their support to a more authoritarian political system, less vulnerable to workers' social demands ("rather Hitler than Blum").[33] Could it be that in 1940 French conservatives and economically dominant groups had not yet overcome the political defeat they had suffered in 1936?

According to this view, dominant fractions of the French bourgeoisie withdrew their allegiance to the democratic setting of the Third Republic when they realized that parliamentary democracy did not guarantee their political dominance. The electoral victory of the Popular Front (May 1936) demonstrated that it was possible for a leftist coalition led by a socialist leader to gain access democratically to the levers of the state. The great fear of May–June 1936 spurred antidemocratic feelings. Class-based motivations for a political revenge went along with a rejection of the political regime that had made political defeat possible (Noiriel 1999, 88–89). The moral condemnation of democracy took a dramatic turn with the realization that democracy could open the door to social revolutions or drastic social reforms.

Hence conservative and bourgeois élites seized on the occasion to discard a

---

33. Similarly, when Weygand in his manifest referred to the devastating consequences of class struggles and the mollifying influence of, again, the "spirit of pleasure," no doubt he had in mind the Popular Front.

political regime that had been unable to protect their economic interests. They had to take revenge, and Laval's political offensive in July 1940 gave them an opportunity to do so. They played the card of an authoritarian regime more likely to consolidate their socioeconomic positions. This reaction to political defeat was a litmus test: French conservatives had not come to terms with the Republic. They were not committed to the republican framework to the point of accepting political challenge within the framework of current institutions (Soucy 1995, 27). Vichy was the revenge of the vanquished (Miquel 1995, 146); it was the revenge of those who blamed their defeat on political institutions.

The Avatars of Pacifism

As Hitler made his territorial claims explicit in the second half of the 1930s, foreign policy gradually took over political debates and controversies. One had to decide which attitude to adopt toward a prospective German Lebensraum that would sanction Germany's political dominance in Europe as well as the expansion of a totalitarian political project. Should Hitler's territorial pretensions in Europe be opposed by a strong demurrer even if this meant the possibility of war? Could peace and stability be saved if concessions were granted on time? By the time of the Anschluss—Germany's annexation of Austria (March 1938)—these questions became very concrete. One could no longer take refuge in vague statements of intention.

The lines of cleavage that emerged in this context were complex and cut across party affiliations (Handourtzel and Buffet 1989, 47). Those on the Left who were resolute to oppose Germany's territorial expansion found their resolution reinforced by their abhorrence of fascism. Those on the Right committed to a policy of firmness reflected a long-term nationalist antagonism toward Germany. Conversely, appeasers from the Left remained in their view faithful to the pacifist tradition that characterized the Left's internationalist inclinations. Appeasers from the Right were not so much concerned by peace as by the expansion of communism and the risk of internal subversion that a war with Germany would occasion. Conflicts over foreign policy were therefore related to internal cleavages. For many proponents of appeasement, war raised the specter of a Bolshevik revolution. Opposition to Germany in the name of antifascism was a cover-up for revolutionary bellicosity.

The First Crisis

Throughout the spring and summer of 1938, these divergent assessments smoldered. The annexation of Austria by Germany was the first warning of future showdowns. It was with the German-Czech crisis of September 1938 that the configuration of positions became clearer. At the beginning of September 1938 Hitler raised the question of the German minorities living in the Sudetenland and requested that territories in which Germans formed the majority of the population be integrated into Germany. Yielding to his demands meant redrawing the map established by the Versailles treaty and jeopardizing the territorial integrity of Czechoslovakia, with which France had treaty obligations. Hitler's demands thus confronted France and Britain with the following dilemma: siding with the Czechoslovakian government against Hitler opened up the possibility of war, and yielding to Hitler's claims meant leaving Eastern Europe in the hands of Nazi Germany.

On 30 September 1938 the leaders of the four European powers (Britain, France, Italy, and Germany) met in Munich and signed an accord which approved the transfer of the Sudetenland to Germany and in effect sanctioned the breakup of Czechoslovakia. These accords had to be ratified by the Chamber of Deputies. The debates which surrounded the Munich accord exacerbated the confrontation between those resolute to check Hitler's demands, by force if necessary, and those willing to promote a policy of appeasement, even if this meant giving a free hand to Nazi Germany in the East, with the hope that Germany and the Soviet Union would neutralize each other. Taking a position for or against Munich meant taking a position for or against the possibility of war.

The crisis and its outcome revealed two heterogeneous camps, for and against a compromise with Hitler (Duroselle 1985, 357–63). The camp which applauded the settlement (the Munichois) encompassed pacifists from the Left and conservatives newly converted to the virtues of peace. Chief among the Munich supporters from the Left were a few intellectual personalities, the majority of the Socialist delegation (led by Paul Faure, the secretary general of the party), and the few self-labeled Socialist groups not affiliated with the SFIO (Union Socialiste Républicaine), as well as groups that occupied a "marginal" (Cointet) position within the spectrum of the parliamentary Left (Gauche indépendante). Members of this camp could legitimately invoke their traditional attachment to a pacifist ideology that was part of the political identity of the Left. In some cases this pacifist reflex did not always disguise a growing anticommunism, especially among the members of the Radical party (Burrin 1986, 266–71; Duroselle 1985, 359; Gombin 1970, 248; Lacaze 1991, 373).

The conservatives' motives for endorsing an appeasement policy with Hitler were diverse. Some, such as Flandin, the leader of the Alliance Démocratique in the Chamber, refused to entertain an "ideological war" between the democratic bloc and the fascist bloc and accepted the possibility of Germany's territorial expansion in Eastern Europe (Duroselle 1985, 361; Lacaze 1991, 323–26). Others, such as representatives of the Fédération Républicaine and the far-right French Social Party (Parti Social Français), viewed the Munich settlement as a respite justified by the lack of French military preparation (Irvine 1979, 191–97; Lacaze 1991, 333; Machefer 1978, 315). Their endorsement of the settlement did not imply an acceptance of Germany's push toward the East. The endorsement was tactical and conditional.

The Communists, a few Socialists, and a few members of the Radical party, convinced that the only way to check Hitler's ambitions was to confront him directly, formed the bulk of the opposition to the Munich accord (Lacaze 1991, 372; Berstein 1982, 548–49).[34] For these actors the "fight against fascism took precedence over the tradition of pacifism" (Duroselle 1985, 361). A few personalities from the Right cast their lot with the anti-Munich camp in the name of combating pan-Germanism: Mandel (minister of colonies in Daladier's government), Reynaud (minister of justice), Champetier de Ribes (minister of war veterans), and Henri de Kerillis (Duroselle 1985, 364; Sherwood 1970, 215).

The relative strength of these camps shifted significantly in the spring when Hitler, trampling international treaties, invaded Czechoslovakia on 15 March 1939. This "coup" justified a posteriori those who had been committed to a policy of firmness. It also stiffened the backs of those who had supported the Munich policies by opportunism. As a result, the ranks of what intransigent pacifists called the "war party" swelled after March 1939. The Republican Federation, which had welcomed the Munich accords a few months earlier, demanded that Daladier's government show "the firmest determination to abandon the policy of weakness and return . . . to a foreign policy worthy of the name of France" (quoted by Irvine 1979, 199). By contrast, Socialists and representatives of the Right who had supported the Munich accords out of intransigent pacifism or anticommunism held firm while keeping a low profile.

There is probably no better illustration of how internal politics captured foreign policy considerations than the reactions to the Nazi-Soviet nonaggression pact of 23 August 1939. The pact appeased the qualms of conservatives who feared that in fighting Nazi Germany they would indirectly work for the interests of the Soviet Union. For these Conservative representatives, the nationalist and republican stance adopted until then by the leadership of the Communist party was primarily motivated by their antifascism, not the defense of French national interests. Once Communists appeared after September 1939 as "the

---

34. The Socialist deputy Moch notes in his memoirs that ten Socialist deputies had initially voted against the motion of confidence (including himself) and had finally agreed to revert their vote in order not to breach party discipline. Moch, *Une si longue vie*, 149.

party of the enemy," the fight against Hitler was devoid of its ambiguities. Fighting Hitler meant fighting Stalin. The Right's anticommunism was again on familiar ground.

The Nazi-Soviet nonaggression pact also transformed the makeup of the appeasement camp by inducing the leadership of the French Communists to adopt a more conciliatory stance. Within a few weeks Communist leaders dropped their attitude of uncompromising opposition to the territorial claims of fascist regimes and endorsed the outfits of the most devoted appeasers. In the second fortnight of September the Communist leadership condemned the war as a conflict between imperialist powers, a war "which it was the duty of Communists to oppose" (Mortimer 1984, 285).

Pacifism and Reaction

Who could be characterized as "pacifist" in the summer of 1939? As the previous remarks indicate, the question is rendered complex by the considerable mutations that the "pacifist" camp underwent in the two years preceding the war. It is nonetheless possible to identify a group of parliamentarians whose commitment to a pacifist stance and a policy of conciliation and agreement with Germany remained consistent and intransigent between Munich (September 1938) and June 1940. These formed a small minority (Wieviorka 2001, 29). In August 1939 fifteen deputies constituted a Committee of Liaison against the War (Burrin 1986, 314). When on 1 September the news broke out that the German troops had entered Poland, twenty-eight deputies signed a statement addressed to the French government, asking it to "associate itself with the spiritual, moral and pacific forces of the world in order to try a last effort at the truce between the belligerents and propose a general conference likely to pacify Europe" (Burrin 1986, 314).[35]

The day after, as parliament convened for an extraordinary session in which the government was to announce general mobilization and request exceptional credits for the war efforts, a group of twenty-two deputies submitted a motion requesting that the chamber meet as a secret committee, instead of holding the session public (Burrin 1986, 314).[36] The purpose of this motion could only be to initiate a debate on the government's policy, and in doing so to allow the supporters of compromise a chance to make their objections to war heard without being accountable to public opinion. Both the membership

---

35. One extract of this letter is reproduced in Montigny, *Le complot contre la paix*, 264.
36. Assemblée Nationale, *Débats de la Chambre*, 1939, vol. 1, 1950.

of the Committee of Liaison against the War and the lists of signatories to the letter of 1 September to the government map out the intransigent pacifist camp. All in all, these intransigent pacifists, resolute to find a peace of compromise with Germany, formed a group of about thirty deputies in the chamber (about 5 percent).

In June 1940, as the government in Bordeaux was considering an armistice with Germany, these diehard pacifists actively opposed any departure of the government for Northern Africa: in their view, a departure from metropolitan France made a continued military struggle more likely (Burrin 1986, 328). Not surprisingly, this small group applauded the conclusion of the armistice. It is also these militant pacifists who in Vichy mobilized early on in favor of Laval's bill (Burrin 1986, 331). Thirteen of the fifteen members of the Liaison Committee against the War were among the twenty promoters of the motion written by the centrist deputy Bergery, which called not only for passing Laval's bill but also for implementing a new political order, authoritarian, national, and social. In brief, those who had been the most consistent in opposing a war with Germany were also elaborating the political rationale for an alignment with totalitarian countries.

This simple observation provides strong support for a continuity of positions between endorsing a policy of appeasement before the war and endorsing Laval's agenda in July 1940. It does suggest, to paraphrase Agulhon (1993, 251), that "the logic which gradually led to the formation of a collaborationist coalition and a resistance coalition" was in place "well before the event" — that is, in the present case, 10 July. Yet if this logic can be factually documented by considering individual trajectories, its ideological significance needs to be spelled out. Why would pacifism lead to authoritarianism?

The answer points to the peculiarity of the pre-war cleavages over foreign issues: a steadfast policy of concessions and appeasement toward Germany's territorial claims in the East had to justify the option of letting Hitler assert its geopolitical domination in the East. Anticommunism provided one of these justifications. Nazi Germany could be a buffer against the spread of communism. In an ideal world, the two totalitarian regimes would fight one another. A less cynical version of conciliation emphasized the legitimacy of Hitler's claims: the Versailles treaty had created artificial boundaries, and peoples had a right to seek self-determination. France had to coexist with a totalitarian regime. Justifying the aggressive plans of these regimes implied some form of positive evaluation, if not of the authoritarian character of these regimes then at least of their expansionary plans. Pacifism could easily accommodate itself with an authoritarian conception of politics if democracy proved unable to find a compromise with fascist regimes. "The relentless fight for peace was going to go along with the shattering and the disintegration of democratic values" (Burrin 1986, 267).

The Socialists and War

In this regard, the split that affected the Socialist party on 10 July may be viewed as a test case of a process that had broader significance. The vote, explains Sadoun (1982), "was not an accidental event, but, on the contrary, the major piece of an evolution, of a continuum that confirms the stands taken since Munich and anticipates actors' future choices" (42). Those who had taken a pacifist stand before and after Munich were more likely to vote for the power transfer. Their commitment to peace had taken precedence over their commitment to republican institutions.

The breakup that occurred in Vichy cannot be understood without reference to the intense confrontation that took place among Socialist representatives in 1938–39. International tensions in the course of the 1930s had led some Socialist representatives to reassert their pacifist commitment and to reject in its name any intervention in the Spanish civil war in 1936. In the spring and summer 1938 the divergence between partisans of appeasement and partisans of resistance to Hitler became explicit (Gombin 1978, 248). The September crisis and the debates which surrounded the ratification of the Munich accord crystallized and sharpened this divergence. One faction, around the secretary general of the party, Paul Faure (the "Faurists"), endorsed the Munich agreement almost without any reservation, and accepted concessions intended to appease Hitler. The other faction, around Blum (the "Blumists"), took the view that France had to defend itself against fascist regimes by strengthening its pacts of mutual assistance with other states, including if necessary with the Soviet Union.

On 30 September 1938 the parliamentary group of the Socialist party (SFIO) in the Chamber of Deputies adopted a resolution which "expressed its gratification that the Munich conference had halted the movement towards war" (Graham 1994, 225). On 4 October, against Blum's recommendation, a majority of the delegation decided to endorse the Munich accord (Greene 1969, 229). A little less than two months later parliamentarians and militants met in Montrouge, in the suburbs of Paris, for an extraordinary congress (24–26 December 1938). Léon Blum and Paul Faure presented separate motions that summarized their positions. Blum's motion won an absolute majority, with one third of the mandates cast for Faure's (Graham 1994, 229). The debate over foreign policy had created a major split which threatened the existence of the party. At the national congress the next May, both factions sought to bridge their differences by voting for a common motion.

When SFIO parliamentarians convened in Vichy in July 1940, the antagonisms of the two previous years had obviously not come to a rest. On 8 July SFIO representatives present in Vichy met separately to discuss their votes. Before the meeting Blum reflected on how it might turn out. The pacifists would probably find in the military disaster an a priori justification for their previous stance. "Would they go as far as to yield over and liquidate the Republic as culprit of the war"?[37] Blum did not believe this. But it remained for him a possibility, and this indicates the extent of his uncertainty about the position of his peers in the delegation.

Among the 126 Socialist representatives who attended the parliamentary session in Vichy on 10 July, 99 of them, according to Sadoun (1982, 41), were affiliated with the pacifist faction: these delegates had previously endorsed party resolutions that far from seeing the territorial claims of totalitarian dictatorships as posing the greatest threat of war, saw the danger as lying in the peace settlements of 1919. Sadoun estimates that sixty-four of these delegates, that is 65 percent, voted "yes" on 10 July. Among SFIO representatives affiliated with the Blum faction only five voted "yes" (Sadoun 1982, 41). All the prominent representatives of the Faurist faction took a stand in favor of Laval's bill. By contrast, most representatives personally close to Blum voted "no" on 10 July. Furthermore, twenty-two members of the Faurist faction signed the Bergery motion, while none of the Blum faction signed it.

Spontaneous Endorsement

The thread that runs from the ideological context of the 1930s to the vote of 10 July seems therefore quite clear. This thread is twofold. One strand relates the "spirit of the thirties" to the political offensive that took place in Vichy. Anti-Semitism and xenophobia had been rising (Marrus and Paxton 1995 [1981], 34–44). Reactionaries were using anti-Jewish feelings as a political tool against the republican state (Birnbaum 1992, 20). Discriminatory legislation directed at foreigners was already in place at the end of the 1930s (Marrus and Paxton 1995 [1981], 55–57; Noiriel 1999, 144–47). The gradual propagation of a national, antiliberal, antimaterialist and anti-Marxist reaction, combined with growing xenophobia in the years preceding the collapse, explains "the ease, the naturalness with which the alternative regime was set [in July 1940] and the wide consensus it enjoyed" (Sternhell 1996 [1986], 292). "Beyond purely conjunctural

---

37. Blum, *Mémoires*, 76.

motivations the vote of a large number of deputies and senators had a clear-cut ideological significance marked by the support for the armistice with Germany and the longing for an authoritarian state" (Sadoun 1982, 41).

The second strand points to the "accommodation" between "pacifists from the Left, determined to dismiss whatever did not fit in their beliefs in international understanding, and pacifists of the Right, who feared the nefarious manipulations of anti-Nazis eager to use the French as a cat's-paws" (Weber 1994, 22). In either case the military defeat acted as a precipitant. It crystallized pervasive feelings and gave them a new impetus (Burrin 1986, 338; Sternhell 1996 [1986], 293). Underlying this interpretation is the claim that the collective endorsement of the bill was more or less spontaneous. There was no resistance simply because no one wanted to resist (Paxton 1972, 32). "The 'victims' had in reality been consenting" (Azéma 1984, 52). Wieviorka (2001) concurs: this was a "vote of adhesion" (66).

PREFERENCES, PUBLIC AND PRIVATE . . .

> I view Laval's plan as dangerous since it can only succeed if 480 senators and deputies agree to commit suicide. — Paul Baudouin, minister of foreign affairs in Pétain's cabinet, end of June 1940[38]

The ideological collusion thesis implies that contamination was widespread. The antiliberal critique of parliamentary democracy had impregnated the political establishment to the point of making it receptive to the prospect of a nondemocratic regime. Undoubtedly this interpretation highlights the ideological drift that many steadfast appeasers underwent in 1940 and the "blurring of previous cleavages" observed at the same time (Laborie 2001 [1990], 91). The small clique devoted to a peace of compromise with Germany at any price was also consistently advocating reconciliation with fascist regimes. Whether they viewed these regimes as a rampart against the spread of communism, or were motivated by the vision of a French-German collaboration ensuring peace in Western Europe, these militant appeasers were not always immune to the surreptitious fascination—the "subterranean attraction" (Burrin 1986, 275)—exerted by fascism. In some cases anti-Semitism provided an additional motivation (Jackson 2001, 107).

What about mainstream parliamentarians? Shall we conclude that their democratic convictions had been crucially perverted by antiliberalism or conciliatory pacifism? Two groups can be easily identified, because they publi-

---

38. "[Je] juge [le projet de Laval] dangereux car il ne peut réussir que si 480 sénateurs ou députés acceptent de se suicider." Baudouin, *Neuf mois au gouvernement*, 227.

cized their preferences. First were those—I estimate about a hundred—who endorsed the prospect of a nondemocratic state. At the opposite end stood a group of roughly the same size willing to publicly state its commitment to democratic institutions (the "republican diehards"). The difficulty concerns those who did not take any public position. Were they leaning toward one of these two poles? One key observation is provided by testimonies describing how parliamentarians of any stripe initially reacted to the content of the bill and Laval's agenda: with stupor, befuddlement, and indignation. The dominant mode was certainly not one of acquiescence, and the reactions were consistent with shared perceptions about the republicanism of the large majority of parliament members.

The Authoritarian Camp

For those who signed the Bergery motion, France had to partake in the establishment of a new political order under German hegemony. This new order implied a change of political institutions, and a change of foreign policy. Political institutions had to be modeled on those of the victor. Even if the future institutions were to remain, as the text of the motion underlined, "distinctively French," the reference to Germany left no doubt about their antidemocratic character. Change in foreign policy resulted from the situation created by defeat. Germany had won the war. France could only expect to escape a humiliating peace if it demonstrated its willingness to faithfully collaborate with the emergence of the new European order. Since the political significance of these two policy recommendations was unmistakable, it makes sense to identify those who subscribe to the Bergery statement as partisans of an authoritarian and antidemocratic option in July 1940. Not surprisingly, all those whose names were listed in support of the motion voted for the bill except one.[39]

Does the Bergery declaration capture all those who professed antidemocratic sentiments? Is there any reason to believe that those who despised democracy did not or could not have a chance to add their signature? The

---

39. The exception is the Socialist deputy Édouard Froment. This deputy had been a member of the Committee of Liaison against War in 1939–40. It remains uncertain whether Froment's name appeared on the Bergery motion because his colleagues in this committee added it without his awareness—believing that his involvement went without saying—or because he signed the motion and then revised his position. Froment denied after the war that he had provided his support to the Bergery declaration. (See Maurice Boulle: "Les parlementaires ardéchois et les pleins pouvoirs au maréchal Pétain le 10 juillet 1940: Deux parcours: Édouard Froment, Xavier Vallat," L'Ardèche dans la Guerre: De la République ... à l'Etat Français, Cahiers Mémoire d'Ardèche et Temps Présent, 15 Mai 1994, 23.)

declaration was widely distributed. People in Vichy were aware of its existence. Some parliamentarians may not have had the opportunity to sign the motion because of their late arrival in Vichy.[40] But the number of parliamentarians who arrived in Vichy just in time for the vote was quite small (see chapter 4) and it is therefore reasonable to assume that with few exceptions, all those present in Vichy on 10 July had taken cognizance of the content of this pro-grammatic and policy statement. On 7 July the Bergery motion was signed by seventy-one parliamentarians. Between 7 July and 10 July, twenty-two mem-bers of the National Assembly added their signatures.

Overall, parliamentarians who signed the Bergery declaration came from all political parties in the chamber of deputies, with the exception of the Independent Group of Popular Action (table 14). The parliamentary group most supportive of the Bergery motion was the far-right Parti Social Français (PSF)—five of its seven delegates, or 71 percent, endorsed the motion. But parties classified on the left and center of the political spectrum taken together did contribute significantly: thirty signatories on the left, thirteen in the center, and fifty-one on the right.[41] This observation is consistent with the hypothesis that the moral disintegration of democratic ideals had been pervasive. More to the point: variations in the frequency of support across party affiliations suggest that the motion provides an adequate picture of the numerical strength of the authoritarian camp in the Assembly.[42]

The Republican Consciousness

Was the "moral disintegration" (Burrin) of democratic values so pervasive that the mainstream parliamentarians no longer cared about republican insti-tutions? Consider Henri Becquart, a deputy of the Fédération Républicaine, which at the end of the 1930s had become far-right (Jackson 2001, 79). In the years preceding the war, Becquart contributed several articles to La Nation

40. For example, the extreme Right senator Jean Fabry arrived in Vichy on 9 July. Fabry, *J'ai connu . . .*, 174.

41. This computation is based on the objectivist classification of positions along the left-right axis discussed in chapter 3.

42. Becquart suggests that we should not overemphasize the political significance of the Ber-gery motion: many related to this motion as if it were an inconsequential pre-war statement (*Au temps du silence*, 141). Fernand Robbe, deputy of the French Social party, makes similar observa-tions (Archives Nationales, Dossiers du jury d'honneur, Paris: dossier Robbe, AL 5328). In short, some parliamentarians signed the motion without fully gauging what they were promoting. It may also be that some signatures were added without their authors' consent (e.g. Bounin and Froment). If so, the list of ninety-four signatories as of 10 July probably overestimates the scope of the authoritarian camp.

Table 14   Parliamentarians Who Signed the Bergery Declaration (List as of 10 July: Bergery Personal Papers)

		Signatures	No Signatures	Total
Left	Union Populaire Française (former communists)	3	7	10
	Parti Socialiste (SFIO)	27	95	122
	Parti Socialiste (SFIO) (Senate)	0	10	10
	Union Socialiste Républicaine (USR)	6	14	20
	Gauche Indépendente	3	8	11
	Groupe Républicain Radical et Radical-Socialiste (Radical party)	4	77	81
	Gauche Démocratique, Radicale et Radicale Socialiste (Senate)	0	128	128
	Gauche Démocratique et Radicale Indépendante	12	19	31
	Groupe Démocrate Populaire	4	9	13
	Union Démocratique et Radicale (UDR) (Senate)	0	25	25
	Alliance Démocratique	7	30	37
	Groupe Agraire Indépendant	1	7	8
	Groupe Indépendent d'Action Populaire	0	10	10
	Républicains Indépendants et d'Action Sociale	8	16	24
	Union Républicaine (Senate)	3	39	42
	Indépendants Républicains	1	5	6
	Action Nationale, Républicaine et Sociale (Senate)	0	11	11
	Fédération Républicane	10	35	45
Right	Parti Social Français	5	2	7
Not affiliated		0	29	29
Total		94	576	670

Source: Déclaration sur l'Assemblée Nationale, juillet 1940, Hoover Institution Archives, Stanford University, Gaston Bergery papers, box 12.

which reflected the political views of the Fédération Républicaine leadership. In his personal testimony he mentioned that he was willing to vote for the bill because it provided an opportunity to get rid of institutions that were "worn out" and had proved their "noxiousness."[43] Bardoux, the conservative senator

43. Becquart, *Au temps du silence*, 183.

from the Union Démocratique et Radicale, is another case in point. A few years earlier Bardoux had written a political pamphlet in which he noted the dynamism of the fascist regimes, condemned Bolshevism and Nazism as nefarious ideologies, and proposed a reform of democratic institutions along corporatist lines. His diary shows that in July 1940 he leaned toward a "yes" vote and feared the possibility that the bill might be collectively rejected. He would have signed Bergery's petition had there not been the references to Germany.[44]

Initial Reactions

Yet a host of personal accounts reveal that *initially* negative reactions to the bill, and to Laval's programmatic agenda, were widespread. The peculiarity of these accounts is that they come from representatives with very different political affiliations and different vote propensities. Even parliamentarians predisposed to vote for the bill, or resigned to do so, recorded their peers' latent opposition to the political agenda that was being set up before their eyes.

"We all arrived from our provinces with the will to resist. . . . The first colleagues whom I meet are . . . irritated . . . : They proclaim that they will refuse to divest themselves [from their constitutional authority] for good,"[45] Paul Ramadier, a former undersecretary in Blum's government of 1936, recalled. Although not formally affiliated with a party delegation in the Chamber of Deputies in 1940, Ramadier was mainly in touch with groups in the Center and on the Left of the parliamentary spectrum. His assessment is corroborated by Blum's observations about the indignation that Laval's plans elicited among those arriving in Vichy: "They were going to fake the overthrow of the Constitution under the guise of constitutional legality. Really, this was too much! Consequently I was not surprised to hear from Dormoy [a Socialist senator and close friend of Blum] and Thivrier that even in the parliamentary milieu of Vichy, the *first reactions* [to the draft bill] were hostile, irritated. . . . A spontaneous resistance was already expressing itself. . . . Dormoy in Montluçon met a few Socialist deputies who . . . hastened from the occupied zone; all were exuding the same indignation" (my emphasis).[46]

Among senators the mood was strikingly similar. Paul-Boncour, a former prime minister and a senator affiliated with the politically moderate Gauche Démocratique, had followed the government to Bordeaux and then Vichy. His personal account describes spontaneous reactions of republican defense:

44. Bardoux, *Journal d'un témoin de la Troisième*, 402.

45. Ramadier, "Vichy (juillet 1940)," notes written in 1941 and published in *Cahiers Paul Ramadier*, no. 1, 49.

46. Blum, *Mémoires*, 72–73.

"Really, in [my] first contacts, I do not recall having met anyone who, at least in the Senate, might have wished this overthrow of regime."[47] His colleague Pichery, who had no group affiliation, was taken aback by the government's proposal to discard the constitutional framework of the Third Republic and exclaimed: "But they are not going to call into question Universal Suffrage!" Paul-Boncour mentions that "all his colleagues who were arriving from their respective province expressed a similar stand to him. . . . All of them seemed very little detached from the concern for individual liberties that would be so little regarded a few days later. They were friends of order, for sure, but certainly not of the 'new order.'"[48] It was the same republican spirit which motivated the conservative Jean Jacquy, the Radical André Maroselli, the Socialist Louis Noguères, and his colleague in the Senate, Georges Pézières, when before leaving for Vichy on 3 July they all agreed that everything had to be done to prevent the regime from being handed over to a "dictator."[49]

Ramadier, Blum, Paul-Boncour, Noguères: theirs are testimonies by parliamentarians who in the end decided to vote against the bill. Being inclined to vote against the power transfer, they may have also have been inclined to overestimate the extent and intensity of their peers' initial willingness to resist. Strikingly, accounts from parliamentarians who ended up in the "yes" camp convey observations that are congruent with those I have just cited. After he heard Laval bluntly asserting his political agenda on 4 July (see chapter 4), Taurines decided to draft a motion asking for guarantees about the devolution of constitutional powers, and to submit this motion to senators who like him were ex-servicemen.[50] Significantly, those whom he convened for this purpose on 6 July—about forty senators attended the meeting—unanimously endorsed his proposal.[51]

Consider also the initial reaction of Pierre-Étienne Flandin, the leader of the conservative Alliance Démocratique. Flandin arrived in Vichy late on 6 July. The next day, around 4:30 P.M. in an informal meeting before a large audience—parliamentarians kept arriving in Vichy—Flandin criticized the government's lack of efforts to counter the propaganda of the Germans.[52] He questioned the appropriateness of a meeting of the National Assembly, suggesting that there were tasks more urgent than revising the Constitution: "Change the Constitution? . . . But why? What need is there to change institu-

47. Paul-Boncour, *Entre deux guerres*, 253.
48. Ibid., 252–53.
49. Louis Noguères's diary, *Événements* VII, 2228.
50. *Événements* VIII, 2330.
51. Ibid., 2333; Paul-Boncour, *Entre deux guerres*, 260–61.
52. Louis Noguères's diary, *Événements* VII, 2236.

tions which we may be blamed above all for not having respected?"[53] Noguères, who attended the meeting, noted in his journal: "I looked at the audience at this very moment. It was obvious that the vast majority of the deputies present was taking sides with Pierre-Étienne Flandin. Besides, their applause bore witness to their support."[54]

Flandin was obviously not isolated among his peers. His defiance toward Laval's bill spontaneously elicited approval. The important point is that many of his colleagues on the Right at first shared the same inclination. The conservative Piétri, who belonged to the same party as Flandin (the Alliance Démocratique), originally wanted to oppose a constitutional revision.[55] Upon his arrival in Vichy the conservative deputy Marcel Héraut (Républicain Indépendant) told his friends that he wanted to intervene to safeguard the Republic (Calef 1988, 277).[56] In the "information meeting," which gathered around eighty deputies, Héraud called into question both the right of the government to modify the constitution by decree and the appropriateness of such an action (Beau de Loménie 1951, 372; Calef 1988, 85).

A group of representatives from Brittany who had traveled together directly therefrom arrived in Vichy on the morning of 8 July. Several independent testimonies describe their initial resoluteness to thwart passage of the bill. Blum describes them as "revolted" by the provisions of the armistice and the plans of Laval's and Pétain's government.[57] The Socialist deputy Noguères mentions these "newcomers" in his diary under the date of 8 July and notes that they were not willing to let themselves be "guillotined by persuasion."[58] The conservative deputy Becquart (Fédération Républicaine) remarked that they "arrived so exasperated by the capitulation and the insulting charges that Laval was starting to bring against Great Britain that we believed for a while that they were going *to crystallize the latent opposition*" (my italics).[59]

Although he did not attend the "information meeting" between Laval and deputies on 8 July, in his diary the conservative senator Bardoux refers to the hostility aroused by Laval's policy statements: "Monday, 8 July (Vichy) . . . Laval had spoken before the Chamber [of Deputies], during a private session and had received a cool reception. The bluntness of his statements: 'France

53. Ibid. See note 48 in chapter 3.
54. Louis Noguères's diary, *Événements* VII, 2237.
55. "When at the beginning of July I learnt that the Marshal government, at Laval's instigation, convened Parliament in Vichy for a constitutional reform, my first reaction was to oppose it." Piétri, *Mes années d'Espagne*, 16.
56. Calef refers to the minutes of the trial of Flandin: Archives Nationales, WIII 174, 175.
57. Blum, *Mémoires*, 83.
58. Louis Noguères's diary, *Événements* VII, 2239.
59. Becquart, *Au temps du silence*, 169.

now must align itself with totalitarian countries; we must implement a totalitarian regime French style'; the brutality of his charges against England and his mentioning of his quarrels with London created an uproar."[60] The observations in the diary of Laurent Bonnevay, a conservative deputy from the Democratic Alliance who attended the meeting, confirms this report: "Laval makes a speech against the war, which was declared in spite of himself, against the English, and against parliament. Deep stir [in the audience]. Open threats that force might be used. Many react."[61]

Diffuse Republicanism

These reactions are consistent with actors' perception of the republicanism of their peers. Take for instance the appraisal of Jules Jeanneney, the chairman of the Senate. On 4 July Jeanneney wrote in his diary: "There is no lack of democrats in the Senate, who remain faithful to republican and parliamentary institutions. . . . It is even probably the case of the great majority."[62] When Boivin-Champeaux, on behalf of the Legislative Commission of the Senate, stated before his peers on 9 July that the "Republic [was] dying less by reason of its own imperfections than by the faults of the men who were charged with assuring its functioning," one could feel, Louis Noguères observed, that "he was reflecting, by his cautious words, the thought of the whole Assembly."[63] These different accounts are consistent with Blum's perception of the vote: "By their votes, the republican assemblies were . . . going to draw up and sign the Republic's death certificate. The men who were going to perpetrate this were nonetheless, for the great majority (*en très grande majorité*), republicans."[64]

60. Bardoux, *Journal d'un témoin de la Troisième*, 400.

61. Archives Départementales du Rhône, Lyon, Archives Laurent Bonnevay, 10 J 20, diary, handwritten notes, "L'Assemblée Nationale du 10 juillet 1940." See also Becquart's account: "Laval's speech on July 8 was very coldly received. Applause was rare. He was interrupted several times by mutterings, in particular when he attacked England" (Becquart, *Au temps du silence*, 174).

62. Jeanneney, *Journal politique*, 88. Jeanneney himself professed to be "more than ever hostile to [Laval's] initiative." He did "not conceal his hostility" (88). Albert Lebrun, the president of the Republic, remarked on the following day that "there [were] a certain number of parliamentarians independent enough to display their discontent in their conversations at restaurants or in corridors" (Lebrun, *Témoignage*, 104). Paul-Boncour observes that among the 569 parliamentarians who in eight days were led to vote the suppression of the Republic, no more than fifty had this intention nor were even resigned to it when they arrived (Paul-Boncour, *Entre Deux Guerres*, 254).

63. Louis Noguère's diary, *Événements* VII, 2244.

64. Blum, *Mémoires*, 90–91. See also the following statement: "Most of the cabinet members, on behalf of whom Laval, from time to time, pretended to speak, were undoubtedly republican"

It is this assumption of republicanism which explains expressions of disbelief at the outcome of the vote. "Thursday, 11 July. . . . This vote stupefies us. All the colleagues whom I meet are, like me, hostile to the passing of the bill. What happened exactly? How come that only eighty parliamentarians voted against the bill? Which pressure was exercised? For sure, many senators and deputies must have voted for the bill while remaining secretly committed to the Republic. My friends and I cannot believe that so many may have made a mistake. We read and read again the bill which was passed."[65] Thus, for the Radical senator Tony-Révillon and his colleagues, the outcome of the vote was incomprehensible. Along with twenty-six other parliamentarians, Tony-Révillon had embarked on the steamer *Massilia*, which left Verdon (near Bordeaux) on 21 June for Algiers, at a time when the Pétain government was considering leaving metropolitan France. Upon their arrival these parliamentarians were placed under house arrest, and despite their protestations were prevented from sailing back to metropolitan France to partake in the Vichy meetings.

The same assumption of republicanism underlies the astonishment of the far-right deputy Henri Becquart (Fédération Républicaine) at the Radical parliamentarians' vote. Among all the political parties the Radical party had identified itself most closely with the Third Republic. Yet almost all its representatives voted "yes" to Laval's bill.[66] The long republican tradition of the Radical party led Becquart to believe that a majority of its members would have rejected the power transfer. In his memoirs the centrist deputy Pomaret makes similar observations: "Among the 'Yes' one finds old intransigent republicans: Schrameck, Hippolyte Ducos, Bédouce, Maupoil, Maroselli, Fourment, Hubert Rouger, William-Bertrand, Aimé Bertrand [sic], William Thorp, and also Bounin, . . . and also Michard-Pélissier. And Joseph Caillaux who, nonetheless, . . . invited senator Pierre Chaumié, who was asking for his advice, to vote 'against.'"[67]

("La plupart des membres du Cabinet, au nom duquel Laval se donnait, de temps en temps, l'air de parler, étaient sans nul doute des Républicains"). Blum, *Mémoires*, 90–91.

65. Tony-Révillon, *Mes carnets*, 116–17.

66. "How can we not be dumbfounded when we observe that among the 113 deputies affiliated with the *Radical* delegation in the Chamber, only 13 voted against the [government] proposal and 3 asserted their abstention?" (Becquart, *Au temps du silence*, 255). But Becquart also notes that the conservatives—those whom he called the *modérés*—did not vehemently express their opposition to Laval's bill. He explains this lack of overt opposition to their ambivalence vis-à-vis republican institutions. Becquart, *Au temps du silence*, 255.

67. Pomaret, *Le dernier témoin*, 281–83. Pomaret mistakenly hyphens William Bertrand and confuses the last name of the Radical senator Aimé Berthod.

Massive Assent or Collective Resignation?

Can we reconcile these observations with the suggestion by Paxton (1972, 31–32) and Azéma (1984, 52) that French parliamentarians widely consented to Laval's bill? The minutes of the parliamentary sessions are silent about numbers. Mention is only made that several members of the Assembly shouted "Let us vote!" (*Aux voix! Aux voix!*) to prevent any debate. Several testimonies, on the other hand, provide numerical estimates. The far-right deputy Becquart speaks of a "bunch of bawlers" (*une bande de braillards*) who were taking the decisions and to whom Laval's agents were giving the pitch. "The others, help-less, desperate, and disgusted were witnessing the collapse of the regime."[68] Blum mentions "around one hundred henchmen, well disciplined and well supervised, [who] formed small groups which occupied dominant positions as the claque in a theatre orchestra, and their hoots stifled in advance any opposition attempt."[69]

Further, the notion of assent imperfectly highlights the motivations at work. On this point Becquart's testimony is again worth close attention, for it points to more complex motivations than a political reading of the event would suggest. Becquart was willing to vote for the bill, and was planning to explain his vote during the discussion which was supposed to precede the vote. To this effect he had prepared a short draft which outlined the main reasons for his vote. With his "yes" vote, Becquart had planned to say, he "remained faithful to his past." He had not awaited the defeat to proclaim the need to deeply reform political institutions that had strongly contributed to the moral degeneration observed in the country, which was an essential cause of the defeat.[70]

The significant point is that even for a far-right deputy such as Becquart who was obviously in favor of more authoritarian institutions, the dominant feeling was one of extreme ambivalence. In his memoirs Becquart does not

68. Becquart, *Au temps du silence*, 243.

69. Blum, *Mémoires*, 87. See also Becquart's account of the close of the July 10 meeting: [several parliamentarians] insisted to be heard, but they soon realized that it was a waste of effort. ... M. Jeanneney [the Chairman of the Senate and of the National Assembly session] could have suspended the session. He realized that the tumult was not due to nervousness caused by an incident, but to a premeditated decision taken by an important minority. ... Resigned, [Jeanneney] consulted the Assembly about the wish to suppress the general discussion [before the vote is taken]. A *few hands* stood up, the other ones stayed still, indicating thereby the disgust with which most of the audience was filled ... M. Jeanneney at least hoped that [the Assembly] would agree to hear a few explanations of vote. ... Yet, the bunch of bawlers refused to satisfy this wish. The racket grew stronger. ... It is in this way that the Assembly, dominated by a minority well organized, acquiesced to a measure [the suppression of deliberation] which conflicted with all regulations, and with justice" (Becquart, *Au temps du silence*, 250–51).

70. Becquart, *Au temps du silence*, 291.

hide the "disgust" and "despair" which the spectacle of the Assembly elicited in him.[71] "I did not expect that this change of regime, which for so long I had been calling for, would take place in cries."[72] This ambivalence, this consent mingled with "disgust" and "despair," can only be understood in light of Becquart's awareness of how the future might look. Becquart disliked the institutions of the Third Republic. He wanted to get rid of them, as he acknowledges in his memoirs. But he did not want and could not want a regime aligned with Germany. Yet Laval's public statements had made clear that such a regime was on the agenda. Hence the dilemma in which Becquart was caught, and the half-heartedness of his consent.

Equally interesting are the testimonies which point to a pervasive feeling of bad conscience among those who voted "yes." On 11 July, the day after the vote, the Socialist deputy Noguères encountered several senators in the Hotel of Ambassadors and observed: "[They] had not slept like myself for almost all had voted for the Government's bill and they had done so half-heartedly (la mort dans l'âme). As early as the previous evening, Pézières [Noguères's colleague from the Socialist party] had noticed like myself that his colleagues did not have the peace of mind we had."[73] The conservative senator Bardoux, who voted "yes," also acknowledged a feeling of regret: "[Immediately after the vote] I meet on the terrace my two Socialist colleagues, Paulin and Andraud, who voted like P. E. Flandin and myself, and who share our sadness."[74] Four weeks later, in a letter to Laval, the Radical deputy Léon Castel described the Assembly as stricken "with considerable grief" (la mort dans l'âme).[75] Sadness,

71. Ibid., 243.

72. Ibid.

73. Louis Noguères's journal, Événements VII, 2256. In a book published in 1941, Anatole de Monzie, member of the centrist Union Socialiste Républicaine and former minister of public works in the Daladier and Reynaud cabinets (August 1938–June 1940), notes regarding his colleagues of the Lot département: "they all voted for the bill removing constitutional authority from parliament. They are not very proud of their vote" (De Monzie, Ci-devant, 262). Speaking about the National Assembly as a whole, de Monzie has this remark: "Never in a French Assembly was there less enthusiasm than in this meeting in Vichy." De Monzie, Ci-devant, 259.

74. Bardoux, Journal d'un témoin de la Troisième, 405. The Socialist deputy Maurice Voirin mentions a vote "with regret" (Archives de la ville de Paris, Paris, Archives Raymond-Laurent, letter by Maurice Voirin to Paul-Boncour, 10 November 1944, D 51 Z 72). In April 1942 Flandin evokes the "disgust" felt in Vichy. Bibliothèque Nationale, Paris, Archives Flandin, Don 31357, box 127, interview with Roger Stéphane.

75. "I am one of the rare parliamentarians who, without balking and with conviction voted the motion which you shrewdly got passed by an Assembly that, for multiple reasons, passed it with considerable grief." Archives départementales de l'Aude, Carcassonne, letter by Léon Castel to Laval, 13 August 1940, M W 3916. Laurent Bonnevay, deputy of Alliance, describes the evolution of his colleagues' state of mind after 8 July: "Many who were clearly hostile [to Laval's plans] became subdued the next day and favorable to it with deep grief ("la mort dans l'âme")

ambivalence, a lack of peace of mind: in acknowledging these feelings, parliamentarians were acknowledging a choice at odds with their political preferences.[76]

Part of the problem is that the picture we get of the modal preference depends on the point in time to which we refer. On 4 July befuddlement prevailed among those who heard Laval announcing political alignment with Germany. Four days later, on 8 July, the republican consciousness was gaining ground. Then, on 10 July, assent was massive. If we take 10 July as the referential point, the dominant picture is that of a rush toward subservience with no serious opposition. This is Paxton's account. If we take 4 and 8 July as referential points, the dominant picture is that of parliamentarians who think in republican terms and are taken aback by the political offensive launched by Laval. These different snapshots offer contradictory representations only if one collapses the time frame into a single unit of time. On 8 July a collective feeling of republican defense emerged in reaction to the prospect of an authoritarian regime. On the afternoon of 10 July assent to Laval's demands was massive, even though it was more resigned and equivocal than Paxton seems to acknowledge. The real issue is the shift from one to the other, and the emergence of a collective stance characterized by consent and ambivalence.

The Issue of Peace

Adamant appeasers were among the fiercest supporters of Laval's bill. This observation applies in the first place to the members of the Committee against War which had formed in August 1939.[77] It also applies to the Socialists, who until September 1939 had been among the most vocal proponents of compromise with Hitler: Gaston Allemane, Justin Arnol, René Brunet, André Février, Jean-Louis Garchery, Louis L'hévéder, Charles Spinasse, Fernand Roucayrol (Gombin 1970, 249–50; Graham 1994, 225). This observation suggests, as I mentioned earlier, the existence of a strong connection between an adamant pacifist stance in 1938–39 and the endorsement of an authoritarian project

the day after [10 July]." His encounter with the Socialist deputy Charles Baron illustrates this point: "Baron . . . meets me the first day. "How will you be voting?—Against.—Ah, you do me much good. You are a great honest man and I am happy to have had a chance to meet you!" The next day [Baron] avoided me and the day after he voted "yes" (Archives Départementales du Rhône, Lyon, Archives Laurent Bonnevay, 10 J 20, "L'Assemblée Nationale du 10 juillet 1940").

76. In the terminology of Kuran (1996, 154–57), these feelings indicate "moral dissonance": actors realize that their behavior is at odds with their normative commitments.

77. See Becquart's remark about the promoters of the Bergery motion: "with two or three exceptions, the first eighteen names [of the Bergery motion] comprised all the distinguished elements (*fine fleur*) of defeatism and treason." Becquart, *Au temps du silence*, 141.

Table 15 Socialist Deputies Cross-Classified by Their Votes on the Blum and Faure Resolutions at the Montrouge Congress (December 1938) and on the Granting of Special Powers to Marshal Pétain, 10 July 1940

Motions (Montrouge Congress, 1938)	Faure Motion	Blum Motion	No Position	Total
"Yes" vote on 10 July 1940	57	7	23	87
"No" vote	16	10	3	29
Abstentions	2	2	2	6
Present in Vichy but did not vote	0	0	1	1
Total	75	19	29	123[a]

[a] Because of incomplete information figures do not take into account the nine Socialist senators except Dormoy who signed the Blum resolution in December 1938.
Source: Based on Greene (1969, 245–46).

under the sign of a moral renovation. Thus we have to ask: Was support for Laval's bill a fallout of the propensity to view a peaceful compromise with Hitler as a political priority in 1938–40? The correlation is well established for militant pacifists. Is it also significant for rank-and-file parliamentarians?

Since the connection has been made more specifically for the left and the center-left (Jelen 1988, 199–212), my focus will be on the influence of pacifism in the Socialist party and the correlation between the Faurists' involvement for peace and their backing of Laval's bill.[78] To assess this point I rely on the data collected by Greene (1969, 245–46 n. 54) on SFIO deputies' adhesions to Faure's and Blum's motions at the Montrouge Congress in December 1938, two months after ratification of the Munich accord by the Chamber of Deputies. Greene listed deputies who signed one of the motions presented at the Congress and deputies who publicly declared their support for one or the other in local Socialist newspapers. This yields a threefold classification: first, deputies who in December 1938 embraced a strong pacifist stance by endorsing Faure's position on international policy; second, the "Blumists," who rejected a policy of concessions to Hitler; third, the deputies who remained silent and did not take any position (table 15).[79]

If we restrict our attention to the contrast between partisans of Faure's pacifist motion and partisans of Blum's motion for firmness toward Hitler,

78. As I indicated earlier in the chapter, the Faurists were Socialist delegates who supported the positions advocated by the secretary general of the Socialist party, Paul Faure, on foreign issues. I describe the emergence of these controversies within the Socialist party in "The Socialists and War."

79. The odds of voting "yes" for Faure's partisans were 3.56 (57/16) and 0.7 (7/10) for the "Blumists."

Table 16   Pre-war Pacifism and Political Stance in Vichy: The case of the Socialist Deputies (Odds ratios of voting "Yes" on 10 July 1940, $N = 122$)[a]

Motions (Montrouge Congress, 1938)	Faure Motion	Blum Motion	No Position
Faure motion		5.09***	0.46
Blum motion			0.09***

[a] Odds for the row category relative to the column category

* $p < .10$,   ** $p < .05$,   *** $p < .01$.

it appears that those who voted for Faure's motion were five times (5.09) as likely to vote "yes" on 10 July (table 16). This observation is consistent with Sadoun's (1982, 25) contention: there is a positive correlation between endorsing a pacifist stance before the war and voting for the power transfer in July 1940. Conversely, the "Blumists" — who opposed a policy of conciliation and compromise with Hitler before the war — were more likely to turn down Laval's demands.

This contrast becomes less obvious, however, when we take into account parliamentarians who did not take any position in the fall of 1938: for these the odds of voting "yes" on 10 July are twice (1/0.46) as high as the odds for the pacifists (the "Faurists") and eleven times (1/0.09) as high as the odds for the "Blumists" (table 16). The difference between the "Faurists" and the "no position" group contradicts the suggestion that pacifism was the key motivation behind a vote to abdicate in July 1940. There is no statistically significant difference between the "Faurists" and the "no position" group with regard to the odds of voting "yes." Rather, having advocated firmness toward Hitler before the war (the "Blumist" position) provided strong immunization against the temptation of endorsing the power transfer to Pétain in Vichy.

This point is confirmed when we consider whether a deputy's electoral district (département) was occupied by the Germans (table 17). If we take the "no position" group as the reference category, it appears that having been a pacifist — that is, endorsing the Faure motion — in the fall of 1938 has no statistically significant impact on the probability of voting "yes" in Vichy. By contrast, having endorsed Blum's motion substantially increases the probability of voting "no." Bellicosity is a clear factor of resistance relative to a "no position" stance, while pacifism is not a significant factor of abdication relative to the "no position" stance.[80] Also note that military occupation has no statistically

80. This empirical assessment spells out the claim by Wieviorka (2001, 48) that the vote of 10 July does not result from "the adhesion to pacifist theses."

Table 17   Logistic Regression of the Vote on 10 July on Military Occupation and
Motions on Peace and War for Socialist (SFIO) Parliamentarians

	Model 1		Model 2	
	Logistic Coefficient	Exponen-tiated Coefficient	Logistic Coefficient	Exponen-tiated Coefficient
Motions				
Faure, December 1938			−0.32	0.73
			(0.62)	
Blum, December 1938			−2.24**	0.11
			(0.73)	
Military occupation	0.55	1.73	0.57	1.78
	(0.45)		(0.49)	
Constant	0.84***		1.48**	
−2 log likelihood	134.4		120.0	
Improvement χ^2	1.52		14.5***	
d.f.	1		2	
N	118		118	

* $p \leq .10$, ** $p < .05$, *** $p < .01$. Standard deviations are in parentheses.

significant impact on the probability of voting "yes" in July 1940 for Socialist
representatives. This observation is consistent with the conclusions of chapter 3 about the impact of coercion.

Political Opportunity

> We bear a solid grudge against the last years of such insane politics. We have
> no liking for the men who led us to this point, nor for the majority that
> supported and followed them. We heard the creaking of the regime long ago,
> well before 6 February, 1934. We know how urgent reform is, assuming that
> there is still time. But this does not mean that we are predisposed to sacrifice
> the republican formula.
> —Déat, beginning of July 1940[81]

Recall the rationale that could induce an ideological drift from a foreign policy
of appeasement to authoritarianism (Burrin 1986, 267; Jelen 1988): Intransigent pacifists were willing to give Hitler a free hand in the East if that could save
Europe from the prospect of war. Not even the fight against fascism could justify war. Compromising with Hitler implied legitimizing some of his demands

81. Déat, *Mémoires politiques*, 536.

and downplaying the threat represented by fascist regimes. For these intransigent pacifists, the advocates of resistance to Hitler were the main enemy. Anticommunists, on the other hand, wanted peace with Hitler because in their view war served the interests of "subversion," and Nazi Germany formed a rampart against Bolshevism. Between these two strands of pacifism convergence was not obvious except on the issue of anticommunism (Hoffmann 1974, 33).

Consider now Flandin's reaction. Flandin had been one of the most prominent pacifists in the two previous years. His letter of congratulation to Hitler after the Munich accord had elicited an uproar, including among his own party colleagues (the Alliance Démocratique).[82] He had been a member of the Committee of Liaison against War and taken part in the meetings of the committee until the spring of 1940. Yet he initially reacted to the government bill by adopting a strong republican stance. His example, as well as that of Piétri, indicates that there was no necessary ideological connection between a committed pacifist stance in 1938–40 and a rejection of democracy. Blum made the same assumption when he went to the meeting of Socialist parliamentarians on the afternoon of 8 July: he knew that among his Socialist colleagues, some had taken an unconditional pacifist stand before the war. But this did not imply that faced with the government bill they would not react as democrats and republicans.[83]

Equally revealing are the testimonies indicating that parliamentarians who actively supported the government bill improvised their action. In his political memoirs Déat points out that when he initially heard about Bergery's proposal, he was not thinking of getting rid of republican institutions. His priority was to build a political alliance.[84] Vallat explains that in the information meeting between Laval and the deputies on 7 July, when Spinasse implored his fellow parliamentarians to crucify themselves, Vallat responded positively to this call on the spur of the moment.[85] This convergence of views between a Socialist

---

82. "Démissions à l'Alliance Démocratique," Le Populaire, 11 October 1938.

83. "There were in this Assembly men affiliate with very divergent currents of the Socialist thought. I had for long known some of them as pure, absolute pacifists . . . Maybe when they heard the armistice news, their first reaction had been to only take into account its immediate outcome, that is, the end of the battle. . . . Anyway, today, the Socialist and republican consciousness stood up among them as among the others." Blum, A l'échelle humaine, 79.

84. Déat, Mémoires politiques, 536, beginning of July 1940.

85. "[6 July] Spinasse then asks to speak. In a moving improvisation, he asks parliamentarians to bring about their 4 August night [in reference to the night of 4 August 1789, during which delegates to the Estates General abolished feudal privileges] . . . on behalf of my colleagues from the Right, since Louis Marin [the chairman of the far-Right Republican Federation] remained silent, I responded to the call of the Socialist deputy." Vallat, Le nez de Cléopatre, 185–86. See also Vallat, Le grain de sable de Cromwell, 139.

(Spinasse) and a man representing the monarchist far Right was unexpected and struck the minds of those present. Such an alliance, however, was forged on the spot, as a perspicacious observer like Becquart did not fail to observe: "It was only an accidental encounter between pacifist elements and the most reactionary elements.[86]

These few remarks suggest that the different factions who actively supported Laval's and Pétain's bill in Vichy had not planned their alliance in advance. Nor had they already elaborated the ideological agenda that they would outline in Vichy. These different groups realized that the defeat and the armistice provided them with an opportunity to oust their political opponents from the political scene and to boost their own political fortunes. They seized their chance, and as they strove to assert their dominance they simultaneously forged the ideological agenda which provided political meaning to their action. Their political project emerged in the context of both the showdowns immediately before the armistice and the National Assembly meetings.[87]

Undoubtedly some men, chief among them Déat and Bergery, had honed for some time the themes which ideologically framed their political offensive: the critique of political institutions, the call for national unity beyond party

86. Becquart, *Au temps du silence*, 134. A few weeks later, the Socialist deputy L. O. Frossard would theorize this ideological convergence: "The worst mistake . . . was to ignore national realities" (*Le Mot d'Ordre*, 30 August 1940, Archives départementales de la Charente, Angoulème, Archive René Gounin, 22 J 11). These observations undercut a broader claim: there was no intrinsic ideological connection between pacifism and the longing for an authoritarian state. Édouard Depreux observes, for instance, that his friend Augustin Malroux reacted unambiguously to the project of a constitutional devolution independent of his pacifist commitment: "[5 July] Malroux reacted with a spontaneous move that I will never forget: 'There is no issue. I am being asked to choose between the Republic and Fascism. I will choose the Republic. I will vote against Pétain' . . . Malroux was being considered a friend of Paul Faure. He had hoped for peace until the end and was not shameful of this" (Depreux, *Souvenirs d'un militant*, 136).

87. Consider for instance how Bergery describes the situation to Jacques Le Roy Ladurie on 8 July: "This is an opportunity for us to grab. We need to wipe out these lost men." Le Roy Ladurie does not hide his surprise: "How can we explain that this man [Bergery], whom one could have classified as vaguely belonging to the pacifist Left, rallied the new regime right away, he who had never had a profascist activity, far from it!" (Le Roy Ladurie, *Mémoires*, 208). Michèle Cointet (1993, 29) captures this sense of opportunism on the part of Laval when she states: "Laval's personal motivations and pragmatic activism provided the essential impulse to the implementation of institutional structures which he had not anticipated and which he improvised being intoxicated by a power which he wanted to fully take over." From this perspective the "ideological ferment" evoked by Handourtzel and Buffet (1989, 83) regarding these few days in Vichy reflects a sense of opportunity. While they experienced the conjuncture as a formidable occasion to advance their interests and move forward their pawns, the promoters of a "new order" came up with ambitious plans for political reforms.

interests, and the call for a spiritual regeneration. But in the political context of July 1940, these active advocates of a new regime promoting national renaissance under German tutelage elaborated an original synthesis. Burrin (1986, 322) notes for instance that even in January 1940, Déat and Bergery rejected totalitarian regimes and did not condemn democracy. "Déat still perceived the 'state of dynamic inferiority' in which democracies found themselves with regard to totalitarian regimes. But [in January 1940] in the intimacy of his diary, he continued to condemn totalitarianism" (322). This synthesis took shape and crystallized on the occasion of a political gamble.[88] The broad echo received by Vallat's response to Spinasse testifies to this point. The exchange was not premeditated, and it made a sensation because it was politically improbable.

It should also be noted that in July 1940 those fully endorsing the prospect of a constitutional devolution were not *publicly* stating their claims under the heading of a racial conception of national identity. Clearly there were ominous signs that some were harboring a racialist agenda. In his exchange with the members of the National Assembly constitutional commission on 10 July, Laval did not hesitate to play on this theme by alluding to race and religion.[89] Noguères in his diary echoed concerns about the status of Jewish citizens.[90] During a brief encounter, the Radical deputy Jean Mistler proferred anti-Semitic insults at Léon Blum in front of his party colleague Vincent Badie. Badie warned Mistler that such insults were unacceptable.[91]

Yet the Bergery motion—which outlined a policy of collaboration with

88. See the diagnosis offered by Pétrus Faure, a Socialist deputy who abstained on 10 July: "these hatreds, these fears, these jealousies that smouldered in the latent state, joined sides with one another against the Third Republic. Then, the men of Bordeaux and Vichy, realizing that everything was possible, decided that the time of a National Revolution had come." Faure, *Un témoin raconte* . . . , 65.

89. "Compte rendu de la séance tenue par la Commission constitutionnelle de l'Assemblée Nationale, le 10 juillet 1940," *Événements IV*, 501.

90. Noguères, *Vichy, juillet 1940*, 69.

91. Badie, *Vive la République*, 45. This is not an isolated instance. "Laval's friends denounce [the] gang of Jews" (Noguères, *Vichy, juillet 1940*, 104). Pétrus Faure records expressions of anti-Semitism toward Mandel (Pétrus Faure, *Un témoin raconte*, 64). Maurice Martin du Gard witnessed Tixier-Vignancourt verbally abusing Blum. Louis L'hévédher vents anti-Semitic feelings toward Blum before Noguères (Noguères, *Vichy, juillet 1940*, 149). These examples show that some among those who harbored the great resentment toward the "bellicists" did not hesitate to play the tune of rabid anti-Semitism. The point applies in particular to Socialists. "The violence of the conflicts among Socialists gets colored by an anti-Semitism "a priori foreign to the ethical values of the Jacobine Left but which is directed at the person and the entourage of Léon Blum" (Handourtzel and Buffet 1989, 47). As the case of Mistler reveals, Radicals were not immune (Berstein 1978, 301).

Nazi Germany—contained no anti-Semitic charge. Its supporters called for a new political regime in the first place to settle accounts with those who had opposed and marginalized them in the past and whom they castigated as "belliciste." They viewed defeat as a political opportunity to assert their claims to power. Their primary goal was to neutralize their opponents in the political realm. These, not the "Jews," were their target. Their main frame therefore was this: "Those responsible for the disaster should be tried and punished. Parliamentary democracy has been the source of our decadence. Our institutions should be changed. We need *carte blanche*."[92]

The thrust of an explanation in terms of ideological affinities is that conjunctures precipitate latent dispositions. Applied to March 1933, this argument states that German Catholics and their religious and political representatives shared with the Nazis a rejection of Marxism. They were inspired by the same critique of the modern world, the same antiliberalism which nurtured a pervasive antidemocratic ethos. German Catholics had never been fully committed to the republican framework of Weimar. Moreover, they were eager to demonstrate that their nationalist credentials were impeccable. Hitler's challenge, in the context of the national mystique of March 1933, brought these dispositions to the fore. As for July 1940, the ideological affinity argument takes the following form. The defeat precipitated antidemocratic proclivities that had been smoldering for years under the conjoint influence of partisan and class antagonisms; the apparently irresistible rise of totalitarian regimes on the European scene; and the development of a pacifist stance toward Nazi Germany nurtured by anticommunist feelings.

I question this interpretation on two grounds. First, the ideological affinity thesis minimizes in retrospect the political distance between the challenger and the groups that are the target of his challenge. Until March 1933 the Center party defined its political agenda by opposition to reactionary conservatives (the Prussian conservatives) and anti-Christian radicals (the Nazis and the Communists). From a doctrinal viewpoint, the Nazis were anti-Christians, and therefore Catholic representatives opposed Nazism on ideological grounds. No ideological modus vivendi between these two political movements was

92. Marrus and Paxton (1995 [1981]) note that "as late as May 1940 one can find, on a list of sponsors of a committee to defend oppressed Jews, the name of ... Déat" (45). The anti-Semitic repertoire came out into the open later on, most explicitly in the fall of 1940, with the decree of October 1940 distinguishing between Jewish and non-Jewish nationals and excluding those labeled as Jewish from state positions. Along consonant lines, while noting that "racial assumptions had infiltrated mainstream opinion" (110), Jackson (2001) observes that "until the arrival of the Germans in 1940, [the] French racial tradition remained marginal" (109).

possible, since they embodied two opposite worldviews: a Christian ethos on the one hand, a racist and hierarchical conception of human relations on the other. Until 1933 Catholic representatives made this point forcefully.

Regarding July 1940, the key observation concerns French parliamentarians' initial reaction to Laval's plans: they reacted with dismay and indignation to the prospect of a diplomatic and institutional alignment with Nazi Germany. They remained imbued with a republican conception of the state. This point applies to conservatives as well. For them, "the battle against the Popular Front had been won by 1938." They "did not need Hitler" (Jackson 2001, 113). There is no indication that at this juncture mainstream parliamentarians went to Vichy with an anti-Semitic or an anti-foreigner interpretive grid, believing that Jews or foreigners bore the responsibility for national decadence. Nor are there indications that once in Vichy these parliamentarians fall back on a racialist understanding of the nation.

The second point is that an interpretation of the vote in terms of ideological predispositions overlooks the extent to which parliamentarians experienced their choice as an excruciating dilemma. Hesitations, uncertainties, doubts about oneself as well as about others, and a harrowing sense of responsibility were rife. This evidence does not fit the hypothesis of a subterranean determination subverting political conceptions to the point of rendering them ineffective. Furthermore, the ideological affinity thesis misses a significant aspect of the collective decision: the vote crystallized fault lines which emerged in the course of the decision process and which, as a result, only imperfectly overlapped with previous political cleavages.

Obviously, in both March 1933 and July 1940 the parliamentarians' vote would not have been conceivable if parliamentarians, independent of their inclinations, had never thought about the likelihood of an authoritarian alternative—if, in other words, the authoritarian scenario had never been part of their political reflection about the future. Ideology mattered as a condition of possibility: it made the authoritarian scenario politically conceivable and consequently prepared the ground for the possible emergence of this scenario on the scene of history.

The existence of this possibility was only a precondition. As such, it did not yield clear-cut determinations. Both Jackson (2001, 113) and Laborie (2001 [1990], 37) emphasize this point about the Vichy regime: "the idea that there exist elements of continuity in attitudes suggests no fatality and rests on no determinism of some kind . . . The behaviors which the [military] defeat is going to elicit are not the implacable sanction of the preceding moral crisis" (Laborie 2001 [1990], 37). A close examination of the political culture of German Catholics in the 1930s and of the mainstream political parties of the French Third

Republic at the end of the same decade suggests that in times of intense political conflicts, the universe of ideological possibilities is much more extensible, malleable, and indeterminate than a retrospective outlook usually leads us to believe.

The "power" of ideological representations lies in their symbolic function: they provide systems of meaning in light of which actors can make sense of their action. This property of ideology explains why, ex post, we can always reconstruct the actors' reasons for their choice. As they rationalize their decisions, actors produce the meaning of their action. It then becomes tempting for an external observer to interpret the "reasons" that actors provide to themselves in the course of, or subsequent to, their decisions as indicators of latent dispositions that awaited the opportune moment to come to the fore. In this chapter I argued that this assumption about latent dispositions is unwarranted when actors experience their decision as a problem and a dilemma.

PART III

The Terms of the Challenge

These are problematic decisions. The previous chapters discussed why. Actors have information allowing them to assess the challenger's agenda (chapter 4). They have, furthermore, no taste for a regime denying basic individual rights (chapter 5). Nor are they naturally convinced of the need to dismiss themselves as politically irrelevant and, by extension, of the need to legitimize the prospect of arbitrary power. The challenger's reliance on threats of various sorts—some dubious, others credible—confirms the authoritarian substance of his agenda. It also suggests that those subject to the challenge might be unwilling to go along. The challenger would not resort to threats and pressures if these actors were predisposed from the outset to endorse his constitutional claims (chapter 3).

Yet the decision is unanimous or quasi-unanimous. Dissent is minimal. Acquiescence in the challenger's demands takes the guise of an almost uniform stance. Not only do actors abdicate. They display consensus in this endeavor. This uniformity recasts the puzzle and provides us with a lead. It suggests that the explanatory key to the outcome is to be found in the collective dimension of the decision. The focus should be on a collective process of decision making. This requires that we simultaneously pay attention to the parameters of the decision and the collective interactions in the context of which individuals make their decision. How do actors assess the terms of the challenge? How do they relate to this assessment as they interact? This focus leads us away from a broad, synoptic and in the end external appraisal of contextual factors and toward a more fine-grained approach to the mechanics of decision.

Recast in this light, the constitutional abdications of March 1933 and July 1940 can be characterized as instances of collective alignment. Actors made their decision by aligning themselves with one another in their behavioral stance. The task is to figure out how alignment takes place. The next chapter explores three processes: sequential alignment, local knowledge, and tacit coordination. The likelihood of each mechanism is a function of group and situational factors pertaining to the distribution of individual sensitivities to risks, the type of information provided through interpersonal contacts, and the identity of actors who take a public stance.

Chapter 6

Collective Alignment: Three Processes

1

The decision is high risk. Consequences are far-reaching and can be very costly. Violence is a possibility in the showdown. Actors know this. The challenger backs up his demand with threats of retaliation. Turning down his demands entails the possibility of being retaliated against. If the opposition has the upper hand, the challenger will not be able to monopolize state power without resorting to illegal means and, if this strategy elicits further opposition, without resorting to force. If he is granted a constitutional mandate without restrictions, arbitrary power lurks on the horizon. Groups and individuals will lose all protections. Opposition is costly since it opens the possibility of a direct showdown with the challenger. Acquiescence is costly since it means institutionalizing arbitrary power.

This last point brings up a second characteristic: the decision will have consequences for those who make the decision *and* for others, many others. The decision concerns in the first place the polity as a whole, its political institutions, and the rights of its members. Second, the delegates commit their stance vis-à-vis those whom they represent in parliament. At stake in the decision are their political representation and, ultimately, their legal and political capacity to defend the interests of a constituency. Third, isolation is the worst possible outcome. The costs of isolation are psychological (sense of identity, ideological commitment, commitment to a constituency, status among peers) and physical (exposure to the challenger's reprisals in the short and long term).

2

High risks, externalities, and the cost of isolation define an abstract class of decision. The notion of collective alignment is premised on the hypothesis that these three characteristics are a priori relevant. A group of individuals facing the same decision undergoes a collective alignment process if (1) initially this decision is, for these individuals, a source of uncertainty and (2) these individuals overcome their uncertainty by aligning their line of conduct. Alignment refers to a process and an outcome. The scope of the process concerns all those who at first are at a loss to determine their line of conduct and make their action conditional on one another's. Unanimity is the collective outcome sanctioning this process.

Each process of alignment analyzed in this chapter implies a mechanism of decision making. Alignment is sequential when actors first observe how many people around them acquiesce in, or oppose, the threat and then choose the line of conduct which they see fit given this information. Local knowledge prevails when actors assess the group stance on the basis of the private information communicated through interpersonal exchange. Coordination is tacit when actors reach a common understanding of their collective behavior in light of the information indirectly revealed by the prominent actors' public stand. They achieve this common understanding without directly exchanging information about their intentions (Schelling 1980 [1963], 54).

All three processes are interactive, but they involve different types of interactions. In sequential alignment, individuals assess the risks they take in light of the decisions already made by others. The interactive character of the decision-making process is confined to the observation of others' behavior. Each individual's adoption of a behavioral stance is the direct consequence of this observation, not the byproduct of an inference-making process. Local knowledge and tacit coordination, by contrast, imply a process of inference making. When individual actors base their decisions on their local knowledge, they form a belief about the preference distribution in light of the sample provided by their interpersonal contacts. Under this type of alignment, actors communicate information about their preferences through direct, private, and face-to-face interactions. Tacit coordination implies a different process of inference making, based not on private communications but on inferences believed to be commonly shared.

Structural and conjunctural factors condition these three alignment processes. Sequential alignment is possible if two conditions are fulfilled. First, actors publicly reveal their choice once made; and second, the distribution of individual thresholds is such that there is no gap in the disclosure process (Granovetter 1978, 1424). Individuals' reliance on their local knowledge depends on the type of information they exchange through their interpersonal contacts and the extent to which they attribute reliability to this information. The possibility of tacit coordination is a function of the public characteristics of those who take a public stand. Individual actors seek to form beliefs about the group's likely stance that they can reasonably assume to be commonly shared within the group. The plausibility of this assumption depends on the extent to which each one can assume the characteristics of the public speaker to be known by everybody.

3

This chapter builds on the observations provided by the critique of the common sense of subservience. I begin by specifying the decision parameters and examine under which conditions individual actors make their choice conditional on the choice of those facing the same problem. This investigation leads me to consider the factors affecting how individual actors define their reference groups as well as the factors affecting the determination of their propensity for action (individual thresholds). I then discuss the conditions under which sequential alignment is likely to take place. Local knowledge and tacit coordination come to the fore as plausible inference mechanisms when these conditions do not obtain.

Later in the chapter I analyze each inference-making mechanism in turn. The discussion of local knowledge focuses on the type of information being exchanged in private encounters and actors' likely use of this information. The analysis of tacit coordination spells out the cognitive process whereby actors form a representation of the group's stance that they view as commonly shared. The tacit coordination argument implies a distinction between two categories of actors: those who lend themselves to common-belief assumptions about their individual characteristics and those who elude such assumptions. I relate this distinction to differences in public visibility. By exposing themselves to the public gaze of their peers, actors who often take a public stand make their individual and political characteristics known to the other group members. In particular, they disclose the extent to which they value their political commitments. Given this information, these actors enable plausible inferences about their dispositions (or thresholds).

Underlying this argument about tacit coordination is the distinction between prominent actors and the rank and file. Prominent actors are focal points. They draw the attention of everyone, and everyone knows it. The source of this focal-point quality is the public resonance of their statements. People talk about the positions they take. This publicity goes along with the common belief that their statements are a focus of attention. In this conceptual framework prominence is not necessarily tied to actors' intrinsic qualities. Rather, it is a property of the group. Prominent actors are actors whom others acknowledge as focusing their attention for reasons that may well turn out to be extrinsic to their competence or intrinsic qualities.

THE OUTCOMES AT PLAY

Any choice implies the determination of two types of preference: an "action preference" and a preference over outcome (Austen-Smith 1992, 45). First, an individual actor—to simplify language, I will hereafter designate this individual actor by "ego"—has to opt for a behavioral stance. This is concomitant with an action preference. This preference, once enacted, will commit ego from a behavioral standpoint. Second, ego determines his action preference in light of the consequences that he expects from his choice. He makes his decision with an eye on different possible outcomes, and his preference among these outcomes influences the line of conduct that he opts for.

We get a sense of the outcomes implicated by the decision when we ask: Whose interests are at stake? Who is concerned by the decision? Who might be affected? Who has something to lose? The decision has consequences for many "others": the polity, since the decision has constitutional consequences; constituents, since the decision calls into question political representatives' capacity to exercise their representative mandate and by extension their capacity to defend their constituents' interests; and parliamentarians, since the decision puts at stake the collective capacity to devise legal regulations. These are collective outcomes. They pertain to collective goods defined by reference to the interests of a group: the polity, constituents, and parliamentarians.

In addition, ego—the individual voter—is putting his individual welfare at stake. The notion of welfare in the present case encompasses different dimensions that reflect the nature of the challenge and the substance of the decision. Given the element of threat, personal security is an obvious dimension. In opposing the authoritarian challenger, ego is exposing himself to possible retaliations. His security is at stake. If security were the only dimension of his welfare, the choice would be easily settled. But ego is not the only one concerned. The decision is political. Beyond the issue of personal security is the issue of commitments, commitment to others and commitment to one's political convictions.

With the polity outcome, ego puts at stake his political convictions. If he decides to vote against his convictions, he jeopardizes his sense of integrity and if he values this integrity, the cost is considerable. The matter is not simply one of ideological commitment. It is also one of collective rights and welfare. Ego is a political representative. He represents a set of constituents. These are members of the polity. A constitutional blank check puts into question these constituents' collective rights as well as the collective rights of the polity. Finally, through his decision, ego puts at stake his relationship with those whom he views as his peers. If his choice is at odds with theirs, his status becomes problematic. All the more so since the stakes are high. The cost of alienating peers is a positive function of the value vested in affiliating with them. The outcomes for ego are therefore fourfold: personal security, ideological consistency (commitment to one's ideological convictions), political consistency (commitment to others), and status among peers.

Preference Order

Each class of events, i.e. each type of outcomes, elicits a preference order. If ego values individual and collective rights he ranks a regime securing these rights above the prospect of arbitrary power. If he values representative institutions, he prefers institutional arrangements that contribute to the permanence of these institutions over arrangements that call them into question. If he values his status among those whom he defines as a reference group, ego prefers an outcome that puts his choice on a par with this reference group's to an outcome that isolates him. The group's decision determines ex post whether he made a mistake or not. And if he values his physical welfare, he prefers an outcome that shields him from direct threats to an outcome that exposes him.

A preference over a possible state of the world in turn implies an action preference — the choice of the line of conduct that ego deems the most appropriate to achieve his preferred outcome. Through his action preference, ego takes a behavioral stance. When the outcomes at stake are the welfare of the polity, the welfare of one's constituents, and the possibility of political representation, opposition prevails. When ego is considering his security, acquiescence prevails since acquiescing fends off immediate threats.

Kaas's presentation of the decision problem before the center delegates on 23 March (morning meeting) lays bare in exemplary fashion this preference structure and the behavioral dilemma that it reveals. Kaas frames the choice as one between two sets of negative consequences. He acknowledges the necessity to "save one's soul." In the present case, saving one's soul means reasserting the Center's political values. The prospect of Hitler's rule is a dreadful one. Endorsing the transfer of constitutional power to Hitler goes against the Center's political ethos. In both respects the adequate behavioral choice is an oppositional stance.

"But," opposition implies "unpleasant consequences." Kaas makes this point right after having stated the necessity to "save one's soul." He remains vague about these "consequences." They could mean a dramatic depletion of the Center's political capacity if the party is repressed. They could also mean a threat to the delegates' personal security. That he is remaining vague can be interpreted as an indication that he is alluding to security rather than political capacity. The notion of "unpleasant" is out of context if the issue is political. Brüning responds to Kaas by denying that security is the key issue, as if interpreting for all those present the claim that Kaas had made implicitly. If so, Kaas's reference to "unpleasant consequences" — "unpleasant" is a euphemism for "dreadful" — implies that with regard to the individual welfare outcome, it is preferable to acquiesce. This assessment of the situation simultaneously points to two conflicting action preferences. Hence "the difficult position in which the Center delegation finds itself."[1]

Nested Games

I sum up these observations as follows. The individual actor's primary confrontation is with the challenger (chapter 2). In choosing between acquiescence and opposition, ego is taking a stand toward the challenger. This game commits his responsibility as a decision maker. Subsumed to this confrontation is another type of game with those who will have to bear the consequences of the decision: (1) parliamentary peers, (2) constituents, and (3) the polity. Ego affects them through his choice. In accordance with the terminology used in chapter 2, I call these groups "target groups." Conversely, through their collective decision — will they acquiesce or oppose? — these groups affect the way ego is affected by his own decision regarding his welfare, his ability to claim a representative mandate, as well as his political commitments.

The group offers a shield against the challenger's retaliation in the case of opposition and against the charge of political renunciation in the case of acquiescence if the group itself acquiesces. For the individual actor, these three games represent degrees of isolation. Isolation is greatest when none of the target groups backs up the actor's stance. In the terminology of Tsebelis (1990, 10): these three games are nested in the game with the challenger. The nested structure is replicated among the three games with target groups. Groups that have the broadest base mediate the impact of "smaller" ones. Thus the game with the polity is nested in the game with constituents and in the game with parliamentary peers. The game with constituents in turn is nested in the game with parliamentary peers (figure 4). The larger the target group, the more substantial the shield.

If this last observation makes intuitive sense, it may not adequately describe how individual actors experience the terms of the challenger. The assumption

---

1. "Im Anschluß weist Dr. Kaas auf die schwierige Stellung der Fraktion im gegenwärtigen Augenblick hin." *Protokolle*, 23 March, parliamentary delegation, morning meeting, no. 750, 630.

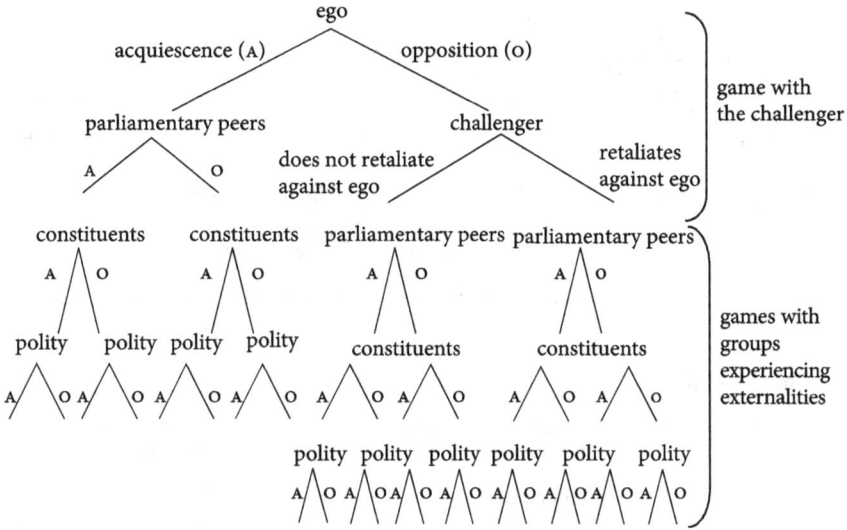

Figure 4   Nested games

that ego *simultaneously* takes into account these different nested relationships and the parameters that go along with them (as figure 4 implies) is cognitively implausible. The hierarchical representation is too complex to allow a simultaneous treatment of the information. Rather, it is more plausible to argue that ego serially addresses these multiple games, successively defining as the nested game the game with the polity, the game with constituents, and the game with parliamentary peers. According to this argument, the adequate graphical representation is a two-level nested game: the game with the challenger and the game with a collective referent—the polity, constituents, and parliamentary peers (figure 5). This point immediately raises the question of the factors determining the choice of a collective referent. I postpone this discussion to the analysis of the notion of reference group.

ACTION THRESHOLDS AND REFERENCE GROUP

In this decisional setting, because the challenge involves not one but multiple actors, payoffs are collectively determined. The decision made by each individual actor affects the welfare of the other target actors. Conversely, for each individual actor payoffs are determined by the other group members' behavioral stance. Isolation carries a cost. The expected cost of opposing the challenger is a function of the size of the opposition. If ego opposes the challenger when everyone else acquiesces, he obviously exposes himself to measures of

ego

acquiescence   opposition

collective referent   challenger

acquiesces   opposes   retaliation   no retaliation

game with
the challenger

collective referent   collective referent

acquiesces   opposes   acquiesces   opposes

game with
the group

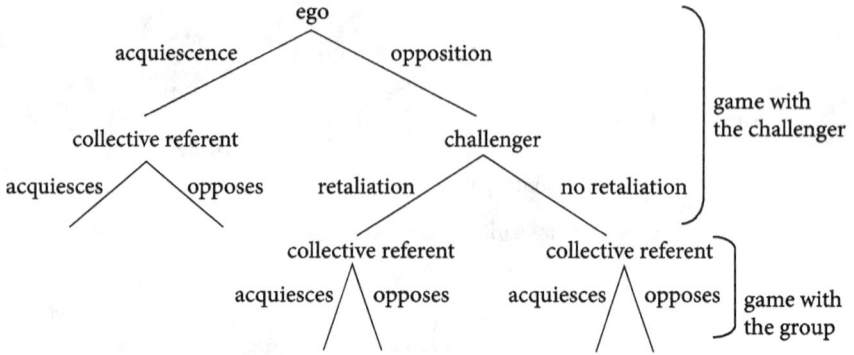

Significance of the outcome for ego:

collective abdication	defection	isolated opposition	collective opposition	isolated opposition	collective opposition

Figure 5   Nested games: generic version

retaliation by the challenger. Isolated opposition is more costly than collective opposition. The risk of having to bear the full cost of repression becomes greater. Similarly, the expected cost of reneging on one's political commitment is a function of the proportion of target actors who renege on their commitment as well. An actor who acquiesces when everyone else opposes becomes a traitor. Abdicating when everyone acquiesces mitigates the cost of reneging on one's commitment.

Ego's expected cost of opposition decreases with the proportion of the target group choosing opposition. His expected cost of acquiescence decreases with the proportion of the target group choosing acquiescence. This interdependence makes the sharing of risks possible and highlights by extension the risks attached to isolation. This point can be recast in terms of individual thresholds—the individual propensities to choose one course of action depending on the number or proportion of those opting for this line of conduct (Granovetter 1978, 1422; Schelling 1972, 160). If defined as a group proportion, this action threshold is between 0 and 1. Ego experiences his decision as a problem if he has a threshold strictly between 0 and 1 and if he does not have perfect information about the group stance (see appendix B).

The Case of Autonomy

The correlate of this analysis is that the values of the decision parameters may be such that ego does not make his action conditional on the choice of those facing the same decision (appendix B). Two cases are possible: (1) Opposition is the dominant option independent of the other group members' choices. The value imputed to the preferred outcome outweighs any other cost consideration. (2) Acquiescence is the dominant option independent of the other group members' choices.

In both cases the choice is unproblematic. Ego acts autonomously without consideration of the group's stance. He makes a choice consistent with his preferred outcome independently of what the other group members do. The benefits and costs of his choice may vary with the proportion of group members who make the same decision. This variation does not, however, affect his utility to the point of making his choice conditional on the choice of the other group members. Ego's threshold therefore is either equal to 0 or 1 or has a value beyond the range of possible values, that is, he would modify his behavior only if the proportion of the group choosing the alternative option reached a point beyond 1 (see appendix B). As terminological shorthand I characterize this type of threshold — outside the]0,1[range — as *absolute* in contrast to the *relative threshold* of actors who make their choice conditional on the collective behavior of the group.

The following remarks by the Socialist senator Georges Pézières to Louis Noguères, a Socialist deputy, illustrate the relevance of this distinction. Noguères narrates this episode in his diary. The exchange takes place on the morning of 10 July before the National Assembly meets in a session closed to the public. "At 8:00 A.M., I was in Pézières' room for a last meeting. Pézières . . . was absolutely convinced that the government's bill would pass without serious opposition, for the senators were falling back. When I asked him: 'And Maroselli?,' he answered: 'Like the others! As for Jacquy, nothing to expect from him . . . 'And Sénès?' — 'Sénès will vote against, whatever happens.' . . . Pézières asked me what Rous and Delcos would do. I told him that I was certain that the former would vote 'No.' As for the latter, he did not disguise his intention to vote 'No,' but I could not have an absolute certitude. I thought nonetheless that he would vote 'No.'"[2]

In Pézières's short survey of attitudes and dispositions, most actors — the senators in general, Maroselli, Jacquy — are making their choice conditional on the stance of their peers. Their opposition threshold is relative. By contrast, "Sénès will vote against, whatever happens." His opposition threshold is absolute. Noguères replicates this distinction when he discusses the probable attitude of two other colleagues, Rous and Delcos. Interestingly, at one point in the discussion Pézières, who clearly expressed his belief that the majority would pass Laval's bill, seems to waver: "Pézières . . . raised an objection. 'We

2. Louis Noguères's diary, *Événements* VII, 2248.

should not take the risk of looking like fools! Imagine that we end up being a dozen to cast a 'no' vote!"[3] In other words, Pézières is willing to oppose Laval, but up to a certain point. If the group of the "no" voters is about a dozen, taking an oppositional stance seems absurd to him. Recast in the language of action thresholds, Pézières is revealing to his party colleague that although his abdication threshold is very high—he will not endorse the power transfer unless 98 percent (658/670) of the delegates acquiesce—this threshold remains nonetheless relative.

Thresholds, Absolute and Relative

The distinction between absolute and relative thresholds is informative in three respects. First, it recasts the distinction between autonomy and heteronomy. An actor who behaves autonomously—without reference to others' action—is an actor with an absolute behavioral threshold. The stance taken by those he defines as peers does not condition his decision. Heteronomy is the behavioral translation of a relative threshold. Second, the notion of absolute threshold invites us to consider the "strength" of the subjective orientation underlying a choice disposition. The value of an absolute threshold is a measure of the "strength" of autonomy, the limit case being an infinite value. By extension, this value sheds light on the likelihood that an actor might shift to a heteronomous mode of decision. The greater the distance from 0 or 1, the lower the likelihood that changes in the decision parameters might affect the decision mode.

Third, and complementary with the point I have just made, this analytical distinction underlines that decision modes (heteronomy versus autonomy) are less individual features than interaction effects of individual and situational characteristics. This observation goes back to a point made by Granovetter (1978, 1436) about the context dependency of individual thresholds. Individuals vary with regard to their risk sensitivity and the extent to which they value their commitments. This value is correlated with actors' self-definition and their identification with peers. An individual threshold is a synthetic measure of these idiosyncratic propensities and social characteristics. These, however, are actualized in specific contexts. Individuals' level of risk sensitivity for instance is context dependent. Thresholds are therefore situation relative. They vary with the situation at play.

Hence thresholds can be relative or absolute depending on the conjuncture. The distinction between absolute and relative thresholds draws attention to the factors affecting the shift from one to the other. An individual threshold may

3. Noguères's diary, *Événements* VII, 2248.

become relative because a change in the value of a situational parameter substantially shifts expected utilities. For instance, an increase in the expected cost of being retaliated against decreases the utility of opposition. It consequently lowers the value of the point at which the utility functions of opposition and acquiescence intersect. Ego initially may have opted for an oppositional stance irrespective of his peers' stance. If the prospect of repression becomes more tangible or threatening, he may decide to relate his action to that of his peers. The distinction between absolute and relative thresholds and the claim about their context dependency are complementary. To say that thresholds are situation relative is to say that an absolute threshold may become relative in some situations and vice versa.

Reference Group

Implied by the notion of threshold is the notion of reference group (Petersen 2001, 23). By relating his decision to others, ego takes these others as referent. An actor's reference group is the collective of individuals with whom this actor identifies for the specific problem he has to face. This relation to others can be addressed from two complementary standpoints along the lines suggested by Merton (1968). First, a reference group provides a basis for comparison (Merton 1968, 285). Its phenomenological relevance is mediated by ego's relation to his own welfare. In the present case, for the type of decisions we are considering, the reference group is the collection of individuals that ego takes as a reference for assessing the risks entailed by his behavioral choices.

Beyond the issue of welfare is the question of how ego frames the situation. A reference group provides a "frame of reference" (Merton 1968, 284), a "point of reference for shaping one's attitudes, evaluations and behaviors" (287). From this perspective, the reference group is the collective entity onto which ego projects a definition of the situation. Ego takes as a reference actors whom he also identifies as peers. Reference groups can be grounded in interpersonal relations or in imagined relations—relations based on an imagined affiliation. In the first case, "individuals take as a basis for self-reference the situation of people with whom they are in direct relation" (286). In the second, the "assumed frame of reference is yielded by social categories" (286). The individual affiliates himself to others with whom he is not in direct relation.

Collective referents can be more or less abstract. This point is particularly relevant in the present case. The decision has externalities of different kinds. Each type of outcome defines a possible collective referent for ego: the polity, constituents, and parliamentary peers. These entities have varying degrees of abstraction. The polity is the most abstract entity. We can only "imagine" the polity in the same way we "imagine" the nation (Anderson 1991, 6). We cannot properly represent it. The polity encompasses all those whose existence is amenable to the system of rights and institutions regulating political interactions. Parliamentary peers, on the other hand, are identifiable. This group has a very concrete existence. Ego knows who they are. He can relate to them. They face the same challenge and are exposed to the same risks. This point about abstraction relates to a question I left pending: if different collective referents are possible, which one does ego define as his primary reference group?

The decision is risky, which means that ego is interested in assessing the potential cost of his decision. If isolation carries a high cost, ego is primarily concerned with getting concrete information regarding the prospect of his isolation. If the group is diffuse and abstract, this endeavor is abstract and very uncertain. If the group is bounded and identifiable, the task is more tractable. Ego can hope to garner information that is directly relevant to the issue of his isolation.

This observation underlies a twofold argument. First, the more concrete the target group, the more tangible ego's assessment of the impact of the collective stance on his own welfare. Second, the greater the risks of isolation, the greater the incentives to relate to identifiable peers. In the present case, this argument implies that given the risks attached to isolation, the parliamentarians' primary reference group is their peers in parliament. The group that provides a basis for comparison and a frame of reference is the one that provides the most concrete assessment of isolation. I probe the empirical soundness of this claim for both March 1933 and July 1940 in chapter 7.

The Dilemma of Public Disclosure

If all group members behave autonomously, the collective outcome is the direct translation of independent individual choices. If heteronomy prevails, actors' choices are interdependent. These experience considerable uncertainty about their own choice as long as they do not know how the group is going to behave. Their uncertainty reflects their ignorance. *Uncertainty* here is understood in a phenomenological sense, to indicate a lack of confidence in one's decision, not to indicate the incapacity to assign probabilities to events.[4] To

4. Epstein and Wang (1996, 1344) distinguish between risk, where probabilities (either objective or subjective) are available to guide choice, and uncertainty, where the information is too vague to be summarized adequately by a probability measure. The notion of phenomenological uncertainty, which I use in this analysis, is compatible with the act of assigning probabilities between 0 and 1 to future events, what Epstein and Wang designate as *risk*. As I indicate in

make their decisions, actors need to assess their peers' future choices. The lessons of the past offer one lead.

Assessing the future becomes a problem when the challenge is unprecedented. In the absence of an established script, individuals who make their action conditional on one another's at first are groping in the dark. Explicit communication a priori offers one way out. They know that they face the same decision. They decide to convene. They state their preference and deliberate. Through this deliberation process, they come to an equilibrium state that sustains both their beliefs about one another and the definition of a behavioral stance. They have no reason to revise their expectations about others' future behavior and, by way of consequence, no reason to reconsider their own behavioral stance. As a result (1) beliefs and behavioral stances are tautological, and (2) individuals know how others are going to collectively behave. They hold the same beliefs about their future collective behavior.

Of course target actors need to have the time to deliberate. That is, they need to have the time to reveal their preferences, let others reveal their preferences, and adjust accordingly. Time constraints may prevent explicit coordination. Problematic decisions, high-risk decisions, decisions that affect the welfare of many others and that are high stakes are often made in emergencies. The larger the group, the greater this time constraint. The time required to set up explicit coordination is indexed on group size: the process becomes more arduous and therefore more time consuming as group size increases.

For the class of decisions under consideration, however, time is not the main reason for the lack of explicit coordination. The more formidable obstacles to this process relate to the nature and scope of the risks involved. Taking a public stance is risky. Individual actors have no incentive to publicly disclose their preference if this disclosure entails individual risks. Rather, they have an incentive to wait and see as long as their threshold is not met. This incentive is proportional to the risks at stake in terms of social cost and exposure to reprisal. To deal with the issue of risk, group members can devise an anonymous procedure of preference revelation such as an impersonal ballot. However—and this is the second problematic factor—the preference distribution revealed by this procedure may not reflect the outcome. If ego suspects that some of his peers might reverse their decision—their threshold is not met—and that others in turn could revise their decision as well, his anticipation of

---

appendix B ("Can Local Knowledge Be a Source of Uncertainty?"), this phenomenological meaning can be complemented by a more probabilistic approach that measures the extent to which ego differentiates his beliefs about the future—represented by probabilities about different possible states of the world.

the outcome remains unstable and uncertain. The procedure misses its goal. How in these conditions can individual actors assess the stance of the group?

SEQUENTIAL ALIGNMENT

One possibility is that individual actors make their decision sequentially. Ego observes others taking positions and discloses his decision when the observed proportion of those publicly taking position for one or the other option reaches his threshold. The group achieves a collective stance when everyone has made his decision. The collective stance of the group is the sequential aggregation of individual decisions. This model assumes that each participant (1) has direct and perfect information about the behavior of all other members of the group, and (2) makes his decision sequentially, each one deciding to join in at the point when he observes the number of participants corresponding to his threshold (Granovetter 1978, 1433). In other words, each one reacts "to some aggregate statistic about the distribution of behaviors in the general population" (Young 1988, 2).

A central hypothesis of this model is that group members have different action thresholds. The sequence takes place because actors with lower action thresholds motivate, through their action, the action of individuals with higher thresholds. Threshold heterogeneity reflects the variance of individual parameters. Individual actors differ with regard to their sensitivity to risk and the value they vest in their political commitments. The first analytical advantage of this model is that it accounts for the possibility of a unanimous stance in light of an explicit heterogeneity hypothesis. The second analytical advantage of this model is that it conceptualizes the group stance as the outcome of an interactive process. This interaction is minimal: group members simply observe one another and record one another's stance.

Students of threshold models point out that it is inaccurate to "infer individual dispositions from aggregate outcomes or to assume that behavior is directed by ultimately agreed-upon norms" (Granovetter 1978, 1420). Collective outcomes can be at odds with the "average level of preferences" (Granovetter 1978, 1425). This does not mean that individual actors let themselves be taken away by the mood of the time, the collective effervescence, and the diffusion of an emotional state. The discrepancy between the outcome and the modal preference is the by-product of the threshold distribution. This point complements the previous one. It is because collective outcomes can be at odds with what group members on average would have preferred to do that we cannot infer individual dispositions from the outcome. In the present case this characteristic of the model is illuminating and consistent with the critique of ideological explanations developed in chapter 5. In March 1933 and July 1940 target actors in parliament would have preferred *not* to abdicate their constitutional authority.

The Possibility of a Sequence

The threshold distribution is key to the theoretical possibility of a full-fledged sequence. Group members sequentially align with one another when the proportion of those who made their decision is always high enough to motivate others in the group to make the jump. This requires in particular that some group members either have absolute thresholds or have a threshold low enough that they can easily coordinate their action and be sure that their threshold is met when they make their decision public. Any "gap" in the distribution that would lead some actors to remain uncertain about their behavioral preference is a stumbling block. The sequence resumes only if individuals who at this point are coming close to adopting a behavioral stance, given the proportion of group members who have already committed themselves, coordinate their decision to overcome the gap. The greater the gap, the greater the stumbling block (appendix B, figure 10).

This distribution requirement is a theoretical precondition. It does not imply that if fulfilled, sequential alignment ensues. If individuals do not reveal their choice or if they do not have the time to do so, a sequential process of alignment can easily be jeopardized. This observation suggests two additional requirements. The first is that individuals publicly reveal their decision. There must be some device or procedure motivating them to disclose their behavioral stance. If not, ego interprets the behavioral stance of those who remain silent as a sign of indecision—their threshold has not been met. Their silence precludes others from sequentially aligning. A further requirement is that this disclosure process not be temporally constrained in a way that prevents some group members from revealing their stance.

Imperfect Information and Coordination Dilemma

If one of these conditional factors does not obtain, individuals who did not sequentially align remain stuck with their uncertainty. They still make their choice conditional on their peers. If they do not know how these others are going to behave, they are left with an indeterminate choice. This collective situation can be paradigmatically described as an N-person "coordination game" (Schelling 1980 [1963], 89–99). Actors who make their behavior conditional on one another's and who, as a result, experience behavioral uncertainty have an interest in coordinating their action, that is, in mutually adjusting their decision to one another's. The purpose of coordination is to achieve agreement about what each one will do given everyone else's decision.

Coordination does not mean that everyone has an interest in doing the same thing. It means that all those experiencing the same behavioral uncertainty have an interest in forming mutually consistent beliefs about what everyone will do. Thus coordination does not imply a unanimous outcome. Actors' interest in coordination results from each actor's need to define a line of conduct in light of what others intend to do. This adjustment comes to a halt when no one has an incentive to change his behavioral stance given the intentions of these other actors. In these situations, "singling out a coordination equilibrium is a matter of concordant mutual expectations" (Mackie 1996, 1007). If actors are unable to coordinate, they experience the situation as a source of behavioral uncertainty. The peculiarity of this situation is that these actors want to form convergent beliefs regarding their collective behavior but have no interest in revealing a behavioral preference. If they are unable to explicitly coordinate their behavior, they need to achieve expectation convergence through other means.

It could be, as Chwe (1999, 141–46) has shown, that individuals overcome their uncertainty by acquiring a common knowledge of their thresholds and preferences through informal contacts among themselves. This common knowledge allows them to converge and settle on a collective stance. The problem here is size. As group size increases, the knowledge provided by interpersonal contacts becomes more localized.[5] Common knowledge is possible under specific conditions regarding the group structure and communication flows.[6] If individual actors cannot hope to achieve a common knowledge of their behavioral preferences, they fall back on a process of inference making. They draw inferences about one another as they interact with one another. The type of inferences they draw is a function of the type of interactions at play.

Interactions may be direct, based on interpersonal contacts. Or they may be based on mutual inferences in the absence of direct communication. This distinction points to two possible mechanisms for dealing with the imperfect information problem. Both mechanisms describe a process of belief formation and both depict actors as strategic in their subjective orientations toward others. The first mechanism describes how actors try to resolve their lack of

5. Chwe (1999, 138) constructs his argument about common knowledge as a requisite of collective action by simulating interpersonal contacts in groups of twenty actors.

6. One plausible hypothesis is that the group is segmented into multiple subgroups interconnected through weak ties.

information about the group's future behavior by drawing on the information provided by their interpersonal contacts (their local knowledge). The second describes how group members tacitly coordinate their beliefs about their own collective behaviors in light of the information provided by public events. In the remainder of this chapter I spell out the hypotheses built into these two mechanisms, their empirical validity, and their observable implications.

LOCAL KNOWLEDGE

Local knowledge designates the assessment of a global statistic based on the information provided by ego's local environment — his interpersonal contacts. As they interact with one another, actors exchange information about themselves and others. They construct their assessment of the preference distribution within the group in light of the information thus communicated. In this model collective alignment results from the convergence of individual assessments based on local knowledge. Actors achieve convergence through interpersonal communication. Three processes are involved in this scenario. One is a communication process. Which type of information is being disclosed? The second is a cognitive process of inference making. How do actors use this information to assess the global preference distribution? The third process is interactive. With whom do actors interact?

Interpersonal Communication

In the course of their private interactions, individuals can communicate three types of information relevant to their assessment of the situation and ultimately to their decision. (1) They can communicate their assessment of the preference distribution based on their local knowledge. (2) They can reveal their preference. (3) They can indicate their propensity to choose one option given their assessment of the situation (their individual threshold). In short, actors can provide information about others (global assessment derived from local knowledge) as well as about themselves (threshold and behavioral preference). The communication of two of these pieces of information sheds light on the third. One can infer ego's behavioral preference in light of his assessment and his threshold. Conversely, one can infer how ego minimally assesses the group's future stance in light of his threshold and preference. If for instance Pézières decides to vote "yes," in light of his remarks to Noguères we can conclude that he expects at least 98 percent of his colleagues in the National Assembly to endorse Laval's bill.

Since individuals can exchange three different types of information, it is worth considering to which type of information they give priority and which factors limit or condition the exchange. Between dispositions and behavioral preferences, the priority is clear. Ego is mostly concerned about his peers' future stance. His primary interest is in assessing which choice they are going to make. Dispositions, on the other hand, have only secondary relevance. Hence actors facing the coordination dilemma will try to guess each other's behavioral preference when they discuss their decision face to face. What about the communication of an assessment of the group stance based on local knowledge versus the disclosure of individual preferences? Pieces of information that are the most relevant to them are those that help them form a global picture of the group stance. The more global the information, the greater its strategic relevance. Ultimately this is the information that ego needs to overcome his uncertainty. Therefore he will want to know what the person he interacts with—let us call this person "alter"—knows about the group's future stance.

When individuals, in addition to exchanging information about their individual preferences, also communicate their assessment of the group as a whole, they have to appraise the extent to which their assessments are reliable. Ego may be confronted with two problems. The first is the possibility that alter falsifies the prediction of the group stance to increase the probability that the outcome mirrors the prediction. For instance, alter is defecting to the challenger's side and seeks to diffuse the announcement by suggesting that the group as a whole is in favor of acquiescence. The second problem lies in the possibility that alter misrepresents the preference distribution: his sample is biased.

In any case individuals will not be able to exchange information about the group before they have interacted with other group members and, on this basis, before they have constituted their own assessment of the preference distribution. As long as their local knowledge is elusive, this type of information exchange is precluded. If ego has no sample, how could he pretend to form a mental image of the group? A second consideration further suggests that individuals will not necessarily try to probe each other's assessments of the group stance as they interact face to face. In seeking out information about the group stance, ego discloses his heteronomy in the presence of peers. Unless he knows that those to whom he is speaking have the same concern, he may not want to reveal the conditional character of his choice. Actors who do not want to reveal their heteronomy are more likely to disclose their behavioral preference (assuming that they are willing to do so) than their local knowledge (assuming that they are able to assess the group stance).

Inference

For now I assume that individuals exchange information about their individual preferences as they informally interact. How do actors form a mental image of the group's stance on the basis of this information? Two cognitive scenarios might be considered. In the first, ego projects the sample onto the group, interpreting his distribution of behavioral preferences as a representation *in reductio* of the group. Ego simply extrapolates from the sample to the group. Unless his sample is very large relative to the size of the group, this naïve extrapolation exemplifies an excessive reliance on what Tversky and Kahneman (1982, 11) call the "availability heuristic." When this happens, ego risks generalizing "certain features of his local environment, wrongly believing them to hold in a wider context" (Elster 1983, 144).

In the second mechanism, ego is aware of the imperfect character of the information thus provided. He treats the sample as a sample, keeping in mind that his knowledge remains an imperfect representation of the group. In this second scenario, the constitution of local knowledge goes along with a certain amount of uncertainty. Ego assesses future outcomes as likely outcomes. The smaller the size of the sample relative to the group's, the greater the probability that it might convey an inaccurate representation of the group. Consequently, ego is less likely to interpret this information at face value and use it as a template of the global distribution.

For some time now, cognitive psychology has drawn our attention to the cognitive biases inherent in different heuristic principles "which reduce the complex tasks of assessing probabilities and predicting values to simpler judgmental operations" (Tversky and Kahneman 1982, 3). Judgments of similarity, for instance, are likely to be insensitive to the size of a sample (Tversky and Kahneman 1982, 5). Accordingly, we cannot a priori dismiss the possibility that individuals interpret the sample literally, as if it were a proxy of the global distribution. For the class of decisions I am discussing, however, I argue that this is the least likely hypothesis.

In experimental situations—which provide the empirical grounding of most of the findings on inferential errors and perception biases—subjects can easily trivialize the stakes. Their welfare is not at stake. They may experience any error as a breach of their self-esteem, but it does not have real consequences. This is a crucial difference with the type of collective decisions I am considering. With these decisions individual actors are crucially aware that their decision does have consequences. This awareness spurs them to correct themselves whenever they can in light of the information available. Hence they are likely to remain aware of the limitations of their sample. To the extent that group members differ with regard to the amount of uncertainty they experience, we should also expect them to differ with regard to their propensity to fall into the fallacy of the local—an undue reliance on the availability heuristic. Similarly, to the extent that situations differ with regard to the amount of behavioral uncertainty they generate, they should also differ in terms of actors' average awareness of the frailty of their local knowledge.

Diffusion

Across time, actors meet more group members and expand the scope of their local knowledge. In the process they converge on a similar assessment of the group. Their local knowledge becomes less and less local and more and more representative of the global distribution of behavioral preferences. The degree to which interpersonal ties are segmented puts limits on this process. If the probability of meeting with another group member is uniform, there is no segmentation. Convergence takes place as group members meet with one another. If, on the other hand, individual actors are embedded in subgroups that operate as informal cliques, their local knowledge is confined to these subgroups. Assessing the group stance requires assessing the stance of each subgroup.

The previous analysis assumes that individuals are able to quench their uncertainty through their local knowledge. This in turn assumes two things. First, individuals reveal their behavioral preferences when they informally interact. They indicate a stance. Ego constitutes his sample by aggregating these pieces of information. Second, the knowledge thus acquired allows ego to make inferences about the group as a whole. Ego appraises that he can reasonably assess the situation and opt for a behavioral stance given the information gathered in the course of these informal contacts. Both assumptions can be questioned.

If uncertainty is widespread, ego is most likely to encounter individuals who, like him, do not know what to think and who, like him, have not made their choice. Why would these actors reveal a behavioral preference? They are at a loss to figure out their line of conduct. The informational content of interpersonal contacts then becomes very thin. Most of those with whom ego interacts do not disclose a behavioral stance for or against acquiescence. Ego then has to decide whether his "sample" is of any use. If he views his local knowledge as being too frail to provide a basis for inference regarding the specific decision at hand, he might then decide to stick to his wait-and-see stance.

Two observations follow. In adopting a wait-and-see mode, ego fosters the indecision of those who interact with him and seek to constitute their local knowledge. Here is a situation in which uncertain group members interacting, by remaining silent about their preference, mutually nurture their uncertainty. This is an alignment process, but one of a special kind. Individuals who go through this process align with one another their indeterminate behavioral stance — wait-and-see. Through their indecision they induce others to remain indecisive as well. What is being diffused through interpersonal contacts is not a representation of the group but a sense of uncertainty.

When, for instance, Jean Froget, a Radical senator, writes to his daughter on 10 July, "What will come out [of the vote]? Opinions are so contrasted that, as far as I am concerned, I have not made up my mind about what to vote yet," he is referring to a process of this kind.[7] Froget is uncertain about his choice because he is uncertain of the collective stance of his peers. René Boudet, a Socialist deputy, offers a consonant description of interpersonal relations: "no sooner had they arrived, [deputies and senators] were dazed by the flow of contradictory news. In these difficult conditions, they had to face the most formidable moral dilemmas and had to make very rapidly grave decisions."[8]

Local knowledge by definition is imperfect. It provides a basis for inference; no more. Ego has to assess the risks he is taking in light of this information. But if this information is too scarce, he may assess the risks to be too high to justify a decision. Consider a situation in which ego informally interacts with ten individuals of whom eight elude the question of their stance, indicating that they are waiting to see how the wind blows before opting for one course of action or another. Ego may ignore these eight undecided individuals and revise his beliefs about the group in light of the information provided by the remaining two. Or he may take into consideration this indecision to appraise the possibility of a scenario at odds with his expectation. In either case he can assess the possible cost of a mistake. As I point out in appendix B, if this cost is too high he will decide to wait and see as well.

Tacit Coordination

The third possible process of alignment takes on its strategic significance in light of these remarks. Like local knowledge, it rests on an inferential mechanism. For lack of a better term, I call this third process tacit coordination. The term does not describe the inference mechanism at work. However, it captures the idea that when group members rely on this inference mechanism, they are aware of a coordination process and of the tacit character of this coordination. Tacit coordination is not an alternative to local knowledge.

7. Quoted by Calef (1988, 432).
8. Archives OURS, Paris, dossier René Boudet.

It can complement or weaken the inference drawn from local knowledge. Its phenomenological force becomes particularly salient when local knowledge is nonexistent or frail.

Awareness and Indecision

Interpersonal interactions are not strategically relevant if people do not disclose their behavioral stance. Ego gets no strategically relevant information about the other group members' behavioral preferences. From this standpoint, interpersonal contacts are a source of incapacity. Ego has too little information to settle his mind on one course of action with some level of confidence. This negative conclusion is, paradoxically, informative. For in the process, ego and his peers have learned that they are experiencing the same uncertainty and that one reason for their uncertainty is their interdependence. The failure of these interactions from a strict behavioral standpoint prepares the ground for a higher-order collective solution. Actors realize that they face the same situation of mutual uncertainty.

Interest in Belief Coordination

Having realized that they experience the same indecision and that this indecision has a common source, actors also become aware of the functional need to devise a collective solution to their dilemma. Their assessment of the situation has therefore two facets. It denotes on the one hand an awareness of collective indecision and on the other hand a realization that they can only get out of this mutual uncertainty if they devise a *collective* solution to this dilemma. Mutual uncertainty highlights one key aspect of this collective experience. Its significance lies in the type of dispositions that it generates. Actors facing mutual uncertainty cannot hope to get away from it without collectively acting upon it. Hence they focus their attention on those who share their dilemma.

To achieve this collective solution, actors need to form mutually consistent beliefs about their own collective behavior, beliefs that if disclosed would give no one an incentive to reconsider his or her line of conduct. In other words, they need to form congruent beliefs about the outcome. This does not mean that target actors seek to coordinate on the same behavioral stance. The threshold distribution may be such that a split vote is an equilibrium, i.e., a situation in which no one has an incentive to change his or her choice given the choice made by the other group members. This means, on the other hand, that actors believe they anticipate the same collective stance.

The Functional Requirement of Common Knowledge

Achieving mutually consistent beliefs about the collective outcome requires some form of coordination. One way to bring about this coordination and to form mutually consistent beliefs is to disclose preferences in the open. I mentioned earlier the factors that make this solution unlikely. If individual actors are extremely reluctant to disclose their behavioral preferences in public, belief coordination can only be tacit, taking place in the absence of explicit communication (Schelling 1980 [1963], 70). This tacit coordination implies an inferential process. Actors need to form beliefs about their peers' beliefs. To do so they rely on inferences which they can reasonably assume to be common beliefs, that is, which they can assume their peers to share as well. Additionally, actors have to rely on pieces of information that are common knowledge, i.e., everyone knows these pieces of information to be known by everybody else (Aumann 1976, 1236; Lewis 1969).[9] Without such pieces of information, the prospect of commonly shared inferences is out of reach.

Tacit Coordination: Two Types

Actors form convergent expectations — convergent from their own subjective point of view — about their future collective stance. How is tacit coordination achieved when explicit communication is obstructed or hushed up? A behavioral script is lacking. Actors seek pieces of information that are common knowledge. A minimal assumption is that they turn their attention to happenings taking place in a public setting in which any happening is common knowledge. A forum is a setting of this kind. Everyone in the forum knows that all those present witness, and therefore become cognizant of, the happening.

How then does a public happening make tacit coordination possible? A public event elicits belief coordination if it provides actors with a piece of information which they deem relevant to their own coordination dilemma and from which they can draw inferences about the behavior of the group as a whole. This is the general claim. Two theoretical scenarios are conceivable. In the first, the happening elicits coordination because actors interpret it as a signal, the significance of which is shared by all group members. The inference is that given this signal, group members will act in a certain way. The happening being the signal, its informational content is the fact of its happening. In the second scenario, actors interpret the happening as disclosing

---

9. I use the term in its game-theory sense as indicating an infinite regress about one's knowledge of others' knowledge and their knowledge of one's knowledge.

strategic information about the distribution of behavioral preferences across group members. The inference is twofold. It concerns the informational content of the happening and the possibility that group members might interpret it similarly.

Each scenario points to a type of inference and a type of coordination. In each case the mechanism works if group members assume that they interpret the event in the same way. Thus both scenarios satisfy the cognitive requirement mentioned above: actors assume these inferences to be commonly shared. For purposes of terminological convenience, let us call the first scenario "presumed coordination" and the second "ad hoc coordination." The first scenario postulates a happening that stands for "something else," this something else being, in the present case, the prospect of collective action. The second scenario postulates a happening that lends itself to a strategic interpretation of the preference distribution and its behavioral consequences.

The Presumption of Coordination

Coordination is presumed if elicited by a signal. This type of coordination requires a coordination of the second order. There must be agreement about the significance of the happening qua signal. Actors need to be sure that they interpret the happening as a signal for action. This agreement may belong to a repertoire of shared understandings that group members regularly activate as they interact with one another and that is constitutive of their culture—the set of codes and categories that group members use as regulative guides for action in their dealings with one another. In this case, as for any case of cultural understanding, the interpretation of the happening can be implicit. This interpretive agreement may also be the outcome of a convention explicitly stated as such: group members coordinated their understanding beforehand for the purpose of coordinating their action.

In any event, actors assume that they share the same behavioral preference. They have no mutual uncertainty about their behavior preference. The only uncertainty concerns timing. The coordination dilemma therefore does not result from uncertainty about the others' behavioral preference. Belief coordination is not a problem because group members know that they have the same behavioral preference. Action coordination is a problem because group members are uncertain of the timing. The coordination problem that group members need to resolve is the problem of action (timing).

Ad Hoc Coordination

If group members lack a behavioral script to deal with the challenge and if they are mutually uncertain of their future collective stance, they cannot a priori presume their coordination. How then can a public happening serve as a co-ordinating device? It does so if it provides group members with crucial information about their behavioral preferences. This information is not symbolic, like a signal; it is strategic, in the sense that it allows actors to assess the consequences of their action. Tacit coordination here is based on strategic inference. A public event generates tacit coordination when it provides information about the preference distribution within the group. The coordinating quality of the event results from its informational content.

The happening that I am considering is a statement made by one member of the group in a public setting—a public statement that the other group members interpret as a statement about the decision the group has to make. Through this statement the actor reveals her stand. She opposes acquiescence, she recommends acquiescence, or she seeks refuge in a wait-and-see position. Along with his peers, ego witnesses this statement.[10] He knows her for having observed her taking positions in the past. Her past public statements and the characteristics of the situation give him a clue about her inclination to oppose, or acquiesce in, the challenger. In short, ego can assess her threshold. This belief is crucial: in light of this threshold, ego can determine how the speaker assesses the group stance. I elaborate this point further below. This argument draws on an observation made earlier concerning the complementary character of the three pieces of information that actors can disclose to their peers through their verbal exchanges.

Induction

Individual actors carry with them three parameters: (1) their action threshold, (2) their assessment of the collective stand, and (3) their behavioral preference. By definition an individual's action threshold and assessment of the group's future behavior determine the individual's behavioral stance. The point worthy of attention is that the knowledge of two of these parameters sheds light on the third. A speaker's behavioral stand and her assessment of the situation indirectly reveal the upper limit of her action threshold. Consider for instance an individual who believes that two-thirds of the group will choose opposition

10. For purposes of expositional clarity and to make the abstract presentation of the model more readable, I adopt the following convention: "she" is prominent; "he" is a rank-and-file.

and who herself chooses opposition. Her belief about the group and her own stance reveal that her opposition threshold is equal to, or below, two-thirds. Were her opposition threshold above two-thirds, she would not choose opposition.

Conversely, her action threshold and her behavioral stance reveal how she assesses the collective situation. To go back to the previous example: assume that this actor's opposition threshold is two-thirds: she does not choose opposition unless at least two-thirds of the group chooses opposition as well. If she takes a stand in favor of acquiescence, group members who know her threshold can infer from her behavioral stance that she expects less than two-thirds of the group to choose opposition.

Unless the speaker is known to be a normative diehard—her opposition threshold is absolute—ego interprets her statements under the presumption that she behaves strategically. From ego's viewpoint, her behavioral stand is motivated by her prognosis of the group's future stance. If ego believes her to have a low opposition threshold and her statement indicates that she prefers acquiescence, then ego can deduce that she expects the proportion of the group opposing the challenger to be too low relative to her threshold to motivate a public stance in favor of opposition. Therefore she decides to acquiesce. Thus her statement provides ego with information about the preference distribution among group members that can be of relevance to his own assessment. If initially he had no clue about how the group might behave, this statement would provide him with a clue. If ego already achieved some assessment, the information thus provided would either confirm this assessment or cast doubt on it. The last section of appendix B formalizes this inference process.

Collective Updating

Two characteristics of the speaker allow group members to coordinate their beliefs about their own collective stance. First, her threshold is relative. Second, group members can reasonably assume this threshold to be common belief. I examine each point in turn.

First, an actor who has an absolute threshold does not make her action conditional on the action of her peers. Therefore her statement reveals nothing about how she perceives the group stance. A statement discloses information about the preference distribution only if the speaker has a relative threshold. In this model, speakers who are perceived to have an absolute threshold have no impact on the group's collective stance. The substantive point is that group members only pay attention to actors who they think experience the same dilemma as they do themselves. Underlying this point is an interesting paradox: normative diehards—or rather actors perceived as normative diehards and whose public behavior confirms this collective perception—are the least qualified to elicit collective shifts.

Second, in addition to being public, the statement needs to have strategic content that is interpreted in the same way by all group members under the assumption that this interpretation is shared. Group members make this common belief assumption only if the speaker has made herself known in the past and in the process of making herself known has revealed her preferences. Only her public statements—words, written and spoken—can provide this knowledge in a way accessible to all. Assuming that her threshold is common belief, ego can expect that his peers will infer from her statement the same strategic information about their own collective stance. This last point is key to the possibility of tacit coordination.

Differential Impact

This tacit coordination argument implies that statements have different impacts depending on the type of common belief attached to the prominent actor making the statement. Statements that have the greatest impact are the most counterintuitive given the public characteristics of those making the statements (see the discussion of proposition 2A.1 in appendix B). For example, an actor believed to have a high opposition threshold—that is, she does not choose opposition unless she expects a high proportion of the reference group to choose opposition as well—makes a statement calling for collective opposition. Since her threshold is relative—she makes her choice conditional on her peers' behavioral choice—her statement reveals that she expects a high proportion of the group to oppose the challenger. Her statement is counterintuitive given the value of her threshold. It has a greater impact than a statement by an actor with a low opposition threshold because it motivates group members to revise more substantially their initial beliefs.

THE CONSTITUTION OF PROMINENCE

Visibility and Resonance

It follows from the previous discussion that not all actors have the capacity to produce tacit coordination, since not all actors can make public statements that group members interpret in the same way as revealing the state of their collective preference. The foremost characteristic of actors who have the capacity to produce tacit coordination is their visibility, which they acquired through their public statements. High visibility provides the cognitive basis for the formation of common beliefs regarding a prominent actor's characteristics as a group member. The actor frequently took a public stand in the past, thereby revealing her preferences and dispositions. These stances being public, she exposed herself to the gaze of her peers, enabling them to form shared beliefs about her political and ideological preferences and her commitment to these preferences.

Visibility is a necessary, not a sufficient, condition for tacit coordination. An actor may be highly visible and yet generate little attention. She made frequent public statements in the past. Group members heard her many times. Yet they do not assume that their peers will spontaneously pay attention to her. Her visibility does not sustain a process of tacit coordination. This observation echoes the point I made earlier regarding the lack of collective impact of statements by actors whose action threshold is commonly perceived to be absolute. Group members do not interpret these statements as revealing strategic information about the group's behavioral preference.

For this to happen, this actor needs to be a focus of attention for the group members. Two factors may explain this attention. First, the actor holds group responsibilities. She has an institutional position in the group. Second, her statements generated attention in the past. People talked about these statements, publicly reacted to them, dissected them, commented on them, made reference to them, thereby implicitly engaging a dialogue and contributing to the shared awareness of their resonance. The immediate past carries with it the resilience of its effects into the present. Actors who attract the attention of their peers conditional on the assumption that this attention is shared are "focal points" (Schelling) for their peers. This focal point quality is the defining feature of prominence.

The Statement of Silence

This analysis of prominence substantially expands the meaning of a "statement." So far I have assumed that the public statements eliciting tacit coordination are verbal ones: they take the form of words, more often spoken than written, and these words are intended for others. This assumption was obvious in my choice of terms: the statements I have been considering are those of a "speaker," and their impact is conditioned by the profile of this speaker in terms of visibility and action threshold. The broad justification for this analytical focus is that only actors can provide information about their own preferences. They do so by making statements about themselves and the group.

Yet there is no reason to restrict the notion of statements to verbal statements. The notion of prominence makes this point clear. In troubled and challenging situations, prominent actors are focal points for their peers. Group members who share an interest in coordination turn their eyes to these prominent actors, expecting them more or less implicitly to take a stand and thereby to provide a clue for their own coordination. As a result of this sustained attention, the public behavior of these prominent actors—whether verbal or not—becomes their statement.

This observation applies in particular to their silence. The silence of a rank-and-file group member in a public setting does not mean much if this actor is not expected to take a position. The silence of a prominent actor is significant for the opposite reason. She is expected to take a public stand as a result of her prominence. Her silence is a public stance, and as such is strategically informative. It means that the actor is too unsure of the collective situation to commit herself. She views the situation as too indeterminate. This observation about silence suggests a broader understanding of "public statement" as any attitudinal stance noted in public that reveals a behavioral preference. An attitudinal definition of statement becomes particularly relevant in public settings when actors know that their behavior is being scrutinized and every gesture can be interpreted as a sign.

* * *

The alignment processes examined in this chapter apply to any risky decision made in a group context in which isolation carries a high cost and individuals have an interest in coordinating their stance. The analytical challenge is to specify how individuals construct their sense of risks in light of the information conveyed by their interactions. Two types of interactions are at play as individuals engage in face-to-face interactions and imagine the consequences of their action upon one another. The first type of interaction involves interpersonal contacts. The interactive process is based on direct communicative exchange. The second type involves actors who interact as they draw inferences about their collective behavior. They assess the consequences of their action in light of these inferences. Beliefs about strategic choices become interdependent even though there are no personal contacts. The interactive dimension of the decision-making process is virtual.

The two inference mechanisms that I have distinguished—local knowledge and tacit coordination—illustrate these two types of interactions. Local knowledge describes a type of interaction in which people communicate through interpersonal relations. Communication is direct and interpersonal. It takes place within the same unit of time and space. Tacit coordination, on the other hand, does not involve interpersonal contact. Actors interact by forming beliefs about others' preferences under the assumption that other actors proceed in the same way vis-à-vis themselves. Interaction in this instance rests on a "speculative mechanism" (Schelling 1972, 174). People reflect on their choice in light of their beliefs about others, knowing that these other actors go through the same process.

The peculiarity of this knowledge is that it is based not on features exogenous to the strategic problem (salience, uniqueness, simplicity) but on an act of communication (a public statement) that expresses a point of view directly relevant to the dilemma. This peculiarity qualifies the "tacit" character of the interactions at work here. Schelling's analogy — "The coordination of expectations is analogous to the coordination of behaviors when communication is cut off" (Schelling 1980 [1963], 71) — only partially applies here. We are considering a situation in which communication is not cut off. Communication does take place. It furthermore helps coordinate expectations. Its coordinating quality is however a derived, not a primary, characteristic of public statements.

Chapter 7

Diffusion

The Grand Salon in the Park Hotel was open like a windmill . . . Everyone
bustles about, . . . gathers the latest news, and diffuses it immediately . . .
— Pierre Nicolle[1]

1

The scene takes place on 20 March 1933. The parliamentary delegates of the
Center party are about to leave for Potsdam, a few miles away from Berlin, for
the opening of the parliamentary session. Right before they take their place in
the cars, police officers who supervise the departure request to check passen-
gers in search of possible weapons. The chairman of the party, Ludwig Kaas,
immediately phones Göring to protest. The incident goes no further. In his
memoirs Brüning summarizes the episode in one sentence: "He who had eyes
to see, knew, that all [Center representatives] were to be submitted to fear and
pressure."[2] Kaas is not exculpated. Brüning depicts him perspiring with fear
three days later, as the two leave the Kroll opera house after the vote.[3]

Let us transpose ourselves to Vichy seven years later, on the morning of
9 July 1940. Léon Blum is staying in the hall of the Grand Casino. Within a few
hours the Chamber of Deputies and the Senate will separately meet to vote on
a bill stating that there is ground to revise constitutional laws. "The men whom
one could see swirling in [the Grand Casino] gathering together, parting ways,
and then looking again for one another, seemed to be plunged in some kind
of terrible mixture. . . . Contagion had taken its effect. . . . Within a few hours,
thoughts, words, even faces had become almost unrecognizable. . . . Each one
had become a seat of infection as soon as reached by contagion."[4]

The plausibility of these accounts rests on their evocative power. They build
on a commonsensical metaphor. Diffusion takes the guise of contagion. Individuals let themselves be "contaminated." Fear spreads like a disease. They are
no longer in their normal state. Interpersonal contacts dissolve their countenance and past resolutions. Blum's vivid depiction of the "venom of fear" offers

1. Nicolle, *Cinquante mois d'armistice*, 12.
2. Brüning, *Memoiren*, 657.
3. Ibid., 660
4. Blum, *A l'échelle humaine*, 83.

a perfect illustration of what Blumer (1939, 224) conceptualizes as "circular reaction," i.e., the affective diffusion and reinforcement of an emotional state among individuals sharing a unit of time and space. Individuals communicate their unrest to one another. As they do so they mutually reinforce their emotional state. Social contagion is one variant of this process. "Social contagion refers to the relatively rapid, unwitting, and non-rational dissemination of a mood, impulse, or form of conduct" (Blumer 1939, 230). Individuals lose their critical sense. They are submerged.

To lay observers this interpretation provides a convenient explanation of otherwise unintelligible patterns of behavior. When they go on with their daily tasks, people usually display a sound and practical understanding of the consequences of their actions. Private or daily occupations elicit practical rationality. In a group context, on the other hand, individuals may engage in collective behaviors that can puzzle external observers, displaying for instance emotions (resignation, penance, fear, effervescence) which give way to erratic mood swings and belie a sober assessment of consequences. The contrast between these two types of behaviors is striking. Accounts of collective behavior in terms of contagion or circular reaction impute this contrast to the difference in context (Blumer 1939, 225–26). This seems, at first sight, a commonsensical move. In one case individuals cope with their own private interests. In the other they are engaged in intense interpersonal interactions. If tensions are widespread, routines break down and emotions get the upper hand.

2

We should be wary of this interpretation. For one thing, it postulates a purely mechanistic diffusion process grounded in the affective transmission of an emotional state. People communicate their emotions as they interact. What remains unclear in this interpretation is why fear and resignation are bound to have the upper hand. If irrationality—the lack of reflexive concern for consequences—is the prevalent feature of such situations, could we not as well expect collective heroism, the willful disregard of costs, threats, and pressures? As long as the interpretation remains confined to an emotional reading of the diffusion process, we cannot adjudicate one outcome versus the other. An exclusive emphasis on individuals' suggestibility (Turner and Killian 1972, 80) lends itself to a circular and tautological diagnosis in which the group context accounts for individuals' suggestibility and individuals' suggestibility accounts for the group context.

A diffusion model of alignment does not prejudge a psychological mechanism. The main hypothesis is simply that alignment takes place through interpersonal contacts. Thus we need not assume that as they interact individual actors primarily communicate their emotional understanding of the situation. There is no reason to conflate diffusion with contagion if by contagion we mean the spread of an affective state. Milling can be a strategic device whereby individuals attempt to assess the distribution of behavioral preferences (Berk 1974, 362–63; Coleman 1990, 224). In this case milling does not simply reflect a state of emotional disarray and inconsistency. Similarly, there is no reason to assume that the diffusion of a behavioral stance necessarily takes place in a mechanical fashion. The point applies to sequential alignment, which easily lends itself to a mechanistic interpretation.

A parliamentary setting institutionalizes interpersonal and collective inter-actions. It defines a forum of constant verbal exchange whereby speakers routinely strive to act upon their audience. It also creates the institutional space in which individuals have the opportunity to establish regular and informal ties with one another. The conjunction of these three types of interactions — interactions between speakers and listeners, interactions among members of the same group of affiliation, interactions among members of different groups — justifies the interactive paradigm presented in chapter 6. In this chapter my focus is on two diffusion mechanisms: sequential alignment and local knowledge. Sequential alignment takes place when group members, observing the choice of their peers, openly endorse one option. Local knowledge describes the process whereby group members individually make up their mind about the collective stance of the group in light of the information they get about the preference distribution through their interpersonal contacts.

3

The question "Is there sequential alignment?" tackles another one: How shall we assess the scope of this sequential process? In other words, what is the relevant universe of reference? In March 1933 the challenge first takes place outside the parliamentary arena. Nazi activists launch their political offensive throughout the country. In this context parliamentary representatives are likely to be sensitive to the attitude of the party's rank and file and constituents. In July 1940, by contrast, parliament is the original scene of the challenge. Taking advantage of the political opportunities created by the defeat, Laval and his supporters define an alternative political agenda to which the members of the French National Assembly are the first exposed. Thus parliamentarians are on the frontline of the challenge. At this point their constituents are not directly involved, and there is little analytical ground to expect that the constituents will decisively influence the decision reached in Vichy. Sequential alignment, if any, is most likely to take place among those who directly partake in the vote.

The scope of the inquiry having been specified for each case, what do we observe? In March 1933 there is no indication of widespread and systematic pressures from below in favor of accommodation with the Nazis. As documented in letters and testimonies, the opinions conveyed by the Center party rank and file to their representatives range from disgust at Nazi brutality to a wish for appeasement and accommodation. The bulk of the Center constituents are awaiting guidelines, wavering between a harrowing feeling of danger and hope. The stances of Catholic organizations display a similar pattern. The peasants' associations are compromising and collaborative. The workers' clubs and Windthorst youth organizations convey their opposition to any compromise. Other groups (the clergy, the civil servants, middle-class groups) oscillate between a wait-and-see attitude, passive resistance, and occasional accommodation. The boldness of the Nazi challenge catches them off guard. They still have to make up their mind about what to do. In this conjuncture they are looking for political and behavioral directives from prominent Center party and Catholic representatives.

In July 1940 only a small proportion of those present in Vichy publicly revealed their preference before the final vote. I described in chapter 5 the content of the three parliamentary motions circulating among deputies and senators in these few days. One—the Bergery motion—hailed the prospect of a power transfer. The other two—the ex-servicemen's motion and Badie's—were oppositional. In signing a motion, parliamentarians took a public stand. About one-fifth of the members of the French National Assembly did so in Vichy. The great majority remained silent. For them collective alignment did not take place in a sequential fashion.

4

This conclusion motivates the second empirical question raised by this chapter: As they interact, do individuals converge on a similar assessment of the group's disposition and through this shared assessment do they reach a common behavioral stance? This question invites us to examine patterns of collective interactions. In March 1933 interpersonal contacts took place primarily within the collective setting of parliamentary delegations. These groups had a history of strong behavioral cohesion and a strong sense of discipline. In Vichy in July 1940 interpersonal contacts were random and informal. Encounters with out-group members were frequent. Parliamentary groups broke down as organizational and political entities. This breakdown was the conjoint effect of the incentive structure created by electoral law, the emergence of cross-party cleavages before the war, and the disorganization prevailing in Vichy at the time of the meeting.

Interaction patterns are thus strikingly different. So is the configuration of reference groups. In March 1933 the party delegation was for parliamentarians the reference group. In July 1940 senators and deputies took as an ultimate reference point the attitude of the Assembly as a whole. Yet independent of these differences, uncertainty remained a pervasive and characteristic feature of the collective situation. Center representatives traveled to Berlin without knowing the content of the enabling bill that would be submitted to them. The government released the text of the bill on 21 March. This publication made the Center party delegates crucially aware of the scope of the challenge and its political implications. Given the issues at stake, they knew that they could not elude their responsibilities. As the moment of the decision came closer on 23 March, their sense of dilemma obliterated their collective experience.

The situation in Vichy bore the mark of the organizational breakdown of parliamentary groups. Parliamentarians felt disoriented because they realized that they would not be able to coordinate their action with other group members. As they interacted with one another, they realized the frailty of opinions and commitments. Things were unsure. Parliament members did not know what to think and what to do. This feeling of mutual uncertainty lingered until a few hours before the vote. They went to the meetings knowing that their perception of the assembly, and the perceptions of others, might easily get reversed. Interpersonal contacts, far from allowing them to cling to a mutually reinforcing assessment of the outcome, also contributed to their disarray.

THE SCOPE OF DEFECTIONS

Within a few days after the elections of 5 March, Nazi activists hoisted the swastika along with the old imperial flag on public buildings. They stormed the headquarters of leftist unions and parties. They harassed, took to custody, and sometimes murdered political opponents. The offensive, which the Nazi press hailed as a "national Revolution," was as brutal as it was swift. Although less exposed than their leftist counterparts to Nazi violence, Center representatives and rank and file witnessed it firsthand. Conjointly with this grassroots offensive, Nazi officials proceeded to dismiss from their position the head executives of regional states (*Länder*) who might resist them. Invoking the preservation of law and order, the Nazi minister of the interior, Frick, appointed executive commissars under the direct authority of the government at the head of the state of Bade on 8 March and of Bavaria on 9 March (Bracher 1962, 140–42).

Such is the context. Which impact does the challenge have on Catholic voters and how do their reactions affect Center representatives? The picture we get from internal reports and testimonies offers a contrasted image. The bulk of the Center constituents is confused by the political developments and awaits political directives. Some group leaderships take a deliberate stance, either playing the card of political compromise or sticking to an oppositional stance. Most organizations do not make their voice heard. The challenge seems to catch them by surprise. Their leading representatives behave as if awaiting guidelines and hanging on to define a political stance. Overall, compared to the fate of the other Weimar parties (the Social Democrats and the State German Party), the Center party holds its ranks remarkably well.

"We state the fact"

The Social Democratic party suffers massive resignations in March 1933. Directly exposed to Nazi violence and retaliations, numerous party activists withdraw from their political engagement (Matthias 1960, 173, 239–41; Harsch 1993, 234). There is no indication of such large-scale defections from the Center party. There are defections, for sure. The Center president of the administrative district of Osnabrück leaves the party on 5 March (Morsey 1977, 117). On 9 March the *Kölnische Volkszeitung* reports resignations of some middle-rank party members. The Nazi press gives considerable publicity to these announcements, with the obvious goal of lending credence to the view that the Center party is breaking apart. However, these defections are isolated cases. Among the rank and file there is no sign of such a trend. The contingent of defectors remains marginal.

Revealing in this regard is the circular letter which the secretary of the Center party for Düsseldorf, Dr. Schreiber, sent out to local party leaders on 25 March: "Secretariat of the Center party for Düsseldorf, March 25, 1933. Circular letter to the chairmen of the party districts. . . . . Our adversary makes use of the rumor that there would be "countless resignations" from the party to report. We state the fact: a few people have joined the adversary. All in all, the number of resignations amounts to about one hundred among more than 17000 registered members."[5] We have no reason to suspect that Schreiber concealed the extent of the defections. In the same letter, after having mentioned how many Center members have resigned since the election, Schreiber indicates that the nominative list of the "losses" will soon be sent to the local cells so that they can actualize their membership lists.[6] This openness and transparency leave little doubt as to the genuineness of his account.

5. Stadtarchiv Düsseldorf, Abteilung XXI-77: Rundschreiben an die Bezirke.
6. Ibid.

Contrasted Voices

Do Center officials assess the situation among their constituents in terms consistent with Schreiber's diagnosis? Consider the reports presented by Joos and Walterbach before the executive committee of the Catholic workers' clubs (KAB) in Düsseldorf on 28 March (Aretz 1978, 80). Joos and Walterbach describe the attitude of Catholic voters and Center constituents in reaction to the Nazi challenge. The information they provide is instructive in two respects. First, their reports document how Center officials assessed the attitudes and morale of their constituents. This information is key for evaluating the hypothesis of sequential alignment between the Center party constituents and their political representatives. Second, these reports distinguish between different socioeconomic groups, allowing us to refine the diagnosis along socioeconomic lines.

"Thursday, March 28, 1933 in Düsseldorf. . . . Joos reports on the situation in West Germany. . . . The executive committee of the association in West Germany convened and has now a picture of the mood in West Germany. Overall academic people collaborate while 'preserving fundamental principles.' The civil servants are fearful, the clerks are confused, the youth under 21 have lost all composure; they let themselves be carried away [*mitgerissen*] and are in part collaborating. Insofar as they remain in the ranks of an association which has kept a firm attitude towards the events, they stand firm. This holds also for those above 21 years old. All in all, the apprentice are confused. The Catholic workers have displayed a clear and sensible attitude. The clergy in Catholic associations remains absolutely intact in the different regions (*Gebieten*), some adopting a reserved attitude, others more willing to come forward."[7]

Walterbach confirms: "In Bavaria, the developments parallel [those in West Germany]. Only the peasants, because of the previous attitude of their organizations, have for the most part executed the swing more easily. The young workers are behaving in an exemplary fashion. . . . The young clergy is oscillating. It is in part royalist."[8] Two points stand out in these reports. First, there is no reference to massive defections. Had there been any, they would not have escaped the attention of party cadres. Center leaders do not believe that they are losing their troops to the enemy. They do not report on a general mood of resignation. This point is consistent with the observation made above about the scope of defections.

7. Kommission für Zeitgeschichte, KAB Archiv, C II 13: Sitzungsbericht der Reichsverbandsvorstandssitzung am 28. März 1933 in Düsseldorf und am 29. März in Köln.
8. Kommission für Zeitgeschichte, Bonn, KAB Archiv, C II 13.

Second, reactions across socioeconomic groups are contrasted. According to Joos and Walterbach, the willingness to compromise with the Nazis in March 1933 is most present among Catholic peasants.[9] In contrast to this collusive stance, Joos and Walterbach mention groups adopting a firm stand toward the Nazis: the clergy, Catholic youth organizations, and Catholic workers. Both rapporteurs point out the exemplary attitude of young Catholic workers. Alternative sources of information confirm these assessments. The representatives of the Catholic workers' clubs take a stand against any compromise on the enabling bill. In Cologne they vote a motion requesting rejection of the bill (Aretz 1978, 77–78). In his report of 28 March Joos indicates that on 20 March the secretaries of the Catholic workers' club association for West Germany had released a statement in which, expressing their profound [*innerlich*] concern about current developments, they condemned the "National Revolution." "The ground motto of the first conference [20 March] was: 'We remain what we are and we will even do better.'"[10]

Equally revealing for assessing the dispositions and attitudes of the Catholic youth organizations—the "Windthorst associations"—is their reaction to passage of the enabling bill. On 25 March the archbishop of Freiburg, Gröber, warned these organizations against any behavior that would disrupt peace and public order (Böckenforde 1962, 232). His warning indirectly acknowledged the stir created within these organizations by the vote of 23 March. In a letter to Heinrich Brüning dated 27 March which explicitly deals with the vote and its aftermath, Friedrich Dessauer makes congruent observations: "there is strong unrest among the youth. But we will be able to justify [the vote for the enabling bill]."[11] The report written in April 1933 by Franz Steber, leader of the Catholic youth association Sturmschar, is consistent with Dessauer's appraisal: Steber explains that the "yes" vote of the Center parliamentary delegation aroused indignation among the political circles of the Catholic youth movement (Morsey 1960, 368; Klönne 1958, 86). Members of the Catholic workers clubs obviously shared this indignation, for Joos remarked in the Düsseldorf meeting on 28 March that for the representatives of the Catholic workers' clubs, "in fifty years the vote for the enabling bill will be depicted as a mistake."[12]

9. Interestingly, both rapporteurs relate this willingness to the position adopted by the leaders of peasants' organizations. Those sympathetic to the Nazis have taken over peasants' representative organizations. The documents available in Hermes's personal archives shed light on this takeover. Konrad Adenauer Stiftung, Nachlaß Hermes, I-090-002, Niederschrift über die Sitzung des Vorstandes der deutschen christlichen Bauernvereine vom 22. März 1933.

10. Kommission für Zeitgeschichte, Bonn, KAB Archiv, C II 13.

11. Ibid., NL Dessauer, FD 12.

12. Ibid., KAB Archiv, C II 13.

AWAITING DIRECTIVES

The picture emerging from these sources is not one of acquiescence, compromise, or large-scale defections. It is not one of spreading panic and contagion. Rather, it is a contrasted picture. Defections are marginal. Reactions to the challenge among Center constituents and Catholic voters run the whole gamut of possible attitudes: some call for accommodation, others call for a resolute opposition, still others are confused and await directives. Center representatives are exposed to this heterogeneous range of attitudes. There is no contagion of fear, and the conditions for the diffusion of a homogenous stance are lacking. These observations are at odds with narratives describing a situation in which the Center representatives are exposed to growing demands for compromise (e.g. Morsey 1977, 120; Scholder 1988, 243).

Pressures from Below?

Historical accounts emphasizing pressures from below rest on two pieces of evidence. One is a letter from Conrad Gröber, the archbishop of Freiburg, to Cardinal Pacelli and dated 18 March, in which Gröber states that in his archbishopric a great number of Catholic communities are joining the ranks of the NSDAP with "flags flying" (Morsey 1977, 258).[13] Another document is a letter dated 31 March 1933 from the head of the department of apologetics at the People's Association for Catholic Germany (Volksverein für das katholische Deutschland), Konrad Algermissen, to Cardinal Bertram. Algermissen reports on the Christian peasants' associations and expresses the fear that Catholics might become ideologically influenced by the Nazis: "The recent events in the Christian peasants' association, conjoint with the experiences of the last weeks, make us fear that growing circles which are still faithful to the church on the long run not only join the National Socialist movement, but also get contaminated by its worldview."[14]

The contrast between these alarmed assessments of the political situation and the reports conveyed by Center officials at the same point in time is striking enough to deserve close scrutiny. Gröber and Algermissen betray a sense of urgency for which we find no equivalent in the testimonies of Center officials, who do not describe their constituents as being on the verge of massive

13. This letter is reproduced in *Akten deutscher Bischöfe, I, 1933–1934,* no. 5, 1. Volk (1972, 71).

14. *Akten deutscher Bischöfe, I, 1933–1934,* no. 17, 43. Scholder (1988) bases his concurrent narrative on the same sources while noting at the same time that "the opinions among the bishops were not uniform" (244).

defections. This difference in assessment can be traced to different factors. For one thing, Gröber and Algermissen assess the situation in light of the peasants' attitudes and, more specifically, the stance taken by their representative organizations. As Joos and Walterbach indicate in their reports, these organizations are compromising with the Nazis. This compromising attitude cannot, however, be held to be characteristic of other social groups.

This contrast in assessment may also reflect a different practical experience of the Catholics' involvement in the fight against the Nazis. Center officials constantly interacted with party activists and sympathizers who were committed to the party's political agenda. They sensed the mood of their troops through these daily contacts. For several weeks the mood was resolutely oppositional. Throughout the electoral campaign Center constituents attended party meetings en masse, applauded public denunciations of Nazi violence, and took an active part in the campaign. They showed no sign of resignation. Quite the contrary. Their "oppositional fervor" (Harcourt 1938, 97–99) communicated to their representatives. If fear and resignation were indeed so rampant in March 1933, to the point of motivating overwhelming pressures in favor of compromise — in other words, if Morsey following Gröber is right — then we are left with a perplexing turnaround. We need to explain how Catholic voters shifted from "oppositional fervor" to widespread fear.

"Oppositional Fervor"

In his personal notes about February–March 1933, Joseph Wirth describes a collective mood marked by a fighting spirit: "Liberals and Democrats were in a state of mind similar to that of November 1918, when the bourgeoisie was paralyzed, as if it had been knocked hard on the head. With the members of the Center, things were different. These members were fairly active. Without considerable effort, in huge meetings and powerful demonstrations, one could light up the Catholic people by indicating what was at stake."[15] Party members drew from meetings a feeling of strength that they were eager to convey to their leaders (Junker 1969, 168). A sort of restlessness against the current of the time was building up. The leadership of the Center responded to these aspirations by putting more emphasis on the ritualized aspects of meetings and demonstrations (Junker 1969, 169). Center members displayed a firm resolution to resist Hitler's abuse of power.

On 16 February Center party newspapers published a statement by Catholic organizations which denounced the prospect of a dictatorship and called

15. Bundesarchiv, Koblenz, Nachlaß Wirth, N1342/134.

for respecting the rule of law ("Germany is at stake").[16] This call prompted Göring, the interior minister for the state of Prussia, to impose a three-day ban on the various Center party newspapers accused of debasing the government's action. Far from abating the Center party rank-and-file's fighting spirit, the bans boosted their resoluteness to confront the Nazis. A letter dated 20 February 1933, signed by fourteen members of the Center party from Freiburg and sent to prominent party representatives (Heinrich Marx, Heinrich Vockel, Eugen Bolz, Ernst Föhr, Heinrich Brüning, and Helene Weber), illustrates this point. The petitioners expressed their total agreement with the call from Catholic organizations a few days earlier and lamented the decision by some Catholic newspapers in the state of Bade to publish only extracts from it. They also negatively reacted to the low profile adopted by the Center leadership in response to the ban on Catholic newspapers.

"We are even more painfully surprised by the fact that on this occasion the chairman of the People's Association for Catholic Germany (Volksverein für das katholische Deutschland) as well as the General Secretariat of the Center party have adopted vis-à-vis the relevant Prussian authorities [i.e., Göring], an attitude which is viewed for sure as a weak retreat among Catholic circles who think independently, and only creates confusion and bewilderment among Catholic circles who do not think independently. One should have had the courage to also assume a ban of several days of the Center press even in Berlin, since thereby the latent Kulturkampf would have broken out in the open and the whole Catholic community would have been roused to a higher unity and a more principled behavior."[17]

At the end of February 1933 the same fighting spirit was pointed out in a confidential four-page memo written most probably by Wilhelm Bormann, chairman of the Center party in Hildesheim and one of the party leaders in the region of Hannover: "Now has come the moment of trial and sacrifice for all of us. There is absolutely no need to become discouraged. Quite the contrary. According to all the reports which arrive here, the stance of our electorate in the country is really excellent and exemplary. . . . Never have we experienced such a fighting spirit and such an eagerness to fight in the Center and among German Catholics as in the present time."[18] Equally revealing are Eugen Bolz's reflections on the political dispositions of the Center constituents at the beginning of March. In public meetings he made allusions to the Center party's willingness to collaborate with Hitler's government in spite of the incidents of

16. "Es geht um Deutschland," *Germania*, 16 February 1933.
17. *Der Nachlaß des Reichskanzlers Wilhelm Marx*, vol. 1, no. 52, 150.
18. Konrad Adenauer Stiftung, Sankt Augustin, Bormann, I-352, Mappe 9.

the previous weeks. These allusions received no positive echo. Bolz concluded that this strategy would be resisted by large segments of the Center constituency (Morsey 1977, 112–13). The man who on 23 March took a stance against a "yes" vote had anticipated at the beginning of March that his proposal for positive collaboration would encounter strong opposition among the party ranks.

Given this readiness to fight among Center members and voters during the electoral campaign, it seems difficult to argue that as soon as the electoral results were known the "oppositional fervor" of the electoral campaign gave way to resignation. On 5 March the Center party proved remarkably resilient from an electoral standpoint. The first commentaries in the Center press emphasized this resilience (Hehl 1977, 27; Morsey 1977, 115). To many, political Catholicism still constituted a resolute front after the elections of March 1933 (Altendörfer 1993, 775). "German Catholicism as a whole continued the closest front against National Socialism which it had formed after the September 1930 elections. . . . Seen as a whole Catholicism still represented an ideological block of imposing unanimity" (Scholder 1988, 239). On 7 March Rumbold, British ambassador in Berlin, commented on the electoral results as follows: "The party is still immune to Hitler's overtures."[19]

One week after the elections Johannes Gronowski, member of the Prussian Landtag and former head of the state of Westfalen, made a similar assessment. In a speech in Osnabrück, Gronowski emphasized the resolution of the Center. "In the political surge the Center party holds steadfast and unmoved like a boulder. Our Center people have stood the test. This is for us the satisfactory result of the last elections."[20] The elections took place under exceptional circumstances marked by unfairness and injustice: "Friends, in my thirty-eight year activity as representative of the Center, I have been through almost a half century of elections—including the Hottentot elections of 1907. But I have never experienced an election with such a disparity of means. That was not a regular fight. We were thrown into fighting, but our weapons were made inoffensive or unfit before the battle."[21]

19. Documents, vol. 4, 446; quoted by Morsey (1977, 248). Analyzing the electoral results in an article published in the *Neue badische Landeszeitung* on 7 March 1933, Ernst Lemmer, German State party parliamentary delegate, emphasized that "the Center party and Social Democracy" remained "totally unshaken" (*völlig unerschüttert*). Archiv der Konrad Adenauer Stiftung, Sankt Augustin, NL Lemmer, I-280, 060.

20. Konrad Adenauer Stiftung, Sankt Augustin, NL Stricher, I-293, 001-1.

21. Ibid.

"There Is No Time to Lose"

If there were no defections en masse and if different groups among Catholic voters voiced their position for and against compromise, what was the median attitude? The members of legalist parties such as the Center party had a hard time asserting their political bearings. The Nazis committed violence in the name of the state and openly trampled the fundamental principles for which the Center party had stood for decades: the rule of law, respect for individual rights, preservation of the federal structure of the polity. For Center members the political conjuncture called for defining a collective stance, as Hermann Joseph Schmitt, the general secretary of the Catholic workers' association (KAB), pointed out in a letter dated 14 March 1933 to a regional leader (Landespräses) of the association: "Today I received a letter from Walterbach in which he said that a meeting of the national executive committee of the association must take place at the soonest after clarification of the present circumstances. I also believe that there is no time to lose."[22] Demands for guidelines were mounting.

We get a sense of the rank and file's demands for directives from the internal correspondence of the Center party. On 18 March 1933 the general secretariat of the Center party for the Rhine region (Cologne) sent out a circular letter: "In this time of political decisions, it is our strongest desire to discuss the consequences that need to be drawn from the present situation as soon as possible with our friends and collaborators. *We ask for your understanding* if this is not possible yet. However, we hope to be able to extend to you an invitation to such a discussion in the next few days, after some negotiations have been settled" (my emphasis).[23] The letter does not say "do not lose your temper" or "do not yield to the sirens of our enemies." Rather it conveys a message that could be worded as follows: we know that in this time in which one has to take sides, you, our constituency, are asking for guidelines. But we cannot provide these guidelines yet. The letter is answering the implicit question: What shall we do? It is a response to a demand for directives.

Only after passage of the enabling bill did leading Center party organizations communicate guidelines and recommendations to the membership. I base this contention on the circular letter sent out to the chairmen of the electoral districts by the secretariat of the Center party for Düsseldorf on 25 March 1933. "On behalf of the party national executive committee which, since

22. Kommission für Zeitgeschichte, Bonn, Nachlaß Hermann Joseph Schmitt, HJS 3, letter to Miller, 14 March 1933.
23. Stadtarchiv Düsseldorf, Abteilung XXI-4: Rheinische Zentrumspartei.

the elections, already held several meetings and consultations, I communicate to the chairmen of the electoral districts the following: 1) The party work must at once be resumed with eagerness even under the changed political circumstances. Insofar as the annual meetings of the districts have not taken place yet, they must immediately be prepared and called for. One needs to get in touch with the secretariat regarding the meeting date and the speaker."[24] The phrasing of this letter is instructive in two respects. First, it suggests that the party leadership set out organizational guidelines for the first time since the elections. Second, the letter betrays a sense of emergency that implicitly reveals the silence of the previous weeks.

The Center parliamentary delegate Heinrich Krone acknowledged this demand for directives when in an article published in the March–April 1933 issue of "The Young Center" (*Das junge Zentrum*), the journal of the youth organization of the Center party, he remarked: "You ask me whether there is a firm point from which one could take position on the events of the last weeks." Krone went on: "In times of the most difficult decision, it is always good to open the book of history and to draw on the lessons of our fathers. The past does not repeat itself. Yet, drawing advice from those who have withstood difficult crises is always recommendable."[25] For this purpose Krone referred to former eminent Center representatives (Ketteler, Windthorst, and Schofer) and from these exemplars concluded that it was necessary to take part in the transition and to continue to fight for fundamental liberties. He summarized his position with the motto of the former chairman of the Center party in the state of Bade, the prelate Schofer: "Forward into the new age with the old flag" (*Mit der alten Fahne in die neue Zeit*).

Krone's statement reveals a demand for guidance: "You ask me . . ." This is consistent with the point I made earlier: the lack of political and organizational directives in March and the concomitant demand for such directives on the part of the rank and file and Center officials at various levels of the party hierarchy. It is equally interesting that Krone characterized the situation in decisional terms, as "times of the most difficult decision" (*In Stunden schwerster Entscheidung*). This expression echoes the characterization used in the circular letter of 18 March from the secretariat of the Center party for the Rhine region and pervades many contemporary statements. Note further that Krone attempts to make ideological sense of the decisions that were made and in which he partook. He acknowledges that this exercise is limited, since the

24. Ibid., Abteilung XXI-77: Rundschreiben an die Bezirke.
25. *Das junge Zentrum*, March–April 1933, nos. 13–14, Konrad Adenauer Stiftung, Sankt Augustin, Nachlaß Niffka, I-034, 001-5.

"past never repeats itself." This synthesis is not a call for collaboration. It is a call for vigilance.

That some people are tempted to change sides in periods of intense challenge and might indeed decide to defect should come as no surprise. Defections in times of turmoil and challenge are inevitable. In any group—whether political or not—the level of commitment to the group's ideological stance represented by the group varies, and it is predictable that members the least committed to this stance should consider switching sides. The key question is whether these centrifugal tendencies are so strong that they jeopardize the existence of the group. The Center party showed no sign of such a breakdown process in March 1933. These observations are consistent with the conclusions of studies of local Catholic communities, such as that by Rauh-Kühne (1991, 362) in Ettlingen. I conclude, along with Hürten (1992, 184), that when on 18 March Gröber explains that some Catholic communities are changing sides with flags flying, he overestimates the extent of the defections.

WHICH REFERENCE GROUP?

The personal accounts and testimonies of Center party deputies do not mention pressures from the rank and file in favor of a compromise with Hitler. Nor is there evidence that their line of conduct was motivated by the attitude of their constituents. Ludwig Kaas chose to play the card of collaboration as soon as the election results became known. Although he approached Papen to this effect in his capacity as party chairman, he did so without consulting his party colleagues and without having been exposed to demands from Center party members. On the face of it, his decision seems to have been independent of such considerations. The heated exchange in Cologne between him and Brüning reported by Karl Bachem makes no reference to the attitudes of the rank and file.[26] The same remark applies to Clara Siebert's personal recollections of these two weeks.[27]

On 20 March Karl Bachem, who had an insider's knowledge of the leading circles of his party, remarked about the mood of his peers: "Since it has been banned [on 10 March], the *Kölnische Volkszeitung* is extremely cautious and low-profile. Many competent party colleagues, including religious ones, interpreted this attitude as cowardly and flabby."[28] Two days later, during a meeting

26. Stadtarchiv Köln, Cologne, Nachlaß Bachem 859, notes dated 22 April 1933, reproduced in Morsey (1960, 434).

27. Kommission für Zeitgeschichte, Bonn, Tagebuchaufzeichnungen von Clara Siebert.

28. Stadtarchiv Köln, Cologne, Nachlaß Bachem 859, handwritten notes dated 20 March 1933.

of the delegation executive committee on the morning of 23 March, Ludwig Kaas mentioned that some business circles complained that the party was not resisting.[29] Although, as I mentioned in chapter 4, Kaas's reference is vague, it indicates that circles in contact with the Center leadership voiced their opposition to a conciliatory stance, and that this oppositional stance was not confined to the Catholic workers' clubs. However, Kaas dismissed the charge that the Center party did not put up enough resistance. There is no other reference to external pressures in the minutes of the meetings of the parliamentary delegation and its executive committee.

These few observations suggest that on 23 March the Center party deputies made their decision independently of the opinions expressed by their constituents. Significant in this regard is the reaction elicited by the vote. In his report of 28 March, Joos mentions that passage of the enabling bill demoralized segments of Catholics (Aretz 1978, 78). This resignation surfaces in an editorial published in the 8 April issue of the *Westdeutsche Arbeiterzeitung*, the newspaper of the Catholic workers' clubs for western Germany: "There must have been grave reasons that led the Center party to vote for the enabling bill."[30] In a letter dated 8 April to Friedrich Dessauer, Respondek refers to the demoralization and disorientation of his constituency, implicitly relating this disorientation to the Center delegation's vote in favor of the enabling bill.[31]

In March 1933, taken aback by the extent of the challenge, the bulk of Center followers and rank and file had lost their bearings. They awaited directives and guidelines. The task of the Center party leadership was to redefine these bearings. As I will show in chapter 8, when delegates met in Berlin for the opening of the parliamentary session, they became acutely aware of the dilemma created by Hitler's constitutional challenge. Conjoint with this awareness was a sense of mutual interdependency. Delegates knew that they would have to collectively take a stand. Whatever their previous exposure to the rank-and-file admonitions—fears or calls for arms—the reference group became the delegation as a whole. Social and regional ties receded to the background.

---

29. *Protokolle*, 23 March 1933, Vorstand, no. 748, 629.

30. "Spiegel der Zeit," *Westdeutsche Arbeiterzeitung* 11–12, 8 April 1933, quoted by Aretz (1978, 78).

31. "Returning from my ward, where I again secured and cheered up those who were faltering and worn out, I found your article in the RMV [*Rhein-Mainische Volkszeitung*].... Panic and disorientation seem to be beyond any proportion" (Kommission für Zeitgeschichte, Bonn, Sammlung Dessauer II, no. 6817).

> Deputies arrive little by little, seating as they wish; their seats are not assigned in advance. There is no longer deputies from the Right, from the Center or from the Left. This is the first expression of the dislocation of the former political parties. —*La Dépêche de Toulouse*, 10 July[32]

In July 1940 parliamentary groups broke down. "There are no longer parties" (Jean Froget, Radical deputy, letter to his daughter dated 10 July 1940).[33] As they gathered in Vichy, parliamentarians realized that their affiliation groups had lost their significance. The far-right deputy Henri Becquart described how on 9 July "deputies [sat] in the boxes of the orchestra as they [were] entering the room. There [is] no longer the Right, the Left, 'reactionary,' Radical or Socialist rows. The room [is] like a palette, the colors of which would have been muddled."[34] The Socialist (SFIO) deputy of Puy-de-Dôme Albert Paulin described political parties as "dislocated."[35] The conservative senator Jacques Bardoux sat on the extreme Left side of the room on 10 July "to show that the old parties are dead."[36]

The breakdown was in the first place organizational. The parliamentary groups did not meet. One exception was the Socialist representatives of the Socialist (SFIO) delegation on 8 July.[37] The meeting of the SFIO delegates, on the other hand, did not prevent them from splitting two days later. Among the 132 SFIO representatives voting on 10 July, 90 endorsed the power transfer, 6 abstained, and 36 opposed the power transfer (chapter 1, table 6). Groups, in other words, did not provide their members with an organizational framework for coordination. As collective entities, they were nonexistent.

Chaos versus Cohesion

The chaos reigning in Vichy contributed in no small part to the lack of organization. Everything had to be improvised. The Radical deputy Lucien Galimand evoked "chaos" (*la pagaïe*), and his colleague from the Socialist party,

32. *La Dépêche de Toulouse*, 10 July, 1.

33. Quoted by Calef (1988, 432).

34. Becquart, *Au temps du silence*, 185. Becquart also observes: "political groups were dead" ("Les groupes politiques étaient morts"). Becquart, *Au temps du silence*, 155.

35. Archives nationales, Paris, Dossiers du jury d'honneur: dossier Albert Paulin, Memorandum for the honor jury, n.d., AL5325.

36. Bardoux, *Journal d'un témoin de la Troisième*, 495. In July 1940 Bardoux is affiliated with the Groupe de l'Union Démocratique et Radicale.

37. If we are to believe Calef (1988, 361), the representatives of the small French Social Party also met in Vichy.

Marcel Guernet, "full panic" (*affolement général*).[38] Scattered all around the city, parliamentarians were looking for their party colleagues, often in vain. They were left to their own. Routine processes of decision making and consultation no longer operated. "The events that took place in Vichy unfolded in an inexpressible confusion" (Jean Beaumont, senator of Allier, member of the centrist Democratic Left, or Gauche Démocratique).[39]

Beyond these circumstantial factors the breakdown sanctioned the conjoint effect of past cleavages over foreign policy issues (chapter 5) and the groups' structural weakness (chapter 1). Whereas the outbreak of the war had put a hold on the opposition between "appeasers" (advocates of conciliation toward Nazi Germany) and "bellicists" (advocates of frontal opposition), the conflicts over the armistice brought this opposition back to the fore. The groups' incapacity to meet and coordinate in Vichy bore the mark of these cross-party cleavages in a context of organizational frailty. Groups did not meet in part because they lacked the behavioral cohesion, discipline and collective identity that would have incited their members to spontaneously expect a meeting.

Time and Space: The Grand Casino and the Park

> In the alleys of the parc, just as encounters happened by chance, we exchanged our impressions . . . —Henri Becquart, deputy of the Republican Federation[40]

The breakdown of organizational groups makes interactions more random, more hectic, more informal, less structured, and less predictable than in routine times. Actors are more likely to interact with people with whom they are not affiliated and whom they do not know. Pierre Nicolle, who represented the employers' union (CGPF) in Vichy, spoke of the "most unexpected encounters."[41] The former Communist deputy Émile Fouchard noted that parliamentarians were meeting in small groups of "three or four, sometimes more."[42] Entering the Hôtel du Parc on 8 July, Jacques Le Roy Ladurie observed an "unbelievable hubbub.[43] Under Blum's pen, parliamentarians' febrile agitation

---

38. Galimand, *Vive Pétain! Vive de Gaulle!*, 43; Archives OURS, Paris, dossier Guerret, mémoire d'explication, n.d.

39. Archives Nationales, Paris, Dossiers du jury d'honneur: Dossier Beaumont, AL5298, letter to the president of the honor jury, 15 May 1945.

40. Becquart, *Au temps du silence*, 177; see also an incidental remark at 191.

41. Nicolle, *Cinquante mois d'armistice*, 12.

42. Fouchard's testimony in Marielle and Sagnès (1993, 56).

43. "A real human tide oscillated from one side to the other, buzzing with any kind of murmurs; busy like an ants' nest, the secret order of its activity eluded me" (Jacques Le Roy Ladurie, *Mémoires*, 203).

became an improvised ballet of erratic moves from group to group. Parliamentarians in the hall of the Grand Casino were "whirling, gathering together, breaking apart and then looking for each other again."[44]

Interpersonal contacts are not purely random, however. Their probability remains pre-structured by past interactions. Delegates are still more likely to interact—that is, to exchange opinions and information—with those whom they personally know rather than those whom they have never met before. The difference with routine times is that encounters channeled through ties that are not based on group membership become more frequent. Concomitant with the increase in randomness is an increase in the frequency of out-group interactions. Deputies and senators activate ties and connections established outside their affiliation group in parliament. As political connections lose their salience, we can reasonably expect nonpolitical connections to come to the fore. In the following analysis my focus will be on occupational and regional ties.

Nonpolitical Ties: Lawyers

Ties formed along occupational lines are probably too loose and infrequent to provide a basis for informal coordination. In most cases political affiliations take precedence over occupational identity. Lawyers represent a peculiar case, for two reasons. First, they have a strong sense of corporatist identity that can be traced to the "old-boy networks" presiding over the placement of graduates as they start professional life (Anceau 2003, 175–76; Le Béguec 1991, 24–28). This sense of group identity is reinforced by the ties that lawyers knot with one another in the course of their practice (Le Béguec 2003, 7–8). Louis Noguères offers a vivid example of this sense of identity: "I had dinner [in Vichy on 7 July] with my former collaborator in the law court, Lucien Lamoureux. You know that in the law court, the tradition is to maintain, *independent of any other consideration*, friendly relation (*confraternité*) between a former patron and his secretaries, even when the latter have become patrons in turn" (my italics).[45] Lawyers knew each other. Most of them practiced in Paris. They frequently interacted. When traditional political affiliations were disrupted or broke down, lawyers formed a socioeconomic group particularly congenial to the activation of interpersonal ties and the diffusion of a behavioral stance.

The second—and complementary—reason that made lawyers a special case in France was their numerical importance in parliament: 110 deputies

44. Blum, *A l'échelle humaine*, 83.
45. Louis Noguères's diary, *Événements* VII, 2235.

Table 18   Votes and Occupation in July 1940:
Lawyers versus Non-lawyers ($N = 640$)

	"No" Vote	"Yes" Vote	Total
Lawyers	19	101	120
Expected	*15*	*105*	
Other occupations	61	459	520
Expected	*65*	*455*	
Total	80	560	640

Note: Nine cases are missing.
Pearson Chi-Square: 1.5; df = 1; $p = .221$

of the sixteenth legislature (1936–40) were registered as barristers, forming the most numerous occupational group in parliament (Gaudemet 1970, 63).[46] When combined with their sense of corporatist ethos, which sometimes enabled them, through informal relationships, to coordinate on an implicit consensus, their numbers provided them with a critical mass.[47]

A first-order correlation shows that being a lawyer had no obvious effect on the likelihood of choosing one option rather than the other. The number of lawyers opting for a "no" vote is slightly greater than what we might have expected given the vote distribution (table 18). However, this observation is anything but robust. When we control for military occupation and political affiliation, on the other hand, lawyers appear twice as likely to have rejected the bill (table 19). We may interpret this finding as indicating a diffusion effect. According to this interpretation, contacts established outside parliament among lawyers contribute to the diffusion of a behavioral stance. The interesting point is that in the present case this diffusion effect, if any, far from going along with the tide, opposed it. Corporatist solidarity contributed to resistance, assuming that it had any impact at all.

The Mobilization of Regional Ties

Parliamentarians often traveled to Vichy with colleagues. "I arrived in Vichy on the ninth in the evening, coming from Nantes, with my colleagues of the

46. Lawyers represented 30 percent of the deputies elected in Aquitaine during the Third Republic, 13 percent in Nord-Pas-de-Calais (Ménager et al. 2001, 102–6), 30 percent in Limousin (El Gammal and Plas 2001, 18), and 20 percent in Normandy (Chaline and Sohn 2000, 9).

47. Both le Béguec (1991, 30; 2003, 114–18) and Anceau (2003, 188) note however the gradual decline in the number of lawyers in parliament in the last decades of the Third Republic.

Table 19   Lawyers' Probability of Voting "Yes" ($N = 640$)

Variables	"Yes" vs. "No" Votes	
	Parameter Estimates	Odds Ratio
Military occupation	.38[t]	1.46
	(.26)	
Political camps		
Left	−2.8***	.06
	(.51)	
Center	−1.75***	.17
	(.49)	
Lawyers	−.68**	.51
	(0.56)	
Intercept	3.65***	
	(.51)	
−2*log likelihood		420.10
χ^2		62.17***
Degrees of freedom		4

*** $p < .001$, ** $p < .05$, [t] $p = .15$

Loire-Inférieure Pageot, Le Roux, Thiéfaine, et Lefèvre"[48] (Roger Vantielke, Socialist deputy of Pas-de-Calais). Henri Becquart traveled by train with Charles Hartmann—"my former Alsacian colleague Hartmann, moved away like myself to Lourdes."[49] The centrist deputy of Moselle, Émile Béron, drove with the Socialist representative of Loire, Pétrus Faure, who hosted him with his wife and three children since the exode.[50] The Socialist deputy of the Pyrénées orientales, Louis Noguères, drove with Jean Jacquy, senator without group affiliation of the Marne. So did the centrist senator André Maroselli of the Haute-Saône and the Socialist senator of the Pyrénées orientales, Georges Pézières.[51] These connections were partly the product of circumstance. Becquart was in Lourdes at the same time as Hartmann. Vantielke contacted his Socialist colleagues in Nantes, where he happened to be after his release from a prisoner-of-war camp. Jacquy and Maroselly found themselves in the Pyrénées after the exode.

In some cases representatives elected in the same département decided to

48. Archives Nationales, Paris, Dossiers du jury d'honneur: Dossier Vantielke, AL5333, memorandum for the honor jury, 9 April 1945.

49. Becquart, *Au temps du silence*, 133.

50. Faure, *Un témoin raconte . . .* , 67.

51. Louis Noguères's diary, *Événements* VII, 2228.

make the trip together. Pierre Lohéac, rightist deputy of the Finistère, went to Vichy with senators of the same county: "on 8 July, I went to Vichy along with MM. Lancier, Le Gorgeu et Lejeune, senators, with the intention of voting against."[52] These regional connections were not incidental. Representatives elected in the same county knew each other. Furthermore, parliamentarians identified themselves and each other by reference to the département in which they were elected.[53] In his diary, whenever he mentions encounters with deputies and senators in Vichy, the Socialist deputy Louis Noguères always specifies the regional affiliation of those he meets. This classification is for him a significant and convenient way of situating his peers.[54] "I did not know Badie, but I knew that he had been elected in *Hérault* against the representative of the Popular Front."[55]

The trip to Vichy reinforced these informal ties. Once in Vichy, parliamentarians realized that political groups would not provide them with an organizational setting for coordinating their behavioral stance. Regional affiliations gain greater significance as political identities dwindle. One indicator of this greater significance is instances of regional coordination. Representatives of the same county deliberate and agree on a collective stance. "I consulted the senators of my *département*, Albert Sarraut, Clément Raynaud, and the doctor Guilhem, as well as my colleagues in the deputy chamber, Bousgarbiès and Mistler, and we decided to vote for the amended bill in the last analysis, after the quasi-unanimous votes of the deputy chamber and the Senate [July 9] in favor of the revision of constitutional laws" (Léon Castel, Radical deputy of Aude).[56] The representatives of the Bouches-du-Rhône are another instance.

52. Archives Nationales, Paris, Dossiers du jury d'honneur: dossier Lohéac, AL5319, letter to the chairman of the honor jury, 8 July 1945.

53. This regional identification is not necessarily confined to the limits of the département. Representatives of adjacent counties may coordinate their efforts for lobbying purposes. "I knew Pierre Laval quite well. He was senator of the Puy-de-Dôme, I was deputy of Cantal. We had quite frequent relations when the common interests of the two *départements* from Auvergne needed to be defended." Maurice Montel, Centrist deputy of the gauche démocratique who voted "no" on 10 July, testimony in Marielle and Sagnès (1993, 59).

54. "Pierre Masse, député modéré de l'Herault" (*Événements*, 2238), Boulet, "député de l'Hérault—comme Barthe" (ibid., 2240), "m'adressant à Rous, (député socialiste des Pyrénées-Orientales comme moi)" (ibid.). There are many instances of identifying parliamentarians this way. I cite only one more example, borrowed from Pétrus Faure's testimony: "Nous vîmes aussi d'autres parlementaires: Froment de l'Ardèche, Lucien Hussel de l'Isère." Faure, *Un témoin raconte . . .* , 68.

55. Louis Noguères's diary, *Événements* VII.

56. Archives Nationales, Paris, Dossiers du jury d'honneur: dossier Léon Castel, AL5303.

They met separately in a room adjacent to the grand Casino and decided to vote "yes."[57]

How many instances of regional coordination can we record and how many delegates are concerned? To answer this question I coded all vote explanations presented to the honor jury that refer to regional contacts as one determinant of the vote decision (see appendix A).[58] Of the 182 explanations available, fewer than 10 percent (seventeen) make reference to the regional factor. In the data set combining the vote explanations presented to the honor jury with other accounts ($N = 223$), the proportion of the regional coordination claims is 11 percent ($N = 24$). These numbers indicate the numerical importance of the process. Several qualifications are in order. First, not all these references to regional affiliations reflect instances of regional coordination strictly speaking. About a quarter refer to an alignment process that goes against the actor's initial preference. The actor wants to vote against. He changes his mind when he realizes that his regional peers are not willing to do so.[59]

Second, several instances of regional alignment take place along the lines of political affiliations. Representatives seek to connect with peers who they believe share similar political longings. "With my three colleagues from the Left, we had several discussions to establish a common vote. . . . Pierre Robert, Drivet and myself, we persuaded A. Sérol to abstain as ourselves so that we have a common vote. The other parliamentarians from the Loire *département* voted for the full powers" (Pétrus Faure, Socialist deputy).[60] The Socialist delegates of the Loire-Inférieure are a case in point. "During the debates and until the moment of the vote, I tried to get from my five Socialist colleagues an opposite

57. "The representatives of the Bouches-du-Rhône convened in the neighboring room to deliberate, for the purpose of taking a decision in common." Gros, *République toujours*, 65.

58. Regarding this data set, see appendix A. These explanations were produced after the war at the request of the honor jury set up to assess individual demands of rehabilitation.

59. Typical in this regard is the testimony of Pierre Colomb, centrist (Gauche Démocratique) deputy of Vienne: "Considering that M. Colomb arrived at the National Assembly as resolute as the senator André to refuse the full powers, but that he faced the opinion of the other parliamentarians of Vienne who observed to him that the armistice being signed . . . one was left with choosing between Pétain and a Gauleiter; considering that the power delegation was to the 'government of Republic,' was signed by president Lebrun, and that there was no danger for the constitution, considering that Pétain was a folding screen to avoid a coup by Weygand (Laval's fib in the corridor); for all these reasons the parliamentarians of Vienne asked Colomb not to break their unanimity; that the most persuasive [of these parliamentarians] was then senator Maurice, today deported (and rehabilitated)." Archives Nationales, Dossiers du jury d'honneur, Paris: dossier Colomb, AL5304.

60. Faure, *Un témoin raconte . . .*, 71.

vote, and Blancho will be able to testify that it is only to fulfill his call of a unitary vote on the part of the Socialist representatives of the *département* that I voted Yes" (Maurice Thiéfaine, deputy of the Loire-Inférieure).[61] His colleague Eugène Le Roux confirms.

Third, one-third of the references to regional contacts are from representatives of border provinces. The case of these representatives, in particular those from Alsace-Lorraine, deserves special consideration. After the armistice Alsace and Lorraine came under the threat of a German annexation. "The situation to which the representatives from Alsace-Lorraine were confronted and the motivations that may have inspired their vote are not the same as those which influenced the representatives of the other counties. The German propaganda would not have failed to interpret a "No" or an abstention vote as a loss of interest of Alsace in France or as a repudiation" (Charles Hartmann, rightist deputy of Haut-Rhin).[62]

The nine vote explanations available from the three départements of Alsace-Lorraine all emphasize this threat as a key motivation of the decision. Half of them point to a process of interpersonal coordination. "All the deputies from Alsace-Lorraine present in Vichy voted like one man for the indefectible attachment to mother patria" (Jean Heid, deputy of Moselle).[63] "I attended the national Assembly and I voted for the full powers for Marshal Pétain, with the full agreement of my Alsace colleagues and because the fact of voting differently than the majority could have been interpreted by the enemy already occupying Alsace as a sign of divorce with our French nationals" (Hubert Andlau, senator of Bas-Rhin).[64]

Savoie, which some may have seen as threatened by Italian annexation, is more problematic. The testimonies available make no obvious reference to a process of regional coordination. Cross-checking these sources, I identify four counties in which some parliamentarians determine their votes by reference to the stance of their regional peers—Aude, Bouches-du-Rhône, Loire-Inférieure, and Sarthe—in addition to the three départements of Alsace (Bas Rhin, Haut-Rhin, Moselle). Not including the border counties, the number of representatives potentially concerned amounts to 6 percent (34) of the "yes" votes. Including the delegates of the border counties, the figure adds up to 10 percent (56). These are absolute estimates, not estimates based on the number

61. Archives Nationales, Dossiers du jury d'honneur, Paris: dossier Thiéfaine, exposé lu devant le CDL, 14 November 1944, AL5332.

62. Archives Nationales, Dossiers du jury d'honneur, Paris: dossier Hartmann, AL5315.

63. Ibid.

64. Archives Nationales, Dossiers du jury d'honneur, Paris: dossier Hubert Andlau, AL5295.

of personal testimonies. Thus in July 1940 parliamentarians did activate regional ties as they searched for a line of conduct. But the actual proportion of representatives who ultimately relied on their regional peers to make up their mind is limited. If there was this sort of reliance, the different sources and estimates I have just mentioned suggest that it involved only a small minority of representatives.

This last observation underscores two points. First, the formation of regional subgroups is an emergent feature of the situation, contingent on the establishment of actual contacts. Representatives need to look for one another and maintain a minimal level of interaction. The representatives of Alsace-Lorraine got in touch in Vichy because of the daunting circumstances under which they had to make their decision. The Socialist representatives of Loire-Inférieure traveled together and stayed together. Regional coordination is unlikely if contacts among regional peers are incidental. Second, it may be that regional coordination is rare because from a strategic standpoint, the relevant reference group is not regional peers but the assembly as a whole. To analyze further these two points we need to pay closer attention to the cognitive dimension of the interactive process.

THE LOSS OF BEARINGS

> The opinion of our colleagues was so little settled . . .
> —Paul-Boncour, Senator of the Radical-Socialist delegation[65]

> [8 July:] Too heavy was the burden of my responsibilities . . . I was only thinking about the vote I had to cast . . . Never had I felt so much the truth of de la Rochefoucauld's maxim: "In troubled times, it is often more difficult to know his duty than to do it."
> —Becquart, deputy from the Republican Federation[66]

The diffusion of a behavioral stance is conditioned by the probability structure of interpersonal interactions *and* the type of information being exchanged by actors as they interact. Analyzing this informational component invites us to adopt a more cognitive approach to the interactive process. The focus on this cognitive aspect brings into relief a pervasive sense of disarray and uncertainty. Why is this so? The answer brings us back to group breakdown. The breakdown of affiliation groups makes individual actors less accountable to their peers. As their sense of group commitment dwindles, so does their sense of reliability.

65. Paul-Boncour, *Entre deux guerres*, 267.
66. Becquart, *Au temps du silence*, 183.

Through their informal contacts, actors realize that their peers have neither firm opinion nor firm preference. Their perception of the collective situation gets pervaded by a sense of frailty, fluidity, and oscillation. Talk is cheap. It is not clear what can happen.

Assessing the Stakes

The parliamentarian newly arrived in Vichy gets updated and seeks advice. He probes the opinions of colleagues, people he knows, people he interacted with in the past as well as peers he informally encounters for the first time in the parc and the corridors. The dominant feeling is a lack of bearings. "Confusion and disarray were general" (François Blancho, Socialist deputy).[67] "The political situation displayed the spectacle of the worst confusion, of the utmost disarray" (Albert Paulin, Socialist deputy of Puy-de-Dôme).[68] In his diary under the date of Monday 8 July, the Socialist deputy Louis Noguères refers to a "general state of uncertainty" among his colleagues.[69] "Disarray persists till the eve of the National Assembly's meeting [i.e., 10 July]: one ponders over, one discusses what course to follow" (François de Saint-Just, far-right deputy affiliated with the Fédération Républicaine).[70] The conditions of deliberations were marked by a feeling of "utter helplessness" (Victor Le Gorgeu, Radical senator who voted "no")—a feeling which Ernest Pezet, deputy of the Parti Démocrate Populaire, related to the lack of coordination among party colleagues (Delbreil 1990, 414).[71]

As parliamentarians probe each other's opinions and dispositions in informal interpersonal contacts, they get contradictory impressions. This confusion in turn accentuates their own uncertainty. Being uncertain about others, they become uncertain about themselves. André Baud, far-right deputy from Jura, made the connection explicit: "One needs to take into account the circumstances [of the time] and recall the disarray which *we* went through in these tragic weeks *to understand the anxiety I was feeling* to form an opinion and determine a vote that seemed to me exceptionally grave" (my italics).[72]

---

67. Archives OURS, Paris: dossier François Blancho, statement delivered in a meeting before Socialist delegates on 19 October 1944.

68. Archives Nationales, Dossiers du jury d'honneur, Paris: dossier Paulin, AL5325.

69. Louis Noguères's diary, *Événements* VII, 2238. "The opponents look for themselves, silently probe one other and despair to be so few and so worn out" (Maurice Martin du Gard, *La chronique de Vichy*, 40).

70. Saint-Just, *Une bataille perdue*, 115.

71. Le Gorgeu, letter to Jean Odin, 17 December 1945, reproduced in Jean Odin, *Les quatre-vingts*, 229.

72. Archives Nationales, Dossiers du jury d'honneur, Paris: dossier Wiedmann-Goiran,

Many personal accounts acknowledge a moral dilemma.[73] "As for my personal vote, I underwent a distressing debate of conscience. What I was observing and hearing, in particular Pierre Laval's maneuvers, incited me to vote against. But at this moment voting against was voting for nothingness since no other solution seemed possible: it would have been a symbolic act, with no effect"[74] (Joseph Laniel, conservative deputy of the Alliance). Alphonse Rio, a Radical senator from Morbihan who would get involved in the Résistance underground, depicted the decision as "a tragic moral dilemma" ("*un cas de conscience tragique*").[75]

Sharing Indecision

Given the risks at stake, parliamentarians are unwilling to disclose a clear-cut preference and do not commit to their talk as long as they remain uncertain about their future stance. They convey their hesitations, turnabouts, qualms, and interrogations, and in so doing disclose the frailty of their behavioral choices. More broadly, they convey their lack of reliability. This is the paradoxical outcome of this interactive process. Disarray breeds mutual uncertainty. In the process of interacting, exchanging impressions, opinions, assessments, and appraisals, these actors communicate their uncertainty to one another.

AJ5334. The Radical senator François Labrousse, who voted "no," speaks of an "atmosphere of anguish" ("*atmosphère d'angoisse*") (letter to Jean Odin, 29 December 1945, reproduced in Jean Odin, *Les quatre-vingts*, 220–27).

73. "A distressing inner struggle": the expression and others like it issue from the pen of representatives of different political stripes. Esnest Esparbes, Socialist deputy: "I was left to myself. Anxiety was griping my heart. I did not know what to do" (Archives Nationales, Dossiers du jury d'honneur, Paris: dossier Esparbes, AL3511); Henri Roy, centrist (Radical) senator of Loiret: "I will not hold forth on the July 10 vote. I cast it only after a grave inner struggle" (Archives Nationales, Dossiers du jury d'honneur, Paris: dossier Roy, Letter to the chairman of the honor jury, 6 May 1945, AL5328). Ernest de la Framond, far-Right deputy of Lozère representing the Republican Federation: "I always loved the Republic. . . . Yet, on 10 July 1940, I voted the power delegation. I did not take part in the consultations of Bordeaux. I arrived in Vichy on the 8th. I voted after a distressing inner struggle (*un débat de conscience douloureux*), after a night of true anguish, which I spent composing a vote explanation which I could not read at the rostrum of the Assembly and which specified that I intended to vote *against alignment with the Axe coalition*" (underlined in text; Archives Nationales, Dossiers du jury d'honneur, Paris: dossier Framond, letter to the chairman of the honor jury, 25 September 1945, AL5313). "This moral crisis ("*crise de conscience*") . . . you cannot deny that it was real since yourself you experienced it" (Maurice Voirin, letter to Léon Blum, 12 June 1945; Archives Départementales de la Seine Maritime, Rouen, archives Montalembert, 160 J 45).

74. Laniel, *Jours de gloire et jours cruels*, 117.

75. Archives Nationales, Dossiers du jury d'honneur, Paris: dossier Rio, AL5328: "Les prochaines élections locales et les représentants de la Nation."

Camille Chautemps summed up the situation in Vichy with a striking formula: "parliamentarians shared prostration."[76]

We get a sense of this process in testimonies which, adopting a synoptic view, offer insights on the dynamic of interpersonal interactions. Louis Gros, a Socialist deputy, notes: "Everyone observed everyone else, for we knew how grave was the hour."[77] Paul-Boncour, a Radical senator, makes the same observation: "It is too bad that some sound technician did not record the sound track of the talks being exchanged during these two hours [10 July, afternoon, intersession] during which everyone *asked others and wondered upon what course to follow*" (my emphasis).[78] Upon his arrival in Vichy on July 8, the Radical deputy Badie is advised by colleagues to be "extremely cautious" ("*il faut se montrer extrêmement prudent*"). These pieces of advice exemplify a "wait-and-see" attitude. There is uncertainty about others. The risks are high. One needs to be very careful in making a decision.

Volatility and Distrust

At the beginning of July before leaving for Vichy, the conservative Jean Jacquy and his Radical colleague in the Senate, André Maroselli, agreed with Louis Noguères and Georges Pézières that everything had to be done to prevent handing over the regime to a dictator.[79] On 10 July both endorsed Laval's bill. The Radical senator Vincent Delpuech expressed public reservations on 8 July and voted "yes" two days later.[80] As the Socialist deputy Louis Gros put it, "The vote took place in a certain hubbub and with real hesitation on the part of a great number of members of the Assembly . . . A lot of colleagues modified their vote several times, and some changed five times their ballot."[81]

Actors who rely on weak ties realize that their interlocutors have no incentives to commit to their talk. The latter can easily renege on their word. Therefore there is no reason to lend much credence to what they say. It is not clear to what extent the information provided through these interpersonal contacts is reliable. Talk is cheap not in the sense that it is casual, informal, and private — it does not cost much to express one's opinion — but in the sense that

76. "Les parlementaires partageaient la même prostration" (Chautemps, *Carnets secrets*, 254).

77. Gros, *République toujours*, 56.

78. Paul-Boncour, *Entre deux guerres*, 286.

79. Louis Noguères's diary, *Événements* VII, 2228.

80. Bardoux, *Journal d'un témoin de la Troisième*, 400.

81. Gros, *République toujours*, 64. "Beaucoup de collègues modifièrent leur vote à plusieurs reprises, et certains changèrent jusqu'à cinq fois leur bulletin de vote" (65).

it lacks reliability. Its informational value is problematic. Actors do not face the prospect of informal sanctions if they relay false information, or rumors. Accountability is diffuse. Words do not commit those who speak them. The parliamentarians' vacillation testifies to their lack of commitment, and those present can sense it. Hence the popularity of rumors, unfounded innuendos, and hearsay (chapter 3).

Face-to-face interactions then lose their dimension of trust. A fortiori, actors are less likely to disclose their preferences when they deal with people whom they do not know very well. The interesting point is that this lack of trust also affects members of the same party. Noguères, for instance, described how the long-standing trust that characterized relationships among Socialist representatives vanished in Vichy in July 1940. "Sunday, 7 July . . . among comrades of the party there is no longer this cordial trust which, beyond personal divergences, made the charm of our relation."[82] Distrustfulness pervades interpersonal relationships and discloses mutual uncertainty in interpersonal interactions.[83]

The far-right deputy Henri Becquart came to the same conclusion. Parliamentarians who wanted to resist "felt isolated and were looking for one another in Vichy. They did not know what were the feelings of those whom they were seeing again. . . . Everyone was distrustful of one's neighbor. Therefore, the proponents of resistance were not able to combine their wills and did not know how to act."[84] Although Saint-Just was not as explicit about his far-right colleagues of the Republican Federation, his observations strike a consonant chord. He points out avoidance strategies that go along with the lack of frank and trustworthy relations: "Everyday now, I go to Vichy, where the national Assembly will convene. Some good colleagues welcome me warmly; others appear to me, but as in a painful dream that is going to dissipate; little by little, they become foreign to me, they mean nothing to me . . . Silence and indifference is the supreme courteousness one can display to them."[85]

　　　■　　▣　　▨

"There were a lot of people in the park in Vichy in the evening of 9 July and during the day on 10 July. I happened to be there, and one could meet a lot of

82. Louis Noguères's diary, *Événements* VII, 2236.

83. François Camel and Paul Ramadier corroborate Noguères's testimony: "in this poisonous atmosphere (*atmosphère empoisonnée*), any trust in anyone seemed to have become impossible. Treason out of corruption or cowardice was at every step, even in men whom one could have deemed above all suspicion" (Camel, *Ultimes paroles*, 33). "The fervor of friendship gets cold" ("*La chaleur des amitiés se refroidit*") (Ramadier, *Vichy [juillet 1940]*, 51).

84. Becquart, *Au temps du silence*, 176. Becquart votes "yes" on 10 July.

85. Saint-Just, *Une bataille perdue*, 113–14.

people. These people were primarily speaking of the sessions of the Assembly and probing the opinions of those present who for the most part were either parliamentarians, or cabinet staff members or some directors of an administrative service" (Paul Boulet, centrist deputy of Gauche Indépendante).[86] "They were probing the opinions of those present": this observation—by a participant-observer—underlines the strategic dimension of interpersonal contacts. In March 1933 and July 1940 the challenge faced by parliamentarians was a risky one. Parliamentarians needed, first, to be updated about the challenger's plans and, second, to assess their peers' dispositions. As they interacted, individuals constantly drew strategic inferences about the behavioral stances taken by others, their implications as well as the implications of their own action. This assessment of consequences is reflexive. Actors are strategic.

This strategic background explains why contagion—the diffusion of an affective state—is a misleading representation of the process. When Léon Blum mentions the contagion of fear, he relies on a metaphorical account. The evocative power of this account rests on an image: individuals contaminate one another by face-to-face contact. Fear gets emulated by fear. The metaphor is apt as long as it remains a metaphor. It is mistaken if taken at face value. For it implies that the process is purely emotional, affective, and mechanical. People do not really know what they are doing. In depicting irrationality as the dominant behavioral mode, these accounts actually leave the process shrouded in mystery. The core phenomenon remains out of touch. Irrationality denotes unintelligibility.

Yet Blum's dramatic account points to crucial insights. Interactions matter. There is a diffusion process. What gets diffused is less an emotional state than a strategic assessment of the situation. Parliamentarians communicate to each other their equivocation, vacillation, sudden shifts in stance, lack of firmness, a sense of delusion, and lack of reliability. Disarray becomes pervasive because actors are strategic. This dubious oxymoron—a strategic disarray—outlines the first insight suggested by this analysis of interpersonal interactions. Actors can be subjectively oriented toward a self-reflexive assessment of consequences—in short, actors can be strategic—and yet may communicate to one another uncertainty, disarray, and confusion. In fact, actors convey to one another their disarray because they are strategic in their assessment of the situation. Confusion is generated by a strategic mode of interaction. As they witness others oscillate, actors become uncertain about themselves. Circular reaction has a strategic meaning.

One word about reference groups: parliamentary representatives are ame-

86. Paul Boulet's testimony, *Événements* VII, 2225 (my italics).

nable to their constituency and to their peers. They can align their preferences with one or the other. In March 1933 and July 1940 parliamentarians were primarily concerned about their parliamentary peers. They referred only marginally to their constituency as the main motivation for their decision. The relationship to the constituency was not decisive. When the delegates met in Berlin their relation to their peers took precedence over the relation to their constituents. In July 1940 formal affiliation groups lost their relevance as organizational and political entities. Parliamentarians reconstructed a reference group that included all those facing the same decision problem as themselves. The assembly became the reference group.

An analysis in terms of alignment through local knowledge depicts a process of collective alignment whereby individual actors assess collective preferences, make their choice on the basis of this assessment, and at some point reinforce each other's choice as they interact. Diffusion is complete when individual positions reach a state of equilibrium consistent with actors' local knowledge. Actors experience uncertainty insofar as they remain aware that their assessment of the preference distribution is based on a local sample. However, the greater the diffusion of one stance, the less inconsistent the information provided by interpersonal contacts across time and the less uncertain the assessment of the future. Diffusion goes along with a decrease in individual and collective uncertainty.

When applied to July 1940, this argument stumbles on the pervasive character of the uncertainty. Mutual uncertainty was a lingering feature of the collective situation. Far from yielding an informal consensus, interpersonal interactions contributed to the mutual character of this uncertainty. As actors sought and exchanged strategically relevant information, they also communicate to one another their fickleness, unreliability, and propensity to shift stance. They revealed that they did not have a definite stance. Instead of being a medium of risk assessment, interpersonal interactions became a medium of mutual uncertainty.

Thus in conjunctures of face-to-face interactions, the effect of diffusion and local knowledge can be undone, canceled, or on the contrary amplified. Depending on the preference distribution, the information provided through interpersonal contacts may undermine inferences about a collective stance. Then face-to-face interactions do not diminish uncertainty: they feed individual irresolution by making group members aware of their peers' vacillation, lack of commitment, and vulnerability to sudden shifts in stance.

PART IV

Collective Stances

The resilience of uncertainty is a striking characteristic of the situation. It invalidates the notion of a linear process and the postulate of a predetermined outcome. Still, actors do coordinate their expectations about themselves. They regain a sense of composure. They achieve a shared understanding of where they are going to stand. The purpose of the two following chapters is to explore the ins and outs of this adjustment process. What makes shared understanding possible? How do group members consolidate the beliefs that will determine their stance?

Chapter 8

The Production of Consent

We cannot explore processes of belief coordination without delving into actors' subjective appraisal of their situation, and we cannot reconstruct the phenomenology of the conjuncture without paying close attention to the temporality of the process. I explore this temporality from different angles. The wide angle covers the time frame of the two weeks subsequent to the German election. I use a more confined lens to reflect upon the meetings in Berlin. The close-up narrows the focus to the meetings of 23 March. As the moment of decision comes closer, actors' sense of dilemma gets exacerbated.

1

Until the newly elected delegates of the Center party meet in Berlin on 20 March, the day before the opening of the parliamentary session, the challenge for them remains relatively abstract. It is unspecified. The government has not released the bill. The Center delegates know that they will convene, and since the delegation has a tradition of group cohesion, they can reasonably expect a collective stance. They may anticipate how difficult this collective stance will be. But at this point they do not have to confront themselves with this difficulty. Suffice it to rely on the anticipation that the group will behave as a collective entity.

The publication of the bill in the evening of 21 March lifts any remnant of abstraction. There is no readily available script for dealing with such a challenge. The decision will be dire. The delegates can no longer elude the constraints of their choice. The context of the Berlin meetings makes them crucially aware of their mutual interdependence and their indeterminacy. The group as a whole has no definite stance. No formal decision is reached until the vote is about to take place on the afternoon of 23 March.

2

Unanimity and acquiescence characterize the Center delegates' ultimate stance. This collective outcome sanctions two processes that unfolded in the final delegation meeting before the vote. One was the coming together of the belief that acquiescence is the modal preference. What was critical to this process was the configuration of public stances of those who had become focal points for their peers as a result of their prominence. Whereas Ludwig Kaas, outlining Hitler's verbal assurance, unmistakably signaled acquiescence, Brüning withheld his reservations. The prominent actor who, in actors' recollections, dramatically and frontally opposed Kaas was someone whom his peers viewed as a maverick, outside the party mainstream, someone whose political career and independence of mind set him apart: Joseph Wirth.

On 23 March Wirth stood for himself in the eyes of the delegation members. He remained what he had always been: an outlier. Kaas, by contrast, stood for the group. Its members deciphered their stance in his, all the more so because he signaled acquiescence without explicitly endorsing it. The second process leading to the Center delegates' ultimate stance brings us back to the notion of sequential alignment. A nominal ballot confirms that the majority in favor of acquiescence was overwhelming—more than 80 percent of the delegation members stated a preference for endorsing Hitler's claims. Kaas explicitly asked the few dissenting delegates to reconsider their position so that they could avoid exposing themselves to the risks of an "isolated vote." Out of a sense of party discipline and in order not to jeopardize the unity of the party, these delegates decided to cast their ballot along with those of the majority. Acquiescence now was unanimous.

Subsumed in this account is a counterfactual. Had Brüning in the last meeting struck the delegates by his resolute opposition, had Kaas wavered or conceded that the deal was trumped, collective opposition was possible. This counterfactual contrasts with any deterministic account of 23 March. A close scrutiny of the dynamic of interactions among the delegates contradicts the suggestion that from the moment Hitler made his demands the outcome was foreclosed.

PAST AND FUTURE

The press mentioned the prospect of an enabling bill a few days after the elections of 5 March. "Today the cabinet decided to ask from the Reichstag an enabling bill allowing for constitutional changes. It is still unknown for how long this bill would be in effect" (*Die Kölnische Volkszeitung*, 8 March).[1] In

1. *Die Kölnische Volkszeitung*, 8 March 1933, 2. See Morsey (1977, 92).

an interview given on 1 February, immediately after the formation of Hitler's cabinet, Wilhelm Frick, the Nazi Reich minister of the interior, explained that "the new government [would] request from parliament an enabling bill since regular full powers [were] not sufficient for the accomplishment of its tasks."[2] During the electoral campaign the Nazis had left the issue dormant. They revived it now that the campaign was over.

Newspapers reported that the content of the bill would be broad enough to allow for constitutional amendments. Enabling bills in the past had not had such scope, and this constitutional provision alone singled out the bill. If the bill opened the way to constitutional changes, it would require a two-thirds majority in parliament, and given the distribution of seats in parliament, the position of the Center delegation would be pivotal (chapter 1). The press widely publicized this point. "The two-thirds majority required to pass [the enabling bill] can only be reached with the help of the Center" (*Die Kölnische Volkszeitung*, 8 March 1933).[3] "To pass this bill, like any other change of the Constitution, the government has to rely on the Center's acquiescence" (*Germania*, 9 March).[4] The Center delegates were therefore aware of the challenge lying ahead. Passage of the bill most likely would rest on their vote.

Anticipating a Conciliatory Stance

For the party rank and file, the silence of the leadership was a factor of indecision and cautious wait-and-see (chapter 7). Shall we draw the same conclusion for the newly elected Center deputies? The Center delegates knew that when the time came, they would have to commit themselves to a decision open to public scrutiny. The pressures begotten by the future decision were more stringent for them than for the party rank and file. However, this concern about the future was mitigated by the prospect of collective coordination. Given their history of discipline, they could reasonably hope to settle on a collective stance. The future looked dire. But they could expect the group to take a stand as a whole.

In mid-March the Center press reported that the Center delegates would collectively take part in the Potsdam celebration for the opening of the parliamentary session on 21 March. Goebbels, the master of the ceremony, staged the event as a celebration of the old imperial Reich. According to the program of the event,[5] parliamentary delegations would meet in the Garrison Church of

2. *Germania*, 1 February 1933, 1.
3. *Die Kölnische Volkszeitung*, 8 March 1933, 2.
4. *Germania*, 9 March 1933, no. 68, 1.
5. *Kölnische Volkszeitung*, 15 March 1933, 1; *Germania*, 17 March, 1.

Potsdam, where the Reich president and the chancellor would deliver a speech over the coffin of Frederick the Great.

With the exception of the Communists, all parliamentary representatives were invited. The Center press reported that Social Democrats were not likely to attend the event.[6] The Center delegation, for its part, would attend: "As reported, the Center *as a whole* will partake in the state celebration of Potsdam" (*Germania*, 17 March 1933, 1) (my emphasis).[7] The decision to partake in the Potsdam celebration was that of neither the delegation nor its executive committee. Both groups met on 20 March for the first time after the elections. This decision was the party chairmanship's. In a letter dated 15 March sent to all delegates, the chairman of the delegation, Ludwig Perlitius, made note of the invitation issued by the managing director of parliament and stated, "the delegation will take part in the Catholic service as well as in the solemn state ceremony."[8]

The Frame of National Concentration

This information was accompanied by editorials and commentaries that underlined the necessity to secure the constitutional state (*Rechtsstaat*) and bring about the "fundamental strengths" (*Grundkräfte*) of Catholicism (Morsey 1977, 125). "That the Center party at the national and state level reiterated its readiness to negotiate indicates that it respects the situation created by the 5 March elections. As a popular and constitutionalist party, the Center must strive that the electoral results of 5 March follow an orderly and constitutional course. These principles will orient the stance of the Center regarding an enabling bill and the constitutional changes it will entail" (*Badische Zentrumskorrespondenz*, 14 March 1933).[9]

6. "The SPD delegation will stay away from the ceremony." *Kölnische Volkszeitung*, 15 March 1933. The front-page article on the opening of the parliamentary session in the 17 March issue of the *Kölnische Volkszeitung* mentions that "Social Democratic parliamentary delegates will examine on the following Monday afternoon (20 March) the question of their participation in the event." This article adds: "it is believed that the [SPD] delegation will not take part in the Potsdam celebrations; however, it will show up in the actual opening of parliament in the Kroll Opera House." *Kölnische Volkszeitung*, 17 March, 1.

7. *Germania*, no. 76, 17 March 1933, 1. These words conclude the article on the opening of the parliamentary session.

8. Kommission für Zeitgeschichte, Bonn, Nachlaß Dessauer, FD 12, no. 6795.

9. *Badische Zentrumskorrespondenz*, 14 March 1933, reported in the 15 March 1933 issue of the *Augsburger Postzeitung*. This article makes reference to two parallel sets of negotiations between Kaas and Papen and between Göring and Esser. Kommission für Zeitgeschichte, Bonn, Nachlaß Wolff I 2 n, file: "März 1933."

About the same time, the Center national press increasingly framed the future position of the Center party by reference to Ludwig Kaas's "call for national concentration" during the campaign for the elections of 5 November 1932 (Münster speech, 17 October, 1932). Many party members, chief among them Brüning, noticed this shift.[10] Particularly significant in this regard was the lead article published by the *Kölnische Volkszeitung* in its issue of 17 March, unsigned and attributed to a "prelate." Several commentators (Volk 1972, 67; Morsey 1977, 122; May 1982, 327) have observed that the style, tone, and content of the article bear Kaas's mark. This article reminds readers of the bishops' condemnation of Nazism in a way that leaves open the possibility of rescinding this condemnation if Nazi leaders take the appropriate measures. Cooperation with Hitler's government is predicated on a revision of the bishops' position. The author of the article clearly signals the necessity of cooperation under certain conditions, expressing the hope that Hitler would not reiterate Bismarck's mistake: to leave out Catholics from the process of state reconstruction.[11]

In a Spirit of Conciliation

These different pieces of information—the announcement of future negotiations about the enabling bill, and the increasing frequency of calls for "national concentration"—point to the prospect of compromise. The call for national concentration gives the Center delegates an interpretive frame with which to make sense of the prospect of a conciliatory stance. "All accounts concur in suggesting that the majority of representatives went to Berlin . . . with the prospect of giving the government, which has been confirmed and reinforced by the national and Prussian elections, a credit of confidence in the spirit of the call for union" (Morsey 1977, 124).

This analysis lends itself to the tacit alignment argument. Center delegates infer the position which their peers are likely to take from information available to everyone. The press announces that there will be negotiations. There is no indication that the Center party leadership is a priori opposing Hitler's demands. The members of the Center parliamentary delegation have no reason to assume otherwise. Furthermore, the delegates can make sense of this conjecture in light of the official posture of their party in the past.

10. In his memoirs Brüning has disparaging remarks about this shift in stance, viewing the turnabout of the *Augsburger Post* "well before 21 March" as "the first signal" of a change in attitude. Brüning, *Memoiren*, 653.

11. *Kölnische Volkszeitung*, 17 March 1933, no. 73, 1.

Conjecture

Yet this anticipation of a conciliatory stance remains pervaded with uncertainty. The party has no official watchword. It did not send out clear-cut organizational and political guidelines. Any position remains conditional on future negotiation with the Nazi leadership. Even if the Center delegates can make a reasonable guess about their colleagues' inclination in light of the information publicly available, this remains a guess subject to the vagaries of future disclosures. They do not know for sure what their future collective stance will be. On the eve of the meetings in Berlin, any anticipation of a conciliatory stance is a conjecture awaiting confirmation.

Eugen Bolz goes to the first meeting of the parliamentary delegation executive committee since the elections, on 20 March, without fully knowing where his peers are standing. He goes to the meeting to get a sense of his colleagues' opinions. "This morning, from 10:00 A.M. until 2:00 P.M., I was in the meeting of the Executive Committee so that I know *to some extent* [*einigermaßen*] *what they think*" (letter to his wife, 20 March; my emphasis).[12] He has a stance in mind, but is unsure whether his colleagues share it. To his relief, they do. "Part of what I learnt is reassuring. I think that the parliamentary delegation and the party are finding a political orientation that is good and keeps the party in movement. This orientation is the ideological stance [*Gedankengut*] of a conservative policy and of the Catholic minority. On this point, we came relatively soon to a consensus within the Executive Committee."[13] This remark specifies a general disposition. It leaves concrete decisions open.

Abstraction and Commitment

Hitler's demands, furthermore, are unspecified. The government has not released the provisions of the bill that will be submitted to parliament. The Center delegates can assume that this bill will most likely entail constitutional changes. But they ignore the scope of these changes. Press announcements provide no information. "About the enabling bill. Still no clarity" (*Germania*, 9 March 1933, 1).[14] The Center delegates know that they will have to face a challenging situation without knowing how challenging the decision will be.

12. Hauptstaatsarchiv, Stuttgart, Nachlaß Eugen Bolz, Q 1-25, 7, handwritten letter dated 20 March, quoted in Miller (1951, 449).

13. Hauptstaatsarchiv, Stuttgart, Nachlaß Eugen Bolz, Q 1-25, 7, handwritten letter dated 20 March, quoted in Miller (1951, 449) and Sailer (1994, 208).

14. *Germania* no. 68, 9 March 1933, 1. Kommission für Zeitgeschichte, Bonn, Nachlaß Wolff G W I 2 n.

How far does Hitler want to go? How much exceptional power can he request from parliament?

The challenge being unspecified, the delegates cannot and do not have to fully commit themselves to one position. They are not directly confronted with their decision yet. At this stage they can still afford to elude this confrontation. A cautious wait-and-see remains a possibility, despite the threats looming. Hence before the content of the bill is published, delegates can expect a compromise without fully committing themselves to it. Their own disposition is not clearly established. It remains conditional on where their peers will stand.

The same remark applies to the call for national concentration. It is consistent with the Center party's political traditions, but devoid of unambiguous behavioral guidelines as long as the provisions of the bill are not known. Eugen Bolz summarizes the political line defined by the delegation executive committee on the morning of 20 March as follows: "the ideological stance of a conservative policy." The consensus on a party line reasserting the conservative creed of the Center leaves the door open to a constructive opposition and to the possibility of compromise. Its policy implications, however, are left indeterminate in the absence of precise decisions yet to be made.

In Clara Siebert's testimony, one statement keeps recurring: "to hold on faithfully to one's post" ("*treu gestanden auf seinem Posten*"). She first mentions this motto in the context of a meeting with Josef Schmitt, the prime minister (*Staatspräsident*) of the state of Bade: "On 23 February, I traveled inland and met the regional prime minister Schmitt. We thought about Schöfer's word: 'to hold on faithfully to one's post and (when necessary) to leave it in honor.' There could be no compromise and there will be none for the Christian."[15] Thus at this point in the electoral campaign, both Josef Schmitt and Clara Siebert agree that they cannot compromise with the Nazis and that this refusal to compromise is grounded in religion and ideology. The reference to Christ can only be understood in this sense. The statement "to hold on to one's post" is associated with resistance.

After the elections of 5 March, Siebert has exchanges with several colleagues (Baumgartner, Josef Schmitt, Josef Ersing) elected in the same state as herself (Bade). She mentions again Schöfer's phrase to a visitor shocked by the events of 11 March. She meets with Baumgartner and Schmitt on Sunday, 12 March. A week later she travels with Schmitt and Ersing to Berlin. Nothing indicates that at this point she is favorably disposed toward endorsing the enabling bill.

15. Kommission für Zeitgeschichte, Bonn, Tagebuchaufzeichnungen von Clara Siebert, 89–90.

Nor does she mention a clearly defined attitude among her colleagues. The exchange with Schmitt and Ersing leaves open the determination of a future stance (see chapter 7). For good reasons: they do not know which political mandate Hitler will seek to extract from parliament.

Political Indeterminacy

In the absence of any official stand, Center delegates have an incentive to reflect on the future in light of the past. The past points to the Center's conservative tradition. This tradition is consistent with compromise. The party is eager to demonstrate its capacity for positive collaboration for the sake of the country. During the first two weeks of the electoral campaign in February, Center representatives emphasized their willingness to take part in a government of "national union," led if necessary by Hitler, and they were careful to leave open the possibility of a future collaboration. They also emphasized that if the Center party promoted conciliation for the sake of political stability, it also opposed the prospect of a party dictatorship.

The speech delivered by Johannes Gronowski on 11 March is a case in point. "The Center has always collaborated and will in the future accomplish national work for the sake of the people. But after the speech of M. Göring in Essen we do not hurry, No, we can endure this phase, as many others, who during and after the war, took 'a noticeable reserve' until they no longer had to fear for their physical and material well-being. . . . We want no party state and no party dictatorship. In the same way we fought against the Terror and the exercise of domination through violence in 1918, similarly we condemn the ugly side effects of the so-called 'national revolution' of 1933. But we recognize all authority, which legitimately occupies its place. The parties of the Right have the majority. But we refuse that the strong minority be treated as second-rank citizens."[16]

INTERPERSONAL TIES

The Practice of Discipline

Group cohesion determines the degree to which individual actors view the group as a collective actor. Two factors affect this variation in group cohesion. One is the organizational basis of the group. Groups in parliament can be ad hoc. Or they can represent parties already constituted outside parliament. Modern parliamentary regulations often provide specific resources to regis-

---

16. Konrad Adenauer Stiftung, Sankt Augustin, Nachlaß Fritz Stricher, I-293 001-1.

tered groups, thereby creating the institutional incentive to form ad hoc affiliation groups. Unless the members of these groups share a specific program
action, there is no reason to expect the groups to display unanimity over time.
Party delegations, on the other hand, can be expected to have a higher degree
of behavioral cohesion.

In the institutional context of the Weimar Republic, this expectation was
indeed borne out: group cohesion was high. Very rarely, deputies voted against
their own parties. The split in the Center delegation about a bill on civil servants' salaries sponsored by the Wilhelm Marx cabinet in December 1927 was
exceptional in this regard: about one third of the Center delegates abstained
from voting and one delegate, Heinrich Imbusch, voted against (Cary 1988,
462; Knapp 1967, 210; Schäfer 1990, 211–15; see chapter 4). Furthermore, when
deputies parted ways with their delegation, their action elicited strong disapproval. For instance, many members of the Center party perceived Joseph
Wirth's vote against a confidence motion for Wilhelm Marx's cabinet in February 1927—Wilhelm Marx was a member of the Center party—as an act of
betrayal (Becker 1961a, 377; Hörster-Philipps 1998, 330–31).

This high level of group discipline and cohesion reflected the delegates'
dependency on their party for their political fortunes. Deputies were elected
according to a district system of proportional representation. The party's state
executive committee nominated the candidates. Dissenting delegates therefore
had little chance to be nominated again. The relation ridden with conflicts between Joseph Wirth and the Center party leadership in Bade is a case in point.
In the second half of the 1920s Wirth increasingly adopted political opinions
at odds with the official party line, and after he voted "no" to the confidence
motion for the Marx cabinet, the executive committee of the Center party in
the state of Bade kept him off the ballot for the parliamentary elections in 1928
(Knapp 1967, 217).

Regional Ties

Thus in the parliamentary landscape of Weimar Germany, party delegations
constituted significant reference groups. That is, the delegates identified themselves with party colleagues in parliament, with whom they coordinated their
actions, and most of their communications with other parliamentarians took
place within the social setting of their delegation. Within each group regional
ties, in addition to political ones, structured interpersonal relations. This salience of regional ties was a by-product of institutional design. The electoral
law of the Weimar Republic combined proportional representation at the district and national levels. Most delegates were elected on party lists at the dis-

Table 20   The Center Delegates: Vote Preferences on the Enabling Bill (23 March 1933) and Election Districts

	Total Votes	Total "No" Votes
Bade	3	1 (Ersing)
Berlin	1	1 (H.-J. Schmitt)
Breslau	2	0
Düsseldorf	11	3 (Fahrenbrach, Kaiser, H. Weber)
Frankfort an der Oder	1	0
Hannover	1	0
Hessen	4	2 (Bockius, Dessauer)
Cologne	5	1 (Teusch)
Koblenz	6	0
Liegnitz	1	1 (Schauff)
Oppeln	4	0
Potsdam	1	0
East Prussia	1	0
Thuringen	1	0
Westphalen	14	1 (Imbusch)
Weser-Ems	2	0
Württemberg	4	1 (Bolz)
National List	8	3 (Brüning, Joos, Wirth)
Total	70	14

trict level. In addition, parties had a small number of representatives elected in proportion to the number of votes received nationally. Those elected in the same state developed interpersonal relations among themselves and affiliated themselves with this regional basis.

Do regional affiliations in March 1933 structure the context of alignment? There is no evidence of this in testimonies and personal accounts. The breakdown of vote intentions by electoral district on the enabling bill (second meeting of the Center delegation, 23 March) is inconclusive (table 20). Apart from the districts of Düsseldorf and Hessen, delegates who in the nominal ballot taken on the afternoon of 23 March advocated a "no" vote were isolated voices. There is no instance of alignment at the regional level in favor of a rejection vote. Deputies identified by their election district display unanimity or quasi-unanimity in opting for acquiescence. This pattern may reflect systematic alignment in favor of abdication among delegates who clustered on the basis of their regional affiliations. But it may also indicate a process of alignment independent of regional ties.

How then did interpersonal interactions affect the delegates' inclinations and dispositions? On the train to Berlin, Clara Siebert met her regional colleagues Josef Schmitt and Josef Ersing. They discussed the situation. No resignation is perceptible in her testimony: "On March 19, I traveled in the evening to Berlin. Dr. Schmitt, Ersing and I sat together in the compartment until about 1 A.M. before we went to the sleeping cars. Again, I admired Dr. Schmitt's sovereign judgment and Ersing's firm [kernfeste] devotion."[17] Once in Berlin, Siebert met with her female delegation colleagues Helene Weber and Else Peerenboom. Peerenboom described the lack of basic freedom in Fascist Italy (see chapter 4). Prognoses were ominous. Center delegates became acutely aware of the dilemma that awaited them, with no possibility of remission.

No Exit

It is worth noting that on 22–23 March 1933 all Center deputies except one attend the delegation meetings and the parliamentary session.[18] True, they went to Berlin without knowing the exact content of Hitler's demands and, by way of consequence, the extent of the challenge that would confront them. But the context was pervaded with enough threats and disruption to let them believe that these demands would challenge their convictions. The decision to attend the meetings in Berlin reveals their commitment to the group. An individual representative who would choose not to take part in the vote would signal that he or she forwent group membership. Unanimous attendance reveals the groups' capacity to forge a consensus.

Once in Berlin, delegates could not decide not to decide. The decision to attend the meetings pre-committed them to a collective stance. In these conditions, individual abstention would make little sense. Interestingly, no one considered abstention in personal accounts. From the actors' point of view, individual abstention seemed out of the question. In deciding to individually abstain, a delegate would renege on the pre-commitment to a collective stance and step out from the group. One can always justify an absence, thereby combining the advantage of not exposing oneself with the preservation of group membership. Individual abstention cannot have this pretense.

17. Kommission für Zeitgeschichte, Bonn, Tagebuchaufzeichnungen von Clara Siebert, 98.

18. The missing delegate is Carl Diez. Andreas Hermes, the peasant unionist, was elected on the Center slate but resigned on 18 March when charged with embezzlement (Morsey 1960, 366; see chapter 4).

THE SENSE OF DILEMMA

Whatever we do, it will be fateful. — Eugen Bolz, letter to his wife, 21 March[19]

Make sure that you can pray once more before a tabernacle. Immensely difficult hours stand before us.
— Kaas to the Center parliamentary delegates, 22 March, in the evening[20]

Kaas acknowledged the challenge on 20 March before his colleagues from the parliamentary delegation executive committee: "Our decision is even more difficult than the one we had to make for the Versailles treaty."[21] Before the delegates two days later, on the evening of 22 March, he evoked "immensely difficult hours" ahead.[22] In an article published in the March–April 1933 issue of the journal of the Windthorst association, "The Young Center" (*Das junge Zentrum*), the Center deputy Heinrich Krone publicly acknowledged the trial: "These were hours of *extreme struggle* [*schwerstes Ringen*] for each one of the delegates. Each one struggled with the arguments for and against" (my italics).[23]

From personal testimonies it is clear that the predicament experienced during these few days took a dramatic turn. Right after taking cognizance of the bill along with his Center colleagues, Eugen Bolz conveyed to his wife in a letter written on 21 March how fateful the alternative was (see the epigraph). In a letter dated 27 March 1933 to Franz Graf von Galen, his colleague in the Prussian Landtag, Bernhard Letterhaus, spoke of the most difficult days of his life.[24] Clara Siebert used similar words to depict the afternoon meeting of the parliamentary delegation on 23 March: "We went to the building of the parliament for the most difficult hour that the [delegation] conference room ever witnessed."[25] On 27 March 1933, four days after the vote, Friedrich Dessauer

19. "Was wir auch tun, ist verhängsnisvoll." Hauptstaatsarchiv, Stuttgart, Nachlaß Eugen Bolz, Q 1-25, 7, handwritten letter dated 21 March, quoted in Miller (1951, 470).

20. Tagebuchaufzeichnungen von Clara Siebert, Kommission für Zeitgeschichte, Bonn, quoted in Das "Ermächtigungsgesetz" vom 24. März 1933, 136.

21. "Unsere Entscheidung ist schwerer als selbst die über den Versailler Vertrag," Protokolle, no. 742, 622, quoted by Morsey (1977, 127).

22. Tagebuchaufzeichnungen von Clara Siebert, Kommission für Zeitgeschichte, Bonn, quoted in Das "Ermächtigungsgesetz" vom 24. März 1933, 136.

23. "Es waren Stunden schwersten Ringens für jeden Einzelnen der Abgeordneten. Ein jeder kämpfte mit sich selber um das Für und Wider." Das junge Zentrum, nos. 3–4, March–April 1933, 14, Konrad Adenauer Stiftung, Sankt Augustin, NL Niffka, I-034, 001-5.

24. Materialen Graf Galen, reproduced in Morsey (1960, 433).

25. Kommission für Zeitgeschichte, Bonn, Tagebuchaufzeichnungen von Clara Siebert, quoted by Becker (1961b, 209).

wrote to Heinrich Brüning: "Now that a few days have passed since our decision, a decision that belongs to the most difficult I ever experienced in my life, I
would like to tell you, dear friend, that you correctly managed the matter."[26]

Why such a struggle? Why such a trial and indecision? Bolz provides the
answer in a letter to his wife on 21 March: "The content of the enabling bill
surpasses all expectations."[27] The Center deputies realized that the challenge
was formidable and without precedent. Never had they been confronted with
such demands. Never had they been asked to devolve constitutional powers
to a political actor who challenged the core of their political philosophy. They
had voted for enabling bills in the past, but never for one like this.

Disclosure

The first meeting of the delegation took place on 20 March, in the afternoon.
Almost all the delegates were present.[28] In this meeting Ludwig Perlitius, the
chairman of the delegation, introduced the delegates elected for the first time
to parliament and spoke of the plan to take part in the Potsdam celebration
scheduled for the following day. Georg Schreiber mentions the measures taken
against the press. Then, according to the minutes of the meeting, it was "decided to defer a political debate in the delegation."[29] Bolz requested a discussion of the consequences of the election in party-politics terms. Joseph Wirth
remarked on the possibilities of a governmental breakup, the Center's principled position vis-à-vis the political developments, and the Catholics' tasks
in a time of high nationalist tide.[30] Kaas devoted the rest of the meeting to
general considerations about the circumstances facing the Center party and
its political line in the future. There was no discussion of delegating executive
and constitutional powers to Hitler. As the *Kölnische Volkszeitung* reported,
"the delegation has not taken any position on and could not pass any resolution regarding the enabling bill since governmental consultations have not
ended yet."[31]

The text of the enabling bill was released the following day, in the afternoon.

26. Kommission für Zeitgeschichte, Bonn, Nachlaß Dessauer FD 12, nos. 6596–97. Similarly,
August Wegmann evokes deep "anxiety" (*Angst*). Konrad Adenauer Stiftung, Sankt Augustin,
NL Wegmann I-366, 040-2, letter to Repgen, 9 July 1966.

27. "Der Inhalt [des Ermächtigungsgesetzes] übertrifft alle Erwartungen." Hauptstaatsarchiv,
Stuttgart, Nachlaß Eugen Bolz, Q 1-25, 7, handwritten letter dated 21 March.

28. *Protokolle*, 623 n. 1.

29. *Protokolle*, 20 March 1933, Fraktion, no. 743, 623.

30. Ibid.

31. *Kölnische Volkszeitung*, 21 March 1933, 1.

"Here We Are, Every Man for Himself" (Bolz, 22 March 1933)

> I cannot come to terms with the events. I no longer have the strength. I can only pray. —Clara Siebert to Georg Schreiber, 21 March 1933[32]

In this time of challenge the delegates reasserted their membership in the group. Only a handful of delegates (Eugen Bolz, Hermann Joseph Schmitt, Joseph Wirth) decided not to take part in the celebrations marking the opening of the parliamentary session in Potsdam.[33] The overwhelming bulk of the Center delegates did not envision their action outside the group setting. A letter dated 14 March 1933 from Friedrich Dessauer to the secretary of the Center party, Vockel, about his participation in the Potsdam celebration is revealing: "I am sending you my answer to the executive office of parliament concerning participation in the celebration for the opening of parliament, because I will of course treat the event like the other delegates. If the other delegates go to Potsdam, I will go."[34]

Individual Decisions, Collective Setting

The delegates realized that they would have to reach a consensus. They also realized that each one ultimately would bear the responsibility of his or her vote. This duality was the source of considerable tension. If the delegates individually confronted their own responsibilities, the challenge would be hardly bearable. If, on the other hand, they exclusively relied on the group, they would forgo their integrity as individual decision makers. The upshot was a constant vacillation between an individual and a collective view. As individuals, the delegates reflected on their own responsibilities. As group members, they made their stance conditional on the determination of a collective stance.[35]

32. Kommission für Zeitgeschichte, Bonn, Tagebuchaufzeichnungen von Clara Siebert, reproduced in Becker (1961b, 208).

33. "The colleague from Württemberg Bolz and myself kept away from the state celebration." Bundesarchiv, Koblenz, Nachlaß Wirth N1342/133, "Die historischen Reichstagssitzungen vom 21. und 23. März 1933," 4, 7. See also Nachlaß Wirth N1342/18, question 29 [p. 2]. On the attitude of Hermann Joseph Schmitt, see Schauff's recollections (Institut für Zeitgeschichte, Munich, Archiv Johannes Schauff, ED 346, Nr. 34).

34. Kommission für Zeitgeschichte, Bonn, NL Dessauer Sammlung 2, FD 12, no. 7128. In his letter to the executive officer of parliament, Galle, Friedrich Dessauer makes the same statement: he will attend the opening ceremony of parliament in Potsdam on 20 March if his colleagues, the deputies of the Center party, decide to do so (Kommission für Zeitgeschichte, Bonn, Nachlaß Dessauer, FD 12 no. 6795, 7127).

35. The meeting context magnifies interdependence and, in the absence of information, contributes to mutual uncertainty. Clara Siebert indirectly relates her uncertainty to her col-

Bolz's private reaction to the disclosure of the enabling bill offers a remark-able expression of this tension. In a letter to his wife written on 22 March, the day before the vote, he refers to the intractable character of the choice facing them: "Here *we* are, *every man for himself*, struggling with the position we should take regarding this unprecedented enabling bill. I cannot write the pros and cons. The constraints we face will probably lead us to vote for the bill" (my italics).[36] The letter is remarkable, for it combines a dramatic emphasis on the ultimate responsibility of each delegate with a longing for a consen-sus. Bolz is suggesting that no one can be expected to cope individually with such a dilemma. Strikingly, as he acknowledges the intractable character of the choice, Bolz simultaneously adopts the perspective of the group ("we"). This oscillation between the collective and the individual points of view was constant throughout the meetings, as long as no formal decision was taken and the group stance remained open.[37]

Hanging On

The delegation meeting on the evening of 22 March was short. It started at 8:00 P.M. and ended at 8:45 P.M. Delegates knew that Ludwig Kaas had met with Hitler earlier during the day. "On 22 March we had a delegation meet-ing—Kaas was again with [Hitler] to discuss the issues of religious guarantees, which we ought to unconditionally request. We hoped for binding explana-tions, without which the enabling bill is not even worth discussing" (Clara Siebert).[38] Ludwig Kaas provided a summary of his own exchange with Hitler to the executive committee right before the meeting with the delegation. When

leagues: "the delegation was to meet at 3:00 P.M. [on 20 March], but because *we* still did not have the text of the enabling bill, the meeting was postponed to 6 P.M. *We* still did not have the text. The questions about the enabling bill were oppressing [*lastende*] questions, it was difficult, very difficult to form opinions and to have answers." Kommission für Zeitgeschichte, Bonn, Tagebuchaufzeichnungen von Clara Siebert, Arch 46, 99. There is no indication in the minutes of the Center delegation meetings that the meeting of 20 March was postponed to 6:00 P.M.: it started at 15:30 and ended at 17:00. *Protokolle*, 623. As the minutes of the meeting suggest, Siebert is most likely referring to the postponement of a debate on the enabling bill. This interpretation is consistent with the report in the 21 March issue of the *Kölnische Volkszeitung*, which Morsey quotes in relation to this issue (*Protokolle*, 623 n. 5).

36. Hauptstaatsarchiv, Stuttgart, Nachlaß Eugen Bolz, Q 1-25, 7, handwritten letter dated 22 March, quoted in Miller (1951, 450).

37. The delegates met four times between 20 March and 23 March: in the afternoon on 20 March, in the evening on 22 March, and twice (morning and afternoon) on 23 March.

38. Kommission für Zeitgeschichte, Bonn, Tagebuchaufzeichnungen von Clara Siebert, quoted in Becker (1961b, 209).

the delegation meeting took place, he made no mention of this exchange. Nor was there any debate on this subject. Kaas brought to the delegates' attention a letter by Göring, the minister of interior for the state of Prussia, about an incident with police officers on the previous day.[39] The rest of the meeting was devoted to organizational issues. The delegation proceeded to validate the nominations of the executive committee for parliamentary committees.[40] The Center press reported: "The delegation's political decision will take place on the next day" (*Kölnische Volkszeitung*).[41]

Significantly, when she described this in-between situation, Clara Siebert confused the content of the enabling bill with the letter that Hitler was supposed to communicate to the Center leadership about the scope of the bill.[42] She remarked: "We still did not have the text of the enabling bill." The confusion is revealing in two respects. Siebert remembered lacking key information about the terms of the alternative. Second, she remembered that the delegates ("we") were awaiting Hitler's written statement. This letter takes precedence over the provisions of the bill. In her recollection, it highlights the deferral of a collective discussion toward defining a collective stance. Thus on 22 March — the day before the vote was scheduled — there was no discussion of the enabling bill. The Center deputies did not take cognizance of the substance of the talks with Hitler, and the prospect of a collective decision was — informally or not — postponed to the next day, Thursday 23 March.

"We Still Could Not Make Any Decision" (Clara Siebert)

The day would be critical. It would start with the Center leadership's attempt to have the vote on the bill deferred by one day. For this purpose Johannes Bell and Albert Hackelsberger met with Frick, the federal minister of the interior. Their colleagues in the executive committee convened at 10:15 A.M., but in their absence the meeting was adjourned at 10:30 A.M., then resumed at 11:00 A.M. Hackelsberger reports Frick's announcement: "the chancellor wants to be done today. . . . The government's explanation is right now being considered by the

39. See chapter 7: as they were about to leave for Potsdam by car in the morning of 21 March, the Center representatives were asked by several people who introduced themselves as police officers if the male representatives could be searched for weapons. The delegates refused to leave their cars and the search was not pursued. The incident prompted Ludwig Kaas to call Göring in protest.

40. *Protokolle*, 22 March, delegation executive committee, no. 747, 628.

41. Quoted by Morsey, *Protokolle*, 23 March, Delegation, no. 747, 628 n. 5.

42. Becker (1961b, 209) points out this confusion by remarking that the text of the enabling bill was published the previous day, on 21 March.

cabinet. It will be submitted to us half an hour before the plenary session. If clarifications are necessary, this should be possible during the afternoon pause."[43] The vote would not be postponed. The Center delegation would have to take a stand on the same day.

The meeting of the parliamentary delegation began at 11:15 A.M. Kaas expounded to the delegation the concessions agreed to by Hitler: no action would be taken against the will of the Reich president; a board would be formed in charge of advising laws adopted within the framework of the enabling bill; equality before the law would be respected, except for the Communists; the government did not intend to suppress the independence of judges; the civil servants' membership to the Center party would not be a ground for retaliatory measures; the Christian influence in education would be protected; and the enabling bill would not deal with matters pertaining to the Church, the existent concordats, and education.[44]

Adam Stegerwald, who took part in the talks with Hitler, expanded on Kaas's report: "parliament will not be excluded [from the political process] if it does not make difficulties for the government."[45] Kaas's and Stegerwald's explanations are positive qualifications of the bill. Hitler's concessions would have a dubious value in Kaas's and Stegerwald's presentation if simultaneously both were calling into question Hitler's word. This was not the case. The reports are matter-of-fact assessments. They sound like factual endorsements.

Doubts and suspicion were raised not by those who had been involved in the talks with Hitler but by someone who remained aloof from them: before the meeting closed, Heinrich Brüning expressed his reservations: there was no guarantee that Hitler's government would keep its promises regarding the points that had been agreed upon.[46] This observation is important: for the first time the delegates witnessed dissent on the specific issue of the enabling bill. They observed Brüning express his qualms, stating that he could "hardly opt for a 'yes' vote even if it is acknowledged that one does not carry a moral responsibility for acquiescence" (meeting transcript).[47] Two days earlier Joseph Wirth had taken a stand in the delegation about the Center party's funda-

---

43. *Protokolle*, 23 March, delegation executive committee, no. 749, 629.

44. Ibid., no. 750, 630.

45. "Dr. Stegerwald: . . . Man wolle [den Reichstag] nicht ausschalten, falls er der Regierung keine Schwierigkeiten mache." *Protokolle*, 23 March, parliamentary delegation, no. 750, 631.

46. "Guarantees for the realization of the government's promises have not been provided." *Protokolle*, 22 March, parliamentary delegation, no. 750, 631. The minutes of the meeting indicate no other speaker than Kaas, Stegerwald, and Brüning.

47. *Protokolle*, 23 March, parliamentary delegation, no. 750, 631; quoted by Morsey (1977, 136).

mental attitude and the Catholics' tasks in a time of high nationalistic tide. The minutes of the meeting suggest that his remarks prompted a reply from Ludwig Kaas. But this debate—assuming that it was, implicitly or not, confrontational—was not specifically on the enabling bill.

Brüning's public reservations were a matter of uncertainty. They unsettled the delegates' expectations about their own collective position. Along these lines, Morsey (1977, 136) suggests that no formal decision was taken in this meeting because of Brüning's public reservations. From Kaas's perspective, however, the purpose of the meeting was neither to determine nor to debate a collective stance. The purpose was mainly to deliver a report about the meetings with Hitler. Kaas had made this point clear earlier before the executive committee (10 A.M.). After Johannes Bell and Albert Hackelsberger reported that the vote would take place during the day and that Frick had turned down the proposal to reschedule it for the following day, Kaas concluded: "it is necessary to clarify the situation in the delegation. For that purpose, [I] will report to the delegates." The subsequent remark is crucial: I "will bring about [*herbeiführen*] the decision during the pause."[48] The "pause" that Kaas referred to was the intersession scheduled *after* Hitler's speech.

In postponing the decision, Kaas made it conditional on the programmatic statements that Hitler would provide before parliament in the early afternoon. The delegates were left hanging on Hitler's assurances and promises. Clara Siebert recollects the meeting in precisely these terms: "The morning [of 23 March] was for the delegation; the text of the enabling bill [i.e. Hitler's letter] was still not there. We still could not make any decision. We dealt with the government's explanation [as reported by Kaas]. In the afternoon, we went to the opera Kroll Opera House."[49]

HITLER'S SPEECH

In this time, in which probably no one had ever been more deeply shaken . . .
—Joseph Wirth, manuscript: The historical sessions of parliament of 21 and 23 March 1933[50]

The Center representatives went to the Kroll Opera House at 2 P.M. for the opening of the parliamentary session. The session began with the vote on a

---

48. *Protokolle*, 23 March, delegation executive committee, no. 749, 629.

49. Kommission für Zeitgeschichte, Bonn, Tagebuchaufzeichnungen von Clara Siebert, reproduced in Becker (1961b, 209).

50. "In dieser Stunde, in der wohl niemand nicht im tiefsten aufgerüttelt war." Bundesarchiv, Koblenz, Nachlaß Wirth N1342/133, "Die historischen Reichstagssitzungen vom 21. und 23. März 1933," 7.

proposal to modify the regulations concerning the parliamentarians' leaves of absence (see chapter 1), which simultaneously excluded absentees without a justification for up to sixty days and considered them "present" for current parliamentary debates.[51] The proposal was adopted with the support of the Center delegation. Hitler then went to the rostrum.

Hitler's programmatic speech simultaneously reasserted the prospect of a dictatorship with distinctive ideological principles — race and blood — and stipulated the centrality of Christianity (see chapter 1). Both Christian confessions were "the most important factors that consolidated nationhood" and Christianity the "unwavering grounding of the ethical and moral life" of the German people. This last claim was intended to reassure Catholics. The new regime would not challenge Christianity. Actually, the "government of national revolution" — Hitler assumed the revolutionary character of his government — would preserve the influence of Christianity. This speech echoed Kaas's presentation of the enabling bill before the Center delegates in the morning.

If the delegates left their meeting unsettled by Brüning's public reservations, Hitler's speech, on the other hand, was consistent with Kaas's announcements. Clara Siebert remarked: "*we* noticed and sensed in the speech [of the chancellor] the influence of prelate Kaas" (my emphasis).[52] This concordance predisposed the delegates favorably toward a "yes" vote. Hitler confirmed previous signals about the anticipation of a compromise. Right before the delegation met again, Brüning was told that two-thirds of his colleagues were ready to vote for the bill.[53]

Shall we then conclude that the game was settled? Hitler in his speech reasserted the centrality of "race and blood," in direct opposition to Christian ethics. As Buchheim (1961, 503) points out, the assertion that the state creates the conditions for a "true, real and internal religiosity" is a blaspheme. When Hitler said, "the government sees in both confessions important factors for the maintenance of our nationhood," he was de facto relativizing the Christian faith and making its right of existence dependent on its function. Equally ominous was the reminder that "the belonging to one confession or one race

51. Paragraph 2a of the new regulation empowered the chairman of Parliament to bar a delegate from access to Parliament for up to sixty days if this delegate did not attend a parliamentary session without a health certificate. In a letter to Repgen dated 9 July 1966, Wegmann discusses the political consequences of the change (Konrad Adenauer Stiftung, Sankt Augustin, Nachlaß Wegmann, I-366, 040-2). Since the eighty-one Communist delegates were amenable to the new regulation, the Nazis needed about fifty more absentees among the non-Nazi parties to be able to pass the enabling bill without the support of the Center party or the BVP.

52. Kommission für Zeitgeschichte, Bonn, Tagebuchaufzeichnungen von Clara Siebert; partially reproduced in Becker (1961b, 210).

53. Brüning, *Memoiren*, 657.

cannot waive an individual from his obligations before the law." Hitler's formulations concerning the issue of schools were broad enough to allow for many
different interpretations: "the national government will grant the Christian
confessions, and secure to them, the influence that is due to them." Who would
then decide about this influence?

These assurances were double-edged. Hitler simultaneously provided lip
service to the issue of religion and alluded to the totalitarian and racist character of his claims to state power. Anyone informed about Hitler's political
goal and the Nazis' ideological worldview had reasons to be suspicious of these
assurances. The speech would produce its intended effects if the delegates concurred in viewing Hitler's word as a valid commitment. This required a considerable amount of self-persuasion. For Joseph Wirth there was no ambiguity:
"Whoever had a look at the room during Hitler's speech, whoever had ears to
listen, could think and did not have a hard pebble in place of the heart must
have seen that a satanical travesty and ape-like foolishness had succeeded in
coming to power with terrifying suggestion."[54] Clara Siebert states that right
after Hitler's speech, she wanted to vote "no."[55]

STANCES AND DECISIONS

During the three-hour recess the Center delegates had to make their decision.
The delegates met in their usual room in the Reichstag building for about two
hours, clearly aware of the historical significance of the moment. The meeting would be decisive and they knew it. Because of the stakes and the risks
involved, the session was the most dramatic, difficult, and challenging that
the Center delegation ever experienced. Debates were stormy. The meeting
became confrontational, and yet the great majority of the delegates agreed on
collective acquiescence. I analyze this outcome in light of the public posture
of the prominent members of the delegation.

"Our Harvest Field Is behind Us" (Kaas)

Kaas overshadowed the meeting. He opened the debates by outlining the Center's defensive position: "our harvest field [literally, the field to be cut: *Schnitt-
feld*] is behind us." . . . "We must accomplish and fulfill God's will wherever

---

54. Bundesarchiv, Koblenz, Nachlaß Wirth, 1342/133, "Die historischen Reichstagssitzungen
vom 21. und 23. März 1933," 9.

55. Kommission für Zeitgeschichte, Bonn, Tagebuchaufzeichnungen von Clara Siebert, reproduced in Becker (1961b, 209).

our place is. However harsh is our fate, it does not free us from accomplishing our duty. The nation is in the greatest danger and we cannot afford to fail."[56] The literal meaning of these statements is not straightforward. Kaas was not explicitly advocating a vote. For an external observer these considerations can easily sound ambivalent and unclear. For the delegates, however, these considerations were fully in line with the stand that Kaas had taken at the morning meeting. They knew where he stood.

As early as 20 March, Kaas had emphasized the necessity for the Center party of a "fundamental reorientation toward the religious dimension."[57] His analysis of the situation—made, according to the minutes, right after some remarks by Wirth on the "Catholics' duties in the conjuncture of high national tide"[58]—could be interpreted as a call for a realist adjustment to the constraints of the time, however ambiguous his formulations might seem: "We need to come to terms with the fact that our past working methods are being restricted. But it is preferable to be restricted than to make moral commitments, which on the long term will deprive us from our rights. We must strive by all means to have legal-constitutional principles back in force again."[59]

Kaas's recommendations at the morning meeting of the delegation, before Hitler delivered his speech, pointed to the same conclusion. While it was important to "save the soul" of the [Center], it was also clear that "the rejection of the enabling bill" would have "unpleasant consequences for the delegation and the party. The only thing left is to protect ourselves from the worst. If a two-thirds majority were not achieved, the government will carry out its plans through other means."[60] His position underscored the necessity of conciliation.

Thus when Kaas stated during the afternoon meeting that the harvest field was behind the Center party and added, "However harsh is our fate, it does not free us from accomplishing our duty," no one in the delegation doubted what he meant. His obvious resignation, as well as his favorable view of Hitler's concessions, left no doubt that he favored consent. The Center needed to acquiesce. The delegates understood his statements as a "recommendation" to endorse Hitler's demands (Morsey 1977, 139).

56. Kommission für Zeitgeschichte, Bonn, Tagebuchaufzeichnungen von Clara Siebert, abridged in Becker (1961b, 209).

57. *Protokolle*, 20 March, parliamentary delegation, no. 743, 623.

58. Ibid.

59. Ibid.

60. Ibid., 23 March, parliamentary delegation, no. 750, 630.

Wirth contra Kaas

Kaas was contradicted, though. There was a clash with Wirth, a violent one according to Wirth himself. "To say plainly the matter, I would have happily thrown at Kaas an inkwell or the small bronze statue of the old Windthorst which lay before him on the table. On this day I was, politically speaking, fed up with prelate Kaas."[61] Wirth provided a dreadful picture of the Nazi takeover and described how Hitler would consolidate his grip. "For more than one hour, more visionary than ever, [Wirth] sketched the future picture of what National Socialism would inflict on Germany" (Hermann Joseph Schmitt, Center Reichstag delegate).[62]

"There was no unanimity of opinion" (Siebert),[63] and in light of the dramatic confrontation between Kaas and Wirth, we might have expected more uncertainty, disarray, or cleavage. Yet the dissent failed to produce these effects. There was no group split. Unless we take this fact for granted, the lack of effect becomes meaningful in light of the theoretical considerations developed in chapter 6 regarding status, thresholds, and shared perceptions of individual dispositions. Three points stand out. First, as a result of his past positions Wirth stood outside the party. His public statements had no strategic value for the group members. Second, Kaas's behavior on 23 March stood in direct contrast to Wirth's, lending credence to the belief that he was making his stance conditional on the delegation's. Hence his statements had considerable relevance for the group members. Third, Kaas framed the conflict with Wirth on 23 March in a way that reinforced the common perception of Wirth as outside the party mainstream. I develop these three points in turn.

Wirth, the Outlier

Both Kaas and Wirth were highly visible actors. Kaas owed his prominence to the party chairmanship, and Wirth his to his past ministerial responsibilities and public positions. While Kaas embodied the party mainstream, Wirth was for his party colleagues a "maverick" (Patch 1985, 134). His political affiliation with the democratic Left and his past clashes with the party leadership contributed to make him a rather isolated voice (Cary 1996, 123; Knapp 1973, 167). As minister of the interior of Brüning's first cabinet (1930–31) he was at the fore-

---

61. Bundesarchiv, Koblenz, Nachlaß Wirth N1342/133, 12.

62. Quoted in Prégardier and Mohr eds. (1991, 94).

63. Wirth makes the same remark: "Die Auffassungen in der Zentrumsfraktion waren nicht einheitlich." Bundesarchiv, Koblenz, Nachlaß Wirth N1342/18, III.29.

front of the political fight against the Nazis. His political career was marked by a sustained and public engagement against the radical and anti-republican Right. Hermann Joseph Schmitt alluded to this peculiar status when, remembering Wirth's statements at the meeting, he described him as a "peculiar and controversial man."[64]

This political and behavioral background, which was common knowledge, shaped Wirth's public profile. The relevance of this information to the delegates' alignment was threefold. First, Wirth's delegation colleagues had reasons to believe that he would resolutely fight the prospect of any compromise with the Nazis if doing so implied abandoning the central tenets of the Center's commitment to democratic institutions. Second, they could expect him to put up a fight even at the risk of political isolation: he had made clear in the past that he did not balk at this prospect. In the abstract language of the theory of collective alignment, they had reasons to presume that at this particular juncture, given the terms of the challenge and his record, his opposition threshold was absolute. As a result, and this is the third point, his public statements revealed no strategic information about the preference distribution. The delegates could not infer the delegation's modal stance from his.

Behavioral Contrast

Nothing in Wirth's behavior on 23 March invalidates the presumption of an absolute threshold. After having recalled his fight against the Spartakists and his commitment for the Weimar Republic, Wirth dramatically left the meeting as if stepping out of the delegation. At the instigation of Josef Schmitt, Clara Siebert ran out into the street to persuade him to come back.[65] At this moment Wirth favored an uncompromising stance against the Nazis, a stance which he was on the verge of assuming alone by quitting the room and the delegation. Everything indicates that despite the risks, he might have disregarded the choice of his party colleagues. The violence of his confrontation with Kaas in the last meeting testifies to this conjecture. His public stand confirmed his status in the party.

The contrast with Kaas is striking. In refusing to make an explicit recommendation for or against the enabling bill, Kaas behaved as if he were making

---

64. "This peculiar and controversial man was making a terrible and realist forecast. He said nothing that did not occur!!" Quoted in Prégardier and Mohr eds. (1991, 94).

65. Siebert reports this episode in her account of the event. "Wirth wept, he leaped to his feet and left." Kommission für Zeitgeschichte, Bonn, Tagebuchaufzeichnungen von Clara Siebert, abridged in Becker (1961b, 209).

his choice conditional on that of the delegation. In retrospect, this refusal may seem characteristic of weak leadership (Morsey 1977, 140). From the standpoint of tacit coordination, however, this reservation was important: the delegates could reflect on Kaas's choice — he consistently pointed to the necessity of a political conciliation with Hitler — as indicating an assessment of the preference distribution within the group. In other words, his threshold was relative. Yet there was no wavering on his part. His shunning an explicit recommendation was as consistent as his call for acquiescence.[66]

Framing Divergence

The meaning and implications of the clash between the two men during the meeting become clearer in light of this background. According to Wirth, Kaas attacked him for his past attempts to establish political ties between the Center and the Socialist Left.[67] The charge may seem misplaced if viewed from afar given the issues at stake and the dramatic circumstances in which the Center delegates are meeting. In this crucial hour, while the delegates are confronting their political fate, Kaas, the party chairman is settling old accounts that hark back to the 1920s!

Yet the charge leveled at Wirth is no longer irrelevant or quaint when we reinterpret it from Kaas's main strategic purpose at this juncture, as an attempt to isolate Wirth further and undercut any support he might receive from other visible delegation members. In attacking Wirth for his affinities with the Socialist Left, Kaas is reminding party colleagues that his critic — Wirth — had always been at the outskirts of the party and that he, by contrast, is standing for the mainstream. Wirth may have been outraged by this charge, as he indicates in his recollections, in part because he sensed what it meant for his ability to sway the delegation.

"Brüning Remained Silent" (Kaiser)

These few considerations explain why Wirth was no match for Kaas and could not have reversed the emergence of a consensus in favor of acquiescence. What about the other prominent members of the delegation? Were they not in a position to counterpoise the impact of Kaas's public stance? In terms of visibility and political profile, Brüning was on a par with Kaas. The prominence gained through his chancellorship was undisputed and made him a natural

---

66. Bundesarchiv, Koblenz, Nachlaß Wirth, N1342/133, 12.
67. Ibid.

focal point for party members. He enjoyed considerable visibility. Further-more, in the eyes of the rank-and-file delegates, he stood for the political me-dian, as did Kaas. "Brüning was a conservative, who from the start strove to bring the new social-Christian conservatism to victory" (Joseph Wirth).[68] Given his prominence and median position, Brüning had the capacity to tip the Center delegates' resolution toward opposition, against Kaas's advice.

Brüning does not figure prominently in the delegates' accounts. He was present by default. They do not remember Brüning opposing Kaas; they re-member Wirth opposing Kaas. Helene Weber's and Hermann Joseph Schmitt's testimonies are exemplary in this regard (Prégardier and Mohr eds. 1991, 94). Jakob Kaiser observes: "Brüning was seating next to Kaas and remained silent."[69] This observation is striking, for Brüning did speak.[70] Clara Siebert quotes some of his words: "I do not have the guarantee for the millions I borrowed." But his stand was low-key, which impressed the delegates. Right after reporting his words, Clara Siebert adds—and the incidental remark is crucial—that during this meeting Brüning "did not speak a lot."[71]

Why is this observation significant? First, it underscores the sensitivity of rank-and-file group members to the silence and discretion of a prominent actor who was a focal point for them. Brüning's discretion was important for the delegation members because of his status. Since their first meeting four days earlier, his attitude had been at odds with his prominence. He had been staying in the background, making "no effort to publicize his reservations" (Patch 1998, 297). His visibility was minimal. The minutes do not report him attending the executive committee meetings on 20 March, 22 March (eve-ning), and 23 March (morning). His presence is recorded only in the morning meeting of the executive committee on 22 March. Nor is there any record of a statement by him until the delegation met on the morning of 23 March.[72]

68. Bundesarchiv, Koblenz, Nachlaß Wirth N1342/18, III.22.

69. Bundesarchiv, Koblenz, Nachlaß Kaiser N1018/246, 53: "Brüning hat geschwiegen."

70. In his memoirs Brüning states that the Center as well as what the party had stood for would be smashed by the Nazis (*Memoiren*, 658). Morsey (1977, 253) remarks that Brüning's account in his memoirs (*Memoiren*, 657–58) describes not the morning meeting of the Center delegates but the meeting that took place in the afternoon, after Hitler delivered his speech. It seems that Brüning is conflating the meetings in his account.

71. "Brüning sprach nicht viel in dieser Stunde." Kommission für Zeitgeschichte, Bonn, Tage-buchaufzeichnungen von Clara Siebert, 111. Bausch reports these words by Helene Weber: "Auf die Abgeordneten, die diesen Versprechungen kritisch gegenüberstanden, habe man nicht ge-hört." Bausch, *Lebenserinnerungen und Erkenntnisse eines schwäbischen Abgeordneten*, 117. This observation implicitly confirms Siebert's remark regarding Brüning's discretion and my point about the impact of this discretion.

72. Given his prominence in the party and his past responsibilities, there is no reason to

Wirth confirms this point: "Brüning at that time was shunning the delegation. He did not come to the delegation meeting. The whole thing was for him so dreadfully grave that he wanted to see no one."[73]

Second, these remarks point out the relative character of the actors' prominence. In a collective context as dramatic as that of the Center delegation meetings in March 1933, an actor's capacity to structure expectations is determined as much by his or her stance as by surrounding stances at different points in time. Prominence is also a function of other prominent actors' willingness to step forward and assume their prominence. At the afternoon meeting of the delegation on 23 March, Brüning's "silence" contributed to Kaas's influence. The delegates could interpret his discretion as an indication that he was throwing down the glove because he was aware of the modal preference in the delegation. Clara Siebert indirectly outlined the collective significance of Brüning's position by pointing to the counterfactual. "Everything, everything could have turned well if Brüning had really stepped in."[74]

UNANIMITY

The last episode sanctions the prevalence of consent. Realizing that a few delegates might still be willing to cast a "no" vote, Kaas proposed a straw vote.[75] If the ballot were anonymous and confidential, a vote would be a convenient procedure to have individuals reveal their preference without getting them exposed to the risk of public disclosure. On 23 March none of these conditions applied. Kaas asked the delegates to *nominally* declare themselves. They would commit their name to a behavioral preference. In so doing, they would situate themselves vis-à-vis their peers. Kaas justified this procedure in light of the stakes. Implicitly, the argument was one of individual responsibility. "The mat-

---

assume that these absences are a lapse in the minutes. Had Brüning been present, his attendance would have been recorded. Brüning is only present in one meeting and he does make a public stand in this meeting.

73. Bundesarchiv, Koblenz, Nachlaß Wirth N1342/18, III.29.

74. "Alles, alles hätte sich noch zum Guten wenden können, wenn Brüning wirklich eingeschaltet worden wäre." Kommission für Zeitgeschichte, Bonn, Tagebuchaufzeichnungen von Clara Siebert, 112. Siebert uses the verb "einschalten" when she describes what Brüning could have done. The verb denotes stepping in as a third party. Implicit in it is the suggestion that a third party's action is necessary in the absence of an alternative.

75. The minutes of the meeting offer no precise information about the sequence. Morsey (1977) suggests that Kaas proposed a vote when it appeared that "a minority was still resolute to vote 'No'" (140). This contention is supported by Kaiser's own account, which recounts the chronology of the meeting, as I indicate in the following note.

ter is so important that a nominal ballot—who is for, who is against—needs to be taken."[76]

In addition, the delegates had reasons to suspect a lack of confidentiality. They believed that Grass (who attended the meetings although he was not a parliamentary delegate in the Reichstag) and Hackelsberger reported to the Nazis (Morsey 1977, 134, 253). Brüning was very clear on this point: "We could no longer have open discussions in delegation meetings."[77] Brüning warned Kaas on this issue.[78] To no effect.[79] "Then came the news that Göring had already my speech [Brüning is referring to his statement before the delegates in the morning meeting] and that he was putting pressure on Hitler not to send the promised letter. Somebody from the delegation must have taken my remarks down in shorthand and communicated them to Göring."[80] Thus through the ballot, the Center delegates faced a decision that engaged their individual responsibility *and* their interdependence. They were being requested to reveal their behavioral preference and to expose themselves.

The ballot revealed quasi-unanimity—about 80 percent of the delegates— in favor of acquiescence. Only fourteen delegates out of seventy-two cast a "no" vote.[81] Kaas reacted to this outcome by asking the opponents to align with the rest of the delegation so that no one bore the responsibility of a personalized

76. Jakob Kaiser reports this request by Kaas and situates it at the end of the meeting: "Schluß der Sitzung war so, daß Kaas sagte, die Angelegenheit ist so wichtig, daß in namentlicher Abstimmung festgelegt werden müsse, wer dafür, wer dagegen ist." Bundesarchiv, Koblenz, Nachlaß Kaiser N1018/246, no. 53. Christine Teusch situates Kaas's request after the discussion "for" and "against." Testimony in Prégardier and Mohr eds. (1991, 73).

77. Brüning, *Memoiren*, 657. Brüning made this point again in a letter to Johannes Maier-Hultschin dated 26 March 1947: he did not discuss the amendment to the enabling bill that he wanted to introduce with the German Nationalists' support in the delegation meetings, because confidentiality could no longer be ensured: "two or three members of our party reported to the Nazis everything discussed in the party room in the Reichstag." Bundesarchiv, Koblenz, Nachlaß Maier-Hultschin, N1043/2, no. 150, letter to Johannes Maier-Hultschin dated 26 March 1947.

78. In his memoirs (656) Brüning speaks of two or three traitors (Morsey 1977, 253). According to him this lack of confidentiality was not confined to the Center delegation (Brüning, *Reden und Aufsätze eines deutschen Staatsmanns*, 257). This seems to have been a general problem. Erich Wienbeck, a German Nationalist delegate in the Reichstag in March 1933, notes that the content of the meeting on 20 March of the DNVP Reichstag delegation was reported to the press the next day (Bundesarchiv, Koblenz, KLE 627 Wienbeck, 272). The Hanneman archives contain one of these press reports (Bundesarchiv, Koblenz, KLE 245 Hanneman).

79. "Kaas did not have the authority to throw out Dr. Grass, who was not invited, or to forbid the negotiations with Papen and Frick which Dr. Hackelberger was conducting on his own. All the warnings were of no help." Brüning, *Memoiren*, 657.

80. Ibid., 658.

81. See chapter 3.

vote. Alignment was now explicit and motivated by the risks inherent to public opposition. "No one can take the responsibility of casting an isolated vote. This responsibility is too heavy—the vote needs to be depersonalized and only a unitary vote [*ein einheitliches Votum*] accepting the enabling bill can achieve this impersonal character in the acceptance of the bill."[82] There should be only one vote for the whole group.

Kaas's call for an impersonal vote laid bare the logic of the dilemma. The delegates could not vote alone. In voting for the bill along with their peers, the members of the minority would avoid being singled out for their opposition. Through their individual opposition votes, on the other hand, these delegates would expose themselves directly to measures of retaliation. But the issue was not simply one of personal security. The vote needed to be depersonalized so that individual responsibilities could dissolve. Ultimately, such is Kaas's message, the vote should sanction the delegates' interdependence.

Alignment, if it now took place, would be explicit and sequential. Relying on the information provided by insiders, Karl Bachem reports that those who had come forward as opponents of the bill "finally bowed to this prospect and agreed to vote along with the others for acceptance. They did so primarily to avoid that the delegation collapse. This, however, was extremely tough for them. Wirth gave his consent with tears in his eyes."[83] In his memoirs, Brüning suggests that Wirth yielded to the pressures of the majority. As a result, Brüning had no other option than to yield as well.[84] Wirth, for his part, in his personal notes describes his decision as ultimately motivated by the union leaders' recommendations. He agreed with them that acceptance of the bill could help their organizations survive for a few more years.[85]

CONTRASTS

Kaas is the reference point of these few days. From the outset of the delegation meetings in Berlin, he was at the forefront of the public scene. The delegates knew that he was involved in the negotiations with Hitler, which made him a natural focal point. In addition, he was actively present in the delegation meetings and constantly took the rostrum, defining the Center party's future political line and providing the tactical and strategic justifications for a "yes" vote. He assumed his prominence. Siebert conveyed this assessment when

---

82. Kommission für Zeitgeschichte, Bonn, Tagebuchaufzeichnungen von Clara Siebert, abridged in *Das "Ermächtigungsgesetz" vom 24. März 1933*, 137.

83. Stadtarchiv, Cologne, Nachlaß Bachem 100, remarks dated 29 April 1933.

84. Brüning, *Memoiren*, 658.

85. Bundesarchiv, Koblenz, Nachlaß Wirth, N1342/133, 12.

she observed right after Hitler's speech: "*We* noticed the influence of prelate Kaas." The "we" is important. Siebert was interpreting Hitler's speech at the same time as she was interpreting her peers' beliefs regarding the significance of the speech.

Not surprisingly, given the configuration of public positions that I have just described, Kaas figures prominently in individual accounts. Brüning portrays him as "elegantly" advocating Hitler's concessions.[86] Wirth admits that Kaas's stance elicited an insuperable anger on his part. Johannes Schauff identifies him as the staunchest supporter of the enabling act.[87] The delegates view him as instrumental in determining their collective stance. Schauff notes that Kaas "knew how to make the vote for the enabling bill tasty with conceited arguments, by alluding to the many conditions and restrictions that had been granted to him."[88]

Helene Weber's resentment toward Kaas was similarly motivated. "Kaas was the main culprit for how things turned out. He had fallen prey to the promises Hitler had made in the parliamentary session."[89] Brüning concurs, mentioning both the "great impact of [Kaas's] statement in the delegation meeting that followed Hitler's programmatic speech on 23 March"[90] and his ability to tip the scales: "For all these reasons, the Center party followed Kaas, against my advice, in voting for the enabling bill."[91]

A similar thread runs through the testimonies of contemporary witnesses. Kaas emerges as the tutelary figure of this collective resolution. A few days after the event Muth, the editor of *Hochland*, most likely reporting the account

86. "Kaas expressed in an elegant form his different conception and reported that a letter [from Hitler] had been promised to him." Brüning, *Memoiren*, 658.

87. To the question "Who seemed to the young members of the delegation the strongest supporter and the strongest opponent of a vote for the enabling bill?" Schauff answers: "predominantly two Catholic religious. For: prelate Kaas, the party chairman. Against: Hermann Joseph Schmitt, the religious general secretary of the Catholic workers' clubs in Berlin." Draft of an interview with Kusch, Institut für Zeitgeschichte, Munich, Archiv Johannes Schauff, ED 346, no. 24.

88. Johannes Schauff 1985 [1934], 94, reproduced in *Das "Ermächtigungsgesetz" vom 24. März 1933*, 135.

89. This indictment is reported by Paul Bausch, former delegate of the CSVP, in his memoirs. Bausch mentions that he was very close to Helene Weber and that she often talked to him about these few days. "Aber immer war sie voll von Erbitterung über den Prälaten Kaas ... Er sei der Hauptschuldige an der ganze Entwicklung gewesen. Er sei auf die Versprechungen Hitlers, die er tatsächlich in der Reichstagssitzung gemacht habe, hereingefallen." Bausch, *Lebenserinnerungen und Erkenntnisse eines schwäbischen Abgeordneten*, 117.

90. Brüning, *Memoiren*, 658.

91. Bundesarchiv, Koblenz, Nachlaß Maier-Hultschin, N1043-2, no. 150, letter to Johannes Maier-Hultschin, 26 March 1947.

of one or several Center delegates, mentions the episode to the SPD member Südekum in a way that portrays Kaas as the main architect of the collective decision.[92] Otto Braun, former SPD prime minister of Prussia, imputes the Center's decision to Kaas's "shortsightedness and wretchedness" (*Kurzsichtigkeit und Jämmerlichkeit*).[93] His SPD colleague Felder depicts Kaas as the leader of the acquiescence camp.[94] Hoegner reports Wirth's words: the delegation is resolute to follow Kaas's lead.[95]

On several occasions Kaas himself acknowledged this fact. Right after the vote, in a letter to Carl Bödiker dated 24 March, he made the point explicit: "In any case I hope that the delegation's decision which I brought about yesterday will be approved."[96] Then in 1935, in a letter to the German Vatican envoy, he described his role as pivotal: "Immediately after the passing of the enabling Act, in the acceptance of which I played a positive role on the basis of certain guarantees given to me by the Reich chancellor (guarantees of a general political as well as a cultural political nature . . .)."[97]

Historiographical accounts often impute the collective outcome to Kaas's "influence."[98] It is unclear how much explanatory power this "explanation" has, as long as it begs the question: Why did Kaas's public position have such impact? What made him able to shape the delegation's stance despite his apparent unwillingness to make an explicit recommendation? We start addressing this question when we inquire into actors' relation to the group, the dynamic of this relation, and its epistemic character. Kaas's public stance was influential to the extent that the delegates determined their position collectively and initially

92. Friedrich-Ebert Stiftung, Bonn, Teilnachlaß Braun, Otto, Mappe 5: "Brief Südekums und Notizen auf April–Mai 1933. 10. April 1933."

93. Braun, *Von Weimar zu Hitler*, 449, quoted by Morsey (1960, 365).

94. Felder, "Mein Weg," 38. Similarly, the German State party Reichstag delegate, Ernst Lemmer, evokes the "strong influence" of the prelate Kaas over the Center decision (Lemmer, *Manches war doch anders*, 171).

95. Hoegner, *Der schwierige Außenseiter*, 93.

96. Bundesarchiv, Koblenz, R 53/71, letter to Bödiker, 24 March 1933, quoted by Scholder (1978, 553–54) and abridged in Das *"Ermächtigungsgesetz" vom 24. März 1933*, 80.

97. Staatliche Akten über die Reichskonkordatverhandlungen, 1933, 496, quoted in Scholder (1988, 247).

98. Günther Lewy states that Kaas "caused the decision of the Center" on 23 March (quoted in Scholder 1977, 554 n. 59). For Junker (1969, 171–72), Kaas's attitude had a decisive influence on the course of events and especially on the acceptance of the enabling bill. Evans (1981, 386) states that "Kaas unquestionably led and influenced the majority vote of yes." Patch (1985, 222) notes that Kaas urged acceptance as the lesser of two evils. Matz (1989, 145) speaks of the "decisive influence of the party chairman Kaas." Scholder (1988) makes the same assessment: "for the majority of the parliamentary group, who were looking for their bearings in this unparalleled situation, he became the man whom they could trust" (249).

were at a loss to figure out what this position should be. He shaped this process because the delegates gave him the possibility to do so given Wirth's adamant opposition and Brüning's quasi-silence.

On this last point, Siebert's notes are particularly enlightening. Her testimony combines two observations congruent with the tacit coordination argument. First, Siebert depicts her decision as an intense dilemma. This is consistent with her personal observations about her peers' state of mind. Second, she attributes the resolution of this dilemma to Brüning's public position and, *simultaneously*, to the prospect of a stance. Brüning mentions that he will take part in the vote, indicating that he agrees to side with his peers and to vote for the bill: "Brüning told *us*: I will be in the Kroll Opera House. . . . Brüning's statement was also my decision. I stopped thinking as a woman, as a mother or a grand mother in whom a painful 'I cannot' cried, and in whom fear smirked at the thought of what would happen, if my name was related to the passing of the enabling bill" (my italics).[99]

Subsumed under Siebert's alignment with Brüning is her alignment with the group. The connection is crucial in her account of this moment. She fuses her vote with the group's through Brüning's public stance. "What I was doing now was an impersonalized action trusting what Brüning was doing. Beyond all subjective considerations, beyond all bitter grief, beyond all the urge to confess 'I cannot' stood now 'I do what Brüning does.' I am nothing else, truly *nothing else than another number for the collective* [im]personal vote for the passing of the enabling bill" (my emphasis).[100] The identification with Brüning ("I do what Brüning does") parallels the identification with the group ("I am

99. "Brüning sagte uns: "Ich werde in der Krolloper sein . . . Die Erklärung Brünings war auch meine Entscheidung. Nun dachte ich nicht mehr als Frau, Mutter u. Großmutter, in der ein leidvolles 'ich kann nicht' aufschrie, in der Furcht grinste, was wird es einmal sein, wenn mein Name verbunden ist mit der Annahme des Ermächtigungsgesetzes." Kommission für Zeitgeschichte, Bonn, Tagebuchaufzeichnungen von Clara Siebert, 112.

100. "Jetzt war, was ich tat, entpersönlichte Handlung im Vertrauen auf das, was Brüning tat. Über allen subjektiven Erwägungen, über allem bittern Leid, über allem drängenden Willen zum Bekenntnis: 'ich kann nicht' stund jetzt 'ich tue was Brüning tut,' ich bin nichts, gar nichts weiter als eine weitere Zahl für das einheitliche [ent]persönlichte Votum zur Annahme des Ermächtigungsgesetzes." Kommission für Zeitgeschichte, Bonn, Tagebuchaufzeichnungen von Clara Siebert, 112–13. The expression in the last sentence of the quote is most likely a lapse on the part of Clara Siebert and should read "einheitliche entpersönlichte" ("collective impersonal"). Several observations support this contention. The expression "a collective impersonal vote" is a leitmotiv of these few pages. Siebert uses it three times in the few passages that she devotes to the vote of the Center delegation. In the statement quoted above Siebert uses this expression to convey Kaas's own words. Furthermore, in this passage there are no substantive reasons for changing from collective impersonal to collective personal. Quite the contrary. In the previous sentence Siebert explains that her action is impersonal ("entpersönlichte Handlung") and that

nothing else, truly nothing else than another number for the collective impersonal vote for the passing of the enabling bill").

    ■   ■   ■

I distinguished two moments in the collective dynamic observed on 23 March. The first was the morning meeting. Kaas reports on the negotiations with Hitler. Brüning expresses his reservations. This divergence of views points to the possibility of a split. "In the morning of 23 March [a few hours before the bill was put to the vote] the decision of the Center delegation was still open" (Morsey 1977, 134). The second moment is one of resolution through Kaas, and indirectly through Hitler. Being directly involved in the negotiations with Hitler, Kaas draws the attention of all the Center delegates. His assessment of the situation and strategic recommendations consistently point to the necessity of conciliation.

There is no wavering on his part. The delegates make their decision conditional on the information that he provides. He is the actor who discloses the group's position. Hence, he is playing a decisive role in the emergence of an informal consensus in favor of acquiescence. This role cannot be assessed independently of the role played by actors who could challenge his prominence to the extent that they too represent a median position within the delegation. Wirth does not have this status because of his past conflicts with the Center leadership and his close association with the Social Democratic Left. Brüning does have it. Yet on the afternoon of 23 March he does not step forward, and his reserve, which could not but impress his delegation colleagues, corroborates the collective significance of Kaas's position.

---

the meaning of this "impersonal action" lies in trust for Brüning, beyond all the personal considerations that would motivate her to oppose the enabling bill.

Chapter 9

Vacillations, Convergence

Uncertainty is general.[1]

On 10 July, I found myself in Vichy and learned that everybody
agreed on doing what was subsequently done.[2]

1

The first quote is from Louis Noguères, a Socialist deputy. The second is from
Paul Benazet, a centrist senator. Juxtaposed, these two judgments are inconsistent. Noguères says: there was indecision, wavering and indeterminacy. Benazet says: there was consensus, in favor of a "yes" vote. The Socialist deputy Pétrus Faure concurs with the centrist senator Benazet: when parliamentarians
were about to vote, everyone had made his decision.[3] In contrast, his Socialist
colleague Maxence Roldes, deputy of Yonne, speaks of an "atmosphere of an-
guished unrest and feverish anxiety."[4]

These inconsistencies are an artifact. Individual accounts contradict one
another only if we freeze their temporality. Parliamentarians successively experience befuddlement, indignation, and resignation. They vacillate, and these
vacillations take place at the same time. When we reconstruct this temporality,
not only do the inconsistencies noted above dissolve—Benazet and Noguères
refer to different moments of these vacillations—they also take on a consistency of their own. Resolutions ebb and flow. Parliamentarians with different
political affiliations and outlooks undergo the same shifts at the same time.
Vacillations are synchronic and collective. Parliament as a whole oscillates.
I reconstruct the temporality of these collective swings by cross-checking
the information that the actors themselves provide about their experience in
Vichy.

Laval's radical agenda initially dumbfounds the delegates. On Monday

1. Louis Noguères's diary, *Événements* VII, 2238.
2. "Je me suis cependant trouvé à Vichy le 10 juillet pour apprendre que tous étaient d'accord
pour faire ce qu'on y a fait." Archives Nationales, Dossiers du jury d'honneur, Paris: dossier
Benazet, AL5298.
3. "Les positions de chacun étaient prises." Faure, *Un témoin raconte . . .* , 67.
4. Archives Nationales, Dossiers du jury d'honneur, Paris: dossier Roldes AL5329.

(8 July) indignation prevails. On Tuesday (9 July), in the evening, renunciation is the order of the day. Deputies and senators anticipate their own collective subservience. The next morning (Wednesday), Laval's edifice is on the verge of crumbling. In the afternoon, as the vote takes place, the outcome looks certain to most. These ups and downs are strikingly peculiar. Twice, on 7 and 9 July, the pendulum swings back, dramatically. The swings are as drastic as they are sudden. Is there a causal pattern underlying these collective swings in mood and expectations?

2

In this chapter I multiply the takes and the perspectives. The first take is chronological. I document the chronology of the oscillations. Detailed narratives help us to identify moments of reversal and provide essential clues for tracing causal connections. The second take focuses on causal imputations inferred from the actors' own accounts. Moments of reversal can be traced to public statements by prominent actors: Spinasse, Flandin, Herriot, and Jeanneney. These prominent members of parliament take stances that are unexpected and surprising given the context and their political profile.

I complement these causal imputations by comparing the frequencies of the different motivational claims that parliamentarians invoke in their accounts of the event. The point of this analysis is to assess, first, whether the reference to prominent actors' public statements is salient in actors' portrayal of their motivations and, second, how salient it is compared to other motivational factors such as the acceptance of Pétain as the man of the hour, the necessity of constitutional reform, subservience to circumstantial constraints, the lack of information, or the deceptive ploys used by the bill's promoters. This is the third take.

Then I narrow the focus. Having shown the salience of public statements in actors' assessments of the situation, I examine to what extent individual accounts and testimonies reveal a process of belief coordination. The focus is on the cognitive hints, implicit or not, disclosed by these accounts regarding actors' beliefs and their decision-making process. The fifth take explores a test case, an episode that could have been a moment of reversal and turned out to be a moment of consolidation: Flandin's dramatic speech on the morning of 10 July. I analyze the impact of this speech on the collective outcome. Finally, I step back and adopt a more synoptic view. I reconsider the frequency assessment of motivational claims within a broader taxonomy, one that contrasts epistemic versus linear arguments. Epistemic arguments describe a process of belief coordination. Linear arguments state the causal impact of exogenous factors (coercive pressures, mistaken beliefs, the ideological zeitgeist).

THE CHRONOLOGY OF UNCERTAINTY

At first there is befuddlement. Laval unveils his game before senators in a meeting held in the small casino on Thursday, 4 July. Outlining the scope of the defeat, he states "right away that 'it is necessary to align our political regime with that of the victor'" (Paul-Boncour, senator affiliated with the Radical party). A constitutional reform will have to be carried out. Parliament should be dissolved. Senators are taken aback. "Laval . . . realized the move of surprise that expressed itself" (Paul-Boncour).[5] He makes the same points before the deputies. "Dumbfounded" (*stupéfaits* in Blum's account), they do not know what to think.[6]

After the first shock, indignation creeps in. It takes those present less than one day to regain their sense of composure (Friday, 5 July). Léon Blum records reactions of "spontaneous resistance."[7] Realizing what is at stake, shocked by Laval's antidemocratic diatribe, twenty-five ex-serviceman senators convene to "examine the situation" in the early afternoon of Friday 5 July. These senators unanimously vote a motion paying tribute to Pétain and reasserting their attachment to the republican framework of the regime. Laval has another "information meeting" with deputies.[8] This time, contrary to the previous meeting, he encounters public opposition. The president of the Republic, Albert Lebrun, notes in his diary: "Several deputies take part in a very stormy debate."[9]

Saturday, 6 July, witnesses the resurgence of a cautious wait-and-see marked by apprehension, puzzlement, and contrition. Meeting with the senators, Laval develops once again his argument in favor of an alignment with totalitarian regimes. Léon Bérard, a rightist senator who chairs the meeting, concludes with a speech which "buried with casualness not only the Republic but also freedom, on which he pretended to shed a tear."[10] The Radical senator Paul-Boncour notes the constrained reserve of those who attend: "too many were remaining silent. . . . They were listening, contrived at heart, without expressing their feelings."[11] Jules Jeanneney, who did not attend these debates, writes in his

5. Paul-Boncour, *Entre deux guerres*, 254.

6. Blum, *A l'échelle humaine*, 68.

7. Ibid., 72.

8. During this meeting Laval tried to exploit the tragedy of the British attack on the French ships anchored at Mers-el-kébir on 3 July (Noguères, *Vichy, juillet 1940*, 29: see chapter 1). This event contributed to further the disarray experienced in Vichy among most parliamentarians (Berl, *La fin de la IIIe République*, 205). Bardoux evokes his "despair" (*Journal d'un témoin de la Troisième*, 399) and Blum his "incredulity" (*A l'échelle humaine*, 81–82).

9. Lebrun, *Témoignage*, 104: "Plusieurs députés prennent part au débat très houleux."

10. Paul-Boncour, *Entre deux guerres*, 267.

11. Ibid., 266.

journal: "I was told that Laval was applauded at intervals. No real opposition. Stupor? Resignation? Contrition?" (92).[12]

On Monday (8 July) the Assembly is displaying a new "state of mind" (*état d'esprit*, in the words of the Socialist deputy Louis Noguères). Noguères who left Vichy for one day, is struck by the change in mood. Around 3:00 P.M. he enters the room where Laval is to address the deputies: "Monday, 8 July. . . . Here we are, meeting once again, during the day, in the Small Casino. The room was the same as on 5 July, but what a difference!"[13] Laval encounters widespread hostility. His outline of the government's motivations is interrupted several times by expressions of discontent. "I went to the small Casino in which the services of the Chamber of Deputies are located. . . . Laval just explained his views: a totalitarian regime to collaborate more easily with Germany. Oppositions quite sharp" (Abbot Desgranges's diary).[14] The Radical deputy Gaston Manent makes the same observation in his account of the meeting: "In substance, Pierre Laval tells us that we need to align with totalitarian countries. There was protest in the room."[15]

The meeting with senators is as inauspicious for Laval. Bardoux observes: "the bad mood and hostile reservations of my colleagues—quite a few of them, around 80—were obvious."[16] Laval's statements about the possibility of a war with England "horrifies" senators.[17] The Radical senators Vincent Delpuech and Pierre Chaumié explain that "they cannot accept that Parliament be considered, and consider itself, a scapegoat and the only one responsible [for the defeat]. Nor can they accept that a personal regime, without limitations, guarantees and supervision be implemented for a while."[18] Jeanneney notes in his diary: "There is great agitation within the Left [of the Senate] against the government's proposal of granting the Marshal absolute power to establish and promulgate a new Constitution."[19] Opposition is gaining momentum. "Resistances were finding themselves, gathering together" (Paul Ramadier, former Socialist deputy).[20]

12. Jeanneney, *Journal politique*, 6 July.

13. Louis Noguères's diary, *Événements* VII, 2239.

14. Desgranges, *Journal d'un prêtre député*, 393. The senator Jacques Bardoux, who did not attend the meeting and relies on hearsay, confirms this observation. Bardoux, *Journal d'un témoin de la Troisième*, 400. On this meeting of 8 July see my remarks in chapter 5.

15. "Une explication de vote," reproduced in *Événements*, 2260.

16. Bardoux, *Journal d'un témoin de la Troisième*, 400.

17. Boivin-Champeaux's testimony, *Événements* VII, 2198–99.

18. Bardoux, *Journal d'un témoin de la Troisième*, 400.

19. Jeanneney, *Journal politique*, 93.

20. Ramadier's letter to Jean Odin, n.d., reproduced in Odin, *Les quatre-vingts*, 237.

The next evening (Tuesday 9 July) "the government's success looked as if it were certain" (Henri Becquart, far-Right deputy, affiliated with the Republican Federation).[21] Within one day the resolution to challenge Laval yielded the ground to widespread resignation. The change was dramatic: "A sizable number of Blum's friends have already shifted sides and were preparing themselves for a vote more shameful for them than for any other fraction of the Assembly. One finds among them many of these revolutionaries who reproached me my moderate stances. . . . On the Left, defections were speeding up" (Paul-Boncour, Radical senator).[22]

The events of Wednesday 10 July confirmed this prognosis. Laval encountered no opposition. The ex-serviceman senators withdrew their counter-motion. At the beginning of the afternoon session "Laval has his majority, but he wants it to be impressive."[23] "In this casino, rien ne va plus! within closed minds. Even those who, still the previous evening, stood firm, are staggering" (Vincent Auriol, Socialist deputy).[24] Louis Gros remarks in his memoirs that Laval "had succeeded . . . in creating an atmosphere favorable to his proposal, which, as a result, seemed to be about to win a large majority."[25] "The game was settled. . . . Abdication was decided; the meeting was but the formality of a signature" (Henri Becquart).[26]

CAUSAL IMPUTATIONS

Is there a logic behind these ups and downs? I focus on moments of reversal: Saturday (6 July), Monday (8 July), and Tuesday (9 July). These are moments when a modal representation of the group recedes and another, with quite different behavioral implications, comes forward. Superimposed on the temporality of these reversals is the temporality of public statements which, because of the shared attention they receive, have great visibility and resonance. In some cases the resonance is explicit. People talk about the statement. In the process they acknowledge its collective significance. Spinasse's call for self-repudiation on 6 July illustrates this process. In other cases the statement needs no comment. Its occurrence is self-sufficient. Flandin, Herriot, and Jeanneney exemplify this second process.

21. Becquart, *Au temps du silence*, 208.
22. Paul-Boncour, *Entre deux guerres*, 273.
23. "Laval [avait] sa majorité, mais il la [voulait] imposante." Auriol, *Hier . . . demain*, 127.
24. Ibid., 135.
25. Gros, *République toujours*, 59.
26. Becquart, *Au temps du silence*, 235.

A Plea for Abjuration

Louis Noguères left Vichy for one day on 6 July (Saturday). He returned in the evening. Upon his return, colleagues kept him abreast of the latest developments. The most striking event was a call for self-repudiation, order, and moral regeneration that explicitly endorsed the prospect of an unconditional power transfer and underlined the necessity of a revolutionary and moral break with the past—a theme already labored by Pétain in his public announcement. The peculiarity of this statement is that it came from a member of the Socialist party: Charles Spinasse was Noguères's party colleague. The contrast between his political identity and the substance of his stance caught actors off guard and confused them. "Parliament will take the blame for the faults of all. This crucifixion is required so that the country do not lapse into violent outbursts of anarchy. Our duty is to allow the Government to carry out a bloodless revolution. . . . We believed in individual liberty and in the independence of man. These were but anticipations of a future that was not within our reach. . . . We must have a new faith built on new values."[27]

Upon learning the content of this statement in the press, the Socialist deputy Vincent Auriol diagnosed it as a speech of "total renunciation."[28] Spinasse's self-repudiation was the event of the day. It created a "sensation" (Aron 1958, 88; Dreyfus 1990, 187). It is not difficult to understand why. Spinasse was minister of the economy in Blum's first cabinet (June 1936–June 1937) and minister of the budget in the second (March 1938). These ministerial responsibilities vested him with political visibility. Given this political background and profile, the substance of his statement is quite surprising. Deputies and senators had no reason to expect a high-profile SFIO Socialist representative to repudiate "individual liberty" and "the independence of man." In the political philosophy and ideological landscape of the SFIO party both themes held a central place. Spinasse was repudiating his political past *and* the political philosophy of his party. "Apparently, the crucifixion formula struck many" (Louis Noguères).[29]

Spinasse's self-denunciation opened the possibility of a reshuffling of political affiliations because it so blatantly called for a break with the past. The far-right deputy Xavier Vallat immediately saw this possibility when, catching the ball on the bounce, he responded to Spinasse with an appeal of his own, an appeal to transcend party boundaries and change both "men" and "institutions."[30] Thus the old herald of the far Right concurred with a young So-

---

27. *Le Temps*, 7 July 1940, trans. adapted from Hare (Aron 1958, 88).

28. Auriol, *Hier . . . demain*, 94.

29. *Événements* VII, 2234. See also Noguères, *Le véritable procès du maréchal Pétain*, 152.

30. "I rejoice at the fact that tomorrow all the parties will be united in one single national

cialist representative, former minister in the Popular Front government. This conjunction of political opposites was too unusual to be left unnoticed. The "sensational" scene of "reconciliation" was the first piece of news that Gaston Manent, Emmanuel Roy, and Isoré took cognizance of upon their arrival.[31] This explains the echo of Spinasse's sortie. "Overall Spinasse's speech had a big impact even on men who were moderately disposed to listen to it favorably" (Louis Noguères).[32] For the conservative deputy Becquart "Spinasse's speech was going to be the signal of a series of 'spontaneous' abjurations."[33]

"What Need Is There . . . ?" (Flandin, 7 July)

How then shall we explain the tendency toward opposition that prevailed on Monday 8 July? Three factors are at play. The most salient, and probably most decisive, was the public stand of Pierre-Étienne Flandin in an informal meeting with deputies the previous evening (Sunday 7 July). Flandin enjoyed considerable visibility. He was premier in November 1934–June 1935, state minister in June 1935–January 1936, and minister of foreign affairs in January–June 1936. The substance of his statement of 7 July, which I quote in chapter 5, is critical. The time is not appropriate for a change in constitution. If the purpose is to grant Pétain the highest political responsibilities to negotiate with the Germans, there is no need to abandon the constitution of 1875. The two chambers can ask the president of the Republic, Albert Lebrun, to resign and appoint Pétain in his place.[34]

In his diary Louis Noguères observes that the audience "unanimously" approved Flandin's observations.[35] In his view the drastic change in the parliamentarians' state of mind, which he contrasts with the mood prevailing two days earlier, can be traced to this public statement.[36] If Flandin is not willing to go along, parliamentarians have grounds to question their peers' future acquiescence. His public opposition provides them with further reasons for their

---

group, in which the misunderstandings that we persistently maintained among us will fade away. Institutions corrupted men: we need to change the institutions. But men also corrupted institutions: we also need to change the men." *Le Temps*, 7 July 1940.

31. Gabriel Manent, "Une explication de vote," reproduced in *Événements*, 226.

32. "Le discours de Spinasse avait, dans l'ensemble, produit un gros effet, même sur des hommes modérément disposés à l'accueillir favorablement." Louis Noguères's diary, *Événements* VII, 2234.

33. Becquart, *Au temps du silence*, 137.

34. According to the constitutional texts of 1875, the two chambers elected the president of the Republic.

35. Louis Noguères's diary, *Événements* VII, 2237.

36. Ibid., 2239.

own. The Radical senator François Labrousse mentions Flandin's public stance in his assessment of the situation on 7 July: Laval would not have been able to command a majority. Simultaneously, Labrousse mentions the ex-serviceman senators: these decided on Sunday to go ahead with their counterproposal.[37] This is the second factor. Noguères, who was deputy, notes this initiative in his diary. That he mentions the decision of the ex-serviceman senators indicates how diffuse this piece of information was at the time.

The third factor is the reaction of the representatives from Brittany as they arrived in Vichy. "An unexpected event almost toppled all the combinations of the schemers. This was the arrival in the morning of an important group of representatives from Brittany coming straightforward from their counties" (Becquart).[38] Numbering seven or eight, they got their pass from the German military authorities at the last minute and traveled together, arriving on the morning of 8 July.[39] Right upon their arrival, they let it be known how strongly they resented Laval's ploys and political goals. Their indignation was noticeable and impressed those present.[40] The stance that they took in interpersonal exchanges crystallized a pervasive feeling of indignation (see chapter 5).

"Veneration, . . . Unity" (9 July)

On Tuesday 9 July resignation had the upper hand. Two facts stand out in actors' accounts. One is the stance of the two assembly chairmen, Édouard Herriot and Jules Jeanneney, in the formal setting of the chambers' meetings. Both occupied the highest posts in the constitutional blueprint of the regime. Because of their credentials and background, their peers commonly viewed them as embodying the "spirit" of the republican regime. The second fact was the unanimity of both assemblies as they voted on the governmental motion stating the need for a revision of the laws of the constitution. Only three votes against the proposal were cast in the Chamber (out of 398). In the Senate the government motion passed by a vote of 230 to 1. To fully assess the political significance of this unanimity, one needs to pay attention to its discursive context.

The Chamber of Deputies met in the morning and the Senate in the after-

37. Reported by Sagnès 1991, 559. This point is confirmed by Paul-Boncour (*Entre deux guerres*, 268), and Taurines (*Tempête sur la République*, 17).

38. Becquart, *Au temps du silence*, 169. See also Blum, *Mémoires*, 83.

39. The Catholic deputy Trémintin writes to the head of the Kommandatur of Plouescat (Brittany) to get a pass for Vichy on 7 July and receives the pass the following day. Archives Départementales du Finistère, Quimper, Archives Pierre Tremintin, 104 J 20.

40. Louis Noguères's diary, *Événements* VII, 2239.

noon. In each session debates were minimal. Herriot opened the morning session by mentioning the names of those killed in action. In light of their sacrifices, Herriot stated, one could not but feel estranged from the passions that could be expressed. The present time ought to be not one of justice, of fixing responsibilities for the disaster, but a time of mourning. Herriot ended this short statement with an homage to the marshal, a call for unity around him—"let us not disturb the harmony which has been established under his authority"—a call for moral regeneration, and an assertion that "republican principles maintain all their virtues."

After a hiatus of one hour, during which the Chamber of Deputies' Commission on universal suffrage discussed the government motion, the session resumed. The Radical deputy Jean Mistler presented the report of the commission, which unanimously endorsed the government motion. Laval then asked that debates be postponed to the next day. According to the Official Journal, a deputy of the far-right French Social Party, Tixier-Vignancourt, requested a vote on a motion calling for an inquiry into the "political, administrative and military responsibilities that led France to disaster."[41] Herriot, acting as chairman of the Assembly, turned down this request, because contrary to the Assembly's regulations the motion had not been printed and distributed before the session.

The Senate's meeting in the afternoon followed the same pattern. Jeanneney, the Senate's chairman, opened the session with a short speech expressing his "veneration" for Pétain and made no reference to republican principles. The meeting was interrupted for one hour to allow the deliberations of the Senate's commission on civil and criminal legislations. Jean Boivin-Champeaux presented the commission's report. The commission endorsed the government motion. Laval then took the rostrum to make the same proposal he had submitted to the deputies in the morning.[42] Jeanneney put the government motion to the vote: 229 to 1.

In actors' detailed narratives, the Assembly chairmen hold center stage and overshadow the meetings. The conservative deputy Henri Ponsard explained that upon his arrival in Vichy on the eve of the National Assembly meeting, the first thing he had been told was the substance of speeches by Herriot and Jeanneney (whom he characterized as "the Republic's second and third highest officials").[43] Not only did Herriot and Jeanneney capture the parliamentarians'

41. *Journal Officiel*, Débats Parlementaires, Chambre des députés, séance du mardi 9 juillet 1940, 815.

42. *Journal Officiel*, Débats Parlementaires, Sénat, séance du mardi 9 juillet 1940, 353.

43. "I get in Vichy on the eve of the famous meeting in which Laval expounds his project,

attention, but deputies and senators understood the chairmen's stance as anticipating collective endorsement. Georges Boully, a Radical senator, described the parliamentarians' last hesitations being "shaken when the two chairmen, Herriot and Jeanneney, emphasized the 'great virtues' of [Pétain] to justify a vote of confidence.[44]

Three factors explain the impact of Herriot's and Jeanneney's statements: the setting, their timing, and their prominence. Herriot and Jeanneney took a public position in the formal setting of official parliamentary sessions that have all the trappings of historical meetings: they are extraordinary sessions. Deputies and senators knew that their colleagues would attend the meeting and attach special importance to it. Second, Herriot and Jeanneney delivered their speeches at the outset of the meeting. The members of each assembly were naturally inclined to grant these statements their utmost attention, assuming that their colleagues felt similarly. Finally, both had institutional visibility and public resonance. In the political hierarchy of the Third Republic, the assembly chairmen had a political status close to that of state dignitaries. A major decision such as the convening of both chambers to revise the Constitution was not conceivable without their assent. Consequently, their speeches had an "official" character that added to their political significance.

FREQUENCIES

Thus the chronologies of public statements and collective reversals are correlated over time, with a time lag. Public statements by high-profile figures preceded moments of reversal in actors' subjective views of their collective stance. These statements had the peculiarity of being unexpected given the political profile of those delivering them. This temporal contiguity presumes a causal relation. It does not demonstrate it. To assess this relation further, we need to get closer to the subjective makeup of the decision process and investigate the participants' reasons and beliefs.

---

which was voted a few hours later. I seek to get some clarification regarding the situation and, to my great amazement, I learn the statements made by the Republic's second and third highest officials of the Republic." Archives Nationales, Dossiers du jury d'honneur, Paris: dossier Ponsard, AL5326.

44. Boully, *Mémoire à mes juges*, 16.

Table 21   References to the Public Stance of Prominent
Actors (N = 223)

	Restrictive Definition (Explicit Statement)	Broad Definition (Including Silence)
No reference	128	114
Percent	57	51
Reference	95	109
Percent	43	49

Statements, Verbal and Nonverbal

More than 40 percent of actors' accounts mention Herriot's and Jeanneney's public statements as an explicit motivation for alignment (table 21).[45] This figure rises to almost 50 percent if we define "public stance" more broadly to include silence, which group members can interpret as a sign that the silent actor is resigned to collective acquiescence (table 21), and if we take into account statements that mention Flandin's public position on 10 July (I will analyze the significance of this event subsequently).

I refine this overview by considering two dimensions of subjective accounts: their timing (retrospective versus contemporary accounts) and their formal structure (synchronic accounts versus narratives). By "contemporary accounts" I mean accounts produced at the time of the event or immediately after it. By "narratives" I mean accounts that have chronological and linear structures. These accounts capture the subjective experience of the event by reconstructing it chronologically. "Synchronic accounts," by contrast, do not (appendix A). Underlying these distinctions is a twofold claim about the way actors relate to their experience and, by extension, the way they transcribe this experience: first, the greater the temporal proximity between accounts and events, the greater the likelihood that accounts provide an unmediated transcript of subjective states; second, the more factually detailed the account, the greater its contribution to our understanding of processes and conditional factors. It appears that the amount of factual details disclosed by a testimony is related to its formal structure. Testimonies that have the structure of a chronological narrative are factually more informative than testimonies without any temporal referent.

In light of this twofold claim, it is worth noting that 76 percent of contem-

45. This proportion holds true whether we consider deputies or senators. For a description of the data set see appendix A.

Table 22   Classification Grids and References to Public Stances (*N* = 223)

	No Reference		Reference to the Public Stance of One or More Prominent Actors		Total
	Number	Percent	Number	Percent	
Timing					
Retrospective	110	53	96	47	206
Contemporary	4	24	13	76	17
Formal Structure					
Synchronic	67	69	30	31	97
Narrative	47	37	79	63	126
Author's decisional stance[a]					
Yes	99	50	98	50	197
No	9	50	9	50	18
Abstention	4	67	2	33	6

[a] The data set includes testimonies from parliamentarians who were in Vichy on 10 July 1940 but decided not to vote (Lagrossillière and Renaitor). As a result, when the focus in on actors' decisional stances, *N* = 221.

porary accounts refer to the public stance—including silence—of prominent actors as a motivational factor. In retrospective testimonies this frequency is 50 percent (table 22). The public stances of prominent actors clearly impressed those who recorded their immediate experience in letters and diaries. Similarly, accounts that have a narrative structure underline the motivational impact of these public stances. The reference is present in more than 60 percent of them. In accounts that lack a chronological structure, by contrast, the frequency is much lower (31 percent).

The reference to the public stances of prominent actors as a decisional factor also appears to be prevalent compared with other mechanisms of alignment (table 23). Among the testimonies that relate the makeup of the decision to heteromous considerations, the reference to the public stance of prominent peers is by far the most frequent one (71 percent). In short, whenever parliamentarians describe an alignment process, public statements figure prominently in their accounts. In addition, a high proportion of parliamentarians (43 percent) mention the state of mind of their peers to situate their decision.[46]

46. These percentages are not additive. The same account can simultaneously refer to the collective mood of the assembly and the impact of public statements.

Table 23   Alignments: Variants and Their Frequencies for All Testimonies ($N = 223$)

	Number	Percent of All Testimonies	Percent of Alignment Claims ($N = 153$)
Statements	109	49	71
Explicit	95	43	62
Silence	43	19	28
Collective state	96	43	63
Mood	86	39	56
Disarray	50	22	33
Local coordination (coordination with regional peers)	24	11	16
Total	153	69	100

They emphasize either a collective mood characterized by resignation (39 percent) or the disarray that reigned at the time (22 percent). Comparatively, the percentage of accounts that refers to interpersonal relations as a source of motivation is low (11 percent). This observation is consonant with the analysis of diffusion through interpersonal ties that I developed in chapter 7.

Comparing Explanatory Types

A more synoptic viewpoint, one that takes into account the three motivational claims discussed in chapters 3–5, confirms this assessment (table 24): when French deputies and senators attempt to explain their own decision as well as that of their peers, they most often invoke the public stances of prominent colleagues or protest their good faith—the vote was a swindle and they were deceived. References to the constraints of the circumstances or the positive characteristics of the decision are significantly less frequent (table 24). As noted in chapter 3, references to the armistice are infrequent (8 percent of all accounts). So is the claim that a constitutional reform was necessary at the time (5 percent). The two most frequent motivational claims are references to explicit public statements (49 percent), references to collective feelings (43 percent), and claims that the vote was a swindle (43 percent).

The swindle argument implies ignorance and blindness. As I pointed out in chapter 4, since Laval and his supporters made it clear what kind of policy decisions they had in mind, this claim is problematic except for the tiny number of parliamentarians who arrived in Vichy right before the vote and may have

Table 24   Explanatory Claims: All Accounts ($N = 223$)

	Frequency	Percent
Alignment	153	69
Reference to public stances (including silence) of prominent actors	109	49
Reference to collective feelings	93	43
Coordination with regional peers	24	11
Pressures of the circumstances	67	30
Presence of the Germans	42	19
Threat of a military coup	38	17
Ideological convictions	51	23
Endorsement of the armistice	27	12
Trust in Pétain, hero of Verdun	12	5
For the sake of the nation	19	9
Constitutional reforms were necessary	11	5
This was a legitimate decision	23	10
Expression of the country's wishes	16	7
Expression of one's constituents' wishes	10	4
Deception	136	61
Lack of information	27	12
Expectation that republican institutional setting would be maintained	69	31
Vote was a swindle	95	43

remained ignorant of Laval's political agenda. The popularity of the deception claim reflects its convenience. Those who invoke it can take it easy with facts. In the absence of cross-checks, the claim seems credible, unless the audience has a precise knowledge of the event. Deception, furthermore, has no precise content. The claim may be fleshed out with good reasons of various sorts. Ego may have been deceived because he unduly believed in the threat of a coup. He may have been deceived because he expected the republican framework to be maintained. Or he may have been deceived because he lent credence to denials and assurances.

Invoking deception helps to obfuscate motivations which ego may not want to acknowledge to himself and to others. Heteronomy is a prime example. Actors concerned about their public image are inclined to cultivate for their own sake and for their own usage a representation of themselves that asserts a principle of sovereignty: they are the sovereigns in their own realm; they know

Table 25   The Swindle Argument and the Reference to Prominent Actors' Public
Stances ($N = 223$)

	No Deception Argument	Deception Argument	Total
No reference to a public stance	39	75	114
Expected	*45*	*69*	
Reference to a public stance	48	61	109
Expected	*43*	*66*	
Total	87	136	223

Pearson Chi-Square: 2.261; df = 1; p = .13

where they stand; they have the capacity to make up their own mind. Even
in troubled and confused times, so goes the argument, they act on their own
terms and do not situate themselves in the wake of others. A deception claim
preserves this self-image. It provides the additional benefit of avoiding self-
confrontation and dissonance. Ego can keep up appearances vis-à-vis others
and vis-à-vis himself. The advantages are psychological as well as social.

Yet a surprisingly high number of accounts ($N = 61$) invoke both the fact
of having been deceived and the influence of prominent actors through their
public stance (table 25). Consider Louis Deschizeaux's explanation: "the bill
implied neither a formal nor a tacit abandon of the republican form of the
state. Finally, I voted 'yes' because Mr. Jeanneney and Mr. Herriot exhorted us
to do so."[47] We would expect actors who claim to have been deceived to indict
those who deceived them in the first place by pointing to false promises and
fallacious guarantees. A reference to Herriot, Jeanneney, and Flandin, or to the
silence of the prominent members of parliament, or both, points to a different
decisional process, one through which ego, initially hesitant and doubtful, lets
himself be convinced that acquiescence is collectively acceptable. The belief
that the power transfer did not jeopardize the republican regime comes afterward. This belief provides a good reason ex post, once ego has resigned himself
to the prospect of collective acceptance.

When we confine the frequency assessment to accounts that have a narrative structure, the reference to the public and explicit statements of prominent actors becomes prevalent: the reference is present in 63 percent of these
accounts against 39 percent for the blunt assertion that the vote was a swindle
(table 26). The discrepancy across explanation types—alignment, coercion,

47. Archives Nationales, Paris, Dossiers du jury d'honneur, dossier Louis Deschizeaux,
AL5308.

Table 26   Explanatory Claims in Narratives (*N* = 126)

	Frequency	Percent
Alignment	108	86
Reference to the public stances (including silence) of prominent actors	79	63
Reference to collective feelings	70	56
Coordination with regional peers	20	16
Pressures of the circumstances	47	37
Presence of the Germans	31	25
Threat of a military coup	29	23
Ideological convictions	29	23
Endorsement of the armistice	16	13
Trust in Pétain, hero of Verdun	6	5
For the sake of the nation	11	9
Constitutional reforms were necessary	6	5
This was a legitimate decision	10	8
Expression of the country's wishes	12	10
Expression of one's constituents' wishes	8	6
Deception argument	79	63
Lack of information	26	21
Expectation that republican institutional setting would be maintained	44	35
Vote was a swindle	49	39

Note: Categories are not exclusive and percentages not additive. Each account can have several motives and explanations.

ideological collusion, and deception — is emphasized more strongly. This observation is consistent with the the twofold claim that I set forth earlier regarding accounts' timing and their formal structure. Accounts with a narrative structure are the most likely to provide a close-up on actors' subjective experience as this experience unfolded in time. The more emphasized this narrative structure, the more likely that ego discloses information about shifting subjective states and the dynamic of collective interactions.

Is there ground to argue that parliamentarians in their accounts invoke the public stance of their prominent peers to exculpate themselves? Motivational claims are more or less costly in terms of self-esteem and public credibility (Sadoun 1986, 53). In the deception argument, ego is not at fault. He was cheated. The fault lies with those who cheated him. In revealing that he took his cues from the public stance of prominent actors, on the other hand, ego is revealing that his choice was not truly his. Indirectly he is at fault, for having been gullible and having lacked independent judgment. Thus in terms of one's public image and self-esteem, citing the public stance of prominent peers as a motivational factor is more costly than the deception argument, all the more so in that ego particularly values his own image and the impression he conveys.

In sum, actors are unlikely to acknowledge that their choice was not theirs and that they were not the agents of their own fate unless they truly experienced their decision as such. The high proportion of references to public statements in contemporary accounts (76 percent; see table 22) bears out this claim. To this first consideration I add a second one that relates to the substance of actors' accounts. A rhetorical posture intended to shift the blame is necessarily perfunctory. It cannot delve into details without taking the risk of being refuted. A striking feature of testimonies outlining the incidence of public stances is that actors provide phenomenological and cognitive features that would be superfluous and unexpected if the claim were mainly perfunctory and rhetorical. These notations bear witness to the original experience. I now explore these features in greater detail.

THICK DESCRIPTIONS: "WE AND I"

In the process of narrating their choice, actors can reveal its epistemic character without being fully aware of it, behind their back. I analyze three hints of this kind. The first is the confusion of viewpoints. Actors go back and forth between the individual's standpoint and the group's. In the process they conflate the two. They assess their situation through the group's eyes. A second hint is the interpretation of public statements in intentional terms. Actors look for coordination devices and interpret public statements as motivated calls addressed at them. The third hint is more explicit. Actors infer collective expectations from public statements without necessarily explaining to themselves the basis for this inference.

The Confusion of Viewpoints

Consider this account by Pierre Pichery, a conservative senator: "What decided *my* vote was the attitude of chairman Jeanneney and general Weygand's opinion. Jeanneney read the offending motion without making any observation." Pichery then shifts the perspective from his own standpoint to that of the Assembly as a whole: "*We* thought that this attitude meant approbation"[48]

48. Archives Nationales, Dossiers du jury d'honneur, Paris: dossier Pichery, AL5325.

(my emphasis).[49] In conflating the two points of view, Pichery discloses the inferential character of his own beliefs: his belief regarding the significance of Jeanneney's public stance goes along with an immediate reference to the stance of his peers. "I" requests "we" as the lens through which events are to be deciphered.

This conflation of standpoints reveals the collective underpinnings of actors' beliefs. Actors make their assessment with an eye on their peers. Abbot Desgranges, a centrist deputy of the Popular Democratic Party, is another illustration: "The two chairmen's speeches describe union around this leader [Pétain] as the condition of salvation. . . . It is in these conditions that *we* voted. Never did I witness my colleagues make up their mind with greater gravity and a greater sense of the country's exclusive interest."[50] Equally revealing is this statement by the Socialist deputy Sabinus Valière, who voted for the power transfer in Vichy and later got involved in the Resistance movement: "I did not know Marshal Pétain. On his civic value I could form no other opinion than the one formulated by the former premiers or the Assembly chairmen who in the past trusted him and who, on his behalf, were asking for our trust. *We* knew that they were not thinking to deceive us and we could not assume that they themselves were mistaken. Hence, the massive votes registered after chairmen Jeanneney's and Herriot's pathetic calls" (my italics).[51]

Focal Points: Imputing Intentions

Conjoint with this confusion of viewpoints is a portrayal of the two chairmen's public statements as intentional calls for collective acquiescence. According to this interpretation, the two chairmen knew what they were doing. Prominence guided collective alignment. Adopting the collective viewpoint of the Assembly, implicitly defined as the reference group, the Radical deputy Victor Rochereau outlines the need for consensus in a situation of imperfect information: "Ignoring the exact situation, *we* heard the pathetic call of the chairmen Jeanneney and Herriot who removed *our* hesitations and who determined us to grant Marshal Pétain the powers he requested to save the country from a catastrophe with no way out. . . . after having taken cognizance of such state-

---

49. A grammatical note: it could be objected that the "we" used in these testimonies disguises the personal voice. It may be that some parliamentarians rely on the old usage of the plural pronoun in French. These testimonies, however, make simultaneous use of "I" and "we," which clearly suggests that the "we" being used here has a collective meaning.

50. Archives Nationales, Dossiers du jury d'honneur, Paris: dossier Desgranges, AL5308.

51. Ibid., dossier Valière, AL5333 (my italics).

ments on the part of so prominent authorities, what else could *we* do except than respond to the *call aimed at us* and what else would have our constituents done?" (my italics).[52]

It is worth noting the choice of words used to characterize these public statements. Rochereau depicts them as loaded with pathos. The Socialist deputy Ferdinand Morin portrays them in similar terms: "The moving and passionate call aimed at us on 9 July by M. Herriot, chairman of the chamber of Deputies, whose information naturally overcame ours, the similar call made by M. Jeanneney, chairman of the senate were, I want to emphasize it, the key determinant of *our* vote" (my italics). These characterizations emphasize the intended impact of these public stands. Alignment—the production of unanimity—was possible because parliamentarians could interpret these statements as calls directed at themselves. Morin adds to the sentence just quoted: "I underline that in the 9 July meeting, all party leaders and the unanimity of the chamber except three votes as well as the unanimity of the senate responded to the calls of MM. Herriot and Jeanneney."[53]

Testimonies reveal that this emotional interpretation of the public statements of 9 July was widely shared. Joseph Massé, a conservative deputy from the Republican Federation, arrived in Vichy in the evening of 9 July after the votes of the Chamber of Deputies and the Senate about the opportunity for constitutional reform. He learned the outcome of these two votes through his colleagues, who told him: "in an emotional speech, *our* chairman, M. Herriot, had said: [we need] 'authority.'" Massé goes on: "That is all I needed to determine my vote, all the more so that I also learnt that Jeanneney had made similar remarks during the Senate meeting. That is why, simply stated, I voted 'for' with 59 of our colleagues."[54] This last figure, which Massé does not explain, most likely refers to the delegation of the Republican Federation, of which Massé was a member.

The Stance of the Group

In light of an epistemic argument, it is significant that when actors mention the impact of prominent actors' public statements, they relate these statements to an assessment of the group stance. I have identified the two previous epistemic hints as discursive features: ego adopts the standpoint of the group as a whole;

52. Ibid., dossier Victor Rochereau AL5328.
53. Ibid., dossier Ferdinand Morin AL5323. This testimony exemplifies the importance granted to the experience of unanimity and the prospect of achieving it.
54. Ibid., dossier Massé, AL5321.

and he interprets the statement as a call for a specific collective outcome. In either case ego experiences the happening through the prism of the group: "The Republic's great names were vouching for Pétain's loyalty imploring us to grant him our votes. So did chairman Jeanneney, senator of my county [*département*] who won over the vote of all the senators and deputies of the Haute Saône" (André Liautey, Radical deputy).[55]

Even more significant are accounts that explicitly infer a distribution of preferences from a statement. The centrist deputy Raymond Bérenger describes a decision process that tied the stance of all to the stance of prominent actors, with this common understanding being "tacit": "I adopted what I thought to be a measure of prudence *tacitly accepted by all*, all the more so that none of our group leaders, usually so prolix, publicly advised against this decision. On the contrary, the short speech of the chairman of the chamber, on 9 July, as well as that of the chairman of the senate, incited *us* to make this move" (my emphasis).[56]

Léon Betoulle, a Socialist senator, and Roger Lefèvre, a Socialist deputy, both explain their decision by referring to the decision of their colleagues, not specifically Socialists "I passed the incriminated motion. I passed it as many colleagues did, disturbed by the events and, like myself, influenced by the speeches of the chairmen of the Chamber of Deputies and of the Senate" (Betoulle).[57] Lefèvre arrived in Vichy after escaping from a German camp for prisoners of war. Once in Vichy, he observed that parliamentary groups were in disarray. "Ultimately" the event that determined his decision was Herriot's "vibrant call in favor of the Marshal." Lefèvre adds that "since it came from a man so respected," it "carried many don't knows away. Chairman Jeanneney showed himself no less eloquent."[58]

The significance and impact which Galimand attributed to Herriot's speech reflected the same cognitive process. Galimand, a Radical deputy who subsequently joined the French Free Forces in England, expected Herriot to reassert his colleagues' republicanism before the whole chamber. Quite telling from an epistemic perspective, Galimand was assuming that this expectation was widely shared: "one could legitimately expect from [Herriot] some surprising harangue with a revolutionary inspiration. This was the hope, the last hope of many." The deception was commensurate to the expectation: "but what did

55. Ibid., dossier André Liautey, AL5319.

56. Ibid., dossier Raymond Bérenger AL5298 (my italics).

57. Ibid., dossier Léon Betoulle, AL5300. Betoulle will be later on involved in the underground resistance movement against the Germans.

58. Ibid., dossier Lefèvre AL5318. Like his colleague Betoulle, Lefèvre will subsequently take part in the resistance movement.

he say? What! Only this! An academic oration in praise of the deputies who had died . . . I had the feeling that, although the Chamber was listening to this farewell with emotion, it showed some impatience . . . *The Assembly was disappointed.* The cry of despair, the burst [of indignation], the pieces of advice, the orders that it had wished for: the president [of the Chamber] had been incapable of this. He was majestic, but resigned"[59] (my italics). Coordination takes place in contrapuntal form, at odds with the deputies' modal preference.

Prominent Silence

I have considered verbal statements. I should also consider the silence of prominent actors as a public statement.

Once they were in Vichy and realized the organizational breakdown of the parliamentary groups (chapter 7), rank-and-file parliamentarians paid close attention to the public behavior of their prominent peers. If salvation had to come in the form of a collective resolution, it had to come from them. Their silence was therefore as noticeable as their public statements, and insofar as this silence revealed an attempt to avoid taking political responsibility, parliamentarians disapproved it, silently. Paul-Boncour, for instance, regretted that Joseph Caillaux, his Radical colleague in the Senate, did not publicly express his opinion about constitutional alternatives to a power transfer.[60] Implicit in Paul-Boncour's disapproval was a belief that Caillaux's public silence did have an impact on the final outcome and that public opposition on his part could have changed the outcome. His silence contributed to the collective resignation.

This imputation is present in descriptive accounts that infer the group stance from the lack of any statement by prominent actors. Consider this testimony by Maxime Fauchon, a rightist deputy. Fauchon is impressed by the low profile of those whom he views as prominent in parliament: "great, huge, colossal was my stupefaction to observe that none of the political leaders was displaying any resistance, and I would even dare to say, was expressing any reservation against the projects expounded by Laval." Immediately after making this observation, Fauchon reveals the subtext and implication of his "stupefaction": "*The majority was acquiescing*" (italics in original). Instead of inferring acquiescence from Herriot's call for unity or Jeanneney's "veneration" for Pétain, Fauchon infers it from the statement of silence.

59. Galimand, *Vive Pétain! Vive de Gaulle!*, 49.
60. See chapter 3.

Parliamentarians convened for the first time as a "National Assembly"—the Chamber of Deputies and the Senate meeting together—on the morning of 10 July behind closed doors, to discuss the bill. The meeting first took up the motion submitted by the ex-servicemen in the Senate. Laval indicated that the bill proposed by the government would contain the sentence "The Constitution will be ratified by the nation and applied by the Assemblies it will have created." Speaking on the behalf of the ex-servicemen, Jean Taurines and Maurice Dormann agreed to withdraw their counterproposal. Then Flandin took the rostrum. "Something worried me in your speech, Mr. Laval: it is this allusion that you made to some sort of necessity to align with other regimes."[61] Flandin expressed reservations about the government's proposal and his fear that France might "become Nazi" (*nazifiée*).

"A Wave of Republican Emotion"

Parliamentarians interpreted Flandin's speech as a pro-republican stance against any alignment with totalitarian regimes. His speech "glorified the democratic spirit and the Republic" (Vincent Badie, Radical deputy).[62] The Socialist deputy Pétrus Faure described it as "an emotional speech for the defense of the Republic and the republican freedoms, which elicited Léon Blum's congratulation when Flandin came from the rostrum."[63] The conservative deputy Henri Becquart pointed out that Flandin "implored the government not to copy foreign institutions with servility."[64] The impact of these warnings on the Assembly was considerable. Irrespective of their political affiliations, actors who report the event agreed on this point.[65] Why such an impact?

Two features stand out in actors' testimonies: Flandin's emotion, as well as

---

61. *Événements* I, 496.

62. Badie's testimony, *Événements* VIII, 2273.

63. Faure, *Un témoin raconte . . .* , 68.

64. "Il adjura le gouvernement . . . de ne pas copier servilement des institutions étrangères." Becquart, *Au temps du silence*, 231. Using the third person to describe himself, Flandin makes the same point about the political content of his speech: "Actually, in these dramatic Vichy events president (i.e., former premier) Flandin was the only one who in a foreseeing move (*par avance*) took a stand against the policy of collaboration." Bibliothèque Nationale, Paris, Archives Flandin, Don 31357, box 127.

65. Gros, *République toujours*, 60. Blum, *Mémoires*, 89–90. Lebrun, *Témoignage*, 108. Becquart, *Au temps du silence*, 231–32. Martin du Gard, *La chronique de Vichy*, 54–55. Noguères's diary, *Événements* VII, 2251–52. Ramadier, *Vichy (juillet 1940)*, 55.

the emotion of those who listened to him, and his eloquence. "Emotion took over the audience as a whole who, suddenly, became silent" (Henri Becquart).[66] The speech was "gripping" (très empoignant; Louis Gros, Socialist deputy).[67] As for eloquence, "Flandin delivered a great speech" (Xavier Vallat, far-right deputy).[68] The rightist senator Georges Pernot praised the "magnificent language" with which "[Flandin] evoked our national traditions, our attachment to the Republic and our will for independence" (letter dated 16 December 1940).[69] The Socialist deputy Félix Gouin offered a similar assessment: the "eloquent and grave speech made a great and strong impression," which Gouin attributed to an "emotional depth that was unusual in this orator most often cold and precise."[70]

Against the Tide

Eloquence carries little weight if it offers no clue to a collective dilemma. I reinterpret the emotional impact of Flandin's speech from the perspective of the collective alignment argument. Flandin's warnings imply a stand against the political agenda motivating the bill. A power transfer geared to this agenda is not acceptable. Such is the political message conveyed by his statement. This stand would not have had such resonance had it been predictable. Flandin's public stance was unexpected in two key respects. First, it went against the tide. Remember the context. Since the previous evening, given the statements of the two assembly chairmen and the separate votes of both assemblies on the principle of a constitutional revision, resignation had been prevailing. Anyone observing the unanimity expressed on the evening of 9 July would have expected the government's plans to go off without a hitch the next day. When deputies and senators were about to meet on the morning of 10 July (Wednesday), the collective mood was "favorable to Laval's bill." It seemed that the bill would "receive a fairly large majority" (Louis Gros).[71]

Flandin's speech struck deputies and senators because it was offbeat. Louis Noguères offered a precise diagnosis of the impact in his diary. Flandin's speech, extolling respect for the human person and the dignity of liberty, "had

66. Becquart, Au temps du silence, 231.
67. Gros, République toujours, 59.
68. "Flandin fit un grand discours." Vallat, Le nez de Cléopatre, 188.
69. Bibliothèque Nationale, Paris, Archives Flandin, Don 31357, box 127: Pernot, letter to Flandin, 16 December 1940.
70. Bibliothèque Nationale, Paris, Archives Flandin, Don 31357, box 127: "France du 2-4-43: Quelques souvenirs sur Flandin par Félix Gouin."
71. Gros, République toujours, 59.

a considerable effect" because it "sounded so different from what [parliamen-tarians] had been hearing for so many days."[72] Flandin himself outlined in his notes the contrapuntal quality of his statement, contrasting it with the public stances of other prominent actors: "[This speech] departed from all the other statements delivered before the Assembly, in particular it departed from the statements delivered by the two Assembly chairmen."[73] The point is important. The impact of a public statement is relative to the collective context, and this context is shaped by the public stances of prominent actors.

Flandin's critical stance was unexpected in another respect. Flandin was not only a prominent rightist but also a prominent representative of pre-war paci-fism, who gained his pacifist credentials and visibility through a public gesture that shocked his contemporaries. Soon after the conclusion of the Munich agreement, Flandin sent a telegram to Hitler congratulating him for it (Sep-tember 1938). This move created a split in Flandin's own party, the Democratic Alliance. Many viewed the gesture as a repellent satisfecit to Hitler. Since in Vichy the promoters of the bill were former intransigent pacifists (chapter 5), parliamentarians could reasonably expect Flandin to side with Laval. His paci-fist credentials and his political affiliation predisposed him to do so.

Translated into the language of individual thresholds, this meant a low ac-quiescence threshold. It is precisely because he had this political profile that Flandin also had the capacity to destabilize a tacit consensus in favor of ac-quiescence. The impact of his political denunciation, which actors precisely record in their writings, fleshes out this point. Consider the political lesson that the far-right deputy Becquart drew from the whole episode: Flandin's speech "demonstrated that a leader with a noble spirit and ardent words could have, most likely, taken the Assembly away from its apathy to set it up against the enemy and its accomplices."[74]

Underlying this impact and the possibility of a reversal was a collective process of belief coordination. Herein lies the decisive link between eloquence and its emotional appeal. Flandin's eloquence impressed his peers because it revealed their modal preference. They invested his pro-republican statement

72. Noguères's diary, *Événements* VII, 2252. See also Pernot, *Journal de guerre*, 97.

73. Bibliothèque Nationale, Paris, Archives Flandin, Don 31357, box 127: "notes de base pour les mémoires."

74. Becquart, *Au temps du silence*, 231. Pezet emphasizes the unexpected character of Flan-din's statement and its impact: "The only speech of high class and high politics, deeply moving and subtle, which got a *standing ovation* from the whole Assembly is the speech by the man who sent a telegram to Hitler. Incredible reversal of psychologies and ... of this man" (emphasis in original) (Fondation Nationale des Sciences Politiques, Paris, Archives Pezet, handwritten notes, "éphémérides," p. 9, P E 6).

with collective significance. The connection surfaces in the most perceptive accounts. The Radical deputy Badie notes that Flandin received the approbation of the audience.[75] Blum captures this collective resonance with particular insight: Flandin conveyed "feelings that, more or less disguised, more or less constrained, persisted nonetheless deep down in our hearts and consciences. The expression he gave of these feelings produced at intervals the temporary effect of relief and almost liberation."[76] His critical stance recreated the possibility of a collective recovery.

Renunciation

This brings us to the second moment of the speech. In tears, Flandin ended his warning with a recommendation to pass the bill: "it is in the name of these profound emotions stemming from the French soul that I beseech my colleagues to yield to those who, like myself and so many others, will be returning tomorrow to the occupied region, . . . , so that we may *all* feel that, having fulfilled our duty here, we are leaving to the government [of France], which will take our place, our country free and strong. (Applause)" (my italics).[77] The Socialist deputy Vincent Auriol commented: "After 'a long inner struggle' which appeases those who were anxious, M. Flandin brings his vote to the government project."[78]

With this recommendation for a power transfer, Flandin thus contradicts himself, twice. He contradicts both his initial reaction to the prospect of a constitutional devolution, delivered three days earlier ("What need is there . . . ?"), and the warnings he has just been delivering. The significance of this turnabout is significant in two key respects. First, his ultimate recommendation kills the resurgence of collective opposition in the bud. With his turnaround Flandin is making clear the vanity of collective opposition. This seesaw motion shuts down the prospect of a collective stance reasserting democratic institutions against the prospect of a power devolution. Blum most likely had this impact in mind when he wrote that Flandin's "final call made the work of Laval's propagandists complete."[79]

Second, Flandin's recommendation consolidated the impact of the stance of the two assembly chairmen, thereby amplifying expectations of collective

75. Badie's testimony, *Événements*, 2273.

76. Blum, *Mémoires*, 89–90.

77. *Événements* I, 496. Trans. by Hare (Aron 1958, 110).

78. Auriol, *Hier . . . demain*, 125.

79. "Son appel final vint consommer l'oeuvre des propagandistes de Laval." Blum, *Mémoires*, 89.

acquiescence. The sequence was now well established, as were the collective inferences which members of parliament derived from the successive public statements. In the short time left before the vote, no one alone could reasonably expect to cancel the cumulative impact of these public stances. Flandin's turn-about sanctioned expectations of collective acquiescence. Laval's success was now quasi-certain. This explains why observers, more or less intuitively and ir-respective of their political affiliation, viewed the moment as decisive. "It is the morning of 10 July, in Vichy Great Casino that the drama unfolded" (Vincent Auriol, Socialist deputy).[80] "These tears will ensure an almost unanimous vote tonight" (Bardoux, conservative senator).[81] "Flandin ensured the government proposal an impressive majority" (Noguères, Socialist deputy).[82]

The moment was one of collective alignment. "The Assembly rose up to ac-claim him."[83] "All the members of the Assembly were deeply moved. It is likely that if the vote had taken place at this moment, the majority would have been even stronger than it turned out to be at the end of the official session" (Gros, Socialist senator).[84] Laval's "accomplices" were "joined by all the don't knows, the cowards, all those whose 'conscience' has been relieved, 'after a long inner struggle' by the elevated conscience of the man who sent a famous telegram to Hitler" (Auriol, Socialist deputy).[85] A journalist reports that "after the meeting, many parliamentarians were anxious to tell Pierre-Étienne Flandin himself that his intervention had changed their vote."[86]

Noguères offers a precise diagnosis of the impact of this public stance on the assembly. "Hence, the government—let us say Pierre Laval—benefited not only from Flandin's and his friends' vote but, and above all, from the moral prestige that [Flandin] had just acquired. More to the point: the fact that three days earlier, Flandin had denounced the government's shortcomings, the fact

---

80. "C'est dans la matinée du 10 juillet, au Grand Casino de Vichy, que le drame s'est dénoué." Auriol, *Hier . . . demain*, 119.

81. "Ces larmes assureront un vote presqu'unanime pour ce soir." Bardoux, *Journal d'un témoin de la Troisième*, 405.

82. "P. E. Flandin . . . assurait au projet gouvernemental une imposante majorité." Noguères, *Le véritable procès du maréchal Pétain*, 160. In his diary Déat acknowledges this impact and estimates that Flandin's final call rallied about one hundred votes. Archives Nationales, Paris, F7 15342: Déat, Journal de guerre, 378, quoted by Burrin (1986, 337).

83. "L'Assemblée se lève pour l'acclamer." Bardoux, *Journal d'un témoin de la Troisième*, 405.

84. Gros, *République toujours*, 61.

85. Auriol, *Hier . . . demain*, 125.

86. Article by Charles Morice in *Le Petit Parisien*, dated 11 July, quoted by Calef (1988, 426). Auriol makes the same point (*Hier . . . demain*, 125).

that he had risen up against any project to change the constitution, and that he had even suggested a procedure that could have avoided it, and that in the last resort, after a laborious meditation which he brought to the fore with noble worlds, he was lending his trust to the same government, without reservation, all this *was increasing tenfold* the impact of his adhesion" (my italics).[87] As Calef (1988, 426) puts it, who in these conditions "would dare to take the responsibility of destabilizing the situation since no man of the first rank steps forward to propose a different solution?"

We often think of tipping points as moments of reversal that establish durable trends. The moments that I have explained in this chapter defy this characterization. Within a short time, collective expectations geared to one outcome shifted to the other side, unexpectedly endorsing the opposite outcome. But the trend was not durable. Resolutions soon faltered and crumbled. Individuals ended up embracing the scenario which they had just repudiated. And if subsequently resolutions seemed stabilized again, this could only be an illusion. A push could have destabilized them again. These tipping points were tentative ones. That is why they are so peculiar and why they call for attention.

There are different ways of dealing with this peculiar character. One contrasts expectations and behaviors. Expectations are beliefs about the future. Such beliefs have no firm standing. They come and go depending on the circumstances, the information available, and more broadly the conjuncture. Their ontological status lies in this constant dependence. Without this exogenous input, they are nothing. They lose their raison d'être. To live on, they need something to grab. No surprise that they come and go and can prove so malleable. Behaviors, on the other hand, commit their authors. The trends that they set cannot easily be reversed once set in motion, because of this commitment effect.

Underlying this contrast is the contrast between two types of collective alignment. Tipping points that signal durable shifts relate to sequential alignment. Reversible tipping points relate to an inferential type of alignment. Both processes point to different modes of decision. Sequential alignment is backward-looking. Actors take their cues from decisions that have already been made. Inferential alignment is forward-looking. Decisions are up in the air. This contrast is fundamental. The clue to the possibility of collective reversals lies in mutual uncertainty. These reversals are actualized through a process of inference making geared to the prospect of collective alignment. The scope

87. Noguères, *Vichy, juillet 1940*, 129.

of the collective swings recorded in this chapter testifies to the scope of mutual uncertainty and the scope of the inferential processes that this uncertainty motivated. Reversibility is inherent in mutual uncertainty.

Concomitant with the argument about reversibility is an argument about the open-ended character of the process. Reconstructing the temporality of the process confirms the diagnosis presented in chapter 7: opinions were not settled. This oscillating mood was prevalent till the last meetings; and until then the collective outcome remained open, not in the sense that actors had no clue about what could happen, but in the sense that expectations about the outcome were reversible for the reasons I have just outlined. Any public event shifting inferences about peers could shift, by the same token, the configuration of the day.

PART V

Coda: Judgments of Significance

Scope and significance go hand in hand. The scope conditions tell us how far we can go. The less confined the argument, that is, the less dependent on the specifics of the case, the greater its analytical significance. I address the scope issue first by examining to what extent the conclusions of the previous chapters — as well as the theory of alignment that provides these observations with their systematic character — owe their validity to three types of contextual parameters: the institutional setting, the configuration of the groups involved, and the specific character of the challenge.

An object of investigation can be significant in a second sense: for what it reveals. Significance in this case is heuristic. Critical decisions lay bare a constitutive dimension of individual preferences. The stakes at play and the actors' awareness of these stakes make these decisions magnifying lenses. The events magnify collective processes in a situation marked by a high-stakes challenge. Actors are caught off guard. Observing their familiar world crumbling, they become acutely aware of the extent to which their own assessments and understanding need to be collectively substantiated. If their peers waver, they waver as well. If their peers doubt, they doubt as well. In this collective experience lies the heuristic significance of the events.

The third prong for assessing significance is historical. So far my judgment has been apodictic. I asserted, rather than demonstrated, the historical significance of these events in light of statements borrowed from historians and contemporary actors (chapter 1). In my defense I could note that these references presume historical significance. Still, this justification is secondhand, and as such can only be provisional. Now that the journey in the labyrinth of facts, hypotheses, and counter-objections is close to an end, am I in a position to turn the apodictic judgment about significance into a demonstrative claim?

Chapter 10

The Consistency of Inconsistency

The worst illusion consisted in imagining that [homo oeconomicus] could form so clear an idea of his interests. — Bloch (1953, 195)

1

Any argument developed through a close confrontation with the empirics of specific cases exposes itself to the charge of being too much indebted to the cases on which it rests. Here this charge is rhetorically easy, since it only needs to take notice of the research design to become plausible. I want to assess in which respects it is grounded. Do the cases — insofar as these cases define a class of research objects — confine the scope of the theory and the conclusions? The empirical focus of this inquiry has been on (1) high-stakes and simultaneous decisions made in a (2) parliamentary setting in which (3) formal groups are the main players. These three characteristics define different facets of the object of inquiry, and by extension different points of entry for assessing how indebted to the cases the theory might be. In this chapter I start as the devil's advocate, considering which rationales could plausibly construe these different facets as limiting factors.

Three objections cast along these lines are possible. The first one concerns the simultaneous character of the decision. This feature is specific to synchronic voting procedures. Most of the time people do not confront a behavioral dilemma with the anticipation that they will have to simultaneously make their choice. Are the alignment mechanisms probed in the previous chapters confined to this specific class of decision? The second objection underlines the formal configuration of the groups involved in the decision. Formal groups imply explicit acts of affiliation and a symbolic closure. Could it be argued that the inference mechanisms I have described have no basis in groups that are diffuse and informal?

The third objection points to the institutional peculiarity of parliament. In this setting oral statements enjoy considerable attention, by definition. Group members organize their experience around the prospect of oral statements. Consequently, an inquiry that sets up its exploration camp in this institutional environment is likely to grant analytical precedence to oral statements. In addition, parliament institutionalizes a forum regulated by rituals, protocols, and arcane procedural rules. The highly ritualized and formalistic environment makes informal interactions secondary in importance. Shall we conclude that the main findings of the study primarily reflect the characteristics of the setting?

2

In the first pages of this chapter I address each of these objections in turn. The discussion specifies the scope conditions of the argument. None of the factors mentioned above—simultaneity, the formal constitution of the groups involved, the institutional salience of verbal statements and of formal interactions in the parliamentary arena—limit the scope of the argument. Simultaneous decisions objectify a sense of constraints that comes to the fore whenever actors are directly confronted with a high-stakes behavioral stance. The question is whether in dealing with such decisions, actors relate to others. The theory of collective alignment applies to actors who experience their behavioral commitment as a dilemma and who relate this dilemma to the behavioral stance of others who they believe are in the same situation as themselves. Mutual interdependence defines the scope of the theory.

Mutual interdependence can be ad hoc—produced by the circumstances—or the byproduct of sustained relations over time. Its nature depends on group configuration. Actors' sense of mutual interdependence is not conditional on a formal definition of the reference group. The formal character of the group, on the other hand, brings to the fore actors' awareness of this collective dimension insofar as it increases the cost of their isolation. If the point is to delve into the dynamic of collective interactions when actors cannot fall back on ready-made behavioral scripts, the formal constitution of the group turns out to be a useful heuristic device. It allows us to investigate moments when individuals who have been accustomed to interacting and relying on shared understandings are at a loss to figure out their next collective move.

This analysis recasts simultaneity and the formal constitution of the group as magnifying lenses. Both features magnify interactive mechanisms that otherwise would remain buried in the web of social processes. Here heuristic significance takes care of the issue of scope. The same remark applies to parliament. For comparative purposes, parliament provides a very convenient observation site: in this setting both informal and formal interactions are equally significant. Furthermore, the forum configuration of the setting lends itself to processes that can be simultaneously based on inferences—the information is available to all—and factual observations. Sequential alignment is a possibility as well as tacit coordination. This is the whole point of the alignment theory.

The heuristic advantage of this site is to offer a vantage point for observing these different processes within the same time frame and the same location.

3

The latter part of this chapter pushes the heuristic significance of the argument one step further by outlining its contributions to our understanding of preference instability and ambivalence. Actors' inability to stabilize their action preference is a striking feature of mutual uncertainty. Actors provide to themselves multiple reasons. These vary across time. There is no constancy. This observation draws attention to the possibility of contradictory preferences. By extension, it invites us to inquire into the source of the instability.

I set out this inquiry in light of the point about externalities discussed in chapter 6. These decisions bear upon multiple types of outcomes or classes of events: (1) political outcomes (the issue of collective rights and the political capacity of parliament), (2) status among peers, and (3) individual security and protection from *immediate* threats. Each type, or class of events, elicits a preference order. The political outcome type elicits a preference for a regime that secures individual rights over a regime institutionalizing arbitrary power. The status issue elicits a preference for alignment over isolation. The preference regarding protection from immediate threats is straightforward: shun these threats rather than get exposed to them.

Each preference order in turn implies a behavioral stance. The preference for a regime securing individual rights calls for an oppositional stance. Immediate threats create an incentive for acquiescence. The issue of status among peers leaves the action preference indeterminate, since this status is decided by whether ego's action is discrepant from those of his peers. An action that isolates him jeopardizes his status. When combined, these action preferences— acquiescence, opposition, indeterminacy—are either contradictory or inconsistent.

Thus when we speak of preference instability, we speak in the first place of an instability of action preferences. Vacillation reflects the oscillation between contradictory action preferences. But this shift from one option to another is itself the derivation of the inability to rank types of outcomes. Ego cannot decide which class of events should have precedence. When he considers political outcomes, he opts for opposition. When he considers protection from immediate threats, he opts for acquiescence. When he considers his status in the group, his choice remains indeterminate. The first contribution of this analytical framework is to lay bare this connection between the difficulty of stabilizing the choice of a behavioral option and a failure of ranking. The second contribution is to point to an alternative explanation: ego oscillates between alternative behavioral options not because he does not know which type of outcome he should prioritize, but because he gives precedence to his status among his peers in a situation where their collective stance is not only uncertain but subject to fluctuations.

4

Armed with these few insights, I go back to the problem of self-deception toward the end of this chapter. The critical discussion of the miscalculation thesis developed in chapter 4 concluded with the observation that when actors suppress information—publicly available—about the challenger's agenda, they collectively deceive themselves. Miscalculation and deception should rather be construed as instances of self-deception. On the other hand, we cannot understand the possibility of self-deception without paying attention to the collective underpinnings of heteronomy. The notion describes in the first place a maxim of action, that is, a rule for conduct. Ego makes his action preference conditional on the actions of his peers. He opts for a heteronomous maxim of action. Given the decision at hand, the stakes, and his own uncertainty about the principles that should guide his action, ego agrees to let others determine his own line of conduct. Mutual uncertainty at once discloses the constitutive role of heteronomy and provides an experimental setting for observing its motivational effects.

In the process of making sense of his behavioral choice, ego needs to come up with plausible reasons for this choice. The reasons are plausible if they are shared. The more commonsensical these reasons appear to those whom ego defines as referential peers—that is, the more frequently they provide an operational grid of interpretation in verbal exchanges—the greater their plausibility: ego constructs his reasons in light of the beliefs that he can plausibly impute to his peers. He derives his beliefs about himself from these shared reasons. That is why these reasons are not mock ones. Heteronomy then takes on a cognitive dimension.

SETTINGS, GROUPS, DECISIONS

In what sense do the specifics of the case qualify the conclusions? The following discussion examines two possible limits. The first is proper to theoretical induction. These cases provide the empirical basis for a set of theoretical inferences. Induction misses the mark when we interpret the specifics of the case as the general properties of a class of events that has no empirical substance or when we base our claims on characteristics of the event which we do not explicitly theorize. The second limit concerns validation. Theory building in the present case is a two-step process. First we infer theoretical claims from the cases. Then we go back to the cases to probe the soundness of the inferences. This move back and forth lends itself to a confirmation bias. Since we constructed the theory from the cases, what evidence is there that the theory is not simply confirming itself? I assess both limits for each of the facets distinguished above: the decision, the group, and the setting.

The Sense of Interdependence

The definition that I elaborate in chapter 6 emphasizes three general characteristics: externalities, high risks, and the cost of isolation. First, the decision has multiple externalities. It puts at stake the welfare of groups and actors who are not the primary decision makers. As a result, these actors have no direct leverage. Second, the decision is risky. Actors have to choose between options that are uncertain and potentially very costly for themselves and for others. Whatever choice they make, the decision involves high costs. These two defining features—risks and externalities—characterize the decision as high-stakes. The stakes are high because the welfare of many groups is at stake and because the costs down the road can be horrendous. Finally, ego expects to pay a cost if his choice isolates him among fellow decision makers.

So far, I cast the argument as if it applied mainly to high-stake decisions: there is an element of high cost that is not purely individual. The risks can be shared. On closer examination, as I elaborate below, this assumption is unwarranted. The theory of alignment is empirically relevant in any situation in which a group of individuals confronts a decision which they know to be collective *and* in which they dread the possibility of their isolation. These individuals may or may not define the stakes of the decision as collective ones. Collective stakes are significant insofar as they heighten actors' sense of responsibility and their awareness of potential costs. These stakes amplify the concern for isolation. I develop the same conclusion for two features of these collective decisions which I did not specifically discuss in the previous chapters: simultaneity and public accountability. This analytical close-up substantially expands the scope of the argument.

Stakes and Isolation

The key issue is whether in weighing the ins and outs of their decision, actors relate their choice to the behavioral stance of others who they think are confronted with the same decision as themselves. The theory of collective alignment applies whenever actors view their decisions as interdependent and assess this interdependence as having behavioral consequences: they make their choice conditional on the decisions of their peers. In the language of chapter 6: their action threshold is relative. This assumes that (1) actors are aware that their decision is collective and (2) they view their isolation as costly. In this formulation, neither externalities nor the scope of these costs per se conditions the empirical relevance of the collective alignment argument. Consequences can affect a large number of people and their potential costs can be very high. Ego will not necessarily view his isolation as costly. Conversely, ego may define the costs involved in purely individual terms. Nevertheless, he makes his choice conditional on the choices of others to assuage his uncertainty about the future.

It is reasonable to assume that the higher the collective stakes, the greater the likelihood that ego anticipates his isolation as costly. Analytically, however, the two should be kept separate. In theory, the collective alignment of selfish egos is possible. Selfish actors do not care about externalities. But they care about their self-confidence and seek to shun the psychological burden of being alone in forming beliefs about the future. This theoretical possibility outlines the main point: the concern for isolation, not the collective dimension of the stakes, is a necessary condition of alignment. Collective alignment at the group level belongs to the realm of the possible when cost avoidance strategies motivated by the fear of isolation is a shared property of the group.

Actors' Exposure

Two additional features deserve close attention: simultaneity and public accountability. First, parliamentarians knew that they would have to simultaneously commit themselves. Time was bounded. Wait-and-see could only be a provisional option. At one point, elusion would no longer be possible, and a decision would have to be made. Second, parliamentarians knew that they would be held accountable for their choice. Through their vote, they would attach their name to one action. Whichever line of conduct they opted for, they engaged their individual responsibility. Is alignment conditional on these two characteristics of the decision? The answer is similar to the one I just provided regarding the collective character of the stakes. Simultaneity and public accountability are not conditional factors. Rather, they exacerbate actors' awareness of the alternative. The decision has a distinctive edge that makes it difficult for actors to shun the constraints of their commitment. The situation is "either-or." There can be no fiddling around.

Group Configuration

Is the formal constitution of the group a prerequisite for a theory of alignment? I reframe this question as follows: Do actors only achieve a sense of mutual interdependence within the organizational framework of a formally defined group? A group enjoys a formal definition when acts of symbolic and explicit recognition define the boundaries of the group. Group members identify one another in light of explicit membership criteria. In informal groups they identify themselves on the basis of categories which they perceive as commonsensical and "natural"—what Bourdieu would call "doxic representations." Actors enact and rehearse these doxic categories through their social interactions.

Ego has no concept of isolation unless he has the concept of a collective from which he might get isolated. He relates his decision to a set of "others" whose future behavior affects the cost of his own decision. This collective can be ad hoc, the byproduct of the circumstances. Or it can exist before the decision and determine who has to make the decision. For each individual actor facing the decision, the prospect of isolation raises the issue of how to relate to these "others." Ego has to decide to what extent these "others" warrant his own welfare. If he decides that given the risks involved, he wants to condition his choice on their future behavior, it is crucial for him to determine what this future behavior will be. The cost of isolation is not necessarily grounded on explicit, or even sustained, relations over time. The formal constitution of the group is not a prerequisite. Ego may relate to others to assuage his uncertainty about the future.

The broader implication is that ego can develop a sense of the collective outside the bearings of a formally defined group. Whether the group is formal or informal, whether it enjoys symbolic closure or not, the decisive factor is whether group members have a sense of boundaries. The issue is therefore whether the group is well defined. Inferential alignment is possible in groups that are well defined: group members have a clear sense of the boundaries of the group.

Interestingly, mutual uncertainty is possible in groups that have different organizational configurations. This point takes on its significance when we adopt the lenses of a comparative analysis that sets contrasts and parallels across the two cases. With regard to the organizational setting, the collective decisions of March 1933 and July 1940 are strikingly dissimilar. At one end is the French parliamentary scene, made up of loosely defined affiliation groups. At the opposite end stands the Reichstag, in which groups are clearly defined and enjoy strong behavioral cohesion. These contrasting organizational and institutional contexts have different implications for patterns of interaction. Whereas the German delegates primarily meet with the members of their own affiliation group, French parliamentarians are involved in out-group ties with a high frequency.

Yet irrespective of these striking differences in terms of group configurations, actors in both cases experience mutual uncertainty (chapters 7, 8). This experience is independent of the groups' formal closure and their degree of behavioral cohesion. This comparative insight suggests that beyond institutional and conjunctural factors, the nature of the decision problem—the type of challenge imposed upon actors—shapes how group members define and frame the situation. Organizational factors affect the probability and intensity of a situation of mutual uncertainty. But this set of parameters neither makes this type of conjuncture inevitable nor rules it out.

In which respects are the groups' formal closure and degree of cohesion thus relevant for the analysis of interactions? I advance two claims. First, the greater the social closure of the group and, concomitantly, the greater the group's cohesion, the greater the cost of social isolation. The implication of this claim is that heteronomy—the decision to make one's choice conditional on the choice of one's peers—is all the more probable across group members when the group is cohesive.

Second, variation in cohesion affects the likelihood that actors will redefine their reference group in the process of experiencing the challenge. Unless there is an explicit and shared attempt to reassert the group's organizational capacity, groups that have little cohesion are likely to dilute in a challenging situation. The contrast between French and German parliamentarians is revealing in this regard. For German parliamentarians the reference group remains their party delegation (chapter 8). For French parliamentarians the reference group is the Assembly as a whole (chapter 7). Whereas German delegates expect to coordinate their action with one another, French parliamentarians remain at a loss to figure out whether such a coordination will effectively take place.

Forum

The explicit function of parliamentary delegations is to deliberate, debate, and make decisions. This brings me to the setting issue. A parliament creates a space for public debates. This forum is highly formal and institutional: formal since explicit rules regulate interaction and decision processes, and institutional insofar as the script, in addition to being well established, is repeated over time. Rules are explicit. There is a protocol. The space for interactions is bounded and ritualized. Furthermore, debating and taking a stand are the main modes of interaction in this setting. The forum gears actors' attention to the significance of public statements. One could object that an inquiry set in this empirical site tips the diagnosis in favor of alignment processes induced by public stances.

I turn the objection on its head. In this setting, all three alignment processes — sequential alignment, local knowledge, tacit coordination — are possible. Informal interpersonal contacts are a salient dimension of the interactive process, as chapters 7–9 point out. Sequential alignment is possible because public statements enjoy considerable visibility and actors observe one another. Similarly, the empirical relevance of inferential alignment induced by public statements is grounded in the forum-like configuration of this interaction space. Hence the heuristic value of the parliamentary setting is that it sets a time frame and a spatial location amenable to all three processes. Because this setting is highly formalized and because it creates a forum for public statements, it provides a magnifying lens for the study of different types of interactions. Yet as chapter 11 points out, these processes are not confined to forum settings.

PREFERENCE INSTABILITY

We may delve into an event because we want to make it intelligible and because at first it eludes our causal imagination. But we may also want to delve into its intricacies for the purpose of laying bare processes that in this context have, because of the exceptional character of the event, a distinctiveness which they lack otherwise. This observation applies in the first place to alignment processes. In the remainder of this chapter I expand this claim to two problems which I left pending: preference instability and self-deception. Actors oscillate. By the same token they provide to themselves varying and at times contradictory reasons for their decision. From an external standpoint, this oscillating character is puzzling. The following remarks draw attention to two modes of preference instability. Both reflect different processes of emergence. The first sanctions ego's inability to rank the different types of outcomes implied by his decision. The second sanctions not ego's inability to rank outcomes but rather a specific rank order characterized by the prevalence of status considerations.

A Failure of Ranking

Multiple types of outcomes are at stake (chapter 6). For each type ego prefers a specific state of the world. These preferences over outcomes have conflicting behavioral implications. Thus ego is experiencing a dilemma because different

outcomes are at issue and these outcomes yield noncongruent action preferences. One way out of this inconsistency is to rank the types of outcomes involved by the decision. In this case ego prioritizes the preference orders elicited
by these different outcomes. He has to decide whether he gives precedence to
his personal security, his status among peers, or political outcomes. By ranking outcomes, he decides which one has priority. If this priority order remains
open, ego oscillates between conflicting action preferences and experiences
his behavioral choice as a dilemma. Ego's oscillation reflects a constant shift
from one action preference to another depending on the type of outcome he
considers.

Since the primary decision is a decision over behavioral options, the decision to order preference over outcomes should be conceived as a metadecision.
This "meta" character points to the problem. Ego needs to be able to step out
from the experience of his dilemma if he wants to figure out where he stands
with regard to the ranking of preference orders. As long as this experience
overwhelms him, ego oscillates. The issue is not simply one of "character." He
may not easily let his course of action be swayed by accidents, circumstances,
and external advice. Rather the issue is whether ego initially imputes similar
degrees of valence to the different types of outcomes implied by the decision.
The greater this valence, the more difficult it will be for ego to step out of the
dilemma. The difficulty of stepping out of the dilemma should rather be viewed
as the byproduct of situational factors.

The order of importance determined by this ranking procedure is also an
order of salience. Ego relates to the most important type of outcome as the one
most worthy of his attention. This point is significant in two respects. First, it
outlines the crucial importance of an interpretive frame. Actors experience a
decision as a problem because they lack a political script—the framing of the
problem and the definition of a line of conduct—that provides them with an
order of salience and a ranking of preference orders telling them which type of
outcomes matters most. The unprecedented character of a challenge is critical
in this respect. Second, the collective significance of a frame points to the possibility of a collective way out. What cannot be accomplished individually may
be accomplished as a collective endeavor. Ego may decide to rely on others to
get out of the dilemma.

The Choice of Others

"Relying on others" provides a clue to the second scenario of preference instability. In this second scenario, ego gives priority to his status among peers.
His affiliation with the group takes precedence. Heteronomy is the dominant

option. Here preference instability results from the decision to align with peers in a context where the group stance remains indeterminate. Vacillating expectations about the group generate behavioral oscillations. This instability is tied up with the chronology of the group's stance. Ego's behavioral choices vacillate depending on the collective stance that he expects from the group.

If heteronomy and mutual uncertainty prevail, any reason for making the choice—from the most trivial to the most "elaborate"—might do. Consequently all reasons are valid, which means that the value of any reason can be easily downplayed. Sadoun (1982) notes this lack of significance in his account of the Socialist delegates' behaviors in July 1940. "Often, insignificant reasons free the parliamentarian's consciousness up and tip the decision" (40). Consistent with this line of reasoning is the contention that where heteronomy prevails, behavioral preferences are most unstable when actors are most uncertain about their peers' ultimate choices. Actors are likely to endorse the flimsiest reasons if they face full uncertainty. Then their choices may hinge on insignificant reasons and their "reasons" for choosing one option may be equivalent to tossing a coin in the air.

THE CASE FOR AMBIVALENCE

These few considerations explain how actors can entertain conflicting reasons at once. Consider the depiction by Morsey (1977, 144) of the Center delegates' state of mind as they were about to make their decision. The delegates feared immediate consequences. They invoked a tradition of political conservatism. They bet on the taming effect of state responsibilities. They imagined their consent as a positive contribution to the solidarity of the nation. And they foresaw a regime based on violence, injustice, and lies. "Some delegates had diagnosed that a time of lie, servitude and injustice was to come. Others had a premonition thereof. Many feared it" (Morsey 1977, 145). Hürten (1992, 186–87) offers a similar account.

Heterogeneous Motives

In this account, Morsey (1977, 145) combines two levels of analysis and conflates two referents. When he states "Some delegates had diagnosed that a time of lie, servitude and injustice was to come. Others had a premonition thereof. Many feared it," he is describing a distribution of motives across individuals. Variance concerns the group as an aggregated whole. When, on the other hand, he writes "The delegates feared immediate consequences. . . . They imagined their consent as a positive contribution to the solidarity of the nation," he is describing multiple motives held by the same actors. Variation here takes place within individual psyches.

This conflation of viewpoints is quite frequent in historical narratives. For instance, Sadoun (1982, 36–40) argues that confusion, the atmosphere of constraint, fear, opportunism, and erroneous judgment entered the complex political equation underlying the Socialists' "yes" vote in July 1940. In this formulation it is not clear whether Sadoun is describing the psychological state of the median Socialist delegate or rather offering a synthetic representation of the group as an aggregation of individual motives. The claim of heterogeneity remains ambiguous as long as we do not specify the referent.

From a diachronic perspective, heterogeneity at the group level denotes individual heterogeneity. With regard to actors' reasons for their choice, heterogeneity is a group *and* individual-level characteristic. Because the chronology of uncertainty is a collective one, the same individual psyches go through different states. Collective oscillations are possible inasmuch as the same individuals shift from one stance or disposition to the opposite. When Michel (1966) observes, "Behavioral consistency was not the rule! Albert Lebrun in particular was an instance of vacillating opinion" (66), he is describing variation within the same individual psyches. We assess consistency and the lack thereof by tracing the successive subjective states which ego experiences.

Conflicting Reasons

The greater this heterogeneity of motives, the greater the likelihood that ego will successively rely on reasons that turn out, when juxtaposed, to be either inconsistent or contradictory. For instance, the account by Morsey (1977, 144) just quoted describes positive reasons hand in hand with negative ones. The delegates endorse the power transfer because they "fear immediate consequences." They also anticipate a regime of "lie, servitude and injustice." These are purely negative considerations. Simultaneously, actors view their decision as contributing to "national unity." Now the motive is a positive one. Acquiescence is a constructive act. A conciliatory stance in the face of Hitler's demands reaffirms a longing for national solidarity. A "yes" vote will conform to the behavior of their party's founding fathers and to their political tradition. There is no betrayal, only the stern assertion of a party tradition under challenging circumstances. How can actors entertain conflicting reasons at once?

Drawing on the analysis of preference instability that I have sketched above, I propose two possible answers. The first is that actors have a hard time figuring out which outcome should have precedence. The second is that actors provide to themselves the reasons which they simultaneously impute to their peers.

These two scenarios complement one another and can be reinterpreted from a sequential point of view as a two-moment process. First moment: realizing that their decision taps into different outcomes, actors are aware of the critical character of their decision. Because these outcomes imply contradictory behavioral stances, they experience the decision as a dilemma. Second moment: the decision to rely on others—the choice for heteronomy—provides a way out of this dilemma. Actors get away from the behavioral oscillation inherent to contradictory action preferences by making their choice conditional on the choice of their peers. In so doing they make themselves amenable to another type of behavioral oscillation, one elicited by heteronomy and shifting expectations regarding the group stance.

THE POSSIBILITY OF SELF-DECEPTION

The inability to rank outcomes is a source of considerable tension. Actors do not make up their mind regarding the behavioral stance they should take. By the same token, they have a hard time deciding what their primary motivation should be. If they exit, they avoid the dilemma altogether by avoiding the decision. Exiting de facto implies a choice about the ranking of preference orders. By exiting, actors reveal that they do not value the group enough to take the risk of a decision. They forgo their affiliation with the group. If they decide not to exit, they face either their irresolution or the possibility of a choice that contradicts their sense of consistency. How do they cope with this tension? Two broad strategies are conceivable: actors may reconsider how they rank outcomes—let us call this strategy "preference rationalization"—or they may deny the political implications of their choice—they engage in denial. Let me examine each strategy in turn.

Assume an individual who has always defined himself as a democrat and who votes for the transfer of constitutional power. His decision implies a renunciation of democracy given the challenger's agenda. To regain a sense of consistency between choice and preference while assuming his choice, two options are possible: either he reconsiders his preferences over political outcomes; or, he reconsiders the ranking of his preference *orders* (status, individual welfare, political outcomes) in a way that makes his choice meaningful and acceptable. The first scenario means that he adjusts the value ascribed by him to the different political outcomes at stake in his choice. He used to be a democrat. He now values a regime of authority. The second scenario implies that he ranks above political outcomes his preferences regarding his status in the group or his individual welfare.

Denial is the alternative strategy. Ego tries to make his behavior acceptable to himself by denying its political implications. Plainly stated: "It is not true that a vote of acquiescence implies renouncing democracy." Ego eludes dissonance and contradiction by making himself blind to the significance of his action. He recasts his belief about outcomes. This is self-deception proper (see chapter 4). But self-deception, like denial, will not carry much ground unless it is a collective endeavor. To elaborate this point, I first go back to the puzzle mentioned by Elster (1983, 149) in his brief discussion of the subject.

Elster states the problem lucidly. One cannot decide to forget what one knows and to believe at will what one knows to be misconceived. Thus self-deception contradicts itself. There is no such thing. It is an oxymoron, an impossible feat. "Self-deception involves the simultaneous entertaining of two incompatible or contradictory beliefs that make it impossible" (149). Shall I then conclude that my previous characterization of miscalculation as self-deception is unwarranted?

Heteronomy provides the clue—not so much behavioral heteronomy, the reliance on others' behavioral choices, but cognitive heteronomy, the reliance on their beliefs. The transition from a state of dubious conviction—Elster's point—to a state in which ego finally is at peace with his false beliefs is possible if it is collective. I forget what I know and I endorse what I know to be wrong because those whom I view as references collectively testify to the soundness of the beliefs that I am now endorsing. The feat happens if I have indications that it is so. Recast in these terms, heteronomy is inherent to self-deception.

Denial is phenomenologically possible and viable when it is collectively sustained by a collective process of belief construction. Actors deceive themselves by aligning their beliefs about the consequences of their action with the beliefs that they impute to their peers. This process can be conceptualized as a coordination game in which actors have to coordinate on one interpretation of their collective behavior. There is consensus when this convergence is crystallized by an event—a public statement—indicating that beliefs and expectations have been coordinated. These public events create the "common awareness" (Berk 1974, 368) that most members of the group are adopting the same solution.

Thus denial is a strategy of meaning-construction. Rationalization along these lines requires more or less work depending on two factors: first, the extent of the discrepancy between what the information available tells ego to believe and what he wants to believe; second, the extent to which ego is compelled to account for his choice. These few remarks outline not only that beliefs are malleable but also in what sense they are malleable. Actors adjust their beliefs to their expected behavioral choice. Some beliefs are more congenial than others to explaining the choice made. However, given the terms of the challenge, the process whereby some alternatives appear to be more desirable than others is a collective one. This means that the perception of the costs and the risks entailed by the decision are endogenous to the process of collective interactions. Actors' sensitivity to the prospect of being retaliated against is also a function of their propensity to bring cost considerations to the fore when they interpret the situation.

      ▨   ▨   ▨

In discussing the scope conditions of the argument, I indirectly disposed of two possible dismissive postures. I use the notion of "posture" on purpose: these are rebuttals that pose as critiques but lack precision and, as a result, remain primarily dismissive. The first posture reflects on the validity of the theory in light of the status of the cases. The cases are too exceptional to lend themselves to a general theory. They stamp the theoretical elaborations made in their behalf. The "theory" is nothing less than a derivation of the cases. The second rebuttal states that motivations are so heterogeneous and fluctuant that the project of a systematic explanation is irrelevant. Junker (1969, 188) summarizes this objection when he claims that historical investigation cannot uncover the reasons why each Center delegate was ultimately motivated to vote in favor of Hitler's enabling bill. Implicit in this claim is the idea that when actors are confronted with a crucial decision, their ultimate motivations are indecipherable. These motivations elude a comprehensive explanatory framework.

    The first posture (let us call it the "scope rebuttal") misrepresents the capacity of the theory to construe an object of investigation as a point of entry to processes of much broader relevance. The field of application of the theoretical claims elaborated in chapter 6 encompasses situations in which a group of actors facing a similar decision experience a sense of mutual interdependence. The second posture (the relevance rebuttal) fails to inquire into the sources of actors' vacillation and overlooks the revealing quality of this instability. Ambivalence reveals a preference structure in which heteronomy holds center stage, and a collective conjuncture loaded with mutual uncertainty. Once we reinterpret actors' conflicting reasons — their ambivalence — from this twofold perspective, actors' reasons can no longer be portrayed as eluding the grasp of a systematic explanation. Inconsistency becomes a symptom and a byproduct.

    This analysis yields two additional insights. The first concerns preference instability and highlights ambivalence as a collective phenomenon. When preference instability sanctions an inability to rank outcomes and the corresponding preferences, we have ambivalence proper, ambivalence in the classical sense of the term. Actors have conflicting motives and do not know on which foot they should dance. These conflicting motives originate behavioral indeterminacy. When preference instability sanctions heteronomy, actors experience ambivalence not as an original motivational state but as a byproduct. They provide reasons to themselves. These reasons oscillate because the actors adopt different action preferences depending on their prevailing expectations about the group stance. Unless they are pure opportunists, they also need to believe in these reasons. Hence their ambivalence.

The second insight relates to self-deception. The impossibility of self-deception loses its puzzling character when we focus on the interactive structure of individual beliefs and cognitive heteronomy. Elster bases his argument on the claim that people do not endorse beliefs which they do not believe plausible. The argument is a logical one. Yet in troubled and contested times, individual actors toy with, and in some cases endorse, beliefs which they originally know to be questionable, dubious, false, or invalid. This shift in belief is possible insofar as individuals construct their beliefs in light of the beliefs they impute to those whom they identify as "peers." Plausibility rests on the assumption of commonality: the belief is widely shared among one's peers. Logic lets phenomenology have its place.

Chapter 11

The Event as Statement

The passing of the enabling bill brought about the transition to a
totalitarian party state. The terror spread further and further.
—Friedrich Stampfer, former SPD delegate[1]

1

When we refer to an "event" such as "the military defeat of June 1940" or "the
breakdown of Weimar," we abstract a multiplicity of actions from the "infinite
reality of what happens" (Koselleck 1973, 560). In a more or less explicit way,
we ascribe temporal boundaries to this bundle of actions. From this perspective a historical event is always a nominal construct. It is constructed by an
act of "synthetic judgment" — to use the Kantian terminology — embedded in a
retrospective view and grounded in the assumption that the actions thus subsumed have, *taken as a whole*, the same significance (Ermakoff 2001, 227).

This construct lends itself to a realist interpretation, however: we conflate
the synthetic understanding of a chronological sequence (the "event") with the
different happenings that constituted the raw fabric of this sequence. Thereby
we reify these happenings as a distinct and relatively autonomous entity, sometimes endowed with the attributes of an acting subject (when we say for instance that an event, such as the French Revolution, "created" the conditions
for subsequent outcomes). By the same token, we reify the temporal boundaries of the event or assume that these boundaries are unproblematic. Yet from
an etiological point of view, we can never take for granted our more or less
implicit, more or less vague, understanding of the chronological closure of the
event.

Consider the chronological starting points that set off the factual narratives
of chapter 1: the reelection of Hindenburg in March–April 1932 and the declaration of war with Germany (September 1939). Underlying these chronological
choices was an implicit reference to proximate causes. Hitler would not have
submitted his enabling bill to the Reichstag had he not been appointed chan-

---

1. "Mit der Annahme des Ermächtigungsgesetzes war der Übergang zum totalitären Partei-
staat vollzogen, der Terror breitete sich weiter und weiter aus." Stampfer, *Erfahrungen und Erkenntnisse*, 268.

cellor. Hindenburg signed this appointment. Hence it makes sense to start with Hindenburg's reelection. Similarly, the French National Assembly would not have convened in Vichy for the explicit purpose of examining a project of constitutional reform without the defeat and the armistice. This truism justifies starting off the chronological exposition with the declaration of war.

These were not the only relevant or possible proximate causes. Papen was instrumental in Hitler's appointment to the chancellorship. Therefore I could have started with Papen's bursting onto the political scene at the end of May 1932, when Hindenburg promoted him to the rank of chancellor. The repeated failures of successive French cabinets to check Hitler's diplomatic foreign policy bluffs in 1935–36 could as well be plausible points of entry for a chronological account of the breakdown of the French Third Republic: these failures ultimately allowed Hitler to develop the military capacity he needed to launch his war.

The implication of these observations is that there is no a priori answer to the question "When shall we start?" There are as many possible starting points for elucidating the causal sequence of the event as there are different motivational factors at play in the collective equation. These motivational factors relate to the types of outcomes at stake in the decision *to the extent* that actors take these outcomes into account in the process of choosing a line of conduct. When the Center delegates emphasize their conservatism to explain their decision, they take a political stand. The type of outcome at stake is political and the relevant temporality harks back to the foundation of the party and the definition of a programmatic agenda. When they refer to the possibility of street battles, the stake is their immediate welfare. Then the electoral campaign and its aftermath set the temporality of the event.

Each type of outcome points to a temporal frame. The boundaries of the event depend on which frame is relevant for the type of outcome under consideration. These temporal frames do not necessarily coincide in chronological terms. The more complex the event — that is, the greater the range of outcomes that this event involves — the less likely it is that these different temporalities will coincide. The implication of a lack of coincidence is that the event has no chronological boundaries proper. These are a nominal construct as much as the event. The geometry of the relevant boundaries is variable. This explains why throughout this inquiry, I have shifted back and forth between different temporal frames to capture the different types of motivations at play.

2

The question "When shall we start?" evokes a retrospective outlook. Taking the event as our reference point, we reckon backward to select plausible chro-

nologies informed by our understanding of causes. Assessing historical significance implies a reversed perspective. Starting with the event, we look forward
to see what happened down the road. Both perspectives are related, though.
If the effects of the event are contained in its causes, that is, if its impact is
perfectly understandable in light of the causes that produced this event, then
the event has little significance. For it has little impact on its own. This impact
is the property of its causes. Structural history accordingly gives short shrift to
the causal impact of events. Causes and effects lie in structural determinations
on which events have little grip.

Judgments of historical significance thus are judgments about effects. In
the present cases these judgments are contrasted. Accounts that invoke a Realpolitik grid of assessment state that the power transfer of 23 March did not significantly alter the balance of forces. The true break with Weimar, the decisive
moment, was the promulgation of the emergency decrees on 28 February (Bracher 1962, 158; Winkler 1989, 906). Assessments that point out, by contrast, the
impact of the bill on Hitler's capacity to consolidate his power view this event
as a decisive contribution to the implementation of an exclusive system of rule:
"Hitler succeeded in decisively consolidating his power through the passing
of the so-called enabling bill by parliament on 23 March 1933" (Schwend 1960,
491).

Personal testimonies display the same divergence irrespective of party affiliations. The enabling act is seen by Friedrich Stampfer, a former Socialist
delegate, as a stepping stone toward a Nazi dictatorship,[2] and by Josef Ersing,
from the Center party, as having consolidated Hitler's domination.[3] August
Weber, a member of the German State Party, states that the endorsement of
the Center party and the liberal parties like his gave way to the "mistaken impression that it was possible to trust [Hitler's] government."[4]

At the opposite end, Theodor Heuss, a former colleague of August Weber
(German State party), explains that he had "no illusion about the weight of a
'Yes' or 'No' vote since . . . the enabling bill was of no significance for the im-
plementation of the National Socialist policies."[5] Stampfer's former colleague
Carl Severing rejects the idea that the enabling bill was a turning point. "Those

2. See the epigraph to this chapter.

3. "[Ich] gestehe zu, daß die Zustimmung seine Herrschaft gefestigt hat." Ersing's testimony
before the inquiry commission of the parliament of Bad-Württemberg, Beilage Nr. 77 vom 1.
April 1947 zu den Sitzungsprotokollen des Württembergisch-Badischen Landtags, Wahlperiode
1946–1950, Beilage-Bd 1, 95.

4. Nachlaß August Weber, Bundesarchiv, Koblenz, Kl.-Erw. 384, Lebenserinnerungen von
Dr. August Weber (1956), 178.

5. Heuss, Die Machtergreifung und das Ermächtigungsgesetz, 25–26.

who criticize the parties that voted 'Yes' miss the point when they pretend that the passing of the bill consolidated Hitler's dictatorship."[6] Hitler would have pursued his agenda anyway. A vote of rejection would have implied the dissolution of the Reichstag and led to street battles. The SA and the SS only waited for this signal. Nothing was to be expected from the Reichswehr. The root of the problem harked back to November 1918. It lay in the fragmentation of the parties that served the interests of the Junker state.[7]

This divergence is striking, and it is worth examining how contradictory these diagnoses turn out to be. For this purpose I propose to zero in on accounts and testimonies that state the important consequences of these decisions. The divergence is most striking with regard to March 1933, to which I will confine my attention. The accounts by Repgen (1967) and Bracher (1962) are particularly helpful in this regard, since they both ponder at length the impact of these collective decisions (or rather, as I mentioned earlier, their lack of impact). The intriguing observation is that both accounts, as they outline the lack of impact on the balance of coercive resources, point to the significance of this political event. Repgen (1967, 24) views the vote as the "cardinal mistake" (*Kardinalfehler*) of political Catholicism in 1933. Similarly, Bracher (1962) notes its decisive character: "it made a *decisive difference* whether the two-thirds majority was reached through the acquiescence of a party like the Center or through the terrorist expulsion of the whole Left including the Social Democratic Party" (160) (my italics).

This duality pervades the judgments of contemporary actors as well. Carl Severing describes the acceptance of the enabling bill as "a blunder [*Rechenfehler*] or—if you want—a convenient escape which all the parties [that voted "yes"] were seeking, with the hope of avoiding the dictatorship through some miracle."[8] In the fragment from his memoirs quoted above, Theodor Heuss reveals that he voted with the acute awareness of making a mistake.[9] Jakob Kaiser, former Center delegate, makes the same point: "Of course the vote for the enabling bill was a political mistake. This remains the case even if [my] parliamentary delegation's refusal to endorse the circumstances that went along with the [Nazi] system would not have changed the slightest thing."[10]

The diagnosis is thus Janus-like: no impact on one side, a decisive differ-

---

6. Archiv der sozialen Demokratie der Friedrich-Ebert-Stiftung, Bonn, Nachlaß Severing, Mappe 28, no. 37, "NWDR Köln," 3: text of a radio broadcast.

7. Ibid.

8. Ibid., letter to Holpe, 31 March 1948.

9. Heuss, *Die Machtergreifung und das Ermächtigungsgesetz*, 23: see the quote in chapter 1.

10. Bundesarchiv, Koblenz, Nachlaß Kaiser N1018/246, 58.

ence and a mistake on the other. If we interpret both claims at face value and juxtapose them for this purpose, they flatly contradict each other. How can a decision be a mistake if it was inconsequential? The antinomy is actually deceptive. When Repgen (1967) claims that a "no" vote could have deprived Hitler of "the beautiful aureole of a two-thirds constitutional majority" and of "the apparent claim of a continuity of rights and institutions, a claim he was eagerly seeking for himself" (13), he is setting forth a conception of power and politics different from a strict conception in terms of coercive resources. Here power is not simply the capacity to impose constraints upon others — that is, the ability to make them pay a cost if they do not behave as requested; power is also the capacity to elicit consent.

3

Several observations emerge from this debate. First, assessing significance is like adjudicating gradients of importance. For the sake of being significant, events compete with other events. Happenings which we deem significant may turn out to be secondary when we compare them with other possible candidates. In March 1933 the competitor to the enabling bill was presidential approval of the emergency decrees of 28 February drafted by Hitler's associates in the immediate wake of the Reichstag fire. The argument is that this bundle of emergency decrees institutionalized a state of emergency and exception allowing the Nazis to exercise arbitrary power, repress their political opponents, and trample basic individual rights and freedoms with impunity. In July 1940 the competing event was the armistice. The decision to terminate the war with Germany sanctioned the political victory of pacifists and opened the way to full-scale political resentment.

Second, judgments of significance often do not make their criteria explicit. It is not entirely clear what the yardstick should be. Consider this equivalence between historical event and moment of rupture: "it would be erroneous to exaggerate the importance of the vote of 10 July, for the armistice itself was a much more decisive break with the past" (Azéma 1984, 53). Unless we make explicit the criteria used for assessing the rupture, the claim of a break remains an argument by assertion. What constitutes a "break with the past"? Is it a shift in institutional design, behavioral patterns, or expectations about the future? The difficulty is compounded by a methodological problem. The claim is only meaningful if it incorporates the knowledge of what comes afterward. We assess ruptures in light of subsequent developments. To figure out how much a development owes to the rupture in question, we need a grid of reading — a roadmap identifying connections and effects.

The statement "a 'No' vote would have changed nothing" and the statement "acquiescence was a political mistake" actually point to different realms of consequences. One is the allocation of coercive capacities—the capacities to sanction opponents—and the other is shifting patterns of expectations. Hitler already controlled all the important venues to political power. A negative vote from the Center party could not have modified this situation. On the other hand, a "no" vote would have undermined the prospect of large-scale allegiance. In this respect the passing of the bill by a constitutional majority did make a difference, and in this respect it was a key political mistake. Bracher restores the significance of this event when he emphasizes that the legal character of the revolution—the subject proper of the enabling bill—was the driving force behind German political developments up to 1934. "The key to understanding the course and character of events in Germany from 1933 to 1934 is the slogan "legal revolution" (Bracher 1966, 115).[11]

We easily view these two realms of consequences as disjointed and assume that one realm—the realm of expectations and beliefs—is either epiphenomenal or subordinate to the realm of coercive capacities. If so, the impact of shifting expectations is "only" psychological. This is the interpretation by Aretz (1978): undoubtedly the passing of the enabling bill by the Center delegation did have "psychological consequences"; but it had no *immediate* consequence for the stabilization of the Hitler regime in terms of power politics" (78) (my italics). Yet if we construe the production of consent and, conversely, the failure to elicit consent as a key aspect of the capacity to exercise power, then these so-called psychological consequences have very concrete effects in terms of power relations. I spell out this point with the help of a counterfactual analysis.

4

What could a "no" vote have achieved? I consider for now the fiction of a negative vote. The situation is the following: Hitler can rely on the emergency decrees of 28 February, but he cannot enact bills without the Reich president's seal of approval. His mandate at the head of the chancellorship rests on the active collaboration of the conservatives in the cabinet. Two scenarios might be considered. In the first, Hitler's official agenda remains within the limits of constitutional legality. The office of the Reich president retains decisional power. Those among his reactionary allies in the cabinet who have realized the threat to their political survival seek to devise a strategy adequate to derailing the prospect of a Nazi state, now that Hitler's demand for constitutional au-

---

11. The remark by Bracher (1962, 160) quoted above, about the "crucial difference" between a legal and a terrorist passing of the bill should also be understood in this light.

thority has been turned down. These actors have political leverage to the extent that they can activate venues of influence in Hindenburg's entourage.

The second scenario is one in which the Nazi leadership reacts to the political affront of a rejection vote with renewed violence. Without a constitutional enabling bill, Hitler can only proceed to transform the state into a Nazi state at the cost of a coup (Buchheim 1961, 502). His reactionary allies then have to decide whether, in the name of the rule of law, they take a stand against a Nazi takeover or endorse this prospect through active collaboration or passivity. Since taking a stand against Hitler means risking a military showdown, this last strategy implies a bet on the loyalty of the state apparatus and, especially, the loyalty of the army.

This counterfactual analysis explores the impact relatively to the attitude of three different groups: Hitler's political allies, state agents including the army, and the non-Nazi polity at large. First, if rejecting the bill could mean an increase in violence, it could also mean a rift in the coalition between the German Nationalists and the Nazis. By March 1933 many of Hitler's reactionary allies were fully aware of the threat that loomed over their head. They had a strong interest in thwarting Hitler's plans. The time was still one of high political contention. At stake in these struggles was the structure of the future state and the role that the Nazis would play in it. The army remained a joker in the president's hands. Hindenburg's entourage probably viewed the army as remaining loyal to the Reich president.[12] Recapitulating the balance of the forces in presence, Buchheim (1961, 502) concludes that forcing Hitler to resort to illegal means was the only reasonable strategic option for the non-Nazi camp in March 1933.

Second, at this juncture the state was not a Nazi state. In the eyes of those state agents who were not ready to carry the banner of a Nazi revolution, however committed they may have been to a reactionary agenda, a "no" vote would have signaled that Hitler's pretensions to absolute state power ought to be checked. Concomitantly, indications of a rift between Hitler and his reactionary allies would have signaled the possibility of confrontation. This meant a test of allegiance for the members of each camp. Third, for the non-Nazi polity at large rejection would have vindicated the decision to take an oppositional

12. After the war the Spruchkammer Zentralgeschäfstelle in Stuttgart developed considerations along these lines when trying to assess the impact of the enabling bill and the political responsibility of one of the non-Nazi "yes" voters in Parliament, Simpfendörfer. A general strike was no longer realistic because the SA was too strong. The power factor was the Reichswehr, less numerous than the SA and the SS, but well armed. The Reichswehr could have acted against the Nazis if they had breached the constitution. NL Maier, Haupstaatsarchiv Stuttgart, Q 1-8 Bü 37, judgment delivered on 1 October 1947 concerning the case of Simpfendörfer, 6.

stance: times are dire, but since the constitutionalist parties dared to say "no" to Hitler, the game is not settled and Hitler may not succeed in his bid to assume control of the state apparatus.

5

These few considerations explain in what sense the enabling bill can be said to have paved the way to a full-fledged Nazi takeover. The fictional scenario of a "no" vote outlines—in the same way the negative of a photograph outlines its main features—the impact of the bill for each of the groups considered above. The bill made the transition formally legal. It provided the legal foundations of the Third Reich (Biesemann 1987, 265–66). Consequently it deprived state agents inclined to oppose Nazi policies of the political resource of legalist claims. State agents envisioning an oppositional stance now had to face even greater risks. This made very precarious any mobilization effort on their part directed at fellow state actors. The overall effect of this lack of legal and political opportunities was to elicit the allegiance of the state apparatus.

The same rationale applies to political opposition outside the state. Opponents had little reason to expect a split among state agents on the issue of obedience to state orders. They also had little reason to expect their fellow opposition members to risk a breach with formal legality. Hence they had strong incentives to toe the line. The power devolution was politically significant to the extent that as a collective statement it signaled the irrelevance of opposition. By way of consequence, the passing of the bill undercut political opposition to Hitler. The third impact, and the broadest in terms of the number of groups and people affected, is a consequence of the first two. Because of the legal constraints imposed on state agents and the irrelevance of political opposition, the power transfer elicited consent to the prospect of a Nazi rule. Its contribution to the implementation of the Nazi regime is crucial in this respect.

In these consolidation effects lies the political impact, and by extension the political significance, of the power devolution as a public statement about the state of the polity. The Nazis understood very well the political gains that they could derive from their legal capacity (Thamer 1986, 280). "Hitler vested considerable value in the appearance of legality for it secured the loyalty of the state apparatus and because it helped disarm opponents even more" (Winkler 1989, 906). Underlying this observation is a broader claim. A contender for exclusive state power relies on a legalist strategy when he or she views an armed insurrection as bound to fail. After the collapse of the Beer Hall Putsch in 1923, Hitler concluded that "a direct assault on the existing order was doomed to failure" (Bracher 1966, 116; quoted by Finn 1991, 169). Historians often make this point with regard to the period preceding his appointment to the chancellorship. The analysis developed in the previous chapters extends the claim to March 1933.

Accounts invoking the "politics of the real" (Realpolitik) against the chimeras of idealism and principled action address the problem in terms of sanctioning capacities. The thrust of these accounts is this: Hitler held all the cards, and therefore a rejection of the enabling bill would have changed nothing. This reasoning assumes that in March 1933 Hitler could basically do whatever he deemed politically appropriate. The diagnosis seems quite sound only if we transpose it to four months later, July 1933, when political parties and union organizations have been dissolved, and growing sectors of the state and the civil society have been absorbed by the Nazi party. In March 1933, however, the conjuncture was a transitional one and the question was whether Hitler would be able to gain absolute power at the expense of his political allies.

6

This assessment of historical significance has two broad analytical implications that deserve close scrutiny. The first concerns the processes underlying the impact of the event. These collective decisions display the characteristics of the public statements that I explored in previous chapters. They were highly visible. They committed those who took part in them. Members of the non-Nazi polity could furthermore interpret these decisions as statements about the condition of their own collective preference: their representatives spoke on their behalf. The theory of collective alignment hence applies. The decision was consequential because it elicited convergent expectations about the future stance of the polity and, by derivation, about future political developments. It molded these expectations by enacting their convergence.

The second implication of this analysis concerns the constitution of power in transition processes that have a fundamental ambiguous character insofar as exclusive claims to state power also revolve around claims of legal validity. In a conflict situation, power amounts to the ability to incapacitate an opponent. This conception informs the definition of politics as the continuation of war by other means. Civil war is the limit case: in a civil war, the only capacity that matters is the capacity to fend off, and inflict, blows. This conception also informs interpretations of the events cast along the lines of a Realpolitik grid of reading: in these interpretations, power is primarily a coercive capacity—the capacity to inflict damage upon opponents and to shield oneself. The camp having more power is the camp that has the greatest capacity to inflict costs upon the other. The balance sheet of costs reflects a differential in sanctioning capacities.

Outside war zones, however, naked force is never the only factor at play. Power is not simply a question of "more" sanctioning capacity. A ruler has the capacity to have others act according to an established plan if he can elicit consent on the part of those subject to his injunctions. If consent is lacking, power loses its efficacy from the moment it no longer demonstrates its sanctioning capacity. This dual constitution of power is never more apparent than in situations where the rules of the game are not clearly established and are the subject of intense, at times violent, confrontation. In these political contexts *both* the capacity to sanction opponents and the capacity to elicit consent are crucial resources. The conception of power induced by this observation relates the efficacy of a practice to the subjective orientations of those subject to the practice. Decisional capacity and the production of consent are two sides of the same coin.

7

I close the circle. At the outset of this inquiry I described these collective decisions as "critical." The notion of "critical decision" is underpinned by a reference to risks, high stakes, and a sense of commitment and responsibility. The decision involves the welfare of a large number of people. Actors cannot decide not to decide, unless they leave the scene and renounce their group affiliation. The decision compels individuals to commit themselves, and through their choice it compels them to commit their responsibility, however costly the consequences might be.

Along these characteristics is a fourth dimension that directly relates to the issue of historical significance: critical decisions bind the future. They close off some possibilities and lay the ground for quasi-certain outcomes. Even more intriguing: actors make their decision with the more or less implicit understanding that they will tie their own hands and commit their responsibility. It is now possible to understand why. The vote is a public statement. For all those who have a stake in the political challenge, this public statement has the value of signaling how much collective willingness there is "out there" to oppose, or acquiesce in, the prospect of arbitrary state power legalized as a ruling principle. As such, the event "states" the collective preference of the polity as a whole. Herein lies its historical significance.

Counts and Accounts

Bourdieu often points out that actors have a practical understanding of their own practices which social scientists, clothed in their certitudes and the certitudes of their models, would be mistaken to dismiss for the sake of their own practice.[1] The sources that I drew on for this inquiry are accounts produced by actors themselves. These accounts differ with regard to their timing, the context of their production, and the characteristics of their formal structure. To capture these different facets of the sources, the taxonomy that I elaborate in this appendix takes into consideration three dimensions. The first relates to conditions of production. Are they contemporary or retrospective? Were they produced on demand or in the absence of a request (*sua sponte*)? The second dimension taps content and formal structure. The third moves away from production and accounts. Here the focus is on actors and, more specifically, on their behavioral stance at the time of the decision.

TIMING AND CONTEXT

By "contemporary accounts" I mean accounts written during or in the immediate wake of the event. They include scribbled notes on paper torn from a notebook, letters written in haste, diaries and accounts written when the impressions left by the event still have the vividness of their temporal presence. For instance, Josef Joos provides an explanation of the Center delegation vote a few days after the event. Kaas publishes an article in the press stating the reasons for a "yes" vote. These are contemporary accounts of the decision. They may be responses to calls for clarification or explanation on the part of colleagues and friends. This observation motivates a second, embedded distinction between

1. See for instance the opening lines of Bourdieu (1977, 1).

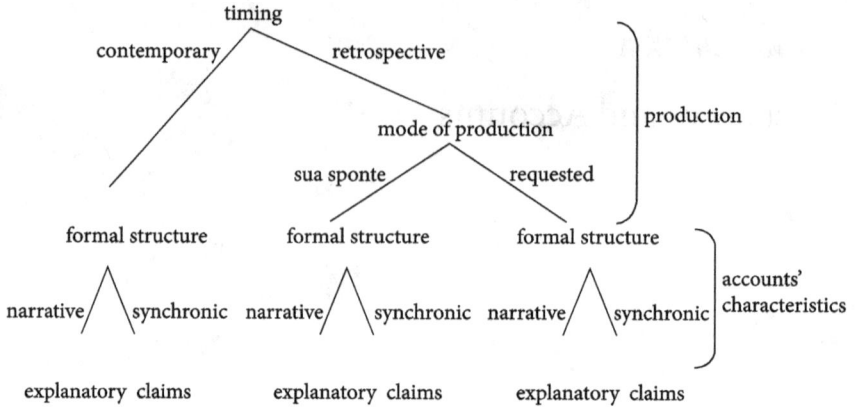

Figure 6   Individual accounts: production, formal structure, and content

accounts produced in response to formal requests and accounts produced sua sponte, in the absence of such requests (figure 6).

Three types of organizations can produce formal requests for vote explanations: inquiry commissions set up by parliament, political party executive committees, and juries. Parliamentary commissions seek to ascertain facts and responsibilities on a broad scale by conducting extended inquiries and analyzing firsthand documents. The purpose is less to determine individual responsibilities than collective ones. The parliament of the state of Württemberg created a commission in 1947 to investigate the passing of Hitler's enabling bill. Similarly, after the war the French parliament mandated several of its members to inquire into the policy decisions made between 1933 and 1940 and to determine the responsibilities that led to the military disaster of May–June 1940 and the installation of the Vichy regime.[2]

The second type of organization, the party executive committee, requests from party members a statement detailing their past conduct, on the assumption that these actors are accountable to their peers. I examined the documents and accounts produced for this purpose by members and former members of the French Socialist party. These documents are held at the archives of the Office Universitaire de Recherches Socialistes (OURS).

The third type of organization, the jury, reviews individual cases independently of political affiliations. The French government created an "honor jury" in the spring of 1945. A decree dated 6 April 1945 excluded from provisional

2. The byproduct of this inquiry was a ten-volume report, *Rapport fait au nom de la commission chargée d'enquêter sur les événements survenus en France de 1933 à 1945.*

representative assemblies those parliamentarians who had voted to delegate constitutional powers to Marshal Pétain. This measure was to be rescinded for parliamentarians who could demonstrate active participation in the resistance against the Germans. For this purpose, the honor jury directly asked former parliamentarians to report on their vote and their activities during the Vichy regime. In addition, the staff of the honor jury asked prefects—the administrative agents of the French government at the département level—to provide them with information on each individual case. The parliamentarians' responses to the request of the honor jury ($N = 293$) vary in terms of length and detail.[3] Some are a few lines long. Others are several pages long and include certificates, letters, and attestations. Not all these accounts include an explanation of the vote of July 1940. Some claimants confine their memoirs to their activities during the Vichy period. A significant number ($N = 182$) mention the vote and provide an explanation.

FORMAL STRUCTURES

Tables 27 and 28 provide a synoptic overview of the primary record in light of the timing of this record (retrospective or contemporary) and the context of production (sua sponte or produced on request). In these tables the unit of analysis is the individual statement. Since some parliamentarians provided several accounts, the number of statements listed in these tables is greater than the number of authors. Among sua sponte accounts I distinguish accounts that the actors decided to publish during their lifetime.

Narratives have a chronological structure. They are punctuated by explicit chronological references which the author orders in a linear fashion. These chronological references can be dates or more abstract temporal markers (for instance conjunctions that point to temporal transitions such as "then" or "after this meeting"). In either case these references indicate that the author is serially organizing happenings along a temporal dimension. The question "Does an account have a narrative structure?" amounts to the question "Does an account specify temporal referents and organize these referents chronologically?" I have coded accounts that have this formal structure as "narratives." Not surprisingly, accounts that have a temporal and linear structure are the most detailed and precise. The most chronological and detailed accounts have the structure of a diary.

3. Olivier Wieviorka (2001, 19) discovered these files in the basement of the Conseil d'État (Paris).

Table 27   Types of Sources, March 1933

Actors' accounts	
Sua sponte	
Unpublished by the author	
Personal notes	12
Letters	25
Diaries	1
Accounts of the event	11
Memoirs	3
Published by the author	
Accounts and memoirs	13
Articles	10
Requested	
Testimonies before an inquiry commission	11
Testimonies before a jury	2
Interviews	7
Total	95
Witnesses and informants	
Sua sponte	
Unpublished by the author	
Personal notes	6
Letters	5
Diaries	1
Accounts of the event	4
Published by the author	
Articles	5
Accounts and memoirs	3
Requested	
Testimonies before a political party executive committee	1
Interviews	1
Total	26

Note: Within the category "Sua sponte" items are ordered from most spontaneous to most formal.

CODING MOTIVATIONAL CLAIMS

In their vote explanations, parliamentarians advance different claims about the factors which in their view decisively influenced their choice. These claims define elementary units of explanation and refer to specific motivations. I identified these explanatory and motivational claims inductively as I gathered the

Table 28   Types of Sources, July 1940

Sua sponte	
Unpublished by the author	
Personal notes	7
Letters	26
Diaries	9
Accounts of the event	10
Memoirs	3
Published by the author	
Diaries	4
Accounts and memoirs	38
Articles	4
Requested	
Testimonies before an inquiry commission	4
Testimonies before a political party	29
executive committee	
Testimonies before a jury	182
Total	316

vote explanations for the data set. For instance, "I was cheated" defines deception as the explanatory scheme: acquiescence was based on false information. This explanation is self-contained and self-sufficient. It is also elementary in the sense that we cannot break it down in additional bits of explanation. For purposes of terminological convenience, I call these elementary units "explanatory semes."

Two qualifications are in order. First, these explanatory claims are not always self-reflexive. In the process of recording the event, their impressions, and factual observations, and more plainly in the process of explaining their behaviors, actors at times also reflect on the behavior of their peers, either because they diagnose their motivations or because they relate their peers' motivations to their own. The search for a diagnosis is often apparent in accounts produced by actors who opposed the power transfer. In testimonies produced by actors who opted for acquiescence, on the other hand, the reference to others most often illustrates an alignment process. Second, the same account can simultaneously refer to different motivational and explanatory factors.

For purposes of presentation, I subsume these elementary claims to the following taxonomy: (1) reference to the public stance of a prominent actor, (2) reference to a collective state of mind, (3) local alignment with acquaintances or regional colleagues, (4) constraints imposed by circumstances, (5) the vote was legitimate and appropriate (positive reasons), and (6) deception. Among these six categories, the last three overlap the three commonsensical explanations of subservience discussed in part II. The reference to the constraints of the situation is the coercion argument: the vote was the lesser of two evils given the constraints of the time. The claim that the vote was appropriate and legitimate illustrates the ideological collusion argument: basically, ego agreed with the prospect of a change of regime. Deception refers to involuntary miscalculation: parliamentarians were misled by false promises and guarantees that were not fulfilled. The power transfer was a swindle.

Public Stances

The reference to the public stance of prominent actors has two variants. One refers to the explicit statements or the public attitude of specific actors—Herriot, Jeanneney, and Flandin—as motivational factors of the vote, whether individual or collective. The other variant refers to the silence of prominent actors as a factor of disarray and confusion. From the perspective of the rank and file searching for directives, guidelines, and bearings, the silence of prominent actors amounts to a statement. Whether the reference is to an explicit statement or to silence, I coded the presence of this explanatory claim when this reference has a motivational subtext. That is, this claim helps to explain either ego's behavior or the collective outcome. A typical and explicit example is this statement by the Socialist deputy Valière: "*We* followed the advice provided by the two Assembly chairmen, whose attachment to the republican regime we could not call into question" (my enphasis).[4] His colleague Ernest Esparbes illustrates the claim about the motivational importance of public silence when he explains: "I did not know what to do. I hoped that in the course of the session, the republican leaders would warn us against the political dangers that lay in [these] manipulations."[5]

Collective State of Mind

Here the reference is to a shared subjective state. Ego relates his behaviors to the state of mind of his peers and colleagues without necessarily specifying

4. "*Nous* avons suivi les conseils donnés par les chefs des deux Assemblées, dont l'attachement au régine républicain ne pouvait être mis en doute." Fondation Nationale des Sciences Politiques, Paris, Archives Blum, AP 570 22, letter from Valière to Léon Blum, 29 May 1945. Valière underlined this statement in the letter. Note the use of the plural first person.

5. Archives Nationales, Dossiers du jury d'honneur, Paris: dossier Esparbes, AL5311.

which colleagues he has in mind. This explanatory seme is of two kinds. One points to a collective mood most often characterized by an informal or implicit consent. For instance: "Basically, if not sometimes formally, we *seemed to all agree*" (Pierre de Courtois, Radical senator; my emphasis).[6] "I adopted what I thought to be a cautious decision *tacitly* endorsed by all" (Raymond Bérenger, deputy from the Union Socialiste Républicaine; my emphasis).[7] A second variant describes widespread confusion. The explanation provided by the Socialist deputy Antoine Dubon illustrates this variant. Dubon relates his confusion to the "disarray in which the parliamentarians of mediocre intelligence [*intelligence moyenne*] were steeped without being able to know the opinions of the great and deep minds of the two chambers gathered together and who, voluntarily or involuntarily, remained silent."[8]

Local Alignment

Local alignment signals the reconfiguration of the reference group on a local basis. Ego coordinates his stance with the stance of those with whom he entertains interpersonal contacts. In some cases his colleagues have already made up their stance, and he aligns with them. "I thought it wise to follow the vote of the quasi-unanimity of my Socialist comrades of the Bouches-du-Rhône" (Toussaint Franchi, Socialist deputy).[9] In other cases ego mentions a meeting among regional peers. For instance: "the representatives of my county convened to issue [*émettre*] an unanimous vote at the département level" (Ernest Pezet, Parti Démocrate Populaire, deputy of Morbihan).[10] "During the intermission, I conversed with my Socialist colleagues from the département [Loire-inférieure] and M. Blancho requested that we maintained a unity of vote and that we voted the order of the day as it was presented. I cast a 'yes' vote not out of cowardliness, but out of solidarity with my friends" (Eugène Le Roux, Socialist deputy).[11]

6. Archives Nationales, Dossiers du jury d'honneur, Paris: dossier Pierre de Courtois, AL5307.

7. Archives Nationales, Dossiers du jury d'honneur, Paris: dossier Raymond Bérenger, AL5298.

8. Archives Nationales, Dossiers du jury d'honneur, Paris: dossier Dubon, AL5309.

9. Archives OURS, Paris, letter to Daniel Mayer, 6 November 1945.

10. Archives de la ville de Paris, Paris, Archives Raymond-Laurent, memorandum by Ernest Pezet: "Déchéance civique: Observations à titre personnel d'un député DP," n.d., D 51 Z 72.

11. Archives Nationales, Dossiers du jury d'honneur, Paris: dossier Eugène Le Roux, AL5319.

The Constraints of the Circumstances

Ernest Esparbes, a Socialist deputy, relates his "yes" vote on 10 July 1940 to—among other things—"the blackmail of the termination of the armistice and of the total occupation of France."[12] René Rollin, a Radical deputy, evokes the "anguish that gripped all genuine men regarding the fate awaiting the country if occupation became total."[13] These vote explanations illustrate the first variant of the pressures-of-the-circumstances argument. The emphasis here is on the situation created by the military defeat and the presence of the Germans. In turning down the power transfer, parliamentarians would have disavowed Pétain and would have brought about German retaliation. The other variant of the pressure argument refers to the possibility of a military coup by the commander in chief, general Weygand. For instance, André Albert, a Radical deputy, explains that he "finally voted for the Pétain proposal out of fear for Weygand."[14] These are negative reasons. Acquiescence was motivated by the prospect of an even worse alternative.

Positive Reasons (Ideological Endorsement)

In contradistinction to this negative assessment, some acknowledge their choice as a positive decision. I identify seven declensions of this stance. All point to an evaluative assessment of the situation, however implicit and self-reflexive this assessment might have been:

1. A transfer of full powers to Pétain was the right decision given the armistice (Émile Béron, deputy of the gauche indépendante: "I viewed the armistice as one step making it possible to reorganize the fight [against the Germans]").[15]
2. Pétain was universally acclaimed. He was the hero of the Battle of Verdun during the First World War. He was the man of the situation (André Lavoinne, conservative senator: "It is without hesitation that in July 1940 along with the great majority of my colleagues I granted

12. Archives Nationales, Dossiers du jury d'honneur, Paris: dossier Ernest Esparbes, AL5311.

13. "L'angoisse étreignait tous les hommes sincères quant au sort attendant le pays si l'occupation devenait totale." Archives Nationales, Dossiers du jury d'honneur, Paris: dossier René Rollin, AL5329.

14. "J'ai finalement voté le projet Pétain, par crainte de Weygand." Archives Nationales, Dossiers du jury d'honneur, Paris: dossier André Albert, AL5295.

15. Archives Nationales, Dossiers du jury d'honneur, Paris: dossier Béron, AL5299.

full powers to Marshal Pétain who at this time inspired me with confidence").[16]

3. The decision was the right one for the sake of the nation (François Milan, Radical senator: "I persist in saying that my vote was in the interest of my country").[17]

4. The country needed reforms (Gaston Henry-Haye: "There happened to be at this time an important majority willing to acknowledge the need to improve a political system that had caused so many setbacks").[18]

5. The decision was legitimate (Henri Lémery, senator without group affiliation: "The standing of the session was beyond reproach. Herriot and Jeanneney expressed the unanimous feeling in extolling the abnegation of Marshal Pétain and in thanking him for accepting power").[19]

6. The vote reflected the wish of the country (Louis Gaillemin, senator from the rightist Union Républicaine: "The whole France at this time was longing for a new constitution and a radical change in our institutions").[20]

7. The vote reflected the wish of one's constituents (Louis Courot, senator from the right: "In voting as I did, I believed that I was expressing the wish of the population of the Meuse").[21]

The Deception Argument

Finally there is the argument that parliamentarians were misled. One claim is to have lacked the information that would have allowed ego to make his decision fully aware of the consequences of a power transfer. Another refers to the text of the bill and argues that a "yes" vote implied a transfer of constitutional authority to the "government of the Republic," not to Pétain. Pétain's subsequent decision to dismantle the republican framework was therefore in blatant contradiction with the text of the bill passed by the National Assembly. Still another claim along these lines is the assertion that Pétain and his associates simply abused the parliamentarians' trust. "Swindle" and "betrayal"

16. Archives Nationales, Dossiers du jury d'honneur, Paris: dossier Lavoinne, AL5318.

17. Archives Nationales, Dossiers du jury d'honneur, Paris: dossier Milan, AL5322.

18. Henry-Haye, *La grande éclipse franco-américaine*, 63.

19. "La séance de l'Assemblée fut d'une tenue irréprochable. Herriot et Jeanneney exprimèrent le sentiment unanime en exaltant l'abnégation du maréchal Pétain et en le remerciant d'accepter le pouvoir" (Lémery, *D'une République l'autre*, 244).

20. Archives Nationales, Dossiers du jury d'honneur, Paris: dossier Gaillemin, AL5313.

21. Archives Nationales, Dossiers du jury d'honneur, Paris: dossier Courot, AL5306.

are the key words of this line of explanation: "My good faith [was] caught off guard . . . [After the vote], I realized that we had been betrayed"[22] (Hyacinthe Carron, Radical deputy).

SYNTHETIC CATEGORIES

To compare alternative types of explanation I collapsed the first three moti-vational claims distinguished above—public stances, reference to a collective state of mind, and local alignment—into a synthetic one which summarizes the alignment argument, since these three explanatory claims are variants of a decision-making process in which heteronomy and the reference to peers prevail. I label this synthetic category "Alignment mechanisms." This more synthetic taxonomy allows me to compare the frequencies of claims amenable to the interactionist paradigm, as I develop it in chapter 6, and claims ame-nable to the framework of common sense and a linear paradigm of causality (chapters 3–5). This synthetic taxonomy has the advantage of subsuming under the same categories claims that exemplify the same type of arguments.

This last point raises the issue of multiple statements. To avoid muddling the comparative analysis, the data set only considers one account for each individual actor. Parliamentarians who produced multiple accounts pose an interesting problem for the construction of the data. I collapsed accounts that belonged to the same genre as defined in table 27. For instance, the personal papers of the Socialist deputy Justin Arnol contain different sets of hand-written notes.[23] One set is about the parliamentary session that took place on the morning of 10 July. Another set is about the significance of the vote. I treated these personal notes as one single account.

When the same individual produced multiple accounts belonging to differ-ent genres, I ranked these accounts according to their formal proximity to the ideal type of a chronological narrative. The rationale underlying this selection criterion draws on the argument about the truth content of formal structures: the more chronological and detailed the account, the more informative it is regarding the decision process. Ernest Laroche, a Socialist deputy, responded to the honor jury on 12 September 1945 with a brief explanatory statement about his vote in which he simply stated his lack of knowledge of the political backdrop of the decision.[24] Ten years later, in November 1955, Laroche wrote a letter in which he provided a full-fledged narrative account of the events in

22. Archives Nationales, Dossiers du jury d'honneur, Paris: dossier Hyacinthe Carron, AL5303.

23. Archives Départementales de l'Isère, Grenoble, Archives Justin Arnol, 37 J 40.

24. Archives Nationales, Dossiers du jury d'honneur, Paris: dossier Ernest Laroche, AL5317.

Vichy with explicit temporal referents. For coding purposes, this second account is the one I included in the data set.

I have described accounts in light of their morphological characteristics (timing, production context, formal structure) and their content, that is, the type of explanatory and descriptive claims that these accounts bring forward. The third descriptive dimension pertains to the data set as a whole: How representative is it? Here the focus shifts from the account's characteristics to the characteristics of whoever produced it. I assess the representative character of the data set in two respects: political affiliation and decisional stance. In both cases the data set covers the whole gamut of political affiliations.

Political Affiliations

For July 1940 the data set provides a representative picture of both assemblies in Vichy. The only exception is the Socialist delegation (Section Française de l'Internationale Ouvrière, or SFIO), which is slightly overrepresented in terms of vote explanations (table 29). The SFIO delegates represent 18 percent of the parliamentarians who cast a ballot in Vichy in July 1940. They account for 24 percent of the personal testimonies in the data set.

Decisional Stances

If we break down accounts with respect to actor's vote ("for," "against," and "abstention"), the frequency of an account appears to be highest among those who endorsed the power transfer (35 percent) and the lowest among those who opposed it (23 percent), with those who abstained representing an intermediate category (29 percent). This discrepancy in terms of sample size (table 30) relates to the context of the production of vote explanations. Opponents write down an account for the record (Blum, Paul-Boncour). Their primary purpose is to reconstitute the event and, through this reconstitution, to highlight the conditions and processes that made it possible. Parliamentarians who did endorse the power transfer at times engage in a similar explanatory project, especially when their resistance credentials during the war demonstrate their political integrity (Becquart, Galimand). But in most cases, these actors produce an account on request. They are being asked to explain their behavioral stance (table 28). Their account takes place in this context.

Table 29   Political Affiliations and Accounts, July 1940

		Accounts	Percent	Number of Votes in Vichy	Percent
Chamber of Deputies					
Left	Union Populaire Française (UPF; former communists)	2	1	10	1
	Socialists (SFIO)	54	24	122	18
	Union Socialiste Républicaine	9	4	20	3
	Gauche Indépendante	4	2	11	2
	Groupe Républicain Radical et Radical-socialiste (commonly called Parti Radical)	24	11	81	12
	Gauche Démocratique et Radicale Indépendante	10	4	31	5
	Groupe Démocrate Populaire	5	2	13	2
	Alliance Démocratique	8	4	37	5
	Groupe Agraire Indépendant	2	1	8	1
	Groupe Indépendant d'Action Populaire	6	3	10	1
	Républicains Indépendants et d'Action Sociale	4	2	24	4
	Groupe des Indépendants Républicains	2	1	6	1
	Fédération Républicaine	11	5	45	7
Right	Parti Social Français	3	1	7	1
No affiliation		1	*	1	*
Senate					
	Socialist Party (SFIO)	3	1	10	1
	Groupe de la Gauche Démocratique, Radicale et Radicale Socialiste	41	18	128	19
	Union Démocratique et Radicale	8	4	25	4
	Union Républicaine	16	7	42	6
	Groupe d'Action Nationale, Républicaine et Sociale	1	*	11	2
No affiliation		9	4	28	4
Total		223	100	670	100

* = less than 0.5 percent

Table 30   Accounts and Decisional Stances, July 1940

Behavioral Stance	Frequency	Percent	Accounts	Percent	Size of Sample Relative to Vote Category
"No" vote	80	12	18	8	0.23
"Yes" vote	569	85	197	89	0.35
Abstention	21	3	6	3	0.29
Total	670	100	221	100	0.33
Present in Vichy but did not vote[a]	8		2		
Total	678		223		

[a] Based on the roll call for 9 July and parliamentarians' own testimonies, I identify eight representatives who were present in Vichy on 10 July 1940 but did not cast a ballot: François Beaudoin, Camille Blaisot, René Héry, Joseph Lagrosillière, Louis Marin, Jean-Michel Renaitour, Jean Philip, Paul Reynaud.

A Two-Pronged Model of Alignment

The purpose of this appendix is to specify in formal terms the claims about processes of alignment and their conditions of possibility expounded in chapter 6. The substantive argument, cast in natural language, stands on its own. It is intelligible as such. Why then have an appendix with a symbolic exposition? The substantive argument is based on claims that have a formal grounding. The purpose of this appendix is to spell out these formal underpinnings. This may seem at times an arcane exercise. Yet there is actually much to learn from formal expressions, not simply because they make terminological rigor a methodological imperative but also because they generate insights of their own. Consequently, the formal exposition is not a redundant duplication of the natural language exposition. This appendix lays out the logic underlying substantive claims and, in the process, makes additional claims.

By convention, superscripts describe actions and subscripts actors. Parameters with no subscript are assumed to be constant across actors. Following the terminological convention adopted in chapter 6, I use the feminine pronoun when the referent is a prominent actor and the masculine pronoun for a member of the rank and file.

RISKS, REFERENCE GROUP, AND THRESHOLDS

Decision Parameters

An authoritarian challenger requests from a collective of individuals an action that violates these individuals' political commitments. He backs up his demand with threats. Actors subject to this challenge face therefore two options: either they fulfill this request and betray their political commitments or they turn it down, remaining consistent with their commitments but exposing themselves to retaliations. To analyze the terms of the challenge I proceed in two steps.

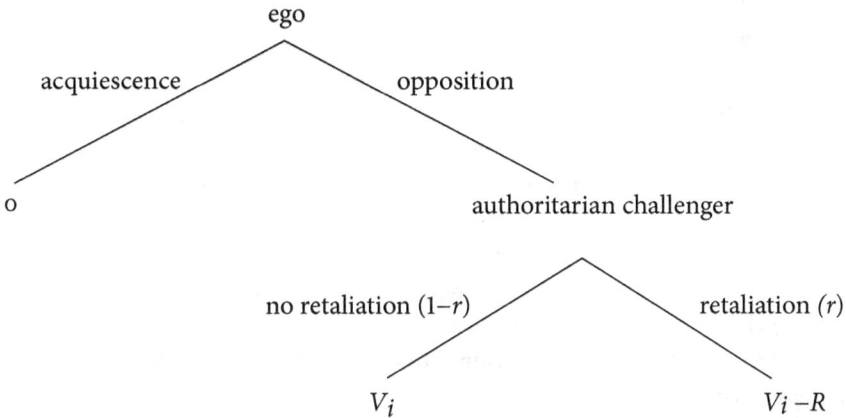

Figure 7   Ego's confrontation with the authoritarian challenger

First, I ignore the fact that the challenge is directed at a group. Ego is alone. Then I factor in the collective dimension.

Ego Alone

Three parameters are at play: the value (V_i) that ego imputes to his commitment, the cost of being retaliated against (R), and the probability (r) that the challenger will put his threat into effect (figure 7). V_i is self-explanatory. Individuals more or less value their political commitments. The cost of being retaliated against (R) ranges from a few days in jail, harassment, public humiliation, and the suppression of economic independence to physical violence or death. There is some uncertainty about whether the challenger will retaliate against ego if ego adopts an oppositional stance. The challenger may decide not to retaliate if ensuring his agents' compliance is too costly or if he expects a backlash.

Given this uncertainty, ego relies on an assessment of the expected cost that he would bear if retaliated against: the absolute cost (R) mitigated by this uncertainty (r): $r \cdot R$. Ego chooses to oppose the challenger when $r < V_i / R$. If ego values his political commitments more than the cost of being retaliated against ($V_i > R$), he makes his decision independent of r. The assessment of the probability of being retaliated against is relevant from a decisional standpoint when the cost of being retaliated against is greater than the value of his commitment. Ego acquiesces when this commitment value is lower than the expected cost of the challenger's reprisals ($V_i < rR$).

The Group Factor

But ego is not the only one on the spot. I assume he is aware that the challenge is a collective one. Consequently, the probability of being retaliated against is a negative function of the number ($n°$) or the proportion ($p°$) of individuals who oppose the authoritarian challenger. Ego assesses this probability in light of this parameter: $r = r(n°)$ or $r = r(p°)$. The challenger has a certain amount of repression available for use. This makes his threats credible. Hence the greater the number or proportion of opponents, the lower the amount of repression he can devote "per head" and the lower the expected cost for ego of being retaliated against. For now, I assume that this expected cost is homogenous across target actors.

Furthermore, if ego's commitment implies a sense of group affiliation, betraying this commitment has a psychological and a social cost. The psychological cost increases with the value that ego vests in his commitment (V_i). The greater this value, the greater the psychological cost of betrayal. The social cost of this betrayal is the cost of being ostracized by the group if the group remains firm, that is, if it makes a collective decision consistent with its initial commitments. This social cost increases with the value that ego vests in the prospect of future interactions with group members and, more broadly, the degree to which ego's ties with the group are exclusive ones (thus increasing the opportunity cost of exit).

The greater the value vested in the individual's affiliation with the group and the opportunity cost of exit, the higher the cost of his isolation if it turns out that his decision is at odds with the decision of the group. The social cost of isolation makes the utility of choosing acquiescence a decreasing function of the number ($n°$) or proportion ($p°$) of group members choosing opposition. This cost is highest when ego is the only one to acquiesce. It is lowest when abdication is collective. I designate this overall cost as the cost of betrayal ($-B_i$).

One issue is left pending in this formulation: Should we define the social cost of isolation by reference to a group proportion or to an absolute number? If the group is well defined and numerically identifiable, I hypothesize that the relevant metric is the group proportion. Ego has a clear notion of the collective referent and relates his propensity to the collective. If the group is not well defined or is diffuse, then ego cannot assess a proportion. His metric is an absolute number. The determination of the threshold metric is therefore a function of ego's ability to identify the group's boundaries. In the following analysis I assume that the group is large ($N > 30$) and well defined. Ego assesses

the social cost of isolation vis-à-vis the group by considering how the proportion of the group members opposing the challenger ($p°$) affects the utility of
each option. I also assume that ego assesses the cost of being retaliated against
by reference to a group proportion.

The Class of Decisions

In opposing the challenger, ego gets the value of his political commitment
(V_i) minus the cost of being retaliated against ($R \cdot r \, (p°)$): the utility of opposition is therefore $U_i° = V_i - R \cdot r(p°)$. In yielding to the challenger, ego faces
the cost of betraying his political commitment: the utility of acquiescence is
$U_i^a = -B_i(V_i, p°)$. Both utility functions vary with the proportion of the group
choosing opposition, and they vary in opposite directions. The utility of opposition is an increasing function of the proportion of the group members who
decide to oppose the challenger. The utility of acquiescence decreases as this
proportion gets higher: the cost of reneging on one's commitments becomes
higher as more group members choose to oppose the challenger's claims to
unrestrained power.

$$U_i° = U_i°(p°) = V_i - R \cdot r(p°)$$
$$U_i^A = U_i^A(p°, V_i) = -B_i(p°, V_i)$$

There is no reason to assume that from ego's viewpoint the cost of being retaliated against and the cost of acquiescence are a linear function of $p°$. A more
plausible assumption is that both costs are logistic functions of this group
proportion. Depending on the size of the group and the amount of repression
available to the challenger, ego perceives the threat of being retaliated against
as substantially more diffuse after a certain proportion of opponents has been
reached. Conversely, depending on the extent to which ego's affiliation with the
group is exclusive, the psychological and social costs of betrayal become more
obvious and tangible after a certain point. Equations (1) and (2) operationalize
both claims.

(1) $$U_i° = V_i - R \cdot r(p°) = V_i - \frac{1}{1 + \exp(\beta(p° - \alpha))}$$

(2) $$U_i^A = -B_i(p°) = \frac{-1}{1 + \exp(\gamma(\delta - p° - \theta \cdot V_i))}$$

For now I do not assume that the threat of being retaliated against by the
challenger differs across group members. This expected cost is the same for

Table 31   Value Parameters for Figure 8

Value Ego Imputes to His Commitment	Slope Parameters		Inflection Point Parameters		
V_i	β	γ	α	δ	θ
0.3	2	5	0.7	2	3

everyone in the group.[1] Parameters α and β are exogenous characteristics of the situation. Parameter β is the slope parameter ($\beta \geq 1$). The greater the value of β, the greater the expected cost of isolated opposition and the lower the expected cost of collective opposition. The slope parameter captures the sense of protection provided by the opposition of the other group members. Parameter α reflects the value of the inflection point and provides a measure of the overall cost of being retaliated against. The greater the value of α, the greater this cost. This parameter may be described as the amount of coercion available to the challenger.

Similar considerations can be made regarding the utility of acquiescence: γ, the slope parameter, captures the sense of protection provided by the other group members' acquiescence. Parameter δ provides a measure of the overall cost of reneging on one's commitment. The greater the value of δ, the lower this cost. The cost of acquiescence is furthermore a function of the extent to which ego values his political commitments (V_i). The higher the value of V_i, the higher the cost of reneging on one's commitments—the cost of renunciation. I account for the scope of this effect in equation (2) with parameter θ. Table 31 illustrates the example of an individual actor who grants relatively low value to his political commitment (V= 0.3) and faces substantial cost if he is the only one to either oppose the challenger or acquiesce in the challenger's demands.

Action Thresholds

The utilities of opposition and acquiescence vary with the group's behavior, and they vary in opposite direction. Consequently they intersect at one point. Three situations are then possible on the [0, 1] interval: (1) Acquiescence is

1. Differences in public visibility call this assumption into question. More visible actors can expect to be easier targets for the wrath of the challenger. This point rests on the distinction between prominent and rank-and-file group members. I will address this issue in subsequent work.

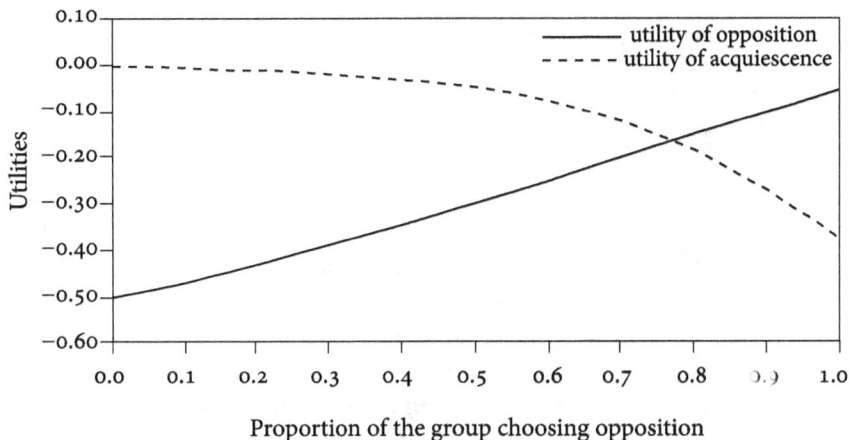

Figure 8   An example of utility functions producing a relative threshold

the dominant choice. Whatever the proportion of those opposing, the utility of acquiescence for ego is greater than the utility of opposition. This is most likely when R is high and the value of ego's commitment (V_i) is quite low. (2) Opposition is the dominant choice. This is the reverse situation: whatever the proportion of those opposing, the utility of acquiescence for ego is lower than the utility of opposition. This situation is most likely when the cost of being retaliated against is expected to be quite low. (3) In the third situation the relative utility of opposition versus acquiescence depends on the proportion of those deciding to oppose the challenger. There is a unique point p_i^{o*} at which the two curves $U_i^o(p^o)$ and $U_i^A(p^o)$ intersect. At this point the difference between the utility of opposition and the utility of acquiescence ($U_i^o(p^o) - U_i^A(p^o)$)) changes sign.

This intersection point (p_i^{o*}) defines ego's threshold. It specifies the proportion of the group which tips ego over from acquiescence to opposition. Opposing becomes the most attractive option for ego when the proportion of those choosing opposition becomes greater than p_i^{o*}. This threshold reflects ego's reliance on the other target actors for the adoption of one course of action. Indirectly ego's threshold reflects the extent to which his utilities vary with the group's behavior. In the example specified in table 31, ego's opposition threshold is quite high ($p_i^{o*} \approx 0.8$) (figure 8). He opposes the challenger only if a large proportion of the group—about 80 percent of the group—opposes him as well.

Thresholds, Absolute and Relative

In theory, an individual threshold can be strictly below 0 or strictly above 1 (Oliver 1993, 289). These unreal values capture the same behavioral traits as the extreme values 0 and 1: ego's choice is unconditional on the choice of the other target actors (autonomy). In addition, these unreal values highlight how close ego is to a heteronomous mode of decision, i.e., they highlight which changes in the parameter values would be required to produce heteronomy. The insight thus provided is akin to that of a counterfactual. Ego is not necessarily indifferent to the decisions made by other target actors. That his utility functions vary with the proportion of the group choosing opposition indicates as much. But he is not sensitive to this variation of utility to the point of making his choice conditional on theirs. Defined relatively to a group proportion, an individual threshold is absolute when it falls strictly outside the]0,1[range.

Decision Rule

Ego makes his decision by comparing the utility of opposition with the utility of acquiescence. He chooses opposition over acquiescence when $V_i - R.r(p°) > -B_i(V_i, p°)$, that is, when the proportion of group members choosing opposition reaches his threshold. This decision rule presumes that ego knows whether this proportion is above, or equal to, his threshold. In the absence of this information, ego has to assess the likelihood of different collective outcomes. His decision rule in this case is based on a comparative assessment of the expected utilities of opposition and acquiescence. He assigns probabilities to different possible collective outcomes and computes his utilities accordingly. Ego chooses opposition over acquiescence when the expected utility of opposition is greater than the expected utility of acquiescence: $\text{Exp}(U_i^o) > \text{Exp}(U_i^A)$.

$$\text{Exp}(U_i^o) = \text{prob}(p° = h) \cdot U_i^o(p° = h) \qquad \text{with } h = \frac{k}{N}, k \in \{0,1,...,N\}$$

$$\text{Exp}(U_i^A) = \text{prob}(p° = h) \cdot U_i^A(p° = h) \qquad \text{with } h = \frac{k}{N}, k \in \{0,1,...,N\}$$

Consider for instance the example summarized in figure 8. Ego's opposition threshold is approximately 0.8. He is considering eleven possible collective outcomes (or states of the world): (1) 0 percent of the group chooses opposition, (2) 10 percent of the group chooses opposition . . . (11) 100 percent of the group chooses opposition. Assume that he is fully uncertain about the outcome. That is, he assigns a uniform probability of 0.09 to each one of the

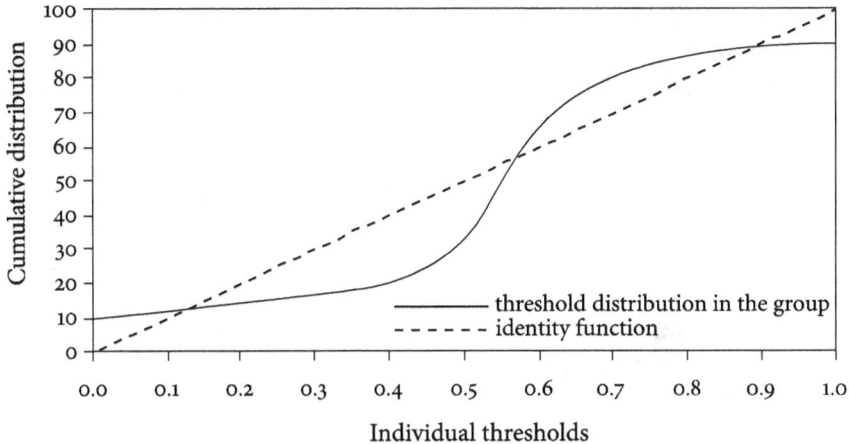

Figure 9   Threshold distribution and sequential alignment

possible states of the world. His expected utility in this case is −0.1 for acquiescence and −0.29 for opposition. He chooses to acquiesce.

SEQUENTIAL ALIGNMENT

Alignment is sequential when actors make their decision given the proportion
of those who already behaviorally committed themselves to one stance. Assuming that individuals who made their choice publicly reveal their decision
and that they have the time to do so, this process diffuses to the whole group
only under a specific condition pertaining to the distribution of individual
thresholds. This distribution must be such that there is only one stable equilibrium point. In graphic terms, this means that the cumulative frequency
distribution intersects the identity function only once. One example illustrates
this point.

Consider the cumulative distribution of opposition thresholds represented
by figure 9. There are two stable equilibria determined by the intersection
points between the $y = x$ curve and the cumulative distribution (Schelling
1972, 164–65). Of the group, 10 percent have a threshold below or equal to zero:
these 10 percent indicate that they oppose the challenger. This public disclosure triggers a process of sequential alignment which will affect 15 percent of
the group. At this point the process of sequential disclosure stops: the group
members who have not yet disclosed their decision have no incentive to do
so: their opposition threshold is greater than the proportion of the group that
has already taken a public stance against the challenger. Since their opposition

threshold has not been met, their decision is still indeterminate and conditional on the decision of other group members.

At the opposite end, let us assume that 10 percent of the group members have an opposition threshold equal or greater than 1—their acquiescence threshold is absolute—and that they publicly state their behavioral stance. This public stance motivates the group members with an acquiescence threshold $(1 - p_i^{\circ*})$ between 0 and 0.1 to state their acquiescence as well. Given the threshold distribution specified in figure 9, the chain reactions at both ends involve a little less than 25 percent of the group. When these individuals have made their position public, no one else discloses acquiescence. This graph represents a situation in which 75 percent of the group remains undecided.

LOCAL KNOWLEDGE

Actors rely on an inferential mechanism if they cannot sequentially align their behavioral stance with one another. Local knowledge is the first possibility. In the course of their face-to-face interactions, actors disclose their behavioral preferences. Interpersonal contacts provide them with a sample of the group. They form a mental representation of the preference distribution within the group in light of this information. Two cognitive mechanisms are conceivable. The first mechanism states that ego interprets his local knowledge as a template of the group. Ego extrapolates the group distribution from his sample, thereby assuming that his sample offers an accurate picture of the global preference distribution. According to the second mechanism, ego does not lose sight of the uncertain character of his knowledge. He uses the information provided by his sample to draw an inference about the global preference distribution, being aware that this inference remains an assessment, subject to possible revisions.

Inference

I specify the likelihood of each mechanism by making two claims. First, ego's behavioral uncertainty—his lack of confidence about his decision—goes along with an acute awareness of the imperfect character of his knowledge. Second, the more clearly ego defines his reference group and assesses the boundaries of this group, the greater his awareness of the local character of his knowledge. By extension, the more ego is aware that his knowledge is local, the greater the likelihood that he will view this knowledge as trail. Bayesian updating—actors update their subjective beliefs about future outcomes in light of Bayes's rule—

offers a convenient way of operationalizing both insights. In this conceptualization, actors think in probabilistic terms. They make inferences rather than extrapolations and they revise their subjective assessment of the group stance in light of the information provided by their local knowledge. In addition, the Bayes formula operationalizes the hypothesis that ego's uncertainty about his inferences—his cognitive uncertainty—is negatively correlated with the relative size of his sample.

In sum, actors are more likely to behave in a Bayesian fashion when they experience behavioral uncertainty and when they clearly define their reference group. Which probability law approximates the mental process whereby ego updates his beliefs about the group? Ego interacts face-to-face with n group members. His sample is of size n. Among these n group members, k indicate that they want to oppose the challenger. Ego differentially assesses the likelihood of meeting with k opponents given different assumptions about the global proportion of opponents in the group. For instance, the probability of meeting randomly with 8 opponents in a sample of 10 is extremely low if the global proportion of opponents in the group is 20 percent. If the group is large, this probability follows a binomial law defined by two parameters: the sample size (in the present case 10) and the proportion of the group choosing opposition (in the present case 0.2).

Ego is considering different possible states of the world defined as different proportions of the group opting for opposition (p°). For the reasons outlined above, ego has imperfect information about the distribution of behavioral preferences across group members. Given the imperfect character of his information, he relies on conjectures—he assigns probabilities to these different states ($\text{prob}(p^\circ = h)$ with $h \in \{0, \dots, k/N, \dots 1\}$ if the size of the group is N). I designate by x the random variable indicating the number of opponents in his sample. His posterior belief takes into account the information provided by his sample as indicated in equation (3):

$$(3) \quad \text{prob}(p^\circ = h \:/\: x = k) = \frac{\text{prob}(x = k \:/\: p^\circ = h) \cdot \text{prob}(p^\circ = h)}{\text{prob}(x = k)}$$

with $0 \leq k \leq n$

A simple example illustrates this inference process. To simplify exposition and represent this updating process in a cognitively realistic fashion, I assume that ego is considering only a limited number of possible states of the world: he considers the possibility that the proportion of opponents might be 0, 0.2, 0.4, 0.6, 0.8, or 1. I also contrast three prior assessments of the group stance. (1) In the first assessment, ego expects that most of the group will acquiesce

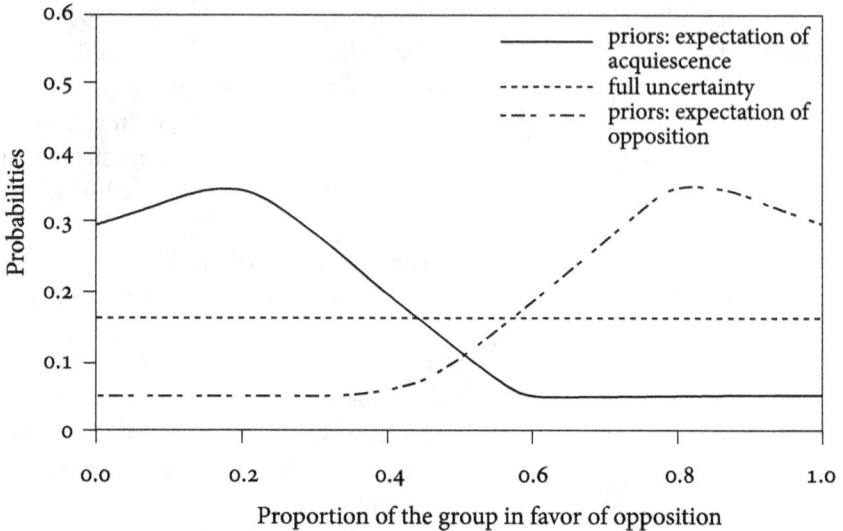

Figure 10   Prior beliefs about the likelihood of opposition: three hypotheses

(prob($p°$ < 0.5) > 0.5). (2) The second assessment states the opposite: ego expects that most of the group will oppose the challenger (prob($p°$ < 0.5) < 0.5). (3) The third assessment displays full uncertainty. Ego is fully uncertain about the outcome. He assesses the different possible states of the world as equiprobable (in the present case 1 / 6 = 0.166): prob($p°$ = h) = 1/6, with h ∈ {0,0.2, … 1} (figure 10).

Let us assume that the size of ego's sample is 10. Among these 10 individuals 6 indicate that they will oppose the challenger. Ego updates his beliefs about the group stance in light of this information. I approximate this updating process with equation (3). The outcome of this process for each of the three priors distinguished above — expectation of acquiescence, full uncertainty, expectation of opposition — is represented in figure 11. Assuming that the utility functions for opposition and acquiescence in ego's case are those specified in figure 8, his expected utilities for each of these three hypotheses lead him to choose acquiescence.[2] This is consistent with what we could have expected given ego's high opposition threshold (approximately 0.8).

2. The expected utilities for opposition and acquiescence are the following: −0.30 and −0.06 when ego updates an expectation of acquiescence, −0.28 and −0.08 when he updates full uncertainty and −0.22 and −0.11 when he updates an expectation of opposition.

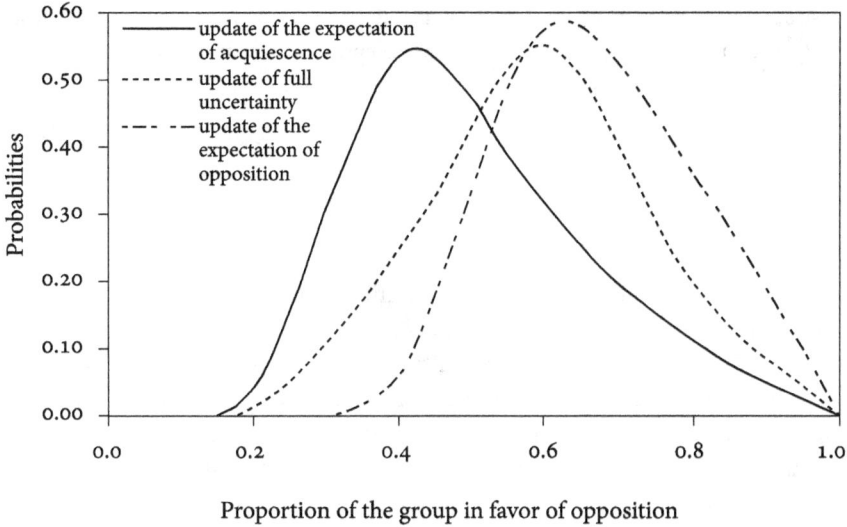

Figure 11   Updated beliefs ($n = 10$, $k = 6$)

Can Local Knowledge Be a Source of Uncertainty?

Uncertainty reflects the extent to which ego is unsure about himself. Ego can be unsure about his judgment (cognitive uncertainty) or his decision (behavioral uncertainty). Uncertainty in cognitive terms reflects the extent to which ego differentiates his beliefs about the future states of the world. Cognitive uncertainty can be translated in probabilistic terms. Assuming as in the previous case that the probability distribution is unimodal, the standard deviation of the distribution provides a measure of this differentiation level. The lower this standard deviation, the greater this lack of differentiation and the greater ego's uncertainty about the future. The standard deviation is zero if all future states of the world are equiprobable.

Behavioral uncertainty is a direct consequence of a risk assessment. Both decisional and individual parameters are involved in this uncertainty. The decisional parameters are the costs involved for each option. These costs are potentially very high depending on the likelihood of future states of the world. Ego's awareness of these potential costs hampers his determination. He oscillates whenever he reflects on them. The individual parameter is the sensitivity to risk. Individuals vary with regard to their willingness to take risks.

These few considerations highlight in which respects ego's local knowledge can be a source of behavioral uncertainty. I distinguish two scenarios. In the first scenario, ego's posterior beliefs about the group increase the potential cost of a mistake. In the second scenario, ego realizes that his peers remain indecisive. This information leads him to reconsider the risks he is taking. I consider each scenario in turn.

Increase in Expected Cost

First scenario: the information that ego gets through his interpersonal inter-actions leads him not only to revise his initial prediction but also to revise upward the risks he is taking. He sticks to his original choice—in accordance to the decision rule of expected utilities—but as a result of his new belief about the group, realizes that because the probability of a mistake is higher, the expected cost of a mistake also becomes higher. This expected cost is the loss that he has to bear for any proportion of the group that does not meet his threshold given the stance he is choosing. If he is opting for acquiescence, for instance, the risk he is taking is the loss he will have to face if the proportion of the group choosing opposition is above his opposition threshold—that is, the expected utility of acquiescence minus the expected utility of opposition for any group proportion above his threshold.

Consider the following example. I assume the utility functions represented in figure 8. Ego's opposition threshold is about 0.8. Let us assume that initially he expects the group to acquiesce: his prior beliefs are those represented by the curve "expectation of acquiescence" in figure 10. He assesses the proba-bility that more than 80 percent of the group opts for an oppositional stance to be 0.10. Then, he interacts with 10 people. Eight of them let him know that they want to oppose the challenger. This information substantially modifies his beliefs about the likelihood that different proportions of the group might choose opposition. Now he assesses the probability that more than 80 percent of the group opts for opposition to be 0.65. Yet he still opts for acquiescence: the expected utility of opposition remains lower than the expected utility of acquiescence (table 32). In other words, his expectations are such that he still prefers to acquiesce rather than adopt an oppositional stance. However, the risks he is taking are now higher, and if he assesses these risks to be too high, he will decide to wait and see.

The Future Is Too Indistinct

The second scenario is one in which ego has too little information about his peers' behavioral preferences to feel confident about his decision. The infor-mational content of his local knowledge is too frail. He decides to wait, if he

Table 32   Updating the Cost of a Mistake

	Prior Beliefs (Expectation of Acquiescence)	Posterior Beliefs ($n = 10, k = 8$)
Expected utility of opposition	−0.39	−0.19
Expected utility of acquiescence	−0.04	−0.14
Decision	acquiescence	acquiescence
Probability ($p° ≥ 0.8$)	0.10	0.65
Loss if $p° ≥ 0.8$ (expected utility of acquiescence if $p° ≥ 0.8$ minus expected utility of opposition if $p° ≥ 0.8$)	−0.0178	−0.0236

can afford to do so. This meta decision — the decision whether to make a decision — is based on the same considerations in terms of risks as the ones I have just outlined. I operationalize this insight in two ways.

First, if the cost of isolation for each option is high for ego and he has little information to differently appraise the likelihood of these different states of the world, then ego realizes that he is likely to face high risks. The following example illustrates this claim. Ego meets with 10 people and only 2 reveal a behavioral stance. One individual indicates that he will endorse the power transfer and the other indicates that she will oppose the power transfer. Initially ego is completely uncertain about the different states of the world, assigning a probability of 0.166 to the six group outcomes he is considering. As he learns from the interaction with these two individuals, it is unlikely that either no one or everyone will choose opposition.

Thus ego is getting some information. But this information is very thin if his purpose was to get a sense of how the group is going to behave. The great majority of those whom he has met with refused to disclose a behavioral preference. Practically, the sample he is considering as a valid source of information about his peers' behavioral preferences is reduced to 2. Had the other 8 people indicated their behavioral preference, his capacity to differently assess the likelihood of different group outcomes would have been greater. With a sample size of 2, ego estimates at about 0.2 the probability that 80 percent or more of the group will choose opposition. With a sample size of 10 — assuming the same 50–50 percent distribution — he estimates this probability to be 0.06. In both cases the expected utility criterion leads him to choose acquiescence. But in the first case there is a 20 percent chance that he may find himself at odds with 80 percent or more of his peers, while in the second case these odds are 6 percent. This difference in estimate is significant if the risks are high.

Who Remains Indecisive?

The second way to operationalize the claim about indecision is to note that in reducing the size of his "valid" sample to 2, ego overlooks a piece of information that indirectly sheds light on the risks he is taking. This information concerns the proportion of those who wait and see. In light of his full sample, ego can assess the likelihood that different proportions of the group will be indecisive. For instance, the fact of encountering 8 people out of 10 who shun a behavioral commitment suggests that the proportion of the group remaining indecisive is quite high. If initially ego had assigned the same probability to different proportions of indecisive group members, now he assesses as 0.7 the probability that 80 percent of the group is indecisive. This inference is based on the same updating process as the one described earlier (assuming six states of the world).

Observing how many group members in private interactions shun any behavioral commitment points to a second way of operationalizing the behavioral impact of the frailty of one's local knowledge. For any given proportion of group members remaining indecisive, the worst possible scenario if ego opts for a behavioral stance is one in which these indecisive group members turn out to make a choice at odds with his. Ego assesses the possible cost of a mistake in light of this scenario. Thus in the present case ego chooses acquiescence. If the 8 group members who shunned a behavioral stance choose opposition, he should be considering instead of a sample of size 2 with a 50–50 percent divide a sample of size 10 with a 90–10 percent divide. This provides ego with a probability distribution on the basis of which he can assess the expected cost of being at odds with his peers given his choice to acquiesce in the challenger's demands (table 33). Depending on his sensitivity to risk, he will then decide whether it is worth taking this behavioral option.

TACIT COORDINATION

Collective Updating

An actor speaks up. She makes a statement signaling an oppositional stance. Ego can infer no strategic information from this statement if he has no clue about this speaker's propensity to make her action conditional on the actions of her peers. If, on the contrary, ego can estimate her propensity to choose one option or the other — that is, if ego can estimate her action threshold with a reasonable degree of confidence — then he can infer informational content from this statement and revise his beliefs about the group accordingly. The statement

Table 33   Assessing the Cost of a Mistake in Light of Indecision

	Updated Beliefs When Ego Only Uses the Information Provided by Those Who Disclose a Behavioral Preference ($n = 2, k = 1$)	Counterfactual If the Indecisive Group Members Choose Opposition ($n = 10, k = 9$)
Expected utility of opposition	−0.29	−0.14
Expected utility of acquiescence	−0.07	−0.22
Decision	acquiescence	
Probability ($p° \geq 0.8$)	0.21	0.90
Loss if $p° \geq 0.8$ (expected utility of acquiescence if $p° \geq 0.8$ minus expected utility of opposition if $p° \geq 0.8$)	−0.0102	−0.0951

becomes strategically relevant from a cognitive viewpoint. For instance: ego has strong reasons to believe that the speaker's opposition threshold is high. She would not make a statement signaling opposition unless she assessed that a lot of group members wanted to oppose the challenger. Her statement sheds light on her assessment of the preference distribution in the group.

This cognitive process can be formally represented in Bayesian terms. Speaker s makes a statement $\sigma_s°$ signaling opposition. Ego imputes an opposition threshold $p_s°*$ to her in light of her past public statements and assesses the probability that she makes a statement advocating opposition given a definite proportion of opponents in the group ($\text{prob}(\sigma_s° \mid p° = h)$). From a strictly logical point of view, ego should consider the probability that speaker s has encountered a number of opponents, leading her to expect the utility of opposition to be greater than the utility of acquiescence. Doing so requires that ego first reconstruct speaker s's utility functions and then compute all the possible numbers k for which $\text{Exp}(U_i°) \geq \text{Exp}(U_i^A)$.

The cognitive complexity implied by this task casts doubt on the relevance of operationalizing the updating process this way. I simplify the process by positing that ego infers from speaker s's statement her local knowledge, assuming that her statement reflects the state of her local knowledge. From this perspective, ego assesses the probability that speaker s makes a statement advocating opposition (given a definite proportion of opponents in the group) as the probability that she gets a sample satisfying her threshold (conditional on this proportion of opponents in the group). The random variable is the number of opponents in speaker s's sample. Actor s interacts with n members of the group. She makes a statement in favor of opposition if among these n individuals, at least $n \cdot p_s^{o*}$ stated that they would oppose the challenger given the proportion h of opponents in the group. This probability follows a binomial law of parameters n and h.

(4) $\text{prob}(\sigma_s^o \mid p^o = h) = \text{prob}(x \geq n \cdot p_s^{o*} \mid p^o = h)$

with $h = \dfrac{k}{N}$, $k \in \{0, 1, \ldots, N\}$

Ego updates his prior beliefs about the different possible states of the world (i.e. different proportions of the group choosing opposition) in light of (1) his belief about speaker s's threshold and (2) the probability that s's sample satisfies her threshold. This updating process can be formally represented according to Bayes's rule. Ego revises his belief about the size of opposition in the group in light of (1) his prior belief about this size ($\text{prob}(p^o = h)$), (2) the probability that speaker s makes a statement if this belief is true ($\text{prob}(\sigma_s^o \mid p^o = h)$) as well as (3) the probability that speaker s makes a statement signaling opposition ($\text{prob}(\sigma_s^o)$).

(5) $\text{prob}(p^o = h \mid \sigma_s^o) = \dfrac{\text{prob}(\sigma_s^o \mid p^o = h) \cdot \text{prob}(p^o = h)}{\text{prob}(\sigma_s^o)}$

By the law of total probability, the probability that speaker s makes a statement signaling opposition $\text{prob}(\sigma_s^o)$ is the sum of the probabilities that she gets a sample satisfying her threshold given a state of the world $\text{prob}(\sigma_s^o \mid p^o = h)$ times the probability of this state of the world $\text{prob}(p^o = h)$

(6) $\text{prob}(\sigma_s^o) = \sum\limits_{h=0}^{1} \text{prob}(\sigma_s^o \mid p^o = h) \cdot \text{prob}(p^o = h)$

with $h = \dfrac{k}{N}$, $k \in \{0, 1, \ldots, N\}$

Figure 12 represents this inferential process. Ego updates his assessment that different proportions of the group will choose opposition by considering the likelihood that speaker s would deliver a statement in favor of opposition depending on these different proportions. Ego assumes that this speaker is basing her judgment on the information provided by the sample of her interpersonal contacts — her local knowledge. To assess the probability of this information given different group proportions choosing opposition, as indicated in equation (4), we need to set a value for n, the size of the sample constituted by speaker s's interpersonal contacts. For this numerical example this sample

reference group

opposition $(1-\phi)$ acquiescence (ϕ)

statement σ_s by speaker with threshold p_s^{o*}

reference group

opposition $(1-\phi')$ acquiescence (ϕ')

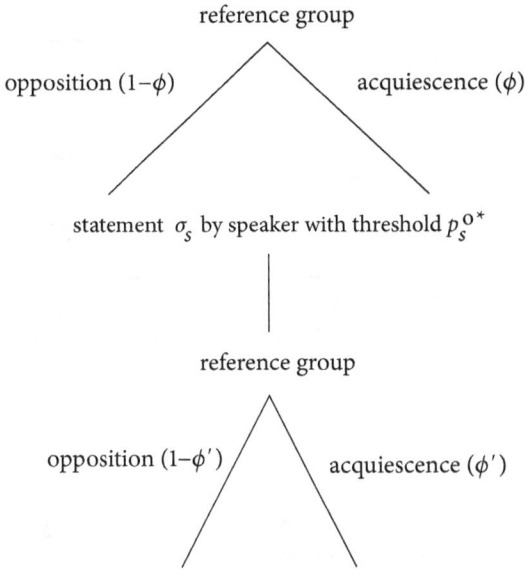

Figure 12   The future stance of the group reassessed from ego's standpoint

size is set at 10. This example assumes that ego imputes an opposition threshold of 0.3 to speaker s and that this speaker makes a statement revealing an oppositional stance. Table 34 and figure 13 indicate the upshot of this update process. The prior beliefs are those indicated in figure 10.

Differential Impact

Proposition: The impact of a statement depends on the action threshold imputed to the speaker. The greater the threshold value, the greater the impact.

This proposition rests on two conjoint effects. (1) The probability distribution of samples satisfying speaker s's threshold, given a proportion of opponents in the group ($\mathrm{prob}(\sigma_s^o / p^o = h)$) gets more skewed toward higher values as her opposition threshold gets higher. (2) Simultaneously, the probability that she makes a statement advocating opposition ($\mathrm{prob}(\sigma_s^o)$) gets lower as her opposition threshold increases: the probability of getting a sample satisfying her threshold becomes lower as her threshold gets higher. This second effect reinforces the skewness of the probability distribution. A simple numerical example illustrates this differential impact. I estimate the impact of s's statement in light of three different threshold values in addition to the one I have already considered. As before, the sample size is assumed to be 10 (figures 14–16).

Table 34 Belief Updating: A Numerical Example

			Revised after Statement by Speaker s in Favor of Opposition	
	$1-\phi$ prob $(p^\circ > 0.5)$	ϕ prob $(p^\circ < 0.5)$	$1-\phi'$ prob $(p^\circ > 0.5)$	ϕ' prob $(p^\circ < 0.5)$
Expectations of acquiescence	0.85	0.15	0.65	0.35
Full uncertainty	0.5	0.5	0.28	0.72
Expectation of opposition	0.15	0.85	0.06	0.94

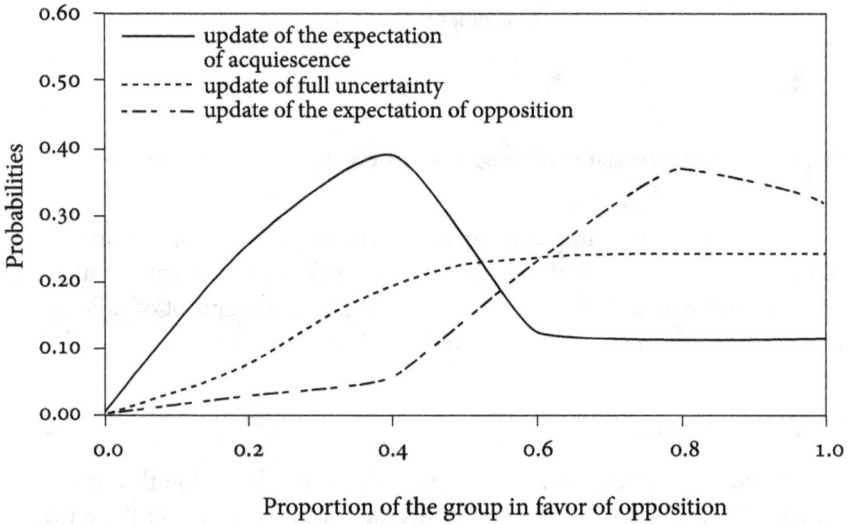

Figure 13 Belief update in light of a threshold value of 0.3

The greater the opposition threshold, the greater the impact on actors' beliefs. The value of an individual threshold captures a behavioral disposition
given the parameters and constraints of the situation. An actor with a high
opposition threshold is assumed to have no taste for opposition. A statement
revealing an oppositional stance is therefore counterintuitive. Restated with
reference to the content of the statement, the claim about the differential impact of a stance becomes: the more counterintuitive the statement, the greater
the impact. Counterintuitive statements have the greatest capacity to produce
convergence. Figure 16 shows the power of the tacit coordination mecha-

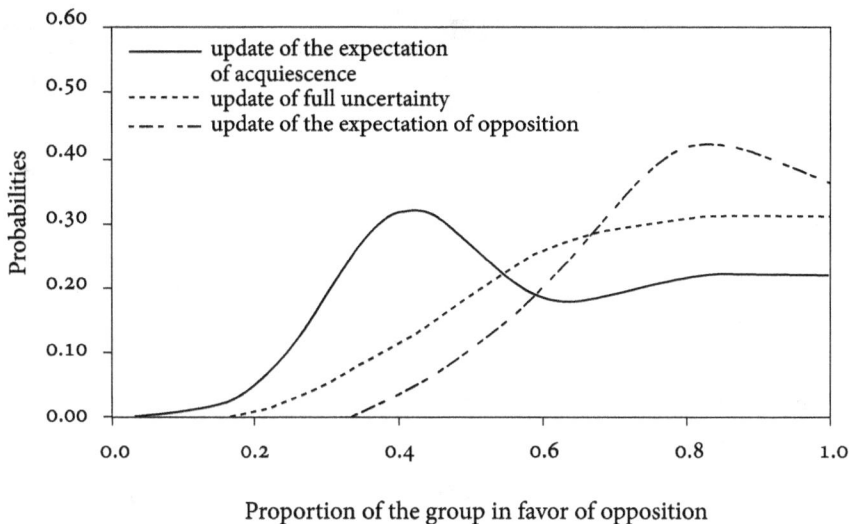

Figure 14   Belief update in light of a threshold value of 0.5

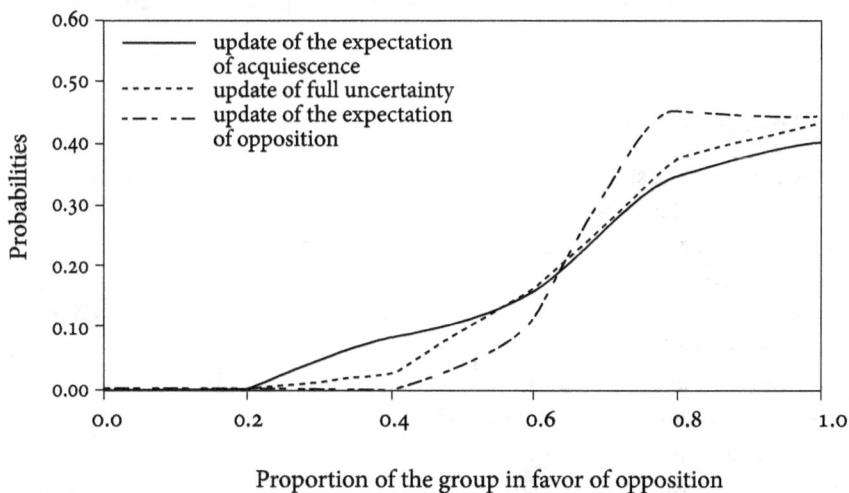

Figure 15   Belief update in light of a threshold value of 0.7

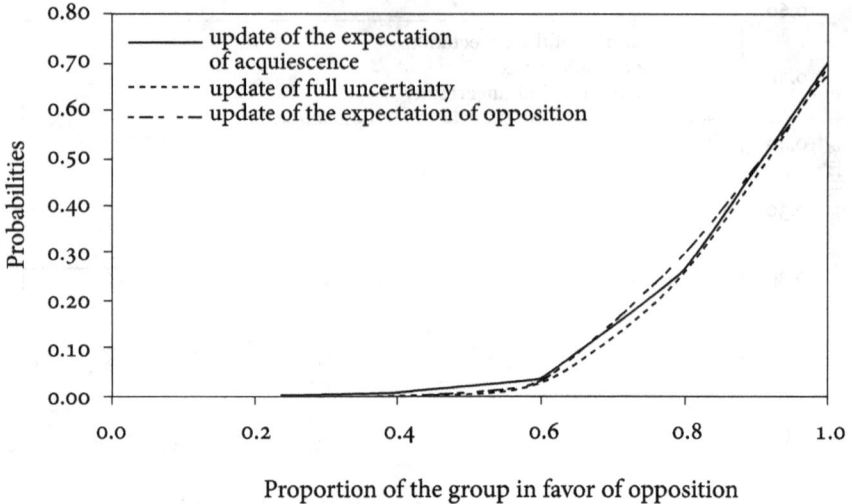

Proportion of the group in favor of opposition

Figure 16   Belief update in light of a threshold value of 0.9

nism to reduce divergent initial beliefs to one single dominant and univocal mode.

The Production of Uncertainty

Depending on the state of the priors, a statement can either produce or reduce uncertainty understood in probabilistic terms. Given a finite number of states of the world, ego's uncertainty is inversely related to the standard deviation of his subjective probabilities. The lower the standard deviation, the greater the uncertainty. A standard deviation of 0 captures full uncertainty. Consider the following example summarized by figure 17. Initially ego is quite convinced that the group will acquiesce: he assesses at 0.8 the probability that either the whole group or a proportion of four-fifths of it will acquiesce. The standard deviation of his belief distribution is quite high (sd = 0.20).[3] An actor with a relatively moderate opposition threshold (0.4) makes a statement indicating opposition. This statement leads ego to revise his beliefs. In the process, his former quasi-certitude crumbles. Ego is now less certain: he assigns a more even probability distribution to different possible states of the world (sd = 0.11).

3. The upper limit defining full certainty is a function of the number of states of the world being considered. In the present case this number is 6, and a state of full certainty—ego imputes a probability of 1 to one state of the world—corresponds to a standard deviation of 0.37.

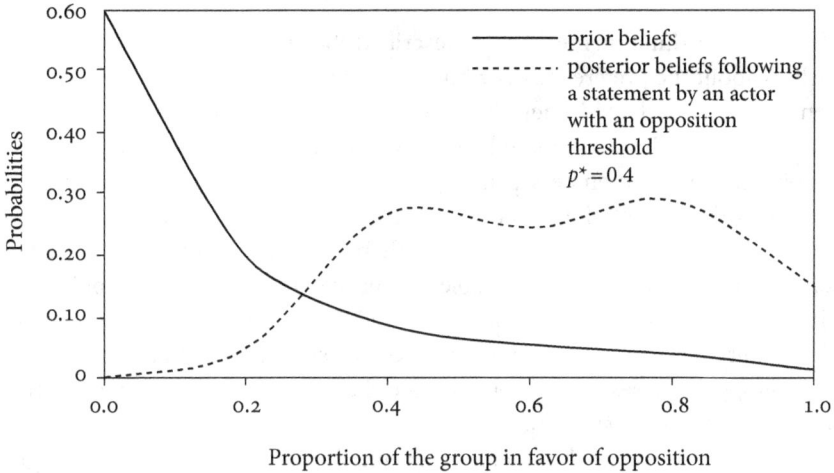

Figure 17   A statement producing greater uncertainty

Sequences

This point about uncertainty draws attention to the issue of sequence. Group members can be exposed to more than one statement from which they can infer strategic information about the group stance. Congruent statements are statements that produce the same type of adjustment: they yield congruent inferences about the group stance and consequently elicit convergent expectations. These statements have necessarily the same behavioral content: speakers advocate the same behavioral stance. Noncongruent statements yield opposite adjustments. The amplitude of this adjustment is determined by the speaker's opposition threshold.

For instance, the correction induced by the oppositional stance of an actor with a low opposition threshold of 0.2 has the same amplitude as the correction induced by the acquiescence stance of an actor with a high opposition threshold of 0.8. These effects do not cancel each other. They may, however, contribute to increasing the amount of uncertainty in the group. The less informative they are—i.e. the lower the action threshold of the actor advocating the specific action—the more they flatten the probability distribution. The least informative statements are the most likely to increase uncertainty. From this perspective, sequences of statements can be conceptualized in terms of (1) the amount of uncertainty that has been reduced and (2) the number of reversals along the way (uncertainty variation).

■   ■   ■

The tacit coordination mechanism described above does not assume that prior beliefs about the preference distribution are common knowledge. If the challenge is unprecedented, there is no reason to assume that at first individual actors know their peers' initial beliefs. However, the process I have described implies that group members' primary motivation for tacitly coordinating their beliefs is the expectation of convergence. As a result, consistent sequences of statements have a reality effect of their own. They produce the reality of the group stance by making subjective probabilities increasingly objective. The dispersion of beliefs gets narrower. Subjective probabilities get aligned. The reality lies in the group members' consensus (Katz and Lazarsfeld 1955, 54). Subjective assessments approximate the behavioral outcome when this outcome attains the status of common belief.

This analysis has two broader implications for the theory of collective alignments. First, it outlines the conditions under which the members of a group may not be able to align their behavior with one another. They lack the information allowing them to assess the stance of their peers with some degree of confidence and remain trapped in their mutual uncertainty. Second, there is no tipping point properly speaking. Any sequence can be reversed as long as group members are not fully certain of the outcome. Sequences therefore are not foreclosed. Congruent beliefs can start unraveling if a prominent actor makes a statement that goes counter to prevailing expectations and that group members cannot ignore given this actor's focal quality.

BIBLIOGRAPHY

ARCHIVAL MATERIAL

Germany

Archiv für Christlich-Demokratische Politik,
Konrad-Adenauer-Stiftung (ACDP), Sankt-Augustin

Nachlaß Paul Bausch
Nachlaß Wilhelm Bormann
Nachlaß Jakob Diehl
Nachlaß Oskar Farny
Nachlaß Franz Feilmayr
Nachlaß Edmund Forschbach
Nachlaß Hanna Gerig
Nachlaß Andreas Hermes
Nachlaß Heinrich Krone

Nachlaß Ernst Lemmer
Nachlaß Erwin Niffka
Nachlaß Joseph Scherer
Nachlaß Albert Schmidt
Nachlaß Arnold Siben
Nachlaß Adam Stegerwald
Nachlaß Fritz Stricher
Nachlaß August Wegmann

Archiv der sozialen Demokratie der Friedrich-Ebert-Stiftung, Bonn

ADGB Restakten
Teilnachlaß Otto Braun
Nachlaß Arthur Crispien
Nachlaß Wilhelm Dittmann

Nachlaß Heinrich Imbusch
Nachlaß Wilhelm Keil
Nachlaß Carl Severing

Bundesarchiv, Koblenz

Nachlaß Paul Bausch
Nachlaß Johannes Bell
Nachlaß Arnold Brecht
Nachlaß Hermann Dietrich
KLE Hanneman
Nachlaß Theodor Heuss
Nachlaß Jakob Kaiser
Nachlaß Wilhelm Külz
Nachlaß Maier-Hultschin

Nachlaß Fritz Schäffer
Nachlaß Otto Schmidt-Hannover
Nachlaß Bernhard Schwertfeger
Nachlaß Martin Spahn
Nachlaß ten Hompel
KLE August Weber
KLE Erich Wienbeck
Nachlaß Joseph Wirth

Haupstaatsarchiv Stuttgart

Nachlaß Eugen Bolz
Nachlaß Reinhold Maier

Historisches Archiv der Stadt Köln

Nachlaß Karl Bachem   Nachlaß Leo Schwering
Nachlaß Wilhelm Marx   Nachlaß Christine Teusch

Institut für Zeitgeschichte, Munich

Nachlaß Johannes Schauff

Kommission für Zeitgeschichte, Bonn (kfz)

KAB Archiv: records of the Reich executive committee of the Catholic workers' clubs
Nachlaß Friedrich Dessauer   Nachlaß Hermann Joseph Schmitt
Nachlaß Wilhelm Fonk   Tagebuchaufzeichnungen von Clara Siebert
Nachlaß Splitter Joos   Teilnachlaß Gustav Wolff

France

Archives Départementales de l'Aude, Carcassonne

Archives Albert Sarraut
Série W

Archives Départementales de la Charente, Angoulême

Archives René Gounin

Archives Départementales de la Charente-Maritime, La Rochelle

Archives William Bertrand

Archives Départementales du Finistère, Quimper

Archives Pierre Trémintin

Archives Départementales de l'Isère, Grenoble

Archives Justin Arnol

Archives de la ville de Paris

Archives Raymond Laurent

Archives Départementales du Rhône, Lyon

Archives Émile Bender
Archives Laurent Bonnevay

Archives Départementales de la Sarthe, Le Mans

Archives Caillaux

Archives Départementales de la Seine-Maritime, Rouen

Archives Montalembert

Archives Nationales, Paris (CARAN)

Archives Paul-Boncour
Archives René Cassin
Archives Daladier
Archives Félix Gouin
Papiers Locquin

Archives Reynaud
Papiers Albert Rivière
Série A G II
Fonds du jury d'honneur: AL5295–5334
F7 15342: Déat, Journal de guerre

Bibliothèque Nationale, Paris

Archives Flandin, Don 31357

Fondation Nationale des Sciences Politiques, Paris

Archives Blum
Archives Ernest Pezet

Office Universitaire de Recherche Socialiste (OURS), Paris

Dossier Gaston Allemane
Dossier François Blancho
Dossier Léon Bon
Dossier René Boudet
Dossier Ernest Esparbes
Dossier Joseph Lagrosillière
Dossier Paul Lambin
Dossier Roger Lefèvre
Dossier Albert Mennecier

Dossier Georges Monnet
Dossier Auguste Muret
Dossier Marcel Régis
Dossier André Rivière
Dossier Charles Saint-Venant
Dossier Albert Sérol
Dossier Marcel Vardelle
Dossier Maurice Voirin

Hoover Institution Archives, Stanford

Gaston Bergery papers

Musée Historique Henri Queuille, Neuvic, Corrèze

Archives Henri Queuille

PUBLISHED DOCUMENTS AND DIRECTORIES

Germany

Akten der Reichskanzlei: Die Regierung Hitler, vol. 1, *1933–34*, part 1, *30. Januar bis 31. August 1933*, ed. Karl-Heinz Minuth. Boppard am Rhein: Harald Boldt.

Akten deutscher Bischöfe über die Lage der Kirche, 1933–1945, ed. Bernhard Stasiewski. Mainz: Matthias-Grünewald. 1968.

Anpassung oder Widerstand? Aus den Akten des Parteivorstands der deutschen Sozialdemokratie, 1932–33, ed. Hagen Schulze. Bonn–Bad Godesberg: Neue Gesellschaft, 1975.

"Der Bericht des Untersuchungsausschusses über die Stellungnahme von Mitgliedern des Württembergisch-Badischen Landtags in ihrer Eigenschaft als Reichstagsabgeordnete zum Ermächtigungsgesetz am 23. März 1933." *Beilage Nr. 77 vom 1. April 1947 zu den Sitzungsprotokollen des Württembergisch-Badischen Landtags, Wahlperiode 1946–1950*, Beilage-Bd 1.

Das "Ermächtigungsgesetz" vom 24. März 1933: Quellen zur Geschichte und Interpretation des "Gesetzes zur Behebung der Not von Volk und Reich," ed. Rudolf Morsey. Düsseldorf: Droste, 1992.

Die Gewerkschaften in der Endphase der Republik, 1930–1933, ed. Peter Jahn and Detlev Brunner. Quellen zur Geschichte der deutschen Gewerkschaftsbewegung im 20. Jahrhundert, vol. 4. Series ed. Hermann Weber, Klaus Schönhoven, and Klaus Tenfelde. Cologne: Bund-Verlag, 1988.

Hitlers Machtergreifung: Dokumente vom Machtantritt Hitlers 30. Januar 1933 bis zur Besiegelung des Einparteienstaates 14. Juli 1933, ed. Josef Becker and Ruth Becker. Berlin: Deutscher Taschenbuch Verlag, 1993.

Inventar zu den Nachlässen der deutschen Arbeiterbewegung: Für die zehn westdeutschen Länder und West-Berlin, im Auftrag des Archivs der sozialen Demokratie der Friedrich-Ebert Stiftung, ed. Hans-Holzer Paul. Munich: K. G. Saur, 1993.

Katholische Kirche und Nationalsozialismus: Dokumente, 1930–1933, ed. Hans Müller. Munich: Nymphenburger, 1963.

MdR: Biographisches Handbuch der Reichstage, ed. Max Schwarz. Hannover: Literatur und Zeitgeschehen, 1965.

MdR: Die Reichtagsabgeordneten der Weimarer Republik in der Zeit des Nationalsozialismus: Politische Verfolgung, Emigration und Ausbürgerung, 1933–1945: Eine biographische Dokumentation, ed. Martin Schumacher. 3rd edn. Düsseldorf: Droste, 1994.

Der Nachlass des Reichskanzlers Wilhelm Marx, ed. H. Stehkämper. Cologne, 1968.

Die Protokolle der Reichstagsfraktion und des Fraktionsvorstandes der deutschen Zentrumspartei, 1926-1933, ed. Rudolf Morsey. Mainz: Matthis-Grunewald, 1969.

Reichsgesetzblatt 1933. Berlin, 1933.

Reichstags-Handbuch VIII. Berlin, 1930-33.

Reinhold Maier: Briefwechsel mit seiner Familie, 1930-1946, ed. Paul Sauer. Stuttgart: W. Wohlhammer, 1989.

Staatliche Akten über die Reichskonkordatsverhandlungen 1933, ed. Alfons Kupper. Mainz: Matthias-Grünewald. 1969.

Verfassungsgesetze des Deutschen Reichs und der deutschen Länder nach dem Stande vom 1. Februar 1926, ed. Otto Ruthenberg. Berlin: Franz Dahlen. 1926.

Verhandlungen des Reichstags, VIII, *Wahlperiode 1933*, vol. 457. Berlin, 1934.

France

Annales de la Chambre des Députés: Débats Parlementaires, 1940: Sessions ordinaires et extraordinaire de 1940. Paris: Imprimerie des Journaux officiels, 1946.

Annales du Sénat: Débats Parlementaires, 1940. Paris: Imprimerie des Journaux Officiels, 1946.

Compte-rendu sténographique de la séance privée des membres de la chambre des députés et du sénat tenue à Vichy le 10 juillet 1940: Séance du 22 juillet 1948 du bureau du Conseil de la République: Chambre des Députés. Paris, 1948.

Dictionnaire des parlementaires français: Notices biographiques sur les ministres, députés et sénateurs français de 1889 à 1940, ed. Jean Jolly. 8 vols. Paris: Presses Universitaires de France. 1960-1977.

France during the German Occupation, 1940-1944. Stanford: Hoover Institution on War, Revolution and Peace, 1958.

Le procès du Maréchal Pétain: Compte rendu sténographique. Paris: Albin Michel, 1945.

Rapport fait au nom de la commission chargée d'enquêter sur les événements survenus en France de 1933 à 1945: Témoignages et documents recueillis par la Commission d'Enquête Parlementaire: Assemblée Nationale: Annexe au procès verbal de la séance du 8 août 1947. Paris: Chambre des Députés, 1951.

NEWSPAPERS AND CONTEMPORARY MATERIAL

Germany

Augsburger Postzeitung
Badischer Beobachter
Der Deutsche

Frankfurter Zeitung
Der Gerade Weg
Germania
Die Glocke
Kaisenberg, Georg. 1933. "Das Ermächtigungsgesetz." *Deutsche Juristen-Zeitung* 38, 458–61.
Kölnische Volkszeitung
Neue Badische Zeitung
Neue Pfälzische Landes-Zeitung
Pfälzische Volkszeitung
Schmitt, Carl. 1933. "Das Gesetz zur Behebung der Not von Volk und Reich." *Deutsche Juristen-Zeitung* 38, 455–58.
Vossische Zeitung
Westdeutsche Arbeiterzeitung
Westfälisches Volksblatt
Das Zentrum

France

La Dépêche de Toulouse
Le Figaro
Le Jour
Le Journal des Débats
Le Midi Socialiste
Le Mot d'Ordre
Le Petit Parisien
Le Populaire du Centre
Le Temps

MEMOIRS, DIARIES, COLLECTED ESSAYS, AND SPEECHES

Germany

Bausch, Paul. 1969. *Lebenserinnerungen und Erkenntnisse eines schwäbischen Abgeordneten*. Korntal: Selbstverlag.
Braun, Otto. 1949. *Von Weimar zu Hitler*. Hamburg: Hammonia Norddeutsche Verlagsanstalt.
Brecht, Arnold. 1967. *Mit der Kraft des Geistes: Lebenserinnerungen: Zweite Hälfte, 1927–1967*. Stuttgart: Deutsche Verlagsanstalt.
———. 1970. *The Political Education of Arnold Brecht: An Autobiography, 1884–1970*. Princeton: Princeton University Press.
Brüning, Heinrich. 1968. *Reden und Aufsätze eines deutschen Staatsmanns*, ed. Wilhelm Vernekohl with collab. of Rudolf Morsey. Münster: Regensberg.
———. 1970. *Memoiren, 1918–1934*. Stuttgart: Deutsche Verlagsanstalt.

Buchwitz, Otto. 1950. *50 Jahre Funktionär der deutschen Arbeiterbewegung*. East Berlin: Dietz.

Felder, Josef. 1982. "Mein Weg: Buchdrucker—Journalist—SPD Politiker." *Abgeordnete des Deutschen Bundestages: Aufzeichnungen und Erinnerungen*, vol. 1, 15–79. Boppard: Boldt.

———. 1992. "Erinnerungen an Weimar, die schwäbische Sozialdemokratie und Hitlers 'Machtergreifung.'" *Von der Klassenbewegung zur Volkspartei: Wegmarken der bayerischen Sozialdemokratie, 1892–1992*, ed. Hartmut Mehringer, 175–86. Munich: Saur.

Heuss, Theodor. 1967. *Die Machtergreifung und das Ermächtigungsgesetz: Zwei nachgelassene Kapitel der Erinnerungen, 1905–1933*. Tübingen: Rainer Wunderlich.

Hoegner, Wilhelm. 1959. *Der schwierige Außenseiter: Erinnerungen eines Abgeordneten, Emigranten und Ministerpäsidenten*. Munich: Isar.

———. 1978. *Flucht vor Hitler: Erinnerungen an die Kapitulation der ersten deutschen Republik*. Munich: Nymphenburger Verlag.

Joos, Joseph. N.d. *Am Räderwerk der Zeit: Erinnerungen aus der katholischen und sozialen Bewegung und Politik*. Augsburg Verlag.

———. 1958. *So sah ich sie, Menschen und Geschehnisse*. Augsburg: Winfried-Werk.

Lemmer, Ernst. 1968. *Manches war doch anders*. Frankfurt: Scheffler.

Maier, Hans. 1964. *Ein Grundstein wird gelegt*. Tübingen: Wunderlich.

Meinecke, Friedrich. 1946. *Die deutsche Katastrophe: Betrachtungen und Erinnerungen*. Wiesbaden: Brockhaus.

Muckermann, Friedrich. 1973. *Im Kampf zwischen zwei Epochen: Lebenserinnerungen*, ed. Nikolaus Junk. Mainz: Matthias-Grünewald.

Quaatz, Reinhold. 1989. *Die Deutschnationalen und die Zerstörung der Weimarer Republik: Aus dem Tagebuch von Reinhold Quaatz, 1928–1933*, ed. Hermann Weiß and Paul Hoser. Munich: R. Oldenburg.

Schauff, Johannes. 1985 [1934]. "Aus meiner beruflichen und politischen Arbeit," ed. Pulheimer. *Beiträge zur Geschichte und Heimatkunde* 9, 93–94.

Schmidt-Hannover, Otto. 1959. *Umdenken oder Anarchie*. Göttingen: Göttinger Verlagsanstalt.

Schreiber, Georg. 1930. *Zentrum und Reichspolitik: Ein politisches Handbuch in Frage und Antwort*. Cologne: *Kölner Görres-Haus*.

Severing, Carl. 1950. *Mein Lebensweg*, vol. 2. Cologne: Greven.

Stampfer, Friedrich. 1957. *Erfahrungen und Erkenntnisse: Aufzeichnungen aus meinem Leben*. Cologne: Politik und Wirtschaft.

Treviranus, Gottfried Reinhold. 1968. *Das Ende von Weimar: Heinrich Brüning und seine Zeit*. Düsseldorf: Econ.

France

Auriol, Vincent. 1945. *Hier . . . demain*. Paris: Charlot.

Badie, Vincent. 1987. *Vive la République: Entretiens avec Jean Sagnes*. Toulouse: Privat.

Bardoux, Jacques. 1957. *Journal d'un témoin de la Troisième: Paris–Bordeaux–Vichy, 1er septembre 1939–15 juillet 1940*. Paris: Arthème Fayard.

Barthe, E. 1945. *La ténébreuse affaire du "Massilia": Une page d'histoire (18 juin 1940–octobre 1940)*. Paris.

Baudouin, Paul. 1948. *Neuf mois au gouvernement, avril–décembre 1940*. Paris: La Table Ronde.

Becquart, Henri. 1945. *Au temps du silence: De Bordeaux à Vichy: Souvenirs et réflexions*. Paris: Iris.

Berl, Emmanuel. 1968. *La fin de la IIIe République, 10 juillet 1940*. Paris: Gallimard.

Blum, Léon. 1955. *L'Oeuvre de Léon Blum, 1940–1945: Mémoires; La prison et le procès; A l'échelle humaine*. Paris: Albin Michel.

Bonnet, Georges. 1971. *Dans la tourmente, 1938–1948*. Paris: Fayard.

Boully, Georges. 1945. *Mémoire à mes juges*.

Bounin, Jacques. 1974. *Beaucoup d'imprudences*. Paris: Stock.

Camel, François. 1985 [July 1940]. "Ultimes Paroles." *Cahier et Revue de l'OURS* 158, 30–34.

Castagnez, Jean. 1945. *Précisions oubliées*. Published by the author.

Chautemps, Camille. 1963. *Cahiers secrets de l'armistice (1939–1940)*. Paris: Plon.

Déat, Marcel. 1989. *Mémoires politiques*. Paris: Denoël.

de Monzie, Anatole. 1941. *Ci-devant*. Paris: Flammarion.

Depreux, Edouard. 1972. *Souvenirs d'un militant*. Paris: Fayard.

Desgranges, Abbé. 1960. *Journal d'un prêtre député, 1936–1940*. Paris: La Palatine.

Fabry, Jean. 1960. *J'ai connu . . . 1934–1945*. Paris: Descamps.

Faure, Paul. 1948. *De Munich à la Libération*. Paris: L'Élan.

———. n.d. *De Munich à la Vème République*. Paris: L'Élan.

Faure, Pétrus. 1962. *Un témoin raconte . . .* Saint Étienne: Dumas.

Février, André. 1946. *Expliquons-nous*. Aspremont, Hautes-Alpes: A. Wast.

Flandin, Pierre-Étienne. 1938. *Paix et liberté (L'Alliance démocratique à l'action)*. Paris: Flammarion.

Galimand, Lucien. 1948. *Vive Pétain! Vive de Gaulle!* Paris: La Couronne.

Gros, Louis. 1945. *République toujours*. Avignon: Édouard Aubanel.

Henry-Haye, Gaston. 1972. *La grande éclipse franco-américaine*. Paris: Plon.

Herriot, Édouard. 1950. *Épisodes, 1940–1944*. Paris: Flammarion.

Jeanneney, Jules. 1972. *Journal politique, septembre 1939–juillet 1942*, ed. Jean-Noël Jeanneney. Paris: Colin.

Laniel, Joseph. 1971. *Jours de gloire et jours cruels, 1908–1958*. Paris: La Cité.

Lebrun, Albert. 1945. *Témoignage*. Paris: Plon.

Lémery, Henry. 1964. *D'une République l'autre*. Paris: La Table Ronde.

Le Roy Ladurie, Jacques. 1997. *Mémoires, 1902–1945*. Paris: Flammarion/Plon.

Manent, Gaston. 1947. *Résistance parlementaire*. Tarbes: A. Hunault.

Maroselli, André. N.d. *Des prisons de la gestapo à l'exil*. Montréal: L'arbre.

Martin Du Gard, Maurice. 1948. *La chronique de Vichy, 1940–1944*. Paris: Flammarion.

Moch, Jules. 1970. *Rencontres avec . . . Léon Blum*. Paris: Plon.

———. 1976. *Une si longue vie*. Paris: Laffont.

Montigny, Jean. 1940. *De l'armistice à l'Assemblée Nationale, 15 juin–15 juillet 1940: Toute la vérité sur un mois dramatique de notre histoire*. Clermont-Ferrand: Mont-Louis.

———. 1966. *Le complot contre la paix, 1935–1939*. Paris: La Table Ronde.

Nicolle, Pierre. 1947. *Cinquante mois d'armistice: Vichy, 2 juillet 1940–26 août 1944: Journal d'un temoin*. Paris: Bonne.

Noguères, Louis. 1972. *Le véritable procès du maréchal Pétain*. Paris: Fayard.

———. 2000. *Vichy, juillet 40*. Paris: Fayard.

Odin, Jean. 1946. *Les quatre-vingts*. Paris: Tallandier.

Paul-Boncour, J. 1946. *Entre deux guerres: Souvenirs sur la Troisième République: Sur les chemins de la défaite, 1935–1940*. Paris: Plon.

Pernot, Georges. 1971. *Journal de guerre (1940–1941)*. Paris: Les Belles Lettres.

Piétri, François. 1954. *Mes années d'Espagne, 1940–1948*. Paris: Plon.

Pomaret, Charles. 1968. *Le dernier témoin*. Paris: La Cité.

Ramadier, Paul. 1967. "Vichy (juillet 1940)." *Cahiers Paul Ramadier* 1, suppl. to *Revue Socialiste* 203, 49–56.

Raymond-Laurent, Jean. 1966. *Le Parti Démocrate Populaire, 1924–1944*, vol. 2, *La politique intérieure et extérieure de la France entre les deux guerres, 1919–1939*. Le Mans: Imprimerie Commerciale.

Renaitour, Jean-Michel. 1952. *La Mémoire fidèle*. Paris: Éditions Latines.

Saint-Just, François de. 1964. *Une bataille perdue . . . 17 mai—10 juillet 1940*. Éditions du Scorpion.

Taurines, Jean. 1944. *Tempête sur la République*. Saint-Étienne: Dubouchet.

Tixier-Vignancourt, Jean-Louis. 1976. *Des Républiques, des justices et des hommes*. Paris: Albin Michel.

Tony-Révillon, M.-M. 1945. *Mes carnets (juin–octobre 1940)*. Paris: Odette Lieutier.

Vallat, Xavier. 1957. *Le nez de Cléopatre: Souvenirs d'un homme de droite (1919–1944)*. Paris: Les Quatre Fils Aymon.

———. 1972. *Le grain de sable de Cromwell: Souvenirs d'un homme de droite*. Paris: Association des Amis de Xavier Vallat.

Voirin, Maurice. 1945. "Le scrutin du 10 juillet 1940." *Questions Actuelles*, 18 July 1945, 43–46.

Weygand, Général. 1950. *Mémoires: Rappelé au service*. Paris: Flammarion.

SECONDARY LITERATURE

Germany

Abraham, David. 1986. *The Collapse of the Weimar Republic: Political Economy and Crisis*, 2nd edn. New York: Holmes and Meier.

Adolph, Hans J. L. 1971. *Otto Wels und die Politik der deutschen Sozialdemokratie 1894 bis 1939: Eine politische Biographie*. Berlin: De Gruyter.

Altendörfer, Otto. 1993. *Fritz Schäffer als Politiker der Bayerischen Volkspartei, 1888–1945*. Munich: Archiv für Christlich-Soziale Politik der Hanns-Seidel-Stiftung.

Aretz, Jürgen. 1978. *Katholische Arbeiterbewegung und Nationalsozialismus: Der Verband katholischer Arbeiter- und Knappenvereine Westdeutschlands, 1923–1945*. Mainz: Matthias-Grünewald.

Becker, Josef. 1961a. "Joseph Wirth und die Krise des Zentrums während des IV. Kabinetts Marx (1927 bis 1928): Darstellung und Dokumente." *Zeitschrift für die Geschichte des Oberrheins* 109, 361–482.

———. 1961b. "Zentrum und Ermächtigungsgesetz 1933." *Vierteljahrshefte für Zeitgeschichte* 9, 195–210.

———. 1963a. "Brüning, Prälat Kaas und das Problem einer Regierungsbeteiligung der NSDAP 1930–1932." *Historische Zeitschrift* 196, 74–111.

———. 1963b. "Das Ende der Zentrumspartei und die Problematik des politischen Katholizismus in Deutschland: Zu einem Aufsatz von Karl Otmar Freiherr von Aretin." *Welt der Geschichte* 23, 149–72.

———. 1969. "Die deutsche Zentrumspartei 1918–1933: Grundprobleme ihrer Entwicklung." *Politische Parteien in Deutschland und Frankreich, 1918–1939*, ed. Oswald Hauser, 59–74. Wiesbaden: Franz Steiner.

———. 1980. "Heinrich Brüning und das Scheitern der konservativen Alternative in der Weimarer Republik." *Aus Politik und Zeitgeschichte*, B22/80, 3–17.

Becker, Winfried, ed. 1986. *Die Minderheit als Mitte. Die Deutsche Zentrumspartei in der Innenpolitik des Reiches, 1871–1933*. Paderborn: Ferdinand Schönigh.

Bendersky, Joseph W. 1983. *Carl Schmitt: Theorist for the Reich*. Princeton: Princeton University Press.

Biesemann, Jörg. 1987. *Das Ermächtigungsgesetz als Grundlage der Gesetzgebung im nationalsozialistischen Staat*. Münster: Lit.

Blackbourn, David. 1980. *Class, Religion and Local Politics in Wilhelmine Germany: The Center Party in Württemberg before 1914*. New Haven: Yale University Press.

Böckenförde, Ernst-Wolfgang. 1961. "Der deutsche Katholizismus im Jahre 1933. Eine kritische Betrachtung." *Hochland* 53, 215–39.

———. 1962. "Der deutsche Katholizismus im Jahre 1933: Stellungnahme zu einer Diskussion." *Hochland* 54, 217–45.

Bracher, Karl Dietrich. 1962. "Stufen der Machtergreifung," *Die nationalsozialistische Machtergreifung: Studien zur Errichtung des totalitären Herrschaftssystems in Deutschland, 1933–34*, ed. Karl Bracher, Wolfgang Sauer, and Gerhard Schulz, 31–348. Cologne: Westdeutscher Verlag.

———. 1964 [1955]. Die *Auflösung der Weimarer Republik: Eine Studie zum Problem des Machtverfalls in der Demokratie*, 3rd edn. Villingen/Schwarzwald: Ring.

———. 1966. "The Technique of the Nationalist Seizure of Power." *The Path to Dictatorship: Ten Essays by German Scholars*, trans. John Conway, 113–32. New York: Frederick A. Praeger.

———. 1970. *The German Dictatorship: The Origins, Structure and Effects of National Socialism*. New York: Praeger.

Brecht, Arnold. 1944. *Prelude to Silence: The End of the German Republic*. New York: Oxford University Press.

Breuning, Klaus. 1969. *Die Vision des Reiches: Deutscher Katholizismus zwischen Demokratie und Diktatur (1929-1934)*. Munich: Max Hueber.

Buchheim, Hans. 1960. "Warum das Zentrum unterging." *Hochland* 53, 15-27.

———. 1961. "Der deutsche Katholizismus im Jahre 1933." *Hochland* 53, 497-515.

Carsten, Francis. 1990. "Der Preußische Adel und seine Stellung in Staat und Gesellschaft bis 1945." *Europäischer Adel, 1750-1950*, ed. Hans-Ulrich Wehler. 112-25. Göttingen: Vandenhoeck.

Cary, Noel D. 1988. "Political Catholicism and the Reform of the German Party System, 1900-1957." Diss., University of California, Berkeley.

———. 1996. *The Path to Christian Democracy: German Catholics and the Party System from Windthorst to Adenauer*. Cambridge: Harvard University Press.

Childers, Thomas. 1983. *The Nazi Voter: The Social Foundations of Fascism in Germany, 1919-1933*. Chapel Hill: University of North Carolina Press.

Craig, Gordon. 1978. *Germany, 1866-1945*. Oxford: Clarendon.

Dessauer, Friedrich. 1931. *Das Zentrum*. Berlin: Pan.

Deuerlein, E. 1961. "Zur Vergegenwärtigung der Lage des deutschen Katholizismus 1933." *Stimmen der Zeit* 168.

Dirks, Walter. 1969. "Geleitwort." *Die Vision des Reiches: Deutscher Katholizismus zwischen Demokratie und Diktatur (1929-1934)*, by Klaus Breuning, 7-12. Munich: Max Hueber.

Eksteins, Modris. 1969. *Theodor Heuss und die Weimarer Republik: Ein Beitrag zur Geschichte des deutschen Liberalismus*. Stuttgart: Ernst Klett.

Eley, Geoff. 1986. *From Unification to Nazism*. Boston: Allen and Unwin.

Evans, Ellen Lowell. 1981. *The German Center Party, 1870-1933*. Carbondale: Southern Illinois University Press.

Evans, Richard J. 2004. *The Coming of the Third Reich*. New York: Penguin.

Eyck, Erich. 1963. *A History of the Weimar Republic*, vol. 2, *From the Locarno Conference to Hitler's Seizure of Power*, trans. P. Hanson and Robert G. L. Waite. Cambridge: Harvard University Press.

Feuchtwanger, E. J. 1993. *From Weimar to Hitler: Germany, 1918-33*. London: Macmillan.

Forster, Bernhard. 2003. *Adam Stegerwald (1874-1945): Christlich-nationaler Gewerkschafter, Zentrumspolitiker, Mitbegründer der Unionsparteien*. Düsseldorf: Droste.

Friedrich, Carl. 1933. "The Development of Executive Power in Germany." *American Political Science Review* 27.

Hamilton, Richard. F. 1982. *Who Voted for Hitler?* Princeton: Princeton University Press.

Harcourt, Robert. 1938. *Catholiques d'Allemagne*. Paris: Plon.

Harsch, Donna. 1993. *German Social Democracy and the Rise of Nazism*. Chapel Hill: University of North Carolina Press.

Hehl, Ulrich von. 1977. *Katholische Kirche und Nationalsozialismus im Erzbistum Köln, 1933–1945*. Mainz.

Heiber, Helmut. 1993. *The Weimar Republik*, trans. W. E. Yuill. London: Blackwell.

Hömig, Herbert. 1979. *Das Preussische Zentrum in der Weimarer Republik*. Mainz: Matthias-Grünewald.

———. 2000. Brüning: Kanzler in der Krise der Republik: Eine Weimarer Biographie. Paderborn: Ferdinand Schöningh.

Hörster-Philipps, Ulrike. 1998. *Joseph Wirth, 1879–1956: Eine politische Biographie*. Paderborn: Ferdinand Schöningh.

Hürten, Heinz. 1992. *Deutsche Katholiken, 1918–1945*. Paderborn: Ferdinand Schöningh.

Jasper, Gotthard. 1986. *Die gescheiterte Zähmung: Wege zur Machtergreifung Hitlers, 1930–1934*. Frankfurt am Main: Suhrkamp.

Jones, Larry Eugene. 1988. *German Liberalism and the Dissolution of the Weimar Party System, 1918–1933*. Chapel Hill: University of North Carolina Press.

Junker, Detlef. 1969. *Die Deutsche Zentrumspartei und Hitler, 1932/33: Ein Beitrag zur Problematik des politischen Katholizimus in Deutschland*. Stuttgart: Ernst Klett.

Kalyvas, Stathis N. 1996. *The Rise of Christian Democracy in Europe*. Ithaca: Cornell University Press.

Klönne, Arno. 1958. *Gegen den Strom: Bericht über den Jugendwiderstand im Dritten Reich*. Hannover: Norddeutsche Verlagsanstalt.

Knapp, Thomas A. 1967. "Joseph Wirth and the Democratic Left in the German Center Party, 1918–1928." Diss., Catholic University of America.

———. 1973. "Joseph Wirth," *Zeitgeschichte in Lebensbildern*, vol. 1, ed. Rudolf Morsey, 160–73. Mainz: Matthias-Grünewald.

Kolb, Eberhard. 1988. *The Weimar Republic*, trans. P. S. Falla. London: Unwyn Hyman.

Kosthorst, Erich. 1967. *Jakob Kaiser: Der Arbeiterführer*. Stuttgart: W. Kohlhammer.

Leiber, Robert. 1960. "Reichskonkordat und Ende der Zentrumspartei." *Stimmen der Zeit* 167, 213–23.

Lepsius, Rainer. 1978. "From Fragmented Party Democracy to Government by Emergency Decree and the National Socialist Takeover: Germany." *The Breakdown of Democratic Regimes: Europe*, ed. Juan J. Linz and Alfred Stepan, 34–79. Baltimore: Johns Hopkins University Press.

Lewy, Günther. 1964. *The Catholic Church and Nazi Germany*. New York: McGraw-Hill.

Lill, Rudolf. 1990. "NS-Ideologie und katholische Kirche," *Die Katholiken und das Dritte Reich*, ed. Klaus Gotto and Konrad Repgen, 151–72. Mainz: Matthias-Grünewald.

Maier, Hans. 1972. *Kirche und Gesellschaft*. Munich: Kösel.

Matthias, Erich. 1954. "Die Sitzung der Reichstagsfraktion des Zentrums am 23. März 1933: Dokumentation." *Vierteljahrshefte für Zeitgeschichte* 4.

———. 1960. "Die Sozialdemokratische Partei Deutschlands." *Das Ende der Parteien, 1933*, ed. Erich Matthias and Rudolf Morsey, 101–278. Düsseldorf: Droste.

————. 1966. "The Social Democratic Party and Government Power." *The Path to Dictatorship: Ten Essays by German Scholars*, trans. John Conway, 50–67. New York: Frederick A. Praeger.

Matthias, Erich, and Rudolf Morsey. 1960. "Die Deutsche Staatspartei." *Das Ende der Parteien, 1933*, ed. Erich Matthias and Rudolf Morsey, 31–97. Düsseldorf: Droste.

Matz, Klaus-Jürgen. 1989. *Reinhold Maier (1889–1971): Eine politische Biographie*. Düsseldorf: Droste.

May, Georg. 1982. *Ludwig Kaas*, vol. 3. Amsterdam: Grüner.

Medicus, Franz Albrecht. 1933. "Vereinfachte Gesetzgebung (Gesetz zur Rettung von Volk und Reich." *Reichsverwaltungsblatt und Preußisches Verwaltungsblatt* 54, 241–42.

Miller, Max. 1951. *Eugen Bolz: Staatsmann und Bekenner*. Stuttgart: Schwabenverlag.

Morsey, Rudolf. 1960. "Die Deutsche Zentrumspartei." *Das Ende der Parteien, 1933*, ed. Erich Matthias and Rudolf Morsey, 281–453. Düsseldorf: Droste.

————. 1961. "Hitlers Verhandlungen mit der Zentrumsführung am 31. Januar 1933." *Vierteljahrshefte für Zeitgeschichte* 9, 182–94.

————. 1966. "The Center Party between the Fronts." *The Path to Dictatorship: Ten Essays by German Scholars*, trans. John Conway, 68–85. New York: Frederick A. Praeger.

————. 1977. *Der Untergang des politischen Katholizismus: Die Zentrumspartei zwischen christlichem Selbstverständnis und "Nationaler Erhebung," 1932–33*. Stuttgart: Belser.

————. 1989. "Zentrumspartei und Zentrumspolitiker im rückblickenden Urteil Heinrich Brünings." *Wege in die Zeitgeschichte: Festschrift zum 65. Geburtstag von Gerhard Schulz*, ed. Jürgen Heideking et al., 49–68. Berlin.

————. 1997. *Von Windthorst bis Adenauer*, ed. Ulrich von Hehl, Hans Günter Hockerts, Horst Möller, and Martin Schumacher. Paderborn: Ferdinand Schöningh.

————, ed. 1973. *Zeitgeschichte in Lebensbildern*, vol. 1. Mainz: Matthias-Grünewald.

Mosse, George. 1964. *The Crisis of German Ideology: Intellectual Origins of the Third Reich*. New York: Grosset and Dunlap.

Neumann, Sigmund. 1965 [1932]. *Die Parteien der Weimarer Republik*. Stuttgart: W. Kohlhammer.

Opitz, Günter. 1969. *Der christlich-soziale Volksdienst: Versuch einer protestantischen Partei in der Weimarer Republik*. Düsseldorf: Droste.

Orlow, Dietrich. 1991. *Weimar Prussia, 1925–1933: The Illusion of Strength*. Pittsburgh: University of Pittsburgh Press.

Patch, William L. 1985. *Christian Trade Unions in the Weimar Republic, 1918–1933: The Failure of "Corporate Pluralism."* New Haven: Yale University Press.

————. 1998. *Heinrich Brüning and the Dissolution of the Weimar Republic*. Cambridge: Cambridge University Press.

Peukert, Detlev. 1992. *The Weimar Republic: The Crisis of Classical Modernity*, trans. Richard Deveson. New York: Hill and Wary.

Prégardier, Elisabeth, and Ann Mohr, eds. 1991. *Helene Weber: Ernte eines Lebens.* Essen: Plöger.

Rauh-Kühne, Cornelia. 1991. *Katholisches Milieu und Kleinstadtgesellschaft: Ettlingen, 1918–1939.* Sigmaringen: Jan Thorbecke.

Repgen, Konrad. 1967. *Hitlers Machtergreifung und der deutsche Katholizismus: Versuch einer Bilanz.* Saarbrücken: Universität des Saarlandes.

———. 1988. *Von der Reformation zur Gegenwart: Beiträge zu Grandfragen der neuzeitlichen Geschichte,* ed. Klaus Gotto and Hans Günter Hockerts. Paderborn: Ferdinand Schöningh.

Richter, Michaela. 1986. "Resource Mobilization and Legal Revolution: National Socialist Tactics in Franconia." *The Formation of the Nazi Constituency, 1919–1933,* ed. Thomas Childers, 104–30. Totowa, N.J.: Barnes and Noble.

Rohe, Karl. 1966. *Das Reichsbanner Schwarz Rot Gold: Ein Beitrag zur Geschichte und Struktur der politischen Kampfverbände zur Zeit der Weimarer Republik.* Düsseldorf: Droste.

Ruppert, Karsten. 1986. "Die Deutsche Zentrumspartei in der Mitverantwortung für die Weimarer Republik: Selbstverständnis und politische Leitideen einer konfessionellen Mittelpartei." *Die Minderheit als Mitte: Die Deutsche Zentrumspartei in der Innenpolitik des Reiches, 1871–1933,* ed. Winfried Becker, 71–88. Paderborn: Schöningh.

Sailer, Joachim. 1994. *Eugen Bolz und die Krise des politischen Katholizismus in der Weimarer Republik.* Tübingen: Bibliotheca Academia.

Schäfer, Michael. 1990. *Heinrich Imbusch: Christlicher Gewerkschaftsführer und Widerstandskämpfer.* Munich: Beck.

Schneider, Hans. 1968 [1953]. "Das Ermächtigungsgesetz vom 24. März 1933." *Von Weimar zu Hitler, 1930–1933,* ed. Gotthard Jasper, 405–42. Cologne: Kiepenheuer und Witsch.

Scholder, Klaus. 1977. *Die Kirchen und das Dritte Reich: Vorgeschichte und Zeit der Illusionen, 1918–1934.* Frankfurt am Main: Ullstein.

———. 1988. *The Churches and the Third Reich,* vol. 1, trans. John Bowden. Philadelphia: Fortress.

Schönhoven, Klaus. 1977. "Zwischen Anpassung und Ausschaltung: Die Bayerische Volkspartei in der Endphase der Weimarer Republik, 1932/33." *Historische Zeitschrift* 224, 340–78.

Schulz, Gerhard 1992. *Von Brüning zu Hitler.* Berlin: Walter de Gruyter.

Schulze, Hagen. 1977. *Otto Braun oder Preussens demokratische Sendung.* Frankfurt am Main: Propyläen.

Schumann, Dirk. 2001. *Politische Gewalt in der Weimarer Republik, 1918–1933: Kampf um die Straße und Furcht vor dem Bürgerkrieg.* Essen: Klartext.

Schwend, Karl. 1960. "Die Bayerische Volkspartei." *Das Ende der Parteien, 1933,* ed. Erich Matthias and Rudolf Morsey, 457–519. Düsseldorf: Droste.

Schwertfeger, Bernhard. 1947. *Rätsel um Deutschland.* Heidelberg: Carl Winter Universitätsverlag.

Sontheimer, Kurt. 1962. *Antidemokratisches Denken in der Weimarer Republik*. Munich: Nymphenburger Verlagshandlung.

———. 1963. Preface. *Katholische Kirche und Nationalsozialismus: Dokumente, 1930–1933*, ed. Hans Müller, viii–xvi. Munich: Nymphenburger Verlagshandlung.

Steinmetz, George. 1993. *Regulating the Social: The Welfare State and Social Politics in Imperial Germany*. Princeton: Princeton University Press.

Stern, Fritz. 1961. *The Politics of Cultural Despair: A Study in the Rise of the Germanic Ideology*. Berkeley: University of California Press.

Stump, Wolfgang. 1971. *Geschichte und Organisation der Zentrumspartei in Düsseldorf, 1917–1933*. Düsseldorf: Droste.

Thamer, Hans-Ulrich. 1986. *Verführung und Gewalt: Deutschland, 1933–1945*. Berlin: Siedler.

Turner, Henry Ashby, Jr. 1985. *German Big Business and the Rise of Hitler*. New York: Oxford University Press.

Volk, Ludwig. 1972. *Das Reichskonkordat vom 20. Juli 1933*. Mainz: Matthias Grünewald.

———. 1987. *Katholische Kirche und Nationalsozialismus: Ausgewählte Aufsätze*, ed. Dieter Albrecht. Mainz: Veröffentlichungen der Kommission für Zeitgeschichte.

———. 1990. "Nationalsozialistischer Kirchenkampf und deutscher Episkopat." *Die Katholiken und das Dritte Reich*, ed. Klaus Gotto and Konrad Repgen, 49–92. Mainz: Matthias-Grünewald.

Wachtling, Oswald. 1974. *Joseph Joos: Journalist, Arbeiterführer, Zentrumspolitiker: Politische Biographie, 1878–1933*. Mainz: Matthias Grünewald.

Watkins, Frederick Mundell. 1939. *The Failure of Constitutional Emergency Powers under the German Republic*. Cambridge: Harvard University Press.

Webersinn, Gerhard. 1970. "Karl Ulitzka." *Jahrbuch der Schlesischen Friedrich-Wilhelms-Universität zu Breslau* 15, 146–205.

Wiesemann, Falk. 1975. *Die Vorgeschichte der nationalsozialistischen Machtübernahme in Bayern, 1932/1933*. Berlin: Duncker und Humblot.

Winkler, Heinrich August. 1989. *Der Weg in die Katastrophe: Arbeiter und Arbeiterbewegung in der Weimarer Republik 1930 bis 1933*. Berlin: J. H. W. Dietz.

France

Agulhon, Maurice. 1993. *The French Republic, 1872–1992*. Oxford: Blackwell.

Anceau, Éric. 2003. "Les écoles du Parlement: Les types de formation des parlementaires." *Les parlementaires de la Troisième République*, ed. Jean-Marie Mayeur, Jean-Pierre Chaline, and Alain Corbin, 167–93. Paris: La Sorbonne.

Aron, Robert. 1958. *The Vichy Regime, 1940–44*, trans. Humphrey Hare. London: Putnam.

Audigier, François. 1995. "L'Alliance démocratique de 1933 à 1937, ou l'anachronisme en politique." *Vingtième Siècle* 47, 147–57.

————. 1997. "Les modérés face au Front Populaire: Les ambiguités de l'Alliance démocratique." *Annales de l'Est*, 47, no. 2, 321–52.

Azéma, Jean-Pierre. 1984. *From Munich to the Liberation, 1938–1944*. Cambridge: Cambridge University Press.

Bankwitz, Philip Charles. 1967. *Maxime Weygand and Civil-Military Relations in Modern France*. Cambridge: Harvard University Press.

Baruch, Marc O. 1997. *Servir l'état français: l'administration en France de 1940 à 1944*. Paris: Fayard.

Beau de Loménie, E. 1951. *La mort de la Troisième République*. Paris: Conquistador.

Bellamy, David. 2006. *Geoffroy de Montalembert (1898–1993): Un aristocrate en République*. Rennes: Presses Universitaires de Rennes.

Bernard, Mathias. 1998. *La Dérive des modérés: La Fédération Républicaine du Rhône sous la IIIe République*. Paris: L'Harmattan.

Berstein, Serge. 1978. "Le parti radical-socialiste, arbitre du jeu politique français." *La France et les français en 1938–1939*, ed. René Rémond and Janine Bourdin, 275–306. Paris: Fondation Nationale des Sciences Politiques.

————. 1982. *Histoire du parti radical*, vol. 2, *Crise du radicalisme, 1926–1939*. Paris: Fondation Nationale des Sciences Politiques.

Birnbaum, Pierre. 1992. *Anti-semitism in France: A Political History from Léon Blum to the Present*, trans. Miriam Kochan. Oxford: Blackwell.

Bloch, Marc. 1990. *L'étrange défaite: Témoignage écrit en 1940*. Paris: Gallimard.

Bonnefous, Edouard. 1967. *Histoire politique de la Troisième République*, vol. 7, *1938–1940*. Paris: Presses Universitaires de France.

Bougeard, Christian. 2002. *Tanguy Prigent, paysan ministre*. Rennes: Presses universitaires de Rennes.

Bouju, Paul M., and Henri Dubois. 1984. *La Troisième République*. Paris: Presses Universitaires de France.

Burrin, Philippe. 1986. *La dérive fasciste: Doriot, Déat, Bergery, 1933–1945*. Paris: Le Seuil.

Calef, Henri. 1988. *Le sabordage de la Troisième République*. Paris: Librairie Académique Perrin.

Chaline, Jean-Pierre, and Anne-Marie Sohn, eds. 2000. *Dictionnaire des parlementaires de Haute-Normandie sous la Troisième République, 1871–1940*. Rouen: Université de Rouen.

Cointet, Jean-Paul. 1978. "Les marginaux de gauche." *La France et les Français en 1938–1939*, ed. René Rémond and Janine Bourdin, 261–74. Paris: Fondation Nationale des Sciences Politiques.

————. 1996. *Histoire de Vichy*. Paris: Plon.

Cointet, Michèle. 1993. *Vichy capitale, 1940–1944*. Paris: Perrin.

Cointet-Labrousse, Michèle. 1987. *Vichy et le fascisme*. Bruxelles: Complexe.

Delbreil, Jean-Claude. 1990. *Centrisme et démocratie-chrétienne en France: Le Parti Démocrate Populaire des origines au M.R.P. (1919–1944)*. Paris: La Sorbonne.

————. 2000. "Parti démocrate populaire, modérés, centrisme et démocratie chrétienne (1919–1940)." *Les modérés dans la vie politique française (1870–1965)*, ed. François Roth, 351–66. Nancy: Presses Universitaires de Nancy.

Dobry, Michel. 1989. "Février 1934 et la découverte de l'allergie de la société française à la 'Révoluton fasciste.'" *Revue française de sociologie* 30, 511–33.

———. 2003. "La thèse immunitaire face aux fascismes." *Le mythe de l'allergie française au fascisme*, ed. Michel Dobry, 17–67. Paris: Albin Michel.

———, ed. 2003. *Le mythe de l'allergie française au fascisme*. Paris: Albin Michel.

Dreyfus, François-George. 1990. *Histoire de Vichy*. Paris: Perrin.

Duroselle, Jean-Baptiste. 1985. *La décadence, 1932–1939*, 3rd edn. Paris: Imprimerie Nationale.

Duverger, Maurice. 1982. Preface. *Les Socialistes sous l'Occupation: Résistance et Collaboration*, by Marc Sadoun. Paris: Fondation Nationale des Sciences Politiques.

El Gammal, Jean, and Pascal Plas eds. 2001. *Dictionnaire des parlementaires du Limousin sous la Troisième République*. Limoges: Presses Universitaire de Limoges.

Ferro, Marc. 1987. *Pétain*. Paris: Fayard.

Fleurieu, Roger de. 1951. *Joseph Caillaux au cours d'un demi-siècle de notre histoire*. Paris: Raymond Clavreuil.

Gauchet, Marcel. 1992. "La droite et la gauche." *Les lieux de mémoire*, vol. 3, *La France: Conflits et partages*, ed. Pierre Nora, 393–467. Paris: Gallimard.

Gaudemet, Yves-Henri. 1970. *Les juristes et la vie politique de la IIIe République*. Paris: Presses Universitaires de France.

Gombin, Richard. 1970. *Les socialistes et la guerre: La SFIO et la politique étrangère française entre les deux guerres mondiales*. Paris: Mouton.

———. 1978. "Socialisme et pacifisme." *La France et les français en 1938–1939*, ed. René Rémond and Janine Bourdin, 245–60. Paris: Fondation Nationale des Sciences Politiques.

Graham, Bruce Desmond. 1994. *Choice and Democratic Order: The French Socialist Party, 1937–1950*. Cambridge: Cambridge University Press.

Greene, Nathanael. 1969. *Crisis and Decline: The French Socialist Party in the Popular Front Era*. Ithaca: Cornell University Press.

Guillaume, Sylvie, ed. 2003. *Le centrisme en France aux XIXe et XXe siècles: Un échec?* Pessac: Maison des Sciences de l'Homme d'Aquitaine.

Handourtzel, Rémy, and Cyril Buffet. 1989. *La Collaboration . . . A gauche aussi*. Paris: Perrin.

Hazareesingh, Sudhir. 1994. *Political Traditions in Modern France*. Oxford: Oxford University Press.

Hilaire, Yves-Marie. 1992. "1900–1945: L'ancrage des idéologies." *Histoire des droites en France*, vol. 1, *Politique*, ed. Jean-François Sirinelli, 519–66. Paris: Gallimard.

Hoffmann, Stanley. 1974. *Decline or Renewal? France since the 1930s*. New York: Viking.

Hohl, Thierry. 2004. *A Gauche! La Gauche socialiste, 1921–1947*. Dijon: Presses Universitaires de Dijon.

Hutton, Patrick H., Amanda S. Bourque, and Amy Staples. 1986. *Historical Dictionary of the Third French Republic, 1870–1940*. New York: Greenwood.

Irvine, William D. 1979. *French Conservatism in Crisis: The Republican Federation of France in the 1930s*. Baton Rouge: Louisiana State University Press.

———. 1991. "Fascism in France and the Strange Case of the Croix de Feu." *Journal of Modern History* 63, 271–95.

Jackson, Julian. 2001. *France: The Dark Years, 1940–1944*. Oxford: Oxford University Press.

———. 2003. *The Fall of France: The Nazi Invasion of 1940*. Oxford: Oxford University Press.

Jeanneney, Jean-Noël. 1978. "La Fédération Républicaine." *La France et les français en 1938–39*, ed. René Rémond and Janine Bourdin, 341–59. Paris: Fondation Nationale des Sciences Politiques.

Jelen, Christian. 1988. *Hitler ou Staline: Le prix de la paix*. Paris: Flammarion.

Laborie, Pierre. 2001 [1990]. *L'opinion publique sous Vichy: Les français et la crise d'identité nationale*. Enlarged edn. Paris: Le Seuil.

Lacaze, Yvon. 1991. *L'opinion publique française et la crise de Munich*. Berne: Peter Lang.

Larkin, Maurice. 1988. *France since the Popular Front: Government and People, 1936–1986*. Oxford: Clarendon.

Larmour, Peter J. 1964. *The French Radical Party in the 1930s*. Stanford: Stanford University Press.

Le Béguec, Gilles. 1977. "L'évolution de la politique gouvernmentale et les problèmes institutionnels." *Édouard Daladier, chef de gouvernement*, ed. René Rémond and Janine Bourdin, 55–74. Paris: Fondation Nationale des Sciences Politiques.

———. 1991. "L'Aristocratie du barreau, vivier pour la République: Les secrétaires de la conférence du stage." *Vingtième Siècle* 30, 22–31.

———. 2001. "La constitution des groupes parlementaires: Questions de méthode." *Associations et champ politique: La loi de 1901 à l'épreuve du siècle*, ed. Claire Andrieu, Gilles Le Béguec, and Danielle Tartakowsky. Paris: La Sorbonne.

———. 2003a. *La République des avocats*. Paris: Armand Colin.

———. 2003b. "Les réseaux." *Les parlementaires de la Troisième République*, ed. Jean-Marie Mayeur, Jean-Pierre Chaline, and Alain Corbin, 241–61. Paris: La Sorbonne.

Lindenberg, Daniel. 1990. *Les années souterraines (1937–1947)*. Paris: La Découverte.

Machefer, Philippe. 1978. "Le parti social français." *La France et les français en 1938–1939*, ed. René Rémond and Janine Bourdin, 307–26. Paris: Fondation Nationale des Sciences Politiques.

Malroux, Anny. 1991. *Avec mon père Augustin Malroux*. Albi: Rives du Temps.

Marielle, Jean, and Jean Sagnès. 1993. *Pour la République: Le vote des quatre-vingts à Vichy le 10 juillet 1940*. Vichy: Centre National de Documentation Pédagogique.

Marrus Michael R. and Robert O. Paxton. 1995 [1981]. *Vichy France and the Jews*. Stanford: Stanford University Press.

Mayeur, Jean-Marie. 1984. *La vie politique sous la troisième République*. Paris: Le Seuil.

———. 2000. "Les modérés et l'Église." *Les modérés dans la vie politique française (1870–1965)*, ed. François Roth, 185–90. Nancy: Presses Universitaires de Nancy.

Ménager, Bernard, Jean-Pierre Florin, and Jean-Marc Guislin, eds. 2001. *Les parlementaires du Nord-Pas-de-Calais sous la IIIe République*. Villeneuve d'Ascq: Université Charles de Gaulle.

Michel, Henri. 1966. *Vichy, Année 1940*. Paris: Robert Laffont.

Milza, Pierre. 1987. *Fascisme français*. Paris: Flammarion.

Miquel, Pierre. 1995. *Les quatre-vingts*. Paris: Fayard.

Mortimer, Edward. 1984. *The Rise of the French Communist Party, 1920–1947*. London: Faber and Faber.

Nobécourt, Jacques. 1996. *Le colonel de la Rocque (1885–1946) ou les pièges du nationalisme chrétien*. Paris: Fayard.

Noiriel, Gérard. 1999. *Les origines républicaines de Vichy*. Paris: Hachette.

Passmore, Kevin. 1995. "Boy Scoutism for Grown-ups? Paramilitarism in the Croix-de-feu and the Parti Social Français." *French Historical Studies* 19, no. 2, 527–57.

———. 1997. *From Liberalism to Fascism: The Right in a French Province, 1928–1939*. Cambridge: Cambridge University Press.

Paxton, Robert O. 1972. *Vichy France: Old Guard and New Order*. New York: W. W. Norton.

Pinol, Jean-Luc. 1992. "1919–1958: 'Le temps des droites?'" *Histoire des droites en France*, vol. 1, *Politique*, ed. Jean-François Sirinelli, 291–390. Paris: Gallimard.

Prélot, Marcel. 1972. "La révision et les actes constitutionnels: La figure politique et juridique du chef de l'état français." *Le gouvernement de Vichy, 1940–1942: Institutions et politiques*, ed. René Rémond and Janine Bourdin, 23–36. Paris: Fondation Nationale des Sciences Politiques.

Prost, Antoine. 1977. "L'éclatement du Front populaire: Analyse factorielle des scrutins de la Chambre des députés, juin 1936–juin 1939." *Édouard Daladier, Chef de gouvernement*, ed. René Rémond and Janine Bourdin, 25–44. Paris: Fondation Nationale des Sciences Politiques.

Puyaubert, Jacques. 2005. "Le centrisme chez les radicaux de l'entre-deux-guerres." *Le centrisme en France aux XIXe et XXe siècles: Un échec?*, ed. Sylvie Guillaume, 105–20. Pessac: Maison des Sciences de l'Homme d'Aquitaine.

Rémond, René. 1982. *Les Droites en France*. Paris: Aubier.

Rimbaud, Christiane. 1984. *L'affaire du Massilia, été 1940*. Paris: Le Seuil.

Rossi, Amilcare. 1948. *Physiologie du PCF*. Paris: Self.

Rossi-Landi, Guy. 1971. *La drôle de guerre: La vie politique en France, 2 septembre 1939–10 mai 1940*. Paris: Fondation Nationale des Sciences Politiques.

Roth, François, ed. 2000. *Les modérés dans la vie politique française (1870–1965)*. Nancy: Presses Universitaires de Nancy.

Sadoun, Marc. 1982. *Les socialistes sous l'occupation: Résistance et collaboration*. Paris: Fondation Nationale des Sciences Politiques.

———. 1986. "Les contraintes de la position." *Vichy, 1940–1944*, ed. Denis Peschanski, 51–67. Paris: CNRS / Milan: Feltrinelli.

Sagnès, Jean. 1991. "Le refus républicain des quatre-vingts parlementaires qui dirent non à Vichy le 10 juillet 1940." *Revue d'Histoire Moderne et Contemporaine*, October–December, 555–89.

Sanson, Rosemonde. 1978. "L'Alliance démocratique." *La France et les Français en 1938–1939*, ed. René Rémond and Janine Bourdin, 327–40. Paris: Presses de la Fondation Nationale des Sciences Politiques.

———. 2000. "L'Alliance républicaine démocratique: Une reformulation du Centre gauche?" *Les modérés dans la vie politique française (1870–1965)*, ed. François Roth, 155–68. Nancy: Presses Universitaires de Nancy.

———. 2005. "Le centrisme dans l'Alliance démocratique." *Le centrisme en France aux XIXe et XXe siècles: Un échec?*, ed. Sylvie Guillaume. Pessac: Maison des Sciences de l'Homme d'Aquitaine.

Schor, Ralph. 1992. *L'antisémitisme en France dans les années trente: Prélude à Vichy.* Brussels: Complexe.

Sherwood, John M. 1970. *Georges Mandel and the Third Republic.* Stanford: Stanford University Press.

Shirer, William. 1969. *The Collapse of the Third Republic: An Inquiry into the Fall of France in 1940.* New York: Simon and Schuster.

Sirinelli, Jean-François, ed. 1992. *Histoire des droites en France*, vol. 1, *Politique*. Paris: Gallimard.

Sirinelli, Jean-François, and Eric Vigne. 1992. "Des droites et du politique." *Histoire des droites en France*, ed. Jean-François Sirinelli, vol. 1, *Politique*, iii–xliii. Paris: Gallimard.

Soucy, Robert. 1995. *French Fascism: The Second Wave, 1933–1939.* New Haven: Yale University Press.

Sternhell, Zeev. 1996 [1986]. *Neither Right nor Left: Fascist Ideology in France*, trans. David Maisel. Princeton: Princeton University Press.

Waline, Jean. 1961. "Les groupes parlementaires en France." *Revue du droit public et de la science politique*, 1170–1237.

Warner, Geoffrey. 1968. *Pierre Laval and the Eclipse of France.* London: Eyre and Spottiswoode.

Weber, Eugen. 1994. *The Hollow Years: France in the 1930s.* New York: W. W. Norton.

Wieviorka, Olivier. 2001. *Les orphelins de la république: Destinées des députés et sénateurs français (1940–1945).* Paris: Le Seuil.

Wileman, Donald G. 1988. "L'Alliance Républicaine Démocratique: The Dead Centre of French Politics, 1901–1947." PhD diss., York University.

———. 1990. "P. É. Flandin and the Alliance Démocratique, 1929–1939." *French History* 4, no. 2, 139–73.

THEORETICAL AND OTHER REFERENCES

Abbott, Andrew. 1988. "Transcending General Linear Reality." *Sociological Theory* 6, no. 2, 169–86.

Anderson, Benedict. 1991. *Imagined Communities: Reflections on the Origin and Spread of Nationalism*, rev. edn. London: Verso.

Aumann, Robert J. 1976. "Agreeing to Disagree." *Annals of Statistics* 4, 1236–39.

Austen-Smith, David. 1992. "Strategic Models of Talk in Political Decision-Making." *International Political Science Review* 13, no. 1, 45–58.

Aya, Rod. 1979. "Theories of Revolution Reconsidered." *Theory and Society* 8, no. 1, 39–99.

Bearman, Peter, Robert Faris, and James Moody. 1999. "Blocking the Future." *Social Science History* 23, no. 4, 501–33.

Berk, Richard A. 1974. "A Gaming Approach to Crowd Behavior." *American Sociological Review* 39, no. 355–73.

Bloch, Marc. 1953. *The Historian's Craft*, trans. Peter Putnam. New York: Vintage.

Blumer, Herbert. 1939. "Collective Behavior." *An Outline of the Principles of Sociology*, ed. Robert E. Park, 220–32. New York: Barnes.

Bourdieu, Pierre. 1977. *Outline of a Theory of Practice*. Stanford: Stanford University Press.

Bueno de Mesquita, Bruce, and David Lalman. 1992. *War and Reason*. New Haven: Yale University Press.

Chwe, Michael Suk-Young. 1999. "Structure and Strategy in Collective Action." *American Journal of Sociology* 105, no. 1, 128–56.

Coleman, James. 1990. *Foundations of Social Theory*. Cambridge: Harvard University Press.

Durkheim, Émile. 1982 [1895]. *The Rules of Sociological Method*, trans. W. D. Halls. New York: Free Press.

Elster, Jon. 1983. *Sour Grapes: Studies in the Subversion of Rationality*. Cambridge: Cambridge University Press.

———. 1984. *Ulysses and the Sirens*, rev. edn. Cambridge: Cambridge University Press.

———. 1985. *Making Sense of Marx*. Cambridge: Cambridge University Press.

Epstein, Larry G., and Tan Wang. 1996. "Beliefs about Beliefs without Probabilities." *Econometrica* 64, no. 6, 1343–73.

Ermakoff, Ivan. 2001. "Strukturelle Zwänge und zufällige Geschehnisse." *Geschichte und Gesellschaft* 19, 224–56.

Fearon, James. 1993. "Ethnic War as a Commitment Problem." Unpublished MS, University of Chicago.

Finn, John E. 1991. *Constitutions in Crisis: Political Violence and the Rule of Law*. New York: Oxford University Press.

Geyl, Pieter. 1964. *The Netherlands in the Seventeenth Century*, vol. 2. London: E. Benn.

Goldthorpe, John H. 1991. "The Uses of History in Sociology: Reflections on Some Recent Tendencies." *British Journal of Sociology* 42, 211–30.

Granovetter, Mark. 1978. "Threshold Models of Collective Behavior." *American Journal of Sociology* 83, no. 6, 1420–43.

Holmes, Stephen. 1993. *The Anatomy of Antiliberalism*. Cambridge: Cambridge University Press.

Israel, Jonathan I. 1995. *The Dutch Republic: Its Rise, Greatness, and Fall, 1477–1806*. Oxford: Clarendon.

Katz, Elihu, and Paul F. Lazarsfeld. 1955. *Personal Influence*. Glencoe: Free Press.

Koselleck, Reinhart. 1973. "Ereignis und Struktur." *Geschichte — Ereignis und Erzählung*, ed. Reinhart Koselleck and Wolf-Dieter Stempel, 560–71. Munich: Wihelm Fink.

Kreuzer, Marcus. 2001. *Institutions and Innovations: Voters, Parties, and Interest Groups in the Consolidation of Democracy: France and Germany, 1870–1939*. Ann Arbor: University of Michigan Press.

Kuran, Timur. 1996. "Social Mechanisms of Dissonance Reduction." *Social Mechanisms: An Analytical Approach to Social Theory*, ed. Peter Hedstrom and Richard Swedberg, 147–71. Cambridge: Cambridge University Press.

Lewis, D. K. 1969. *Convention*. Cambridge: Cambridge University Press.

Linz, Juan J. 1978. *The Breakdown of Democratic Regimes: Crisis, Breakdown and Reequilibration*. Baltimore: Johns Hopkins University Press.

Lipset, Seymour M. 1981. *Political Man: The Social Bases of Politics*, enlarged edn. Baltimore: Johns Hopkins University Press.

Mackie, Gerry. 1996. "Ending Footbinding and Infibulation: A Convention Account." *American Sociological Review* 61, 999–1017.

Marwell, Gerald, and Pamela Oliver. 1993. *The Critical Mass in Collective Action*. Cambridge: Cambridge University Press.

Merton, Robert K. 1968. *Social Theory and Social Structure*. New York: Free Press.

Moore, Barrington, Jr. 1966. *Social Origins of Dictatorship and Democracy: Lord and Peasant in the Making of the Modern World*. Boston: Beacon.

North, Douglass C., and Barry R. Weingast. 1989. "Constitutions and Commitment: The Evolution of Institutions Governing Public Choice in Seventeenth-Century England." *Journal of Economic History* 49, no. 4, 803–32.

Oliver, Pamela. 1993. "Formal Models of Collective Action." *Annual Review of Sociology* 19, 271–300.

Olson, Mancur. 1965. *The Logic of Collective Action*. Cambridge: Harvard University Press.

Petersen, Roger D. 2001. *Resistance and Rebellion: Lessons from Eastern Europe*. Cambridge: Cambridge University Press.

Pfaff, Stephen. 2006. *Exit-Voice Dynamics and the Collapse of East Germany: The Crisis of Leninism and the Revolution of 1989*. Durham: Duke University Press.

Popper, Karl. 1961. *The Poverty of Historicism*. London: Routledge.

Przeworski, Adam. 1987. "Democracy as a Contingent Outcome of Conflict." *Consti-*

tutionalism and Democracy, ed. Jon Elster and Rune Slagstad, 59–80. Cambridge: Cambridge University Press.

———. 1991. *Democracy and the Market*. Cambridge: Cambridge University Press.

Rossiter, Clinton L. 1948. *Constitutional Dictatorship: Crisis Government in the Modern Democracies*. Princeton: Princeton University Press.

Schelling, Thomas C. 1972. "A Process of Residential Segregation: Neighboring Tipping." *Racial Discrimination in Economic Life*, ed. A. Pascal, 157–84. Lexington, Mass.: D. C. Heath.

———. 1980 [1963]. *The Strategy of Conflict*. Cambridge: Harvard University Press.

Schumpeter, Joseph A. 1976 [1942]. *Capitalism, Socialism and Democracy*. London: Allen and Unwin.

Sewell, William H., Jr. 1996. "Three Temporalities: Toward an Eventful Sociology." *The Historic Turn in the Human Sciences*, ed. Terrence J. McDonald, 245–80. Ann Arbor: University of Michigan Press.

Tilly, Charles. 1975. "Revolutions and Collective Violence." *Handbook of Political Science III*, ed. Fred Greenstein and Nelson Polsby. Reading, Mass.: Addison-Wesley.

Trotsky, Leon. 2001 [1932]. *History of the Russian Revolution*. New York: Pathfinder.

Tsebelis, George. 1990. *Nested Games: Rational Choice in Comparative Politics*. Berkeley: University of California Press.

Turner, Ralph, and L. M. Killian. 1972. *Collective Behavior*. Englewood Cliffs, N.J.: Prentice Hall.

Tversky, Amos, and Daniel Kahneman. 1982. "Judgment under Uncertainty: Heuristics and Biases." *Judgment under Uncertainty: Heuristics and Biases*, ed. Daniel Kahneman, Paul Slovic, and Amos Tversky, 3–20. Cambridge: Cambridge University Press.

Weber, Max. 1978 [1922]. *Economy and Society*, ed. Guenther Roth and Claus Wittich. Berkeley: University of California Press.

Young, Peyton H. 1998. "Diffusion in Social Networks." Manuscript, Department of Economics, Johns Hopkins University.

INDEX

Abbott, Andrew, xxvii, 81n

Abdication: formal groups and, 315; organizational setting and, 316; theory of, 106–8. *See also* Collective abdications

Abdication game, 38, 46; assumptions of, 51, 53; empirical accuracy of, 59; formal analysis of, 54–57

Abraham, David, 107–8, 110–11, 130

Abstention, 71–72

Accounts: contemporary vs. retrospective, 335–36; narrative vs. synchronic, 337; representativeness of, 345–47; requested, 336–37; *sua sponte*, 335–36; voting explanations and, *see* Voting explanations

Acerbo bill, xxi

Action threshold. *See* threshold

Affective diffusion. *See* diffusion

Agulhon, Maurice, 155

Albert, André, 342

Algermissen, Konrad, 219–20

Alignment, xv. *See also* collective alignment

Allemane, Gaston; 125n, 169

Alliance, 26, 27, 86, 87

Altendörfer, Otto, 222

Ambivalence, 320–21

Anceau, Eric, 229

Anderson, Benedict, 192

Andlau, Hubert, 234

Anschluss (March 1938), 151

Antiliberalism, 134–35

Antisemitism, 147, 157, 175–76

Aretz, Jürgen, 73n, 217–18, 226, 330

Armistice, between France and Germany, 30; implications for constitutional abdication of, 76–78

Arnol, Justin, 344

Audigier, François, 26, 87

Aumann, Robert, 203

Auriol, Vincent, 89, 121–22, 128, 282–83, 302–3

Autonomy, 188–91, 192

Aya, Rod, 36

Azéma, Jean-Pierre, 30, 45n, 158, 167, 329

Bachem, Karl, 68, 109, 225, 273

Badie, Vincent, 76, 77, 175, 299, 302

Bankwitz, Philip Charles, 89n

Bardoux, Jacques, 45, 123, 148, 161–62, 164, 168, 227, 238, 280–81, 303

Barthe, Edouard, 89n, 125n, 127

Baruch, Marc O., xx

Baud, André, 236

Baudouin, Paul, 46

Bausch, Paul, 23, 71, 102, 270n

Bavarian Peasants' League (BBB), 10

Bavarian People's Party (BVP), 10, 13, 16, 19, 20, 72

Bearman, Peter, 3

Beaumont, Jean, 227

Becker, Johannes, 115

Becker, Josef, 40–41, 69, 101, 136, 139, 142, 144, 146, 253

Becquart, Henri, 43, 117–18, 119n, 122, 125n, 128, 160–61, 166–67, 227–28, 230, 235, 239, 282–85, 289, 300–301

Belgium, 76

Bell, Johannes, 96, 146, 262

Benazet, Paul, 278

Bérard, Léon, 280

Bérenger, Raymond, 297, 341

Bergery, Gaston, 174–75

Bergery declaration, 123–24, 158–59, 172, 175–76

Berk, Richard A., 322

Berl, Emmanuel, 77–78

Berlin, xi, xx, 17, 211

Bernard, Mathias, 85n

Béron, Emile, 230–31, 342

Berstein, Serge, 27, 87, 175n

Besse, René, 42

Biases, 199–200

Ivan Ermakoff is an associate professor of sociology
at the University of Wisconsin, Madison.

Library of Congress Cataloging-in-Publication Data
Ermakoff, Ivan.
Ruling oneself out : a theory of collective abdications / Ivan Ermakoff.
p. cm. — (Politics, history, and culture)
Includes bibliographical references and index.
ISBN-13: 978-0-8223-4143-7 (cloth : alk. paper)
ISBN-13: 978-0-8223-4164-2 (pbk. : alk. paper)
1. Authoritarianism. 2. Dictatorship. 3. Legitimacy of governments.
4. Germany—Politics and government—1933–1945. 5. France—Politics
and government—1940–1945. I. Title.
JC481.E685 2008
321.09—dc22   2007039435

www.ingramcontent.com/pod-product-compliance
Lightning Source LLC
Chambersburg PA
CBHW051947270326
41929CB00015B/2561